The Victoria History of the Counties of England

EDITED BY H. ARTHUR DOUBLEDAY

A HISTORY OF
WORCESTERSHIRE

VOLUME I

THE
VICTORIA HISTORY
OF THE COUNTIES
OF ENGLAND
WORCESTERSHIRE

PUBLISHED FOR

THE UNIVERSITY OF LONDON

INSTITUTE OF HISTORICAL RESEARCH

REPRINTED FROM THE ORIGINAL EDITION OF 1901

BY

DAWSONS OF PALL MALL

FOLKESTONE & LONDON

1971

Issued by
Archibald Constable and Company Limited
in 1901

Reprinted for the University of London
Institute of Historical Research
by
Dawsons of Pall Mall
Cannon House
Folkestone, Kent, England
1971

ISBN: 0 7129 0479 4

Printed in Great Britain
by Photolithography
Unwin Brothers Limited
Woking and London

INSCRIBED
TO THE MEMORY OF
HER LATE MAJESTY
QUEEN VICTORIA
WHO IN HER LIFETIME GRACIOUSLY
GAVE THE TITLE TO
AND ACCEPTED THE
DEDICATION OF
THIS HISTORY

THE ADVISORY COUNCIL
OF THE VICTORIA HISTORY

GENERAL ADVERTISEMENT

THE VICTORIA HISTORY of the Counties of England is a National Survey showing the condition of the country at the present day, and tracing the domestic history of the English Counties back to the earliest times.

Rich as every County of England is in materials for local history, there has hitherto been no attempt made to bring all these materials together into a coherent form. There are, indeed, histories of English Counties; but many of them—and these the best—are exceedingly rare and costly; others are very imperfect; all are out of date.

THE VICTORIA HISTORY will trace, county by county, the story of England's growth from its prehistoric condition, through the barbarous age, the settlement of alien peoples, and the gradual welding of many races into a nation which is now the greatest on the globe. All the phases of ecclesiastical history; the changes in land tenure; the records of historic and local families; the history of the social life and sports of the villages and towns; the development of art, science, manufactures and industries—all these factors, which tell of the progress of England from primitive beginnings to large and successful empire, will find a place in the work and their treatment be entrusted to those who have made a special study of them.

Many archæological, historical and other Societies are assisting in the compilation of this work, and the editor also has the advantage of the active and cordial co-operation of The National Trust, which is doing so much for the preservation of places of historic interest and natural beauty throughout the country.

The names of the distinguished men who have joined the Advisory Council are a

guarantee that the work will represent the results of the latest discoveries in every department of research. It will be observed that among them are representatives of science; for the whole trend of modern thought, as influenced by the theory of evolution, favours the intelligent study of the past and of the social, institutional and political developments of national life. As these histories are the first in which this object has been kept in view, and modern principles applied, it is hoped that they will form a work of reference no less indispensable to the student than welcome to the man of culture.

Family History will, both in the Histories and in the supplemental volumes of chart pedigrees, be dealt with by genealogical experts and in the modern spirit. Every effort will be made to secure accuracy of statement, and to avoid the insertion of those legendary pedigrees which have in the past brought discredit on the whole subject. It has been pointed out by the late Bishop of Oxford, a great master of historical research, that 'the expansion and extension of genealogical study is a very remarkable feature of our own times,' that 'it is an increasing pursuit both in America and England,' and that it can render the historian useful service.

Heraldry will also in this Series occupy a prominent position, and the splendours of the coat-armour borne in the Middle Ages will be illustrated in colours on a scale that has never been attempted before.

The general plan of Contents, and the names of the Sectional Editors (who will co-operate with local workers in every case) are as follows :—

Natural History. Edited by AUBYN B. R. TREVOR-BATTYE, M.A., F.L.S., etc.

    Geology. By CLEMENT REID, F.R.S., HORACE B. WOODWARD, F.R.S., and others

    Palæontology. Edited by R. L. LYDEKKER, F.R.S., etc.

    Flora ⎰ Contributions by G. A. BOULENGER, F.R.S., F. O. PICKARD-CAMBRIDGE, M.A., H. N. DIXON, F.L.S.,
              G. C. DRUCE, M.A., F.L.S., WALTER GARSTANG, M.A., F.L.S., HERBERT GOSS, F.L.S., F.E.S.,
    Fauna ⎱ R. I. POCOCK, REV. T. R. R. STEBBING, M.A., F.R.S., etc., B. B. WOODWARD, F.G.S., F.R.M.S.,
              etc., and other Specialists

Prehistoric Remains. Edited by W. BOYD DAWKINS, M.A., F.R.S., F.S.A.

Roman Remains. Edited by F. HAVERFIELD, M.A., F.S.A.

Anglo-Saxon Remains. Edited by C. HERCULES READ, F.S.A., and REGINALD A. SMITH, B.A.

Ethnography. Edited by G. LAURENCE GOMME, F.S.A.

    Dialect. Edited by JOSEPH WRIGHT, M.A., Ph.D.

    Place Names ⎫
    Folklore   ⎬ Contributed by Various Authorities
    Physical Types ⎭

Domesday Book and other kindred Records. Edited by J. HORACE ROUND, M.A.

Architecture. By Various Authorities. The Sections on the Cathedrals and Monastic Remains Edited by W. H. ST. JOHN HOPE, M.A.

Ecclesiastical History. Edited by R. L. POOLE, M.A.

Political History. Edited by W. H. STEVENSON, M.A., J. HORACE ROUND, M.A., Prof. T. F. TOUT, M.A., JAMES TAIT, M.A., and C. H. FIRTH, M.A.

History of Schools. Edited by A. F. LEACH, M.A., F.S.A.

Maritime History of Coast Counties. Edited by J. K. LAUGHTON, M.A.

Topographical Accounts of Parishes and Manors. By Various Authorities

History of the Feudal Baronage. Edited by J. HORACE ROUND, M.A., and OSWALD BARRON, F.S.A.

Family History and Heraldry. Edited by OSWALD BARRON, F.S.A.

Agriculture. Edited by SIR ERNEST CLARKE, M.A., Sec. to the Royal Agricultural Society

Forestry. Edited by JOHN NISBET, D.OEC.

Industries, Arts and Manufactures ⎫
Social and Economic History   ⎬ By Various Authorities
Persons Eminent in Art, Literature, Science ⎭

Ancient and Modern Sport. Edited by the DUKE OF BEAUFORT

    Hunting   ⎫
    Shooting ⎬ By Various Authorities
    Fishing, etc. ⎭

    Cricket. Edited by HOME GORDON

    Football. Edited by C. W. ALCOCK

Bibliographies

Indexes

Names of the Subscribers

With a view to securing the best advice with regard to the searching of records, the Editor has secured the services of the following committee of experts :—

RECORDS COMMITTEE

Sir Edward Maunde Thompson, K.C.B.	Wm. Page, F.S.A.
Sir Henry Maxwell-Lyte, K.C.B.	J. Horace Round, M.A.
W. J. Hardy, F.S.A.	S. R. Scargill-Bird, F.S.A.
F. Madan, M.A.	W. H. Stevenson, M.A.
F. Maitland, M.A., F.S.A.	G. F. Warner, M.A., F.S.A.

ILLUSTRATIONS

Among the many thousands of subjects illustrated will be castles, cathedrals and churches, mansions and manor houses, moot halls and market halls, family portraits, etc. Particular attention will be given to the beautiful and quaint examples of architecture which, through decay or from other causes, are in danger of disappearing. The best examples of church brasses, coloured glass, and monumental effigies will be depicted. The Series will also contain 160 pictures in photogravure, showing the characteristic scenery of the counties.

CARTOGRAPHY

Each History will contain Archæological, Domesday, and Geological maps ; maps showing the orography, and the Parliamentary and Ecclesiastical divisions ; and the map done by Speed in 1610. The Series will contain about four hundred maps in all.

FAMILY HISTORY AND HERALDRY

The Histories will contain, in the Topographical Section, manorial pedigrees, and accounts of the noble and gentle families connected with the local history ; and it is proposed to trace, wherever possible, their descendants in the Colonies and the United States of America. The Editor will be glad to receive information which may be of service to him in this branch of the work. The chart family pedigrees and the arms of the families mentioned in the Heralds' Visitations will be issued in a supplemental volume for each county.

The Rolls of Arms are being completely collated for this work, and all the feudal coats will be given in colours. The arms of the local families will also be represented in connection with the Topographical Section.

In order to secure the greatest possible accuracy in the descriptions of the Architecture, ecclesiastic, military and domestic, a committee has been formed of the following students of architectural history, who will supervise this department of the work :—

ARCHITECTURAL COMMITTEE

J. Bilson, F.S.A., F.R.I.B.A.	W. H. St. John Hope, M.A.
R. Blomfield	W. H. Knowles, F.S.A., F.R.I.B.A.
Harold Brakspear, A.R.I.B.A.	J. T. Micklethwaite, F.S.A.
Prof. Baldwin Brown	Roland Paul
Arthur S. Flower, F.S.A., A.R.I.B.A.	J. Horace Round, M.A.
George E. Fox, M.A., F.S.A.	Percy G. Stone, F.S.A., F.R.I.B.A.
J. A. Gotch, F.S.A., F.R.I.B.A.	Thackeray Turner

A special feature in connection with the Architecture will be a series of coloured ground plans showing the architectural history of castles, cathedrals and other monastic foundations. Plans of the most important country mansions will also be included.

The issue of this work is limited to subscribers only, whose names will be printed at the end of each History.

W. Hyde.

Worcester from the Severn.

Swan Electric Engraving Co.

THE
VICTORIA HISTORY
OF THE COUNTY OF
WORCESTER

VOLUME ONE

PUBLISHED FOR
THE UNIVERSITY OF LONDON
INSTITUTE OF HISTORICAL RESEARCH
REPRINTED BY
DAWSONS OF PALL MALL
FOLKESTONE & LONDON

County Committee for Worcestershire

THE RT. HON. THE EARL OF COVENTRY, P.C.
Lord Lieutenant, Chairman

J. W. WILLIS-BUND, ESQ., F.S.A., F.L.S., *Chairman of the Quarter Sessions and County Council, Editor.*

THE RT. HON. THE EARL OF PORTSMOUTH
THE RT. HON. THE EARL OF CAMPERDOWN
THE RT. HON. THE VISCOUNT COBHAM
THE RT. HON. THE VISCOUNT LIFFORD
THE RT. REV. THE LORD BISHOP OF WORCESTER
THE RT. REV. THE LORD BISHOP OF HEREFORD
THE RT. HON. THE LORD WINDSOR
THE RT. HON. THE LORD SANDYS
THE RT. HON. THE LORD HAMPTON
THE HON. GEORGE HIGGINSON ALLSOPP, M.P.
THE RT. HON. SIR RICHARD TEMPLE, BART., P.C., G.C.S.I.
SIR RICHARD HARINGTON, BART.
SIR HARRY FOLEY VERNON, BART.
SIR THOMAS LEA, BART., M.P.
SIR BENJAMIN HINGLEY, BART.
GEN. SIR CHARLES C. JOHNSON, K.C.B.
THE VERY REV. THE DEAN OF WORCESTER
JOHN AMPHLETT, ESQ.
ISAAC AVERILL, ESQ.
ALFRED BALDWIN, ESQ., M.P.
ERNEST J. BIGWOOD, ESQ.
R. W. BINNS, ESQ., F.S.A., F.R.H.S.
JOHN BRINTON, ESQ.
REV. J. R. BURTON, F.G.S.
AUSTIN CHAMBERLAIN, ESQ., M.P.
FREDERICK CORBETT, ESQ.
LIEUT.-GEN. H. F. DAVIES
COL. R. P. DECIE
DR. H. E. DIXEY
REV. E. R. DOWDESWELL
REV. R. R. DUKE, F.S.A.
W. H. EDWARDS, ESQ.

REV. F. J. ELD, F.R.A.S.
T. FITZROY FENWICK, ESQ.
EDGAR FLOWER, ESQ.
REV. J. K. FLOYER, F.S.A.
G. W. GROSVENOR, ESQ.
MAJOR WILLIAM C. HILL
G. B. HINGLEY, ESQ.
J. H. HOOPER, ESQ.
REV. HAMILTON KINGSFORD
CHARLES P. LANE, ESQ.
G. E. MARTIN, ESQ.
R. B. MARTIN, ESQ., M.P.
J. T. MIDDLEMORE, ESQ., M.P.
REV. JOHN L. MOILLIET
FRANK S. PEARSON, ESQ.
CHARLES W. DYSON PERRINS, ESQ.
REV. CANON A. S. PORTER, F.S.A.
REV. DAVID ROBERTSON
B. ROBINSON, ESQ., M.P.
SAMUEL SOUTHALL, ESQ.
ROBERT F. TOMES, ESQ.
M. TOMKINSON, ESQ.
E. V. WHEELER, ESQ.
REV. J. BOWSTEAD WILSON, F.S.A.
ROBERT WOODWARD, ESQ.
ALFRED W. WORTHINGTON, ESQ., F.S.S.
REV. ROBERT WYLDE
THE WORSHIPFUL THE MAYOR OF BEWDLEY
THE WORSHIPFUL THE MAYOR OF DROITWICH
THE WORSHIPFUL THE MAYOR OF DUDLEY
THE WORSHIPFUL THE MAYOR OF EVESHAM
THE WORSHIPFUL THE MAYOR OF KIDDERMINSTER
THE WORSHIPFUL THE MAYOR OF WORCESTER

CONTENTS OF VOLUME ONE

CONTENTS OF VOLUME ONE

LIST OF ILLUSTRATIONS

LIST OF MAPS

⋆ *Not reproduced in this edition owing to technical difficulties.*

† *Reproduced in black and white in this edition.*

PREFACE

IN the preparation of this first volume of the *Victoria History of Worcestershire* the editors have had to contend against many difficulties. In the field of Natural History with which this volume is largely concerned the workers have been comparatively few, and their energies have been directed mostly in certain channels. While the popular orders of the flora and fauna have attracted a good deal of attention, those that are less interesting to the collector have been almost entirely unexplored. It has therefore been extremely difficult to preserve anything like a proper balance in the parts which go to make up the first section of this volume.

In the department of Archæology also Worcestershire has been less fortunate than many other parts of the country. The absence of any very striking archæological features such as would attract antiquaries from far and near has perhaps led to a greater neglect of its earliest history than the county deserves. There is every reason to believe that systematic excavation would reveal much of interest in the pre-Norman period of the county's history. But without an extensive use of the spade the early story of Worcestershire must remain scanty and conjectural.

With the Domesday Survey of 1086 we enter upon the period of written history, in which the county possesses many features of exceptional interest and importance. And here the editors venture to claim for this work a distinct advance on anything that has been done hitherto. With the exception of a translation and of the facsimile reproductions of the historian Nash and of the Ordnance Survey Office, the Worcestershire section of Domesday Book has received no serious attention. It is doubtful indeed whether a purely local student would be well equipped for an adequate study of the Survey, which, to be understood, must be dealt with as a whole. The editors consider themselves fortunate therefore in having secured the services of Mr. J. Horace Round, who has made the great national document a life-study.

In the General Advertisement will be found a description of the

PREFACE

aim and scope of this work. The succeeding three volumes, although containing certain general articles, will be mainly devoted to the history of the parishes and manors of the county. A detailed consideration of the work of past historians in this department, and of the methods and achievement of the present undertaking, will more suitably find a place in those volumes.

The editors desire to thank the members of the County Committee and others who have in various ways assisted in the collection and arrangement of materials. Particularly would they express their indebtedness to Mr. Edwards, the Curator of the Museum of the Victoria Institute at Worcester.

A HISTORY OF
WORCESTERSHIRE

GEOLOGY[1]

THE records of the ancient history of the earth are written in the various clays, sandstones, limestones, and other stony materials of which its solid surface is composed. These are classified for convenience into larger and smaller groups, according to their order of position, and the fossilized remains of plants and animals which they contain. Each group may comprise strata of very diverse mineral character, but the larger divisions mark the chief life epochs of which records more or less complete are preserved in all parts of the world, while the smaller groups indicate the more local conditions of natural history. Thus we refer to the Silurian period as one of the great epochs of geological history, and to the Woolhope Limestone or Ledbury Shales as one of the more or less local conditions in that great epoch.

Geological history is for the most part deciphered from ancient sea-beds. The great oceans and the shallow seas are areas in which are ever being deposited various accumulations of sand and shingle, mud or clay, of shell, coral, or organic ooze. The land-surfaces are areas mainly of waste, from which materials are carried away by streams and rivers, or by the sea itself, to be spread over the ocean-bed along with remains of plants and animals that may be carried out to sea, or which live and die in the ocean. The chief areas of deposition on the land are along the courses of rivers and in lakes.

In the course of ages all the land-areas would have been wasted away had not disturbances, which have happened again and again, brought old sea-beds or old lake-beds to the surface. There they have been acted upon by rain, and rivers, and glaciers, and have been worn down or eroded. Through subsequent depression, marine and sometimes extensive lacustrine deposits have been spread over the eroded surfaces of the older strata. This has occurred again and again in the area which now forms Worcestershire, and it will be understood that the intervals during which the strata were upheaved to form land are for the most part breaks in geological time, locally unrepresented by strata.

Thus it is that while Worcestershire contains a most interesting and varied series of geological records—records which date from the earliest known geological times—yet there are great gaps unrepresented in the county by any geological formation.

The following table shows the stratified formations and the igneous rocks which appear at the surface in different parts of the county :—

[1] In the parts relating to the Lias and Rhætic Beds the writer has had the advantage of some MS. Notes prepared by Mr. R. F. Tomes, F.G.S., whose observations are duly acknowledged.

Period	Formation	Character of the strata	Approximate thickness in feet
Recent	Alluvium	Silt, clay, peat, gravel	20
Pleisto-cene	Valley Gravel and Brickearth .	Gravel, sand and loam	20 and more
	Glacial Drift	Sand, gravel and stony clay . .	up to 50
Jurassic	Great Oolite Series	Limestone and clay	15 to 25
	Inferior Oolite Series	Mainly oolitic limestone, with clay, sand and calcareous sandstone .	up to 180
	Lias { Upper	Clay and shale, with subordinate limestone	100 to 120
	Lias { Middle	Hard ferruginous limestone, sands and shales	250
	Lias { Lower	Clays and shales ; argillaceous limestones	950
Triassic	Rhætic	Limestone, black shale, sandstone and marl	30 to 55
	Keuper { Marl	Red and variegated marl and clay, with sandstone	700 to 1,000
	Keuper { Sandstone	Red sandstone	200 to 400
	Bunter	Red and variegated sandstones, with pebble-beds	250 to 900
Permian	Permian	Breccia, sandstone and marl, with conglomerate	500 to 800
Car-boniferous	Coal Measures	Sandstones and shales, with thin beds of limestone, seams of coal, fire-clay and ironstone	1,000 to 2,000
Old Red Sandstone	Lower Old Red Sandstone . .	Sandstone and marl, with bands of cornstone	3,000 to 4,000
Silurian	Ludlow Series { Ledbury Shales . .	Red and purple shales, marls and sandstones	300
	Ludlow Series { Downton Sandstone	Yellow sandstones	100
	Ludlow Series { Upper Ludlow Shales	Sandy shales and thin limestones .	200
	Ludlow Series { Aymestry Limestone	Concretionary limestones . . .	40
	Ludlow Series { Lower Ludlow Shales	Sandy shales	750
	Wenlock Series { Wenlock Limestone	Nodular limestones and shale . .	280
	Wenlock Series { Wenlock Shales . .	Sandy shales	600
	Wenlock Series { Woolhope Limestone	Impure limestone	150
	Llandovery Series { Tarannon Shales .	Purple shales	350
	Llandovery Series { May Hill Sandstone	Grey and purple sandstone and calcareous bands	600
Cambrian	Tremadoc and Lingula Flag Series { Malvern Shales . .	Grey and black shales	1,000
	Tremadoc and Lingula Flag Series { Hollybush and Lickey Sandstone and Quartzite	Green and brown sandstone and quartzite	500
Archæan	Chiefly Igneous and Metamorphic { Uriconian . .	Various volcanic rocks and some flaggy and slaty beds	unknown
	Chiefly Igneous and Metamorphic { Malvernian . .	Gneiss and schists	
Of various ages	Igneous Rocks { Basalt, Dolerite, Diabase, Andesite, Diorite, Rhyolite		

GEOLOGY

The county of Worcester consists for the most part of a wide undulating plain of red Triassic marls and sandstones, and of grey Liassic clays and limestones, overspread in places with sundry superficial gravels. It is bordered on the west by the bold though somewhat tiny mountain range of the Malverns, which rises to a height of 1,394 feet in the Worcestershire Beacon, and extends northwards to the Abberley Hills, which attain a height of 779 feet. On the north the county comprises portions of the Forest of Wyre and South Staffordshire coalfields, while towards the north-east there is again a remnant of a mountainous region in the Lickey Hills, and in the older rocks of Dudley, which appear from beneath coverings of the newer strata. Hence three great groups of rocks are represented; (1) the older rocks of Malvern, Abberley, the Lickey and Dudley, together with the coalfields; (2) the Red rocks and Lias of the plains; and (3) the superficial gravels. With the Lias we may include the Oolitic series, which is represented on Bredon Hill and in some isolated portions of Worcestershire in the northern Cotteswold Hills.

It has been shown in recent papers by Prof. T. T. Groom that the Malvern Hills exhibit all the characteristic features of a folded mountain range. There the older rocks have been disturbed and bent into anticlinal folds, and these inverted and faulted have become 'thrust-planes,' whereby older strata have in places been thrust or pushed over newer rocks. In his opinion this ancient range first arose during late Carboniferous times, and was much faulted and denuded before the Permian and Triassic and succeeding deposits were spread over and against it. Consequently there is a great break between the older rocks and the ' New Red ' strata [1] which rest irregularly on any of them, filling hollows in their worn surfaces. Along the ranges of the older rocks the denuded anticlines exhibit portions of formations the most ancient anywhere known. These, Archæan or Pre-Cambrian in age, occur on Malvern, at Martley, and at Barnt Green in the Lower Lickey Hills, and they truly form portions of what have been termed by Prof. Bonney ' the Foundation-stones of the Earth's Crust.'

ARCHÆAN

The geology of the Malvern Hills has naturally attracted the attention of geologists. The earliest description of the hills was that of Leonard Horner (1811), and the next important account was that of Murchison in his great work on 'The Silurian System' (1839). To John Phillips, however, we are indebted for the earliest elaborate account of this and adjoining tracts.[2] Since then the researches of a Worcester man, Dr. Harvey B. Holl,[3] of the Rev. W. S. Symonds (formerly Rector of

[1] This term is conveniently applied to both Permian and Triassic rocks, as they consist mainly of *red* strata.
[2] 'The Malvern Hills, compared with the Palæozoic districts of Abberley,' etc., *Mem. Geol. Survey*, vol. ii., pt. 1, 1848; see also *Geology of Oxford*, etc., 1871, p. 58.
[3] *Quart. Journ. Geol. Soc.* vol. xxi. p. 72.

3

Pendock), of Dr. C. Callaway, Mr. F. Rutley, and Prof. T. T. Groom[1] have most largely added to our knowledge.

The most ancient rocks of Malvern are those which form the main ridge and consist of hornblendic gneiss, with numerous dykes of diorite. So long ago as 1865 Dr. Holl suggested that the crystalline schists and gneiss which had before been regarded as altered Cambrian rocks, were of Pre-Cambrian age, while shortly afterwards the Rev. J. H. Timins showed by chemical analyses that the rocks could not have resulted from the metamorphosis of any known Cambrian rocks. These views are now generally accepted. These 'Malvernian' rocks form the nucleus of the Malvern and Abberley range and they are faulted against or overlain unconformably by Cambrian, and again by Silurian rocks. The whole group was subsequently bent into an anticline, which is faulted on the east against the New Red rocks. Westwards the successive beds of Silurian strata dip beneath the Old Red Sandstone of Herefordshire.

In 1880 Dr. Charles Callaway recognized on the eastern side of the Herefordshire Beacon certain compact felspathic and brecciated rocks, evidently of volcanic origin, and similar to those named 'Uriconian' in the Wrekin area. These, although newer than the Malvern gneiss, are of very great antiquity. This volcanic series, as observed by Prof. Groom, consists of rhyolites, andesites, basalts and tuffs, while the bedding has a prevailing easterly dip. The junction with the Malvernian is nowhere actually exposed, and at present it is 'impossible to determine whether this junction is a fault or a surface upon which the Uriconian series was originally deposited.'[2]

Prof. Lapworth has observed that the best localities for studying the essential characters of the Malvern rocks are the quarries of the North Hill and the Wych, and the eastern slopes of the hills between Malvern Wells and the Herefordshire Beacon.[3]

The Archæan rocks thus consist to a large extent of crystalline schists, for the most part highly altered or metamorphosed igneous materials, whose precise method of formation cannot be told, at any rate at present. Belonging to the same Pre-Cambrian period there are also beds of volcanic grit and shale, and in some parts of Britain sandstones not unlike Old Red Sandstone. None but obscure traces of organic remains have been found in any of these rocks, and then but rarely ; nor are they to be expected. In the region with which we have now to deal, and in most other localities, the rocks have undergone such pressure-metamorphism that the materials of which they were originally composed have crystallized afresh. Moreover, the schistose structure produced by mechanical movements, the twistings and foldings, the faults and thrust-planes, would tend to obliterate any evidences of organic structure. In some cases the rocks have been penetrated by intrusive igneous rocks prior to the latest great earth-

---

[1] *Quart. Journ. Geol. Soc.*, vol. lv. p. 129, and vol. lvi. p. 138. (References to other workers are given in these papers.)

[2] *Ibid.*, vol. lvi. p. 140.

[3] Article 'Geology' in *Handbook of Birmingham* (Brit. Assoc.) 1886, p. 222.

movements, whereby the whole group has been modified. Hence in one sense these Archæan rocks are a complex of many ages.

The Malvern rocks are notably dislocated and shattered. As Phillips remarked in 1848, 'Brecciated rocks are abundant on the eastern face of the Malvern Chain, as at North End, in the Wych road, on the east side of the Raggedstone Hill, and round the east and north of Key's-end [Chase End] Hill. They consist of slightly displaced portions of the adjoining masses, or else appear to be only crushed parts of these masses, crushed *in situ* by the force which displaced and broke the chain, as it is on the line of the great fault, and in places where much movement may be believed to have happened, that these rocks appear.'[1]

Further attention was drawn to these brecciated rocks by Prof. Hughes in 1887, and he then pointed out ' that we may in certain cases have a conglomeratic-looking mass composed of rounded pieces of rock differing in lithological character both from the matrix and from one another, occurring along what looks like the strike of the rocks, and yet may be able to make out that it is entirely a superinduced structure due to brecciation in place and subsequent decomposition of the broken rock.'[2]

Noteworthy springs occur at various points along the hill range, for while, as pointed out by Phillips, the surface of the hills is exceedingly dry, and the rain sinks into the many fissures, it reappears 'in many springs at or about the level where the steep slopes of the hills end and the Malvern rocks are covered by the strata of the lower ground.'[3] Thus we find St. Ann's Well on the eastern side of the Worcestershire Beacon, also the Holy Well (Malvern Wells), between Great and Little Malvern. Again, Walms Well issues on the western side of the Herefordshire Beacon.

The hill-range is one of mixed woodland and pasture, the thin soil varying much according to the nature of the rocks. The gneissic tracts are for the most part grassy, and the steep slopes of the Worcestershire Beacon are slippery indeed in hot, dry weather. The more prominent of the heights naturally formed strongholds in ancient times, and we find encampments that were used by Britons, Romans and Danes. Some of the hills too have at various times proved useful as beacons. Phillips mentions that across the ridge between the Worcestershire Beacon and the Wych ' runs a sort of vein of mica, giving origin to the only even supposed mine in the Malverns—but a gold mine !' Many years ago, indeed, a shaft was sunk to raise the gold, which was thought to be present, but no traces of the precious metal were found.[4]

The occurrence of Archæan rock near Martley has for some time been recognized. The structure of the region is a complicated one, and according to the observations of Prof. Groom, the old rocks have appar-

---

[1] *Mem. Geol. Survey*, vol. ii., pt. 1, p. 44.
[2] *Geol. Mag.* for 1887, p. 502 ; see also Groom, *Quart. Journ. Geol. Soc.*, vol. lv. p. 151.
[3] *Mem. Geol. Survey*, vol. ii., pt. 1, p. 16.
[4] C. Hastings, *Nat. Hist. Worcestershire*, 1834, p. 89.

ently been thrust on to the Cambrian quartzite, and the overthrust series has been subsequently folded along a north-and-south axis, together with the Old Red Sandstone. He adds that the Coal Measures were subsequently deposited unconformably on the faulted and folded series, while in later times the old rocks covered by the Trias were let down on the eastern side. Thus 'we appear to have in this small area an epitome of the history of the Malvern and Abberley Ranges.'[1]

Near Barnt Green Junction, towards the southern end of the Lickey Hills, there is an inlier of ancient tuffs and volcanic grits ; rocks described by Prof. Lapworth as probably deposited in water during a time of contemporaneous igneous action. They comprise also green, grey and purple, flaggy and micaceous shaly beds, penetrated by diorites. These Barnt Green rocks are apparently overlain by the Cambrian Lickey quartzite, but, as Mr. Walcot Gibson remarks, 'the actual relations of the two formations are not visible.'[2]

CAMBRIAN

Practically speaking the Cambrian rocks are the oldest known fossiliferous strata, for the obscure records, at present found in earlier sediments, simply indicate that life existed. In the Cambrian period, however, we find evidence, not merely of fucoids, sponges, and worm-burrows, but of bryozoa, brachiopods, mollusca, and notably of trilobites. The Cambrian rocks have proved to be locally divided into,—

Malvern Shales { Grey Shales with *Dictyonema sociale.*
{ Black Shales with *Olenus.*
Hollybush Sandstone with conglomerate and quartzite at base.

The Hollybush Sandstone is a greenish, micaceous sandstone, occasionally calcareous, and it contains at its base pebbles which have been derived from Archæan rocks. Upon these it probably in some places rests unconformably, although the junction, according to Prof. Groom, is mainly a faulted one. It occurs in a highly inclined position at White-leaved Oak, to the south of Raggedstone Hill (839 feet high), and along the western borders of that hill and Midsummer Hill (937 feet). For many years only obscure worm-tracks and fucoidal remains had been found in the Hollybush Sandstone, but there have now been recorded remains of the brachiopods, *Kutorgina cingulata* and *Obolella salteri*, and of the pteropod *Hyolithus.* The pebbles in the Hollybush conglomerate differ in character from any of the local Archæan rocks, and thus support Prof. Groom's view that the Malvern Hills did not form a coast-line in Cambrian times.[3]

The Malvern Shales overlie the Hollybush Sandstone, and in the lower (black) portion a number of trilobites occur, such as *Peltura*

---

[1] Groom, *Quart. Journ. Geol. Soc.*, vol. lvi. p. 163 ; see also C. St. A. Coles, *Geol. Mag.*, 1898, p. 304 ; and Symonds, *Records of the Rocks*, p. 38.
[2] See Lapworth, *Proc. Geol. Assoc.*, vol. xv. p. 328 ; and Gibson in *Summary of Progress of Geol. Survey* for 1897, p. 67.
[3] *Rep. Brit. Assoc.* for 1900.

GEOLOGY

(*Olenus*) *scarabæoides* and *Agnostus pisiformis*. In the higher (grey) shales, on the borders of Chase End Hill, the Rev. W. S. Symonds first found the characteristic 'hydroid zoophyte' *Dictyonema*.

Prof. Lapworth in referring to the numerous intercalated igneous rocks which occur both in the Hollybush Sandstone and Malvern Shales remarks that the majority are certainly intrusive.[1] Prof. Groom remarks that they include basalts and ophitic diabases, and were probably intruded in Ordovician times.

Much of the ground occupied by these Cambrian rocks is pasture land.

The famous quartzite of the Lower Lickey, described in 1821 by Buckland, is well seen at Bilberry Hill, and further north at Rubery, where it is flanked by May Hill Sandstone. It has been compared with the quartzite of Hartshill, near Nuneaton, and like that rock it is extensively used for road-metal. According to Prof. Lapworth, however, the Lickey quartzite represents only the lower and middle portions of the Hartshill rock, the upper portion not being recognized at Lickey, although represented at Malvern by the Hollybush Sandstone. The only traces of fossils found in the Lickey rock are worm-burrows. The sequence of events at Lickey, according to the observations of Mr. W. Gibson, indicates that after the volcanic era of the Barnt Green rocks, a long period may have intervened before the laying down of the quartzite.

SILURIAN

Among the fossiliferous strata of Worcestershire none have proved more attractive than the Silurian, whether at Malvern or Dudley. The collections formed by the late Dr. R. B. Grindrod (of Townshend House, Malvern), and by the late John Gray (of Hagley), were remarkably rich, and many other important sets of fossils have been gathered together.

The rocks appear in broken anticlinal ridges at the Lickey Hills and Dudley, and again along the Malvern and Abberley ranges, but they do not occupy a large superficial area in the county. A great break separates them from the Cambrian, for we have no representatives in place of any of the Ordovician (or Lower Silurian) strata.

The oldest subdivision known as the May Hill (or Upper Llandovery) Sandstone consists at Malvern of purple and grey grits and brown sandstones, some of them calcareous, some pebbly. Evidently a shore deposit, the May Hill Sandstone appears to rest indifferently on the older rocks whether Archæan or Cambrian, but we have to be cautious as Prof. Groom remarks in distinguishing between the normal overspread of the newer formation, and the displacements due to subsequent earth-movements.

Among the fossils of the May Hill Sandstone are *Pentamerus*

[1] *Proc. Geol. Assoc.*, vol. xv. p. 338 ; Groom, *Rep. Brit. Assoc.*, 1900.

7

oblongus, *Stricklandinia lens*, *Orthis calligramma*, *Atrypa reticularis*, *Lingula parallela*, *Ctenodonta*, *Encrinurus punctatus*, etc.

Prof. Groom remarks that the May Hill beds on the north of Midsummer Hill are separated from the gneissic series by a well-marked band of hard Cambrian conglomerate and quartzite, which he terms the Hollybush Conglomerate and Quartzite.[1] Further north the May Hill beds occur at Swinyard Hill, south of the Herefordshire Beacon. Overlying them at Malvern the Rev. W. S. Symonds observed a group of grey and purple shales, 'Woolhope Shales,' about 350 feet thick, which probably represent the Tarannon Shales of Montgomeryshire.

In the Lickey Hills, as at Malvern, a long period elapsed after the deposition of the Cambrian quartzite, 'of which no record remains in the form of sediments, but during some portion of which the quartzite and Barnt Green rock were compressed and folded by earth-movements,' followed by faulting. Slow subsidence set in when the May Hill or Upper Llandovery grits and Wenlock Shales were laid down.[2] Here the May Hill beds, which occur at Rubery, consist of coarse reddish sandstone with casts of *Pentamerus* and other fossils, and they are overlaid by the Lower Wenlock shales and flags, including a band of limestone from which Mr. W. Wickham King obtained a number of fossils. These indicate a local representative of the Woolhope Limestone.[3]

The Woolhope Limestone which takes its name from Woolhope, near Hereford, comprises impure and nodular limestone and shale. It occurs at North Malvern and has been well exposed near the Wych. Many trilobites of the genera *Illænus*, *Phacops*, *Acidaspis*, *Encrinurus* and *Calymene* occur, and fine specimens were obtained during the excavation of the Malvern and Ledbury tunnels.

In the region near Dudley the rock is known as the Barr Limestone, from Great Barr near Walsall, a locality from which the characteristic trilobite, *Illænus barriensis*, was first brought into notice.

The Wenlock Shales consist mainly of soft grey shales, but they contain thin nodular layers of limestone. As a rule they are highly fossiliferous and yield the corals, *Favosites gothlandica* and *Heliolites interstincta*; the brachiopods, *Orthis elegantula*, *Strophomena rhomboidalis* and *Atrypa reticularis*; and the trilobites, *Phacops caudatus*, *Encrinurus punctatus*, etc. Many examples were obtained from near the mouth of the Malvern and Ledbury tunnels, where, as observed by Prof. Groom, the shales are faulted against the Old Red Sandstone.[4] The shales are usually exposed on the slopes and borders of the valleys.

The Wenlock Limestone is a more or less concretionary limestone, and it contains large nodules of carbonate of lime. It is in many places exceedingly fossiliferous, as in the quarries at Colwall Coppice and the Winnings near Malvern, and in other exposures on Watts Hill and near

[1] *Quart. Journ. Geol. Soc.*, vol. lv. p. 139.
[2] W. Gibson, *Summary of Progress of Geological Survey* for 1897, p. 69.
[3] Lapworth, *Proc. Geol. Assoc.*, vol. xv. p. 357.
[4] *Quart. Journ. Geol. Soc.*, vol. lvi. p. 147.

GEOLOGY

Martley. It yields corals, such as *Halysites catenularia*, and *Favosites gothlandica*; crinoids; the brachiopods, *Strophomena depressa* and *S. euglypha*; also the pteropod, *Conularia*. Among trilobites, *Calymene blumenbachi*, *Phacops caudatus* and *P. downingiæ* (the last named generally curled up) are characteristic forms.

Referring to the interesting exposures of the strata at Dudley Castle and the Wren's Nest, Prof. Lapworth remarks that 'the Silurian limestone rises up in steep dome-like forms. This limestone, which is that of the Wenlock [Dudley Limestone] of Siluria, is here composed of two calcareous bands—the higher about 28 feet in thickness, and the lower about 42 feet—separated from each other by an intermediate zone of about 90 feet of grey shales. The limestone has been worked for centuries as a flux for the ironstones of the [South Staffordshire] coalfield. The hills have been mined to a great depth, and all the best limestone rock extracted. The intervening and enveloping shales have been allowed to remain, and the present structure of the hills is that of a central dome surrounded by two enveloping shells separated from each other by two more or less empty spaces. Where the dip of the rock is higher, and these excavated parts are exposed, they form deep moat-like hollows bounded by walls of shale. Where the dip is low, and the overhanging rocks are supported by the vast pillars left by the workmen, these excavations form magnificent caverns of peculiar weirdness and beauty. In the heart of the hill at greater depths they form damp gloomy chasms of enormous extent, which can only be seen to perfection when lit up by artificial light.'[1]

At one time fine slabs of limestone with beautiful weathered-out examples of trilobites and crinoids, brachiopods and corals, were obtainable from the Wren's Nest.

The Wenlock Limestone passes upwards into the Lower Ludlow Beds, which consist for the most part of grey shales. Here remains have been found of the oldest known fish, *Scaphaspis*; also cephalopods, such as *Orthoceras* and *Lituites*; starfishes, graptolites, etc.

The Aymestry Limestone, which takes its name from a village north-west of Leominster, is a blue and grey concretionary limestone of somewhat inconstant character. It is characterized by such fossils as *Pentamerus knighti* and *P. galeatus*, *Lingula*, *Cardiola*, etc. The rock has been exposed at Hales End quarry, Malvern, and is represented also at Abberley.

The Aymestry Limestone passes up into the Upper Ludlow Beds. These comprise shales with calcareous bands and thin-bedded sandstones. They yield brachiopods such as *Chonetes lata* and *Discina*; also *Serpulites*, trilobites and other fossils. The strata are capped in places by a thin layer known as the Ludlow bone-bed, which contains coprolites, minute scales and fin-rays, and other remains of fishes, including *Onchus*, *Scaphaspis*, etc.; also remains of the crustacea *Eurypterus*, *Pterygotus*, etc.

[1] Article 'Geology' in *Handbook of Birmingham* (Brit. Assoc.), 1886, p. 229.

9

The Downton Sandstones are yellow and grey sandstones which are quarried in places for building purposes. They yield *Lingula cornea*, and also remains of fishes and crustacea as in the Upper Ludlow rocks.

From the Upper Ludlow Beds to the Old Red Sandstone the series, which includes in ascending order the Downton Sandstones and Ledbury Shales, is a transitional one, and the strata are often spoken of as 'Passage Beds.' The Ledbury Shales comprise red and mottled marls and sandy beds, as well as shales, and they were well exposed in the Ledbury tunnel on the Worcester and Hereford railway. Together with equivalent Tilestones, they were grouped by the Rev. W. S. Symonds with the Silurian, as they contain fossils which for the most part have Silurian affinities, although the fishes serve to connect them with the Old Red Sandstone. Certain gritty beds yielded *Auchenaspis salteri*, while from the Tilestones of Trimpley, near Bewdley, many fossils have been obtained, such as *Pterygotus, Cephalaspis, Auchenaspis*, etc.[1] It is interesting to notice that the Silurian passage-beds have been proved in a boring near Halesowen.[2]

In Silurian times we have evidence of conditions that were entirely marine, and generally those of warm regions. We have distinct evidence of old coral-growths, and in the later deposits we find the earliest traces of land-plants and also of fishes. Among the newer strata also shallower water conditions prevailed ; and we pass in the Worcestershire region gradually from marine into what are regarded as the continental conditions of the Old Red period.

OLD RED SANDSTONE

The Old Red Sandstone, to which especial charm is attached through the writings of Hugh Miller, tells of huge lakes tenanted by curious fishes and still stranger crustacea.

The Rev. W. S. Symonds questioned whether the formation was laid down in *freshwater* areas, because some of the characteristic genera, both of fishes and crustacea, occur in association with marine forms in the later Silurian strata.[3] Be this as it may, the region was probably a subsiding one, as the higher beds of the Old Red Sandstone extend over a wider tract than do the lower portions. In the Worcestershire area we have, however, to deal only with the Lower Old Red Sandstone ; and it may be observed that a considerable portion of the formation is composed of red and mottled marls, resembling many beds in the Permian and Triassic or 'New Red Sandstone' series, and that such coloured strata are usually associated with freshwater or estuarine conditions.

Notwithstanding all that has been written about its organic remains, the Old Red Sandstone is not a very fossiliferous formation.

[1] Symonds, *Quart. Journ. Geol. Soc.*, vol. xvii. p. 152 ; Murchison, *Siluria* ; and G. E. Roberts, *Geologist*, vol. ii. p. 117.

[2] Lapworth, *Proc. Geol. Assoc.*, vol. xv. p. 354.

[3] See also E. Ray Lankester, *Geol. Mag.*, vol. vii. p. 399.

GEOLOGY

It is only in certain localities and at certain horizons that fossils have been obtained in abundance.

The Lower Old Red Sandstone comprises red marls and sandstones, and beds of impure concretionary and unfossiliferous limestone, known as cornstones; and it has yielded remains of *Pteraspis* and *Cephalaspis* among fishes; also *Pterygotus* and *Stylonurus* among crustacea.

The rocks are exposed along the western side of the Malvern range, and along the borders of the Teme at Tenbury. At Cradley, west of Malvern, the sandstones have been quarried for building-stone.

The soil is variable, but much of it is a fertile loam suitable for hop-gardens and orchards. East of Tenbury there are masses of tufa or travertin derived from the cornstones of the Old Red Sandstone, and which have been accumulated in narrow dells at the Southstone Rock and near Spouthouse Farm.[1]

The Lower Old Red Sandstone, as previously remarked, is quite conformable with the Silurian. The earth-movements affected both formations; but Prof. Groom is of opinion that the Malvern range arose later on between the Middle and Upper Coal Measures.[2] Near Bewdley, in the Trimpley anticline which may be regarded as a northerly prolongation of the Malvern-Abberley range, the Old Red Sandstone has been folded and probably to some extent thrust over the Coal Measures. According to Mr. T. C. Cantrill the movement advanced from the south-east, and was effected apparently during the period of the Upper Coal Measures.[3]

The Upper Old Red Sandstone, which contains beds of quartzose conglomerate as well as sandstone, is not exposed in our district.

COAL MEASURES

Portions of the Forest of Wyre coalfield are included in Worcestershire, and they comprise a wooded tract extending westwards from Bewdley and southwards towards the Abberley Hills.

The formation is made up of a series of sandstones, grits and shales, with bands of *Spirorbis*-limestone and a few seams of coal and ironstone. The beds rest irregularly on the Old Red Sandstone, and attain a thickness of from 200 to about 1,700 feet. The strata are much disturbed, and they are locally altered by the intrusion of a sill or dyke of fine-grained basalt, an igneous rock which forms a ridge at Shatterford, and occurs for some distance in the country east of Upper Arley.

The coal-seams are thin, sulphurous, and of poor quality in the Worcestershire region, where the beds belong mainly to the Upper Coal Measures, but they have been worked at Pensax, Abberley, Mamble, Arley Wood and Shatterford. A boring near Dowles Brook was carried

---

[1] Murchison, *Proc. Geol. Soc.*, vol. ii. p. 78.
[2] *Quart. Journ. Geol. Soc.*, vols. lv. p. 157, lvi. p. 165.
[3] 'A Contribution to the Geology of the Wyre Forest Coalfield,' 8vo, *Kidderminster*, 1895, pp. 13, 16, 36.

to a depth of 1,200 feet with unsatisfactory results : salt water filled the bore-hole. Another boring at Arley Colliery, near Bewdley, was carried to a depth of 1,350 feet, and then reached a basaltic rock like that of Shatterford.[1]

Sections of the sandstones and shales are exposed on the banks of the Severn between Bewdley and Upper Arley. At Shatterford the basalt dyke is quarried for road-metal, while some of the sandstones furnish good building-stone.

Attention was first called by E. W. Binney to the occurrence of *Spirorbis*-limestone : this comprises thin grey, black and brown lime-stones, which contain the Annelide *Spirorbis pusillus*.

In the sandstones, and more particularly in the shales, remains of ferns, also *Stigmaria*, *Calamites*, and fish-remains occur.

Exposures of Upper Coal Measures occur on either side of Rubery Hill in the Lower Lickey, resting on the Cambrian quartzite and Silurian rocks, but they are not of particular economic importance. In this region strata of the age of the Coal Measures probably occur over a larger area than is shown on the map, as certain so-called Permian strata, are now recognized as Coal Measures.[2]

Portions of the South Staffordshire coalfield, the 'Black Country,' occur in the county of Worcester, between Dudley, Halesowen and Stourbridge. Here the general sub-divisions are thus noted by Prof. Lapworth :[3]—

		Feet.
Upper Coal Measures	Red and grey shales and sandstones with *Spirorbis*-limestone . . . . Halesowen Sandstones . . . . Red clays with sandstone and conglomerate	600 to 1,000
Lower Coal Measures	Grey and white sandstones, clays, shales, and beds of coal and ironstone .	500 to 1,050

Of special interest is the great Ten-yard seam or Thick coal, which in the southern part of the coalfield is made up of about fourteen seams of coal, elsewhere parted by unproductive strata, and attaining 500 or 600 feet in total thickness.

Some dykes and sills of igneous rock (dolerite) occur in the Coal Measures near Dudley, as at Rowley Regis, but these are rather outside the boundaries of the county.

In this important coalfield, as in the case of the Forest of Wyre, the Coal Measures rest in part directly on Old Red Sandstone, and in part on the Silurian rocks. Prior to the general disturbance of the strata and the production of the anticline of Dudley, the Coal Measures rested in places on the tilted and worn surface of the Silurian, and, as remarked by

---

[1] See D. Jones, *Trans. Manchester Geol. Soc.*, vol. x. p. 37 ; *Geol. Mag.* for 1871, p. 200, for 1873, p. 350 ; and *Trans. Fed. Inst. Mining Eng.*, vol. vii. p. 287 ; G. E. Roberts, *Geologist*, vol. iv. pp. 421, 468 ; T. C. Cantrill, 'Geol. Wyre Forest,' *op. cit.*, and *Coll. Guard.*, vol. lxxi. (1896) p. 351 ; Symonds, *Records of the Rocks*, p. 385.

[2] See W. Gibson in *Summary of Progress of Geological Survey* for 1898, p. 124.

[3] *Proc. Geol. Assoc.*, vol. xv. p. 366 ; see also J. B. Jukes, 'The South Staffordshire Coal-field,' *Mem. Geol. Survey*, ed. 2, 1859.

Jukes, the unconformity was distinct, although the discordance was not very striking.

Of especial importance in the region is the Fire-clay, mined at King's Swinford and Old Swinford, near Stourbridge, for the manufacture of fire-bricks, saggers, crucibles, etc. Fire-clay is one of the kinds of impure clay in the Coal Measures, and is usually regarded as an ancient exhausted soil. The clay, in consequence, will bear intense heat without melting, because of the small amount of lime, protoxide of iron and alkalies contained in it.[1]

Many plant-remains have been obtained in the South Staffordshire coalfield from the shaly beds, notably giant club-mosses (*Lepidodendron* and *Sigillaria*), horse-tails (*Calamites*), and sundry ferns. Freshwater or estuarine mollusca such as *Anthracosia* also occur ; and there are marine fossils, such as *Aviculopecten*, *Lingula*, etc., as well as fishes, such as *Megalichthys*, which have been found in some of the ironstone bands belonging to the Lower Coal Measures.

PERMIAN

Throughout the greater part of the country there is a marked break between the Coal Measures and the succeeding deposits of Red rocks, the lowest portion of which is grouped as Permian. This unconformity is conspicuous along the eastern side of the exposed coal-fields of Derbyshire, Yorkshire and Durham. In the Dudley district we find that the so-called Permian rocks are nowhere distinctly unconformable to the Coal Measures, and at one time they generally overspread the area.

The Permian is divided into :—

	Feet.
Upper Sandstones and marls (local)	300
Breccia, sandstones and marls, with beds of calcareous conglomerate	200 to 500
Lower Sandstones and marls	500 to 850

The mass of the Lower Sandstones and marls and some higher beds have in recent years been proved to contain not only occasional layers of limestone with *Spirorbis*, but also thin coal-seams. They evidently constitute a portion of the Upper Coal Measures. Mr. T. C. Cantrill indeed is inclined to regard the whole series up to the Upper Sandstones and marls, a series which may be 1,500 feet thick, as belonging to the Upper Coal Measures.[2]

The breccia of the Clent Hills, which is reckoned to be about 450 feet thick, forms a bold range of hills rising to a height of 1,028 feet. The breccia is overlaid by the Bunter pebble-beds and the range extends by Romsley to Bromsgrove Lickey, which is about 900 feet high. At Northfield the strata are well exposed.

[1] See Analysis in Percy's *Metallurgy*, vol. i. p. 98.
[2] *Quart. Journ. Geol. Soc.*, vol. li. pp. 530–533, and *Coll. Guard.*, vol. lxxiii. (1897) p. 581 ; see also W. W. King, *Quart. Journ. Geol. Soc.*, vol. lv. p. 97.

Phillips, in describing the Malvern and Abberley region, gave to the breccia the name Haffield Conglomerate, from the locality west of Bromesberrow and south of Ledbury, where the rock is well exposed. It occurs at Warshill Camp, west of Kidderminster, Stagbury Hill, west of Stourport, at Abberley Hill, Woodbury Hill, near Knightsford Bridge, at Alfrick and Howlers Heath at the southern end of the Malvern range. In this region it rests partly against Silurian and older rocks, partly on Coal Measures, but everywhere unconformably. Elsewhere in places it is underlain by red marls and sandstones, and overlain with apparent conformity by the upper Permian Marls and the Bunter Sandstone and pebble-beds.

Geologically, the greatest interest attaches to the breccia. It was originally termed 'Trappoid Breccia,' because the included fragments are mostly igneous rocks. It comprises a red and purplish marly matrix with angular and sub-angular blocks up to 2 feet in diameter, mainly of volcanic grits and lavas, with also quartzite, sandstone and limestone.

Ramsay in 1855 expressed the opinion that the Permian breccias of the Bromsgrove Lickey and Clent Hills were the morainic matter of glaciers scattered in the Permian sea by icebergs.[1]

Jukes at the time hesitated to accept this view, believing that the fragments might have been derived from adjacent rocks now concealed under the red rocks of the neighbourhood[2]; so likewise did the Rev. W. S. Symonds.[3] Their views are supported nowadays. By Mr. W. Wickham King and Mr. R. D. Oldham[4] the breccias are considered to have been derived from scree-material and the stones to have been more or less rolled by streams and torrents which bore them away from the hill slopes. Whether part of the talus was of glacial origin, or whether the striæ found on the stones were produced during the slipping of scree-material, or were derived from ancient slickensided surfaces may be questioned. We need not, however, restrict our explanations to one mode of action.

It is held by Prof. Groom and others that the fragments were not mainly derived from the old rocks of Malvern and Abberley, nor were the strata deposited against a shore line of those hills. Land may have existed east of the Malverns and the talus may thence have been derived. Prof. Lapworth states that the prevalent rock-fragments resemble the old Uriconian volcanic series, representatives of which occur at Barnt Green and on the Herefordshire Beacon.[5] Other fragments may have come from the Lickey quartzite and the May Hill Sandstone.

In the calcareous conglomerates, which were formed somewhat earlier than the breccias, there are many limestone pebbles derived from Carboniferous and Silurian rocks.

---

[1] *Quart. Journ. Geol. Soc.*, vol. xi. p. 186.
[2] 'The South Staffordshire Coal-field,' *Mem. Geol. Survey*, ed. 2, 1859, p. 15.
[3] *Records of the Rocks*, p. 409.
[4] King, *Midland Nat.*, vol. xvi. p. 25; *Quart. Journ. Geol. Soc.*, vol. lv. p. 97; and R. D. Oldham, *ibid.* vol. l. p. 470.
[5] *Proc. Geol. Assoc.*, vol. xv. p. 373.

GEOLOGY

In the opinion of Phillips, the movement affecting the relations of the Malvern ridge and adjacent New Red rocks was not completed until after the deposition of much of the New Red series.   He saw marks of movement like 'the scratchings and smoothings of glaciers' on some of the North Malvern rocks and on the stones of the Haffield Conglomerate[1]; and it may be noted that the great fault which was traced along the eastern margin of Malvern by Mr. H. H. Howell is evidently one of a date subsequent to the Lias.

In the region of the Lickey Hills, Mr. Walcot Gibson found evidence of earth-movements older than the Trias, and later than the Coal Measures.

TRIAS

The Triassic beds have been divided as follows :—

Rhætic.

Keuper { Red and variegated marl, with bands of sandstone.
{ White and brown sandstone, with calcareous conglomerate at base.

Bunter { Upper brick-red and mottled sandstone.
{ Pebble-beds.
{ Lower brick-red and mottled sandstone.

Of these rocks the Keuper and Bunter occur over a large area in Worcestershire.

The Bunter Sandstones are usually soft and unsuitable for building-stone ; they are fine-grained, false-bedded sandstones, brick-red in colour, but mottled with yellow or white.   Some of the lower beds are locally hardened by carbonate of lime, and they stand out in rocky form at Kinver Edge, west of Stourbridge, just beyond the confines of the county. The lower beds appear at Wribbenhall, and the upper beds extend from Stourport by Churchill to Stourbridge, and again from near Hagley to Blackwell, on the north of Bromsgrove.

The Pebble-beds, which form a middle division in the series, comprise for the most part a mass of brown and liver-coloured quartzites. The beds form an escarpment in the area from Bewdley to the west of Kidderminster and Blakeshall north of Wolverley ; and they occur south of the Clent and Lickey Hills.   The soil as a rule is light and sterile.

Fossils of Ordovician (Lower Silurian) age have been found in the pebbles.   One form is *Orthis budleighensis*, which occurs also in the quartzites of the Triassic pebble-bed of Budleigh Salterton, in Devonshire. There is evidently a variety of stones in the Bunter beds.   Some apparently are of May Hill Sandstone, some are Devonian, and some may belong to the Lickey and Hartshill quartzites.   The locality whence they have been mainly derived and their method of formation are questions concerning which there is great diversity of opinion.[2]

---

[1] Pamphlet on *The Geology of the Malvern Hills*, 8vo (Worcester), 1855, p. 13.
[2] See Lapworth, *Proc. Geol. Assoc.*, vol. xv. p. 382 ; and T. G. Bonney, *Quart. Journ. Geol. Soc.*, vol. lvi. p. 299.

On the whole the Bunter beds rest unconformably on all the rocks below them, less conspicuously so on the Permian, the discordance between these not being of very pronounced character, although in places the Permian was no doubt uplifted and denuded prior to or during the Bunter period. There is no evidence, according to Prof. Groom, that the Malvern and Abberley ranges ever formed the margin of Triassic waters; but it is maintained by Mr. Gibson that in the Lickey region the older rocks then formed a ridge around which the red rocks were accumulated.[1]

The Bunter Sandstone occurs over a considerable area at and near Stourport, Kidderminster and Stourbridge, and also to the south of the Clent Hills.

The Keuper Sandstone, which is largely quarried as a building-stone, forms an escarpment above the softer Bunter Sandstones, due as observed by Mr. T. C. Cantrill to its greater power of resisting denudation.[2] He describes the lower part as a coarse, thick-bedded, reddish-brown sandstone, with occasional quartz pebbles and hard calcareous bands. It is generally conformable to the Bunter, and occurs over a large area at Bromesberrow south of the Malvern range, and again near Martley, Ombersley, and east of Stourport to Hagley and Clent, and around Bromsgrove.

Remains of the fish *Dipteronotus* have been recorded from the Lower Keuper Sandstone of Bromsgrove, and elsewhere remains of the amphibian *Labyrinthodon*. Other fish-remains, plant-remains, and *Estheria minuta* have been discovered. Fossils, however, are exceedingly rare.

Both the Bunter and Keuper Sandstones, as well as the Bunter Pebble-beds, are water-bearing strata, and considerable supplies are usually obtainable from them. The ground in general is light and dry at the surface, and the scenery is pleasantly diversified with woodland and pasture, orchard and ploughed land. As a residential district it is much to be preferred to the area of the red marls.

The Keuper Marls form an undulating plain, for the most part under cultivation, of meadow and pasture lands, orchards and ploughed fields. The village of Redmarley d'Abitot, which is partly on Old Red Sandstone and partly on Keuper Marl, evidently takes its name from the nature of the soil. The Keuper Marl extends along the eastern side of Malvern over Malvern Chase and the country near Upton-on-Severn, Kempsey, Worcester and Droitwich, to Redditch and Moseley near Birmingham. The strata consist of red and variegated marls or clays, analysis showing but a small proportion of carbonate of lime.[3]

Occasional and impersistent bands of sandstone occur in the marls, as at Longdon, Eldersfield and Inkberrow, and these are of sufficient importance to be quarried in places. Scattered over the surface of the vale of the Severn are numerous patches of gravel and sand, and these yield

[1] *Summary of Progress of Geological Survey* for 1898, p. 125.
[2] *Geol. Mag.* for 1895, p. 265.
[3] G. Maw, *Quart. Journ. Geol. Soc.*, vol. xxiv. p. 371.

the local supplies of water to the villages and farm-houses, sources which are liable to pollution in populous places through surface contamination.

Pseudomorphous crystals of rock salt have been occasionally found in the Keuper Sandstones, while in the Keuper Marls the presence of rock salt is indicated by the occurrence of brine springs.

These springs in Worcestershire have been known since the Roman occupation, but the deeper-seated and stronger springs were not proved until much later, that of Droitwich in 1725, and Stoke Prior in 1829. At Stoke Prior a shaft was sunk and a small amount of rock salt obtained; subsequently a boring was carried to a considerable depth. At Droitwich a shaft has been sunk 80 feet and a boring carried to a total depth of 210 feet through soil, drift, red marl and gypsum, and red marl with rock salt. Here as at Stoke Prior the deeper borings now extend to about 1,000 feet. At both localities the brine is copious, and when not kept down by pumping, it rises to the surface. At Droitwich the town and neighbourhood have been affected by the pumping from the brine-pits, and subsidences have occurred through the loss of material underground.[1]

H. E. Strickland in 1842 drew attention to some old salt works on Defford Common, mentioning that seventy years previously (about 1770) a shaft was sunk to a depth of 175 feet, and that brine then overflowed. The lowest bed penetrated was the grey marl of the Triassic series, which occurs on top of the red marl.[2] Saline water has been encountered at Aberton, north-east of Pershore, the village being situated on a faulted junction between the Red Marl and Lower Lias. A salt well to the south of Dudley, known as Lady Wood Saline Spa, is situated on the Coal Measures.

The red marls and sandstones were deposited in desert regions with inland salt lakes, the area being subject to wet and dry seasons; in the former the clayey or marly sediments were laid down, in the latter the rock salt was precipitated.[3] It is not unlikely that some of the sandy Triassic layers were drifted by winds, especially those which are remarkably false-bedded.

On top of the Keuper Marls we find a series of passage-beds which connect the Triassic with the Liassic formations. These are the Rhætic Beds, so named from the Rhætian Alps in the Tyrol, and they indicate the incoming of marine conditions, perhaps locally in the form of a large inland sea like the Caspian.

The Rhætic Beds occur in the outliers south of Upton-on-Severn, and at Bushley on the right bank of the Severn.

Their main outcrop lies on the left bank of the Severn from Hill Crome northwards to Norton near Worcester, and Dunhampstead, where the beds are shifted by faults. They occur also north and west of

[1] J. Dickinson, *Report on Landslips in Salt Districts*, 1873.
[2] *Proc. Geol. Soc.*, vol. iii. p. 732.
[3] See T. Ward, *Trans. Manchester Geol. Soc.*, vol. xviii. p. 396.

Evesham and near Cleeve Prior, as well as in outlying portions of the county further east.

The general sequence of the strata is as follows :—

Rhætic	Thin limestone and shale.
	Black shales with pyrites and bands of white or brown micaceous sandstone, which locally become thicker at or near the base ; with *Pullastra arenicola, Pecten valoniensis*, about 20 feet.
	Grey or green marls, 20 to 35 feet.
Keuper.	Red and variegated marl.

The occurrence of the 'Bristol Bone Bed' in the shaft previously mentioned at Defford was noticed by Strickland[1]; and specimens indicating its occurrence were found in a well-sinking at Hoblench.

This Bone bed is well seen at Aust Cliff on the Severn shores in Gloucestershire, where it yields bones of saurians and teeth of *Gyrolepis, Acrodus, Ceratodus*, and other fishes.

The best sections that have been observed in Worcestershire are those at Bushley and the railway-cutting at Dunhampstead, described by Strickland, while further interesting details of Dunhampstead have been noted by Mr. W. J. Harrison.[2] Sections of Rhætic beds, near Church Lench, Wood Norton, Cleeve Prior and South Littleton, have also been observed by Mr. R. F. Tomes.

The uppermost beds and their junction with the Lower Lias were exhibited at Croome d'Abitot,[3] and also at Churchill Wood, near Spetchley, as noted by Mr. Harrison. The fossils which mostly occur in the black shales, include the characteristic *Avicula contorta*, also *Cardium rhæticum* and *Pecten valoniensis*.

In the upper beds *Ostrea liassica, Modiola minima, Monotis decussata* and *Estheria minuta* var. *brodieana* have been met with. Locally in eastern Worcestershire the highest bed is a more or less nodular limestone containing the variety of *Estheria minuta*, and in the *Estheria* bed at Garden Cliff, Westbury-on-Severn, the writer has noticed arborescent markings akin to those of the Landscape or Cotham Marble.

The upper layers of the Rhætic beds, and sometimes the lowest beds of the Lias, have in places yielded remains of insects, and the term 'Insect Limestones' was applied to them by the Rev. P. B. Brodie.[4]

In the outlying portion of Worcestershire which extends northwards from Shipston-on-Stour, beds of White Lias locally form the upper part of the Rhætic formation. They occur at Armscot and Newbold Fields near Alderminster, at Whitchurch and Lower Eatington, where according to Mr. Tomes they have been quarried for building-purposes, road-metal, and lime-burning.

Whether the grey or green marls that lie on top of the red and variegated Keuper Marls should be regarded as Keuper or Rhætic, is

---

[1] *Proc. Geol. Soc.*, vol. iii. pp. 314, 586 ; *Trans. Geol. Soc.*, ser. 2, vol. vi. p. 551.
[2] *Proc. Dudley Geol. Soc.*, vol. iii. p. 115.
[3] H. B. Woodward, 'Lias of England and Wales,' *Geol. Survey*, p. 147.
[4] *A History of the Fossil Insects*, pp. 56, etc., 1845.

one of those vexed questions that is really of little consequence. There is not the least doubt that the Rhætic Beds are passage-beds between the Trias and Lias, but they are generally grouped in this country, as abroad, with the Trias. Curiously enough there is evidence in the vicinity of Bridgend in South Wales of red marly beds on the horizon of the black Rhætic shales, showing that conditions similar to those which attended the deposition of the Keuper Marls locally occurred in Rhætic times. This fact has lately been brought into notice by Mr. R. H. Tiddeman.

It is worthy of remark that while beds of White Lias occur near Shipston-on-Stour, as they do at Bath and towards the Mendips, they are nevertheless absent or poorly represented over great part of Gloucestershire and South Worcestershire. A peculiar layer, called the 'Guinea Bed,' has been observed by Mr. Tomes in Warwickshire,[1] and this contains an admixture of Lower Lias with Rhætic fossils. It is not improbable, therefore, that there was locally an irregular overlap of the Rhætic Beds, accompanied by reconstruction of some layers, during the changing conditions which ushered in the Lower Lias.[2]

LIAS AND OOLITES

Following the Rhætic Beds we have the three divisions of the Lias.

A considerable portion of Worcestershire is occupied by the Lower Lias, which consists of a group of argillaceous limestones, overlain by a thick mass of blue and grey clays with only occasional bands of limestone. The basement limestones are exposed along the scarps from Strensham, Hill Croome, Croome d'Abitot, to Stoulton and Hanbury, east of Droitwich, and they extend near the surface over the northern portions of the Lias area in the county, and again at Hasler Hill, near Evesham, Cleeve Prior, and the neighbourhood. Numerous quarries have been opened in the beds, though fewer are now worked than was the case in past times. Outliers occur at Bushley and at Berrow to the south-east of the Malvern range.

These lower beds of limestone, which are interbanded with shales, are not much more than 20 feet in thickness, and some of the layers are fissile and banded. They yield plant-remains, crustacea, such as *Eryon*, also *Ammonites johnstoni*, and in the lowest layers *Pleuromya crowcombeia*, and many examples of *Ostrea liassica*. Remains of the large reptiles *Ichthyosaurus* and *Plesiosaurus* are also found, as well as the fishes *Dapedius* and *Pholidophorus*.

The stone is burnt for lime, while some smooth and even-grained slabs are used for inside paving, others for steps, tombstones, etc. In several localities the surface beds of limestone have been disturbed, a feature to which further reference will be made.

[1] *Quart. Journ. Geol. Soc.*, vol. xvi. p. 394 ; vol. xxxiv. p. 182.
[2] 'Lias of England and Wales,' *Mem. Geol. Survey*, p. 151.

The Lower Lias Clay extends over the vale of Evesham, around Pershore and Great Comberton, to the foot of Bredon Hill, and the northern end of the Cotteswolds. Here fertile meadows and pastures characterize the land, but the stiffness of the calcareous clay is much ameliorated by superficial coverings of sand and gravel ; hence the rich fruit grounds and market gardens near Evesham and Pershore.

Judging by a deep boring at Mickleton in Gloucestershire the full thickness of the Lower Lias is over 950 feet.[1] The several beds are distinguished by successive groups of fossils, as noted in 1840 by Strickland.[2] These groups are characterized by species of Ammonites, and although there is nowhere any definite plane of division in the strata, yet it is convenient to subdivide them into zones, because the relative order of succession of the fossils is maintained over wide areas while the lithological characters and the thicknesses of the strata are subject to change.

Thus above the limestones before-mentioned, which are characterized by *Ammonites planorbis* (or *A. johnstoni*), we have beds characterized by *Ammonites angulatus*, *A. bucklandi*, and *A. semicostatus*. These occur further east of the scarp as at Bredon, Defford, and Besford, and again at Evesham and Hampton, at Chadbury, and east of the Littletons. Higher stages yield *Ammonites obtusus*, *A. oxynotus*, and *A. jamesoni*, as near Pershore, Honeybourne, and Aston Magna ; and again *A. capricornus* should be found along the northern base of Bredon Hill.

A fine series of Lower Lias fossils many of which are now in the British Museum was locally obtained by the late T. J. Slatter, of Evesham.[3] Among the more noteworthy of the Worcestershire fossils are *Lima gigantea*, *Gryphæa arcuata*, fine examples of *Cardinia*, and the rugged bivalve *Hippopodium ponderosum*, also corals of the genus *Heterastræa*.

Saline waters have been encountered in shallow wells at Evesham and Hampton Spa. The villages in most cases are supplied from water held in gravel which occurs in patches over the Lias clay, so that the supplies are not always safe from surface pollution.

The Middle Lias occupies but small areas in Worcestershire, on the northern and eastern slopes of Bredon Hill, and on the slopes of the Cotteswolds near Broadway and Blockley. In these situations it is much obscured by debris from the heights above. It is a somewhat variable formation, 250 feet thick, or more, the lower part comprising micaceous loams, clays and sands, while the upper part is a rock bed of ferruginous and sandy limestone, sometimes termed the Marlstone.

The clays and loams are characterized by *Ammonites margaritatus*, and the rock bed by *A. spinatus*. In this upper bed, which is 8 or

[1] H. B. Woodward, 'Lias of England and Wales,' *Mem. Geol. Survey*, p. 156.
[2] *Proc. Geol. Soc.*, vol. iii. p. 314 ; see also Murchison, *Geol. Cheltenham.* edit. 2, by J. Buckman and H. E. Strickland, 1845
[3] See also Wright, 'Lias Ammonites' (*Palæontographical Soc.*), p. 375 ; and R. Tate, *Quart. Journ. Geol. Soc.*, vol. xxvi. p. 396.

10 feet thick, fossils as a rule are well preserved. Here *Rhynchonella acuta*, *R. tetrahedra* and *Gryphæa cymbium* occur.

Springs are thrown out by clayey beds which often occur at the base of the marlstone rock bed, and again at lower levels when sandy beds rest on loams or clays. The waters are usually somewhat ferruginous. The rock bed is much quarried in some localities for road-metal, and the loams and clays are serviceable for brick-making. The soil is generally fertile, and is well suited for orchards.

The Upper Lias is for the most part a clay formation, having occasional nodules of limestone. A few more persistent bands of limestone occur at the base, and these are associated with about 20 feet of paper shales which are slightly bituminous. The Upper Lias occurs above the marlstone in Bredon Hill and in the Cotteswold Hills, but is seldom well exposed. Its thickness varies from 100 to 120 feet, and it is characterized by *Ammonites serpentinus*, *A. bifrons* and *A. communis*.

The lower beds of the Upper Lias have attracted much attention on the borders of Worcestershire, especially at Alderton (Dumbleton), and our knowledge is largely due to the researches of the Rev. P. B. Brodie,[1] Mr. R. F. Tomes,[2] and others. The beds have yielded saurians, also fishes, such as *Leptolepis*, *Pachycormus* and *Tetragonolepsis*, insects including forms allied to *Libellula*, corals, and cephalopods with the ink-bag preserved.

That the lower beds of the Lower Lias were formed in comparatively shallow water is indicated by the presence of insects and plant remains, as well as large saurians. Mr. Tomes has noted rain-spots on some of the limestone layers, and in one instance he discovered the large wing of a dragon-fly which had been broken through by a spot of rain when lying on an exposed surface of soft calcareous mud. He has also observed distinct evidence of dust having been blown on to these ancient mud-flats. The clayey beds indicate a deeper sea, but this became shallower during the deposition of the Middle Lias and the basement portions of the Upper Lias, and again deeper when the main mass of the Upper Lias clay was spread out.

The dark shales of the Lias sometimes led in old times to fruitless trials for coal as was the case at Hasler Hill, near Evesham, and at Bretforton.[3]

The Inferior Oolite series which forms great part of Bredon Hill, and of the northern Cotteswolds, as at Broadway, Cutsdean and Blockley, comprises at its base a group of sandy and ferruginous beds with concretions of calcareous sandstone. These lower strata form the passage-beds between the Upper Lias and Inferior Oolite, they include the zones of *Ammonites jurensis* and *A. opalinus*, and are known as the Midford Sands, or locally in the Cotteswold Hills as the Cotteswold Sand and Cephalopoda bed. *Rhynchonella cynocephala* is a characteristic fossil.

[1] *Fossil Insects*, p. 55 ; *Quart. Journ. Geol. Soc.*, vol. v. p. 32.
[2] *Geol. Mag.*, 1886, p. 108.
[3] *Memoirs of H. E. Strickland*, pp. 83, 88.

In Worcestershire we have no precise information concerning these strata as they are obscured by a talus of oolitic rubble. Nor have we present the entire mass of the Inferior Oolite which includes not only beds of oolite freestone and marl, but occasional layers of sand and clay, as at Snowshill, south of Broadway, and thick beds of ragstone further south.

The freestone has been quarried in several places on Bredon Hill, and there are good exposures west of Overbury. Much of it is in a very shattered and broken condition, due to excessive weathering which probably dates back to glacial times, when thick accumulations of oolitic rubble were formed along the slopes of the Cotteswold Hills. Some of these shattered masses have been re-cemented by carbonate of lime, an example of which is seen in the Bambury stone.[1]

The freestone which is quarried is a brown more or less shelly and oolitic limestone, in places largely made up of crinoidal fragments. *Ammonites* and *Belemnites* are occasionally met with, also *Trigonia*, *Pecten personatus*, *Terebratula plicata* and *T. perovalis*. The beds probably belong to the zone of *Ammonites murchisonæ*.[2]

Near the Fish Inn, Broadway, the freestones, about 30 feet thick, have also been quarried, and here higher strata are locally faulted against the freestone. These comprise sandy beds, greenish-grey clay, and rubbly limestone with *Clypeus*, *Nerinæa*, etc.

Thick and heavy stone tiles were formerly obtained from the Inferior Oolite at Hyatt's Pitts, near Snowshill. The formation yields a brashy and loamy soil, forming good land for corn and roots, and yielding also much pasture for the famous Cotteswold sheep.

The formation is water-bearing, and copious springs are given out in places, as at Seven Wells, east of Snowshill, at the junction with the Upper Lias clays.

At Daylesford, in an outlying portion of Worcestershire, there are small areas of Lower, Middle, and Upper Lias, Inferior Oolite, and even Great Oolite. In this region the Inferior Oolite has undergone changes, and is represented apparently by only the lowest and highest stages of the formation. There are thin layers of pebbly sand and calcareous sandstone which approximate to the Northampton Sands, and these are overlaid by high beds of Inferior Oolite with *Clypeus ploti* and *Terebratula globata*, and again by hard and somewhat sandy limestones 10 or 12 feet thick, known as the Chipping Norton limestone.

Above this local bed of Inferior Oolite, near Daylesford, there is a small area of Great Oolite, comprising about 3 feet of marly clays with *Ostrea sowerbyi* and *Rhynchonella concinna*, overlaid by flaggy and rubbly oolitic limestones with *Terebratula maxillata* and *Nerinæa*.[3]

---

[1] G. F. Playne, *Proc. Cotteswold Club*, vol. vi. p. 225.
[2] H. B. Woodward, 'Lower Oolitic Rocks of England,' *Mem. Geol. Survey*, pp. 138, 140, 462, etc.
[3] H. B. Woodward, 'Lower Oolitic Rocks of England,' *Geol. Survey*, pp. 153, etc.

GEOLOGY

An immense break in the series occurs between the Great Oolite and the succeeding deposits which are now found in Worcestershire. We miss all the Middle and Upper Oolites, the whole of the Cretaceous and Tertiary strata, and our next records are those of a time when man had probably appeared on the scenes.

In the meanwhile the changes that took place must have been enormous, both as regards the deposition of great masses of strata and their subsequent removal by rain, rivers and sea. There can be little doubt that the Oolites were spread over the Malvern and Lickey areas, in fact over the entire county ; and that they suffered denudation during Upper Cretaceous times, when the Chalk extended far and wide over the country in general. Since then the Chalk has been removed, and the great vale between Malvern and the Cotteswold Hills carved out.

GLACIAL DRIFT, VALLEY DEPOSITS AND ALLUVIUM

We have at present but very imperfect knowledge of the Drift deposits of Worcestershire, or indeed of the Vale of Severn. The latest deposit, the ordinary Alluvium, is composed of silt and mud and gravel brought down by the river since it commenced to flow, much in its present form. It is now liable to be swollen by heavy rains and by rapid thaw after snow, though it is more hampered than at one time by the works of man.

Bordering the river at higher levels are beds of gravel, which extend in patches over a wide area in the Vale of Severn and in the Vale of Evesham.[1] The gravels are made up of quartzite, quartz, slaty rock, flint and Jurassic material.

Some of these patches are old river gravel and brickearth ; they contain *Unio* and other freshwater mollusca, as well as hippopotamus, rhinoceros, mammoth and other mammalian remains. Sections have been opened up at Cropthorne, Fladbury, Bengeworth, Little Comberton, Eckington, Defford, and Pull Court, near Bushley.

Remains of mammoth have been found at Droitwich, and of reindeer at Upton Snodsbury. Again, in what Prestwich has called the ' Rubble Drift,' remains of mammoth and rhinoceros were found in digging the foundations of the Imperial Hotel at Malvern.[2]

Other deposits of gravel and sand in the Severn Vale contain marine shells, or fragments of marine shells, as well as mammalian remains. Among the shell-fragments are those of *Cyprina islandica*, *Cardium edule*, *Lucina borealis*, *Rissoa*, *Turritella terebra* and *Purpura lapillus*. One of the localities is Beckford, and here have been found remains of mammoth, *Rhinoceros antiquitatis*, *Bos taurus* var. *primigenius* and reindeer. At Kempsey, near Worcester, and other places along the Severn Valley below Bewdley, both mammoth and rhinoceros have been found. It is by no means unlikely

---

[1] See T. G. B. Lloyd, *Quart. Journ. Geol. Soc.*, vol. xxvi. p. 204.
[2] *Quart. Journ. Geol. Soc.*, vol. xlviii. p. 317 ; see also *Life and Letters of Prestwich*, 1899, p. 262.

that the fragments of marine shells at these localities are in some, if not all, cases derived from older Glacial gravels, together with many quartzite pebbles and derived Jurassic fossils.

In 1836, Murchison, from the evidences afforded by the recent species of mollusca, suggested 'that the sea must at the time have covered the valley of the Severn from Bridgnorth to the Bristol Channel, thus separating Wales and Siluria on one side from England on the other.'[1] Later on the view of 'The Ancient Straits of Malvern' formed the theme of an essay by James Buckman.[2]

Prestwich, in 1892, remarked: 'There can be little doubt that the sea of the Raised Beach period stretched northward up the Valley of the Severn; but whether it formed a deep bay or estuary, or whether at that time it was prolonged through to the Irish Channel, forming the "Severn Straits" of Murchison, seems uncertain. It is probable that the marine beds at the higher levels should be referred to an earlier stage of the Glacial period.'[3] Mr. W. J. Harrison, however, considers that these recent marine shells were originally derived from a lobe of the 'Irish Sea Glacier' which invaded Shropshire, and which had scraped up the shells from the bed of the Irish Sea.[4] Be this as it may, we can still regard those shell-fragments which we find with the mammoth in the valley drifts as having been redistributed from earlier Drift deposits.

The district, however, is of considerable interest as being on the borders of the large region which was mantled by the ice-sheet during the accumulation of the Great Chalky Boulder Clay of the midland and eastern counties, and which was not affected by any marked glaciation during the later phases of the Glacial period.

The southern limits of the Boulder Clay must be sought to the north of Bredon Hill, the evidences of the ice action being discernible here and there in the Vale of Evesham and in the vale at Aston Magna and Mickleton, where Boulder Clay was observed in 1853 by G. E. Gavey.[5] At the time Mr. R. F. Tomes obtained glaciated Chalk from this Drift. In connection with the discovery, it is interesting to note that pebbles of hard red and white Chalk were found by Buckland in 1821, to the south-east of Shipston-on-Stour.

'Modified Drifts,' in the form of thin scattered drifts with quartzite pebbles, and of valley gravels and loams, succeeded the Boulder Clay, or the melting of the ice which brought it; and these deposits appear to merge into the old alluvial, and, perhaps in part, estuarine deposits of the great Severn Valley.

That the Cotteswolds themselves have not been glaciated, is shown by the thick accumulations of oolitic rubble which flank their slopes.

[1] *Proc. Geol. Soc.*, vol. ii. p. 334.
[2] 8vo, London [1849]; see also W. S. Symonds, *The Severn Straits*, 8vo, Tewkesbury, 1884, and E. Witchell, *Proc. Cotteswold Club*, vol. iv. p. 216.
[3] *Quart. Journ. Geol. Soc.*, vol. xlviii. p. 287.
[4] *Proc. Geol. Assoc.*, vol. xv. p. 404.
[5] *Quart. Journ. Geol. Soc.*, vol. ix. p. 29; see also S. V. Wood, Jun., *ibid.* vol. xxxvi. p. 483; and H. B. Woodward, *Geol. Mag.* for 1897, p. 485.

GEOLOGY

Even the Bredon outlier of Inferior Oolite exhibits at the surface 30 or 40 feet of rubble. The rock, indeed, is irregularly weathered, and the resulting gravelly detritus contains in its midst isolated masses and pinnacles of unweathered limestone.

W. C. Lucy connected the distribution of the rubble with soil-movements, the weathered rock slipping down the hill-sides during times of thaw after severe frost. In Witchell's opinion, this Rubble Drift was ' due to storm-waters or surface-drainage, which brought the detritus down the hill upon a frozen surface, and deposited it in those places where the frost usually disappeared in spring before it left the higher ground.'[1] Both explanations may be to a certain extent true and they accord much better with the facts than does the explanation of Prestwich, whereby this Rubble Drift would be due to the effects of wide submergence.[2]

At Church Honeybourne, east of Evesham, the Lower Lias Clay is contorted, and again at South Littleton the exposed beds of limestone and clay have been nipped up on the surface in a series of sharp folds. As far west as Croome d'Abitot, near Pershore, in Worcestershire, similar evidences of surface disturbance were observed.[3] Probably the ' Lias clay with contorted beds of Lias limestone,' noted in the railway-cutting at Dunhampstead by Strickland in 1840, exhibited features of the same character. At Halford, north of Shipston-on-Stour, the beds of White Lias are much disturbed in places.

In this region, although the disturbances are similar to those produced by glacial action, we have (with the exception of the Aston Magna Drift) no distinct evidence of Boulder Clay, the superficial deposit being a few feet of reddish-brown clay with pebbles of quartz and quartzite. This Drift occurs here and there over a wide area, and may be a result of the denudation of Boulder Clay. Near Birmingham, on the borders of Staffordshire and Worcestershire, there are abundant evidences of Boulder Clay and other Glacial Drifts. At Moseley and on Frankley Hill there are considerable beds of sand and gravel which belong to the Glacial period.

Until the Drifts are separately mapped, it is impossible to deal adequately with the diverse deposits which are scattered over the surface of the country, for the most part in patches, although much has been written on the subject by Strickland, Brodie, W. C. Lucy, H. W. Crosskey, and others.[4]

In the modern Alluvial deposits peaty layers are sometimes met with, and T. G. B. Lloyd noted a bed 8 feet thick, resting on gravel, at Chadbury. In it many antlers of red deer were found. The Alluvial clays have been used for brick-making, while the land in general forms fertile meadows and pasture.

[1] *Proc. Cotteswold Club*, vol. v. p. 43 ; vol. vi. p. 150 ; and H. B. Woodward, *Lower Oolitic Rocks of England*, p. 462.

[2] *Quart. Journ. Geol. Soc.*, vol. xlviii. p. 314.

[3] H. B. Woodward, *Jurassic Rocks of Britain*, vol. iii. pp. 146, 150, 310.

[4] See W. J. Harrison, ' A Bibliography of Midland Glaciology,' *Proc. Birmingham Phil. Soc.*, vol. ix. p. 116 ; also *Proc. Geol. Assoc.*, vol. xv. p. 400.

From what has already been said, it may be inferred that the broad vale forming great part of Worcestershire, which lies between the Malvern and Abberley Hills on the west, the Lickey Hills on the north, and the Cotteswold Hills on the south, has been excavated during Tertiary and subsequent times. We cannot say whether or not any of the Lower Tertiary (Eocene) strata ever extended over the region ; but we may feel confident that since Eocene times the area has more generally been subject to waste by rain and rivers. The Oligocene and Miocene periods were times of warmth and, perhaps, of tropical rains ; while in the Glacial period the scenes had changed to intense cold, with local floods, due to the melting of glacial ice. These changes were gradually brought about during the intervening Pliocene epoch, when the climate was temperate. The material derived from the waste of the Red rocks, Lias and Oolites, in the vale has been mostly borne away to other regions, and the only relics are the scattered Drifts to which we have called attention.

PALÆONTOLOGY

TO the student of the past history of vertebrate life Worcestershire is lacking in the interest which attaches to many English counties, since it possesses no peculiar extinct vertebrate fauna of its own. Indeed, vertebrate remains of any description are comparatively rare within the limits of the county ; this being to some extent accounted for by the circumstance that many of the Worcestershire formations were laid down at a period when vertebrates had not yet made their appearance, while others were deposited when fishes seem to have been the highest type in existence.

Perhaps the greatest palæontological interest in the county is centred in the circumstance that within its borders are found some of the oldest fossils in England, several of which were first determined from Worcestershire specimens. These oldest fossils occur in the Hollybush Sandstone of the Malvern Hills, which belong to the upper division of the Cambrian epoch. The species known are comparatively few in number, and all indicate low types of invertebrate life ; with the exception of worm-tracks, they are comparatively rare, and require much patience to find. Certain transversely wrinkled or plaited flexible tubes, which are usually found crossing the strata obliquely or vertically, have been regarded as indicating tube-dwelling worms, or annelids, for which the name *Trachyderma antiquissimum* has been proposed. Other tubes of a smoother type of structure have been described as *Serpulites fistula*, and apparently indicate a second type of marine tube-dwelling worms. The brachiopods, or lamp-shells, were represented by several small forms. Most of these pertain to totally extinct genera, but the minute *Lingula* (*Lingulella*) *squamosa* belongs to a genus still existing in modern seas. The fossil form (which is distinguished by the presence of a groove in the beak) is very minute, but the existing type, which is a flattened bivalve triangular shell of a green colour and horny consistence, with a flexible stem for attachment, attains a couple of inches in length. An allied family is represented by *Kutorgina cingulata,* a species common to the Upper Cambrian of Canada ; the genus *Kutorgina* differing from the nearly related *Obolella* by the straight hinge-line.[1]

In the overlying black Malvern shales the same species of *Kutorgina* occurs, but the *Lingula* was distinguished by Dr. Holl as *L. pygmæa.*

---

[1] The Hollybush species is described by Dr. H. B. Holl in the *Quart. Journ. Geol. Soc.,* vol. xxi. p. 89, as *Obolella phillipsi* ; the other fossils from this horizon being mentioned in the same paper.

Here, too, are met with several small representatives of those remarkable Palæozoic crustaceans known as trilobites, which take their name from the circumstance that the body, or middle portion of the carapace, is more or less distinctly divided into three longitudinal lobes. Externally trilobites present a distant resemblance to woodlice, but they were marine creatures related to the existing king-crabs of the Moluccas. They are very important to the palæontologist, as their occurrence always indicates that he has to do with Palæozoic rocks. The trilobites from the Malvern shales belong to the genera *Olenus*, *Conocoryphe*, *Sphær-ophthalmus*, and *Agnostus*. In some of the shales the small *Olenus humilis* occurs in such profusion as to have suggested the name of 'Olenus shales' for these particular beds. The green shales overlying the black shales in the neighbourhood of Hayes Copse contain a curious net-like fossil named *Dictyonema socialis*. This presents a considerable superficial resemblance to the modern lace-corals, but since its skeleton is not calcareous, and bears cups for the reception of polyps, it is considered to belong to the same group as the recent sertularians, or hydroid polyps.

The invertebrate Silurian fossils of Worcestershire, although much more numerous in species than those of the Cambrian (and in certain localities exceedingly abundant in individuals), require somewhat less detailed notice than those of the last-named period for the reason that they are for the most part identical with those of the neighbouring counties. A large series of these fossils were collected by the late Dr. Grindrod, of Malvern, which are now in the Museum at Oxford, and there is also a fine collection in the Museum of the Malvern Field Club.

Like those of other counties, the Silurian rocks of Worcestershire are characterized by the abundance of brachiopods, or lamp-shells, and cephalopods, or chambered molluscs ; gastropods, or ordinary univalve molluscs, and bivalves[1] being much less abundant. In the May Hill Sandstone (Upper Llandovery), which takes its title from the hill of that name in Gloucestershire, two very characteristic fossils are *Pentremites oblongus* and *P. lens*, both easily recognizable by having vertical partitions within the valves ; they often occur in the form of casts. Other brachiopods from this formation are *Atrypa reticularis*, *Orthis protensa*, *O. calli-gramma*, *Strophomena compressa*, *S. antiquata*, and *Stricklandinia*. Of these *Atrypa* and *Stricklandinia* are the most common. The two species of *Pentamerus* and *Orthis calligramma* occur in the May Hill Sandstone of the Lickey Hills, near Bromsgrove. Gastropods are represented by the nautilus-like *Bellerophon* and the spiral *Murchisonia* ; while the cephalopods include the long, straight *Orthoceras barrandei* and the less common *Tretoceras bisiphonatum*. Among tube-dwelling worms we have *Tentaculites ornatus* and *Cornulites serpularia*. Trilobites, too, are abundant, but none are peculiar to this particular formation, such forms as *Calymene blumenbachi* and *Phacops stokesi* having a large vertical

---

[1] Strictly speaking, lamp-shells are also bivalves, but in these the two valves are front and back, instead of right and left.

PALÆONTOLOGY

range in the Silurian. At Dudley *Calymene blumenbachi* is very numerous, and locally known as 'the locust.' Of the corals, it will suffice to mention the simple cup-shaped *Petræa elongata* and the more complex *Favosites* and *Heliolites*.

Of the Woolhope limestone the fossils are generally the same as those of the overlying Wenlock beds, but there are two peculiar trilobites, respectively known as *Homalonotus delphinocephalus* and *Illænus barriensis* ; whether, however, these actually occur within the limits of the county it is difficult to ascertain. On the western flanks of the Malverns the Wenlock limestone and shale, especially the latter, are exceedingly rich in fossils, but since Worcestershire is not the typical area for this formation, mention need be made of only a few. In the limestones the sponge-like *Stromatopora*, and corals of the genera *Omphyma* (cup-coral), *Heliolites*, *Halysites* (chain-coral), *Favosites*, and *Cyathophyllum* are exceedingly abundant. Those curious Palæozoic organisms known as graptolites also occur ; they consist of a tubular shaft on one or both sides of which are small cups for the reception of the polypites. Echinoderms of a primitive type, many of which were stalked (stone-lilies), are also common. Trilobites are represented by the genera *Acidaspis*, *Encrinurus*, *Calymene*, *Lichas*, *Phacops*, *Homalonotus*, etc. ; and many curious jaws of annelid worms have also been discovered. Among the lamp-shells we have representatives of the straight-hinged genera *Strophomena*, *Pentamerus*, *Spirifera*, *Orthis*, *Atrypa*, etc., but in the absence of figures there would be little use in enumerating the various species by which these and other generic types are represented. A few genera of bivalve molluscs occur, as well as gastropods of the Palæozoic genera *Euomphalus*, *Murchisonia*, *Bellerophon*, etc.

Since the Ludlow and Aymestry beds, forming the top of the Silurian, as well as the Old Red Sandstone, are but poorly represented in the county, no special mention need be made of their fossils. Neither would any advantage be gained by referring in detail to the vegetable and other fossils of the Forest of Wyre coalfield, which are, at least for the most part, identical with those of the English Coal Measures generally. It may be mentioned, however, that ferns presenting a network arrangement of the veins (a somewhat rare type) have been described by the late Professor John Morris[1] from a shaly sandstone near Kidderminster, and assigned to the genus *Woodwardites*. A shale bed near Dowles Brook is remarkable for the number of impressions of fern-leaves it contains.

The Permian beds of the county appear mostly unfossiliferous ; while the Triassic (inclusive of Rhætic) strata contain very few invertebrate fossils. The Upper Keuper Sandstone of Pendock yields, however, the bivalve-like shells of the little crustacean known as *Estheria minuta*. As regards the Lower Lias of the county, it must suffice to say that its fossils are for the most part those of this formation generally. An exception must, however, be made with regard to the so-called

[1] *Quart. Journ. Geol. Soc.*, vol. xv. p. 80.

Strensham group, which takes its title from the village of that name east of Upton-on-Severn. From these particular beds the late Rev. P. B. Brodie succeeded in obtaining a number of insect remains of great interest.[1]

Of the vertebrate fossils of Worcestershire by far the most important are the primitive fishes of the lower portion of the Old Red Sandstone. Since, however, only a very small area of the county is occupied by this formation, the number of species of these fishes that have actually been discovered within its limits falls considerably short of those known from Ledbury and Cradley, in Herefordshire, where excellent sections of these strata are exposed. On the other hand, all these Old Red Sandstone fishes may really be regarded as pertaining to the Worcestershire fauna, since it must be largely due to accident that specimens of the whole of them have not hitherto been found within its borders ; and some of the Cradley section runs into the county.

Most of these fishes belong to an entirely distinct group, which ceased to exist before the close of the Palæozoic epoch, and are characterized by the head and body being enveloped in a bony cuirass, and the imperfect ossification of the internal skeleton. The group is collectively known as the Ostracodermi, but is divided into three sections. Among the first section, in which the head and fore part of the body were protected by a bony shield while the hinder half of the body and tail were covered by small angular plates or scales, remains of *Pteraspis rostrata* have been discovered at Heightington and Trimpley, and those of *Pt. crouchi* at the first-named place. This second section, in which the head assumes a different form, and is shaped like a bent cheese-cutter, is represented by *Cephalaspis lyelli* and *C. salweyi* in the Lower Old Red Sandstone of Heightington ; the former being typically a Scottish species, while the latter is confined to the west of England. A totally different Palæozoic group of fish-like creatures is that of the berry-bone fishes, or Arthrodira, of which the typical representative is the well-known *Coccosteus* of the Scottish Old Red Sandstone. In these strange creatures the armour, which is confined to the head and fore part of the body, has the external surface like coarse shagreen ; and although there were no pectoral fins, the pelvic pair were well developed. The group is represented in the Old Red Sandstone of the county by *Phlyctænaspis anglica*, a species first described on the evidence of Herefordshire specimens. Another Herefordshire Old Red Sandstone fish, *Climatius ornatus*, belonging to a group of primitive sharks known as Acanthodii, also occurs in the corresponding formation of the county.

In the Carboniferous rocks fish remains appear to be very scarce, but a tooth from Bewdley in the British Museum indicates a pavement-toothed shark belonging to the family *Cochliodontidæ*. In the Keuper such remains are less uncommon, and the species *Acrodus keuperinus*, a pavement-toothed shark of the family *Cestraciontidæ*, has been named on the evidence of Worcestershire specimens which occur at Pendock, Ripple,

---

[1] See Brodie, *Fossil Insects* (1845).

PALÆONTOLOGY

and Burgehill. A tooth in the British Museum from the upper Ripple has been described as a new species of barramunda, under the name of *Ceratodus lævissimus*, but is now regarded as probably identical with the continental *C. kaupi*. The existing barramunda, it may be observed, is a large air-breathing fish restricted to the rivers of Queensland. A fossil fish from the Keuper of Bromsgrove, now preserved in the Museum of the Geological Survey, has been described as a new genus and species of ganoid under the name of *Deuteronotus cyphus*, but is now believed to be referable to some member of the genus *Chlithrolepis*. The list of fishes closes with *Phæbodus brodiei*, a primitive shark of the group Ichthyotomi, named after the late Rev. P. B. Brodie. This species is known only by two teeth in the British Museum, one of which (the type) was obtained from the Upper Keuper of Warwickshire, and the second from the Lower Keuper of Pendock.

So far as the writer is aware, reptilian remains do not appear to have been obtained from the Worcestershire Keuper, but certain tracks met with in these beds may have been made by the Triassic lizard *Rhynchosaurus*. From the Lower Lias of Brockeridge and Defford Commons, which are situated on the southern side of the county near Tewkesbury, numerous bones of *Ichthyosaurus*, and perhaps also of *Plesiosaurus*, have been obtained, but these reptilian remains seem never to have been specifically determined. The British Museum has, however, part of the skeleton of an *Ichthyosaurus* from near Tewkesbury which has been assigned to *Ichthyosaurus tenuirostris*, and may possibly have been obtained in Worcestershire. In any case, it may be taken as certain that these Worcestershire *Ichthyosauri* belong to the same species as those whose remains are so common in the Lower Lias of Dorsetshire.

The only other vertebrate remains met with in the county appear to be those of Pleistocene mammals from the river gravels of the Severn valley. These doubtless belong to the ordinary species of the epoch. Mr. D. Mackintosh[1] recording the mammoth (*Elephas primigenius*), woolly rhinoceros (*Rhinoceros antiquitatis*), and reindeer (*Rangifer tarandus*) from a bed of estuarine sand and gravel, and the straight-tusked elephant (*Elephas antiquus*) and the Pleistocene hippopotamus (*Hippopotamus amphibius major*) from an underlying deposit.

[1] *Quart. Journ. Geol. Soc.*, vol. xxxvi. p. 181 (1880).

BOTANY

GENERAL PHYSICAL CHARACTER OF THE COUNTY WITH RELATION TO THE FLORA

THE outline of Worcestershire is exceedingly irregular, and not only is this the case, but several detached portions lie outside the main body as islands in neighbouring counties, the largest of these being Dudley in the north and Shipston and Blockley in the south-east. The county may not inaptly be compared in shape to that of a vine-leaf, of which a few fragments have been broken off and scattered near it. And this simile is the more apt because with slight exceptions the whole of the county lies in the watershed of the Severn, which river, running roughly from north to south, divides it into two unequal parts ; and if we place the leaf with the stem downwards, the venation may roughly represent the tributary streams. Those portions of the county which are not within the basin of the Severn are the extreme north-east, including the north-eastern slopes of the Lickey, where the water runs into the Rea, and so into the Trent ; and the detached portions in the south-east, which are drained by the Evenlode, and are in the valley of the Thames. Another peculiarity may be noticed. Nearly all round, with the exception of the north-west, where the Severn enters the county, the north-east, where the county borders upon Warwickshire, and the south-west, where the Severn leaves it, the margin is higher than the centre ; so we may carry our simile further, and place our vine-leaf in a saucer, parts of the lip of which have been broken away.

While the central portion of the county, the wide vale of the Severn, consists of marl overlaid in places with gravelly drift, the higher land towards the margins is mostly of different geological formations. On the west is the long range of the Malvern Hills, rising to the height of 1,394 feet, and composed of plutonic rock with Silurian deposits on their western sides. The county boundary runs for the most part along the summits of these hills, but extends sometimes down the western slopes. Towards Abberley in the north the Malvern range meets the Old Red Sandstone of Herefordshire, on which is situated the district towards Tenbury in the north-west of the county. To the east of Abberley is an extent of New Red Sandstone stretching out to Clent, where the Clent Hills, composed of Permian breccias and sandstones, rise to a height of over 1,000 feet, and are bounded on the north by the coal measures, through which the Silurian rocks of Dudley protrude. Hence

to the north-eastern extremity of the county the boundary sweeps round over New Red Sandstone in a wide semicircle, between the points of which, on Warwickshire soil, stands the city of Birmingham. From the north-eastern corner the boundary turns suddenly in a nearly southerly direction over the Red Marl, until in the neighbourhood of Inkberrow it passes on to the Lias formation, having enclosed the Bromsgrove Lickey, with all its curious variety of geological structure, where the Beacon Hill rises to a height of 956 feet. Below Inkberrow the boundary meets the Avon, and, crossing the river, plunges into the hilly district of the Cotswolds, becoming extremely irregular, and stretching down to the south-east, where a number of isolated portions of the county reach to within some fifteen miles of Oxford. Here a section of the Oolitic system is brought within the limits of Worcestershire. The south-eastern promontory of the mainland of the county is Broadway, which rises at the Beacon to 1,024 feet. The southern boundary of the county is perhaps the most irregular of all, Worcestershire and Gloucestershire penetrating each other in great lobes ; it crosses Bredon Hill, 848 feet high, and, sinking down to the level of the Severn at Tewkesbury, bends sharply back to leave the parish of Twyning to Gloucestershire ; and after more irregularities, having crossed the Severn, turns to the north at Redmarley d'Abitot, and meets again the Malvern Hills.

The surface of Worcestershire generally is undulating and diversified, the only portion of comparatively flat land being that known as the Vale of Evesham, largely occupied at the present time with market gardens. In the south and west of the county hops are largely cultivated, a few hopyards only being found to the east of Worcester. Apple and pear orchards are a feature of the same districts ; and these trees grow not only in orchards, but are scattered thickly in the hedgerows. No orchards, however, occur in the north and east of the county, and with them disappear also hedgerow trees of the same kind. Here also the mistletoe, so plentiful in the orchards of the west, and on poplars and other kinds of trees, is quite unknown. The feature of the hedgerow timber of Worcestershire is the small-leaved elm, *Ulmus campestris*, which flourishes to such an extent in the red marl and sandstone that it has gained the name of the ' Worcestershire weed.'

In the north-east of the county the general level rises considerably, and encloses the Lickey Hills, which are an island of altered Cambrian rock rising out of Red Sandstone and Permian formations. The aspect of this part of the county, with that of the Permian and coal measures further to the north, is markedly bleaker and colder than that of the valley of the Severn. On the Lickey the bilberry flourishes, and the hills are clothed with ling and heather, all plants that are unknown in south-east Worcestershire. The holly grows extensively on the lower slopes of these hills, and the hedgerows sometimes for considerable distances are formed exclusively of this plant. *Ulex Gallii* flourishes abundantly on this high land, as it does throughout the county where the height is some 500 feet above the sea, except in the Cotswold district.

BOTANY

The place of the elm as hedgerow timber is taken by the oak, which however does not usually grow to any great size. Sycamores grow finely on the southern slopes of the hills, and the hornbeam occurs occasionally in the neighbourhood of Bromsgrove. Traveller's joy, *Clematis Vitalba*, which plentifully decks the hedgerows where the soil is at all calcareous, seldom strays on to the New Red Sandstone of the northern parts. Primroses, absolutely abounding in the valley of the Teme, and general˜ elsewhere, thin out as the northern part of the county is approached, where they lurk only on hidden banks and in the thickets of woods, while in the extreme north-east they hardly occur ; but the woods and dingles which clothe the hills in this district are the chosen home of the bluebell and wood-anemone. The roadside wastes and hedgerow banks show little floral decoration after speedwell, stitchwort, and wild parsley have disappeared with the first burst of spring. A feature of the sandstone banks of the north is *Saxifraga granulata*, sometimes occurring most abundantly ; but *Cotyledon Umbilicus*, even in places which seem typical habitats, is unknown except in Habberley Valley and Wolverley near Kidderminster. In many localities on the Red Sandstone, and occurring more sparsely elsewhere, are two somewhat rare plants—*Arabis perfoliata* and *Campanula patula*. The former is especially abundant on the sides of the railway to the north of Kidderminster ; and the latter fringes in quantity the deep railway-cutting through the water-stones to the south of Stourbridge, but entirely disappears to the north-east of the Clent Hills.

There are no natural lakes in Worcestershire, the largest sheets of water being that in Westwood Park, some 60 acres, and Pirton Pool, a few miles to the south of Worcester. But the brooks coming down towards the Stour from the high land at Clent have been formed into chains of pools, usually of no great size. Some large reservoirs have been constructed in the neighbourhood of the Lickey and at Tardebigge to feed the Birmingham Canal. Many marshy spots have been drained, and the plants that love such spots have vanished. Especially is this the case with Longdon Marsh, near Upton-on-Severn, in the south of the county, which in rainy seasons used to assume the appearance of a vast lake. Here grew, and possibly some of them still linger in lesser quantity, *Butomus umbellatus*, *Carex disticha*, *Cnicus pratensis*, *Hippuris vulgaris*, *Lathyrus palustris*, *Lysimachia vulgaris*, *Œnanthe Lachenalii*, *Œ. Peucedanifolia*, *Phragmites communis*, *Poterium officinale*, *Rumex maritimus* and *Scirpus maritimus*. In the far north of the county Moseley Bog, the drainage of which ultimately found its way into the Trent, but the site of which is now nearly covered by extending Birmingham, once produced many rare plants, including *Anagallis tenella*, *Cnicus pratensis*, *Drosera rotundifolia*, *Equisetum sylvaticum*, *Eriophorum vaginatum*, *Hypericum elodes*, *Menyanthes trifoliata*, *Molinia cœrulea*, *Narthecium ossifragum*, *Osmunda regalis*, *Parnassia palustris*, *Pedicularis palustris*, *Potentilla Comarum*, *Rhyncospora alba*, *Vaccinium Oxycoccus* and *Viola palustris*. Some eight miles to the east of Droitwich there formerly existed a tract

of land called Feckenham Bog, long since brought under cultivation. Here have been recorded *Alisma ranunculoides, Anagallis tenella, Cnicus pratensis, Carex distans, Cladium Mariscus, Pinguicula vulgaris, Schœnus nigricans* and *Zannichellia palustris*. All these plants have disappeared. Cradley Park, between Stourbridge and Halesowen, before it became absorbed into the Black Country, nourished some rare plants so lately as 1832, among them *Carex distans, C. strigosa, Pyrola media* and *Sambucus Ebulus*. Of a list of plants growing at the Lickey in 1834, the following, through drainage or other causes, have vanished, *Andromeda polifolia, Erica Tetralix, Parnassia palustris, Potentilla comarum, Vaccinium Oxycoccus* and *Scirpus cæspitosus*. *Anagallis tenella* remained here up to 1890.

In its course through the county the Severn has worn for itself a deep channel in the red marl of the district through which it flows, while above Holt precipitous banks of red sandstone in places bound its course. Below Worcester flat meadows stretch out on either side of the river. The sandstone cliffs are frequently clothed with woodland, notably at Shrawley and Stagbury, below and above Stourport respectively, on its right bank. The red marl banks are not productive of any especially rare plants, except in the case of the Mythe Toot at Tewkesbury, on which precipitous cliff *Isatis tinctoria* flourishes abundantly. This locality, however, though nearly surrounded by Worcestershire territory, is locally in Gloucestershire, and the former county can lay no claim to the plant. At Tewkesbury the Severn receives on its left side the river Avon, which comes down in wide meanders from the Lias country to the north and west of the Cotswolds. No other stream of any size joins the river on the same side till Hawford, some miles above Worcester, is reached. Here it receives the Salwarpe, and by its side the canal from Droitwich, which follows the course of the river. The Salwarpe comes down from the western slopes of the Lickey some fifteen miles away, and is joined below Salwarpe Church by Dordale Brook, which rises in Pepperwood and receives streams from the Randans and Chaddesley Woods. Further to the north, at Stourport, the Stour falls into the Severn on the same side, having been joined at Hoobrook, below Kidderminster, by a number of streams that converge there coming from the higher land in the neighbourhood of Clent ; and on the same side of the Stour, just above Kidderminster, at Broadwaters, more streams from the same district join its course. These streams flow through a country nearly entirely situated on the new red sandstone, except the highest portions of the Clent Hills, where Permian sandstones and breccia are met with. Above Kidderminster the Stour, leaving on its right bank the sandy district of Blakeshall Common, passes out of this county into Staffordshire, joining Worcestershire again near Stourbridge, whence for some distance it forms the boundary of the county, with the detached portion of Dudley to the north of it. At Halesowen the Stour again enters Worcestershire, passing over the coal measures to find its sources on the north-eastern slopes of the Clent Hills. We have here reached the easternmost part of the watershed of the Severn ; further on

in this direction the streams run into the Rea, while Yardley, the extreme north-easterly parish of Worcestershire, drains into the Cole. A little to the south are the large reservoirs connected with the Birmingham Canal, whose waters run into the Arrow, and so into the Avon

On the right bank of the Severn its most northern tributary is Dowles Brook, which divides Worcestershire from Shropshire. Following up Dowles Brook, the water-parting dividing it from the basin of the Teme is arrived at, on the other side of which the Rea flows into that river at Newnham Bridge. Following down the course of the Teme, which runs in a most picturesque valley, at Eastham, on the right bank, some rare orchids have been observed. The tributary brooks in this district are highly charged with lime, which in places is deposited as masses of travertine, so plentiful at Southstone Rock and elsewhere that it forms a useful building material in the neighbourhood. The soil of this district appears favourable to the growth of orchidaceous plants, and the following have occurred, some very abundantly : *Epipactis latifolia*, *E. palustris*, *Habenaria bifolia*, *H. conopsea*, *H. viridis*, *Neottia nidus-avis*, *Orchis pyramidalis*, *O. Morio*, *Ophrys apifera*, *O. muscifera* and *Spiranthes autumnalis*. Just outside the county boundary on the Herefordshire side of Sapey Brook, which runs into the Teme, a single plant of *Epipogum aphyllum* was gathered in 1854, unknown before to the flora of Britain, but the plant has not again rewarded the most diligent search in the locality. Near here, and as close to the county boundary, but in Herefordshire, grows *Eryngium campestre*.

On the left, or east, bank of the Teme rise the Abberley Hills reaching a height of over 800 feet, and possessing quite a sub-alpine appearance ; and to the south of them is Woodbury Hill, nearly the same height. But these hills are curiously barren botanical ground, and little of any interest has been observed in the locality. To the north of Abberley is a little tract of carboniferous measures forming the Pensax coalfield, which also is not a prolific botanical district. At Knightsford Bridge the Teme breaks through a ridge of high land, leaving Ankerdine Hill on the left bank and Rosebury Rock, a mass of Permian breccia, on the right. Henceforward the Teme runs through broad meadows to its confluence with the Severn below Worcester, receiving on its way two tributary brooks—Leigh Brook, coming up the from south-west and the high land which forms the continuation northwards of the Malvern chain, and falling into the Teme at Leigh ; and Laughern Brook, which for some miles pursues a parallel course to the Severn, often not a mile away from that river, and falls into the Teme at Powick Bridge.

In the northern part of its course through the county the Severn, in comparatively quite recent times, flowed over a wider bed than at present contains it, and this at a time when its waters were at least brackish. Lagoons seem to have been left in many places by the retreating waters, which were first marshes and are now dry sandy wastes or valleys. Habberley Valley, near Kidderminster, is a well-marked instance, and of the same nature is Hartlebury Common. Maritime plants

still exist in some of these localities. On Hartlebury Common *Convolvulus Soldanella* has been gathered, and *Erodium maritimum* occurs there and at Habberley. The valley in which the Salwarpe runs from Droitwich to the Severn at Hawford was probably an arm of the river of a similar character, and in it is found a remarkable collection of maritime plants, including *Apium graveolens*, *Spergularia salina*, *Glaux maritima*, and abundantly on the banks of the river at Droitwich, *Lepidium latifolium*, which are perhaps survivals of the former flora kept from disappearing by some brackish quality in the water of the neighbourhood.

Worcestershire possesses two considerable tracts of native woodland, which have possibly never suffered more at the hand of man than thinning and felling. The Randans and the nearly adjoining wood of Pepperwood stretch from some three miles from north-east to south-west in the neighbourhood of Bromsgrove, and Wyre or Bewdley Forest covers a much more considerable tract of land in the north-west of the county, extending over into Shropshire, Dowles Brook, which runs through the forest, forming the county boundary. The latter wood is composed nearly entirely of oaks (*Quercus Robur*) and scattered yews, but possesses few large specimens, the timber being usually cut down as soon as it grows to a size fit for poles. In Wyre Forest grew the historic sorb tree, *Pyrus domestica*, possibly the only wild tree of the species in Britain. This tree, noticed in the *Philosophical Transactions of the Royal Society* in 1678, and then old, continued to exist until 1862, when it was burned down by a fire kindled by a vagrant at its foot. It had become very decrepid and was alive only at the ends of its gaunt branches, but it produced flowers within a few years of its destruction. Grafts taken from it are flourishing trees in the arboretum at Arley Castle near Bewdley. Wyre Forest yields several plants not to be found in other parts of Worcestershire, including *Cephalanthera ensifolia*, *Geranium sylvaticum*, *Pyrola minor*, *Rubus saxatilis*, *Spiranthes æstivalis*, now probably extinct, and *Thalictrum minus*. The undergrowth of Shrawley Wood, by the side of the Severn, consists to a large extent of the small-leaved lime, *Tilia parvifolia*. In the neighbourhood of Pershore are several large woods, and a considerable amount of woodland, though in scattered portions, covers the hilly district that forms a northern continuation of the Malvern range. In the extreme east are the Slads and Yield Woods, and between them and Evesham is Craycombe Hill and the wooded heights behind Woodnorton. In the more southern portion of the county there is but little woodland, nor are there any large woods in the extreme south-east. About Halesowen deep ravines have been cut in the softer measures by the numerous streams that descend from the hills, and for the most part these are shaded by belts of woodland, which sometimes join on to large expanses, as in the case of Ufmore Wood. In these dingles are *Campanula latifolia*, *Chrysosplenium alternifolium*, *Geum rivale* and *Paris quadrifolia*, pretty generally distributed.

The Malvern Hills run parallel with the average course of the Severn for a distance of nine miles, some four miles to the west of the

river, and rise suddenly from the lower land, which was formerly unenclosed, and known as Malvern Chase. The Worcestershire Beacon, the hill immediately behind Great Malvern, is the highest point in the range, which is chiefly composed of syenite. To the north of the Malverns is a series of eminences composed of Upper Silurian rocks, capped in places with Permian, which includes the hills of Ankerdine, Berrow and Woodbury, and curves round by the Abberley Hills to the east, while to the west of this range is the Old Red Sandstone district of Worcestershire. Lime-loving plants are found on these eminences, including *Clematis Vitalba*, *Anthyllis Vulneraria* and *Onobrychis sativa*, which do not stray far on to the red marl. Malvern Hills themselves are bare, and covered with close-cropped turf, affording little that is peculiar to their circumstances. *Sedum album* was found only in the county in a native condition on these hills, and *Potentilla verna* is also thus limited. The bilberry grows only sparsely, and heather is uncommon. On the different commons on the low ground that still represent Malvern Chase several damp spots afford aquatic plants, but many have disappeared on account of the enclosure and cultivation of the greater part of the district.

In the south-east part of Worcestershire a country of quite a different character is entered upon. Most of it is on the Lias formation, while Broadway and Bredon Hills are capped with Oolite. Through this district meanders the Avon, differing from Severn and Teme in the fact that its waters are always bank high, while the other two rivers have cut for themselves deep channels in which they flow. The valley of the Severn is bounded on the east in the middle part of its course through the county by a bold escarpment of marl on which rest Lias limestones and shales, and behind which the limestone crops out in lower ridges, the western faces of which are usually thickly clothed with trees and underwood, in which *Viburnum Lantana* is plentiful. The plants of the higher parts of the district about Bredon and Broadway belong nearly entirely to the flora of the Cotswolds. Such are *Astragalus hypoglottis*, *Hippocrepis comosa* and *Asperula cynanchica*. *Cnicus acaulis*, *Reseda lutea* and *Linaria minor* are also characteristic of the same locality. The Lias stretches as far north in the county as Hanbury, and penetrates the Red Marl in two tall narrow peaks, which join towards the south, and widen out into a broad belt of surface.

NOTES ON THE BOTANICAL DISTRICTS

Worcestershire is divided into four botanical districts : (i.) Avon ; (ii.) Severn ; (iii.) Malvern ; (iv.) Lickey. In a great measure these divisions are purely artificial ; they are formed without regard to geological structure, and their boundaries are difficult to follow, and pay no respect to the water-partings of the several rivers.

(i.) The AVON district comprises the south-eastern portion of the county. Its northern limit on the county boundary is reached at Headless Cross, near Redditch, and continues north-westerly along the Bromsgrove road to the point where this crosses the Birmingham canal, along which the boundary proceeds in a south-westerly direction as far as Oddingley.

From Oddingley the line of demarcation stretches nearly due south, roughly following the boundary of the Lias formation on the west as far as Tewkesbury, a distance of sixteen miles. The district is a roughly triangular area, with its apex to the north, very irregular in the south-east, and its southern base extending from point to point, with many breaks and interruptions, some twenty-five miles from Tewkesbury to Daylesford.

In itself the district falls into three divisions : the valley of the Avon, where the marl of the New Red Sandstone is met with ; the Lias division ; and the hills of Broadway and Bredon, capped with inferior Oolite. At the northern apex of the Avon division, some three miles to the east of Bromsgrove, there is at Tardebigge a large reservoir by the side of the Birmingham canal, where a series of plants occurs remarkable enough to merit special mention. It comprises *Bidens tripartita, Butomus umbellatus, Campanula latifolia, Lepidium ruderale, Lysimachia Nummularia, Malva moschata, Nasturtium amphibium, Paris quadrifolia, Sedum Telephium, Sium angustifolium, Spiranthes autumnalis* and *Typha angustifolia.* This is a part of the district which is upon the measures of the New Red Sandstone, and the spot, though locally in the Avon division, from its characteristics should more properly belong to the Lickey division, which it adjoins.

The Lias district is separated from the marls of the valley of the Severn by a bold escarpment facing westwards, behind which the limestone crops out in lower ridges possessing a similar aspect, the faces of which are usually thickly clothed with trees and underwood, in which *Viburnum Lantana* is plentiful. About Himbleton the meadows display *Genista tinctoria* and *Spiræa Filipendula.* The Trench woods in this neighbourhood is an interesting botanical locality, where are to be found *Allium vineale, Bupleurum rotundifolium, Pimpinella major* and *Poterium muricatum.* At Crowle *Lathyrus Aphaca* has been gathered, and *Lotus tenuis* occurs frequently ; while in the neighbourhood are to be found *Cichorium Intybus, Colchicum autumnale, Daphne Laureola, Dipsacus sylvestris, Linaria Elatine* and *Sparganium ramosum.* About the Lenches, more to the east, occur *Anthyllis vulneraria, Cnicus acaulis, Cnicus eriophorus, Hypopitys multiflora* and *Rosa rubiginosa* ; and at the Slads, among *Juniperus communis,* far removed from human habitation, grows *Asparagus officinalis. Hippocrepis comosa, Ophrys apifera,* and *Picris hieracioides* are also to be found here, while in the neighbourhood *Anagallis cærulea* almost replaces *A. arvensis.* Between Evesham and Fladbury, Craycombe Hill rises on the right bank of the Avon, and here have been gathered *Astragalus glycyphyllos, Cuscuta Epithymum, Galium tricorne, Lathyrus Aphaca, Lathyrus Nissolia* and *Samolus Valerandi.* At Tiddesley Wood, near Pershore, *Agrimonia odorata* and *Lathyrus sylvestris* occur. The conspicuous vegetation of the Avon itself includes *Butomus umbellatus, Iris Pseud-acorus, Lysimachia vulgaris, Lythrum Salicaria, Nuphar luteum, Polygonum amphibium, Phragmites communis, Rumex hydrolapathum, Sagittaria sagittifolia* and *Scirpus lacustris* ; while *Limnanthemum peltatum* is found in the river near Eckington. In some low places in the Lias district saline springs yet occur, the remains, perhaps, of a great salt marsh in times gone by. On Defford Common *Spergularia media* occurs, and *Scirpus maritimus* has been gathered there. *Smyrnium olusatrum* occurred at Badsey, but has now disappeared ; *Apium graveolens,* however, still lingers in the ditches in the locality.

The far south-east of the county is pure Cotswold country. At Blockley, a detached portion of the shire, *Habenaria chlorantha* and *Neottia Nidus-avis* occur ; and at Evenlode, a more distant isolated portion, which and Daylesford, still further to the south-east, are the only parts of Worcestershire which touch Oxfordshire and are in the watershed of the Thames, *Thlaspi perfoliatum* has been noticed. Another detached portion in this vicinity includes Alderminster and Tredington, with the town of Shipston-upon-Stour, and here *Cuscuta Trifolii, Galium erectum, Gentiana amarella* and *Valerianella carinata,* the latter perhaps extinct, have been found, with other plants typical of the Lias formation.

At Broadway, situated on the Oolite, *Arenaria tenuifolia, Brassica alba, Cerastium arvense* and *Specularia hybrida* have been recorded. There also occur here *Anthyllis Vulneraria, Campanula glomerata, Carlina vulgaris, Reseda lutea* and *Scabiosa Columbaria* ; while *Cnicus acaulis* grows commonly on the hilly wastes. Close to Broadway, at Snowshill, which however is in Gloucestershire, *Anemone Pulsatilla* and *Polypodium Robertianum* occur, but it is doubtful if they have ever overleapt the county boundary into Worcestershire. In its course towards the Severn the Avon leaves on its left bank Bredon Hill, an outlier of the Cotswolds belonging to the Oolitic formation. Characteristic of this eminence are *Asperula cynanchica, Astragalus hypoglottis, Brachypodium pinnatum, Calamintha Nepeta, Campanula glomerata, Cnicus acaulis, Cnicus eriophorus, Hippocrepis comosa, Linaria minor, Onobrychis sativa, Potamogeton densus, Reseda lutea, Scabiosa Columbaria, Spiræa Filipendula* and *Viburnum Lantana.*

BOTANY

The following twenty-one plants are peculiar to the Avon district, not having been found elsewhere in Worcestershire, and the first and last of them only doubtfully recorded. *Anemone Pulsatilla, Ranunculus tripartitus, Glaucium luteum, Thlaspi perfoliatum, Linum angustifolium, Astragalus hypoglottis, Hippocrepis comosa, Saxifraga hypnoides, Lythrum hyssopifolia, Asperula cynanchica, Cnicus acaulis, Limnanthemum peltatum, Cuscuta epithymum, Calamintha Nepeta, Chenopodium hybridum, Euphorbia platyphyllos, Buxus sempervirens, Alisma ranunculoides, Cladium Mariscus, Festuca uniglumis* and *Polypodium Robertianum.*

(ii.) The SEVERN district is a strip down the centre of the whole of the county, broad in the north, where it extends from the western limit of Bewdley Forest to the point where the Stour becomes the county boundary in the east; from this point to Tardebigge it abuts on the Lickey district; and then turning south it is bounded as far as Tewkesbury by the Avon district. Of the western side, the northern portion is irregular until the boundary meets the Teme, after which it follows southward the course of that river and of the Severn, and the district ends in a narrow point opposite Tewkesbury. The northern part is chiefly on the New Red Sandstone, but by far the greater portion consists of the Red Marl.

There are several interesting botanical localities in this district. On the left bank of the Severn at Hawford, the canal from Droitwich falls into the river. Between Hawford and Dodderhill church may be found on its banks, or near thereto, *Apium graveolens, Atriplex laciniata, Carum segetum, Geranium perenne* (in quantity on the railway embankments near Droitwich railway station), *Glaux maritima, Glyceria distans, Lepidium latifolium* (abundantly by the Salwarpe at Droitwich), *Lepidium ruderale, Medicago maculata, Myosurus minimus* (1852), *Pimpinella major, Ranunculus parviflorus, Saponaria officinalis, Senebiera Coronopus, Spergularia salina, Triglochin palustre* and *Verbascum nigrum. Daphne Laureola* and *Lonicera Xylosteum* occur by the lake in Westwood Park. *Valisneria spiralis,* the occurrence of which cannot be accounted for, was found shortly before 1877, inhabiting a pond in a brickyard at Northwick near Worcester, but none remains in the county except in the form of specimens in the Museum at Worcester.

Following up the left bank of the Severn to Stourport, in the angle between it and the river Stour is Hartlebury Common, a wild space of land consisting of two distinct tracts—a sandy waste at the top of a steep bluff, and a moor-like expanse at the bottom of it. The sandy summit is covered with *Calluna vulgaris,* and here grow *Botrychium Lunaria, Diplotaxis tenuifolia, Erodium maritimum, Hypochæris glabra, Lycopodium clavatum, L. inundatum, Ornithopus perpusillus, Plantago Coronopus, Silene conica, Spergularia rubra* and *Teesdalia nudicaulis.* The lower portion of the common is a pallid similitude of a Highland moor, with similar peaty cracks filled with stagnant water, and nourishing weak specimens of similar plants. Here are to be found *Drosera rotundifolia* in abundance reddening the ground, *Eriophorum polystachion, Hydrocotyle vulgaris, Pedicularis palustris,* and *Viola palustris.* One small pool is entirely filled with a mass of *Potentilla Comarum* and *Menyanthes trifoliata.* On the drier parts of the low ground, *Anthemis nobilis, Marrubium vulgare, Sedum acre, Sisymbrium Sophia, Trifolium striatum, T. scabrum* and *Viola canina* are to be found.

At Hoobrook, below Kidderminster, several streams converge on their way to the Stour. One of these comes from Stanklin Pool, the one locality in the county where *Parnassia palustris* still flourishes, and in abundance. About the pool grow also *Agrimonia odorata, Menyanthes trifoliata, Myriophyllum spicatum, Pedicularis palustris, Potentilla Comarum* and *Typha angustifolia,* and an *Orchis* once held to be *O. incarnata,* but now referred to *O. latifolia.* By the side of the stream from this pool was the last known locality for *Osmunda regalis* in the county. Another stream passes through the wild dingle called Fenny Rough, in which the vegetation is most luxuriant. Here are *Aquilegia vulgaris, Cardamine impatiens, Carex Bœnninghauseniana, Convallaria majalis,* and *Polygonatum multiflorum.* Above Kidderminster a chain of pools stretches out towards the high land in the north-east; *Nuphar luteum* occurs in several of them, but *Nymphæa alba* is entirely absent. It was in one of these pools that *Elatine hexandra* and *E. hydropiper* were once found. Near the northern boundary of the county in the neighbourhood of Blakeshall a sandy, heather-covered common extends for some distance, near which *Cotyledon Umbilicus* and *Erodium maritimum* are to be found. Habberley Valley, some two miles north-west from Kidderminster, is an interesting spot; *Cotyledon Umbilicus* is found here also, and in the neighbourhood *Botrychium Lunaria, Erodium maritimum* and *Verbascum virgatum* are recorded.

The banks of the Severn and its neighbouring pools afford *Brassica nigra, Carex Pseudo-cyperus, Geranium pratense, Hypericum quadrangulum, Œnanthe Phellandrium, Scirpus sylvaticus*

and *Thalictrum flavum*. Sometimes these banks are fringed with woods, in which *Pyrus torminalis* occurs. *Nasturtium sylvestre* is often conspicuous by the water's edge, and many rare *Carices* lurk in the ditches near the river, such as *Carex ampullacea, C. axillaris, C. binervis, C. canescens, C. disticha, C. elongata, C. fulva, C. strigosa* and *C. vesicaria*. Among the grasses of the meadows by the Severn are found *Avena pubescens, Bromus commutatus, Bromus madritensis, Festuca loliacea, Hordeum pratense, Phalaris canariensis, Poa compressa* and *Setaria glauca*. The western bank of the river above Worcester shows several large woods. In Astley Wood *Galanthus nivalis* has been found, and near Shrawley church *Tulipa sylvestris*. In Shrawley Wood occurs *Aquilegia vulgaris, Convallaria majalis, Dipsacus pilosus, Orobanche major, Pyrola minor, Sedum Telephium,* and *Vicia sylvatica* ; while *Tilia parvifolia* forms much of the undergrowth. Higher up the river near Stourport *Geranium phœum* occurs ; and still more to the north, above Bewdley, *Coronilla varia* is plentiful by the river side, where it has been known for fifty years or more, in a spot which by the alteration of the county boundary has lately been taken into Worcestershire.

Here, on the confines of the county, is situated Bewdley or Wyre Forest, spreading over both sides of Dowles Brook, which divides Worcestershire from Shropshire. *Geranium sanguineum* occurs on the Shropshire side of the brook, but has not been known for many years to have crossed the stream into Worcestershire. Among the plants which have been found in this district are *Aquilegia vulgaris, Botrychium Lunaria, Carex montana, Convallaria majalis, Cephalanthera ensifolia, Doronicum Pardalianches, Echium vulgare, Epipactis palustris, Eriophorum latifolium, Gentiana campestris, Geranium sylvaticum, Hyoscyamus niger, Lithospermum officinale, Lycopodium clavatum, Melica nutans, Narthecium ossifragum, Ornithogalum umbellatum, Pyrola rotundifolia, Rosa rubiginosa, Rubus saxatilis, Thalictrum minus, Triglochin palustre* and *Tulipa sylvestris*. *Spiræa salicifolia* formerly grew in a naturalized condition by the side of Dowles Brook, but has now disappeared ; and *Spiranthes æstivalis* has also gone from the locality.

Some eighty plants have been recorded for the Severn district which have not been found elsewhere in Worcestershire ; and among them, besides several of those mentioned in the above lists, are *Ranunculus Lingua, Crepis paludosa, Lactuca virosa, Wahlenbergia hederacea, Verbascum Lychnitis, Utricularia minor, Crocus vernus, Sparganium natans, Carex digitata, Festuca sylvatica* and what has been recorded as *Lycopodium complanatum*, though it is now contended that no true *L. complanatum* has been found in Britain.

(iii.) The MALVERN district is a band of uneven width, following the western boundary of the county down its entire length from north to south, possessing a varied geological structure, and comprising, as well as the heights of Malvern, a considerable portion of the valley of the Teme after that river enters the county in the north. The eastern limit of this district is the western boundary of the Severn district for the whole of its length. The Malvern Hills run parallel with the average course of the Severn for a distance of nine miles, some four miles west of the river ; they rise suddenly from the lower land, which was formerly unenclosed and known as Malvern Chase. Though the greater part of the chase has been enclosed and cultivated much of it is still wet and waste. *Apium inundatum, Bupleurum tenuissimum, Epilobium roseum, E. virgatum, Heleocharis acicularis, H. multicaulis, Limosella aquatica, Lemna gibba, Mentha piperata, M. pulegium, Myriophyllum alterniflorum, Œnanthe Lachenalii, Œ. peucedanifolia, Peplis Portula, Polygonum minus, Pulicaria vulgaris, Scirpus Caricis, S. fluitans, S. setaceus, Triglochin palustre* and *Zannichellia palustris* have been recorded for this district. On the hills themselves, which are for the most part bare of any conspicuous vegetation, are *Cardamine impatiens, Corydalis claviculata, Cotyledon Umbilicus, Geranium lucidum* and *Spergularia rubra*. *Digitalis purpurea* is sometimes a feature in the summer, and *Myosotis versicolor* is plentiful in the spring ; while *Ornithopus perpusillus* and *Hypericum humifusum* are common. Both *Erica cinerea* and *E. tetralix* are wanting on the Malvern Hills, and *Culluna vulgaris* becomes rare in the southern part of Worcestershire ; the southernmost station in the county for *Erica tetralix* is Broadheath near Worcester. *Narcissus Pseudonarcissus* is plentiful in the meadows on the west and south of the hills. On the north hill *Sedum album* occurred, but is now almost certainly gone. Rarer plants that have been met with in the district are *Centunculus minimus, Gagea lutea, Lactuca scariola, Lathyrus sylvestris* and *Orobanche elatior*. The high land to the north of the Malvern chain is in many places thickly covered with wood, which consists chiefly of oak and hazel, but contains also a considerable quantity of *Tilia parvifolia* and *T. platyphyllos*. *Betula alba* predominates in some places. *Prunus Avium* is very common, and *Populus tremula* is generally distributed. *Fagus sylvatica, Pyrus Aria* and *Carpinus Betulus* are entirely absent as native trees from the Malvern

district. *Daphne Laureola* occurs in these woods; and also *Habenaria chlorantha*, *Neottia Nidus-avis*, and *Paris quadrifolia*.

Up the valley of the Teme the county extends an arm to the west which enters Herefordshire. At Berrington, near the extreme western point, *Inula Helenium* flourishes. *Damasonium stellatum* has been found by the side of a pool near Tenbury, and *Aconitum Napellus* is recorded from Eastham. About Pensax, on the left bank of the Teme, *Narcissus Pseudo-narcissus* occurs in an apparently indigenous condition. Further to the south, on the same bank of the river, is Martley, where *Anthyllus vulneraria*, *Bromus erectus*, *Onobrychis sativa* and *Ophrys apifera* occur, the two former in considerable quantity. At Rosebury Rock are to be found *Cotyledon Umbilicus*, *Lathræa Squamaria* and *Pulmonaria officinalis*; below Knightsford Bridge the valley of the Teme opens out; at Broadwas *Trifolium ochroleucum* and *Lathyrus Aphaca* have been gathered, and at Leigh *Epipactis purpurata* is by no means rare in the neighbourhood. Besides the plants that have been mentioned, the following occur in the district : *Aquilegia vulgaris*, *Campanula Trachelium*, *Cardamine impatiens*, *Chrysosplenium alternifolium*, *Helleborus fœtidus*, *H. viridis*, *Hesperis matronalis*, *Mentha viridis*, *Myrrhis odorata*, *Narcissus biflorus*, *Rumex acutus* and *Vinca minor*, the latter in some quantity.

Including varieties there are 114 plants which have been recorded for the county only in the Malvern division, but of two of them, *Eriophorum gracile* and *Polypodium Phegopteris*, the record is doubtful. Many casuals are brought into the district with the manures used in the hop-yards.

(iv.) The LICKEY district is formed of the north-eastern corner of the county, and is of varied geological structure, its southern boundary starting at Headless Cross near Redditch, continuing in a direction a little to the north of west by Bromsgrove to Chaddesley Corbett, and thence passing north to Stourbridge. The Randans and Pepperwood are in this district, large extents of woodland in a natural state. In the Randans a struggling plant of *Lycopodium clavatum* was observed some years ago; and in Chaddesley Wood, part of the larger Randans, occurs *Pulmonaria officinalis*, apparently in a perfectly wild condition, with *Paris quadrifolia*, *Viola Reichenbachiana* and *Viola palustris*. In one locality *Lathræa Squamaria* is fairly abundant.

The Lickey Hills, whence the Salwarpe river rises, form a portion of the water-parting of central England, the streams to the west reaching the Severn, those to the north-east reaching the Trent, and those from the south-eastern portion joining the Arrow, and so flowing into the Avon. Several rare plants still linger on the hill-sides and about the large reservoirs which feed the Birmingham Canal, and whose overflow runs into the Arrow. The hills are densely covered with *Calluna vulgaris*, *Erica cinerea* and *Vaccinium Myrtillus*, among which occurs *Rubus Sprengelii*; and in the locality occur *Equisetum maximum*, *Geranium lucidum*, *Hydrocotyle vulgaris*, *Myosotis repens*, *Solidago virgaurea* and *Trifolium filiforme*. The woods contain *Betula alba*, *Pyrus Aucuparia*, and quantities of *Ilex aquifolium*. Several forms of *Rubus* are to be found, with some quantity of *Rubus Idæus*. In the neighbourhood are *Callitriche verna*, *Corydalis claviculata*, *Epilobium angustifolium*, *Epipactis purpurata*, var. *media*, *Equisetum sylvaticum*, *Geranium columbinum*, *Geum rivale*, *Habenaria viridis*, *Lomaria Spicant*, *Malva moschata*, *Myrrhis odorata*, *Nephrodium Oreopteris* and *Viola palustris*. Near the reservoirs have been found *Heleocharis acicularis*, *Limosella aquatica*, *Littorella lacustris*, *Rumex Hydrolapathum*, *Salix triandra* and *Sagittaria sagittifolia*; while about Alvechurch *Anagallis tenella*, *Equisetum sylvaticum*, *Euphorbia amygdaloides*, *Fritillaria meleagris*, *Hydrocotyle vulgaris*, *Lathyrus Nissolia*, *Veronica Anagallis* and *Viola palustris* have been noticed.

One of the streams which fall into the Stour below Hoobrook comes from Harvington Hall, in the moat about which grows *Acorus Calamus*. In the more northern parts of this district the characteristic plants are *Arabis perfoliata*, *Campanula patula*, *Erysimum cheiranthoides*, *Geranium columbinum*, *Ornithopus perpusillus*, *Potentilla argentea*, *Saxifraga granulata*, *Senecio sylvaticus*, *Spergularia rubra*, *Trifolium arvense* and *Verbascum nigrum*. On the hills of Clent are *Cerastium quaternellum*, *Chenopodium Bonus-Henricus*, *Cytisus scoparius*, *Hypericum humifusum* and *Linaria repens*. On parts of this range of hills *Ranunculus parviflorus* occurs in the greatest abundance, sometimes forming large tufts; of late years it has been spreading along the higher parts, towards the north-east, in great quantity. *Doronicum Pardalianches* occurs at Hagley and Clent, and with it at Hagley flourished *Borago officinalis*, which has now perhaps disappeared; and in Hagley Hall garden *Chenopodium rubrum* is always present as a weed. There is no heather of any kind on the Clent hills, though heaths flourish in the sandy lanes at their feet to the southward. Nor on the higher parts of this district is any *Ulex Europæa*

to be found. In the valleys between the hills occur *Adoxa Moschatellina, Allium ursinum, Asperula odorata, Campanula latifolia, Cardamine amara, C. impatiens, Chrysosplenium alternifolium, Epipactis purpurata,* var. *media, Geum rivale* and *Myosotis sylvatica.* On the upland pastures is *Ophioglossum vulgatum,* which, however, is not confined to the hills, but grows freely in several localities. In the valley between Clent and Walton hills *Scrophularia umbrosa* has been located, and at its mouth *Cotyledon Umbilicus* and *Erodium maritimum* recorded, neither of which is now to be found there. Deep ravines have been cut through the softer measures by the numerous streams, and for the most part these are shaded by belts of woodland. Here are to be found *Agrimonia odorata, Carex pallescens, Chlora perfoliata, Erythræa Centaurium, Dipsacus pilosus, Geum rivale, Genista tinctoria, Habenaria conopsea, Lathræa squamaria, Ononis spinosa, Paris quadrifolia, Senecio Erucæfolius* and *Trifolium medium. Equisetum Hyemale* occurs at Frankley, *Carlina vulgaris* on nearly the highest part of the slope near St. Kenelm's church, and *Sagittaria sagittifolia* and *Butomus umbellatus* in the canal at Halesowen.

The island of Worcestershire constituting Dudley, situated outside the north-west portion of this district, is chiefly given up to pit mounds and ironworks, forming part of the Black Country, and therefore it does not afford good botanizing ground. In the north part of this island an intrusive arm of Staffordshire includes the limestone hill on which Dudley Castle is situated, and robs this district of *Atropa Belladonna,* which is always to be found in the Castle courtyard.

On the north-eastern slopes of the Clent Hills the streams run into the Rea, while Yardley, the extreme north-easterly parish of Worcestershire, drains into the Cole. This parish formerly contained many rare plants, but the proximity of growing Birmingham has changed its character. There have been found there *Butomus umbellatus, Cardamine amara, Carex Goodenovii, Carex vesicaria, Nasturtium amphibium,* and *Ranunculus heterophyllus,* vars. *peltatus* and *pseudo-fluitans.*

Twenty-nine plants are peculiar to the Lickey district, not having been recorded elsewhere in the county ; one of them, *Claytonia perfoliata,* probably by this time having established itself in the other districts also, has lately been seen near Worcester.

ACOTYLEDONES

FERNS, HORSETAILS AND CLUB-MOSSES

Some few of these plants have been mentioned while dealing with the Botanical Districts into which Worcestershire is divided. Twenty-five kinds of ferns have been recorded for Worcestershire, but of these several are now extinct, and one, *Polypodium Phegopteris,* is only doubtfully reported from the Teme valley, and another, *Polypodium Robertianum,* quite as doubtfully from Broadway. *Polypodium Dryopteris* is possibly extinct in all its old Worcestershire localities, but one plant has lately been seen in Pepperwood, Belbroughton. *Osmunda regalis* once grew at Moseley, and to a later time maintained its existence near Kidderminster, but has now disappeared. *Cryptogramme crispa* was at one time to be found on the Herefordshire Beacon at Malvern, but only one plant remained in 1851. *Cystopteris fragilis,* recorded in all the districts except Malvern, has possibly disappeared, or lingers only on Bredon Hill. *Asplenium viride* grew on Ham Bridge across the Teme up to 1853, when it was destroyed during some repairs to that structure. Near Bell End, in the Lickey district, *Nephrodium Oreopteris* flourishes exceedingly, the fronds in some instances being four feet long. One fine patch of this fern was unfortunately discovered some years ago by a peripatetic fern-gatherer, and was entirely swept away, doubtless to be sold for sixpence a root in Birmingham Market Hall. This fern occurs in all the districts except Avon, but is quite rare. *Asplenium Ceterach* is a rare fern throughout the county, but in the Lickey district is widely distributed, though growing only sparsely where it is found. *Asplenium Ruta-muraria* is common, and reaches an abundant development on the wall that surrounds Lea Castle, in Wolverley. The hart's-tongue, *Scolopendrium vulgare,* is by no means common, but grows finely at Rosebury Rock, in the valley of the Teme. In the northern part of the county it is only to be seen in a stunted condition on some dry wall, or lining the inside of a well in the Red Sandstone, while in the extreme north-east it is nearly unknown. *Asplenium Adiantum-nigrum,* though generally distributed, is seldom seen ; and *Lomaria Spicant,* which formerly occurred abundantly in the Lickey district, and on the higher parts of the district of Severn and Malvern, is becoming less frequent. It is not reported from the Avon district. *Aspidium lobatum* is becoming rare

in all its localities, but *Aspidium angulare* is finely developed in some of the water-worn ravines that are found in the Lickey district.

The more common ferns of Britain are very abundant, especially *Nephrodium Filix-mas*, *Polypodium vulgare*, and *Pteris aquilina*. Polypody sometimes fringes in great quantities the banks of the deep-cut lanes in the red sandstone, and bracken grows to a great height in many of the woods in the Severn district. *Nephrodium dilatatum* is common in moist woods, and *Nephrodium spinulosum* occurs frequently in coppices on drier soil. The lady-fern, *Asplenium Filix-fœmina*, is frequently found in such damp places as it loves; but the most widely diffused fern in the county is the male-fern, *Nephrodium Filix-mas*. *Ophioglossum vulgatum* is common in the upland meadows of the Lickey district, and is fairly abundant elsewhere. *Botrychium Lunaria* has also been recorded in every district. This fern formerly grew in quantity and very finely on the upper Lickey, but disappeared; it has just been rediscovered in its former locality after an absence of twenty-three years. It exists also in other places in the same neighbourhood.

The Horse-tails are well represented in Worcestershire, *Equisetum arvense* indeed in many cases too much so, being an ineradicable field weed, especially in the sandy districts. *Equisetum maximum* perhaps attains its highest development in Fenny Rough in the Severn district, where its luxuriance is truly tropical. *Equisetum hyemale* is reported in all the districts except Avon; in the Lickey district it has been discovered in two localities, and as well grew formerly at Moseley Bog.

Of the four club-mosses recorded for Worcestershire two are extinct. These are *Lycopodium Selago*, which formerly grew at Moseley, and *Lycopodium complanatum*, which was gathered in 1836 on Hartlebury common, and of which the specimen still exists, though it is now contended that it is not true *L. complanatum*. The stag's-horn club-moss, *Lycopodium clavatum*, grows also on Hartlebury common, but is less abundant than formerly was the case. It has also been found on the upper Lickey, in Bewdley Forest, and at the Randans; and on Walton Hill, in Clent, it maintained a struggling existence till 1882, when the turves on which it was growing were taken by a rustic to mend a neighbouring hedge-bank. *Lycopodium inundatum* still occurs on Hartlebury Common.

A COMPLETE LIST OF THE PLANTS OF WORCESTERSHIRE

OBSERVATIONS

The order and nomenclature of this list are those of Sir J. D. Hooker's *Student's Flora*, 3rd edition, 1884. The numbers after the names of species are taken from the *London Catalogue of British Plants*, 9th edition, 1895, and are intended to form a scale of rarity, or frequency, in relation to Britain as a whole, expressing the number of counties or county divisions, 112 in all, in which the species has been reported to occur, as set out in Watson's *Topographical Botany*, 2nd edition, 1883. The letter C or I indicates that the plant occurs in a wild state only in the Channel Islands or Ireland respectively.

A, Avon District; *S*, Severn District; *M*, Malvern District; *L*, Lickey District.

* Extinct plants; † Doubtful for any cause; ‡ Not native; § Require recent confirmation.

These marks when necessary are affixed to the localization of the plants in the several districts, but must not be taken to be exhaustive in any sense.

The numbers before the names of orders are those of the *Student's Flora*.

This list of Worcestershire plants has been taken chiefly from Mr. Edwin Lees's *Botany of Worcestershire* (1867), so carefully analyzed by Mr. William Mathews in vols. x. to xvi. (1887-93) of the *Midland Naturalist*, with additions from the *Transactions of the Worcestershire Naturalists' Club*, and the *Reports of the Botanical Exchange Club*; and from the observations of Mr. J. E. Bagnall, Mr. John Humphreys, Mr. Carleton Rea, and Mr. R. F. Towndrow, from all of whom I have received great assistance in forming this list.

There are six plants marked in this list as belonging to Worcestershire for which no districts are assigned. These are *Arabis hirsuta*, *Cerastium pumilum*, *Cerastium tetrandrum*,

Cicuta virosa and *Valerianella Auricula*.   These do not appear in the list given in Mr. Lees' book, though they are all located in Worcestershire, four of them with Mr. Lees' name appended, in Watson's *Topographical Botany*.   Another plant which requires special mention is *Potamogeton prælongus*.   This is not marked in Mr. Lees' list, but with a note of interrogation after it is given for Worcestershire in the *Topographical Botany*.   *Ranunculus marinus*, *Rosa stylosa* and *Betula glutinosa*, also have no districts assigned to them, since only the varieties given are found in the county.   In appendix B, for the most part, only the varieties are localized.

In three appendixes are given : (A) those species excluded by Sir Joseph Hooker, but placed by him in an appendix to his *Flora*, which have been recorded for Worcestershire ; (B) Plants and some *Rubi*, not mentioned by Sir Joseph Hooker, but given in the 9th edition of the *London Catalogue*, being chiefly hybrids and varieties found in the Malvern district, the records having been supplied by Mr. R. F. Towndrow ; and (C) a list of casuals and a few hybrids not mentioned either in the *Student's Flora* or the *London Catalogue*.   The Malvern district records in this also have been supplied by Mr. R. F. Towndrow.

This list is complete to the end of December, 1900.

1. Ranunculaceæ					Helleborus fœtidus, L.—16		S	M	L^*
Clematis, L.					Eranthis, Salisb.				
— Vitalba, L.—49	A	S	M		— hyemalis, Salisb.	$A\ddagger$	$S\ddagger$	$M\ddagger$	$L\ddagger$
Thalictrum, L.					Aquilegia, L.				
— minus, L.—36		S			— vulgaris, L.—60		S	M	L
— flavum, L.—69	A	S	M	L	Delphinium, L.				
var. sphærocarpum, Lej.			M		— Ajacis, Reichb.	$A^*\ddagger$	$S^*\ddagger$	$M\dagger^*$	$L\ddagger^*$
Anemone, L.					Aconitum, L.				
— Pulsatilla, L.—18	$A\dagger$				— Napellus, L.—7			$M\S$	
— nemorosa, L.—108	A	S	M	L					
Adonis, L.					2. Berberideæ				
— autumnalis, L.—6			M^*		Berberis, L.				
Myosurus, L.					— vulgaris, L.—82		S	M	
— minimus, L.—44		S	M						
Ranunculus, L.					3. Nymphæaceæ				
— heterophyllus, Fries.—43			M	L	Nuphar, Smith				
var. peltatus, Fries.	A	S	M	L	— luteum, Sm.—91	A	S	M	L
var. pseudo-fluitans, Bab.		S		L	Nymphæa, L.				
— marinus, Fries.					— alba, L.—88	$A\ddagger$	$S\ddagger$	$M\ddagger$	$L\ddagger$
var. Baudotii, Godr.—45			M	L					
— fluitans, Lamk.—56	A	S	M	L	4. Papaveraceæ				
— trichophyllus, Chaix.—52	A	S		L	Papaver, L.				
var. Drouettii, F. Schultz ?			M	L	— hybridum, L.—40		S		
— circinatus, Sibth.—60	A	S	M	L	— Argemone, L.—87	A	S	M	L
— tripartitus, DC.—13	A				— dubium, L.—104	A	S	M	L
— lenormandi, F. Schultz—54				L	var. Lecoqii, Lamotte—22			M	
— hederaceus, L.—105	A	S	M	L	— Rhœas, L.—104	A	S	M	L
— Lingua, L.—81		S	M^*		var. strigosum, Bœnn.			M	
— Flammula, L.—112	A	S	M	L	— somniferum, L.		$S\ddagger$		
— auricomus, L.—87	A	S	M	L	Chelidonium, L.				
— sceleratus, L.—100	A	S	M	L	— majus, L.—96	A	S	M	L
— acris, L.—112	A	S	M	L	Glaucium, Hall				
— repens, L.—112	A	S	M	L	— luteum, Scop.—52	$A\dagger$			
— bulbosus, L.—102	A	S	M	L					
— hirsutus, Curtis			M		5. Fumariaceæ				
— arvensis, L.—68	A	S	M	L	Fumaria, L.				
— parviflorus, L.—58	A	S	M	L	— capreolata, L.—32		S	M	L
— Ficaria, L.—110	A	S	M	L	sub-sp. confusa, Jord.—47			M	
var. incumbens, F. Schultz			M		sub-sp. muralis, Sonder			M	
Caltha, L.					— officinalis, L.—106	A	S	M	L
— palustris, L.—112	A	S	M	L	— parviflora, Lam.—21		S		
var. Guerangerii, Boreau				L	sub-sp.Vaillantii,Lois.—13			M	
Helleborus, L.					Corydalis, DC.				
— viridis, L.—28		S^*	M	L	— claviculata, N.E.Br.—87		S	M	L

	A	S	M	L
Corydalis lutea, Scop.	A‡		M‡	
— solida, Hook.			M‡	

6. CRUCIFERÆ

	A	S	M	L
Cheiranthus, L.				
— Cheiri, L	A‡	S‡	M‡	L‡
Nasturtium, L.				
— officinale, Br.—112	A	S	M	L
var. siifolium, Reichb.			M	
— sylvestre, Br.—63	A	S	M	
— palustre, DC.—84.	A	S	M	L
— amphibium, Br.—46.	A	S	M	L
Barbarea, Br.				
— vulgaris, Br.—97	A	S	M	L
var. arcuata, Reichb.—?		S		
sub-sp. stricta, Andrz.—12		S	M	L
sub-sp. intermedia, Boreau —13		S	M	
— præcox, Br.		S‡	M‡	
Arabis, Linn.				
— hirsuta, Br.—96				
— perfoliata, Lam.—38.		S	M	L
Cardamine, L.				
— hirsuta, L.—110	A	S	M	L
sub. sp. flexuosa, With.—101	A	S	M	L
— pratensis, L.—112	A	S	M	L
— amara, L.—75.	A	S	M	L
— impatiens, L.—27.		S	M	L
Sisymbrium, L.				
— Thalianum, J. Gay—99.	A	S	M	L
— Irio, L.—1.			M	
— Sophia, L.—64		S	M	
— officinale, Scop.—110	A	S	M	L
— Alliaria, Scop.—99	A	S	M	L
Erysimum, L.				
— cheiranthoides, L.—38	A	S	M	L
Hesperis, L.				
— matronalis		S‡	M‡	L‡
Brassica, L.				
— campestris, L.	A	S	M	L
var. Napus, L.	A‡	S‡	M‡	L‡
var. sylvestris, H. C. Wats.			M	
var. Briggsii, H. C. Wats.			M	
— monensis, Huds.—16.		S		
sub-sp. Cheiranthus, Vill. —C.		S‡		
— nigra, Koch.—112	A	S	M	
— Sinapis, Visiani.—82.	A	S	M	L
— alba, Boiss.—82	A	S	M	
Diplotaxis, DC.				
— tenuifolia, DC.—41		S		
— muralis, DC.—53.			M	L
Erophila, DC.				
— vulgaris, DC.—104	A	S	M	L
— brachycarpa, Jord.—33			M	
Alyssum, L.				
— calycinum, L		S‡	M‡	
— maritimum, L.		S‡		
Cochlearia, L.				
— Armoracia, L	A‡	S‡	M‡	L‡
Camelina, Crantz				
— sativa, Crantz		S‡	M‡	L‡
Capsella, Mœnch				

	A	S	M	L
Capsella Bursa-Pastoris, Mœnch —112	A	S	M	L
Senebiera, DC.				
— didyma, Persoon—45.			M	L
— Coronopus, Poiret—81	A	S	M	L
Lepidium, L.				
— latifolium, L.—19.		S		
— ruderale, L.—38	A	S	M	L
— campestre, R. Br.—86	A	S	M	L
sub-sp.Smithii,Hook.—88		S	M	
— Draba, L.		S‡	M‡	
Thlaspi, L.				
— arvense, L.—84	A	S	M	L
— perfoliatum, L.—4	A			
Iberis, L.				
— amara, L.—14.		S‡	M‡	
Teesdalia, Br.				
— nudicaulis, Br.—72	A	S	M	L
Raphanus, L.				
— Raphanistrum, L.—110.	A	S	M	L

7. RESEDACEÆ

	A	S	M	L
Reseda, L.				
— Luteola, L.—95	A	S	M	L
— lutea, L.—53	A	S	M	
— alba, L.		S‡		L‡

8. CISTINEÆ

	A	S	M	L
Helianthemum, Tourn.				
— vulgare, Gærtn.—92	A	S	M	L

9. VIOLACEÆ

	A	S	M	L
Viola, L.				
— palustris, L.—104		S		L
— odorata, L.—80	A	S	M	L
— hirta, L.—72	A	S	M	L
— canina, L.—67	A	S	M	L
— sylvatica, Fries.—100	A	S	M	L
sub-sp. Reichenbachiana, Bor.		S	M	L
— tricolor, L.—112	A	S	M	L
sub-sp. arvensis, Murr.—100?		S	M	L

10. POLYGALEÆ

	A	S	M	L
Polygala, L.				
— vulgaris, L.—79	A	S	M	L
sub-sp. oxyptera, Reichb.—35			M	L
sub-sp. depressa, Wend.—91			M	L

12. CARYOPHYLLEÆ

	A	S	M	L
Dianthus, L.				
— Armeria, L.—48	A	S	M	
— prolifer, L.—8.			M	
— deltoides, L.—55.				L
Saponaria, L.				
— officinalis, L.		S	M	L
Silene, L.				
— Cucubalus, Wibel.—104.	A	S	M	L
var. puberula, Syme			M	
— conica, L.—11		S		
— anglica, L.—57		S		L

Species	A	S	M	L
Silene nutans, L.—16				L
— noctiflora, L.—44		S	M	
Lychnis, L.				
— Flos-cuculi, L.—112	A	S	M	L
— diurna, Sibth.—111	A	S	M	L
— vespertina, Sibth.—102	A	S	M	L
Githago, Desfont.				
— segetum, Desfont.—100	A	S	M	L
Cerastium, L.				
— quaternellum, Fenzl.—51		S	M	L
— tetrandrum, Curtis—75				
— pumilum, Curtis—10				
— semidecandrum, L.—87	A	S	M	L
— glomeratum, Thuill.—112	A	S	M	L
— triviale, Link—112	A	S	M	L
— arvense, L.—69	A	S		
Stellaria, L.				
— aquatica, Scop.—57	A	S	M	L
— nemorum, L.—47		S		L
— media, Vill.—112	A	S	M	L
sub-sp.umbrosa,Opiz.—22		S	M	
var. neglecta, Weihe			M	L
— Holostea, L.—109	A	S	M	L
— palustris, Ehrh.—54		S		
— graminea, L.—109	A	S	M	L
— uliginosa, Murr.—110	A	S	M	L
Arenaria, L.				
— tenuifolia, L.—34	A		M	L
— trinervia, L.—100	A	S	M	L
— serpyllifolia, L.—110	A	S	M	L
var. leptoclados, Guss.		S	M	
Sagina, L.				
— apetala, L.—70	A	S	M	L
sub-sp. ciliata, Fr.—66		S	M	L
— procumbens, L.—112	A	S	M	L
— nodosa, Fenzl.—98			M	
Spergula, L.				
— arvensis, L.—112	A	S	M	L
var. sativa, Bœnn.			M	
Spergularia, Persoon				
— rubra, Pers.—97		S	M	L
— salina, Pers.—45	A†	S		
— media, Pers.—44	A	S		

13. Portulaceæ

Species	A	S	M	L
Montia, L.				
— fontana, L.—108		S	M	L
var. minor, Gmel.		S		
Claytonia, L.				
— perfoliata, Don.		S‡		L‡

14. Elatineæ

Species	A	S	M	L
Elatine, L.				
— hexandra, DC.—21		S*		
— Hydropiper, L.—3		S*		

15. Hypericineæ

Species	A	S	M	L
Hypericum, L.				
— Androsæmum, L.—80	A	S	M	L
— calycinum, L.			M‡	
— perforatum, L.—101	A	S	M	L
var. angustifolium, Bab.			M	
— quadrangulum, L.—76	A	S	M	L
— tetrapterum, Fries.—102		S	M	

Species	A	S	M	L
Hypericum humifusum, L.—98	A	S	M	L
— pulchrum, L.—111	A	S	M	L
— hirsutum, L.—89	A	S	M	L
— montanum, L.—45	A	S	M	
— elodes, L.—61				L*

16. Malvaceæ

Species	A	S	M	L
Malva, L.				
— sylvestris, L.—96	A	S	M	L
— rotundifolia, L.—83	A	S	M	L
— moschata, L.—88	A	S	M	L

17. Tiliaceæ

Species	A	S	M	L
Tilia, L.				
— parvifolia, Ehrh.—18		S	M	
— platyphyllos, Scop.—3		S	M	L
— vulgaris, Hayne		S‡	M‡	L‡

18. Lineæ

Species	A	S	M	L
Linum, L.				
— catharticum, L.—112	A	S	M	L
— angustifolium, Huds.—36	A			
— usitatissimum, L.	A‡	S‡	M‡	L‡
Radiola, Gmelin				
— linoides, Roth—84	A	S		L

19. Geraniaceæ

Species	A	S	M	L
Geranium, L.				
— sanguineum, L. 63		S		
— sylvaticum, L.—56		S		L
— pratense, L.—90	A	S	M	L
— perenne, Huds.—58	A	S	M	
— phæum, L.		S‡	M‡	L‡
— molle, L.—112	A	S	M	L
— rotundifolium, L.—21	A	S	M	L
— pusillum, L.—79	A	S	M	L
— columbinum, L.—76	A	S	M	L
— dissectum, L.—110	A	S	M	L
— Robertianum, L.—111	A	S	M	L
— lucidum, L.—93		S	M	L
Erodium, L'Hérit.				
— cicutarium, L'Hérit.—104	A	S	M	L
— moschatum, L'Hérit.—11	A		M	L
— maritimum, L'Hérit.—33		S	M*	L
Oxalis, L.				
— Acetosella, L.—109	A	S	M	L

20. Ilicineæ

Species	A	S	M	L
Ilex, L.				
— Aquifolium, L.—105	A	S	M	L

22. Celastrineæ

Species	A	S	M	L
Euonymus, L.				
— europæus, L.—74	A	S	M	L

23. Rhamneæ

Species	A	S	M	L
Rhamnus, L.				
— catharticus, L.—57	A	S	M	L
— Frangula, L.—63		S		L

24. Sapindaceæ

Species	A	S	M	L
Acer, L.				
— campestre, L.—62	A	S	M	L
— Pseudo-platanus, L.	A‡	S‡	M‡	L‡

BOTANY

25. LEGUMINOSÆ

	A	S	M	L
Genista, L.				
— anglica, L.—86		S	M	
— pilosa, L.—6			M*	
— tinctoria, L.—76	A	S	M	L
Ulex, L.				
— europæus, L.—112	A	S	M	L
— nanus, Forster—27		S		L
sub-sp.Gallii, Planch.—55	A	S	M	L
Cytisus, L.				
— scoparius, Link—109	A	S	M	L
Ononis, L.				
— spinosa, L.—71	A	S	M	L
sub-sp. repens, L.—100	A	S	M	L
Trigonella, L.				
— ornithopodioides, DC.—29			M	
Medicago, L.				
— sativa, L.	A	S	M	
— lupulina, L.—105	A	S	M	L
— denticulata, Willd.—20		S	M	L
var. apiculata, Willd.			M	
— maculata, Sibth.—43		S	M	
Melilotus, Hall				
— altissima, Thuill.—72	A	S	M	L
— alba, Desr.—40			M	
— officinalis, Desr.		S*	M*	L*
Trifolium, L.				
— arvense, L.—94	A	S	M	L
— incarnatum, L.		S‡		
— ochroleucum, L.—11		S‡		
— pratense, L.—112	A	S	M	L
var. parviflora, Bab.			M	
— medium, L.—106	A	S	M	L
— striatum, L.—74	A	S	M	
— scabrum, L.—49		S		
— hybridum, L.	A‡	S‡	M‡	L‡
— repens, L.—112	A	S‡	M	L
— fragiferum, L.—72	A	S	M	L
— procumbens, L.—105	A	S	M	L
— dubium, Sibth.—109	A	S	M	L
— filiforme, L.—64	A	S	M	L
Anthyllis, L.				
— Vulneraria, L.—105	A	S	M	L
Lotus, L.				
— corniculatus, L.—112	A	S	M	L
sub-sp. tenuis, Waldst. & Kit.—66	A	S	M	L
— uliginosus, Schkuhr.—100	A	S	M	L
Astragalus, L.				
— hypoglottis, L.—41	A			
— glycyphyllos, L.—64	A	S	M	
Ornithopus, L.				
— perpusillus, L.—83		S	M	L
Hippocrepis, L.				
— comosa, L.—45	A			
Onobrychis, L.				
— sativa, Lamk.—30	A	S	M	
Vicia, L.				
— tetrasperma, Mœnch—74	A	S	M	L
— hirsuta, Gray—109	A	S	M	L
sub-sp. gracilis, Loisel.—24		S	M	
— Cracca, L.—112	A	S	M	L
— sylvatica, L.—78	A	S	M	L
— sepium, L.—110	A	S	M	L

	A	S	M	L
Vicia sativa, L.	A‡	S‡	M‡	L‡
— angustifolia, L.—92		S	M	
var. Bobartii, Koch.		S	M	
— lathyroides, L.—54		S	M†	
— bithynica, L.—18		S	M	
Lathyrus, L.				
— Aphaca, L.—27	A	S	M	
— Nissolia, L.—40	A	S	M	
— pratensis, L.—112	A	S	M	L
— sylvestris, L.—62	A	S	M	
— palustris, L.—20			M	
— macrorrhizus, Wimm.—107	A	S	M	L

26. ROSACEÆ

	A	S	M	L
Prunus, L.				
— communis, Huds.—108	A	S	M	L
sub-sp. insititia,Huds.—65	A	S	M	L
sub-sp. domestica, L.	A‡	S‡	M‡	L‡
— Cerasus, L.—33		S	M	
— Avium, L.—97	A	S	M	L
Spiræa, L.				
— Ulmaria, L.—112	A	S	M	L
— Filipendula, L.—63	A	S	M	
— salicifolia, L.		S*	M*	L‡
Rubus, L.				
— saxatilis, L.—67		S		
— Idæus, L—110	A	S	M	L
— fruticosus, L.				
sub-sp. suberectus, Anders.				L
var. plicatus, W. and N.				L
sub-sp.rhamnifolius,W.&N.				L
var. incurvatus, Bab.			M	
sub-sp. Lindleianus, Lees			M	
sub-sp. corylifolius, Sm.	A	S	M	L
var. sublustris Lees			M	
var. Balfourianus, Blox	A	S	M	L
sub-sp. cæsius, L.	A	S	M	L
var. tenuis, Bell. Salt.			M	
sub-sp. discolor, W. and N.		S	M	L
var. thyrsoideus, Wimm.			M	
sub-sp. leucostachys, Sm.	A		M	L
sub-sp. villicaulis, Weihe				L
sub-sp. Salteri, Bab.		S	M	
sub-sp. umbrosus, Arrh.		S		L
sub-sp.macrophyllus,Weihe		S	M	L‡
sub-sp.mucronulatus,Boreau				L
sub-sp. Sprengelii, Weihe				L
sub-sp. dumetorum,Weihe	A	S	M	L
var. tuberculatus, Bab.				L
var. diversifolius, Lindl.			M	L
sub-sp. radula, Weihe				L
sub-sp. Bloxami, Lees		S		
var. scaber, Weihe		S		
var. fusco-ater, Weihe				L
sub-sp. Kœhleri, Weihe				L
var. infestus, Weihe				L
sub-sp. Hystrix, Weihe		S		
var. rosaceus, Weihe		S		
sub-sp. pallidus, Weihe		S		
var. foliosus, Weihe		S	M	
var. hirtus, Weihe		S		
sub-sp. glandulosus, Bell				L
var. bellardi, Weihe		S		L
var. rotundifolius, Blox.		S	M	L
sub-sp. pyramidalis, Bab.		S		

	A	S	M	L
Geum, L.				
— urbanum, L.—107 . . .	A	S	M	L
— rivale, L.—93	A	S	M	L
— intermedium, Ehrh.—57 .			M	L
Fragaria, L.				
— vesca, L.—111 . . .	A	S	M	L
— elatior, Ehrh.	A‡		M‡	
Potentilla, L.				
— Comarum, Nestl.—99 . .		S		
— Tormentilla, Scop.—112	A	S	M	L
sub-sp. procumbens, Sibth. —78			M	L
— reptans, L.—95 . . .	A	S	M	L
— verna, L.—22			M	
— anserina, L.—112. . .	A	S	M	L
— Fragariastrum, Ehrh.—106 .	A	S	M	L
— argentea, L.—57 . . .		S	M	L
Alchemilla, L.				
— arvensis, Scop.—111 . .	A	S	M	L
— vulgaris, L.—107 . . .	A	S	M	L
Agrimonia, L.				
— Eupatoria, L.—105 . .	A	S	M	L
sub-sp. odorata, Mill.—44	A	S	M	L
Poterium, L.				
— Sanguisorba, L.—74 . .	A	S	M	L
— muricatum, Spach. . .	A		M	
— officinale, Hook, fil.—64	A	S	M	L
Rosa, L.				
— spinosissima, L.—94 . .	A	S	M	L
— villosa, L.				
sub.-sp. mollis, Sm. . .	A†	S†	M†	L†
sub-sp. tomentosa, Sm. .	A	S	M	L
var. scabriuscula, Sm. . .			M	L
— involuta, Sm. . . .	A	S	M	L
var. Sabini, Woods . .	A	S	M	L
var. Doniana, Woods . .	A	S	M	L
— rubiginosa, L.—62 . .	A	S	M	L
sub-sp. micrantha, Sm. .	A	S	M	
sub-sp. agrestis, Savi. .			M	
var. inodora, Fries. .	A	S	M	L
— canina, L.—112 . .	A	S	M	L
— f. lutetiana, Leman . .	A	S	M	L
— f. urbica, Leman . . .		S	M	L
var. arvatica, Baker . .				L
— f. dumetorum, Thuill. . .			M	L
— f. andevagensis, Bast. . .			M	
var. verticillacantha, Merat			M	L
— arvensis, Huds.—69 . .	A	S	M	L
var. bibracteata, Bast. . .			M	
sub-sp. stylosa, Bast. . .				
var. systyla, Bast. . . .	A	S	M	L
Pyrus, L.				
— torminalis, Ehrh.—50 . .	A	S	M	L
— Aria, Ehrh.—50	A	S	M	
— Aucuparia, Ehrh.—108 .		S	M	L
— communis, L.—49 . .	A	S	M	L
var. Pyraster, L. . . .			M	
var. Achras, Gært. . .			M	
— Malus, L.—88 . . .	A	S	M	L
var. acerba, DC. . . .		S	M	
var. mitis, Wallr. . . .			M	
Cratægus, L.				
— Oxyacantha, L.—111 . .		S	M	
sub-sp. monogyna, Jacq. .	A	S	M	L

27. SAXIFRAGEÆ

	A	S	M	L
Saxifraga, L.				
— umbrosa, L.—I.		S‡		
— tridactylites, L.—81 . .	A	S	M	L
— granulata, L.—78 . . .	A	S	M	L
— hypnoides, L.— ? . . .	A			
Chrysosplenium, L.				
— oppositifolium, L.—107 .		S	M	L
— alternifolium, L.—70 . .		S	M	L
Parnassia, L.				
— palustris, L.—82	A*	S		L*
Ribes, Linn.				
— Grossularia, L.	A‡	S‡	M‡	L‡
— alpinum, L.—35			M	L
— rubrum, L.— ?		S‡	M‡	L‡
— nigrum, L.— ? . . .		S	M‡	L

28. CRASSULACEÆ

	A	S	M	L
Cotyledon, L.				
— Umbilicus, L.—54 . . .		S	M	L*
Sedum, L.				
— Telephium, L.—75 . . .		S	M	L
— album, L.— ?	A‡	S‡	M	
— dasyphyllum, L. . . .	A‡	S‡	M‡	
— acre, L.—107 . . .	A	S	M	L
— rupestre, Huds.—12 . .			M‡	
— reflexum, L.	A‡	S‡	M‡	L‡
Sempervivum, L.				
— tectorum, L.	A‡	S‡	M‡	L‡

29. DROSERACEÆ

	A	S	M	L
Drosera, L.				
— rotundifolia, L.—109 . .		S	M	L*

30. HALORAGEÆ

	A	S	M	L
Hippuris, L.				
— vulgaris, L.—90 . . .		S	M	
Myriophyllum, L.				
— verticillatum, L.—49 . .		S	M	
— alterniflorum, DC.—80 . .			M	
— spicatum, L.—78 . . .		S	M	L
Callitriche, L.				
— verna, L.— ?				
sub-sp. platycarpa, Kuetz. —93	A	S	M	L
sub-sp.hamulata,Kuetz.— ?			M	

31. LYTHRACEÆ

	A	S	M	L
Peplis, L.				
— Portula, L.—98	A	S	M	L
Lythrum, L.				
— Salicaria, L.—92 . . .	A	S	M	L
— hyssopifolia, L.—6 . . .	A§			

32. ONAGRARIEÆ

	A	S	M	L
Epilobium, L.				
— angustifolium, L.—96 . .		S	M	L
— hirsutum, L.—96 . . .	A	S	M	L
— parviflorum, Schreb.—103 .	A	S	M	L
— montanum, L.—112 . .	A	S	M	L
— roseum, Schreb.—46 . .		S	M	L
— tetragonum, L.—42 . .			M	
sub-sp. obscurum, Schreb. —97			M	L

BOTANY

	A	S	M	L
Epilobium palustre, L.—110 .	A	S	M	L
Œnothera, L.				
— biennis, L.	A‡		M‡	
Circæa, L.				
— lutetiana, L.—103 . . .	A	S	M	L

33. CUCURBITACEÆ

	A	S	M	L
Bryonia, L.				
— dioica, Jacq.—59	A	S	M	L

34. UMBELLIFERÆ

	A	S	M	L
Hydrocotyle, L.				
— vulgaris, L.—110 . . .	A	S	M	L
Astrantia, L.				
— major, L.			M‡*	
Sanicula, L.				
— europæa, L.—109 . . .	A	S	M	L
Conium, L.				
— maculatum, L.—104 . . .	A	S	M	L
Smyrnium, L.				
— Olusatrum, L.—63 . . .	A	S		
Bupleurum, L.				
— rotundifolium, L.—39 . .	A	S	M	L
— aristatum, Bartl.—2 . . .	A*			
— tenuissimum, L.—23 . .	A	S	M	
Apium, L.				
— graveolens, L.—58 . . .	A	S	M	
— nodiflorum, Reichb. fil.—82	A	S	M	L
var. repens, Hook. fil.—1	A	S		
— inundatum, Reichb. fil.—96		S	M	L*
Carum, L.				
— Carui, L.		S‡	M‡	
— segetum, Benth. & Hook. fil. —45	A	S	M	
— Petroselinum, Benth. & Hook. fil.		S‡	M‡	
Sison, L.				
— Amomum, L.—54 . . .	A	S	M	L
Cicuta, L.				
— virosa, L.—37.				
Sium, L.				
— latifolium, L.—42 . . .		S*		
— angustifolium, L.—81 . .	A	S	M	L
Ægopodium, L.				
— Podagraria, L.—100 . . .	A	S	M	L
Pimpinella, L.				
— Saxifraga, L.—102 . . .	A	S	M	L
var. dissecta, Retz . . .			M	
— major, Huds.—51 . . .	A	S	M	
Conopodium, Koch				
— denudatum, Koch—108 .	A	S	M	L
Myrrhis, L.				
— odorata, Scop.—65 . . .			M	L
Scandix, L.				
— Pecten-Veneris, L.—93 . .	A	S	M	L
Chærophyllum, L.				
— temulum, L.—99 . . .	A	S	M	L
Anthriscus, Bernh.				
— vulgaris, Bernh.—79 . .	A	S	M	L
— sylvestris, Hoffm.—107 . .	A	S	M	L
— Cerefolium, Hoffm. . . .		S‡		L‡
Seseli, L.				
— Libanotis, Koch—3 . . .		S‡		
Fœniculum, L.				

	A	S	M	L
Fœniculum officinale, All. . .	A‡	S‡	M‡	
Œnanthe, L.				
— fistulosa, L.—68	A	S	M	L
— pimpinelloides, L.—16 . .	A	S	M	
— peucedanifolia, Poll.—22 .		S	M	
— Lachenalii, C. Gmel.—72 .	A	S	M	
— crocata, Linn.—92 . . .		S	M	
— Phellandrium, Lam.—56 .		S	M	L
Æthusa, L.				
— Cynapium, L.—96 . . .	A	S	M	L
Silaus, Bess.				
— pratensis, Bess.—68 . . .	A	S	M	L
Angelica, L.				
— sylvestris, L.—111 . . .	A	S	M	L
Peucedanum, L.				
— sativum, Benth. & Hook. fil. —57	A	S	M	L
Heracleum, L.				
— Sphondylium, L.—112 . .	A	S	M	L
Daucus, L.				
— Carota, L.—109	A	S	M	L
Caucalis, L.				
— daucoides, L.—28 . . .	A*	S		
— arvensis, Huds.—57 . . .	A	S	M	L
— Anthriscus, Huds.—107. .	A	S	M	L
— nodosa, Scop.—73 . . .	A	S	M	L

35. ARALIACEÆ

	A	S	M	L
Hedera, L.				
— Helix, L.—112	A	S	M	L

36. CORNACEÆ

	A	S	M	L
Cornus, L.				
— sanguinea, L.—67 . . .	A	S	M	L

37. CAPRIFOLIACEÆ

	A	S	M	L
Viburnum, L.				
— Lantana, L.—45	A	S	M	L
— Opulus, L.—101 . . .	A	S	M	L
Sambucus, L.				
— Ebulus, L.—77 . . .		S	M	L
— nigra, L.—109	A	S	M	L
Adoxa, L.				
— Moschatellina, L.—91 . .	A	S	M	L
Lonicera, L.				
— Periclymenum, L.—112 . .	A	S	M	L
— Xylosteum, L.		S‡	M‡	
— Caprifolium, L.		S‡		

38. RUBIACEÆ

	A	S	M	L
Gallium, L.				
— verum, L.—111	A	S	M	L
var. ochroleucum, Syme .			M	
— Cruciata, Scop.—97 . . .	A	S	M	L
— palustre, L.—112 . . .	A	S	M	L
var. Witheringii, Sm. . .			M	
— uliginosum, L.—93 . . .	A	S	M	L
— saxatile, L.—111 . . .	A	S	M	L
— sylvestre, Poll.—28 . . .			M	
— Mollugo, L.—77 . . .	A	S	M	L
sub-sp. erectum, Huds.— 29	A		M	
— Aparine, L.—112 . . .	A	S	M	L
— tricorne, Stokes—43 . .	A	S	M	L

	A	S	M	L
Gallium anglicum, Huds.—10 .			M	
Asperula, L.				
— odorata, L.—106	A	S	M	L
— cynanchica, L.—40	A			
Sherardia, L.				
— arvensis, L.—109	A	S	M	L
39. VALERIANEÆ				
Valeriana, L.				
— dioica, L.—73	A	S	M	L
— officinalis, L.— ?	A	S	M	L
var. sambucifolia, Mikan	A		M	L
Centranthus, DC.				
— ruber, DC.		S‡		
Valerianella, Mœnch				
— olitoria, Mœnch—99	A	S	M	L
— carinata, Loisel.—15	A§	S§	M‡	
— auricula, DC.—37	A			
— dentata, Poll.—82	A	S	M	L
var. mixta, Dufr.		S		
— eriocarpa, Desv.—5			M§	
40. DIPSACEÆ				
Dipsacus, L.				
— sylvestris, Huds.—74	A	S	M	L
— pilosus, L.—52	A	S	M	L
Scabiosa, L.				
— succisa, L.—112	A	S	M	L
— Columbaria, L.—72	A	S	M	
— arvensis, L.—98	A	S	M	L
41. COMPOSITÆ				
Eupatorium, L.				
— cannabinum, L.—98	A	S	M	L
Erigeron, L.				
— acre—65	A	S	M	L
— canadense, L.			M	
Solidago, L.				
— Virgaurea, L.—109		S	M	L
Bellis, L.				
— perennis, L.—112	A	S	M	L
Inula, L.				
— Conyza, DC.—58	A	S	M	L
— Helenium, L.— ?	A	S	M	L
Pulicaria, Gærtn.				
— dysenterica, Gærtn.—79	A	S	M	L
— vulgaris, Gærtn.—25			M	
Gnaphalium, L.				
— sylvaticum, L.—102	A	S	M	L
— uliginosum, L.—111	A	S	M	L
Filago, L.				
— germanica, L.—96	A	S	M	L
var. apiculata, G. E. Sm. —19		S		
— minima, Fr.—91		S	M	L
Bidens, L.				
— cernua, L.—82	A	S	M	L
— tripartita, L.—84	A	S	M	L
Anthemis, Mich.				
— arvensis, L.—73	A	S	M	L
— Cotula, L.—74	A	S	M	L
— nobilis, L.—49		S	M	
Achillea, L.				
— Ptarmica, L.—110	A	S	M	L
Achillea Millefolium, L.—112	A	S	M	L
Matricaria, L.				
— Chamomilla, L.—64	A	S	M	L
— inodora, L.—111	A	S	M	L
Chrysanthemum, L.				
— segetum, L.—110	A	S	M	L
— Leucanthemum, L.—112	A	S	M	L
— Parthenium, Pers.	A‡	S‡	M‡	L‡
Tanacetum, L.				
— vulgare, L.—105	A	S	M	L
Artemisia, L.				
— Absinthium, L.—72	A	S	M	L
— vulgaris, L.—110	A	S	M	L
Petasites, L.				
— vulgaris, Desf.—105	A	S	M	L
Tussilago, L.				
— Farfara, L.—112	A	S	M	L
Doronicum, L.				
— Pardalianches, L.		S‡	M‡	L‡
Senecio, L.				
— vulgaris, L.—112	A	S	M	L
— sylvaticus, L.—107	A	S	M	L
— viscosus, L.—33	A*	S		
— Jacobæa, L.—112	A	S	M	L
— erucifolius, L.—67	A	S	M	L
— aquaticus, Huds.—111	A	S	M	L
— squalidus, L.		S‡		
Arctium, L.				
— majus, Bernh.—43	A	S	M	L
sub-sp. minus, Bernh.—91	A	S	M	L
var. intermedium, Lange —36?		S	M	
var. nemorosum, Lej.— 28?			M	
Carlina, L.				
— vulgaris, L.—83	A	S	M	L
Centaurea, L.				
— nigra, L.—111	A	S	M	L
var. decipiens, Thuill.	A	S		L
— Scabiosa, L.—82	A	S	M	L
— Cyanus, L.—95	A	S	M	
— paniculata, L.—C.			M‡	
— Calcitrapa, L.—17		S		
— solstitialis, L.			M‡	
Serratula, L.				
— tinctoria, L.—64	A	S	M	L
Carduus, L.				
— nutans, L.—75	A	S	M	L
— crispus, L.—87			M	L
var. acanthoides, L.	A	S		L
— pycnocephalus, L.—70		S		
Cnicus, L.				
— lanceolatus, Willd.—112	A	S	M	L
— eriophorus, Roth.—48	A	S	M	L
— acaulis, Willd.—44	A	S		
var. dubius, Willd.	A			
— arvensis, Hoffm.—112	A	S	M	L
sub-sp. setosus, Bess.			M	
— palustris, Willd.—112	A	S	M	L
— Forsteri, Sm.		S		
— pratensis, Willd.—49	A	S	M	L
Onopordon, L.				
— Acanthium, L.—60	A	S	M	L
Silybum, Gærtn.				

	A	S	M	L
Silybum Marianum, Gærtn. . .	A‡	S‡	M‡	L‡
Cichorium, L.				
— Intybus, L.—65 . . .	A	S	M	L
Arnoseris, Gærtn.				
— pusilla, Gærtn.—23 . .	A*	S*		
Lapsana, L.				
— communis, L.—112 . .	A	S	M	L
Picris, L.				
— hieracioides, L.—60 . .	A	S	M	L
— echioides, L.—65. . . .	A	S	M	L
Crepis, L.				
— virens, L.—110	A	S	M	L
— biennis, L.—27			M	
— fœtida, L.—15			M	
— taraxacifolia, Thuill.—31 .		S	M	
— setosa, Hall, fil.			M‡	
— paludosa, Mœnch—62 . .		S		
Hieracium, L.				
— Pilosella, L.—110 . . .	A	S	M	L
— aurantiacum, L.			M‡	
— murorum, L.—68. . . .	A	S	M	L
— sylvaticum, Sm.—90 . . .	A	S	M	L
sub-sp. tridentatum, Fries —6			M	
— umbellatum, L.—88 . . .	A	S	M	L
— boreale, Fries—96 . . .	A	S	M	L
Hypochæris, L.				
— glabra, L.—43.	A*	S	M	
— radicata, L.—111. . .	A	S	M	L
Leontodon, L.				
— hirtus, L.—71.	A	S	M	L
— hispidus, L.—92 . . .	A	S	M	L
— autumnalis, L.—110 . . .	A	S	M	L
Taraxacum, Hall				
— officinale, Web.—112. . .	A	S	M	L
var. erythrospermum, Andrz.			M	
var. lævigatum, DC. . .			M	
var. palustre, DC.—74 .		S	M	
Lactuca, L.				
— virosa, L.—51.		S		
— Scariola, L.—6			M §	
— saligna, L.—9.		S*		
— muralis, Fresen.—69. . .	A	S	M	L
Sonchus, L.				
— arvensis, L.—111. . . .	A	S	M	L
— oleraceus, L.—111 . . .	A	S	M	L
sub-sp. asper, Hoffm.—104	A	S	M	L
Tragopogon, L.				
— pratense, L.—84	A	S	M	L
var. minor, Fries . . .		S	M	
— porrifolius, L.			M‡	

42. CAMPANULACEÆ

	A	S	M	L
Jasione, L.				
— montana, L.—80		S	M	L
Wahlenbergia, Schrad.				
— hederacea, Reichb.—46 . .		S*		
Campanula, L.				
— rotundifolia, L.—111 .	A	S	M	L
— Rapunculus, L.—31 . . .		S	M	
— patula, L.—29.	A	S	M	L
— latifolia, L.—61	A	S	M	L

	A	S	M	L
Campanula rapunculoides, L.—24	A‡	S‡	M‡	L‡
— Trachelium, L.—59 . . .	A	S	M	L
— glomerata, L.—51 . . .	A		M	L
Specularia, Heist.				
— hybrida, A. DC.—47 . .	A	S	M	

43. ERICACEÆ

	A	S	M	L
Vaccinium, L.				
— Myrtillus, L.—101 . . .		S	M	L
— Vitis-Idæa, L.—67 . . .				L
— Oxycoccos, L.—68 . . .		S*		L*
Erica, L.				
— Tetralix, L.—110	A	S		L
— cinerea, L.—108		S		L
Calluna, Salisb.				
— vulgaris, Salisb.—111 . .	A	S	M	L
Pyrola, L.				
— minor, L.—68.		S		
— media, Sw.—42		S*		L*
— rotundifolia, L.—29 . . .		S		

44. MONOTROPEÆ

	A	S	M	L
Hypopitys, Scop.				
— multiflora, Scop.—46 . .	A	S		

46. PRIMULACEÆ

	A	S	M	L
Primula, L.				
— vulgaris, Huds.—111. . .	A	S	M	L
var. caulescens, Koch . .	A	S	M	L
× veris		S	M	
— veris, L.—89	A	S	M	L
Lysimachia, L.				
— vulgaris, L.—78	A	S	M	L
— nemorum, L.—109 . .	A	S	M	L
— Nummularia, L.—70. . .	A	S	M	L
Glaux, L.				
— maritima, L.—71. . . .		S		
Centunculus, L.				
— minimus, L.—64			M	L
Anagallis, L.				
— arvensis, L.—99	A	S	M	L
var. pallida			M	
var. cærulea, Schreb.—48	A	S	M	
— tenella, L.—97	A	S	M	L
Hottonia, L.				
— palustris, L.—48		S	M	
Samolus, L.				
— Valerandi, L.—82. . . .	A	S		

47. OLEACEÆ

	A	S	M	L
Ligustrum, L.				
— vulgare, L.—83	A	S	M	L
Fraxinus, L.				
— excelsior, L.—109. . . .	A	S	M	L

48. APOCYNACEÆ

	A	S	M	L
Vinca, L.				
— minor, L.—73.		S	M	L
— major, L.	A‡	S‡	M‡	L‡

49. GENTIANEÆ

	A	S	M	L
Chlora, L.				
— perfoliata, Huds.—60 . .	A	S	M	L

	A	S	M	L
Erythræa, Pers.				
— Centaurium, Pers.—102.	A	S	M	L
sub-sp. pulchella, Fries—43			M§	
Gentiana, L.				
— campestris, L.—85		S		
— Amarella, L.—81	A	S	M	L
Menyanthes, L.				
— trifoliata, L.—110.		S		L
Limnanthemum, S. P. Gmel.				
— peltatum, S. P. Gmel.—10	A			

50. POLEMONIACEÆ

	A	S	M	L
Polemonium, L.				
— cæruleum, L.—5				L‡§

51. BORAGINEÆ

	A	S	M	L
Echium, L.				
— vulgare, L.—92	A	S	M	L
Borago, L.				
— officinalis, L.	A‡	S‡	M‡	L‡
Symphytum, L.				
— officinale, Linn.—86	A	S	M	L
Anchusa, L.				
— arvensis, Bieb.—105	A	S	M	L
— sempervirens, L.		S‡	M‡	L‡
Lithospermum, L.				
— officinale, L.—77	A	S	M	
— arvense, L.—86	A	S	M	L
Pulmonaria, L.				
— officinalis, L.—1		S‡	M‡	L‡
Myosotis, L.				
— palustris, With.—104.	A	S	M	L
— cæspitosa, F. Schultz—107	A	S	M	L
sub-sp. repens, D. Don—92		S	M	L
— sylvatica, Hoffm.—45	A	S	M	L
— arvensis, Lam.—112	A	S	M	L
var. umbrosa, Bab.		S		
— collina, Hoffm.—92		S	M	L
— versicolor, Reichb.—108.		S	M	L
Cynoglossum, L.				
— officinale, L.—76.	A	S	M	L
— montanum, Lamk.—17	A	S	M	

52. CONVOLVULACEÆ

	A	S	M	L
Convolvulus, L.				
— arvensis, L.—96	A	S	M	L
— sepium, L.—94	A	S	M	L
— Soldanella, L.—46		S		
Cuscuta, L.				
— europæa, L.—31	A	S	M	
— Epithymum, Murr.—46.	A			
var. Trifolii, Bab.	A‡		M‡	L‡
— Epilinum, Weihe		S‡	M‡	

53. SOLANACEÆ

	A	S	M	L
Hyoscyamus, L.				
— niger, L.—79	A	S	M	L
Solanum, L.				
— Dulcamara, L.—97	A	S	M	L
— nigrum, L.—64	A	S	M	L
Atropa, L.				
— Belladonna, L.—54		S		L

54. PLANTAGINEÆ

	A	S	M	L
Plantago, L.				
— major, L.—112	A	S	M	L
var. intermedia, Gilib.			M	
— media, L.—81.	A	S	M	L
— lanceolata, L.—112	A	S	M	L
var. Timbali, Jord.			M‡	
— maritima, L.—78.		S§		
— Coronopus, L.—96	A	S	M	L
Litorella, L.				
— lacustris, L.—94			M	L

55. SCROPHULARINEÆ

	A	S	M	L
Verbascum, L.				
— Thapsus, L.—91	A	S	M	L
— Lychnitis, L.—12.		S		
— nigrum, L.—43		S	M	L
— Blattaria, L.—?		S*	M*	
sub-sp. virgatum, With—?	A	S	M	
Linaria, Tournf.				
— Cymbalaria, Mill.	A‡	S‡	M‡	L‡
— spuria, Mill.—43	A	S	M	
— Elatine, Mill.—55	A	S	M	L
— repens, Mill.—21		S		L
— vulgaris, Mill.—99	A	S	M	L
— minor, Desf.—62.	A	S	M	
Antirrhinum, L.				
— Orontium, L.—47		S	M	
— majus, L.	A‡	S‡	M‡	
Scrophularia, L.				
— nodosa, L.—109	A	S	M	L
— aquatica, L.—72	A	S	M	L
var. cinerea, Dum.			M	
sub-sp. umbrosa, Dum.—20		S	M	L
— vernalis, L.				L‡
Mimulus, L.				
— luteus, L.		S‡		L‡
Limosella, L.				
— aquatica, L.—43	A		M	L
Digitalis, L.				
— purpurea, L.—107	A	S	M	L
Veronica, L.				
— agrestis, L.—110	A	S	M	L
sub-sp. polita, Fries—89.	A	S	M	L
— Buxbaumii, Ten.—90	A‡	S‡	M‡	L‡
— hederæfolia, L.—100	A	S	M	L
— arvensis, L.—111	A	S	M	L
— serpyllifolia, L.—112	A	S	M	L
— officinalis, L.—111	A	S	M	L
— Chamædrys, L.—111	A	S	M	L
— montana, L.—89	A	S	M	L
— scutellata, L.—107	A	S	M	L
— Beccabunga, L.—112	A	S	M	L
— Anagallis, L.—100	A	S	M	L
— spicata, L.—3		S§		
Bartsia, L.				
— Odontites, Huds.—111	A	S	M	L
var. verna, Reichb.			M	
var. serotina, Reichb.			M	
Euphrasia, L.				
— officinalis, L.—112	A	S	M	L
Rhinanthus, L.				
— Crista-galli, L.—112	A	S	M	L

Pedicularis, L.				
— palustris, L.—110 . . .	A	S		L
— sylvatica, L.—112 . . .	A	S	M	L
Melampyrum, L.				
— pratense, L.—107 . . .	A	S	M	L
var. montanum, Johnst. .				L
— cristatum, L.—10. . . .		S*		
Lathræa, L.				
— squamaria, L.—62. . . .		S	M	L

56. OROBANCHEÆ

Orobanche, L.				
— major, L.—61.		S	M	L
— elatior, Sutton—28 . . .	A§		M	
— minor, Sm.—32 . . .	A	S	M	

57. LENTIBULARINEÆ

Pinguicula, L.				
— vulgaris, L.—93 . . .	A*		M	L*
Utricularia, L.				
— vulgaris, L.—86			M	
— minor, L.—72 . . .		S		

58. VERBENACEÆ

Verbena, L.				
— officinalis, L.—67. . .	A	S	M	L

59. LABIATÆ

Mentha, L.				
— sylvestris, L.—59 . . .		S	M	
— rotundifolia, Huds.—52 . .		S	M	
— viridis, L.		S‡	M‡	L‡
— piperita, L.—68 . . .	A	S	M	L
var. officinalis, Hull . .			M	
var. vulgaris, Sole . . .			M	
— aquatica, L.—111. . .	A	S	M	L
var. subglabra, Baker . .			M	
var. citrata, Ehrh. . . .		S		
var. palustris, Sole . . .			M	
— sativa, L.—82 . . .	A	S	M	L
var. paludosa, Sole . .			M	
var. subglabra, Baker . .			M	
sub-sp. rubra, Sm.—? .	A		M	
sub-sp. gentilis, L.—? .		S	M	
— arvensis, L.—105 . . .	A	S	M	L
var. agrestis, Sole . . .		S	M	
— Pulegium, L.—52 . .	A	S	M	L
Lycopus, L.				
— europæus, L.—95 . .	A	S	M	L
Origanum, L.				
— vulgare, L.—90 . . .	A	S	M	
Thymus, L.				
— Serpyllum, Fries—112 . .	A	S	M	L
sub-sp. Chamædrys, Fries				
—40		S	M	L
Calamintha, Lam.				
— officinalis, Mœnch—62 . .	A	S	M	L
sub-sp. Nepeta, Clairv.—9	A			
sub-sp. sylvatica, Bromf.				
—3		S§		
— Clinopodium, Benth.—89 .	A	S	M	L
— Acinos, Clairv.—74 . .	A	S	M	
Melissa, L.				
— officinalis, L.		S‡	M‡	

Salvia, L.				
— Verbenaca, L.—64	A	S	M	L
— pratensis, L.—3		S	M	
Nepeta, L.				
— Cataria, L.—58		S	M	L
— Glechoma, Benth.—103 .	A	S	M	L
Brunella, L.				
— vulgaris, L.—112	A	S	M	L
Scutellaria, L.				
— galericulata, L.—103 . .	A	S	M	L
— minor, Huds.—72 . . .		S	M	L
Melittis, L.				
— Melissophyllum, L.—9 . .				L*
Marrubium, L.				
— vulgare, L.—66	A	S	M	L
Stachys, L.				
— sylvatica, L.—112 . . .	A	S	M	L
— palustris, L.—111 . . .	A	S	M	L
— ambigua, Sm.			M	
— arvensis, L.—99 . . .	A	S	M	L
— Betonica, Benth.—82 . .	A	S	M	L
Galeopsis, L.				
— Ladanum, L.—?	A	S	M	L
sub-sp. angustifolia, Ehrh.				
—?			M	
— Tetrahit, L.—112 . . .	A	S	M	L
sub-sp. speciosa, Miller—				
80.	A	S	M	L
Leonurus, L.				
— Cardiaca, L.		S‡		
Lamium, L.				
— purpureum, L.—112 . . .	A	S	M	L
sub-sp. hybridum, Vill.—				
76.		S		
— amplexicaule, L.—96 . .	A	S	M	L
— album, L.—101	A	S	M	L
— maculatum, L.		S§	M	
— Galeobdolon, Crantz—66 .	A	S	M	L
Ballota, L.				
— nigra, L.—77	A	S	M	L
Teucrium, L.				
— Scorodonia, L.—110 . . .	A	S	M	L
Ajuga, L.				
— reptans, L.—109 . . .	A	S	M	L

60. ILLECEBRACEÆ

Scleranthus, L.				
— annuus, L.—100 . . .	A	S	M	L

61. CHENOPODIACEÆ

Chenopodium, L.				
— Vulvaria, L.—37			M	L
— polyspermum, L.—49 . .		S	M	L
— album, L.—111 . . .	A	S	M	L
var. viride, Syme. . . .			M	
— ficifolium, Sm.—18 . .		S		
— urbicum, L.—39 . . .		S	M	
— murale, L.—42 . . .		S		
— hybridum, L.—25 . . .	A			
— rubrum, L.—64 . . .	A‡	S‡	M‡	
— Bonus-Henricus, L.—100 .	A	S	M	L
Beta, L.				
— maritima, L.—57 . . .		S‡		

	A	S	M	L
Atriplex, L.				
— patula, L.—92 ?	A	S	M	L
var. erecta, Huds.		S	M	
var. angustifolia, Sm.		S	M	
sub-sp. hastata, L.—95	A	S	M	L
var. deltoidea, Bab.—53		S	M	
sub-sp. Babingtonii, Woods —70	A	S		
— laciniata, L.—43		S		
62. POLYGONACEÆ				
Polygonum, L.				
— Bistorta, L.—74		S	M	L
— amphibium, L.—108	A	S	M	L
— lapathifolium, L.—103	A	S	M	L
sub-sp. maculatum, Trim. & Dyer—33		S	M	
— Persicaria, L.—112	A	S	M	L
— mite, Schrank.—20		S		
— Hydropiper, L.—105	A	S	M	L
— minus, Huds.—52			M	
— aviculare, L.—111	A	S	M	L
var. agrestinum, Jord.		S	M	
var. arenastrum, Bor.			M	
sub-sp. Roberti, Loisel—39		S		
— Convolvulus, L.—111	A	S	M	L
Rumex, L.				
— obtusifolius, L.—109	A	S	M	L
— acutus, L.—59		S	M	
— pulcher, L.—42	A	S	M	
— maritimus, L.—39	A	S	M	L
sub-sp. palustris, Sm.—26			M	L
— crispus, L.—111	A	S	M	L
— sanguineus, L.—90			M	
var. viridis, Sibth.	A	S	M	L
— conglomeratus, Murr.—96	A	S	M	L
— Hydrolapathum, Huds.—71	A	S	M	L
— Acetosa, L.—112	A	S	M	L
— Acetosella, L.—112	A	S	M	L
63. ARISTOLOCHIACEÆ				
Aristolochia, Tournef.				
— Clematitis, L.		S‡	M‡	
64. THYMELÆACEÆ				
Daphne, L.				
— Laureola, L.—51	A	S	M	L
— Mezereum, L.—9	A		M	
66. LORANTHACEÆ				
Viscum, L.				
— album, L.—40	A	S	M	L
68. EUPHORBIACEÆ				
Euphorbia, L.				
— Helioscopia, L.—112	A	S	M	L
— platyphyllos, L.—28	A*			
— amygdaloides, L.—51	A	S	M	L
— Peplus, L.—105	A	S	M	L
— exigua, L.—83	A	S	M	L
— Esula, L.			M‡	
— Lathyris, L.		S‡§	M‡§	
Buxus, L.				
— sempervirens, L.—?	A‡			

	A	S	M	L
Mercurialis, L.				
— perennis, L.—107	A	S	M	L
69. URTICACEÆ				
Ulmus, L.				
— montana, Stokes—98	A	S	M	L
— campestris, Sm.—60	A	S	M	L
var. suberosa, Ehrh.				L
var. glabra, Mill.		S		L
Urtica, L.				
— dioica, L.—112	A	S	M	L
— urens, L.—108	A	S	M	
Parietaria, L.				
— officinalis, L.—94	A	S	M	L
Humulus, L.				
— Lupulus, L.—86	A	S	M	L
71. CUPULIFERÆ				
Betula, Tournef.				
— alba, L.—109	A	S	M	L
sub-sp. glutinosa, Fries				
var. pubescens—71			M	
Alnus, Tournef.				
— glutinosa, Gærtn.—110	A	S	M	L
Quercus, L.				
— Robur, L.—105	A	S	M	L
var. pedunculata, Ehrh.—67	A	S	M	L
var. intermedia, D. Don		S	M	
var. sessiliflora, Salisb.—65		S	M	
Fagus, L.				
— sylvatica, L.—67	A‡	S‡	M‡	L‡
Corylus, L.				
— Avellana, L.—111	A	S	M	L
Carpinus, L.				
— Betulus, L.—37		S	M	L
72. SALICINEÆ				
Populus, L.				
— alba, L.—60	A	S	M	L
sub-sp. canescens, Sm.—48	A	S	M	L
— tremula, L.—105	A	S	M	L
— nigra, L.	A‡	S‡	M‡	L‡
Salix, L.				
— triandra, L.—68	A	S	M	L
— pentandra, L.—58	A	S		L
— fragilis, L.—90	A	S	M	L
var. Russelliana, Sm.			M	
— alba, L.—92	A	S	M	L
var. vitellina, L.	A	S	M	L
var. cœrulea, Sm			M	
— Caprea, L.—106	A	S	M	L
sub-sp. cinerea, L.—106	A	S	M	L
— aurita, L.—106	A		M	L
— viminalis, L.—88	A	S	M	L
var. Smithiana, Willd.	A	S	M	L
var. acuminata, Sm.			M	
— purpurea, L.—76	A	S	M	L
73. CERATOPHYLLEÆ				
Ceratophyllum, L.				
— demersum, L.—?	A	S	M	L
sub-sp. submersum, L.	A	S	M	L

74. CONIFERÆ				
Pinus, L.				
— sylvestris, L.—17	A‡	S‡	M‡	L‡
Juniperus, L.				
— communis, L.—77	A	S	M	
Taxus, Tournef.				
— baccata, L.—52	A	S	M	L
75. HYDROCHARIDEÆ				
Hydrocharis, L.				
— Morsus-ranæ, L.—47		S	M	
Elodea, Michx.				
— canadensis, Michx.	A‡	S‡	M‡	L‡
76. ORCHIDEÆ				
Neottia, L.				
— Nidus-avis, L.—86	A	S	M	L
Listera, Br.				
— ovata, Br.—105	A	S	M	L
Spiranthes, Rich.				
— autumnalis, Rich.—59		S	M	L
— æstivalis, Rich.—2		S*		
Cephalanthera, Rich.				
— pallens, Rich.—30		S*	M	
— ensifolia, Rich.—34		S		
Epipactis, Adans.				
— latifolia, Sw.—86	A	S	M	L
sub-sp. purpurata, Sm.—6 ?			M	
var. media, Fries—38 ?	A	S	M	L
— palustris, Crantz—64		S	M	
Orchis, L.				
— mascula, L.—106	A	S	M	L
— latifolia, L.—105	A	S	M	L
sub-sp. incarnata, L.—67		S		
— maculata, L.—108	A	S	M	L
— Morio, L.—63	A	S	M	L
— ustulata, L.—43		S	M	
— pyramidalis, L.—63	A	S	M	
Ophrys, L.				
— apifera, Huds.—59	A	S	M	L
— muscifera, Huds.—43			M	
Habenaria, Br.				
— conopsea, Benth.—98	A	S	M	L
— albida, Br.—48				L§
— viridis, Br.—97	A	S	M	L
— bifolia, Br.—89		S	M	L
— chlorantha, Bab.	A	S	M	
77. IRIDEÆ				
Crocus, L.				
— vernus, All.		S‡		
Iris, L.				
— Pseudacorus, L.—112	A	S	M	L
— fœtidissima, L.—49	A	S	M	
78. AMARYLLIDEÆ				
Narcissus, L.				
— Pseudo-narcissus, L.—76	A	S	M	L
var. lobularis, Haw.			M‡†	
— biflorus, Curtis		S‡†	M‡†	
Galanthus, L.				
— nivalis, L—?		S	M	
Leucojum, L.				
— æstivum, L.—7				L

79. DIOSCOREÆ				
Tamus, L.				
— communis, L.—69	A	S	M	L
80. LILIACEÆ				
Ruscus, L.				
— aculeatus, L.—29			M‡	
Asparagus, L.				
— officinalis, L.—5	A‡		M‡	
Polygonatum, Tournef				
— multiflorum, All.—32		S	M	
Convallaria, L.				
— majalis, L.—58		S	M	L
Allium, L.				
— vineale, L.—79	A	S	M	
var. compactum, Thuill.	A		M	
— oleraceum, L.—51	A	S	M	
— carinatum, L.—3		S‡		
— ursinum, L.—108	A	S	M	L
Scilla, L.				
— nutans, Sm.—112	A	S	M	L
Ornithogalum, L.				
— pyrenaicum, L.—9		S		
— umbellatum, L.		S‡	M‡	
— nutans, L.		S‡	M‡	
Fritillaria, L.				
— Meleagris, L.—20		S‡		L‡
Tulipa, L.				
— sylvestris, L.—?		S	M	
Gagea, Salisb.				
— lutea, Ker.—42			M	
Colchicum, L.				
— autumnale, L.—40	A	S	M	L
Narthecium, Mœhr.				
— Ossifragum, Huds.—95		S		L
Paris, L.				
— quadrifolia, L.—73	A	S	M	L
81. JUNCEÆ				
Juncus, L.				
— effusus, L.—112	A	S	M	L
var. conglomeratus, L.—112	A	S	M	L
— glaucus, Leers—90	A	S	M	L
var. diffusus, Hoppe—36			M	
— squarrosus, L.—107	A	S	M	L
— compressus, Jacq.—14		S§	M	
sub-sp. Gerardi, Loisel—99	A	S	M	
— obtusiflorus, Ehrh.—58	A		M	
— articulatus, L.—111	A	S	M	L
sub-sp. supinus, Mœnch—107	A	S	M	L
sub-sp. lamprocarpus, Ehrh.—110	A	S	M	L
— bufonius, L.—112	A	S	M	L
Luzula, DC.				
— maxima, DC.—108	A	S	M	L
— vernalis, DC.—108	A	S	M	L
var. Borreri, Bromf.			M	
— Forsteri, DC.—29		S	M	
— campestris, DC.—107	A	S	M	L
var. erecta, Desv.—107	A	S	M	L

83. TYPHACEÆ

	A	S	M	L
Sparganium, L.				
— ramosum, Huds.—108	A	S	M	L
— simplex, Huds.—99		S	M	L
— natans, L.—54		S		
Typha, L.				
— latifolia, L.—81	A	S	M	L
— angustifolia, L.—58	A	S	M	L

84. AROIDEÆ

	A	S	M	L
Arum, L.				
— maculatum, L.—84	A	S	M	L
Acorus, L.				
— Calamus, L.—31	A	S	M	L

85. LEMNACEÆ

	A	S	M	L
Lemna, L.				
— minor, L.—106	A	S	M	L
— trisulca, L.—73	A	S	M	L
— gibba, L.—53	A	S	M	L
— polyrhiza, L.—56		S	M	L

86. ALISMACEÆ

	A	S	M	L
Alisma, L.				
— Plantago, L.—100	A	S	M	L
var. lanceolatum, With.			M	
— ranunculoides, L.—87	A*			
Elisma, Buchenau.				
— natans, Buch.—14		S		
Damasonium, Mill				
— stellatum, Pers.—13			M*	
Sagittaria, L.				
— sagittifolia, L.—58	A	S		L
Butomus, L.				
— umbellatus, L.—60	A	S	M	L

87. NAIADACEÆ

	A	S	M	L
Triglochin, L.				
— palustre, L.—110	A	S	M	L
Potamogeton, L.				
— natans, L.—100	A	S	M	L
— polygonifolius, Pourr.—107		S	M	L
— plantagineus, Du Croz.—32		S		
— rufescens, Schrad.—70		S		L
— heterophyllus, Schreb.—71	A	S	M	L
— lucens, L.—75	A	S	M	L
— prælongus, Wulf.—47		S		
— perfoliatus, L.—93	A	S	M	L
— crispus, L.—94	A	S	M	L
— densus, L.—59	A			
— zosterifolius, Schum.—20	A	S		
— obtusifolius, Mert. & Koch —54	A	S	M	L
— pusillus, L.—101		S	M	
— pectinatus, L.—83	A	S	M	L
sub-sp. flabellatus, Bab. —48 ?	A	S	M	
Zannichellia, L.				
— palustris, L.—71	A	S	M	L
sub-sp. brachystemon, J. Gay— ?			M	
sub-sp. pedunculata, Reichb.—21			M	

88. CYPERACEÆ

	A	S	M	L
Heleocharis, R. Br.				
— palustris, R. Br.—111	A	S	M	L
— multicaulis, Sm.—88			M	
— acicularis, R. Br.—73	A		M	L
Scirpus, L.				
— lacustris, L.—101	A	S	M	L
sub-sp. Tabernæmontani, Gmel.—57		S	M	
sub-sp. carinatus, Sm.—7		S	M	
— maritimus, L.—84	A	S	M	L
— sylvaticus, L.—75		S	M	
— setaceus, L.—108	A	S	M	L
— fluitans, L.—86	A	S	M	L
— Holoschœnus, L.—1	A†			
— cæspitosus, L.—104			M	L
— pauciflorus, Lightf.—91		S	M	L
— Caricis, Retz.—53	A		M	
Eriophorum, L.				
— vaginatum, L.—90				L
— polystachion, L.—109	A	S	M	L
sub-sp. latifolium, Hoppe —54		S	M	
— gracile, Koch—4			M†	
Rynchospora, Vahl				
— alba, Vahl—75		S		L
Schœnus, L.				
— nigricans, L.—76	A*			L†
Cladium, P. Brown				
— Mariscus, Br.—39	A			
Carex, L.				
— pulicaris, L.—107		S	M	L
— dioica, L.—79			M*	L*
— disticha, Huds.—81	A	S	M	L
— paniculata, L.—92		S	M	L
— teretiuscula, Good.—56				L†
— muricata, L.—78	A	S	M	L
sub-sp. divulsa, Good.—50	A	S	M	L
— vulpina, L. 86	A	S	M	L
— echinata, Murr.—110		S	M	L
— remota, L.—87	A	S	M	L
var. axillaris, Good.—57		S	M	
var. Bœnninghauseniana, Weihe—17		S		
— leporina, L.—112	A	S	M	L
— canescens, L.—76		S		
— elongata, L.—17		S		
— stricta, Good.—44		S†	M†	L†
— acuta, L.—72	A	S	M	L
— Goodenovii, J. Gay—110	A	S	M	L
— limosa, L.—26				L§
— glauca, Murr.—109	A	S	M	L
— pallescens, L.—90	A	S	M	L
— panicea, L.—111	A	S	M	L
— pendula, Huds.—75	A	S	M	L
— præcox, Jacq.—96	A	S	M	L
— pilulifera, L.—104		S	M	
— montana, L.—9		S		
— digitata, L.—13		S		
— hirta, L.—98	A	S	M	L
— flava, L.—65	A	S	M	L
sub-sp. Œderi, Retz.	A†	S†		L†
— distans, L.—58	A*	S*	M*	
sub-sp. fulva, Good.—84		S	M	L

BOTANY

	A	S	M	L
Carex binervis, Sm.—98.	A	S	M	L
— sylvatica, Huds.—87.	A	S	M	L
— strigosa, Huds.—35.		S	M	L
— vesicaria, L.—79.	A	S	M	L
— ampullacea, Good.—103		S	M	L
— Pseudo-cyperus, L.—48.		S	M	L
— paludosa, Good.—77	A	S	M	L
— riparia, Curtis—76.	A	S	M	L

89. Gramineæ

	A	S	M	L
Setaria, Beauv.				
— viridis, Beauv.—34		S§		
Phalaris, L.				
— canariensis, L.	A‡	S‡	M‡	L‡
— arundinacea, L.—110	A	S	M	L
Anthoxanthum, L.				
— odoratum, L.—111	A	S	M	L
— Puelii, Lecoq & Lamotte—13		S‡	M‡	
Alopecurus, L.				
— agrestes, L.—67	A	S	M	L
— pratensis, L.—105	A	S	M	L
— geniculatus, L.—112	A	S	M	L
sub-sp. fulvus, Sm.—27		S	M	L
Milium, L.				
— effusum, L.—88	A	S	M	L
Phleum, L.				
— pratense, L.—108	A	S	M	L
var. nodosum, L.			M	
Agrostis, L.				
— canina, L.—101	A	S	M	L
— alba, L.—104	A	S	M	L
— vulgaris, With.—112	A	S	M	L
var. pumila, L.			M	
var. nigra, With.	A	S	M	L
Polypogon, Desf.				
— monspeliensis, Desf.—7		S		
Calamagrostis, Adans.				
— epigeios, Roth—60	A	S	M	L
— lanceolata, Roth—39.				L†
Gastridium, Beauv.				
— lendigerum, Gaud.—24		S		
Apera, Adans.				
— Spica-venti, Beauv.—17				L
Aira, L.				
— caryophyllea, L.—110	A	S	M	L
— præcox, L.—111	A	S	M	L
Deschampsia, Beauv.				
— flexuosa, Trin.—107.	A	S	M	L
— cæspitosa, Beauv.—111	A	S	M	L
Holcus, L.				
— lanatus, L.—111	A	S	M	L
— mollis, L.—107	A	S	M	L
Trisetum, Pers.				
— flavescens, Beauv.—93	A	S	M	L
Avena, L.				
— fatua, L.—77	A	S	M	L
— pratensis, L.—76	A	S	M	
— pubescens, Huds.—91	A	S	M	
Arrhenatherum, Beauv.				
— avenaceum, Beauv.—112	A	S	M	L
var. bulbosa, Lindl.	A	S	M	L
Sieglingia, Bernh.				
— decumbens, Bernh.—108	A	S	M	L

	A	S	M	L
Phragmites, Trin.				
— communis, Trin.—104	A	S	M	L
Cynosurus, L.				
— cristatus, L.—112	A	S	M	L
Koeleria, Pers.				
— cristata, Pers.—89	A	S	M	L*
Molinia, Schrank.				
— cærulea, Mœnch.—108		S	M	L
Catabrosa, Beauv.				
— aquatica, Beauv.—94.	A	S	M	L
Melica, L.				
— nutans, L.—49		S		
— uniflora, Retz.—96	A	S	M	L
Dactylis, L.				
— glomerata, L.—112	A	S	M	L
Briza, L.				
— media, L.—108	A	S	M	L
— minor, L.—7		S		
Poa, L.				
— annua, L.—111	A	S	M	L
— compressa, L.—69	A	S	M	L
— nemoralis, L.—90		S	M	L
— pratensis, L.—110	A	S	M	L
— trivialis, L.—110.	A	S	M	L
Glyceria, R. Br.				
— aquatica, Sm.—79.	A	S	M	L
— fluitans, R. Br.—110.	A	S	M	L
var. plicata, Fries—72.	A	S	M	L
var. pedicellata, Townsend	A		M	
— distans, Wahlenb.—55	A	S		
Festuca, L.				
— elatior, L.—95	A	S	M	L
var. arundinacea, Schreb.—84		S		L
— sylvatica, Vill.—30		S§		
— ovina, L.—111	A	S	M	L
sub-sp. rubra, L.—100			M	
— Myuros, L.—52	A	S	M	L
sub-sp. sciuroides, Roth—104	A	S	M	
— uniglumis, Soland.—19	A			
— rigida, Kunth—91	A	S	M	L
— loliacea, Curt.	A	S	M	L
— gigantea, Vill.—98	A	S	M	L
var. triflora, Syme	A		M	
Bromus, L.				
— asper, Murr.—96	A	S	M	L
— erectus, Huds.—49	A	S	M	L
— sterilis, L.—108	A	S	M	L
— madritensis, L.—11		S†		
— mollis, L.—112	A	S	M	L
— racemosus, L.—14	A	S	M	
var. commutatus, Schrad.—92	A	S	M	L
— secalinus, L.—80.	A	S	M	L†
var. velutinus, Schrad.		S		
Brachypodium, Beauv.				
— sylvaticum, R. and S.—111.	A	S	M	L
— pinnatum, Beauv.—37	A	S	M	L
Lolium, L.				
— perenne, L.—112.	A	S	M	L
var. multiflora, Lam.		S††		
var. italicum, A. Br.	A‡	S‡	M‡	L‡

	A	S	M	L
Lolium temulentum, Linn.—64			M	
var. arvense, With. .			M	
Agropyrum, J. Gært.				
— caninum, Beauv.—90. .	A	S	M	L
— repens, Beauv.—111 . .	A	S	M	L
var. barbatum, Duval-Jouve			M	
sub-sp. acutum, Roem. & Schult.		S		
Nardus, L.				
— stricta, L.—107 . . .		S	M	L
Hordeum, L.				
— sylvaticum, Huds.—27 .			M	
— pratense, Huds.—62 . .	A	S	M	L
— murinum, L.—78. . .	A	S	M	L

CRYPTOGAMS

90. FILICES

	A	S	M	L
Pteris, L.				
— aquilina, L.—112. . .	A	S	M	L
Cryptogramme, Br.				
— crispa, Br.—58. . . .			M*	
Lomaria, Willd.				
— Spicant, Desv.—111 . .		S	M	L
Asplenium, L.				
— Ruta-muraria, L.—109 .	A	S	M	L
— Trichomanes, L.—108 .	A	S	M	L
— viride, Huds.—46 . .			M*	
— Adiantum-nigrum, L.—107.	A	S	M	L
— Filix-fœmina, Bernh.—110.	A	S	M	L
— Ceterach, L.—68 . . .	A	S	M	L
Scolopendrium, Sm.				
— vulgare, Sm.—101 . .	A	S	M	L
Cystopteris, Bernh.				
— fragilis, Bernh.—82 . .	A	S*		L*
Aspidium, Sw.				
— aculeatum, Sw. . . .		S	M	L
sub-sp. lobatum, Sw.—104		S	M	L
sub-sp. angulare, Willd. —63		S	M	L

	A	S	M	L
Nephrodium, Rich.				
— Filix-mas, Rich.—112 . .	A	S	M	L
— spinulosum, Desv.—83 . .	A	S	M	
sub-sp. dilatatum, Desv.—77	A	S	M	L
— Oreopteris, Presl.—102 . .		S	M	L
Polypodium, L.				
— vulgare, L.—112 . . .	A	S	M	L
— Phegopteris, L.—76 . .			M†	
— Dryopteris, L.—73 . . .		S	M	L
sub - sp. Robertianum, Hoffm.—24	A†			
Osmunda, L.				
— regalis, L.—89.		S*		L*
Ophioglossum, L.				
— vulgatum, L.—87. . . .	A	S	M	L
Botrychium, Sw.				
— Lunaria, Sw.—103 . . .	A	S	M	L

91. EQUISETACEÆ

	A	S	M	L
Equisetum, L.				
— arvense, L.—111	A	S	M	L
— maximum, Lam.—83. . .	A	S	M	L
— sylvaticum, L.—106 . . .	A	S	M	L
— palustre, L.—106. . . .	A	S	M	L
var. polystachya . . .			M	
— limosum, Sm.—107 . . .	A	S	M	L
var. fluviatile, L. . . .			M	
— hyemale, L.—41		S§	M§	L

92. LYCOPODIACEÆ

	A	S	M	L
Lycopodium, L.				
— Selago, L.—88.				L
— inundatum, L.—57 . . .		S		
— clavatum, L.—94 . . .		S		L
— complanatum, L.—55 . .		S*†		
sub-sp. Alpinum, L. . .			M	

APPENDIX A

Plants placed by Sir Joseph Hooker in the Appendix of Excluded Species in *The Student's Flora* which have been recorded for Worcestershire :—

	A	S	M	L
Anemone appenina, L. . . .		S		
Epimedium alpinum, L. . . .		S		
Glaucium phœniceum, Crantz .			M	
Alyssum incanum, L. . . .			M	
Erysimum orientale, Br. . . .			M	
Lepidium sativum, L.. . . .		S	M	
Silene Armeria, L.		S		
Saponaria Vaccaria, L. . . .		S		
Geranium nodosum, L. . . .			M	
— striatum, L.		S		
Coronilla varia, L.		S	M	
Melilotus parviflora, Lamk. . .		S	M	
Lathyrus latifolius, L.. . . .		S		
Rosa cinnamonea, L.		S		
Pyrus domestica, Sm.		S		

	A	S	M	L
Archangelica Angelica, L. . .		S		
Asperula arvensis, L.		S		
Xanthium spinosum, L. . . .		S	M	
Anthemis tinctoria, L. . . .			M	
Petasites fragrans, Presl. . . .			M	
Crepis nicæensis, Balb. . . .			M	
Symphytum peregrinum, Ledeb.			M	
Plantago arenaria, L.			M	
Amaranthus Blitum, L. . . .		S		
Polygonum Fagopyrum, L. . .	A	S	M	L
Castanea vulgaris, Lamk. . .		S	M	L
Narcissus incomparabilis, Curt. .			M	
— poeticus, L.		S		
Lilium pyrenaicum, Gouan . .		S		
Setaria glauca, Beauv.			M	

BOTANY

APPENDIX B

Plants (including some *Rubi*), varieties and hybrids, given in the 9th edition (1895) of the *London Catalogue*, and not mentioned by Sir Joseph Hooker, which have been recorded for Worcestershire :—

	A	S	M	L
Ranunculus peltatus				
var. floribundus, Bab.. .			M	
Papaver dubium, L.				
var. Lamottei, Bor. . .			M	
Sisymbrium officinale, Scop.				
var. leiocarpum, DC.. .			M	
Camelina sativa, Crantz				
var. fœtida, Fr. . . .			M	
Sisymbrium pannonicum, Jacq. .			M	
Viola odorata, L.				
f. alba (Lange)			M	
× hirta			M	
Viola Riviniana, Reich.				
f. villosa (Newm. W. & M.)	A	S	M	L
var. nemorosa (Newm. W. & M.) . . .			M	
Sagina apetala, L.				
var. prostrata, Bab. . .			M	
— Reuteri, Boiss.. . . .		S	M	
Acer campestre, L.				
var. leiocarpon, Wallr. .			M	
Trifolium pratense, L.				
var. sativum, Schreb. . .		S		
Anthyllis vulneraria, L.				
var. coccinea, L. . . .		S		
Prunus communis, Huds.				
var. macrocarpa, Wallr. .			M	
Spiræa Ulmaria				
var. denudata, Bœnn.. .	A	S	M	L
Rubus carpinifolius, W. & N. .				L
— erythrinus, Genev. . . .			M	
— nemoralis, P. J. Muell . .		S		L
— pulcherrimus, Neum.. . .	A	S	M	L
— villicaulis				
var. Selmeri, Lindeb. . .		S	M	L
— argentatus, P. S. Muell . .			M	
— pyramidalis, Kalt.. . .				L
— leucostachys, Schleich. . .		S		L
— anglosaxonicus, Gelert. . .		S		L
— Radula				
var. anglicanus, Rogers .				L
— echinatus, Lindl.			M	L
— fuscus, W. & N.		S		L
— rosaceus				
var. infecundus, Rogers .		•	M	
— adornatus, P. J. Muell . .				L
— Kœhleri				
var. pallidus, Bab. . . .			M	L
— hirtus, W. & K.		S		
var. rotundifolius, Bab. .				L
— dumetorum				
var. ferox, Weihe . . .		S		L
— cæsius				
var. aquaticus, W. & N. .			M	
var. arvensis, Wallr. . .			M	
Potentilla norvegica, L. . . .			M	

	A	S	M	L
Rosa tomentosa, Sm.				
var. pseudo-mollis, E. G. Baker.			M	
— sempervirens, L.			M	
Epilobium parviflorum, Screb.				
× hirsutum			M	
× roseum			M	
× montanum			M	
× obscurum			M	
× palustre			M	
Epilobium montanum, L.				
× roseum			M	
— Lamyi, F. Schultz . . .		S	M	
Coriandrum sativum, L. . . .			M	
Sambucus nigra, L.				
var. laciniata, L. . . .			M	
Anaphilis margaritacea, Benth. & Hook. fil.. . . .		S		
Artemisia vulgaris, L.				
var. coarctata, Forcell. . .		S		
Hieracium sciaphilum, Uechtritz			M	
Sonchus arvensis, L.				
var. glabrescens, Hall . .			M	
var. angustifolia, Mey. . .			M	
Calluna vulgaris, Salisb.				
var. glabrata, Seem. . .		S		
var. incana, auct. . . .		S		
Fraxinus excelsior, L.				
var. diversifolia, Art. . .		S		
Veronica scutellata, L.				
var. hirsuta, Weber. . .		S		
Ballota nigra, L.				
var. ruderalis, Koch . .		S		
Chenopodium polyspermum, L.				
var. spicatum, Moq. . .			M	
var. cymosum, Moq. . .			M	
— album, L.				
var. incanum, Moq. . .			M	
var. iridescens, St. Arn. .			M	
Polygonum Convolvulus, L.				
var. subulatum, V. Hall.. .			M	
— Persicaria, L.				
var. elatum, Gren. & Godr.			M	
— amphibium, L.				
var. terrestre, Leers. . .			M	
Euphorbia Esula, L.				
var. Pseudo - cyparissias (Jord.)		S		
Salix fragilis, L.				
var. britannica, F. B.White			M	
— Caprea, L.				
× aurita (capreola, J.Kern)			M	
× cinerea (Reichardti, A. Kern).			M	
— cinerea, L.				
× aurita (lutescens, A. Kern).			M	

Orchis latifolia, L.					
× maculata		S	M		
Luzula erecta, Desv.					
var. congesta	A		M		
Sparganium ramosum, Huds.					
var.microcarpum,Newman			M		
— neglectum, Beeby . . .			M		
Carex muricata, L.					
var. virens, Koch . . .			M		
— leporina, L.					
var. bracteata, Syme . .			M	L	
— flava, L.					
var. elatior, Schlec. . .					
Aira caryophyllea, L.					
var. multicaulis, Dunn .				M	
Avena fatua, L.					
var. pilosissima, Gray . .				M	
var. intermedia (Lindgr.).				M	
Festuca rottbœllioides, Kunth .			S		
Bromus mollis, L.					
var. glabratus, Doell . .				M	
Asplenium Filix-fœmina, Bernh.					
var. erectum, Syme . .				M	
Aspidium lobatum, Sw.					
var. genuinum, Syme . .				M	

APPENDIX C

Casuals, being plants not mentioned either in the *London Catalogue* or Sir Joseph Hooker's *Student's Flora*, which have been recorded for Worcestershire :—

Aquilegia alpina			L†		
Anemone fulgens	S				
— nemoralis					
var. rubra, Pritzel . . .		M			
Papaver rhœas					
var. Pryorii, Druce . .		M			
Lunaria biennis	S				
Lepidium perfoliatum . . .		M			
Impatiens Roylei					
var. macrochila. . . .		M			
Medicago lupulina					
var. Wildenowiana . .		M			
Rubus corylifolius					
var. fasciculatus, P.J.Muell		M			
— rusticanus					
var. pubigerus, Bab. . .		M			
Rosa stylosa					
var. systyla					
× arvensis		M			
Anagallis Indica				M	
Mentha gentilis					
× arvensis				M	
Salvia verticillata				M	
Rumex conglomeratus					
× crispus				M	
— obtusifolius					
var. sylvestris					
× crispus				M	
— sanguineus					
var. viridis					
× obtusifolius				M	
Cannabis sativa.				M	L
Luzula albida			S		
Carex vulpina					
× divulsa				M	
— flava					
var. minor, Townsend .				M	
Valisneria spiralis			S		

THE MOSSES (*Musci*)

The study of the geological and physical features of Worcestershire would naturally lead a moss student to anticipate a more varied moss flora than has at present been found to exist there. Probably this paucity of species is largely due to artificial, and not to natural causes. The absence of many species may be accounted for by the changes incidental to the growth of centres of industry, and the reclamation of what were in past times uncultivated waste places, such as the extensive bogs and marshes in various portions of the county. As instances Moseley Bog and Feckenham Bog may be named, both places having been the home of the rare *Hypnum scorpioides*, *Sphagnum squarrosum*, and other bog-loving species ; and Longdon Marsh and several other like places which were at one time rich in mosses. Then, too, the reclamation of the peaty

heathlands of the northern portion of the county ; the high state of cultivation that exists throughout the larger portion of its area ; the influence
of the smoky surroundings of the northern and eastern portions, an influence most fatal to the healthy growth of both mosses and lichens, and
prevailing over a wider area than would probably be supposed ; all these
are influences that tend to make the existence of many of our mosses an
impossibility.   Still, there are localities in the county in which there are
remains of a former rich moss flora ; such, for instance, as the peaty
heathlands near Hartlebury.   Here are found *Sphagnum tenellum, S.
subsecundum* and species of *Campylopus* and *Dicranum*.   Again by large
marshy pools such as Stanklin Pool, near Kidderminster, are to be found
Climacium dendroides, Hypnum cordifolium, H. giganteum and other moisture-
loving species.   Other interesting localities exist in the primitive woodlands of Wyre Forest, where the rapid streams are liable to flooding,
and have marshy moss-clad surroundings.   Here are found *Sphagnum
acutifolium* and several of its varities, *Philonotis fontana, Heterocladium
heteropterum*, the beautiful *Pterogophyllum lucens*, several of the *Harpidioid
hypna*, the rare *Weissia mucronata* and *Aulacomnium palustre* ; and somewhat
remote from this, the very rare weird-looking *Buxbaumia aphylla*, a
singular sporadic plant growing on the rotting trunks of old trees,
resembling at first glance some of the more minute fungi.   The stem is
bulb-like, and covered with very small thread-like processes which are
the leaves.   This is surmounted by a short fruit stalk, terminating in
an apophysis, and above it is the oblique reddish brown, saddle-like
capsule.   South of the forest are outlying wild thickety woods, watered
by rapid streams, splashing over rocks and boulders, often through deep
ravines, worn out of the solid rocks, creating a degree of humidity rare
in Worcestershire woods.   Here are found *Tortula mutica, Orthotrichum
rivulare, Amblestegium varium, Hypnum palustre* and *Mnium rostratum* ; and
on the marly banks *Mnium stellare, Thuidium tamariscinum*, rich in fruit,
dark tree-like masses of *Porotrichum alopecurum, Hypnum Patientiæ, Fissidens
exilis, F. Lylei* and its more robust congener *F. decipiens*, whilst on the
overhanging branches are tufts of *Ulota crispa, U. crispa* var. *intermedia,
Orthotrichum leiocarpum* and *O. Lyellii*.

Watering the western portion of the county is the Teme, which
near Stockton-on-Teme is a rapid stream, full of charm for the botanist,
overhung with willow and alder, upon whose river-washed roots is the
alluvial mud of years, forming a matrix most congenial to moss life.
Trailing from these roots are the long feathery stems of *Hypnum riparium*
var. *longifolium, Brachythecium rivulare* and *Hypnum palustre* var. *hamu-
losum*, whilst on the upper portions of the roots are *Brachythecium
cæspitosum, Mnium punctatum, Orthotrichum affine* var. *rivale*, and *Cinclidotus
Brebissoni*.   Other gorge-like streams, such as that of North Wood, near
Bewdley, where is found the very rare *Heterocladium heteropterum* var.
fallax and *Hypnum palustre* var. *sub sphærocarpon*, are worthy of record.
The bare surface of some of the isolated rocks of the county are worthy
of attention, such as Blackstone Rock near Bewdley, a precipitous rock,

constantly splashed by the waters of the Severn, where is found *Cynodontium Bruntoni*. In the Teme valley there is a mass of travertine, called Southstone Rock, and here are found *Weissia verticillata, Eurhynchium pumilum, Leptobryum pyriforme* and *Campylopus flexuosus*. But the richer field for these lime-loving species is in some of the old limestone quarries, where there is a good exposure of broken rock surface, as at Martley and Raven's-hill Wood, near Alfrick. Here are found *Hypnum molluscum, H. chrysophyllum, Ditrichum flexicaule, Pottia lanceolata, Camptothecium lutescens* and the more rare *Trichostomum crispulum*. At intervals in the Lias districts, small exposures of rock surface yield species special to limestone, as at Wolverton near Worcester ; here are found the rare *Thuidium recognitum* and the more common *Anomodon viticulosum*. At Habberley Valley there is a large exposure of sandstone rock, where are found *Eucalypta vulgaris* and *Tortula marginata*, and a rich growth of *Brachythecium albicans*, richly in fruit, and on similar rocks in the railway cutting near Bewdley are found a fine form of *Ptychomitium polyphyllum* and *Grimmia trichophylla*, which is very rare in Worcestershire.

Brick walls are a noticeable feature in many Worcestershire districts, but are rarely a home for any but the more common species such as *Bryum cæspiticium* and *Grimmia pulvinata* ; but occasionally a rare or local species is found on these habitats, as at King's Norton, where are found *Bryum pendulum* and *B. inclinatum*, and near Alfrick the rare *Bryum murale*.

But in many places the walls and fences are of sandstone, capped with mud or mortar. This forms a favourable matrix, and is usually well covered with mosses, as about Frankley and Rubery, where are found *Tortula aloides, T. ambigua*, and several of the Grimmiaceæ usually rare in the county, such as *Grimmia apocarpa, G. pulvinata* var. *obtusa, Racomitrium fasciculare, R. lanuginosum* and *R. canescens* ; but as these walls are of recent origin, and the species enumerated above are rarely seen on the exposed rock surfaces in Worcestershire, possibly these plants are merely colonists.

The rarest moss (excluding *Buxbaumia*) found in the county occurs on banks in a lane near Halesowen ; here is found *Tortula cuneifolia*. This is usually a maritime species, and scarcely to be expected from a smoky inland locality, but it was in abundance and in good fruiting condition. It is also found abundantly near Malvern.

The ordinary grass-grown banks of our lanes offer but faint hope in the struggle for existence for lowly plants like the mosses, the grasses and other flowering plants crowding out all but the more robust Hypna and Bryums. But in some of the deep cuttings of canals and railways are marly, shaly banks, where there is a constant drip of water ; here many species flourish, as at Hopwood. Here is found *Amblyodon dealbatus*, usually a native of boggy alpine and sub-alpine districts, with *Hypnum commutatum, H. falcatum* and *Mnium undulatum* in good fruit, one of our most stately species ; and again at Rubery, where are found the

BOTANY

rare *Bryum uliginosum*, *Mnium subglobosum*, *Philonotis calcarea* and *Weissia tenuis*, all richly fruiting, and *Hypnum stellatum* var. *protensum*, in abundance.

The highlands of Worcestershire are not rich in either rupestral, that is rock-inhabiting mosses, or in montane species ; none of the Andreæa have been found within its limits, and the Racomitriums, Grimmias, and rupestral Dicranums are poorly represented. The Abberley, Clent and Rowley hills have no characteristic mosses ; the Bilberry Hill of the Lickey range is the home of some of the more rare bog-loving species. Here are found *Sphagnum cuspidatum*, *S. intermedium*, *Pogonatum urnigerum* and *Plagiothecium undulatum*, all apparently rare in the county. The Malvern range, which offers such varied rock surfaces, yields, so far as present experience serves, but few of the mosses found on such rocks. Here are found *Hedwigia ciliata*, *Racomitrium aciculare*, *Zygodon Mougeotii*, *Grimmia subsquarrosa*, *Dicranoweissia crispula*, *Webera cruda* and *Eurhynchium crassinervium*.

The fallow fields, which offer a home for the short-lived species such as the Pottia and Phascoid groups, whose whole existence is bounded by the interval between autumn and spring, can only be partially recorded ; their haunts are often inaccessible to the botanist, the plants minute and scattered, and hence they are frequently overlooked. The more frequent species are *Pottia truncata* and *Phascum cuspidatum* ; but in the more retentive soils some of the rarer species are found, as at King's Norton and Moseley, where are found *Acaulon muticum*, *Pottia intermedia*, the rare *P. Wilsoni*, *Ephemerum serratum* and *Physcomitrella patens*.

The woodlands of Worcestershire are extensive, but add little to the rarer moss flora of the county. Usually only such mosses as the larger hypna, *Mnium hornum* and *Catharinea undulata* are found ; but in some of the woods, watered by small streams, and where the surroundings are more humid, as in the woods about Frankley and Pensax, the moss growth is more varied. Here are found *Pleuridium alternifolium*, *Brachythecium illecebrum*, *Hypnum loreum*, *Brachythecium plumosum* and *B. glareosum*, and in Shrawley Wood the rare *Dicranum montanum* and *Bryum roseum*.

The arboreal species, that is those mosses growing on tree trunks above the roots, are rare. The more frequent are *Tortula lævipila* and *Dicranoweissia cirrhata*, which are plentiful over a wide area. The more rare species are found in those districts where the soil is either rich marl or lias and the surroundings more humid, as near Shipston-on-Stour and Tidmington, where are found the very rare *Orthotrichum obtusifolium*, *Tortula papillosa* and *Cryphæa heteromalla*.

The total moss flora of Worcestershire, so far as is yet known, numbers 238 species, but this is scarcely an exhaustive list. Only a limited time has been given to the work, and probably a more thorough investigation of the southern portion of the county will materially increase the record.

The following are the more rare species not included in the preceding notes :—

Archidium alternifolium, Schp. *Malvern, Lees*
Dicranella secunda, Ldb. *Malvern*, Griffiths
Leucobryum glaucum, Schp. *Lickey Hill*
Fissidens crassipes, Wils. Near *Halesowen*
Pottia Starkeana, C. M. ⎱
Tortula pusilla, Mitt. ⎰ *Malvern, Lees*
Weissia crispa, Mitt. ⎰
Orthotrichum anomalum, var. saxatile, Milde. *Malvern, Lees*
O. cupulatum, Hoffm. *Newbould-on-Stour*

Funaria fasciculare, Schp. *Malvern*, Lees
Bryum lacustre, Brid. *Harborne*
Neckera pumila, Hedw. *Malvern*, Lees
Brachythecium salebrosum, B. & S. Near *Alfrick*
Eurhynchium tenellum, Milde. *Malvern*, Lees
Hypnum vernicosum, Ldb. *Wyre Forest*
H. uncinatum, Hedw. *Moseley*
Hylocomium brevirostre, B. & S. *Malvern*, Lees

Comparing the moss flora of Worcestershire with that of the bordering counties, we find that—

Herefordshire has 280 species. But Herefordshire has a larger area, a more humid climate, extensive heathlands, marshes and bogs, and a range of mountains prolific in montane species, and has been more thoroughly examined.

Shropshire has 251 species. This county has nearly twice the area, and a very much greater area of waste and woodland. It has not been exhaustively investigated, and will probably be found to have as large a moss flora as Herefordshire.

Staffordshire has 273 species. This county, nearly twice the size of Worcestershire, has twice the area of wood and waste land, has extensive moorlands and bogs, and numerous rapid streams abounding in mosses.

Warwickshire has 245 species. This county has about the same area as Worcestershire, but has no high hills, is poor in limestone rocks, but its northern woodlands are more boggy, and yield many species not yet observed in Worcestershire. It has been more systematically worked, and is probably more fully recorded.

LIVERWORTS (*Hepaticæ*)

These plants are closely allied to the mosses, and would be included with them by unbotanical observers. But they differ in having capsules opening by valves, and with the exception of Riccia, in the presence of spiral bodies (*elaters*) among their spores. Although found in every sort of habitat, they are on the whole more dependent on the presence of moisture than the mosses, and on the softer soils they are crowded out by the more vigorous growth of the flowering plants ; hence in a highly-cultivated district like Worcestershire, where bogs, marshes and waste heath-lands are few and far between, the hepatic flora is a very meagre one, only forty species being recorded for the county. The richest localities are the marshy banks of streams like Dowles Brook in Bewdley Forest. Here is found the singular but beautiful *Trichocolea tomentella* and *Cephalozia bicuspidata*, *C. multiflora*, *Pellia epiphylla* and *Aneura sinuata*. On the water-splashed rocks of some of the streams near

BOTANY

Pensax the dark green fronds of *Marchantia polymorpha*, *Conocephalus conicus* and *Chiloscyphus polyanthos* are abundant; and on the marly banks and in the more humid recesses of the woods a rich growth of the pretty *Lepidozia reptans*, *Scapania nemorosa*, *Nardia scalaris*, *Plagiochila asplenioides* and other woodland species. Other woods, such as those near Redditch, where the soil is retentive and the surroundings more favourable, yield such hepatics as *Diplophyllum albicans*, *Kantia trichomanes*, *Lophocolea cuspidata*, its congener *L. bidentata*, *Jungermannia crenulata*; and on the tree roots *Lophocolea heterophylla* is often to be found. The softer soils of the cultivated lands are little favoured by these plants, except when lying fallow; but in such fields near Churchill and Clent the stellate fronds of *Riccia glauca* and the barren fronds of *Lunularia cruciata* are abundant.

But the richest hunting-grounds for these plants are the Malvern Hills and the adjacent common lands. The rills, the bare rocks, the heath lands, and fine holly woods afford a home for several of the more local species, and here are found *Scapania resupinata*, *S. irrigua*, *Saccogynia viticulosa*, *Fossombronia pusilla*, the tree-loving *Frullania Tamarisci*, *F. dilatata*, *Lejeunea serpyllifolia*, *Radula complanata*, *Blepharozia ciliaris*, the horn-bearing *Anthoceros punctatus*, and the singular and rare *Targionia hypophylla*.

LICHENS (*Lichenes*)

These are a large and well-known class of plants, usually abundant where the air is pure and uncontaminated by the smoke and poisonous gases of towns and other industrial centres. They are found in all regions, tropic or arctic, and at all elevations, from sea-level to the snow-line of the highest alps; they can endure every degree of cold, and revive after the drying heat of even tropical climates; and their length of existence as individuals is almost indefinite.

Formerly they were considered to be a distinct class of plants intermediate between the algæ and the fungi. But the researches of some of our more learned botanists, as Schwendener and others, have proved them to be in reality fungi, allied to the Ascomycetes, parasitical on certain of the Algæ—Protococcus, Chroococcus, Nostoc—and some of the Confervaceæ. Some are crustaceous as in *Cladonia*, others foliaceous as in *Parmelia*, and others fruticose as in *Usnea barbata*. In the neighbourhood of large towns, or where the atmosphere is charged with smoke, they are rarely found, or only in an abnormal state, forming dust-like or filamentous patches on walls or trees, etc., and known by the older botanists by the pseudo-generic name Lepraria.

In the north-eastern portion of the county lichens are rarely found, save in the abnormal state referred to above, but at Hartlebury Common there are still in existence the remains of a lichen flora, such as *Cladonia rangiferina*, *C. furcata*, *C. uncialis* and *Urceolaria scruposa*; and at Bewdley *Lecidea dispansa* has been found. The Clent Hills have not been fully worked, and do not appear to have any special species. The Lickey Hills, which lie a little south of this, have within recent times

been rich in some of the more common species. Here are found *Cetraria aculeata*, the black-fruited *Verrucaria epigæa*, *V. nigrescens* and *V. rupestris*. But as soon as we approach the more sylvan portions of the Severn Valley near Worcester, lichens are not only more frequent but more noticeable ; trees, walls, the stone coping of bridges, and wild waysides each yield their quota of lichens, some of them rare, such as *Leptogium lacerum*, var. *pulvinata*, *L. subtile*, *Sphinctrina turbinata*, *Calicium phæocephalum*, *C. curtum*, *C. trichiale*, *Sticta pulmonaria*, *Lecidea incompta*, *L. rosella*, the singular parasitical *L. Parmeliarum* and *Opegrapha Turneri*.

But the richest district in the county is that of the Malvern Hills and the adjacent common lands, where the lichens are numerous and often rare. Here are found the beautiful coral-like *Sphærophoron compressum* and *S. coralloides*, *Bæomyces rufus*, *B. roseus*, *Stereocaulon nanum*, *Platysma glaucum*, *Parmelia saxatilis*, var. *omphalodes*, *Umbilicaria pustulata*, *Amphiloma lanuginosa*, *Lecanora ferruginea*, *L. hæmatomma*, *Lecidea tenebrosa*, *L. tricolor*, *L. muscorum*, *L. truncigena*, *Opegrapha vulgaris*, *O. lyncea* ; and on the hollies of Holly Bush Hill are several of that curious genus *Graphis*, as *G. elegans*, *G. scripta*, *G. horizontalis*, *G. serpentina*, *Verrucaria gemmata*, *V. biformis* ; on calcareous rocks, *Verrucaria Salweii* and *Endocarpon hepaticum*. On heathy places on or about the hills the singular family *Collema* are numerous, such as *C. flaccidum*, *C. crispum*, *C. nigrescens*, and their allies, *Leptogium lacerum*, *L. tenuissimum* ; and on old oaks in Cowleigh Park, *Trachylia tigillaris*.

As we travel farther south to the Avon Valley, the trees are more richly clad in their grey clothing of Lichens ; and in the outlying portion of the county—Broadway and the high land about Bredon, where the rocks are capped with oolite, and the fences are of stone from the neighbouring quarries—the lichens are abundant and some of them rare, such as *Lecanora calcarea*, *Verrucaria immersa*, *V. rupestris*, and its variety *muralis*. In some places the broken rock is curiously stained inky black with the thallus of *Pannaria nigra*, and in others a yellow tinge prevails from the abundant thallus of *Placodium murorum*, and now and again on the higher rocks is *Lecidea geographica* and other more common species. The total lichen flora of Worcestershire is 228 species and varieties, and the following are some of the more rare, not recorded in the foregoing notes :—

Leptogium sinuatum, Huds.	Parmelia conspersa, Ehrh.	Lecanora epixantha, Ach.
— turgidum, Ach.	— acetabulum, Neck.	Lecidea lucida, Ach.
— Schraderi, Bernh.	Psoronia hypnorum, Vahl.	— canescens, Dicks.
Coniocybe furfuracea, Ach.	Placodium citrinum, Ach.	— Ehrhartiana, Ach.
Alectoria jubata, Linn.	— candicans, Dicks.	— rubella, Ehrh.
Peltigera rufescens, Hoffm.	Lecanora tartarea, Linn.	— tantilla, Nyl.
Parmelia fuliginosa, Dub.	— circinata, Pers.	Graphis dendritica, Ach.

My principal authorities for the foregoing notes are Mr. E. Lees' *Botany of Worcestershire and Malvern* ; and Dr. Holl's records in Leighton's *Lichen Flora of Great Britain, Ireland and the Channel Islands*, 3rd edition, 1879.

BOTANY

FRESHWATER ALGÆ

The plants belonging to this group have been very imperfectly recorded. Mr. Lees, in his *Botany of the Malvern Hills*, has a list of only about twenty—mostly common species. The following list is all he records, and the nomenclature is that of Gray's *Handbook*, 1864 :—

Tetraspora lubrica, Callithamnion aureus, C. barbatus, Batrachospermum atrum, Lemanea torulosa, L. fluviatilis, Cladophora fracta, Chætophora rivularis, C. capillaris, Enteromorpha intestinalis, Prasiola calophylla, Lyngbya muralis, Ulva crispa, U. bullosa, Oscillatoria limosa, Strigonema atrovirens, Nostoc commune, N. muscorum, Botrydina vulgaris, Palmella cruenta.

In the *Transactions of the Worcestershire Naturalists' Club*, 1897–99, p. 3, the occurrence of *Tetraspora explanata*, Agardh., at Lower Wick, is recorded for the first time in Britain.

The *Desmidiaceæ* and *Diatomaceæ* appear to have been totally neglected.

FUNGI

The fungus flora of the county has been investigated very little owing to few botanists taking up the study of mycology. Notwithstanding this neglect, and the meagre dimensions of the county list, a few noteworthy plants have been gathered in Worcestershire. Amongst these we may enumerate *Amanita aureola*, Habberley Valley, *Lepiota submarasmioides*, near the Valley of the White-leaved Oak, *Lepiota leucothites*, near the Holly Bush Pass, *Tricholoma glaucocanum*, Wyre Forest, and *Coprinus squamosus*, Hanbury Park. All of these were recorded as British for the first time, whilst the following species were entirely new and unknown before, *Collybia veluticeps*, Claines, *Flammula rubicundula*, Wyre Forest, and *Coprinus roseotinctus*, Ash Plantation, Temple Laughern.

The authority for the following list is *Cooke's Handbook of British Fungi*, with emendations from *Fries, Lister, Massee, Plowright, Grevillea*, and the *Transactions of the British Mycological Society*.

BASIDIOMYCETES

HYMENOMYCETES

I. *Agaricineæ*

Amanita phalloides, Fr.
   var. verna, Bull.
— mappa, Fr.
— pantherina, D.C.
— muscaria, Fr.
— aureola, Kalch.
— rubescens, Fr.
— spissa, Fr.
— nitida, Fr.
Amanitopsis vaginata, Roze.
— strangulata, Fr.
— adnata, W. G. Smith

Lepiota procera, Scop.
— permixta, Barla.
— rachodes, Vitt.
   var. puellaris, Fr.
— prominens, Viv.
— excoriata, Schæff.
— acutesquamosa, Weinm.
— Friesii, Lasch.
— Badhami, Berk.
— clypeolaria, Bull.
— submarasmioides, Speg.
— felina, Pers.
— metulæspora, B. & Br.
— cristata, A. & S.
— erminea, Fr.
— holosericea, Fr.

Lepiota leucothites, Vitt.
— cepæstipes, Sow.
— carcharias, Pers.
— granulosa, Batsch.
— amianthina, Scop.
— illinita, Fr.
Armillaria mellea, Vahl.
Tricholoma sejunctum, Sow.
— spermaticum, Fr.
— resplendens, Fr.
— acerbum, Bull.
— flavo-brunneum, Fr.
— albo-brunneum, Pers.
— ustale, Fr.
— rutilans, Schæff.
— columbetta, Fr.

69

Tricholoma scalpturatum, Fr.
    var. chrysites, Jungh.
— murinaceum, Bull.
— terreum, Schæff.
    var. atrosquamosum,
      Chev.
— saponaceum, Fr.
— cartilagineum, Bull.
— cuneifolium, Fr.
    var. cinereo-rimosum,
      Batsch.
— sulphureum, Fr.
— carneum, Bull.
— gambosum, Fr.
— album, Schæff.
— leucocephalum, Fr.
— personatum, Fr.
— glaucocanum, Bres.
— nudum, Bull.
— panæolum, Fr.
— melaleucum, Pers.
    var. polioleucum, Fr.
— grammopodium, Bull.
— brevipes, Bull.
— sordidum, Fr.
Clitocybe nebularis, Batsch.
— clavipes, Pers.
— odora, Sow.
— rivulosa, Pers.
— cerrusata, Fr.
— phyllophila, Fr.
— pithyophila, Fr.
— tornata, Fr.
— candicans, Pers.
    var. minor, Cke.
— gallinacea, Scop.
— decastes, Fr.
— aggregata, Schæff.
— fumosa, Pers.
— maxima, Gärtn. & Mey.
— infundibuliformis, Schæff.
— incilis, Fr.
— sinopica, Fr.
— geotropa, Bull.
— inversa, Scop.
— flaccida, Sow.
— cyathiformis, Bull.
— brumalis, Fr.
— metachroa, Fr.
— ditopa, Fr.
— diatreta, Fr.
— fragrans, Sow.
Laccaria laccata, Berk.
    var. amethystina, Bolt.
    var. tortilis, Bolt.
Collybia radicata, Relh.
— longipes, Bull.
— veluticeps, Rea.
— platyphylla, Fr.
    var. repens, Fr.

Collybia semitalis, Fr.
— fusipes, Bull.
— maculata, A. & S.
— prolixa, Fl. Dan.
— butyracea, Bull.
— velutipes, Fr.
— vertiruga, Cke.
— stipitaria, Fr.
— confluens, Pers.
— conigena, Pers
— cirrhata, Fr.
— tuberosa, Bull.
— xanthopoda, Fr.
— esculenta, Wulf.
— tenacella, Pers.
    var. stolonifer, Jungh.
— acervata, Fr.
— dryophila, Bull.
    var. funicularis, Fr.
— extuberans, Fr.
— ocellata, Fr.
— rancida, Fr.
— ambusta, Fr.
Mycena strobilina, Fr.
    var. coccinea, Sow.
— pura, Pers.
— zephira, Fr.
— lineata, Bull.
— flavo-alba, Fr.
— luteo-alba, Bolt.
— lactea, Pers.
— parabolica, Fr.
— polygramma, Bull.
— galericulata, Scop.
    var. calopoda, Fr.
— sudora, Fr.
— rugosa, Fr.
— tenuis, Bolt.
— ammoniaca, Fr.
— alcalina, Fr.
— plicosa, Fr.
— filopes, Bull.
— amicta, Fr.
— vitilis, Fr.
— acicula, Schæff.
— sanguinolenta, A. & S.
— galopoda, Fr.
— leucogala, Cke.
— epipterygia, Scop.
— clavicularis, Fr.
— vulgaris, Pers.
— rorida, Fr.
— stylobates, Pers.
— tenerrima, Berk.
— discopoda, Lév.
— pterigena, Fr.
— hiemalis, Osbeck.
— capillaris, Schum.
Omphalia hydrogramma, Fr.
— Postii, Fr.

Omphalia rustica, Fr.
— muralis, Sow.
— umbellifera, Linn.
— pseudo-androsacea, Bull.
— camptophylla, Berk.
— grisea, Fr.
— umbratilis, Fr.
— fibula, Bull.
    var. Swartzii, Fr.
— integrella, Pers.
Pleurotus corticatus, Fr.
— dryinus, Pers.
— ulmarius, Bull.
— subpalmatus, Fr.
— ostreatus, Jacq.
    var. columbinus, Quélet.
    var. glandulosus, Bull.
— serotinus, Schrad.
— mitis, Pers.
— limpidus, Fr.
— tremulus, Fr.
— chioneus, Pers.
Volvaria Taylori, Berk.
— speciosa, Fr.
— parvula, Fr.
— media, Schum.
Pluteus cervinus, Schæff.
    var. Bullii, Berk.
— ephebius, Fr.
— chrysophæus, Schæff.
Entoloma sinuatum, Fr.
— prunuloides, Fr.
— jubatum, Fr.
— sericellum, Fr.
— clypeatum, Linn.
— costatum, Fr.
— sericeum, Fr.
— nidorosum, Fr.
Clitopilus prunulus, Scop.
— orcella, Bull.
— cancrinus, Fr.
— stilbocephalus, B. & Br.
Leptonia lampropoda, Fr.
— solstitialis, Fr.
— euchroa, Pers.
— lazulina, Fr.
— incana, Fr.
Nolanea pascua, Pers.
— pisciodora, Cesati.
— icterina, Fr.
— picea, Kalch.
Claudopus variabilis, Pers.
Pholiota togularis, Bull.
— dura, Bolt.
— præcox, Pers.
— radicosa, Bull.
— leochroma, Cke.
— ægerita, Fr.
— squarrosa, Müll.
— spectabilis, Fr.

Pholiota adiposa, Fr.
— Cookei, Fr.
— mutabilis, Schæff.
— marginata, Batsch.
Inocybe hirsuta, Lasch.
— lanuginosa, Bull.
— pyriodora, Pers.
— incarnata, Bres.
— flocculosa, Berk.
— mutica, Fr.
— carpta, Fr.
— rimosa, Bull.
— asterospora, Quélet.
— eutheles, B. & Br.
— geophylla, Fr.
— scabella, Fr.
— tricholoma, Fr.
Hebeloma musivum, Fr.
— fastibile, Fr.
— glutinosum, Lindgr.
— mesophæum, Fr.
— sinapizans, Fr.
— crustuliniforme, Bull.
    var. minor, Cke.
— elatum, Fr.
— longicaudum, Pers.
— nauseosum, Cke.
Flammula gummosa, Lasch.
— carbonaria, Fr.
— fusa, Batsch.
— rubicundula, Rea.
— alnicola, Fr.
— flavida, Schæff.
— inopoda, Fr.
— sapinea, Fr.
— picrea, Fr.
— ochrochlora, Fr.
Naucoria melinoides, Fr.
— badipes, Fr.
— striæpes, Cke.
— pediades, Fr.
— semiorbicularis, Bull.
— tabacina, DC.
— myosotis, Fr.
— temulenta, Fr.
— escharoides, Fr.
Galera tenera, Schæff.
— campanulata, Mass.
— spartea, Fr.
— hypnorum, Batsch.
    var. sphagnorum, Fr.
Tubaria furfuracea, Pers.
    var. trigonophylla, Fr.
— paludosa, Fr.
— stagnina, Fr.
— autochthona, B. & Br.
— crobula, Fr.
— inquilina, Fr.
Crepidotus mollis, Schæff.
— calolepis, Fr.

Crepidotus epigæus, Pers.
Agaricus augustus, Fr.
— campestris, Linn.
    var. silvicola, Vitt.
    var. pratensis, Vitt.
    var. hortensis, Cke.
    var. rufescens, Berk.
— arvensis, Schæff.
— xanthoderma, Genev.
— silvaticus, Schæff.
— hæmorrhoidarius, Schulz.
— comptulus, Fr.
Stropharia æruginosa, Curt.
— albo-cyanea, Desm.
— inuncta, Fr.
— coronilla, Bull.
— melasperma, Bull.
— squamosa, Fr.
    var. thrausta, Fr.
— stercoraria, Fr.
— semiglobata, Batsch.
— scobinacea, Fr.
Hypholoma sublateritium,
    Schæff.
— capnoides, Fr.
— fasciculare, Huds.
— hypoxanthum, Phil. &
    Plow.
— lachrymabundum, Fr.
— velutinum, Pers.
— pyrotrichum, Holmsk.
— cascum, Fr.
— appendiculatum, Bull.
— hydrophilum, Bull.
Psilocybe sarcocephala, Fr.
— bullacea, Bull.
— semilanceata, Fr.
    var. cærulescens, Cke.
— spadicea, Fr.
    var. hygrophila, Fr.
— fœnisecii, Pers.
Psathyra corrugis, Pers.
— bifrons, Berk.
    var. semitincta, Phil.
— semivestita, B. & Br.
— fibrillosa, Pers.
Anellaria separata, Karst.
— fimiputris, Karst.
Panæolus phalænarum, Fr.
— sphinctrinus, Fr.
— papilionaceus, Fr.
— campanulatus, Linn.
Psathyrella gracilis, Fr.
— atomata, Fr.
— disseminata, Pers.
Coprinus comatus, Fr.
— atramentarius, Fr.
— squamosus, Morg.
— picaceus, Fr.
— fimetarius, Fr.

Coprinus fimetarius
    var. cinereus, Schæff.
— niveus, Fr.
— roseotinctus, Rea.
— micaceus, Fr.
— papillatus, Fr.
— deliquescens, Fr.
— Hendersonii, Berk.
— radiatus, Fr.
— stercorarius, Fr.
— ephemerus, Fr.
— plicatilis, Fr.
— filiformis, B. & Br.
Bolbitius flavidus, Bolt.
— fragilis, Fr.
— tener, Berk.
Cortinarius
(Phlegmacium) varius, Fr.
— largus, Fr.
— anfractus, Fr.
— talus, Fr.
— glaucopus, Fr.
— cærulescens, Fr.
— purpurascens, Fr.
    var.subpurpurascens,Fr.
— scaurus, Fr.
— emollitus, Fr.
— cristallinus, Fr.
— porphyropus, Fr.
(Myxacium) collinitus, Fr.
— mucifluus, Fr.
— elatior, Fr.
— pluvius, Fr.
(Inoloma) argentatus,
    Krombh.
— violaceus, Linn.
— albo-violaceus, Fr.
(Dermocybe) ochroleucus, Fr.
— tabularis, Fr.
— caninus, Fr.
— anomalus, Fr.
— lepidopus, Cke.
— miltinus, Fr.
— sanguineus, Fr.
— anthracinus, Fr.
— cinnamomeus, Fr.
    var. semisanguineus, Fr.
— cotoneus, Fr.
— raphanoides, Fr.
(Telamonia) torvus, Fr.
— quadricolor, Fr.
— limonius, Fr.
— hinnuleus, Fr.
— injucundus, Weinm.
— flexipes, Fr.
— psammocephalus, Fr.
— incisus, Fr.
— hemitrichus, Fr.
— rigidus, Fr.
— paleaceus, Fr.

(Hygrocybe) castaneus, Bull.
— bicolor, Cke.
— pateriformis, Fr.
— dolabratus, Fr.
— leucopus, Bull.
— erythrinus, Fr.
— decipiens, Fr.
— acutus, Fr.
Gomphidius glutinosus,
    Schæff.
— viscidus, Fr.
— roseus, Fr.
— gracilis, Berk.
Paxillus giganteus, Fr.
— lepista, Fr.
— lividus, Cke.
— involutus, Fr.
    var. excentricus, Fr.
Hygrophorus
(Limacium) chrysodon, Fr.
— eburneus, Bull.
— cossus, Sow.
— penarius, Sow.
— glutinifer, Fr.
— arbustivus, Fr.
— discoideus, Fr.
— olivaceo-albus, Fr.
— hypothejus, Fr.
(Camarophyllus) nemoreus,
    Fr.
— pratensis, Fr.
— virgineus, Wulf.
    var. roseipes, Mass.
— niveus, Fr.
— russo-coriaceus, B. & Br.
— fornicatus, Fr.
— ovinus, Bull.
(Hygrocybe) lætus, Fr.
— vitellinus, Fr.
— ceraceus, Wulf.
— coccineus, Schæff.
— miniatus, Fr.
— turundus, Fr.
— puniceus, Fr.
— obrusseus, Fr.
— conicus, Fr.
— calyptræformis, Berk.
    var. niveus, Cke.
— chlorophanus, Fr.
— psittacinus, Schæff.
— unguinosus, Fr.
— nitratus, Pers.
Lactarius (Piperites) interme-
    dius, Krombh.
— torminosus, Schæff.
— turpis, Fr.
— controversus, Pers.
— pubescens, Fr.
— insulsus, Fr.
— blennius, Fr.

Piperites trivialis, Fr.
— circellatus, Fr.
— uvidus, Fr.
— pyrogalus, Bull.
— chrysorrheus, Fr.
— pargamenus, Fr.
— piperatus, Fr.
— vellereus, Fr.
(Dapetes) deliciosus, Fr.
(Russularia) pallidus, Fr.
— quietus, Fr.
— aurantiacus, Fr.
— theiogalus, Bull.
— vietus, Fr.
— rufus, Scop.
— helvus, Fr.
— glyciosmus, Fr.
— fuliginosus, Fr.
— volemus, Fr.
— serifluus, Fr.
— mitissimus, Fr.
— subdulcis, Fr.
— camphoratus, Fr.
— minimus, W. G. Smith
Russula nigricans, Fr.
— adusta, Fr.
— albo-nigra, Krombh.
— densifolia, Secr.
— delica, Fr.
— olivascens, Fr.
— furcata, Fr.
— rosacea, Fr.
— depallens, Fr.
— cærulea, Fr.
— drimeia, Cke. = expallens,
    Gillet
— lactea, Fr.
    var. incarnata, Quélet
— virescens, Fr.
— lepida, Fr.
— rubra, Fr.
— xerampelina, Fr.
— vesca, Fr.
— azurea, Bres.
— cyanoxantha, Fr.
— galochroa, Fr.
— consobrina, Fr.
    var. intermedia, Cke.
    var. sororia, Fr.
— fœtens, Fr.
— fellea, Fr.
— emetica, Fr.
— ochroleuca, Fr.
— granulosa, Cke.
— citrina, Gillet
— fragilis, Fr.
    var. nivea, Cke.
    var. violacea, Quélet.
    var. fallax, Cke.
— integra, Fr.

Russula aurata, Fr.
— nitida, Fr.
    var. pulchralis, Britz.
    var. cuprea, Cke.
— puellaris, Fr.
— alutacea, Fr.
— armeniaca, Cke.
— lutea, Fr.
— chamæleontina, Fr.
Cantharellus cibarius, Fr.
— aurantiacus, Fr.
— carbonarius, Fr.
— tubæformis, Fr.
— infundibuliformis, Fr.
— cinereus, Fr.
— muscigenus, Fr.
Nyctalis parasitica, Fr.
— asterophora, Fr.
Marasmius peronatus, Fr.
— porreus, Fr.
— oreades, Fr.
— prasiosmus, Fr.
— erythropus, Fr.
— archyropus, Fr.
— calopus, Fr.
— Vaillantii, Fr.
— fœtidus, Fr.
— ramealis, Fr.
— candidus, Bolt.
— alliaceus, Fr.
— rotula, Fr.
— graminum, Berk.
— ardrosaceus, Fr.
— epiphyllus, Fr.
Lentinus lepideus, Fr.
— cochleatus, Fr.
Panus torulosus, Fr.
— rudis, Fr.
— stypticus, Fr.
Lenzites betulina, Fr.
— flaccida, Fr.
— sæpiaria, Fr.

II. *Polyporeæ*

Boletus luteus, Linn.
— elegans, Schum.
— granulatus, Linn.
— tenuipes, Cke.
— aurantiporus, Howse
— bovinus, Linn.
— badius, Fr.
— piperatus, Bull.
— variegatus, Sw.
— chrysenteron, Fr.
    var. nanus, Mass.
— subtomentosus, Linn.
— pachypus, Fr.
— edulis, Bull.
    var. lævipes, Mass.
    var. crassus, Mass.

BOTANY

Boletus impolitus, Fr.
— satanas, Lenz.
— luridus, Schæff.
    var. erythropus, Pers.
— purpureus, Fr.
— laricinus, Berk.
— duriusculus, Schulz.
— versipellis, Fr.
— scaber, Fr.
    var. aurantiacus, Bull.
— felleus, Bull.
— alutarius, Fr.
— castaneus, Bull.
Strobilomyces strobilaceus,
    Berk.
Fistulina hepatica, Fr.
Polyporus rufescens, Fr.
— squamosus, Fr.
— picipes, Fr.
— varius, Fr.
— elegans, Fr.
    var. nummularius, Fr.
— intybaceus, Fr.
— giganteus, Fr.
— sulphureus, Fr.
— dryadeus, Fr.
— hispidus, Fr.
— quercinus, Fr.
— nidulans, Fr.
— mollis, Fr.
— destructor, Fr.
— betulinus, Fr.
— adustus, Fr.
— chioneus, Fr.
— cæsius, Fr.
— spumeus, Fr.
— fragilis, Fr.
Fomes lucidus, Fr.
— ulmarius, Fr.
— populinus, Fr.
— connatus, Fr.
— fomentarius, Fr.
— igniarius, Fr.
— annosus, Fr.
— applanatus, Wallr.
Polystictus perennis, Fr.
— versicolor, Fr.
— radiatus, Fr.
— hirsutus, Fr.
— abietinus, Fr.
Poria vaporaria, Fr.
— medulla-panis, Fr.
— vitrea, Pers.
— Hibernica, B. & Br.
— blepharistoma, B. & Br.
— obducens, Pers.
— terrestris, Fr.
— sanguinolenta, A. & S.
Trametes suaveolens, Fr.
— serpens, Fr.

Dædalea quercina, Pers.
— cinerea, Fr.
— unicolor, Fr.
Merulius tremellosus, Schrad.
— corium, Fr.
— lachrymans, Fr.

III. *Hydneæ*

Hydnum repandum, Linn.
    var. rufescens, Pers.
— auriscalpium, Linn.
— ochraceum, Pers.
— viride, Fr.
— udum, Fr.
— niveum, Pers.
— farinaceum, Pers.
Caldesiella ferruginosa, Sacc.
Irpex obliquus, Fr.
Radulum orbiculare, Fr.
— quercinum, Fr.
Phlebia merismoides, Fr.
— radiata, Fr.
Grandinia granulosa, Fr.
— crustosa, Fr.

IV. *Thelephoreæ*

Craterellus cornucopioides,
    Pers.
— clavatus, Fr.
Thelephora caryophyllea,
    Pers.
— palmata, Fr.
— laciniata, Pers.
Soppittiella sebacea, Mass.
— cæsia, Mass.
— fastidiosa, Mass.
— crustacea, Mass.
Stereum Sowerbeii, Mass.
— hirsutum, Fr.
— ochroleucum, Fr.
— purpureum, Pers.
— sanguinolentum, Fr.
— rugosum, Fr.
— spadiceum, Fr.
Coniophora arida, Karst.
— sulphurea, Fr.
— puteana, Fr.
Peniophora quercina, Cke.
— gigantea, Mass.
— rosea, Mass.
— incarnata, Mass.
— ochracea, Mass.
— cinerea, Cke.
— velutina, Cke.
Hymenochæte rubiginosa,
    Lév.
— tabacina, Lév.
Corticium calceum, Fr.
— læve, Pers.
— nudum, Fr.

Corticium sambuci, Fr.
— sanguineum, Fr.
— cæruleum, Fr.
— comedens, Fr.
Cyphella muscicola, Fr.
Exobasidium vaccinii, Wor-
    onin
Solenia anomala, Fr.

V. *Clavarieæ*

Sparassis crispa, Fr.
Clavaria amethystina, Bull.
— fastigiata, Linn.
— muscoides, Linn.
— coralloides, Linn.
— cinerea, Bull.
— cristata, Holmsk.
— rugosa, Bull.
— pyxidata, Pers.
— formosa, Pers.
— abietina, Schum.
— flaccida, Fr.
— fusiformis, Sow.
— inæqualis, Fl. Dan.
— vermicularis, Scop.
— fragilis, Holmsk.
— dissipabilis, Britz.
— pistillaris, Linn.
Typhula erythropus, Fr.
— phacorrhiza, Fr.
— muscicola, Fr.
Pistillaria tenuipes, Mass.
— quisquiliaris, Fr.
— puberula, Berk.

VI. *Tremellineæ.*

Tremella frondosa, Fr.
— lutescens, Pers.
— mesenterica, Retz.
— tubercularia, Berk.
— sarcoides, Sm.
Exidia glandulosa, Fr.
— recisa, Fr.
— albida, Brefeld
Hirneola auricula-Judæ,
    Berk.
Auricularia mesenterica, Fr.
— lobata, Sommerf.
Dacryomyces deliquescens,
    Duby.
— stillatus, Nees.
Calocera viscosa, Fr.
— cornea, Fr.
Tremellodon gelatinosum,
    Pers.

GASTROMYCETES

II. *Sclerodermeæ*

Scleroderma vulgare, Fr.
— verrucosum, Pers.
— geaster, Fr.

III. *Nidularieæ*

Cyathus striatus, Hoffm.
— vernicosus, DC.
Crucibulum vulgare, Tul.
Sphærobolus stellatus, Tode.

IV. *Lycoperdeæ*

Lycoperdon Hoylei, Berk.
— excipuliforme, Scop.
— saccatum, Vahl.
— gemmatum, Batsch.
— pyriforme, Schæff.
— perlatum, Pers.
— cælatum, Bull.
— bovista, Linn.
— plumbeum, Pers.
— nigrescens, Vitt.
— pusillum, Fr.
Geaster fornicatus, Fr.
— fimbriatus, Fr.

V. *Phalloideæ*

Ithyphallus impudicus, Fisch.
Mutinus caninus, Fr.

MYXOMYCETES

I. *Exosporeæ*

Ceratiomyxa mucida, Schrœt.

II. *Endosporeæ*

Badhamia macrocarpa, Rost.
Physarum nutans, Pers.
Fuligo septica, Gmelin
Leocarpus vernicosus, Link.
Chondrioderma spumarioides, Rost.
Didymium farinaceum, Schrad.
— effusum, Link.
Spumaria alba, DC.
Stemonitis fusca, Roth.
— ferruginea, Ehrenb.
Comatricha ? Sp.
Tubulina fragiformis, Pers.
Reticularia Lycoperdon, Bull.
Trichia scabra, Rost.
— varia, Pers.
— fallax, Pers.
Arcyria punicea, Pers.
— incarnata, Pers.
Lycogala miniatum, Pers.

HYPHOMYCETES

I. *Mucedineæ*

Fusidium griseum, Link.
Monilia fructigena, Pers.
Cylindrium flavo-virens, Bon.
Polyscytalum fungorum, Sacc.

Oidium leucoconium, Desm.
— farinosum, Cke.
— aceris, Rabach.
— balsamii, Mont.
— monilioides, Link.
Trichoderma lignorum, Harz.
Aspergillus glaucus, Link.
— candidus, Link.
Sterigmatocystis dubia, Link.
Penicillium glaucum, Link.
Acremonium verticillatum, Link.
Rhinotrichum repens, Preuss.
— Thwaitesii, B. & Br.
Botrytis vulgaris, Fr.
— cinerea, Pers.
Sepedonium chrysospermum, Fr.
Asterophora agaricicola, Corda.
Verticillium agaricinum, Corda.
Diplocadium penicillioides, Sacc.
Trichothecium roseum, Link.
Dactylium dendroides, Fr.
Ramularia calcea, Ces.

II. *Dematieæ*

Torula monilioides, Corda.
Acrospeira mirabilis, B. & Br.
Zygodesmus fuscus, Corda.
Bispora monilioides, Corda.
Fusicladium dendriticum, Fckl.
— pyrinum, Lib.
Polythrincium trifolii, Kze. & Schm.
Cladosporium fulvum, Cke.
— herbarum, Link.
Heterosporium epimyces, C. & M.
Macrosporium commune, Rabh.
— tomato, Cke.
Fumago vagans, Pers.

III. *Stilbeæ*

Stilbum erythrocephalum, Ditm.
— fimetarium, B. & Br.
Isaria farinosa, Fr.
— arachnophila, Ditm.
— citrina, Pers.
Graphium subulatum, Sacc.
Stysanus stemonites, Corda.

IV. *Tuberculariæ*

Tubercularia vulgaris, Tode.
— brassicæ, Lib.

Ægerita candida, Pers.
Sphacelia segetum, Lév.
— typhina, Sacc.
Cylindrocolla urticæ, Bon.
Epicoccum micropus, Corda.

UREDINEÆ

Uromyces fabæ, Pers.
— polygoni, Pers.
— geranii, DC.
— valerianæ, Schum.
— dactylidis, Otth.
— poæ, Rabh.
— ficariæ, Schum.
Puccinia asparagi, DC.
— calthæ, Link.
— lapsanæ, Schultz.
— variabilis, Grev.
— pulverulenta, Grev.
— violæ, Schum.
— pimpinellæ, Strauss
— menthæ, Pers.
— primulæ, DC.
— graminis, Pers.
— coronata, Corda.
— glumarum, Sch.
— coronifera, Kleb.
— poarum, Nielsen
— caricis, Schum.
— phragmitis, Schum.
— Trailii, Plow.
— persistens, Plow.
— agrostidis, Plow.
— suaveolens, Pers.
— hieracii, Schum.
— lychnidearum, Link.
— chrysanthemi, Roze.
— tragopogi, Pers.
— betonicæ, Alb. & Schw.
— ægopodii, Schum.
— umbilici, Guép.
— fusca, Relham.
— malvacearum, Mont.
Triphragmium ulmariæ, Schum.
Phragmidium fragariastri, DC.
— sanguisorbæ, DC.
— violaceum, Schultz.
— rubi, Pers.
— subcorticatum, Schrank.
Xenodochus carbonarius, Schlecht.
Endophyllum euphorbiæ, DC.
— leucospermum, Sopp.
Gymnosporangium sabinæ, Dicks.
— clavariæforme, Jacq.

BOTANY

Melampsora helioscopiæ, Pers.
— lini, Pers.
— populina, Jacq.
Coleosporium senecionis, Pers.
— sonchi, Pers.
— campanulæ, Pers.
Uredo symphyti, DC.
— mulleri, Schröt.
Milesia scolopendri, B. White
Cæoma euonymi, Gmelin
— mercurialis, Pers.

USTILAGINEÆ

Ustilago hypodytes, Schlecht.
— segetum, Bull.
— scabiosæ, Sow.
— flosculorum, DC.
— tragopogi, Pers.
Urocystis violæ, Sow.
Entyloma ranunculi, Bon.

SPHÆROPSIDEÆ

Phyllosticta primulæcola, Desm.
Phoma samarorum, Desm.
— longissimum, Berk.
Sphæronema subulatum, Tode.
Diplodia vulgaris, Lév.
— herbarum, Lév.
Ascochyta scabiosæ, Rabh.
— ribis, Lib.
Septoria ulmi, Kze.
— hippocastani, B. & Br.
— fraxini, Desm.

MELANCONIÆ

Glœosporium fructigenum, Berk.
Nemaspora crocea, Pers.

PHYCOMYCETES

Pilobolus crystallinus, Tode.
Mucor mucedo, Linn.
    var. caninus, Pers.
Spinellus fusiger, Van Tiegh.
Sporodinia aspergillus, Schröt.
Cystopus candidus, Lév.
— tragopogonis, Schröt.
Phytophthora infestans, De Bary
Peronospora parasitica, De Bary
— urticæ, De Bary
Leptomitus lactens, Ag.
Saprolegnia ferox, Nees.
Empusa muscæ, Cohn.
Protomyces macrosporus, Unger.

ASCOMYCETES

I. *Perisporiaceæ*

Lasiobotrys loniceræ, Kze.
Sphærotheca pannosa, Wallr.
— castagnei, Lév.
Phyllactinia guttata, Lév.
Uncinula adunca, Lév.
— bicornis, Lév.
Erysiphe graminis, DC.
— Montagnei, Lév.
— communis, Schl.
Chætomium elatum, Kze.
Eurotium herbariorum, Lk.
Capnodium Footii, Berk. & Desm.

II. *Gymnoascaceæ*

Ascomyces pruni, B. & Br.
— deformans, Berk.

III. *Hysteriaceæ*

Hysterium pulicare, Pers.
Hysterographium fraxini, De Not.

IV. *Discomycetes*

Coccomyces coronatus, Sacc.
Phacidium multivalve, Kze. & Schmidt
Trochila ilicis, Crouan
Rhytisma acerinum, Fr.
— punctatum, Fr.
Propolis faginea, Karst.
Cenangium furfuraceum, De Not.
— populneum, Rehm.
Tympanis conspersa, Fr.
Bulgaria polymorpha, Wettstein
Ombrophila brunnea, Phil.
Orbilia leucostigma, Fr.
— inflatula, Karst.
Calloria fusarioides, Fr.
Coryne sarcoides, Tul.
— atrovirens, Sacc.
Ascobolus vinosus, Berk.
— furfuraceus, Pers.
Pseudopeziza trifolii, Fckl.
Mollisia cinerea, Karst.
— lignicola, Phil.
Helotium claroflavum, Berk.
— citrinum, Fr.
— luteolum, Currey
— virgultorum, Karst.
    var. fructigenum, Rehm.
— calyculus, Berk.
— renisporum, Ellis

Ciboria echinophila, Sacc.
— ochroleuca, Mass.
Sclerotinia tuberosa, Fckl.
— sclerotiorum, Mass.
Chlorosplenium æruginosum, De Not.
Sphærospora trechispora, Sacc.
Lachnea stercorea, Gill.
— scutellata, Gill.
— hemispherica, Gill.
Dasyscypha virginea, Fckl.
— nivea, Mass.
— leuconica, Mass.
— hyalina, Mass.
— calycina, Fckl.
Neottiella nivea, Sacc.
Geopyxis coccinea, Mass.
— cupularis, Sacc.
Sepultaria semiimmersa, Mass.
Barlæa Crouani, Mass.
Humaria carbonigena, Sacc.
    var. fusispora, Mass.
— omphalodes, Mass.
— granulata, Sacc.
— violacea, Sacc.
Peziza vesiculosa, Bull.
    var. cerea, Rehm.
— sepiatra, Cke.
— venosa, Pers.
— ampliata, Pers.
    var. tectoria, Mass.
— mellea, Cke. & Plow.
— badia, Pers.
Otidea leporina, Fckl.
— cochleata, Fckl.
— onotica, Fckl.
— aurantia, Mass.
Acetabula vulgaris, Fckl.
Helvella crispa, Fr.
— lacunosa, Afzel.
— atra, König.
— elastica, Bull.
— macropus, Karst.
Leotia lubrica, Pers.
— acicularis, Pers.
Morchella crassipes, Pers.
    var. Smithiana, Cke.
— esculenta, Pers.
Mitrula viride, Karst.
Spathularia clavata, Sacc.

V. *Pyrenomycetes*

Cordyceps militaris, Fr.
— ophioglossoides, Tul.
— capitata, Fr.
Claviceps purpurea, Tul.
Epichlœ typhina, Berk.
Hypocrea rufa, Fr.

Hypomyces chrysospermus, Tul.
— asterophorus, Tul.
— rosellus, Tul.
— aurantius, Tul.
Nectria pulicaris, Tul.
— cinnabarina, Fr.
— aquifolia, Berk.
— ditissima, Tul.
Polystigma rubrum, Pers.
Sphæria aquila, Fr.
— tristis, Tode.
— ovina, Pers.
— spermoides, Hoffm.
— pulvispyrius, Pers.

Sphæria arundinacea, Sow.
— millepunctata, Grev.
— herbarum, Pers.
— rubella, Pers.
Sphærella punctiformis, Pers.
Cucurbitaria laburni, Pers.
Stigmatea robertiani, Fr.
Valsa nivea, Fr.
— salicina, Fr.
Phyllachora trifolii, Pers.
Dothidella betulina, Fr.
— ulmi, Duv.
— graminis, Fr.
Diatrype quercina, Tul.
— stigma, Fr.

Diatrype disciformis, Fr.
Xylaria polymorpha, Grev.
— digitata, Grev.
— hypoxylon, Grev.
Poronia punctata, Fr.
Ustulina vulgaris, Tul.
Daldinia concentrica, Sacc.
Hypoxylon coccineum, Bull.
— multiforme, Fr.

VI. *Tuberaceæ*

Elaphomyces variegatus, Vitt.
— granulatus, Fr.
Onygena equina, Pers.

CLIMATE

FROM its conformation and the fact that a large portion of the county is included in the lower Severn basin, the main meteorological features of Worcestershire do not differ from those of the rest of the West Midland district. On each side of the county the hills rise to a considerable elevation, Malvern reaching to nearly 1,500 feet and Birmingham to 585 feet. The rest of the county does not attain to much over 400 feet, except some of the hills on the Abberley and Lickey ranges. In the river basin Stourport, near where the Severn enters the county, is only about 100 feet above sea level. The result is a moderate rainfall, varying from 26·00 at Malvern to about 21·00 in the river basin. The mean for the county would be about 23·00.

To show the meteorological features of the county the figures are given on a line drawn across it from east to west at Malvern at a point about 500 feet above sea level, at Worcester at an elevation of 180 feet, and at Birmingham, or rather Edgbaston, at about 500 feet. Although spots may be found that are both wetter and drier, yet on the whole the line fairly represents the county meteorology.

The figures given are, except when otherwise stated, for the mean of five years ending December 31, 1900, and they give the rainfall, barometric pressure and temperature at the three stations.

(a) RAINFALL

The mean annual rainfall is 23·18 inches. At Malvern it is 24·88 inches, at Worcester 20·47 inches, at Birmingham 24·21 inches. Having regard to the series of dry years included in the last five, 1896–1900, it is probable that if taken over a longer period the mean annual rainfall would be higher.

The monthly rainfall figures are—

	Malvern	Worcester	Birmingham		Malvern	Worcester	Birmingham
January .	2·35	1·84	1·66	July . .	1·60	1·47	2·19
February	1·44	1·22	1·20	August .	2·41	1·93	2·90
March .	1·87	1·49	1·65	September	2·23	1·54	1·90
April .	1·75	1·37	1·66	October .	2·75	2·14	2·55
May . .	1·65	1·45	2·00	November	2·35	1·84	2·32
June . .	1·68	1·94	1·97	December	2·80	2·25	2·26

It will thus be seen that the autumn is wetter than the spring, the wettest months being October, November and December, the last the wettest of all. Probably however it is hardly fair to take the dry cycle which the last five years cover as in any way showing what the real

rainfall is. In the case of Worcester the rainfall over a series of years would be from 21·00 to 24·00 inches, and that would probably be the real rainfall of the lower Severn basin. In the five years under notice the actual Worcester rainfall was—

1895, 22·94   1896, 18·33   1897, 24·14   1898, 18·21   1899, 23·36

(b) Barometric Pressure

The readings of the barometer give a mean for the county of 29·68 inches, Malvern showing 29·45 inches, Worcester 29·63 inches, and Birmingham 29·98 inches.

The monthly means are as follows—

	Malvern	Worcester	Birmingham		Malvern	Worcester	Birmingham
January .	29·44	28·86	30·04	July . .	29·55	30·06	29·98
February	29·50	28·82	30·07	August .	29·51	30·10	29·94
March .	29·30	29·02	29·88	September	29·57	29·85	30·03
April .	29·40	29·82	29·95	October .	29·29	29·85	29·89
May . .	29·55	30·94	29·94	November	29·44	29·83	29·93
June . .	29·55	29·58	30·03	December	29·30	29·73	29·95

These figures are not really properly comparable, for the Birmingham figures have been corrected to sea level, which neither the Malvern nor Worcester have been. The Birmingham figures are for the twelve years ending December 31, 1899, while the Malvern and Worcester are only for the five years, hence probably the variation in the figures. The Worcester figures are taken at an elevation of 180 feet above sea level, the Malvern at about 500 feet, the Birmingham at 541 feet, so that the figures at best are only indications of the real state of things.

(c) Temperature

The temperature is subject to considerable variations. In the low grounds near the rivers there is in the spring great liability to hoar frosts to such an extent that in planting fruit trees it becomes necessary to ascertain the line of the hoar frost. This limit is in many places well known and clearly defined ; above it fruit can be grown with comparative safety, below it the risk of the crop being destroyed by spring frosts is greatly increased. The mean of the annual temperature for the county is 47·9, that is the mean of the maximum and minimum readings. For Malvern it is 49·7, for Birmingham 46·1.

The monthly figures are—

	Malvern at 9 a.m.	Worcester at noon	Birmingham at 9 a.m.		Malvern at 9 a.m.	Worcester at noon	Birmingham at 9 a.m.
January .	37·9	42·5	36·6	July . .	63·7	78·0	59·0
February	38·0	44·0	37·9	August .	65·5	66·2	58·8
March .	42·2	51·0	40·6	September	58·5	68·4	55·6
April .	47·3	56·2	45·1	October .	47·8	56·2	47·4
May . .	53·7	65·2	51·3	November	44·2	48·1	42·9
June . .	61·5	73·2	57·9	December	40·2	43·5	38·4

CLIMATE

It is unfortunate that the Worcester temperature was taken at a different hour from those of Malvern and Birmingham, so as to make any comparison quite impossible and useless, but it will be seen that Malvern is warmer than Birmingham. It seems hardly worth giving the other temperatures for all three places, but the figures for Malvern and Birmingham will enable a good idea to be formed of the temperature of the two sides of the county.

The mean monthly *maximum* temperature at Malvern and Birmingham is as follows—

	Malvern	Birmingham			Malvern	Birmingham
January .	42·4	58·0	July . .		71·1	84·6
February .	43·8	61·9	August . .		69·9	85·6
March .	49·0	64·8	September .		65·8	82·8
April . .	54·0	79·0	October .		54·9	70·0
May . .	61·3	77·6	November .		49·0	61·6
June . .	67·6	82·8	December .		44·3	56·0

The minimum temperature at Worcester and Birmingham is as follows—

	Worcester	Birmingham			Worcester	Birmingham
January .	11·0	10·8	July . .		35·0	39·5
February .	8·03	8·0	August . .		41·0	41·2
March .	16·0	21·3	September .		27·0	33·0
April . .	20·0	27·0	October .		22·0	27·9
May . .	21·0	31·0	November .		16·0	23·5
June . .	38·0	38·3	December .		7·0	14·5

So far as is known there are no observations as to the earth temperature in Worcestershire, but some observations on the temperature of the river Severn have been taken which give the monthly mean temperature of that river near Worcester at 9 a.m.—

January . .	36·0	May . . .	50·0	September .	58·0
February . .	37·0	June . . .	57·0	October . .	51·3
March . .	39·0	July . . .	60·0	November .	43·7
April . . .	45·0	August . .	60·0	December . .	40·2

It will be observed that the temperature, as would be expected, is slightly lower than that of the air. When the tideway is reached the temperature falls considerably, and is subjected to much greater fluctuation. But there is no doubt that the comparatively high temperature the above figures show is due to two causes, both of which are to some extent exceptional : (1) the dry weather reducing considerably the volume of water, causes, especially in the summer months, the temperature to rise ; and (2) the absence of freshets also tends to keep up the temperature, as the large mass of cold water caused the river to be at

a lower figure, although it is probable it made the temperature far less uniform.

It is only at Birmingham that there are any recorded observations as to solar radiation, sunshine and wind.

The solar radiation is ascertained by taking the maximum temperature given by a blackened bulb thermometer *in vacuo* exposed to the direct rays of the sun. The figures given are for the twelve years ending December 31, 1899—

	Solar radiation	Date of greatest		Solar radiation	Date of greatest
January . .	93·7	21, 1898	July . . .	138·0	2, 1893
February .	100·7	23, 1897	August . .	133·0	12, 1898
March . .	117·3	26, 1897	September .	130·0	7, 1898
April. . .	125·7	21, 1893	October . .	113·9	5, 1896
May . . .	132·6	31, 1892	November .	97·9	2, 1894
June . . .	133·8	16, 1896	December .	88·5	11, 1898

The amount of sunshine is measured by a Jordan's sunshine recorder, which is placed on the top of the monument, about 100 feet above the ground. It gives the following figures for the twelve years—

	Hours and minutes of sunshine for the months		Hours and minutes of sunshine for the months		Hours and minutes of sunshine for the months
January .	35·29	May .	143·19	September	113·39
February	55·22	June .	146·23	October .	69·30
March .	91·15	July .	130·53	November	36·36
April . .	112·3	August	127·51	December	32·57

As to the wind, the pressure is ascertained by Osler's anemometer. The pressure plate presents a surface to the wind of 2 feet superficial.

	Total velocity in miles	Extreme pressure in lb. per sq. ft.		Total velocity in miles	Extreme pressure in lb. per sq. ft.
January .	9,800	20·0	July . .	8,571	11·0
February .	9,334	27·5	August . .	8,762	12·0
March .	10,426	37·0	September .	8,142	15·0
April . .	9,014	17·0	October .	8,961	17·0
May . .	9,184	18·0	November .	9,435	19·0
June . .	7,908	10·0	December .	10,221	24·0

The prevailing winds when they blow heaviest are south-west to west, in January, February, March and December. The easterly winds are of longer duration when they come, but do not equal the west or south-west either in velocity or pressure.

ZOOLOGY

MOLLUSCS

Ninety-eight species of non-marine mollusca have been recorded from Worcestershire out of a total of 139 known to inhabit the British Isles, and this, when the scanty number of published lists is taken into account, is a very good number.

In this estimate no note is taken of four species (*Helicella barbara, Pupa anglica, Clausilia biplicata, Unio margaritifer*) which find their place in one list, but are apparently due to erroneous determinations.

The occurrence of *Pupa secale* in the Malvern district, if correct, is of interest, since the species is not as a rule met with so far inland.

Testacella maugei is presumably an importation with garden or hot-house plants : for the rest the assemblage is a typically British one.

Several of the localities mentioned in the list are probably no longer habitats for mollusca, since owing to the rapid increase of buildings some of them have become parts of towns : *e.g.* Acock's Green, Selly Oak and Hall Green.

A. GASTROPODA

I. PULMONATA

a. Stylommatophora

Testacella maugei, Fér.   Worcester
— *haliotidea*, Drap. Worcester ; Stourbridge
— *scutulum*, Sby.
Limax maximus, Linn.
— *flavus*, Linn.
— *arborum*, Bouch.-Chant. Worcester ; Malvern.
Agriolimax agrestis (Linn.)
— *lævis* (Müll.).   Stourport ; Lincomb
Amalia sowerbii (Fér.).   Stourport
— *gagates* (Drap.)
Vitrina pellucida (Müll.)
Vitrea crystallina (Müll.)
— *alliaria* (Miller)
— *glabra* (Brit. Auct.).   Lincomb
— *cellaria* (Müll.)
— *nitidula* (Drap.)
— *pura* (Ald.).   Acock's Green
— *radiatula* (Ald.).   Lincomb

Vitrea nitida (Müll.)
— *fulva* (Müll.)
Arion ater (Linn.)
— *hortensis*, Fér.
— *circumscriptus*, John. Lincomb
— *subfuscus* (Drap.). Stourport
Punctum pygmæum (Drap.).   Malvern district ; Henwick Mill, near Worcester
Pyramidula rupestris (Drap.).   Malvern district ; Bredon Hill
— *rotundata* (Müll.)
Helicella virgata (Da C.).
— *itala* (Linn.)
— *caperata* (Mont.)
— *cantiana* (Mont.)
Hygromia granulata (Ald.)
— *hispida* (Linn.)
— *rufescens* (Penn.)
Acanthinula aculeata (Müll.).   Malvern district, near Worcester
Vallonia pulchella (Müll.).   Base of the Worcestershire Beacon

Helicigona lapicida (Linn.)
— *arbustorum* (Linn.)
Helix aspersa, Müll.
— *nemoralis*, Linn.
— *hortensis*, Müll.
Buliminus obscurus (Müll.)
Cochlicopa lubrica (Müll.)
Azeca tridens (Pult.). Near Worcester; Malvern district; Acock's Green; Dudley
Cæcilianella acicula (Müll.)
Pupa secale, Drap. Malvern
— *cylindracea* (Da C.)
— *muscorum* (Linn.)
Sphyradium edentulum (Drap.). Malvern; Acock's Green
Vertigo antivertigo (Drap.). Malvern district
— *pygmæa* (Drap.). Malvern district; Selly Oak
Balea perversa (Linn.). Malvern district
Clausilia laminata (Mont.)
— *bidentata* (Ström.)
Succinea putris (Linn.)
— *elegans*, Risso. Stourport; Acock's Green

b. BASOMMATOPHORA

Carychium minimum, Müll. Malvern; near Worcester
Ancylus fluviatilis, Müll.
Velletia lacustris (Linn.)
Limnæa auricularia (Linn.)
— *pereger* (Müll.)

Limnæa palustris (Müll.)
— *truncatula* (Müll.)
— *stagnalis* (Linn.)
— *glabra* (Müll.). Hartlebury Common
Planorbis corneus (Linn.)
— *albus*, Müll.
— *glaber*, Jeff. Malvern.
— *nautileus* (Linn.)
— *carinatus*, Müll.
— *marginatus*, Drap.
— *vortex* (Linn.)
— *spirorbis*, Müll.
— *contortus* (Linn.)
— *fontanus* (Lightf.)
— *lineatus* (Walker). Stinton Pool, Crossway Green; Malvern
Physa fontinalis (Linn.)
— *hypnorum* (Linn.)

II. PROSOBRANCHIATA

Bithynia tentaculata (Linn.)
— *leachii* (Shepp.). Malvern
Vivipara vivipara (Linn.)
— *contecta* (Millett). River Severn; Worcester and Birmingham Canal
Valvata piscinalis (Müll.). Malvern; River Severn
— *cristata*, Müll. Near Worcester
Pomatias elegans (Müll.). Malvern; Bewdley
Neritina fluviatilis (Linn.). Malvern; River Severn

B. PELECYPODA

Dreissensia polymorpha (Pall.). River Severn; Worcester and Birmingham Canal
Unio pictorum (Linn.). River Teme (very abundant at Powick); near Worcester; River Avon; Worcester and Birmingham Canal
— *timidus*, Retz.
Anodonta cygnæa (Linn.)
Sphærium rivicola (Leach). Malvern
— *corneum* (Linn.)

Sphærium ovale (Fér.)
— *lacustre* (Müll.)
Pisidium amnicum (Müll.)
— *pusillum* (Gmel.). Malvern; near Worcester
— *nitidum*, Jenyns
— *fontinale* (Drap.). Near Worcester; Moseley. [The variety *Henslowianum* has been found at Hall Green and near Worcester.]

INSECTS

The insects of Worcestershire have unfortunately been only partially studied. In this, as in most counties, the Lepidoptera seem to have engaged the attention of collectors to the exclusion of most of the other orders, and consequently it is impossible to give here lists or notes of the Orthoptera, Diptera or Hemiptera. The physical features and climate of the county are favourable to a fairly representative insect fauna, for with the exception of coast, fen, high altitude and extreme northern or southern species the entomologist has every chance of obtaining types of any of our English genera. Its surface is undulating and diversified, but in taking a comprehensive view of the whole county its lowest level is in the centre, across the vale of the Severn, and it rises gradually towards the surrounding boundary until it reaches in most directions to a considerable height, especially towards the west where the Malvern Hills rise to a height of 1,394 feet. Throughout the county the woods are well distributed, and the Randans in the neighbourhood of Bromsgrove, and the primeval Wyre or Bewdley Forest in the north-west, consisting chiefly of scrub oak, birch, hazel and alder, with an occasional beech and some Scotch firs, are tracts of native woodland which offer a wide field for research to the collector. Wild heathy or sandy wastes and commons are also plentifully dispersed ; such are Hartlebury Common, Kempsey Common, Defford Common, Habberley Valley, Blakedown, Dodderhill, Castle Morton and Malvern Link amongst others. The bogs of Wyre Forest, Hartlebury Common and West Malvern have also their particular interest for the collector ; and in the neighbourhood of Longdon Marsh, which was of considerable extent before it was drained and divided up many years ago, may be found a few insects lingering in the old haunts, whither they used to be drawn by their favourite plants. The county is well watered by its rivers and natural pools, such for instance as are formed by the brooks running down into the Stour ; and also to a great extent artificially by its reservoirs and canals. Man has also added to the variety of the county's flora and extended the entomologist's field by cultivation. Besides the usual pasture and arable lands, the pear and apple orchards and the hop-yards cover an extensive area in the south and west, and in the neighbourhood of Pershore and Evesham large districts are devoted to market gardening.

The diversified physical character of the county, affecting as it does the insect fauna to so large an extent, should offer a strong inducement

to entomologists in the future to work up the different orders which are inadequately treated here.

There is little variation to be noted in the insects generally captured, but amongst the Lepidoptera melanistic examples have been secured of the Coronet (*Acronycta ligustri*), the Treble Lines (*Caradrina trigrammica* var. *bilinea*), the Marbled Rustic (*Hadena strigilis* var. *aethiops*), the Brindled Crescent (*Miselia oxyacanthæ* var. *capucina*), the Peppered Moth (*Biston betularius* var. *doubledayarius*), the Mottled Beauty (*Selidosema repandata* var. *destrigaria*), the Dark Arches (*Hadena polyodon*).

From my own personal observation in the county it seems that a considerable number of the females of the Oak Beauty (*Biston stratarius*) are crippled in nature, and this forms some ground for supposing that the female of this species is tending towards an imperfectly winged condition. The season 1900 was marked by a considerable migration of the Clouded Yellow (*Colias edusa*) and the great number of the larvæ and pupæ of the Death's Head (*Acherontia atropos*).

NEUROPTERA

The list of *Psocidæ* contains some twenty-two examples and is of average length. The *Planipennia* present a fairly strong list, but the *Odonata*, or dragonflies, commonly called 'horse-stingers,' have not been well worked up to the present and are poorly represented. From my own personal observation in the county I have noticed that *Calopteryx virgo* passes through a notable early stage. After emerging from the water, and when its wings have become firm enough for flight, it rises and flies slowly over the meadows to the top of some low tree, where it settles in the sun. At this period it is of a reddish-brown colour, with sooty wings. In this state it used to be considered a distinct species, and was named *C. vesta*. When it becomes mature its colour is lighter, and its wings to a very great extent have lost their sooty hue.

ODONATA

Sympetrum vulgatum, L. Woods and lanes
— scoticum, Don. *Dodderhill Common* (Rea)
Libellula depressa, L. Woods and lanes
— quadrimaculata, L. *Tibberton*
Gomphus vulgatissimus, L. Woods and lanes
Cordulegaster annulatus, Latr. *Broadwas, Wyre Forest*
Æschna cyanea, Müll. Woods and lanes
— grandis, L. *Shrawley, Cotheridge*
Calopteryx virgo, L. *Himbleton, the Teme*
— splendens, Harr. *Laughern Brook*
Platycnemis pennipes, Pall. Meadows by the *Teme*
Pyrrhosoma nymphula, Sulz. Lanes outside woods
Ischnura elegans, Lind. Pool at *Cotheridge*
Agrion puella, L. Lanes and wood sidings

PSOCIDÆ

Atropos divinatoria, Müll. } Indoors
Clothilla pulsatoria, L.

Psocus nebulosus, Stph.
— variegatus, F.
— fasciatus, F. } By beating trees and hedges
— bifasciatus, Latr.
— 4-maculatus, Latr.

Stenopsocus immaculatus, Stph.
— stigmaticus, McLach. } By beating hedges
— cruciatus, L.

Cæcilius pedicularius, L. Often indoors
— flavidus, Stph. } Beating oaks, etc.
— vittatus, Latr.

Peripsocus alboguttatus, Dahn. } Indoors
— subpupillatus, McLach.
— phæopterus, Stph. From a hedge, *Cotheridge*

INSECTS

Elipsocus unipunctatus, Müll. By beating
— westwoodi, McLach. On Pinus sylvestris
— hyalinus, Stph. On Abies excelsa, *Old Hills*
— flaviceps, Stph. On A. excelsa
— cyanops, Rostock. By beating fir trees

EPHEMERIDÆ

Ephemera vulgata, L. *Severn*
— danica, Müll. *Avon*
Cænis macrura, Stph. *Teme*
Cloëon dipterum, L. To 'light,' *Worcester*
Heptagenia semicolorata, Curt. *Teme*
— venosa, F. *Severn*
— longicauda, Stph. *Teme*

PLANIPENNIA

Sialis lutaria, L. All rivers and brooks
— fuliginosa, Pict. The *Teme*
Raphidia xanthostigma, Schum. *Trench Woods*
Sisyra fuscata, F. By rivers and brooks
— terminalis, Curt. By the *Teme*
Micromus variegatus, F. Lanes and thickets
— aphidivorus, Schr. *Leigh* and *Bransford*
— paganus, L. Lanes and thickets

Hemerobius elegans, Stph. *Grimley*
— pellucidulus, Walk. *Middleyards Copse*
— nitidulus, F. On Pinus sylvestris, *Old Hills*
— micans, Oliv. On Abies excelsa, *Old Hills*
— humuli, L. *Lower Wick, Worcester*
— limbatus, Wesm. *Old Hills*
— subnebulosus, Stph. *Hallow*
— nervosus, F. Bred from oak apples
Chrysopa flava, Scop. *Crown East Wood*
— vittata, Wesm. *Hallow*
— alba, L. *Monkwood*
— flavifrons, Brau. *Pitmaston*
— tenella, Schn. Bred from cone of Abies, *Witley*
— vulgaris, Schn. In garden, *Worcester*
— septempunctata, Wesm. Gardens
— aspersa, Wesm. *Bransford*
— ventralis, Curt. *Ockeridge Wood*
— phyllochroma, Wesm. *St. John's, Worcester*
— perla, L. *Monkwood, Crown East Wood*
Coniopteryx psociformis, Curt. *Pitmaston*
— tineiformis, Curt. } *Wyre Forest*
— aleurodiformis, Stph. }
Panorpa communis, L. Among flowers
— germanica, L. *Achen Hill Wood*

TRICHOPTERA

Caddis-flies seem to be fairly represented in this county in a list of seventy-eight species. The only example of terrestrial Caddis-fly (*Enoicyla pusilla*) known in this county has probably not been detected outside Worcestershire. Another species (*Allotrichia pallicornis*) seems also not to have been found elsewhere.

Neuronia ruficrus, Scop. One or two; seldom seen
Phryganea grandis, L. Comes to 'light'; not common
— varia, F. One or two
Colpotaulius incisus, Curt. In marshy places, *Grimley*
Glyphotælius pellucidus, Retz. In low fields near brooks
Limnophilus rhombicus, L. *Temple Laughern*
— flavicornis, F. By *Severn, Grimley*
— marmoratus, Curt. *Hallow*
— stigma, Curt. *Grimley, Camp*
— lunatus, Curt. *Bransford, Mudwall*
— centralis, Curt. *Middleyards*
— vittatus, F. *Broadheath*
— affinis, Curt. *Shrawley Wood*
— auricula, Curt. *Cotheridge*
— extricatus, McLach. *Laughern Brook*
— sparsus, Curt. *Monkwood*
— fuscicornis, Ramb.
Anabolia nervosa, Curt. *Laughern Brook*

Stenophylax stellatus, Curt. *Ronk's Wood*
— concentricus, Zett. *Bransford*
— vibex, Curt. *Pitmaston*
Micropterna sequax, McLach. ⎫
— lateralis, Stph. ⎬ *Dine's Green*
Halesus radiatus (Leach), Curt. ⎭
— digitatus, Schrk. *Bransford*
Chætopteryx villosa, F. By a brook, *Cotheridge*
Enoicyla pusilla, Burm. By a rill, *Little Eastbury*
Sericostoma personata, Latr. The *Teme, Cotheridge*
Notidobia ciliaris, L. *Laughern Brook*
Goëra pilosa, F. The *Severn, Grimley*
Silo pallipes, F. *Thorngrove* and *Temple Laughern*
Brachycentrus subnubilus, Curt. By the *Teme*
Lepidostoma hirta, F. ⎫ The *Teme,*
Lasiocephala basalis, Kol. ⎭ *Bransford*
Molanna angustata, Curt. *Laughern Brook*

Leptocerus alboguttatus, Hag. By a brook, *Cotheridge*
— aterrimus, De G., Stph. A pool, *Cotheridge*
— cinereus, Curt. } By the *Severn*
— albifrons, L. }
— bilineatus, L. By *Laughern Brook*
— dissimilis, Stph. The *Severn*
Mystacides nigra, L. The *Teme* and the *Avon*
— azurea, L. The *Teme*
Triænodes bicolor, Curt. By a pool, *Cotheridge*
— consperta, Ramb. Bank of *Teme*
Œcetis lacustris, Pict. Comes to 'light'; by nearly stagnant water
— notata, Ramb. Two, by *Severn*, *Lenchford*
— testacea, Curt. Banks of *Teme*, *Cotheridge*
Setodes tineiformis, Curt. By the *Severn*, *Camp*
— interrupta, F. *Severn* and *Teme*
— punctata, F. One, by the *Severn*, *Grimley*
Beræa pullata, Curt. A brooklet, *Cotheridge*
Beræodes minuta, L. *Laughern Brook*
Hydropsyche pellucidula, Curt. By the *Teme*
— augustipennis, Curt. *Teme*, *Cotheridge*
— guttata, Pict. The *Teme*, *Bransford*
— instabilis, Curt. *Broadwas*
— lepida, Pict. *Severn* and *Avon*

Wormaldia subnigra, McLach. By a rill out of bank of *Teme*
Plectrocnemia conspersa, Curt. *Comer Gardens*
Polycentropus flavomaculatus, Pict. *Teme*
— multiguttatus, Curt. The *Teme*, *Powick*
Holocentropus dubius, Ramb. The *Teme*, *Bransford*
— picicornis, Stph. Pond, *Grimley*
— stagnalis, Albarda. Marsh, *Grimley*
Cyrnus trimaculatus, Curt. By rivers generally
Tinodes wæneri, L. *Laughern Brook*
Lype phæopa, Stph. *Avon* and *Severn*
Psychomyia pusilla, F. The *Teme*, *Cotheridge*
Chimarrha marginata, L. Two or three, by the *Teme*
Rhyacophila dorsalis, Curt. By the *Teme*
Agapetus fuscipes, Curt. By rills generally
— comatus, Pict. One or two, *Teme*
Agraylea multipunctata, Curt. To 'light,' *Worcester*
Allotrichia pallicornis, Eaton. One at 'light,' *Pitmaston*
Hydroptila sparsa, Curt. The *Severn*, near *Worcester*
— forcipata, Eaton. By the *Teme*, *Bransford*
Oxyethira costalis, Curt. To 'light,' *Worcester*

HYMENOPTERA

It would seem that this order of insects has not been worked at in this county until my time, so there is little to be said in a preliminary way. The order contains creatures only second in interest to the human species. Parthenogenesis is very common among the Sawflies, and a similar case came under my notice in the Ants. A small ant (*Leptothorax tuberum*), consisting of but a few individuals in any one community, chooses for its nest some rather prominent piece of bark, more or less hollowed on the inner side (if indeed the creature does not form the cavity), on a tree in a retired thicket—poplar and maple are the only trees I have found it on—in which to set up its home. In the beginning of April, 1887, I came across such a piece of bark on a scrubby maple, which with my trowel I chipped off, exposing to view a little group of twenty or thirty of these creatures. As I had no males and only one wingless female in my collection, it occurred to me to carry these ants home and try what could be done with them in captivity.

I tried to get the ants into a tin box, but only succeeded with the greater part; the female, owing to the rough bark and projecting shoots of the tree, escaped me and fell to the long grass at the roots and was lost. On reaching home I took a short piece of green willow, the thickness of a man's arm and some 10 inches long, and stood it up in a large

garden pot containing about 4 inches of prepared soil. On the soil around the willow I laid some close-growing moss and a tuft of grass. I took a suitable piece or two of bark, which I fastened to the willow with three or four strong pins, to serve the ants for a nest. Over all I raised a bag of close-woven white leno, resting on a contrivance of wire, and fastened tightly below the rim of the pot by string. Having made this improvised home ready, I placed on the moss two or three scraps of fresh meat, some moist sugar and preserved fruit. The ants were turned into it and after a day or two of unrest they took up their abode in the nest and settled down. The meat and other edibles were often replaced by fresh. The ants were often watched and seen to be using the food and foraging. In July, seeing but little of them, I unpinned a part of the nest and was surprised to see several larvæ, upon and around which the ants were gathered. Three weeks later I again looked into the nest and was pleased to see several cocoons. During the last third of September, twenty-one males were bred from these cocoons.

ACULEATA

HETEROGYNA

FORMICIDÆ

Formica rufa, Linn. (the Horse Ant). *Shrawley, Trench Woods, Wyre Forest,* etc.

— sanguinea, Ltr. *Wyre Forest* ; common (Martineau)

— exsecta, Nyl. *Bewdley* (Blatch)

— fusca, Ltr. *Temple Laughern, Worcester,* etc. ; common in most localities

Lasius fuliginosus, Ltr. *Lathe Lane* (Fletcher) ; *Trench Woods* (Martineau)

— umbratus, Nyl. In bank of *Severn, Lenchford* (Fletcher) ; *Bewdley* (Blatch)

— flavus, De Geer. At foot of tree, *Cotheridge* (Fletcher) ; common in fields everywhere

— niger, Linn. (the Garden Ant); common generally

Formicoxenus nitidulus, Nyl. *Bewdley* (Blatch)

Stenamma westwoodii, Westw. *Hallow*

Leptothorax tuberum, Fab. Sides of *Teme, Powick, Bransford*

Myrmica rubra, Linn., race lævinodis, Nyl. *Hallow, Stoulton*

—   ruginodis, Nyl. *Stoulton, Little Eastbury*

—   scabrinodis, Nyl. *Old Hills, Monkwood*

FOSSORES

MUTILLIDÆ

Myrmosa melanocephala, Fab. *Crown East Wood* (Fletcher) ; *Moseley* (Bradley)

SAPYGIDÆ

Sapyga clavicornis, Latr. On a wooden rail, *Crown East*

POMPILIDÆ

Pompilus cinctellus, Spin. *Wyre Forest* (Martineau)

— plumbeus, Fab. *Crown East*

— niger, Fab. *Moseley* ; common (Bradley)

— viaticus, Linn. *Wyre Forest* (Bradley)

— spissus, Schiödte. *Wyre Forest*; common (Martineau)

— gibbus, Fab. *Wyre Forest, Droitwich, Moseley,* etc. (Bradley)

— unguicularis, Thoms. *Moseley* (Bradley)

— pectinipes, V. de Lind. *Wyre Forest* (Martineau) ; *Moseley* (Bradley)

Salius (*S. G. Priocnemis,* Schiödte), *fuscus,* Linn. *Hallow* (Fletcher) ; *Wyre Forest, Malvern, Droitwich* (Martineau)

— affinis, V. de Lind. *Oldbury Road*

— exaltatus, Fab. *Grimley*

— notatulus, Saund. *Wyre Forest* (Martineau) ; *Moseley* (Bradley)

— obtusiventris, Schiödte. *Middleyards*

Agenia variegata, Linn. *Monkwood*

SPHEGIDÆ

Trypoxylon figulus, Linn. In garden, *Worcester* (Fletcher) ; *Moseley* (Bradley)

— clavicerum, Lep. *Hallow*

— attenuatum, Sm. *Crown East*

Spilomena troglodytes, V. de Lind. Indoors, *Worcester*

Stigmus solskyi, Moraw. *Hallow*

Pemphredon lugubris, Latr. *Powick* (Fletcher) ; *Wyre Forest, Moseley* (Bradley)

SPHEGIDÆ (*continued*)

Pemphredon shuckardi, Moraw. *Moseley* (Bradley)
— lethifer, Shuck. *Wyre Forest* (Martineau)
— morio, V. de Lind.
Diodontus minutus, Fab. } *Moseley* (Bradley)
— tristis, V. de Lind.
Passalœcus insignis, V. de Lind. *Thorngrove* (Fletcher) ; *Bewdley* (Blatch) ; *Moseley* (Bradley)
— gracilis, Curt. *Worcester* (Fletcher) ; *Bewdley* (Blatch)
— monilicornis, Dahlb. *Bewdley* (Blatch)
Mimesa dahlbomi, Wesm. *Wyre Forest* (Martineau) ; *Moseley* (Bradley)
Psen pallipes, Panz. *Moseley* (Bradley) ; *Worcester*
Arpactus tumidus, Panz. *Moseley* (Bradley)
Gorytes mystaceus, Linn. *Bewdley* (Blatch); *Crown East*
Nysson spinosus, Fab. *Wyre Forest* (Bradley)
Mellinus arvensis, Linn. *Worcester* (Fletcher) ; *Moseley* (Bradley)
Oxybelus uniglumis, Linn. *Hallow* (Fletcher) ; *Moseley* (Bradley)
Crabro clavipes, Linn. *Worcester* (Fletcher); *Moseley* (Bradley)
— tibialis, Fab. *Hallow*
— leucostomus, Linn. Bred, larva in old willow, *Cotheridge* (Fletcher) ; *Moseley* (Bradley)
— podagricus, V. de Lind. *Middleyards*
— gonager, Lep. In garden, *Worcester*
— palmipes, Linn. *Moseley* (Bradley)
— varius, Lep. *Little Eastbury* (Fletcher); *Wyre Forest* (Bradley)
— anxius, Wesm. *Crown East* (Fletcher); *Wyre Forest* (Bradley)
— wesmaeli, V. de Lind. *Wyre Forest*
— elongatulus, V. de Lind. *Worcester* (Fletcher) ; *Moseley* (Bradley)
— quadrimaculatus, Dhlb. *Wyre Forest* (Martineau)
— dimidiatus, Fab. *Moseley* (Bradley)
— vagabundus, Panz. *Wyre Forest* (Martineau)
— cephalotes, Panzer. *Crown East*
— cavifrons, Thoms. *Moseley* (Bradley)
— chrysostomus, Lep. *Wyre Forest* (Fletcher) ; *Moseley* (Bradley)
— vagus, Linn. *Wyre Forest* (Martineau)
— cribrarius, Linn. *Moseley* (Bradley)
— interruptus, De Geer. *Worcester* (Fletcher) ; *Moseley* (Bradley)
— albilabris, Fab. *Bransford*
Entomognathus brevis, V. de Lind. *Wyre Forest* (Martineau)

DIPLOPTERA

VESPIDÆ

Vespa crabro, Linn. *Temple Laughern* (Fletcher) ; *Cleeve Prior* (Blatch)
— vulgaris, Linn. Generally common
— germanica, Fab. *Cotheridge, Worcester* (Fletcher) ; *Droitwich*, etc.
— rufa, Linn. *Bransford* (Fletcher) ; *Wyre Forest, Droitwich* (Martineau)
— sylvestris, Scop. *Crown East, Wyre Forest*
— norvegica, Fab. *Wyre Forest* (Martineau)

EUMENIDÆ

Odynerus spinipes, Linn. *Lane, Sinton Green* (Fletcher) ; *Wyre Forest, Moseley* (Bradley)
— melanocephalus, Gmel. *Middleyards* (Fletcher) ; *Bewdley* (Blatch)
— lævipes, Shuck. Bred from bramble stems, *Crown East* (Fletcher) ; *Malvern, Wyre Forest* (Martineau)
— callosus, Thoms. Common in gardens, *Worcester, Pershore, Malvern, Wyre Forest, Moseley*
— parietum, Linn. Common in gardens, *Worcester, Moseley*, etc.
— pictus, Curt. *Worcester* (Fletcher) ; *Wyre Forest, Moseley* (Bradley)
— trimarginatus, Ztt. *Moseley* (Bradley)
— trifasciatus, Oliv. *Bransford* (Fletcher); *Moseley* (Bradley)
— parietinus, Linn. *Moseley* (Bradley)
— antilope, Panz. About an old wall, *Grimley*
— gracilis, Brullé. *Crown East* (Fletcher) ; *Ran Dan Woods* (Wainwright)
— sinuatus, Fab. *Cotheridge* (Fletcher) ; *Wyre Forest, Moseley* (Bradley)

ANTHOPHILA

COLLETIDÆ

Colletes succincta, Linn. *Wyre* (Martineau)
— fodiens, Kirby. Flowers of tansy, *Grimley*
— Daviesana, Sm. *Moseley*, common (Bradley)
Prosopis communis, Nyl. *Peghouse Wood* (Fletcher) ; *Moseley* (Bradley)
— hyalinata, Sm. In garden, *Worcester* (Fletcher) ; *Moseley* (Bradley)
— confusa, Nyl. *Worcester* (Fletcher) ; *Wyre Forest* (Martineau)
— brevicornis, Nyl. *Worcester* ; in garden

ANDRENIDÆ

Sphecodes gibbus, Linn. *Sinton Green* (Fletcher) ; *Moseley* (Bradley)
— subquadratus, Sm. *Moseley* (Bradley)
— puncticeps, Thoms. *Monkwood*

INSECTS

ANDRENIDÆ (*continued*)

Sphecodes pilifrons, Thoms. *Wyre Forest, Malvern* (Martineau) ; *Moseley* (Bradley)

— semilis, Wesm. *Moseley* (Bradley)

— variegatus, V. Hag. *Hallow* (Fletcher) ; *Wyre Forest* (Martineau)

— dimidiatus, V. Hag. *Moseley* (Bradley)

— affinis, V. Hag. *Wyre* (Martineau) ; *Moseley* (Bradley)

Halictus rubicundus, Christ. *Bransford* (Fletcher) ; *Wyre Forest, Malvern, Droitwich,* etc.

— leucozonius, Schrank. *Hallow* (Fletcher); *Moseley* (Bradley)

— zonulus, Sm. *Monkwood*

— lævigatus, Kirby. *Tibberton*

— cylindricus, Fab. *Bransford* (Fletcher); *Wyre Forest, Moseley* (Bradley)

— albipes, Kirby. *Crown East* (Fletcher) ; *Wyre Forest* (Martineau)

— subfasciatus, Nyl. *Middleyards*

— villosulus, Kirby. *Hallow* (Fletcher) ; *Wyre Forest, Moseley* (Bradley)

— punctatissimus, Schrenck. *Wyre Forest* (Martineau)

— nitidiusculus, Kirby. *Grimley*

— atricornis, Smith. *Wyre Forest* (Martineau) ; *Moseley* (Bradley)

— tumulosum, Linn. *Hallow, Grimley* (Fletcher) ; *Wyre Forest* (Martineau)

— smeathmanellus, Kirb. *Worcester*

— morio, Fab. *Pole Elm* (Fletcher) ; *Wyre Forest* (Bradley)

— leucopus, Kirby. *Hallow* (Fletcher) ; *Wyre Forest* (Bradley)

Andrena albicans, Kirby. *Powick* (Fletcher) ; *Wyre Forest, Droitwich, Malvern, Moseley*

— pilipes, Fab. *Cotheridge*

— rosæ, Panz. *Martley* (Fletcher) ; *Wyre Forest, Malvern, Droitwich, Moseley,* etc. (Bradley)

— var. trimmerana, Kirb. *Old Hills* (Fletcher) ; *Wyre Forest, Malvern, Droitwich, Moseley,* etc. (Bradley)

— nitida, Fourc. *Bransford* (Fletcher); *Wyre Forest* (Martineau) ; *Trench Woods* (Bradley)

— cineraria, Linn. *Old Hills, Oldbury Farm* (Fletcher); *Wyre Forest* (Martineau)

— fulva, Schr. *Generally distributed*

— clarkella, Kirby. *Wyre Forest* (Martineau)

— nigroænea, Kirby. *Wyre Forest*

— gwynana, Kirby. *Wyre Forest* (Bradley)

— augustior, Kirby. *Moseley* (Bradley)

ANDRENIDÆ (*continued*)

Andrena præcox, Scop. *Wyre Forest* (Martineau)

— varians, Rossi. On pathway, *Hallow* (Fletcher) ; *Wyre Forest* (Martineau)

— fucata, Sm. *Wyre Forest* (Martineau)

— cingulata, Fab. *Crown East* (Fletcher) ; *Bewdley* (Martineau)

— albicrus, Kirb. *Moseley* (Bradley)

— chrysosceles, Kirby. *Middleyards* (Fletcher) ; *Droitwich* (Martineau)

— analis, Panz. *Wyre Forest* (Martineau)

— humilis, Imhoff. *Wyre Forest* (Wainwright)

— labialis, Kirb. *Stanbrook* (Fletcher) ; *Wyre Forest, Moseley* (Bradley)

— minutula, Kirby ⎱ *Wyre Forest* (Martineau)
— nana, Kirby
— similis, Sm. ⎰

— wilkella, Kirby. *Old Hills* (Fletcher) ; *Wyre Forest* (Martineau)

— afzeliella, Kirby. *Old Hills*

Nomada solidaginis, Panz. *Wyre Forest* (Martineau)

— succincta, Panz. *Sinton Green* (Fletcher); *Wyre Forest, Droitwich, Malvern, Moseley*

— alternata, Kirby. *Bransford* (Fletcher) ; *Wyre Forest, Droitwich, Moseley, Malvern*

— lathburiana, Kirby. *Moseley* (Bradley)

— ruficornis, Linn. *Sinton Green* (Fletcher); *Wyre Forest, Malvern, Droitwich, Moseley*

— borealis, Ztt. *Wyre Forest* (Martineau)

— lateralis, Panz. *Old Hills*

— ochrostoma, Kirby. *Achen Hill Wood* (Fletcher) ; *Wyre Forest, Moseley* (Bradley)

— fabriciana, Linn. *Wyre Forest* (Fletcher); *Droitwich* (Martineau)

— flavoguttata, Kirb. *Middleyards*

— furva, Panz. *Sinton Green* (Fletcher) ; *Droitwich* (Martineau)

APIDÆ

Epeolus rufipes, Thoms. *Wyre Forest* (Bradley)

Chelostoma florisomne, Linn. *Martley* (Fletcher) ; *Moseley* (Bradley)

— campanularum, Kirby. *Hallow*

Cœlioxys quadridentata, Linn. *Wyre Forest* (Martineau)

— elongata, Lep. In garden, *Worcester*

— acuminata, Nyl. *Wyre Forest* (Martineau)

Megachile Willughbiella, Kirby. *Moseley* (Bradley)

— circumcincta, Lep. *Wyre Forest* (Martineau) ; *Trench Woods* (Bradley)

— ligniseca, Kirby. *Evesham* (Bradley)

APIDÆ (*continued*)

Megachile centuncularis, Linn. *Worcester* (Fletcher) ; *Wyre Forest, Moseley* (Bradley)

Osmia rufa, Linn. In gardens, *Worcester, Bewdley, Moseley,* etc.

— xanthomelana, Kirby. *Trench Woods* (Bradley) ; *Middleyards* (Fletcher)

— cærulescens, Linn. In gardens (Fletcher) ; *Wyre Forest, Droitwich,* etc.

— fulviventris, Panz. *Moseley* (Bradley)

— bicolor, Schk. *Middleyards*

— leucomelana, Kirb. *Wyre Forest* (Martineau)

Anthidium manicatum, Linn. At labiate flowers, *Worcester*

Eucera longicornis, Linn. *Middleyards, Birchen Groves* [1] (Fletcher) ; *Bewdley* Martineau)

Melecta armata, Panz. *Wyre Forest, Grimley*

Anthophora retusa, Linn. *Wyre Forest, Shrawley*

— pilipes, Fab. At flowers in town and country

— furcata, Panz. One, *Middleyards* (Fletcher) ; *Wyre Forest* (Martineau)

Psithyrus rupestris, Fab. At thistles, *Monkwood* (Fletcher) ; *Moseley* (Bradley)

— vestalis, Fourc. *Crown East, Middleyards* (Fletcher) ; *Moseley* (Bradley)

APIDÆ (*continued*)

Psithyrus barbutellus, Kirby. *Bransford*

— campestris, Panz. *Monkwood* (Fletcher) ; *Moseley* (Bradley)

— quadricolor, Lep. *Moseley* (Bradley)

Bombus venustus, Sm. *Claphill Lane, Martley Road* (Fletcher) ; *Pershore, Wyre Forest, Moseley*

— agrorum, Fab. *Crown East, Wyre Forest,* etc. ; common generally

— hortorum, Linn. *Grimley, Oldbury Farm* (Fletcher) ; *Wyre Forest, Moseley* (Bradley)

— — var. subterraneus. *Moseley* (Bradley)

— — var. harrisellus. *Wyre Forest, Moseley* (Bradley)

— latreillellus, Kirby. *Bransford* (Fletcher); *Wyre Forest* (Martineau)

— sylvarum, Linn. Thistle flowers, *Temeside, Powick, Malvern, Droitwich, Wyre Forest*

— derhamellus, Kirb. *Stanbrook* (Fletcher); *Malvern* (Martineau)

— lapidarius, Linn. Generally common.

— pratorum, Linn. *Powick* ; in garden, *Worcester*

— terrestris, Linn. *Stanbrook* ; generally common

Apis mellifica, Linn. *Grimley* ; generally common

PHYTOPHAGA

This county is fairly well represented in the phytophagous Hymenoptera. The sawflies number 172 species, some of which are recent discoveries. The gall-raisers also are fairly represented.

In collections of sawflies many species are represented by females only. The deficiency of males might in some instances be remedied were careful breeding pursued by energetic young collectors ; or failing in that aim, further evidence would be gained of the unisexuality of the creatures experimented on.

Among the gall-raisers, notwithstanding Dr. Adler's discoveries, many species remain very imperfectly known. Here a young and intelligent man gifted with a spirit of inquiry might do much good service.

TENTHREDINIDÆ

Tenthredo livida, L. *Wyre Forest, Monkwood*

— colon, Klug. One, *Bransford*

— rufiventris, Pz. *Tibberton*

— dispar, Klug. *Oldbury Farm*

— atra, L. Meadows by the *Teme, Cotheridge*

— mesomela, L. *Crown East*

TENTHREDINIDÆ (*continued*)

Rhogogastera punctulata, Klug. *Bransford*

— viridis, L. *Cotheridge*

— lateralis, F. *Whitehall,* in *Worcester*

— picta, Klug. *Callow End*

— aucupariæ, Klug. *Powick*

Tenthredopsis cordata, Fourc. In garden, *Worcester*

— nigricollis, Lep. *Crown East*

[1] This wood was stubbed up many years ago and so the records here inserted therefor will have to be again verified in the adjacent Crown East Woods.

INSECTS

TENTHREDINIDÆ (continued)

Tenthredopsis scutellaris, F. *Mudwail*
— tristis, Steph. *Wyre Forest*
— raddatzi, Kow. *Shoulton*
— dorsalis, Sep. *Crown East*
Pachyprotasis rapæ, L. In garden, *Worcester*
Macrophya neglecta, Klug. *Bredon*
— albicincta, Schr. *Sling Lane, Worcester*
— punctum-album, L. *Comer Lane*
Allantus scrophulariæ, L. The *Severn side*, near *Bewdley*
— arcuatus, Forst. Common in meadows generally
— bicinctus, F. *Oddingley*
Sciopteryx costalis, F. One, by *Laughern*
Soderus vestigialis, Klug. *Bransford*
Dolerus madidus, Konow. *Broadheath*
— fulviventris, Scop. *Thorngrove*
— anticus, Klug. *Middleyards*
— palustris, Klug. *Grimley*
— gonagra, F. *The Grove Farm*
— hæmatodes, Schr. *Powick*
— fissus, Hart. *Old Hills*
— æneus, Hart. *Pole Elm*
— elongatus, Cam. *Crown East*
Selandria serva, F. *Hallow*
— sixii, Voll. *Cotheridge, New Bromsgrove*
— stramineipes, Klug. In garden, *Worcester*
— analis, Thoms. In garden, *Worcester*
— morio, F. *Powick*
— cinereipes,[1] Klug. *Grimley*
Taxonus equiseti, Fall. By the *Teme, Bransford*
— glabratus, Fall. *Earl's Court Farm*
— albipes, Thoms. One, *Hallow*
Pœcilosoma luteola, Klug. *Shrawley Woods*
— pulverata, Retz. *Grimley*
— guttata, Fall. One, near *Worcester*
— carbonaria, Scop. *Cotheridge*
— excisa, Thoms. *Old Hills*
Eriocampa ovata, L. *Laughern side*, near *Worcester*
Eriocampoides annulipes, Klug. *Achen Hill Wood*
— varipes, Klug. *Crown East*
— limacina, Retz. *Lathe Hill*
— cinxia, Klug. One, near *Worcester*
— rosæ, Harris. *Middleyards*
Blennocampa nigrita, F. One, near *Worcester*
— geniculata, Hart. ⎫ *Bransford*
— albipes, Gmel. ⎭
— lineolata, Klug. *Middleyards*
— fuscipennis, Fall. *Crown East Wood*
— ephippium, Pz. *Stanbrook*
— fuliginosa, Schr. *Teme-side, Bransford*

[1] According to Cameron this is the same as Blennocampa cinereipes, Klug.

TENTHREDINIDÆ (continued)

Blennocampa cinereipes, Klug. *Bransford*
— subserrata, Thoms. *Middleyards*
— subcana, Zach. *Wyre Forest*
— betuleti, Klug. *Crown East*
— quercus, Cam. *Monkwood*
— assimilis, Fall. *Middleyards*
Hoplocampa testudinea, Klug. Garden and orchards
— pectoralis, Thoms. *Temple Laughern*
Emphytus togatus, Pz. *Crown East*
— cinctus, L. Sloe-hedges, generally
— cingulatus, Steph. *Sinton Green*
— ruficinctus, Ratz. *Middleyards*
— calceatus, Klug. *Grimley*
— tibialis, Pz. *Wyre Forest, Wichenford*
— serotinus, Klug. *Wyre Forest*
— grossulariæ, Klug. *Hallow*
— tener, Fall. *Camp*
— perla, Klug. *Camp, Bransford*
Phyllotoma nemorata, Fall. *Crown East*
— ochropoda, Klug. *Wyre Forest, Monkwood*
— vagans, Fall. *Laughern sides*
— microcephala, Klug. *Grimley*
Fenella nigrita, Westw. *Cotheridge*
Fenusa melanopoda, Thoms. *Laughern sides*
— pumila, Klug. Among birches
— ulmi, Sundeval. Among elms
— hortulana, Klug. On black poplars generally
— pygmæa, Klug. Among oaks
— pumilio, Hart. Among Rubus idæus; uncommon
— nigricans, Klug. Among birches
Athalia ancilla, Sep. *Little Eastbury*
— rosæ, Fall. Among flowers everywhere
— lugens, Klug. *Leigh*
— annulata, F. One, *Middleyards*
Hemichroa alni, L. On alders, *Thorngrove*
— rufa, Pz. Among alders
Dineura virididorsata, Retz. Among birches, *Monkwood*
— stilata, Klug. *Monkwood, Wyre Forest*
— verna, Klug. *Middleyards*
— despecta, Hart. One, *Bransford*
Camponiscus luridiventris, Fall. Among alders
Cladius pectinicornis, Fourc. Among rose, in gardens and hedges
— viminalis, Fall. On poplars; not common
— rufipes, Sep. On elms, generally
— eradiatus, Sep. *Camp*
— drewseni, Thoms. *Cotheridge*
— padi, L. Among hawthorns, and in gardens
— brullæi, Dbm. Among Rubus idæus, in gardens

91

TENTHREDINIDÆ (*continued*)
Crœsus septentrionalis, L. *Wyre Forest*
— latipes, Villaret. On birch trees, *Monkwood*
— varus, Fall. On alders, *Laughern sides*
Nematus compressicornis, F. On black poplars, near *Worcester*
— fletcheri, Cam. *Oldbury Road*
— crassus, Fall. *Broadheath*
— cæruleocarpus, Hart. *Broadwas*
— lucidus, Pz. *Crown East*
— histrio, Lep. *Monkwood*
— humeralis, Zett. One, on palings, near *Worcester*
— hæmorrhoidalis, Fall. On sallows, *Middleyards*
— capreæ, Pz. *Camp*
— pallidiventris, Fall. *Bransford*
— obductus, Hart. *Broadmoor Green*
— conductus, Ruthe. *Powick*
— leucogaster, Hast. *Cotheridge*
— lacteus, Thoms. On willows generally
— maculiger, Cam. *Laughern Brook*, near *Worcester*
— orbitalis, Cam. *Bransford*
— palliatus, Dbm. *Boughton*
— curtispina, Thoms. *Bransford*
— glutinosæ, Cam. Among alders
— salicivorus, Cam. Wherever willows grow
— consobrinus, Voll. *Worcester* ; in gardens
— myosotidis, F. *Claphill Lane*
— zetterstedti, Dbm. *Monkwood*
— subbifidus, Thoms. One, *Bransford*
— croceus, Fall. *Hallow*
— flavescens, Steph. *Thorngrove*
— abdominalis, Pz. One, near *Worcester*
— bilineatus, Br. & Zad. } *Hallow*
— ruficapillus, Gmel. }
— salicis, L. *Grimley*
— melanocephalus, De G. *Grimley*
— ribesii, Scop. *Worcester* ; in garden
— pavidus, Lep. *Wyre Forest*
— bipartitus, Lep. }
— xanthogaster, Foër. } *Bransford*
— rumicis, Fall. }
— leucostictus, Hart. *Wyre Forest*
— purpurææ, Cam. *Grimley*
— nigrolineatus, Cam. *Thorngrove*
— baccarum, Cam. *Powick*
— salicis-cinereæ, Retz. *Grimley*
— gallicola, Steph. Wherever willows grow
Euura flavipes, Cam. *Cotheridge*
— nigritarsis, Cam. *Wichenford*
— angusta, Hart. *Middleyards*
— saliceti, Fall. *Hallow*
CIMBICIDÆ
Trichiosoma vitellinæ, L. Larvæ on willow

CIMBICIDÆ (*continued*)
Trichiosoma betuleti, Kl. Larvæ on hawthorn
Abia sericea, L. *Longdon*
HYLOTOMIDÆ
Hylotoma pagana, Pz. *Achen Hill Wood*, *Wyre Forest*
— cyaneocrocea, Fourc. *Thorngrove*
— cæruleipennis, Retz. *Wyre Forest*
— enodis, L. *Cotheridge*
LYDIDÆ
Pamphilius flaviventris, Retz. Larva on hawthorn near *Worcester*
— sylvaticus, L. *Hallow*
XYELIDÆ
Xyela julii, Breb. One, at *Old Hills*
CEPHIDÆ
Cephus linearis, Schr. *Middleyards*
— arundinis, Gir. From rushes, *Monkwood*
— phthisicus, F. *Crown East*
— pygmæus, L. *Claphill Lane, Lovington*
— pusillus, Steph. *Wyre Forest*
SIRICIDÆ
Sirex gigas, L. Two or three, near *Worcester*
— juvencus, L. One specimen, near *Worcester*
Xiphydria dromedarius, F. One, from willow, near *Worcester*
CYNIPIDÆ
Sarothrus canaliculatus, Hart. *Pitmaston*
Amblynotus opacus, Hart. *Monkwood*
Anacharus eucharoides, Dalm. *Comer Lane*
— immunis, Walk. *Powick*
Eucoela mandebularis, Zett. *Crown East*
Kleditoma picicrux, Gir. *Perry Wood*
Rhodites eglanteriæ, Gir. Lanes and woods
— rosæ, L. Borders of woods and thickets
Aulax glechomæ, Hart. *Pole Elm*
Xestophanes potentillæ, De Vill. *Powick*
Periclistus caninæ, Hart. Bred from Rhodites eglanteriæ
Synergus incrassatus, Hart. Bred from several galls
— pallicornis, Hart. Bred from several galls
— vulgaris, Hart. „ „ „
— facialis, Hart. „ „ „
Diastrophus rubi, Hart. *Powick*
Andricus ostreus, Gir. Woods and thickets
— fecundatrix, Hart. Woods generally
— globuli, Hart. „ „
— radicis, F. „ „
— corticis, Hart. „ „
— collaris, Hart. „ „
— ramuli, L. „ „
— quadrilineatus, Hart. „ „
— cirratus, Adler. „ „
— albopunctatus, Mayr. „ „
— glandulæ, Schenck. „ „

INSECTS

CYNIPIDÆ (*continued*)

Andricus solitarius, Fourc. Woods generally

Cynips kollari, Hart. Scrubby oaks generally

Trigonaspis megaptera, **Pz.** *Middleyards Copse*

Biorhiza terminalis, F. Scattered oaks

Dryophanta folii, L. Woods and thickets

CYNIPIDÆ (*continued*)

Dryophanta longiventris, Hart. Woods and thickets

— divisa, Hart. Woods and thickets

Neuroterus lenticularis, Oliv. „ „

— fumipennis, Hart. „ „ „

— læviusculus, Schenck. „ „ „

— numismatis, Oliv. „ „ „

— aprilinus, Gir. „ „ „

ENTOMOPHAGA

Few species of insects are wholly free from attack by some of the entomophagous Hymenoptera, and many are subject to attack by one, two or more species. Some of these parasites are themselves subject to attack by other parasites (hyper-parasitism). No stage that insects pass through is free from parasitism, beginning with the egg state. Here is a wide field for investigation.

I am indebted to the Rev. T. A. Marshall, M.A., and to the late Mr. J. B. Bridgman of Norwich, for the determination of many of the following species. The *Pinacographia* of Snellen van Vollenhoven has been very useful to me.

CHRYSIDIDÆ

Cleptes semiaurata, Latr. A parasite of sawfly larvæ

Homalus auratus, Dahlb. Two, in garden

Chrysis ignita, L. ⎫ About walls and fences ;
— cyanea, L. ⎭ common

— neglecta, Dahlb. Parasite of Odynerus spinipes

ICHNEUMONIDÆ

Chasmodes motatorius, F. One, by the *Teme*

— lugens, Gr. One, under bark of willow, *Hallow*

Ichneumon fuscipes, Gmel. *Lathe Hill*

— pistorius, Gr. Under garden refuse, *Worcester*

— trilineatus, Gmel. *Cotheridge*

— multiannulatus, Gr. Ex p. Palimpsestis octogesima

— vaginatorius, L. *Crown East Wood*

— xanthorius, Forst. *Old Hills*

— luctatorius, L. *Hallow*

— latrator, F. *Nunnery Wood*

— saturatorius, F. *Worcester* ; in garden

— fabricator, F. Side of *Teme, Powick*

— curvinervis, Hlmz. *Lovington*

— lanius, Gr. *Crown East*

— albolarvatus, Gr. *Crown East Woods*

— lepidus, Gr. *Honeybourne*

— albicinctus, Gr. *Monkwood*

— albifrons, Seph. *Achen Hill Wood*

Amblyteles armatorius, Forst. *Crown East*

— oratorius, F. *Bransford*

— subsericans, Gr. *Middleyards*

ICHNEUMONIDÆ (*continued*)

Amblyteles castanopygus, Steph. *Honeybourne*

— castigator, F. *Cotheridge*

Probalus alticola, Gr. *Bransford*

Platylabus pedatorius, F. *Crown East*

Herpestomus brunnicornis, Gr. Ex Yponomeuta cognatellus

Dicœlotus pumilus, Gr. In moss, *Hallow*

— ruficoxatus, Gr. *Worcester* ; indoors

— parvulus, Gr. *Hallow*

— rufilimbatus, Gr. *Bransford*

Æthecerus discolor, Wesm. In moss, *Crown East*

Alomyia debellator, F. *Grimley*

CRYPTIDÆ

Stilpnus gagates, Gr. In moss, *Tiddesley Wood*

Phygadeuon fulgens, Bridg. *Grimley*

— probus, Tasch. *Teme-side, Bransford*

— flavimanus, Gr. *Hallow*

— variabilis, Gr. Near *Bromsgrove*

— fumator, Gr. Near *Droitwich*

— troglodytes, Gr. *Grimley*

— jejunator, Gr. *Bransford*

— vagans, Gr. *Worcester* ; indoors

— brevis, Gr. *Oldbury Farm*

— prophligator, F. In osier bed, *Camp*

— semipolitus, Tasch. *Worcester* ; in gardens

— vagabundus, Gr. *Bransford*

— sodalis, Tasch. *Hallow*

— quadrispinus, Gr. *Wadborough*

— congruens, Gr. *Middleyards*

93

CRYPTIDÆ (*continued*)

Phygadeuon curvus, Schr. *Middleyards*
— abdominator, Gr. *Shrawley Wood*
— jucundus, Gr. *Mudwall*
— basizonius, Gr. *Hallow*
— oviventris, Gr. *Grimley*
— procerus, Gr. *Comer Lane*
— erythrinus, Gr. *Oddingley*
Cryptus erythropus, Bridg. *Bow Wood*
— cimbicis, Tschek. Near *Worcester*
— tarsoleucus, Schr. *Bransford*
— moschator, F. *Temple Laughern*
— minator, Gr. *Middleyards*
— obscurus, Gr. }
— analis, Gr. } *Crown East*
— rufiventris, Gr. Near *Worcester*
— migrator, F. *Pitmaston*
— pygoleucus, Gr. *Crown East*
Nematopodius ater, Brischké. Mixed hedge, *Lower Wick*
Hemiteles brevicaudatus, Bridg. *Worcester*; indoors
— ruficinctus, Gr. *Trench Woods*
— furcatus, Tasch. Osier bed, *Thorngrove*
— micator, Gr. *Shoulton*
— oxyphimus, Gr. *Oldbury Farm*
— similis, Gr. *Broadheath*
— fulvipes, Gr. Ex. larva of Pieris rapæ
— tristrator, Gr. *Worcester*; in gardens
— ridibundus, Gr. }
— æstivalis, Gr. } *Worcester*; in gardens
— areator, Pz. From Abies excelsa, *Boughton*
— castaneus, Tasch. *Hallow*
— cingulator, Gr. } *Worcester*; in-
Cecidonomus rufus, Bridg.} doors
Orthopelma luteolator, Gr. Ex Rhodites rosæ
Aptesis nigrocincta, Gr. Roots of a tree, *Ketch*
— microptera, Gr. Sides of *Severn* and *Teme*
Pezomachus palpator, Gr. *Trench Woods*
— fasciatus, F. On eggs of spider
— rufulus, Forst. *Worcester*; indoors
— bellicosus, Forst. Side of *Teme*, *Bransford*
— detritus, Forst. *Worcester*; indoors
— insertus, Forst. *Bransford*
— corruptor, Forst. *Cotheridge*
— analis, Bridg. *Middleyards*
— transfuga, Forst. *Worcester*; indoors
— viduus, Forst. *Cotheridge*

OPHIONIDÆ

Ophion obscurus, F. Comes to light in autumn
— luteus, L. *Old Hills*
Anomalon xanthopus, Schr. *Cotheridge*
— cerinops, Gr. *Hallow*

OPHIONIDÆ (*continued*)

Agrypon flaveolatum, Gr. *Middleyards*
— tenuicorne, Gr. *Monkwood*
— canaliculatum, Ratz. *Crown East*
Paniscus testaceus, Gr. *Eastbury*
Campoplex mixtus, Gr. Near *Worcester*
— pugillator, L. *Crown East*
— cultrator, Gr. *Crown East Wood*
Limneria crassicornis, Gr. *Camp*
— erucator, Zett. Near *Worcester*
— femoralis, Gr. Ex Coleophora solitariella
— ruficornis, Bridg. Ex Elachista cerusella, *Worcester*
— mutabilis, Holmz. Ex Gracilaria stigmatella, near *Worcester*
— nana, Gr. *Peg-house Wood*
— obscurella, Holmz. *Crown East*
— rufiventris, Gr. *Camp*
— unicincta, Gr. Ex Acronycta psi
— vienensis, Gr. Ex Gracilaria stigmatella
— interrupta, Holmz. *Worcester*; indoors
— vestigialis, Ratz. Ex Nematicus gallicola
— cursitans, Holmz. Ex Camponiseus luridi-ventris
— hyalinata, Holmz. Ex Crœsus varus
— lugubrina, Holmz. *Peg-house Wood*
Cremastus albipennis, Zett. *Wyre Forest*
Atractodes vestalis, Hal. *Eastbury*
— arator, Hal. *Cotheridge*
— bicolor, Gr. In outhouse, *Worcester*
— gilvipes, Bridg. *Worcester*, at light
Exolytus lævigatus, Gr. *Cotheridge*
Mesochorus confusus, Holmz. Ex Nematus salicivorus
— vittator, Zett. *Wyre Forest*
— sylvarum, Hal. Ex. shoot of larch
— fuscicornis, Brischké. Ex Spanteles glomeratus
— incidens, Thoms. *Middleyards*
Plectiscus albipalpis, Gr. *Monkwood*
Thersilochus truncorum, Gr. *Grimley*
Collyria calcitrator, Gr. *Wyre Forest*
Pristomerus vulnerator, Pz. From privet, *Worcester*
Exetastes osculatorius, F. } *Worcester*; in
— femorator, Desv. } garden
— albitarsus, Gr. *Wyre Forest*

TRYPHONIDÆ

Mesoleptus truncatus, Bridg. *Crown East*
— testaceus, F. *Worcester*; at light
— cingulatus, Gr. *Bransford*
— sulphuratus, Gr. }
— femoralis, Bridg. } *Monkwood*
Catoglyptus fortipes, Gr. *Bransford*
— pulchricornis, Holmz. *Worcester*; indoors
Euryproctus defectivus, Gr. *Monkwood*

INSECTS

TRYPHONIDÆ (*continued*)

Euryproctus geniculosus, Gr. *Cotheridge*
— chrysostomus, Gr. *Temple Laughern*
— annulator, Steph. *Monkwood*
— sinister, Brischké. Ex Eriocampa varipes
Prionopoda stictica, F. *Middleyards*
Perilissus filicornis, Gr. By the *Teme, Bransford*
— subcinctus, Holmz. *Leigh*
— prærogator, Gr. *Hallow*
— bucculentus, Holmz. *Cotheridge*
— pictilis, Holmz. Ex Fenusa melanopoda
— gorskii, Ratz. Ex Melanopygla phyllotoma
Mesoleius aulicus, Gr. *Worcester* ; indoors
— dubius, Holmz. *Worcester* ; in garden
— caligatus, Gr. Ex Nematus salicis
— opticus, Gr. Ex Nematus pavidus
— sanguinicollis, Gr. *Crown East*
— hæmatodes, Gr. *Cotheridge*
— pubescens, Bridg. By the *Teme, Bransford*
— armillatorius, Gr. *Cotheridge*
— formosus, Gr. Ex Nematus sp.
— insolens, Gr. *Monkwood*
— brevispina, Thoms. Ex Nematus purpureæ
— filicornis, Holmz. *Leigh*
— lateralis, Gr. } *Monkwood*
— napæus, Bridg. }
— buccatus, Bridg. *Cotheridge*
— calcaratus, Bridg. *Martley Wood*
— dives, Bridg. *Crown East*
— difformis, Bridg. Ex Cladius brullii
— fallax, Bridg. *Monkwood*
Trematopygus erythropalpus, Gmel. By the *Teme*
Tryphon elongator, F. *Cotheridge*
— brachyacanthus, Gmel. *Crown East*
— vulgaris, Holmz. *Cotheridge*
— trochanteratus, Holmz. By the *Teme, Bransford*
— incestus, Holmz. *Bransford*
— nigripes, Holmz. *Cotheridge*
— signator, Gr. *Eastbury*
— albipes, Gr. *Crown East*
— bicornutus, Holmz. }
Monoblastus femoralis, Holmz. } *Bransford*
— lævigatus, Holmz. Ex Eriocampa ovata
Polyblastus varitarsus, Gr. *Hallow*
— mutabilis, Holmz. *Eastbury*
— carinatus, Bridg. Ex Nematus ribesii
— pyramidatus, Bridg. By the *Teme.* Ex Nematus salicivorus
Erromenus frenator, Gr. Ex Nematus xanthogaster
— analis, Brischké. Ex Nematus curtispina

TRYPHONIDÆ (*continued*)

Atractomus xanthopus, Holmz. *Camp*
— lucidulus, Gr. *Worcester* ; in gardens
Cteniscus lituratorius, L. Ex Nematus consobrinus
— dahlbomi, Holmz. *Bransford*
Triclistus congener, Holmz. *Monkwood*
Metacœlus mansuetor, Gr. *Worcester* ; indoors
Exochus femoralis, Fourc. *Monkwood*
— gravipes, Gr. *Camp*
— curvator, F. *Middleyards Copse*
— pectoralis, Hal. *Swinesherd*
— decorator, Holmz. In marsh, *Grimley*
— tibialis, Holmz. *Grimley*
— pictus, Holmz. *Worcester* ; indoors
Chorinæus cristator, Gr. *Middleyards Copse*
Orthocentrus discolor, Bridg. *Monkwood*
Bassus lætatorius, F. *Wyre Forest*
— albosignatus, Gr. *Bransford*
— nemoralis, Holmz. Osier bed, *Eastbury*
— lateralis, Gr. *Broadmoor Green*
— flavomaculatus, Gr. *Tiddesley Wood*
— cinctus, Gr. *Camp*
— pectoratorius, Gr. *Boughton*
— flavolineatus, Gr. *Wadborough*
— pictus, Gr. *Tiddesley Wood*
— strigator, F. By *Bow Brook*
— nigritarsus, Gr. *Wyre Forest*
— areolatus, Gr. *Camp*
— pulchellus, Holmz. *Bransford*
— cognatus, Holmz. }
— signatus, Gr. } *Camp*
— gracilentus, Holmz. Near *Pershore*
— similis, Bridg. *Crown East*
— rufonotatus, Bridg. *Bransford*
— bimaculatus, Bridg. By the *Teme, Powick*
— exsultans, Bridg. *Middleyards*
— tibialis, Bridg. *Eastbury*
— holmgreni, Bridg. Near *Evesham*
— sundevalli, Holmz. *Grimley*

PIMPLIDÆ

Rhyssa persuasoria, Gr. On Pinus, *Comer Lane*
Ephialtes rex, Gr. *Trench Woods*
Pimpla stercorator, F. *Crown East*
— detrita, Holmz. *Cotheridge*
— instigator, F. *Worcester*; in garden
— examinator, F. Ex Orthosia citrago
— turionellæ, L. *Middleyards Copse*
— rufata, Gmel. *Cotheridge*
— flavonotata, Holmz. *Monkwood*
— scanica, Vill. Bred from a geometerid on oak
— oculatoria, F. *Worcester* ; indoors
— grammellæ, Schr. *Bransford*
— brevicornis, Gr. *Hallow*
— opacellata, Desv. *Worcester* ; in garden

95

PIMPLIDÆ (*continued*)

Pimpla nucum, Ratz. Willows, in *Worcester*
Ischnoceras rusticus, Fourc. *Whitehall*
Polysphincta tuberosa, Gr. *Monkwood*
Clistopyga incitator, F. *Eastbury*
Glypta monoceros, Gr. *Camp*
— ceratites, Gr. *Eastbury*
— hæsitator, Gr. *Tibberton*
— teres, Gr. *Hallow*
— scalaris, Gr. Among peas, *Worcester*
— bifoveolata, Gr. *Bransford*
— resinanæ, Hart. *Middleyards*
— parvicaudata, Bridg. *Monkwood*
— evanescens, Ratz. *Tiddesley Wood*
— parvicornuta, Bridg. *Oddingley*
— similis, Bridg. *Monkwood*
— mensurator, Gr. *Cotheridge*
Lycorina triangulifera, Holmz. *Monkwood*
Lampronota caligata, Gr. ⎫
Lissonota femorata, Holmz. ⎬ *Bransford*
— fletcheri, Bridg. Ex b. Gelechia lentiginosella
— bellator, Gr. *Crown East*
— commixta, Gr. *Hallow, Bransford*
— cylindrator, Vill. *Monkwood*
— segmentator, F. From fungus on oak
— sulphurifera, Gr. *The Ketch*
— semirufa, Desv. *Hallow*
— distincta, Bridg. Near *Worcester*
Meniscus catenator, Pz. *Leigh*
— impressor, Gr. *Temple Laughern*
Phytodiætus segmentator, Gr. Among oaks
— obscurus, Desv. *Kempsey*
— scabriculus, Gr. Among oak
Odontomerus dentipes, Gmel. *Temple Laughern*

BRACONIDÆ

Bracon mediator, Nees. *Grimley*
— discoideus, Wesm. *Middleyards*
— atrator, Nees. *Old Hills*

BRACONIDÆ (*continued*)

Spathius clavatus, Schr. In garden, *Worcester*
Rhogas reticulator, Spin. Ex larva of Odonestis potatoria
— circumscriptus, Nees. *Monkwood*
Colastes braconius, Hal. Ex larva of Tischeria dodonæa
Chelonus sulcatus, Juline. *Worcester*
Ascogaster varipes, Wesm. Ex Eucosma gentianana
Apanteles candidatus, Hal. *Worcester*
— lacteipennis, Curt. *Trench Woods*
— glomeratus, L. Ex cocoon of Abraxas
— ruficrus, Hal. Ex cocoon of Plusia gamma
Microplitis spectabilis, Hal. *Worcester*
— ingrata, Hal. *Middleyards*
— annulipes, Curt. *Tibberton*
Orgilus obscurator, Nees. *Wyre Forest*
Earinus nitidulus, Nees. *Little Eastbury*
Therophilus cingulipes, Nees. *Crown East*
Zemiotes albiditarsis, Curt. Among wild carrot
Perilitus pendulator, Latr. At light, *Worcester*
Zele testaceator, Curt. From oak, *Trench Woods*
Macrocentrus marginator, Nees. Ex Trochilium tipuliforme
Biosteres carbonarius, Nees.
Alysia manducator, Nees. Parasitic on dipterous larvæ

OXYURA

Proctotrypes gravidator, L. *Temple Laughern*
Lagynodes pallidus, Boh. *Crown East*, in moss
Perisemus triareolatus, Walk. *Middleyards*
Belyta dorsalis, Thoms. *Bransford*

COLEOPTERA

So far as is ascertained no one has worked up the beetles of this county. The late Mr. W. G. Blatch worked more or less in the northern part, especially in the Severn valley. Accounts of his discoveries were published from time to time in the *Entomologist's Monthly Magazine*. Others must have worked in different localities if we are to judge by occasional references to Worcestershire in Fowler's *Coleoptera of the British Islands*.

The species found here hitherto number about a thousand. The following list includes the less common species only :—

Cychrus rostratus, L. *Wyre Forest, Crown East*
Carabus arvensis, F. *Broad Heath*
Notiophilus substriatus, Wat. *Hartlebury*

Notiophilus rufipes, Curt. *Kempsey Grove*
Leistus rufescens, F. *Leigh*
Elaphrus uliginosus, F. *Hallow*
Clivina collaris, Herbst. Banks of *Teme*

INSECTS

Dyschirius æneus, Dej. *Bewdley*
Badister unipustulatus, Bon. *Kempsey*
— sodalis, Duft. *Hallow*
Chlænius nigricornis, F. Margin of *Teme*
Harpalus azureus, F. *Malvern Hills*
— rubripes, Duft. *Bransford*
— ignavus, Duft. *Oldbury Farm*
Stomis pumicatus, Pz. *Crown East*
Platyderus ruficollis, Marsh. *Malvern*
Pterostichus anthracinus, Ill. *Diglis*
— picimanus, Duft. Banks of *Teme*
Amara consularis, Duft. ⎱ *Ivy House Farm*
— bifrons, Gyll. ⎰
— ovata, F. *Wichenford*
— lunicollis, Schiöd. *Laughern Hill*
— communis, Pz. *Ivy House Farm*
Taphria nivalis, Marsh. *Hallow*
Anchomenus sexpunctatus, L. *Monkwood*
— scitulus, Dej. *Temple Laughern*
— gracilis, Gyll. *Northwick*
— puellus, Dej. *Grimley*
Bembidium quinquestriatum, Gyll. Near *Worcester*
— mannerheimii, Sahl. *Hallow*
— gilvipes, Sturm. *Kempsey*
— fluviatile, Dej. Banks of *Severn*
— punctulatum, Drap. Banks of *Teme*
— prasinum, Duft. Among shingle by the *Teme*
— adustum, Sturm. Banks of *Teme*
Trechus micros, Herbst. *Hallow*
— secalis, Payk. Banks of *Teme*
Dromius agilis, F. *Northwick*
Metabletus truncatellus, L. *Little Eastbury*
— obscuro-guttatus, Duft. *Martley*
Haliplus confinis, Steph. Pond, *Temple Laughern*
— cinereus, Aubé. Pond, *Croome*
— fluviatilis, Aubé. In the *Severn*
Pelobius tardus, Herbst. Pond, *Temple Laughern*
Noterus clavicornis, De G. Pond, *Grimley*
— sparsus, Marsh. Pond, *Shoulton*
Laccophilus interruptus, Pz. In the *Teme*
Hydroporus granularis, L. Pond, *Moorcroft*
— dorsalis, F. Pond, *Hartlebury*
Agabus paludosus, F. Streamlet, *Severn Stoke*
Ilybius fenestratus, F. Pond, *Leigh*
Rhantus exoletus, Forst. Pond, *Grimley*
Orectochilus villosus, Müller. Among stones by the *Teme*
Philhydrus nigricans, Zett. In ditch, *Grimley*
Paracymus nigroæneus, Sahl. Pond, *Middleyards*
Chætarthria seminulum, Herbst. *Powick*
Helophorus rugosus, Ol. Near *Worcester*
— nubilus, F. *Birchen Grove*
— dorsalis, Marsh. In a ditch, *Hallow*
— arvernicus, Muls. Banks of *Teme*

Octhebius bicolon, Germ. *Monkwood*
Cercyon quisquilius, L. *Witley*, near *Stourbridge*
— nigriceps, Marsh. Near *Evesham*
— minutus, F. *Wyre Forest*
Aleochara bipunctata, Ol. In dung, *Wadborough*
— mœsta, Grav. In moss, *Wyre Forest*
— mœrens, Gyll. In fungi, *Leigh Sinton*
Microglossa pulla, Gyll. *Crookberrow Hill*
Oxypoda annularis, Sahlb. Moss, *Peg-house Wood*
Thiasophila inquilina, Mærk. Moss, *Pirton*
Ocyusa picina, Aubé. Moss, *Cotheridge*
Ilyobates nigricollis, Payk. Under a stone, *Crown East*
— propinquus, Aubé. *Crown East*
Chilopora longitarsis, Er. *Pitmaston*
Callicerus rigidicornis, Er. Garden rubbish, *Worcester*
Homalota insecta, Thoms. Bank of *Teme*, *Bransford*
— pavens, Er. Vegetable refuse, *Leigh*
— hygrotopora, Kr. Bank of *Severn*, *Bewdley*
— oblongiuscula, Sharp. Moss, *Crown East*
— sylvicola, Fuss. Moss, *Peg-house Wood*
— occulta, Er. In dung, *Cotheridge*
— boletobia, Thoms. Fungus, *Powick*
— testudinea, Er. Dung, *Old Hills*
Tachyusa constricta, Er. Banks of *Teme*
— umbratica, Er. Bank of *Severn*, *Holt*
Encephalus complicans, Westw. Moss, *Peg-house Wood*
Bolitochara lucida, Grav. Fungi, *Monkwood*
Oligota atomaria, Er. Moss, *Wyre Forest*
Myllæna dubia, Grav. Moss, *Cotheridge*
Tachyporus solutus, Er. Moss, *Leigh Sinton*
— tersus, Er. Moss, *Wyre Forest*
Tachinus laticollis, Grav. Fungus, *Shrawley Wood*
Megacronus inclinans, Grav. Moss, *Birchen Grove*
Mycetoporus splendens, Marsh. Moss, *Trench Woods*
Quedius cruentus, Ol. Dead leaves, *Wyre Forest*
— fuliginosus, Grav. Vegetable refuse, *Shoulton*
— umbrinus, Er. Moss, *Malvern Wells*
— suturalis, Kies. Moss, *Whittington*
— rufipes, Grav. Dead leaves, near *Evesham*
— attenuatus, Gyll. Moss, *Wyre Forest*
— semiæneus, Steph. Moss, *Severn Stoke*
Leistotrophus nebulosus, F. On the wing, *Hallow*
— murinus, L. *Bromsgrove, Kempsey*
Staphylinus cæsareus, Ceder. *Oldbury Farm*
Ocypus fuscatus, Grav. On dry dung, *Ombersley*

Ocypus compressus, Marsh. Under dead leaves, *Shoulton*

Philonthus intermedius, Boisd. In dung, *Lathe Hill*

— proximus, Kn. Vegetable refuse, *Crowle*

— atratus, Grav. Moss, *Leigh*

— decorus, Grav. Moss, *Crown East*

— albipes, Grav. *Bransford*

— agilis, Grav. Moss, etc., *Moseley Heath*

— vernalis, Grav. Vegetable refuse, *Norton*

— fumarius, Grav. Flood refuse, *Lenchford*

— fulvipes, F. Banks of *Teme*

Xantholinus tricolor, F. At roots of poplar, *Wadborough*

— distans, Kr. Near *Martley*

Lathrobium longulum, Grav. *Lenchford*

— quadratum, Payk. Near *Dudley*

Achenium depressum, Grav. *Cotheridge*

— humile, Nic. *Leigh*

Medon fusculus, Mann. *Malvern Wells*

— obsoletus, Nord. Moss, *Cotheridge*

Sunius intermedius, Er. Haystack refuse, *Severn Stoke*

Evæsthetus scaber, Grav. Vegetable refuse, *Sapey Bridge*

Stenus biguttatus, L. Margin of *Severn*, near *Bewdley*

— bipunctatus, Er. ⎱ By the *Severn*, near
— atratulus, Er. ⎰ *Bewdley*

— fuscipes, Grav. Moss, *Leigh*

— vafellus, Er. By the *Teme*, *Cotheridge*

Platystethus capito, Heer. Haystack refuse, *Kempsey*

— nodifrons, Sahlb. *Upton-on-Severn*

Oxytelus inustus, Grav. Among dead leaves, *Powick*

Ancyrophorus homalinus, Er. Damp moss, *Stoulton*

Trogophlœus arcuatus, Steph. Bank of *Teme*, *Cotheridge*

— rivularis, Mots. *Forest of Wyre*

— fuliginosus, Grav. By the *Teme*, *Bransford*

Syntomium æneum, Müll. Moss, *Middle-yards*

Deliphrum tectum, Payk. Vegetable refuse, *Crown East*

Coryphium angusticolle, Steph. On old wall, *Worcester*

Omalium iopterum, Steph. On flowers near *Worcester*

— deplanatum, Gyll. Haystack refuse, *Severn Stoke*

Proteinus macropterus, Gyll. Fungus, *Stoulton*

Megarthrus denticollis, Beck. Fungus, *Hallow*

Bythinus validus, Aubé. Sparingly in moss

— curtisii, Leach. In moss, *Peg-house Wood*

Batrisus venustus, Aubé. One, in moss near ants' nest

Bryaxis hæmatica, Reich. Moss, *Crown East*

Clambus minutus, Sturm. Moss, *Peg-house Wood*

Agathidium nigrinum, Sturm. *Peg-house Wood*

Anisotoma dubia, Kug. One, moss, *Hallow*

Necrophorus vestigator, Hers. Carcase of mouse, *Hallow*

Necrodes littoralis, L. At foot of tree, *Cotheridge*

Silpha sinuata, F. Carcase, *Thorngrove*

Choleva angustata, F. Under a stone, *Crown East*

— kirbyi, Spence. One, in agaric, *Monk-wood*

Colon serripes, Sahl. Field refuse, *Hallow*, *Temple Laughern*

— latum, Kr. Moss, *Crown East Wood*

Hister merdarius, Hoff. In loose decayed wood, one, *Cotheridge*

Meligethes lugubris, Sturm. *Leigh*

— obscurus, Er. *Pole Elm*

Cryptarcha strigata, F. *Callow End*

Tenebrioides mauritanica, L. In an old house

Corticaria denticulata, Gyll. Moss, *Perry Wood*

Antherophagus pallens, Ol. *Grimley*

Cryptophagus acutangulus, Gyll. Vegetable refuse, *Martley*

Atomaria nigripennis, Payk. Haystack refuse, *Wichenford*

— basalis, Er. Moss, *Lenchford*

Scaphidium quadrimaculatum, Ol. *Monk-wood*

Triphyllus suturalis, F. Fungus, *Bransford*

— punctatus, F. Fungus, *Leigh*

Attagenus pellio, L. One in old house, *Worcester*

Megatoma undata, L. Two in a grocery store

Tiresias serra, F. One, *Trench Woods*

Anthrenus claviger, Er. On flowers, *Monk-wood*

Georyssus pygmæus, F. Banks of *Severn*, *Bewdley*, banks of *Teme*

Elmis æneus, Müll. In the *Teme*

— volkmari, Pz. Margin of *Severn*, *Lenchford*

— nitens, Müll. In the *Teme*; one specimen

Heterocerus lævigatus, Pz. Banks of *Severn*, *Bewdley*

Lucanus cervus, L. *Longdon*

Onthophagus cœnobita, Herbst. Cow dung, *Cotheridge*

— fracticornis, Preys. Cow dung, *Shoulton*

Aphodius fœtens, F. Dung, *Oldbury Farm*

— granarius, L. Vegetable refuse, *Worcester*

Aphodius sordidus, F. In dung, *Powick*
— rufescens, F. In dung, *Bransford*
— fœtidus, F. In dung, *Holt*
— obliteratus, Pz. In dung, *Grimley*
Geotrupes spiniger, Marsh. In dung, *Broadheath*
Trox scaber, L. Flying at dusk, near *Worcester*
Hoplia philanthus, Füss. On flowers, *Wyre Forest*
Cetonia aurata, L. On flowers, sparingly
Cryptohypnus riparius, F. Banks of *Teme*, etc.
— quadripustulatus, F. By the *Teme*
Athous longicollis, Ol. *Cotheridge*
Limonius minutus, L. *Lord's Wood*
Adrastus limbatus, F. *Monkwood*
Corymbites pectinicornis, L. *Malvern Hills, Wyre Forest*
— cupreus, F. *Malvern Hills*
— tessellatus, F. *Trench Woods*
— æneus, L. *Malvern Hills*
— metallicus, Payk. *Monkwood*
— bipustulatus, L. One, *Thorngrove*
Helodes marginatus, F. *Cotheridge*
Cyphon coarctatus, Payk. Herbage, by the *Teme*
— pallidulus, Boh. *Monkwood*
Scirtes hemisphæricus, L. Water herbage, *Camp*
Lampyris noctiluca, L. Occasionally, in woods
Telephorus hæmorrhoidalis, F. *Lathe Hill*
— oralis, Germ. Marshy place, *Camp*
— thoracicus, Ol. *Camp*
Malthodes flavoguttatus, Kies. *Grimley*
— dispar, Germ. *Lenchford*
— fibulatus, Kies. *Worcester*, one
— misellus, Kies. *Bransford*
Malachius æneus, L. *Little Oldbury*
Axinotarsus ruficollis, Ol. *Grimley*
Anthocomus fasciatus, L. In hedges
Haplocnemus impressus, Marsh. One, at *Trench Woods*
Tillus elongatus, L. *Trench Woods*
Opilo mollis, L. On elms, occasionally, near *Worcester*
Thanasimus formicarius, L. One, under bark of ash, *Powick*
Necrobia violacea, L. On flowers, *Trench Woods*, and among skins
Ptinus sexpunctatus, Pz. Occasionally in houses, *Worcester*
Hedobia imperialis, L. On flowers, near *Worcester*
Priobium castaneum, F. Hawthorn bloom
Anobium denticolle, Pz. In old house, *Worcester*
— fulvicorne, Sturm. Hawthorn hedge
Xestobium tessellatum, F. Old house, *Worcester*

Ochina hederæ, Müll. Ivy, *Powick*
Dinoderus substriatus, Payk. In moss on old stump, *Perry Wood*
Lyctus canaliculatus, F. Herbage, *Powick*
Cis micans, Herbst } From polyporus on willow, *Powick*
— hispidus, Payk. }
— bidentatus, Ol. Tree fungus, *Crown East*
Rhopalodontus fronticornis, Pz. } *Kempsey*
Ennearthron affine, Gyll. }
Callidium alni, L. *Boughton*, near *Worcester*
Clytus mysticus, L. On flowers of Heracleum, *Hallow*
Rhagium bifasciatum, F. *Dine's Green*
Pachyta collaris, L. *Thorngrove*
Strangalia quadrifasciata, L. *Monkwood*
Pogonochærus bidentatus, Thoms. *Dine's Green*
Mesosa nubila, Ol. *Monkwood*
Stenostola ferrea, Schr. *Shrawley Wood*
Bruchus rufimanus, Boh. *Monkwood*
Orsodacna cerasi, L. Hawthorn, near *Trench Woods*
Lema erichsoni, Suffr. One, by *Laughern Brook*
Crioceris asparagi, L. *Worcester*
Clythra quadripunctata, L. *Birchen Grove, Trench Woods*
Cryptocephalus bipunctatus, L. *Trench Woods*
— aureolus, Suffr. *Monkwood*
— fulvus, Goeze. *Crown East*
— frontalis, Marsh. *Bransford*
Lamprosoma concolor, Sturm. Moss, *Middleyards*
Chrysomela gœttingensis, L. Flood refuse, by the *Severn*
— didymata, Scriba. } *Wyre Forest*
— hyperici, Forst. }
Melasoma æneum, L. *Monkwood*
— longicolle, Suffr. *Trench Woods*
Phytodecta rufipes, De G. *Monkwood*
— olivacea, Forst. *Wyre Forest*
— pallida, L. Near *Malvern*
Phyllodecta cavifrons, Thoms. *Cotheridge*
Batophila rubi, Payk. Moss, *Flyford Flavel*
Blaps mucronata, Latr. Cellars, etc.
Bolitophagus reticulatus, L. One, fungus on willow, *Kempsey*
Scaphidema metallicum, F. Under bark on old stump near *Worcester*
Tenebrio obscurus, F. One, indoors
Cistela ceramboides, L. In decayed bark of oak tree, near *Worcester*
Orchesia micans, Pz. Woody fungus on ash, *Bransford*
Hypulus quercinus, Quens. *Crown East*
Œdemera nobilis, Scop. *Cotheridge*
— lurida, Marsh. *Trench Woods*
Metœcus paradoxus, L. In wasps' nest

Brachytarsus varius, F. *Trench Woods*
Byctiscus populi, L. *Monkwood*, etc.
Rhynchites æneovirens, Marsh. *Wyre Forest*
Apion difforme, Ahr. *Birchen Grove*
— varipes, Germ. *Crown East*
— ebeninum, Kirby. *Monkwood*
— filirostre, Kirby. *Peg-house Wood*
Otiorrhynchus ligneus, Ol. *Crown East*
Polydrusus teretricollis, De G. *Shrawley Wood*
Tanymecus palliatus, F. By beating hedge, *Bransford*

Grypidius equiseti, F. From horsetail, *Teme Bank*
Dorytomus vorax, F. Base of poplar, *Camp*
— tremulæ, Payk. *Broadmoor Green*
Acalles roboris, Curt. *Trench Woods*
Baris lepidii, Germ. Among herbage by the *Teme*
Magdalis barbicornis, Latr. *Temple Laughern*
Scolytus multistriatus, Marsh. Beaten from hedge, *Bransford*
Hylastes palliatus, Gyll. *Pitmaston*
Cissophagus hederæ, Schmidt. *Bransford*

LEPIDOPTERA

In enumerating the following list of Worcestershire Lepidoptera we have been compelled to adopt a broad boundary line in order that we might incorporate therein the records of fellow entomologists whose reports merely state Malvern, West Malvern, Wyre Forest, Broadway or Bredon, without definitively setting out the county wherein the captures were made. This omission we think cannot much affect the value of the list as a county record, seeing that insects are not likely to be restricted to the boundary line of the map, but would in all probability occur on both sides of it.

In 1834 Charles Hastings, M.D., published *Illustrations of the Natural History of Worcestershire*, which, in appendix C. entitled ' A Catalogue of some of the rarer Lepidopterous Insects found in Worcestershire,' by Edwin Lees, enumerated some 230 species, and the specimens were represented in the cabinet of A. Edmunds. This list is referred to hereafter as I.N.H.W.

In 1870 the Rev. E. Horton recorded 328 species in a paper entitled ' List of Malvern Lepidoptera,' which is printed in *The Transactions of the Malvern Naturalists' Field Club*, part iii. pp. 175–184. This is more of a county list than a local one, seeing that it includes Bredon, Bow Wood, Trench Woods, Monk Wood, Martley, Shrawley, etc. It is cited herein as T.M.N.F.C.

In 1899 appeared by far the most reliable list that has hitherto been published for a portion of the county. It is entitled *The Butterflies and Moths of Malvern*, by the veteran and esteemed entomologists, W. Edwards and R. F. Towndrow. It enumerates 590 species. This list embraces a circle, as the crow flies, round Malvern of six miles, and thus renders, where the locality is not definitely stated in another county, the task of the present writers harder. This list is referred to as E. & T.

Worcestershire is referred to in the systematic works of the following, and will be quoted as follows :—

H. T. Stainton, *A Manual of British Butterflies and Moths*, 1857–1859 : St.

E. Newman, *The Natural History of British Moths ana Butterflies*, 1869 : N.

E. Meyrick, *A Handbook of British Lepidoptera*, 1895 : M.

INSECTS

The Transactions of the Worcestershire Naturalists' Club, 1847-1899 : T.W.N.C.

It is by the kind assistance of Messrs. W. Edwards, W. H. Edwards, Rev. E. C. Dobrèe Fox, Messrs G. D. Hancock, J. Peed and R. F. Towndrow that we are enabled to place the following list before the reader.

Amongst the Rhopalocera (Butterflies) the following are very rare and almost extinct : *Apatura Iris, Nemeobius lucina, Lycæna corydon* and *ægon, Pieris daplidice* and *Aporia cratægi ;* whilst amongst the Heterocera (Moths) *Œonistis quadra, Lithosia deplana, Miltochrista senex, Coscinia cribrum, Diacrisia urticæ, Arctia villica, Leucania turca, L. vitellina, Agrotis lunigera, A. subrosea, Caradrina oo, Hadena flammea, H. pabulatricula (connexa), Boletobia fuliginaria, Plusia orichalcea* and *bractea, Eustrotia uncula, Ocneria dispar, Leptomeris marginepunctata, Pseudopanthera pictaria,* and *P. hippocastanaria* and *Leucophthalmia orbicularia* have either entirely disappeared or are of very rare occurrence.

The subjoined list includes 57 *Rhopalocera,* 254 *Caradrinina,* 233 *Notodontina,* 14 *Lasiocampina,* 76 *Pyralidina,* 8 *Psychina,* 124 *Tortricina,* 141 *Tineina,* and 9 *Micropterygina,* making a grand total of 916. This exceeds by 326 the number of species enumerated by Edwards and Towndrow in the latest list that has appeared for Worcestershire or a part thereof.

Under the headings of various well-favoured haunts the more local insects have been formed into groups which have been appended to the following list.

RHOPALOCERA

IV. *PAPILIONINA*

1. NYMPHALIDÆ

Argynnis paphia, L. *Wyre Forest,* July 18, 1895, July 30, 1896 ; *Shrawley,* July, common (T.M.N.F.C. p. 175, Fletcher); *Monk Wood* (G. D. Hancock)

— adippe, L. *Monk Wood* and *Shrawley Wood* (N. p. 33) ; *Wyre Forest,* July 18, 1895 ; *Malvern Woods, Ockeridge* (T.M.N.F.C. p. 175) ; *Bredon Hill* (W. H. Edwards, Fletcher)

— aglaia, L. *Monk Wood* (N. p. 29; T.M.N.F.C. p. 175) ; *Wyre Forest* (W. H. Edwards) ; one specimen, *Monk Wood* (Fletcher)

— lathonia, L. (T.M.N.F.C. p. 175)

— euphrosyne, L. *Worcester* (St. p. 43); *Trench Woods,* May 18, 1895 ; *Tiddesley Wood,* May 22, 1894 ; *Wyre Forest, Monk Wood* ; generally distributed (W. H. Edwards, Fletcher)

— selene, Schiff. *Worcester* (St. p. 43) ; *Monk Wood* (N. p. 39, Fletcher) ; *Malvern Woods, Crown East,* June (T.M.N.F.C. p. 175) ; *Wyre Forest*

Melitæa aurinia, Rott. *Worcester* (St. p. 48) ; *Himbleton* (Fletcher) ; *Oddingley, Great Malvern,* but disappeared (N. p. 42) ; rare (W. Edwards, T.M.N.F.C. p. 175) ; *Cowleigh Park* and other marshy places, formerly on *Malvern Link Common* (E. & T. p. 4) ; not common, *Trench Woods* ; a specimen taken on the wing in *Friar Street, Worcester,* April, 1834 (I.N.H.W. p. 137) ; *Wyre Forest* (W. H. Edwards) ; formerly common at *Cradley,* specially in a field in *Leigh Sinton Road* (Rev. E. C. Dobrèe Fox)

Vanessa c-album, L. *Worcester* (St. p. 40, and N. p. 51) ; *Worcester,* June 29, 1896 ; *Wyre Forest,* July 30, 1896 ; *Craycombe, Monk Wood* ; generally distributed (W. H. Edwards) ; fields, lanes and hopyards (Fletcher)

— urticæ, L. Common (Fletcher)

— polychloros, L. *Worcester* (St. p. 39) and *Malvern* (N. p. 58) ; chiefly about *Mathon* and *Cradley,* but occasionally elsewhere (E. & T. p. 3) ; *Nunnery Wood, Northwick,* etc., scarce

(I.N.H.W. p. 137) ; *Worcester*, 1874 ; *St. John's, Worcester* (W. H. Edwards) ; *Castle Morton* (Rev. E. C. Dobrèe Fox) ; among elm trees (Fletcher)

Vanessa io, L. *Wyre Forest*, July 30, 1896, common (Fletcher)

— antiopa, L. *Worfield House, Malvern*, thirty years ago (R.F.T.) ; two *Malvern* (W.E.), near College grounds (C. F. Grindrod) ; *Upton* (Sewell, E. & T. p. 3) ; very uncommon, but has been captured at *Barbourne*, close to *Worcester* (I.N.H.W. p. 137)

— atalanta, L. *Hanbury Churchyard*, Sept. 22, 1895 ; common (Fletcher)

— × cardui. *West Malvern* (W.E. 1876, E. & T. p. 3)

— cardui, L. Occasionally common (Fletcher)

Limenitis sibilla, L. *Worcester* (St. p. 34) ; not confirmed (N. p. 70, M. p. 335) ; *Cradley*, 1861 (R.F.T.) ; *Croft Banks* (W.E., E. & T. p. 2) ; one taken near *Worcester* (I.N.H.W. p. 138)

Apatura iris, L. One near *Park Wood, West Malvern*, 1864 (W. Edwards, T.M.N.F.C. p. 176) ; observed at *Perdiswell*, but is very rarely taken (I.N.H.W. p. 138)

2. SATYRIDÆ

Melanargia galathea, L. *Worcester* (St. p. 26) ; *Himbleton* (Fletcher) ; *Monk Wood, Malvern* (N. p. 80) ; *The Slads*, July 25, 1899 ; *Malvern Woods, Eldersfield, Bow Wood, Bredon, Trench* (T.M.N.F.C. p. 176) ; once or twice *Croft Banks* (W.E., Goodyear) ; *Cowleigh Park* (E. & T. p. 2) ; *Bredon*, July 14, 1895

Pararge ægeria, L. ⎫
— megæra, L. ⎬ Common (Fletcher)

Satyrus semele, L. *Worcester* (St. p. 28) ; *Malvern Hills* (W. Edwards, July, T.M.N.F.C. p. 176) ; rocks near *Winds Point* and elsewhere about the hills (E. & T. p. 2) ; *Bewdley Forest* (I.N.H.W. p. 138)

Epinephele tithonus, L. ⎫
— janira, L. ⎬ Common (Fletcher)
— hyperanthus, L. ⎭

Cœnonympha tiphon, Rott. Not common (I.N.H.W. p. 138)

— pamphilus, L. Common (Fletcher)

3. ERYCINIDÆ

Nemeobius lucina, L. *Worcester* (St. p. 49) ; sparingly 2 miles from *Great Malvern* (N. p. 105) ; at foot of *Berrow Hill, Martley* (T.M.N.F.C. p. 176) ; *Trench Woods* and *Craycombe* (I.N.H.W. p. 137)

4. LYCÆNIDÆ

Thecla rubi, L. *Worcester* (St. p. 54) ; *Wyre Common*, June 12, 1899 ; *Croft Wood, Oddingley* (Fletcher)

— pruni, L. (T.M.N.F.C. p. 176) ; rare (I.N.H.W. p. 138)

— w.-album, Kn. *Worcester* and formerly *Great Malvern* (N. p. 110) ; *Cowleigh Park*, rare (T.M.N.F.C. p. 176) ; *Malvern Link* (R.F.T.) ; *Cowleigh Park* (W.E., E. & T. p. 4) ; *Trench* and *Warndon Woods* (A. Edmunds, I.N.H.W. p. 138) ; *St. John's, Worcester* and *Bransford* (W. H. Edwards) ; among elms, *Cotheridge* (Fletcher)

— betulæ, L. *Worcester* (St. p. 52) ; *Trench Woods* (N. p. 114, and Fletcher) ; August, scarce (T.M.N.F.C. p. 176) ; *Cowleigh* (E. & T. p. 4) ; *Wyre Forest* (W. H. Edwards)

— quercus, L. *Worcester* (St. p. 54) ; *Monk Wood, Crown East, Middleyards* and *Trench*, July (T.M.N.F.C. p. 176) ; *Cowleigh Park* and *Malvern Link* (R.F.T., E. & T. p. 4) ; larvæ, *Wyre Forest*, 1899 (W. H. Edwards, Fletcher)

Chrysophanus minimus, Fuesl. *The Slads*, June 16, 1898, May 31 and July 25, 1899 ; *Broadway*, June 23, 1898 ; lime pits, *Croft Farm*, common (T.M.N.F.C. p. 176) ; *The Wyche*, 1898 (W.E., E. & T. p. 4) ; *Oddingley* (Fletcher)

— semiargus, Rott. One seen, July, 1855, near *Croft Farm* (T.M.N.F.C. p. 176) ; extinct (E. & T. p. 4) ; *Hawford*, near *Worcester* and *Trench Woods* (I.N.H.W. p. 139) ; *Hilly Fields* (Fletcher)

— astrarche, Bgstr. Not uncommon (T.M.N.F.C. p. 176) ; *Broadway*, June 23, 1898 ; *West Malvern*, June 8, 1899 ; *Bredon, Oddingley* (Fletcher)

— phlæas, L. Common (Fletcher)

— var. Schmidtii. (R.F.T., E. & T. p. 4)

— dispar, Hw. Very rare in this county ; a solitary individual has been taken (I.N.H.W. p. 138)

Lycæna argiolus, L. *Midsummer Hill*, 1895, and May 14, 1899 ; *Bilberry Hill*, June 10, 1899 ; *Worcester* ; generally distributed

— corydon, Pod. *Helbury Hill, Worcester* (E. Lees, T.M.N.F.C. p. 176)

— ægon, Schiff. *Trench Woods* (I.N.H.W. p. 139)

— icarus, Rott. Common (Fletcher)

INSECTS

5. PIERIDÆ

Colias hyale, L. One near *Bransford*, 1878 (W.E., E. & T. p. 1); several at *Craycombe*, 1874 (W. H. Edwards)
— edusa, F. *Norton*, near *Evesham*, August, 1874; *Worcester* (N. p. 146); *Croft lime quarries* (W. Edwards, T.M.N.F.C. p. 175); very uncertain in appearance. In 1878 fairly distributed, one at *Newland* and one on the hills 1894, rare, (E. & T. p. 1); *Craycombe*, plentiful, 1874, and *Trench Woods*, 1887 (W. H. Edwards); near *Knightsford Bridge*, August 13, 1900, and several at *Worcester*; clover fields, pea fields, etc. (Fletcher)
— var. Helice. One (Goodyear); very rare (E. &. T. p. 1)
Gonepteryx rhamni, L. } Common (Fletcher)
Euchlœ cardamines, L. }
Leucophasa sinapis, L. Locally abundant, *Monk Wood, Middleyards, Ockeridge, Worcester* (N. p. 156, St. p. 20); in woods sparingly (Fletcher)
Pieris daplidice, L. *Worcester* (St. p. 19); 'once at *Malvern*' (*Malvern Field Handbook*)
— napi, L. } Common (Fletcher)
— rapæ, L. }

Pieris brassicæ, L. Common (Fletcher)
Aporia cratægi, L. *Great Malvern*, scarce (W. Edwards, N. p. 168); *Worcestershire* (St. p. 18); *Wyre Forest*, August 24, 1852 (T.W.N.C. p. 10, June 20, 1851); *Craycombe* (T.W.N.C. p. 11); *Malvern* and *Cradley*, in woods, scarce (T.M.N.F.C. p. 175; one, *Malvern Link*, about 1858 (R.F.T.); in June, 1876, larvæ near *Cradley*, and in 1877 two on the wing near there (W.E., E. & T. p. 1); woods near *Worcester* (I.N.H.W. p. 137)

6. PAPILIONIDÆ

Papilio machaon, L. Near *Worcester*, but very rare (I.N.H.W. p. 136); near *Martley* (Dr. Grindrod, 1900)

7. HESPERIADÆ

Hesperia malvæ, L. } Common (Fletcher)
— tages, L. }
Cyclopædes palæmon, Pall. *Berrow Hill, Martley* (W.E., E. & T. p. 5); *Craycombe*, June 20, 1854 (T.W.N.C. p. 11)
Pamphila thaumas, Hufn. } Common
— sylvanus, Esp. } (Fletcher)

HETEROCERA

I. *CARADRININA*

1. ARCTIADÆ

Œonistis quadra, L. *St. John's*, near *Worcester* (T.M.N.F.C. p. 178, E. & T. p. 11)
Lithosia complana, L. Common, July (T.M.N.F.C. p. 178, E. & T. p. 10); *Bredon* (W. H. Edwards); scarce (Rev. E. C. Dobrèe Fox)
— lurideola, Zk. *Bransford*, July 28, 1899, 34, *Foregate Street*, August 1, 1899; *Monk Wood* (W. H. Edwards)
— deplana, Esp. About *Malvern* (W. Edwards, T.M.N.F.C. p. 178)
— griseola, Hb. *Middleyards* (T.M.N.F.C. p. 178); *Castle Morton*, common some years (Rev. E. C. Dobrèe Fox)
— sororcula, Hufn. *Middleyards*, scarce, May (T.M.N.F.C. p. 178); *Monk Wood*, June, 1899 and 1900; sparingly in woods (Fletcher); *Ockeridge* (G. D. Hancock)
Gnophria rubricollis, L. *Malvern Woods* (T.M.N.F.C. p. 178); *Crumpend Hill*, June 17, 1882 (Mr. F. Powell);

Birchwood (W.E.); rather rare (E. & T. p. 11); *Nunnery Wood* (I.N.H.W. p. 142); one specimen at *Cradley* (Rev. E. C. Dobrèe Fox)
Cybosia mesomella, L. *Monk Wood*, May 30, 1896 and June 28, 1898; *Wyre Forest*; singly in woods (Fletcher)
Miltochrista miniata, Forst. *Monk Wood*, June 13 and 16, 1898; *Tiddesley*, July 6, 1899; *Middleyards* and near *Bromsgrove*, etc. (T.M.N.F.C. p. 178); *Nunnery Wood* (I.N.H.W. p. 142), and July 17, 1900; one specimen, *Longdon* village (Rev. E. C. Dobrèe Fox)
— senex, Hb. Rather rare (W. Edwards, E. & T. p. 11)
Nudaria mundana, L. *Malvern, Worcester*, etc., July, not uncommon (T.M.N.F.C. p. 178); *Bredon*, July, 1897; *Broadway*, larvæ, June 23, 1898
Roeselia (Nola) confusalis, H.S. *Wyre Forest* June 17, 1899, July 8, 1900; *Malvern Woods, Shrawley Wood*, etc., scarce (T.M.N.F.C. p. 178); rather rare (E. & T. p. 35); *Middleyards*, one specimen (Fletcher)

Nola cucullatella, L. Fairly common, *Water-works*, *Worcester*, June 29, 1896; *Foregate Street*, *Worcester*, July 18, 1898, July 13, 1899; rare (E. & T. p. 35)

Uraba (Nola) strigula, Schiff. Rare (E. & T. p. 35)

Sarrothripus undulana, Hb. *Ribbesford*, Sept. 21, 1860 (T.W.N.C. p. 62); *Monk Wood*, July 25, 1900; singly in woods (Fletcher)

Hylophila bicolorana, Fuesl. Rather common (E. & T. p. 36); *Crown East Wood* (W. H. Edwards); *Monk Wood*, July 11, 1895; *Bransford*, larvæ, June 2, 1899, on oaks (Fletcher); *Elm Hill* and *Temple Laughern*

Halias prasinana, L. *Monk Wood*, *Trench Woods*, *Storridge Woods*, *Perry* and *Nunnery Woods* (A. Edmunds, T.M.N.F.C. p. 184); rather common (E. & T. p. 36); *Wyre Forest*

Tyria (Euchelia) jacobææ, L. Common

Utetheisa (Deiopeia) pulchella, L. One, *Madresfield* (W. Edwards, 1886; E. & T. p. 11)

Coscinia (Eulepia) cribrum, L. Very local (A. Edmunds, T.M.N.F.C. p. 178); a very local insect, *Bewdley Forest* (I.N.H.W. p. 142)

Phragmatobia fuliginosa, L. *Bredon*, June 3, 1897; *Wyre Forest*, June 10, 1899; *Old Storridge*, not common, May (T.M.N.F.C. p. 178); *Malvern Link* and *Newland Common*, etc. (E. & T. p. 11); *Trench Woods* (I.N.H.W. p. 142); *Tibberton* (W. H. Edwards); *Oddingley*, larvæ (Fletcher); *Holly-bush Hill* (G. D. Hancock)

Diacrisia (Spilosoma) mendica, Cl. *Monk Wood*, *Trench Woods*, *Wyre Forest*, *Ockeridge*

— urticæ, Esp. Rare (I.N.H.W. p. 142)
— menthastri, Esp. } Common
— lubricipeda, L. }
— russula, L. *Wyre Forest*, June, 1896, 1899, 1900 (W. Edwards, T.M.N.F.C. p. 178); near the obelisk, *Eastnor* (W. E., E. & T. p. 11); *Craycombe* (I.N.H.W. p. 141)

Arctia plantaginis, L. *Bredon*, June 3, 1897; *Malvern Hills*, *Randan Woods*, *Bilberry Hills*, etc., June, not common (T.M.N.F.C. p. 178); *Nunnery Wood* (I.N.H.W. p. 141); one specimen (Fletcher)

— villica, L. Uncommon (T.M.N.F.C. p. 178); *Perry Wood* (I.N.H.W. p. 141)?
— caja, L. Common

2. CARADRINIDÆ
Sub-Fam. 1. POLIADES

Cucullia chamomillæ, Schiff. (W. Edwards, T.M.N.F.C. p. 182); at rest; more plentiful than usual 1897 (W.E., E. & T. p. 22); *Castle Morton*, scarce (Rev. E. C. Dobrée Fox)

— umbratica, L. Common
— asteris, Schiff. Of rare occurrence (W. Edwards, T.M.N.F.C. p. 182)
— scrophulariæ, Cap. Larvæ, *Hanley Castle*, 1897 (W.E.); rare (E. & T. p. 22, I.N.H.W. p. 144)
— verbasci, L. Common

Polia exoleta, L. *Worcester* (St. p. 282); larva, *Temeside*, *Powick*, June 21, 1896; *Bredon* (W. H. Edwards); in gardens (Fletcher); *Monk Wood* (G. D. Hancock)

— vetusta, Hb. (W. Edwards, T.M.N.F.C. p. 182)
— semibrunnea, Hw. *Worcester* (St. p. 283); *Boughton Park*, October, 1899 (J. Peed, W. H. Edwards, T.M.N.F.C. p. 182); *Castle Morton* (Rev. E. C. Dobrée Fox); one at sallow and one at ivy bloom (Fletcher)
— socia, Rott. *Worcester* (St. p. 283); *Henwick*, *Worcester*, October 17, 1899; *Boughton* (W. H. Edwards, W. Edwards, T.M.N.F.C. p. 182); one on railings (Fletcher); *Grimley*, 1896 (G. D. Hancock); *Wyre Forest* (J. Peed)
— ornithopus, Rott. *Worcester* (St. p. 283, I.N.H.W. p. 144); *Monk Wood* (J. Peed and W. H. Edwards); larvæ, *Monk Wood*
— areola, Esp. *Worcester* (St. p. 280); *Wyre Forest*, April 3, 1897, April 21, 1898; *Crown East* and *Bransford* (W. H. Edwards); *Trench Woods* (J. Peed); *Grimley* (G. D. Hancock)
— viminalis, F. *Worcester* (St. p. 266); *Monk Wood*, July 11, 1895; *Perry Wood* (W. H. Edwards); *Middleyards*, larvæ, May 28, 1900; generally distributed
— lichenea, Hb. Rather common (E. & T. p. 21)
— protea, Bkh. *Bransford*, *Madresfield* and *Grimley* (W. H. Edwards); common
— aprilina, L. Common, *Nunnery Wood*, *Monk Wood*, *Grimley*, *Ketch*
— chi, L. *Malvern*, July 12, 1895; at rest on rocks and walls, rather common (E. & T. p. 21)
— flavicincta, F. *Worcester* (St. p. 264, W. Edwards, T.M.N.F.C. p. 181); at rest on walls, rather common (E. & T.

p. 21); *Castle Morton* (Rev. E. C. Dobrée Fox)

Miselia oxyacanthæ, L. *Henwick*, October 14, 1899; *Boughton and The Slads*, larvæ (W. H. Edwards); *Grimley and Holt* (J. Peed and G. D. Hancock)

Diloba cæruleocephala, L. Common

Asteroscopus sphinx, Hufn. *Worcester*, November 9, 1895; *Spetchley Avenue*, November 3, 1895; by pupæ digging (Fletcher); *Grimley* (G. D. Hancock); *Boughton* (J. Peed)

Aporophyla lutulenta, Bkh. *Worcester* (St. p. 266); *Wyre Forest*, September, 1898 (Rev. E. C. Dobrée Fox, E. & T. p. 21); *Boughton and Wyre Forest*, 1899 (W. H. Edwards); *Grimley* (G. D. Hancock and J. Peed)

— lunosa, Hw. *Worcester* (St. p. 248); *Worcester*, common

Orthosia xerampelina, Hb. *Worcester* (St. p. 254); *Henwick*, pupa, August, 1895; *Boughton and St. John's* (eleven in 1887), *Henwick* (W. H. Edwards); *Castle Morton* (Rev. E. C. Dobrée Fox); on ash trees (Fletcher); *Temple Laughern*, 1898 (J. Peed)

— croceago, F. *Worcester* (St. p. 251); *Wyre Forest* (W. H. Edwards)

— citrago, L. *Worcester* (St. p. 252); larvæ, *Ockeridge*, May 27, 1899, June, 1900; *Shrawley and Boughton* (W. H. Edwards); on lime trees (Fletcher); *Grimley*, 1897 (G. D. Hancock and J. Peed)

— aurago, F. *Worcester* (St. p. 253); *Boughton Park*, October 12, 1895, and 1899; *Wyre Forest* (W. H. Edwards); *Castle Morton* (Rev. E. C. Dobrée Fox)

— flavago, F. ⎫
— fulvago, L. ⎬ Common

— gilvago, Esp. *Worcester* (N. p. 376); *Foregate Street*, September 12, 1896; *Castle Morton* (Rev. E. C. Dobrée Fox); two at 'light' (Fletcher); *Grimley* (G. D. Hancock and J. Peed)

— circellaris, Hufn. *Riddells Farm*, September 18, 1895; *Boughton Park*, October 12, 1895; *Wyre Forest* (W. H. Edwards)

— helvola, L. *Worcester* (St. p. 247, W. Edwards); ivy bloom (T.M.N.F.C. p. 181); *Wyre Forest and Boughton* (W. H. Edwards); *Castle Morton*, rare (Rev. E. C. Dobrée Fox); *Grimley* (G. D. Hancock)

— litura, L. *Boughton Park*, October 22, 1895; *Foregate Street*, September 12, 19, 1895; *Wyre Forest and Crown East* (W. H. Edwards)

Orthosia pistacina, F. ⎫
— macilenta, Hb. ⎬ Common
— lota, Cl. ⎭

— ypsilon, Bkh. *Worcester* (J. Peed, I.N.H.W. p. 143); *Castle Morton* (Rev. E. C. Dobrée Fox)

— satellitia, L. Common

Conistra (Dasycampa) rubiginea, F. *Worcester* (St. p. 251, N. p. 372); ivy bloom (W.E., E. & T. p. 20); very rare, a single specimen, *Nunnery Wood* (A. Edmunds, I.N.H.W. p. 143); one specimen at sallow, *Castle Morton* (Rev. E. C. Dobrée Fox)

— (Glæa) ligula, Esp. ⎫
— vaccinii, L. ⎬ Common at ivy

Sub-Fam. 2. MELANCHRIDES

Leucania turca, L. (A. Edmunds, T.M.N.F.C. p. 180); rare (I.N.H.W. p. 143)

— lithargyria, Esp. Common

— conigera, F. *Worcester* (St. p. 187); *Perry Wood*, July 4, 8, 1895; *Bransford*, July 9, 1895; *Monk Wood* (W. H. Edwards); occasionally to 'light' (Fletcher)

— vitellina, Hb. (T.M.N.F.C. p. 180)

— comma, L. Common

— impudens, Hb. Rather rare (E. & T. p. 14)

— impura, Hb. Common (E. & T. p. 14); *Castle Morton*, common (Rev. E. C. Dobrée Fox)

— pallens, L. Common

Monima (Tæniocampa) incerta, Hufn. Common at sallows

— opima, Hb. *Wyre Forest* (P. W. Abbott); *Castle Morton* (Rev. E. C. Dobrée Fox); *Grimley* (G. D. Hancock)

— gracilis, F. *Worcester* (St. p. 244); *Trench Woods*, April 3, 1896; *Nunnery Wood*, April 4, 1896, March 31, 1897; *Perry Wood and Wyre Forest*

— stabilis, View. Common

— populeti, Tr. *Worcester* (N. p. 360); *Ockeridge* (W. H. Edwards); coppice, *Elm Hill* (G. D. Hancock, T.M.N.F.C. p. 181); rather rare (E. & T. p. 19); at sallow bloom (Fletcher)

— miniosa, F. *Crown East*, March 23, 1896; *Perry Wood*, March 27, 1896; *Trench Woods*, April 3, 1896; *Nunnery Wood*, April 4, 1896; *Wyre Forest and Malvern* (W. H. Edwards); *Ockeridge* (G. D. Hancock)

— pulverulenta, Esp. Common

— munda, Esp. *Middleyards*, April 4, 1895, March 19, 1896; *Crown East*, March 23, 31, 1895; *Nunnery*, April 3, 1895, March 31, 1899; *Trench Woods*, April

5, 1895; *Monk Wood, Ockeridge* and *Wyre Forest*

Monima gothica, L.　Common

Charæas graminis, L.　*Worcester* (St. p. 204); *Foregate Street, Worcester,* at 'light,' August 20, 1895, August 3, 1897

Neuronia popularis, F.　Common at 'light'

Harmodia (Dianthoecia) nana, Rott.　At rest on walls (E. & T. p. 20)

— carpophaga, Bkh.　*Castle Morton,* scarce (Rev. E. C. Dobrèe Fox); *Bredon* (W. H. Edwards, 1898); larvæ abundant, *Hartlebury Common,* July, 1899, 1900

— capsincola, Hb.　*Worcester* (St. p. 262); *Elm Hill* (G. D. Hancock)

— cucubali, Fuesl.　*Worcester* (St. p. 262); *Bransford* and *Boughton* (W. H. Edwards); one specimen, *Castle Morton* (Rev. E. C. Dobrèe Fox); at lychnis bloom (Fletcher)

Melanchra cespitis, F.　*Foregate Street, Worcester,* May 16, 1896; lanes near *Worcester* (I.N.H.W. p. 142); *Castle Morton,* rare (Rev. E. C. Dobrèe Fox); *Elm Hill* (G. D. Hancock)

— reticulata, Vill.　Two, *Foregate Street, Worcester,* June 2, 4, 1896; two at 'light' (Fletcher)

— serena, F.　*Wyre Forest,* June 10, 1899; *Bredon,* June 15, 1899 (Goodyear and W.E.); rather rare (E. & T. p. 21); *Blackstone Rock,* June, 1900; *Worcester* (G. D. Hancock)

— chrysozona, Bkh.　*Worcester* (St. p. 263, M. p. 82)

— trifolii, Rott.　*Worcester* (St. p. 276); *Perry Wood,* July 22, 1895; *The Denes,* May 14, 1896; *Foregate Street,* May 31, 1899; *Waterworks Road* and *Boughton* (W. H. Edwards)

— dentina, Esp.　*Monk Wood,* May 30, 1896; *Foregate Street,* June 14, 1896; *Wyre Forest,* June 6, 1897, June 27, 1898, June 17–19, 1899

— glauca, Hb.　*Worcester* (N. p. 415, W. Edwards, T.M.N.F.C. p. 182)

— conspicillaris, L.　*Worcester* (St. p. 202); *Monk Wood,* May 25, 1899; *St. John's* (W. H. Edwards); one specimen, plum blossom, *Castle Morton* (Rev. E. C. Dobrèe Fox); on tree trunks (Fletcher) var. melaleuca (W.E., E. & T. p. 15)

— contigua, Vill.　*Foregate Street, Worcester,* June 4, 1896; *Wyre Forest,* June 18–24, 1899

— genistæ, Bkh.　*Worcester* (N. p. 423); *Foregate Street, Worcester,* May 16, 19, 26, 30, 1896, June 2, 3, 4, 1896; *Wyre Forest,* June 21, 1898; *Trench Woods,* June 15, 1895; *Knightwick* and *Monk Wood*; on palings (Fletcher); *Elm Hill* (G. D. Hancock)

Melanchra thalassina, Rott.　Common

— dissimilis, Kn.　*Foregate Street, Worcester,* May 16, June 2, 1896; I have met with this once and believe others have occurred (R.F.T., E. & T. p. 22, Rev. E. C. Dobrèe Fox); *Wyre Forest* (W. H. Edwards); *Elm Hill* (G. D. Hancock)

— oleracea, L.　Common

— pisi, L.　*Worcester* (St. p. 277); on the hills (T.M.N.F.C. p. 181); larvæ common on the *Malvern Hills,* September, 1900; and *Wyre Forest* (W. H. Edwards); two at 'sugar' (Fletcher)

— tincta, Brh.　*Worcester* (St. p. 272, N. p. 409); *Wyre Forest,* June 26, 27, July 10, 1898, June 17, 24, 1899

— advena, F.　*Foregate Street, Worcester,* June 11, 1896, June 8, 1897 (Rev. E. C. Dobrèe Fox, E. & T. p. 21); *Wyre Forest* and *Monk Wood* (W. H. Edwards); *Laughern Bank* (G. D. Hancock)

— nebulosa, Hufn. }　Common
— brassicæ, L.

— persicariæ, L.　*Worcester* (St. p. 209, T.M.N.F.C. p. 181, R.F.T., E. & T. p. 16); once bred from pupæ dug at *St. John's* (W. H. Edwards); one specimen, *Castle Morton* (Rev. E. C. Dobrèe Fox); *Wyre Forest,* 1899 (J. Peed)

— albicolon, Hb.　(Goodyear and W.E., E. & T. p. 16)

— myrtilli, L.　*Wyre Forest,* June 11, 1898, June 12, 17, July 9, 1899; woods, rare (W. Edwards, T.M.N.F.C. p. 182)

Sub-Fam. 3.　CARADRINIDES

Agrotis corticea, Hb.　*Worcester* (St. p. 225); *Wyre Forest,* June 17–19, 1899; *Bransford* (W. H. Edwards); two or three at 'light' (Fletcher); *Laughern Bank* (G. D. Hancock)

— segetum, Schiff.　*Wyre Forest,* June 17–19, 1899; generally common

— ypsilon, Rott.　*Worcester* (J. Peed, I.N.H.W. p. 143); *Castle Morton* (Rev. E. C. Dobrèe Fox); *Grimley* (G. D. Hancock)

— lunigera, Stph.　(T.M.N.F.C. p. 181); rare (E. & T. p. 17); *Lowesmoor* (I.N.H.W. p. 142)

— exclamationis, L.　Common

— nigricans, L.　Rather rare (E. & T. p. 17, I.N.H.W. p. 143); *Castle Morton,*

two or three specimens (Rev. E. C. Dobrèe Fox); *Wyre Forest* (J. Peed); *Elm Hill* (G. D. Hancock)

Agrotis saucia, Hb. *Worcester* (St. p. 224); common (E. & T. p. 17); *Castle Morton*, erratic in appearance (Rev. E. C. Dobrèe Fox); one among dandelion (Fletcher); *Wyre Forest* (W. H. Edwards); *Holt Castle* and *Elm Hill* (J. Peed and G. D. Hancock)

— tritici, L. (T.M.N.F.C. p. 181); common (E. & T. p. 17); *Lowesmoor* (I.N.H.W. p. 142)

— augur, F. *Cowleigh*, June 22, 1895; *Trench Woods*, June 11, 1895; *Monk Wood*, July 31, 1899; *Wyre Forest* (W. H. Edwards)

— subrosea, Stph. Very rare (I.N.H.W. p. 143)

— simulans, Hufn. *Worcester* (St. p. 228, N. p. 336)

— obscura, Brh. *Worcester* (St. p. 228); occurred freely in *Castle Morton Vicarage* and farmhouse adjoining for two years, and also came freely to 'sugar'; it is apparently very erratic in its appearance (Rev. E. C. Dobrèe Fox); *Grimley* (G. D. Hancock)

— putris, L. *Worcester* (St. p. 198); *Foregate Street, Worcester*, June 14, 1896; *Bransford, Monk Wood, Wyre Forest* (W. H. Edwards)

— c-nigrum, L. *Foregate Street, Worcester*, August 22, 27, September 8, 12, 14, 1895, September 8, 1898; *Trench Woods*, June 15, 1895; *Bransford* and *Monk Wood* (W. H. Edwards)

— triangulum, Hufn. ⎫
— pronuba, L. ⎬ Common
— comes, Hb. ⎭

— orbona, Hufn. *Malvern* (W. Edwards, 1899, E. & T. p. 42)

— brunnea, F. ⎫ Common
— xanthographa, F. ⎭

— umbrosa, Hb. *Worcester* (St. p. 237); *Nunnery Wood* (I.N.H.W. p. 142); *Castle Morton* (Rev. E. C. Dobrèe Fox); *Elm Hill* (G. D. Hancock)

— rubi, View. Common (E. & T. p. 18) *Castle Morton* (Rev. E. C. Dobrèe Fox); *Elm Hill* (G. D. Hancock)

— dahlii, Hb. Rather rare (E. & T. p. 18); *Wyre Forest* (Peed and Hancock)

— festiva, Hb. Common

— stigmatica, Hb. *Worcester* (St. p. 235, T.M.N.F.C. p. 181)

— glareosa, Esp. *Monk Wood*, September 9, 1898; at rest on rocks (W.E.); rather rare (E. & T. p. 18)

— depuncta, L. *Worcester* (N. p. 344)

Agrotis typica, L. Common

Triphæna fimbria, L. *Worcester* (St. p. 230); *Wyre Forest*, July 8, 14, 1899; *Trench Woods* (I.N.H.W. p. 142); *Bransford* and *Monk Woods* (W. H. Edwards); *Worcester*, July, 1900; *Cotheridge* (Fletcher)

— janthina, Esp. *Foregate Street, Worcester*, August 2, 1897, August 18, 1898; *Bransford*

— interjecta, Hub. *Worcester* (St. p. 230, T.M.N.F.C. p. 181); rather rare (E. & T. p. 18); *Castle Morton*, rare (Rev. E. C. Dobrèe Fox); four or five by mothing (Fletcher)

— baja, F. *Perry Wood*, July 22, 1895; *Bransford*, July 29, 1895; *Wyre Forest, Trench Woods, Monk Wood* (W. H. Edwards); rather rare (E. & T. p. 18)

— rubricosa, F. Common.

— leucographa, Hb. *Bright's Wood, West Malvern*, April 12, 20, 1895, April 20, 1900; *Nunnery Wood* (I.N.H.W. p. 142); *Ockeridge* (W. H. Edwards)

— prasina, F. *Worcester* (St. p. 271); *Monk Wood*, June 24, 1895; *Foregate Street*, June 14, 1896; *Wyre Forest*, June 17, 24, 1899; *Crown East* (W. H. Edwards); two or three at 'sugar' (Fletcher)

Heliothis armigera, Hb. One at rest (W.E., E. & T. p. 23)

— peltigera, Schiff. Three at rest (W.E., E. & T. p. 23)

— dipsacea, L. *Worcester* (St. p. 292)

Ochria (Gortyna) ochracea, Hb. *Worcester* (St. p. 197); *Henwick* and *Worcester*, September 5, 7, 1898

Nonagria arundinis, F. *Worcester* (St. p. 194); common

Luperina testacea, Hb. *Worcester* (St. p. 206); common at 'light'

Rusina tenebrosa, Hb. Common

Amphipyra pyramidea, L. *Worcester* (St. p. 311); *Bransford*, July 29, August 30, 1895; *Wyre Forest, Trench Woods, Monk Wood* (W. H. Edwards)

— tragopogonis, L. Common

Caradrina pyralina, View. *Worcester* (St. p. 258, N. p. 383); sparingly (W. Edwards, T.M.N.F.C. p. 181); one at 'light,' *Dine's Green* (Fletcher)

— diffinis, L. *Worcester* (St. p. 258, N. p. 383); sparingly (W. Edwards, T.M.N.F.C. p. 181); rather rare (E. & T. p. 20); *Boughton* and *Bransford* (W. H. Edwards); *Castle Morton* (Rev. E. C. Dobrèe Fox); *Elm Hill* (G. D. Hancock)

— affinis, L. *Worcester* (St. p. 259, N.

p. 384); *Middleyards,* July 18, 25, 1899; *Elm Hill* (G. D. Hancock)

Caradrina trapezina, L. Common

— subtusa, F. *Worcester* (St. p. 256); larvæ near *Monk* and *Ockeridge Woods* (J. Peed); mothing (Fletcher); *Laughern Brook* (G. D. Hancock)

— retusa, L. *Worcester* (St. p. 256); generally distributed; *Grimley, Claines* and *Bransford*; mothing (Fletcher)

— oo, L. *Worcester* (St. p. 257, M. p. 118)

— paleacea, Esp. Rather rare (E. & T. p. 20); *Shrawley Wood,* once at 'sugar' (Fletcher)

— umbra, Hufn. *Worcester* (St.); local (W. Edwards, T.M.N.F.C. p. 182); *Bransford* (W. H. Edwards); *Castle Morton,* scarce (Rev. E. C. Dobrèe Fox)

— micacea, Esp. *Worcester* (St. p. 198); *Foregate Street,* August 20, 1895; *St. John's* (W. H. Edwards)

— petasitis, Dbld. Rare (E. & T. p. 15)

— lutosa, Hb. *Worcester* (St. p. 194); *Foregate Street,* August 1895

— fulva, Hb. *New Pool* (W. Edwards); damp meadows, *Castle Morton,* September (Rev. E. C. Dobrèe Fox)

— arcuosa, Hw. *Worcester* (St. p. 213); *Monk Wood,* July 3, 1895, June 28, 1898

— quadripunctata, F. In woods at 'sugar,' common (E. & T. p. 17); *St. John's* and *Bransford* (W. H. Edwards); *Castle Morton* (Rev. E. C. Dobrèe Fox)

— morpheus, Hufn. *Worcester* (St. p. 217); *Worcestershire* (W. H. Edwards); *Castle Morton* (Rev. E. C. Dobrèe Fox)

— alsines, Brh. *Wyre Forest,* June 26, July 8, 1899 (Rev. E. C. Dobrèe Fox, E. & T. p. 17)

— taraxaci, Hb. Common (E. & T. p. 17); *Castle Morton* (Rev. E. C. Dobrèe Fox)

— var. redacta. (I.N.H.W. p. 143)

— trigrammica, Hufn. *Worcester* (St. p. 215); common

— var. bilinea. *Cowleigh Park* (E. & T. p. 17); *Wyre Forest, Monk Wood*

— matura, Hufn. *Worcester* (St. p. 205); *Perry Wood,* July 22, 1895; *Bransford,* July 29, 1895; *Monk Wood* and *Crown East* (W. H. Edwards); two at 'light' (Fletcher)

Hadena meticulosa, L. ⎫
— lucipara, L.   ⎬ Common
                      ⎭

— flammea, Esp. (T.M.N.F.C. p. 182)

— maura, L. Common

— scabriuscula, L. *Worcester* (St. p. 201); *Wyre Forest* (J. Peed); June, 1899; *Farley Wood,* June 21, 1900

— adusta, Esp. *Foregate Street,* May 11,

1895 (W. Edwards, T.M.N.F.C. p. 182)

Hadena gemina, Hb. *Wyre Forest* (J. Peed); June, 1899 (T.M.N.F.C. p. 181)

— polyodon, L. ⎫
— lithoxylea, F. ⎬ Common
                 ⎭

— sublustris, Esp. *Wyre Forest* (J. Peed); June, 1899 (T.M.N.F.C. p. 180); one at 'light' *Bow Wood* (Fletcher)

— rurea, F. Common

— scolopacina, Esp. Generally distributed, but in small numbers; rather rare (E. & T. p. 15, I.N.H.W. p. 144)

— hepatica, Hb. *Worcester* (St. p. 200); *Monk Wood,* June 24, 1895; *Crown East, Wyre Forest,* etc.

— furva, Hb. *Worcester* (N. p. 300; *Malvern Wells* (Rev. E. C. Dobrèe Fox); *Wyre Forest* (W. H. Edwards)

— abjecta, Hb. *Castle Morton,* rare, probably more common in former years (Rev. E. C. Dobrèe Fox)

— sordida, Bkh. *Worcester* (St. p. 208); *Wyre Forest,* June 18, 24, 1899; *Castle Morton,* not noticed for some years (Rev. E. C. Dobrèe Fox)

— basilinea, F. *Trench Woods,* June 15, 1895, June 4, 1896; *Wyre Forest, Monk Wood* (W. H. Edwards)

— pabulatricula, Brh. Taken at 'sugar,' but now disappeared or very rare (E. & T. p. 16)

— didyma, Esp. Common

— nictitans, Bkh. *Worcester* (St. p. 197); *Trench Woods* (W. H. Edwards), 1899; *Severnside,* 1900

— literosa, Hu. Common (E. & T. p. 16); *Castle Morton,* two or three specimens (Rev. E. C. Dobrèe Fox); occasionally to 'light' (Fletcher)

— bicoloria, Vill. *Powick,* July 25, 1895; *Bransford* (W. H. Edwards)

— strigilis, Cl. Common

— fasciuncula, Hu. *Worcester* (St. p. 212); *Cowleigh Park,* June 22, 1895; *Crown East, Bransford, Wyre Forest,* etc.

Metachrostis (Bryophila) perla, F. *Worcester* (St. p. 177); *Malvern,* June 22, 1895; *Henwick* (W. H. Edwards)

— muralis, Forst. *Worcester* (St. p. 177; T.M.N.F.C. p. 180), near *Clatter's Cave,* 1897 (W.E.), rare (E. & T. p. 13)

Acronycta leporina, L. Pupæ *Laughern Brook, Wyre Forest,* June 10, 1899; *West Malvern* (W. H. Edwards); *Temeside* (J. Peed)

— alni, L. *Worcester* (St. p. 182); *The Tything, Worcester* (W. H. Edwards, T.M.N.F.C. p. 180); *Spetchley, Grimley* and *Cotheridge* (Fletcher)

Acronycta strigosa, F. At rest on apple trees (W.E.); rare (E. & T. p. 14); three specimens taken at *Castle Morton*; it has not occurred lately; probably more common before *Longdon Marsh* was drained (Rev. E. C. Dobrèe Fox)

— tridens, Schiff. *Worcester* (St. p. 180, T.M.N.F.C. p. 180); rather rare (E. & T. p. 13); larvæ not rare on hawthorn (Fletcher)

— psi, L. Common

— megacephala, F. Generally distributed

— ligustri, F. *Worcester* (St. p. 182); *Middleyards*, June 16, 1896; *Wyre Forest, Monk Wood* (W. H. Edwards)

— rumicis, L. Common

— menyanthidis, View. (W. Edwards, T.M.N.F.C. p. 180)

3. PLUSIADÆ

Sub-Fam. 1. HYPENIDES

Boletobia fuliginaria, L. *Worcester* (N. p. 69, M. p. 147)

Æthia tarsipennalis, Tr. (Rev. E. C. Dobrèe Fox, E. & T. p. 34); *Wyre Forest* (W. H. Edwards)

— nemoralis, F. *Nunnery Wood*, May 31, 1895; *Monk Wood*, May 26, 1895; *Crown East, Bransford* and *Wyre Forest* (W. H. Edwards)

— derivalis, Hb. Rather common (E. & T. p. 34). Wants confirmation (J. Peed and G. D. Hancock)

Herminia barbalis, Cl. *Worcester* (St. vol. ii. p. 131); common

Hypenodes costistrigalis, Stph. *Monk Wood* (Fletcher)

— albistrigalis, Hw. *Bransford*, July 18, 1899

Hypena rostralis, L. *Worcester* (St. vol. ii. p. 128, W. Edwards, T.M.N.F.C. p. 182); *Crown East, Bransford* and *Wyre Forest* (W. H. Edwards)

— proboscidalis, L. Common

Colobochyla (Madopa) salicalis, Schiff. (W. Edwards, T.M.N.F.C. p. 182, E. & T. p. 33)

Aventia flexula, Schiff. (Rev. E. C. Dobrèe Fox; E. & T. p. 28); *Tiddesley Wood, Tibberton*, by mothing (Fletcher)

Sub-Fam. 2. PLUSIADES

Ophiusa pastinum, Tr. (W. Edwards, T.M.N.F.C. p. 182); taken by Rev. Day (R. F. Towndrow), July 12, 1900

Scoliopteryx libatrix, L. Generally distributed, but not common

Plusia chrysitis, L. Common

— orichalcea, F. Rare (W. Edwards, T.M.N.F.C. p. 182)

Plusia bractea, F. *Worcester* (N. p. 453, W. Edwards, T.M.N.F.C. p. 182); *Dudley Castle Hill* and near *Bromsgrove* (I.N.H.W. p. 145)

— festucæ, L. *Worcester* (St. p. 307); *Foregate Street*, June 2, 1896; about the pool in *Nunnery Wood*, also in *Bewdley Forest* (I.N.H.W. p. 145)

— iota, L. Common

— pulchrina, Hw. *Worcester* (St. p. 308); *Wyre Forest*, 1899 (J. Peed); at flowers of lychnis (Fletcher)

— gamma, L. Common

— tripartita, Hufn. *Worcester* (St. p. 305); *Foregate Street*, July 22, August 21, 1895; *Boughton* and *Bransford* (W. H. Edwards)

— triplasia, L. *Worcester* (St. p. 305); *Bransford*, June 3, 1895; *Foregate Street*, July 25, 1898

Catocala nupta, L. *Worcester* (St. p. 313); *Perry Wood*, August 20, 1898; *Bransford, Powick, Ombersley*, etc.

Euclidia mi, Cl.⎱ Common
— glyphica, L.⎰

Erastria fasciana, L. *Worcester* (St. p. 299); *Middleyards*, May 29, 1895; *Nunnery Wood*, May 27, 1896; *Monk Wood*, June 4, 1899; *Wyre Forest, Monk Wood* (Fletcher); *Ockeridge Wood* (J. Peed)

Eustrotia uncula, Cl. Rather rare (E. & T. p. 23)

— luctuosa, Esp. *Sheriff's Lench*, July 5, 1900; *Bredon* (W. H. Edwards), July 22, 1900

Rivula sericealis, Sc. *Nunnery Wood*, August 4, 1898; *Monk Wood*, July 12, 1899; *Shrawley* (Fletcher)

4. OCNERIADÆ

Orgyia gonostigma, L. *Wyre Forest*, larva, July 23, 1897; common, August (T.M.N.F.C. p. 179)

— antiqua, L. Common

Dasychira fascelina, L. Woody places rare (T.M.N.F.C. p. 179, A. Edmunds p. 184); *Trench Woods* but rare (I.N.H.W. p. 141)

— pudibunda, L. Common

Colocasia (Demas) coryli, L. *Wyre Forest*, June 17, 1900; *Malvern Woods* among hazel (T.M.N.F.C. p. 180); *Bewdley Forest* (I.N.H.W. p. 141); *Trench Woods, Ockeridge Wood*

Porthesia similis, Fuesl. Common

Euproctis chrysorrhœa, L. Not uncommon (A. Edmunds, T.M.N.F.C. p. 179)

Stilpnotia salicis, L. Common

Ocneria monacha, L. *Monk Wood* (W. H. Edwards) ; *Shrawley Wood* (Fletcher) ; *Ockeridge Wood* (J. Peed)
— dispar, L. *Powick* (T.M.N.F.C. p. 179)

II. *NOTODONTINA*

1. HYDRIOMENIDÆ

Trichopteryx (Lobophora) viretata, Hb. *Castle Morton*, one specimen (Rev. E. C. Dobrèe Fox) ; *Wyre Forest*, June, 1900
— carpinata, Bkh. *Wyre Forest*, April 3, 1897, April 21, 1898 ; *Wyre Forest* (Fletcher)
— polycommata, Hb. Rather rare (E. & T. p. 31) ; *Comer Lane*, one specimen (Fletcher)
Lobophora halterata, Hufn. *The Denes*, May 14, 1896 ; *Monk Wood*, May 30, 1896 ; *Wyre Forest*, June 7, 1896
Chloroclystis (Eupithecia) coronata, Hb. *Monk Wood*, May, 1900
— rectangulata, L. *Wyre Forest*, July 9, 1900 ; *Ribbesford*, *The Lickey* and *St. John's* (W. H. Edwards)
Gymnoscelis pumilata, Hb. *Malvern Hills*, scarce (Rev. E. C. Dobrèe Fox)
Tephroclystis venosata, F. *Wyre Forest Station*, June 7, 1897 ; larvæ *Hartlebury Common*, July 13, 1899
— pimpinellata, Hb. Larvæ, in flowers of harebell, rather common (E. & T. p. 30)
— vulgata, Hw. Common (E. & T. p. 30); common at gas lamps, *Worcester* (W. H. Edwards) ; *Castle Morton* (Rev. E. C. Dobrèe Fox)
— oblongata, Thnb. *Bransford*, May 26, July 29, 1895 ; *Dodderhill Common*, July 14, 1896
— subfulvata, Hw. *Castle Morton* (Rev. E. C. Dobrèe Fox); *Dine's Green* (Fletcher)
— satyrata, Hb. Common (E. & T. p. 30) ; *Wyre Forest* (Rev. E. C. Dobrèe Fox)
— pulchellata, Stph. *Malvern Hills* (Rev. E. C. Dobrèe Fox)
— linariata, F. *Wyre Forest*, larvæ, 1899 (W. H. Edwards) ; at 'light,' *Oldbury* (Fletcher) ; *Severnside* (J. Peed)
— castigata, Hb. Rare (E. & T. p. 30) ; *West Malvern* (Rev. E. C. Dobrèe Fox)
— lariciata, Frr. *Abberley*, May 23, 1895 ; *Broadway*, June 23, 1898 ; *Bredon*, June 15, 1899 ; *Ockeridge* (J. Peed)
— plumbeolata, Hw. *Eymore Wood*, May 15, 1863 (T.W.N.C. p. 79) ; *West Malvern* (Rev. E. C. Dobrèe Fox)

Tephroclystis tenuiata, Hb. Larvæ from the catkins of sallow (E. & T. p. 30)
— abbreviata, Stph. *Wyre Forest*, April 4, 1897, April 21, 1898 ; *Monk Wood*, April 16, 1898
— exiguata, Hb. Sallow heads gathered *Trench Woods*, April 22, 1899
— insigniata, Hb. *Castle Morton* (Rev. E. C. Dobrèe Fox)
— fraxinata, Crewe. At 'light,' *St. John's* (Fletcher) ; pupæ near *Worcester* (J. Peed)
— sobrinata, Hb. Larvæ beaten from juniper, *The Slads*, May 31, 1899
— nanata, Hb. *Hartlebury Common*, July 15, 1897, July 20, 1898, July 13, 1899
Eucymatoge (Phibalapteryx) vitalbata, Hb. *Bredon*, June 18, 1896, June 15, 1899 ; *West Malvern* (W. H. Edwards)
— tersata, Hb. *Perry Wood*, June 7, 1895 ; *Bredon*, June 15, 1899 ; *West Malvern*, (W. H. Edwards)
Eucestia (Chesias) spartiata, Fuesl. *Foregate Street*, October 27, 1898 ; *Ribbesford*, September 21, 1860 (T.W.N.C. p. 62)
— rufata, F. *Malvern Hills* (Rev. E. C. Dobrèe Fox)
— (Anaitis) plagiata, L. Common
Calocalpe (Scotosia) certata, Hb. (W. Edwards, T.M.N.F.C. p. 183) ; *Tything*, *Worcester*, at 'light,' and larvæ near Bewdley, 1900 (W. H. Edwards)
— undulata, L. *Croft Wood*, June 22, 1895 ; *Ribbesford*, June 22, 1896 ; *Storridge*, June 22, 1899 ; *Cowleigh Park* and *Wyre Forest* (W. H. Edwards) ; *Monk Wood* (G. D. Hancock)
Philereme (Scotosia) vetulata, Schiff. Larvæ near *Ockeridge*, May, 1899 ; *Bransford*, 1900
— rhamnata, Schiff. Rather common (E. & T. p. 32) ; once at 'light,' *St. John's* and *The Tything* (W. H. Edwards)
Eustroma (Cidaria) prunata, L. Common (E. & T. p. 33) ; *Boughton* (W. H. Edwards)
— associata, Bkh. Common
— populata, L. *Worcester*, 1898 ; rather common (E. & T. p. 33)
— testata, L. *Nunnery Wood*, July 28, 1895 ; *Monk Wood* (W. H. Edwards)
Plemyria (Melanippe) bicolorata, Hufn. *Henwick Road*, July 13, 1896 ; *Bransford*
— hastata, L. *Wyre Forest*, June 11, 12, 1898, June 11, 13, 17, 19, 25, 26, 1899 ; *Eymore Wood* (T.W.N.C. p. 79); *Himbleton* (Fletcher)
— tristata, L. Rather common (E. & T. p. 31)

INSECTS

Plemyria rivata, Hb. The Slads (W.H. Edwards)
— sociata, Bkh. Common
— galiata, Hb. Common (E. & T. p. 31)
Hydriomena (Melanthia) ocellata, L. *Middle-yards*, May 14, 29, 1895; *Foregate Street*, July 10, 1895; *Trench Woods*, June 11, 1896; *Wyre Forest*, June 6, 7, 1896; *Monk Wood*
— (Thera) variata, Schiff. *Westwood*, May 14, 1896; common (E. & T. p. 31); *Ockeridge* and *Trench Woods* (W. H. Edwards)
— (Cidaria) fulvata, Forst. Common
— dotata, L. *Middleyards*, July 9, 1895; *Boughton, Monk Wood* (W. H. Edwards)
— miata, L. *Lench*, May 7, 1895; *Boughton*, and at 'light,' *St. John's* (W.H. Edwards)
— (Cidaria) siterata, Hufn. Very common (E. & T. p. 32); *Boughton* (W. H. Edwards)
— (Hypsipetes) sordidata, F. Common
— trifasciata, Bkh. Pupæ, *Laughern Brook*, 1898; *Wyre Forest*, June 18, 1899
— (Cidaria) truncata, Hufn. Common
— silaceata. *Bredon*, June 15, 1899; *Middleyards* (Fletcher); *Ockeridge* (J. Peed)
— corylata, Thnb. Generally distributed
— suffumata, Hb. *Monk Wood*, June 20, 1895; generally distributed; *Laughern Brook* (J. Peed)
— dubitata, L. (Rev. E. C. Dobrèe Fox); *Boughton* and *Bransford* (W. H. Edwards); *Grimley* (G. D. Hancock)
— (Anticlea) badiata, Hb. *Bransford*, April 4, 1895, March 19, 1896; *Perry Wood*, April 19, 1895; *Trench Woods*, April 3, 1896; *Crown East* and *Monk Wood* (W. H. Edwards); *Ockeridge* (J. Peed)
— nigrofasciaria, Gz. *Middleyards*, May 14, 1895, May 9, 13, 1896; *Crown East*, May 12, 1898; *Abberley Hill*, May 18, 1898; *Wyre Forest* (W. H. Edwards)
— rubidata, F. Rather rare (E. & T. p. 31); *Castle Morton*, scarce (Rev. E. C. Dobrèe Fox); *Laughern Bank* and *Wyre Forest* (G. D. Hancock)
— berberata, Schiff. *Worcester* (M. p. 216)
— (Melanthia) albicillata, L. *Ockeridge*, May 30, 1896; *Wyre Forest*, June 26, 1897, June 13, 1898, June 19, 1899; *Crown East* (W. H. Edwards)
— unangulata, Hw. Common (E. & T. p. 31)
— adæquata, Bkh. *Worcester* (M. p. 218); *Wyre Forest*, June, 1900
— (Emmelesia) alchemillata, L. *Monk Wood*, July 11, 1895, July 16, 1898; *Bredon*, June 15, 1899; *Wyre Forest*, June 20, 25, 1899
— affinitata, Stph. *The Denes*, May 14, 1896; *Wyre Forest*, 1900

Hydriomena decolorata, Hb. *The Denes*, May 14, 1896; *Knightwick*, June 22, 1899; *Wyre Forest*
— albulata, Schiff. *Powick Ham*, June 4, 1895; fields, *Malvern Link*, June 8, 1899; *Wyre Forest, Trench Woods, Boughton* (W. H. Edwards)
— (Melanthia) procellata, F. *Bredon*, July 14, 1895, July 29, 1898
— (Camptogramma) bilineata, L. Common
— fluviata, Hb. Very rare (E. & T. p. 32); at 'light,' *Oldbury* (Fletcher)
Operophtera (Cheimatobia) brumata, L. Common
— boreata, Hb. Very common (E. & T. p. 29)
Euchœca (Asthena) luteata, Schiff. *Croft Wood*, June 10, 1895; *Tiddesley*, July 6, 1899; *Bransford, Lord's Wood, Monk Wood, Wyre Forest*
— obliterata, Hufn. *Monk Wood*, May 30, 1896; *Wyre Forest*, June 17, 19, 1899; *Stanklyn*, June 23, 1899; *Alfrick*, June 22, 1899; *Broadway*, June 23, 1898
— sylvata, Hb. *Tiddesley Wood*, July 6, 1899; *Wyre Forest* (Rev. E. C. Dobrèe Fox and W. H. Edwards); *Shrawley Wood* (Fletcher)
— blomeri, Curt. Wood behind Camp, *Bredon*, June 15, 1899; *Purlieu Lane* (W. H. Edwards)
Asthena candidata, Schiff. Common
— murinata, Sc. *Monk Wood*, May 23, 26, 1895; *Ockeridge, Wyre Forest, Trench Woods*, etc.
— (Oporabia) dilutata, Bkh. *Trench Woods*, October 26, 1894; *Nunnery Wood, Grimley, Bransford*
Xanthorhoe (Phibalapteryx) vittata, Bkh. Taken twice (W.E., E. & T. p. 32)
— (Eubolia) cervinata, Schiff. Larvæ on hollyhock (W.E., E. & T. p. 33); *Trench Woods* (W. H. Edwards)
— (Eubolia) limitata, Sc. Common
— plumbaria, F. Common
— bipunctaria, Schiff. *Bredon*, June 15, 1899
— (Larentia) multistrigaria, Hw. *Malvern*, April 12, 1895, March 24, 1896, April 1, 8, 1899
— didymata, L. Common
— spadicearia, Bkh. *Bransford*, May 13, 1896; *Westwood*, May 14, 1896; *Monk Wood*, etc.
— ferrugata, L. *Bransford*, May 14, 29, 1895, May 13, 1896; *The Denes*, May 14, 1896; *Monk Wood*, June 8, 1898

111

Xanthorhoe designata, Rott. *Wyre Forest*, June 6, 7, 1896; *Lickey*, June 1, 1899; *Ockeridge*, etc.
— munitata, Hb. Rather common (E. & T. p. 32)
— quadrifasciaria, Cl. *Hartlebury*, July 15, 1897
— montanata, Bkh. ⎱ Common
— fluctuata, L. ⎰
— salicata, Hb. *Middleyards* (Fletcher)
— viridaria, F. Common

2. STERRHIDÆ

Eois (Acidalia) virgularia, Hb. (Rev. E. C. Dobrèe Fox, E. & T. p. 27)
— straminata, Tr. *Hartlebury Common*, July 15, 1897, July 20, 1898, July 13, 1899; *Wyre Forest*
— holosericata, Dup. *Worcester* (N. p. 78)
— dilutaria, Hb. Rare (E. & T. p. 27)
— subsericeata, Hw. *Cowleigh Park*, May 21, 1896; *Wyre Forest*, June 5, 1896, June 3, 1897
— inornata, Hw. *Monk Wood*, July 16, 1898, 1900 (also G. D. Hancock)
— aversata, L. Common
— emarginata, L. *Middleyards*, July 25, 1898
— dimidiata, Hufn. *Bredon*, July 14, 1895; *Wyre Forest*, etc.
— trigeminata, Hw. *Knightwich*, May 22, 1897; *Monk Wood*, etc.
— bisetata, Hufm. *Perry Wood*, July 22, 1895; *Croft Wood*, August 11, 1899; *Monk Wood*, etc.
Leptomeris (Acidalia) remutaria, Hb. Common
— marginepunctata, Gz. Rare (E. & T. p. 27)
— ornata, Sc. *Bredon*, June 18, 1896; *Trench Woods* (I.N.H.W. p. 146)
— imitaria, Hb. One *Worcestershire* specimen, but locality uncertain, and *Claines* (W. H. Edwards)
— strigilaria, Hb. Rather common (E. & T. p. 27)
Leucophthalmia (Ephyra) orbicularia, Hb. (M. p. 245); *Monk Wood* (Fletcher)
— pendularia, Cl. *Monk Wood*, May 26, 1895; *Trench Woods*, June 11, 1896; *Wyre Forest*, May 25, 1899
— porata, F. *Middleyards*, May 28, June 4; *Trench Woods*, June 11, 1898; *Wyre Forest, Monk Wood*
— punctaria, L. *Perry Wood*, May 13, 21, 1895; *Middleyards*, May 13, 1896; *Trench Woods*, June 11, 1896; *Wyre Forest*, June 5, 7, 1897; *Monk Wood*, August, 1900
— trilinearia, Bkh. Common (E. & T. p. 26)

Leucophthalmia annulata, Schulze. *Croft Wood*, June 10, 1895, June 8, 1899
Calothysanis (Timandra) amata, L. Common

3. GEOMETRIDÆ

Nemoria strigata, Müll. Common
— viridata, L. *Worcester* (N. p. 71); rather rare (E. & T. p. 26); *Broad-heath* (Fletcher)
Euchloris (Phorodesma) pustulata, Hufn. *Monk Wood*, June 20, 24, 1895; *Wyre Forest*, May 25, 1896; *Croome Perry*, July 1, 1897; *Perry Wood*, June 19, 1895; *Tiddesley*, June 18, 1896; *Wyre Forest, Middleyards* (Fletcher)
— (Iodis) vernaria, Hb. *Bredon*, June 18, 1896; *Martley*, June 22, 1897
— lactearia, L. Common
Geometra papilionaria, L. *Perry Wood*, July 8, 1895; *Wyre Forest*, July 18, 1895; *Monk Wood* and *Dine's Green* (Fletcher)
Pseudoterpna pruinata, Hufn. *Hartlebury Common*, July 15, 1897; *Monk Wood*, July 6, 1898

4. MONOCTENIADÆ

Baptria (Tanagra) atrata, Linn. *Elmley Castle*, June 18, 1896; formerly in *Cowleigh Park* (E. & T. p. 33)
Erannis (Anisopteryx) æscularia, Schiff. *Monk Wood, Crown East, Bransford, St. John's* (W. H. Edwards)
Brephos parthenias, L. *Worcester* (St. p. 30); *Trench Woods*, April 19, 1899, and *Wyre Forest* (Fletcher); *Monk Wood* (J. Peed)
— notha, Hb. *Monk Wood*, March 30, 1897, April 8, 16, 1898; *Trench Woods*, April 17, 19, 1899

5. SELIDOSEMIDÆ

Opisthograptis (Macaria) liturata, Cl. *Trench Woods*, May 18, 1896; *Wyre Forest*, June 6, 7, 1897; *Farley Wood*, 1900; *Whitehall* (Fletcher); *Ockeridge* (W. H. Edwards)
— clathrata, L. *Bredon*, July 14, 1895, June 15, 1899; *The Slads* (W. H. Edwards); *Crowle* (Fletcher); *Wyre Forest* (J. Peed)
— (Rumia) luteolata, L. Common
Diastictis (Halia) wauaria, L. *Foregate Street*, July 19, 1895; *Boughton, Bransford*, etc. (W. H. Edwards)
— (Boarmia) roboraria, Schiff. *Wyre Forest*, July 9, 14, 1899; scarce, *Trench Woods* (I.N.H.W. p. 146); a rare in-

INSECTS

sect (A. Edmunds, T.M.N.F.C. p. 184); *Shrawley Wood* (Fletcher)

Diastictis consortaria, F. At rest (W.E.); rare (E. & T. p. 26)

Ectropis (Tephrosia) luridata, Bkh. *Monk Wood*, June 8, 1898, June 3, 1899; *Wyre Forest*, June 12, 1898, June 10, 1899; *Ockeridge* (J. Peed)

— punctularia, Hb. *Trench Woods*, May 19, 1895; *Monk Wood*, June 1, 1899; *Wyre Forest*, June 12, 1898; *Ockeridge* (J. Peed)

— biundularia, Bkh. *Wyre Forest*, April 21, 1898; *Abberley Hill*, May 18, 1898; *Ockeridge*, May 27, 1899; *Lickey*, June 1, 1899; *Malvern Hills* (Rev. E. C. Dobrée Fox)

Cleora lichenaria, Hufn. *Monk Wood*, May 26, 1895; rare (E. & T. p. 25)

Selidosema (Boarmia) repandata, L. Common

— gemmaria, Brk. Common

Bupalus piniarius, L. *Trench Woods*, June 15, 1895; *Wyre Forest*, June 6, 1896, June 27, 1898; *Crown East* (W. H. Edwards)

— atomarius, L. *Wyre Forest*, common

— limbarius, F. *Vine's End Bank*; very rare (E. & T. p. 28)

Synopsia (Hemerophila) abruptaria, Thnb. At 'light,' *Worcester*; fairly common.

Abraxas grossulariata, L. Common

— sylvata, Sc. *Croft Wood*, June 10, 1895; *Bredon*, June 18, 1896; *Lincombe* (W. H. Edwards); *Crown East* (Fletcher)

— adustata, Schiff. *Middleyards*, May 29, 1895, May 11, 1896; *Crown East*, *Trench Woods*, *Monk Wood* (W. H. Edwards)

— marginata, L. Common

Pseudopanthera (Corycia) punctata, F. *Croft Wood*, June 10, 1900; *Trench Woods* (W. H. Edwards)

— pictaria, Curt. Rare (E. & T. p. 27)

— (Venilia) macularia, L. Common

— (Gnophos) obscuraria, Hb. Rare (E. & T. p. 26); *Malvern Wells* (Rev. E. C. Dobrée Fox); *Wyre Forest* (G. D. Hancock)

— (Pachycnemia) hippocastanaria, Hb. Rare (E. & T. p. 28)

— (Panagra) petraria, Hb. *Perry Wood*, May 13, 1895; *Wyre Forest*, May 25, 1896; *Hollybush Hill* (W. H. Edwards); *Monk Wood* and *Ockeridge* (G. D. Hancock)

Crocota (Selidosema) belgiaria, Hb. Rather rare (E. & T. p. 28)

— (Aspilates) strigillaria, Hb. *Wyre Forest*, June 7, 1895, June 17, 19, 1899

Crocota gilvaria, F. Rather rare (E. & T. p. 28)

Theria (Hybernia) rupicapraria, Hb. *Kempsey Road*, February 12, 1899; *Hallow* (G. D. Hancock)

Hybernia leucophæaria, Schiff. *Westwood Park*, March 7, 1895; *Monk Wood*, *Trench Woods* and *Bransford* (W. H. Edwards)

— marginaria, Bkh. *Bransford*, April 4, 1895; *Crown East*, April 9, 1895; *Spetchley* (W. H. Edwards)

— aurantiaria, Esp. *Foregate Street*, November 25, 1899; *Cotheridge* (Fletcher)

— defoliaria, Cl. Common

Apocheima (Nyssia) hispidaria, F. (W. Edwards); *Blackmore Park* (T.M.N.F.C. p. 183); pupæ at elms (E. & T. p. 25)

— pedaria, F. From pupæ dug January 20, February 8, 1896; *Grimley*, *Spetchley*, *Bransford* (W. H. Edwards)

Biston hirtarius, Cl. Woods, rare (A. Edmunds, T.M.N.F.C. p. 184); larvæ, *Ribbesford*, September 21, 1860 (T.W.N.C. p. 62); *Spetchley*, 1898 (W. H. Edwards); *Crown East* (J. Peed)

— stratarius, Hufn. Pupæ dug at *Spetchley*, February 19, 1897; *Boughton*, *Grimley* and at 'light' (W. H. Edwards)

— betularius, L. *Foregate Street*, June 15, 1898; *Spetchley*, *Boughton*, etc. (W. H. Edwards)

— — var. doubledayaria. *Foregate Street*, May 16, June 9, 1896, June 16, 1898, May 31, 1899

Deilinia (Cabera) pusaria, L. }
— exanthemata, Sc. } Common
Ourapteryx sambucaria, L. }

Metrocampa (Ellopia) prosapiaria, L. *Sapey Brook*, *Henwick*, at 'light' (W. H. Edwards)

— margaritaria, L. Common

— (Numeria) pulveraria, L. *Monk Wood*, May 26, 1895, May 17, 1896, June, 1899; *Crown East*, *Wyre Forest* and *Trench Woods* (W. H. Edwards)

— (Eurymene) dolobraria, L. *Wyre Forest*, June 6, 1897, June 18, 1896, June 25, 1899; *Monk Wood*, June 4, 1899; *Tiddesley*, June 18, 1896; *St. John's* (W. H. Edwards); *Dine's Green* (Fletcher)

Euchlæna (Angerona) prunaria, L. *Monk Wood*, June 20, 24, 1895; *Tiddesley*, June 18, 1896, and *Wyre Forest*

— (Epione) apiciaria, Schiff. *Henwick*, July 13, 1896; *Monk Wood*, July 28, 1897; *Foregate Street*, July 31, 1897; *Laughern Brook*, August 23, 1898

Selenia bilunaria, Esp. } Common
    var. juliaria. }

113

Selenia lunaria, Schiff. *Bransford*, July 29, 1895; *Foregate Street*, June 11, 1896; *Wyre Forest* and *St. John's* (W. H. Edwards); *Grimley* (G. D. Hancock)
— tetralunaria, Hufn. *Monk Wood*, July 24, 1900; around *Malvern* (T.M.N.F.C. p. 183); *Wyre Forest* (J. Peed); *Laughern Bank* (G. D. Hancock)
Hygrochroa (Pericallia) syringaria, L. *Monk Wood*, June 20, 1895, July 15, 1898; *Wyre Forest*, July 11, 1898; *Boughton* and *Bransford* (W. H. Edwards); a few by mothing (Fletcher)
Cepphis (Epione) advenaria, Hb. *Croft Wood*, June 8, 22, 1899, June 3, 15, 1900; *Wyre Forest* once only (W. H. Edwards)
Colotois (Himera) pennaria, L. *Foregate Street*, November 10, 1895; *Henwick* at 'light' and larvæ *Monk Wood* (W. H. Edwards)
Ennomos erosaria, Bkh. *Bransford*, July 29, 1900; *Monk Wood* (G. D. Hancock)
— fuscantaria, Hw. *Perry Wood*, August 16, 1895; *Foregate Street*, July 30, 1897, August 6, 1899, September 5, 1899; *Oldbury Road* (Fletcher)
— alniaria, L. Rare (E. & T. p. 25); *St. John's*, *Henwick* (W. H. Edwards); *Grimley* (G. D. Hancock)
— quercinaria, Hufn. Rather common (E. & T. p. 25); *St. John's* (W. H. Edwards)
Gonodontis (Odontopera) bidentata, Cl. *Bransford*, *Crown East*, *Monk Wood* (W. H. Edwards); *Ockeridge* (J. Peed)
— (Crocallis) elinguaria, L. *Perry Wood*, July 22, 1895; *Bransford*, July 29, 1895; *Foregate Street*, July 25, 30, 1897

6. POLYPLOCIDÆ

Habrosyne (Thyatira) derasa, L. *Worcester* (St. p. 173); *Foregate Street*, July 25, 1898; *Wyre Forest*, June 19, 21, July 8, 1899; *Middleyards*, July 18, 1899; *Sheriff's Lench*, July 24, 1899; *Crown East* and *Monk Wood* (W. H. Edwards); two by mothing (Fletcher)
Thyatira batis, L. *Worcester* (St. p. 174); *Wyre Forest*, June 17, 19, 1899; *Crown East*, *Monk Wood* and *Middleyards* (W. H. Edwards); by 'sugaring' in woods (Fletcher)
Palimpsestis (Cymatophora) fluctuosa, Hb. *Worcester* (St. p. 175); *Wyre Forest*, June 6, 1897, June 26, 1898, June 11, 13, 17, 19, July 8, 1899
— duplaris, L. *Worcester* (St. p. 174); *Wyre Forest*, June 7, 1897, June 25, 1898

Palimpsestis or, F. *Worcester* (St. p. 175); *Wyre Forest*, June 6, 1897, June 11, 25, 1898
— octogesima, Hb. *Worcester* (St. p. 175); *Wyre Forest*, June 18, 1899; *Perry Wood*, June 7, 1895; *Cotheridge* (Fletcher)
Polyploca (Asphalia) diluta, F. *Worcester* (St. p. 175); *Bransford*, August 30, 1895, etc.; *Ockeridge* (G. D. Hancock)
— flavicornis, L. Larvæ, *Monk Wood*, May 25, June 5, 1899; *Wyre Forest*, June 16, 1900; *Malvern Hills* (Rev. E. C. Dobrée Fox); *Trench Woods* (W. H. Edwards)
— ridens, F. *Worcester* (St. p. 176, T.M.N.F.C. p. 180); from pupæ dug recently (W. H. Edwards); *Elm Hill* and *Ockeridge* (J. Peed and G. D. Hancock)

7. SPHINGIDÆ

Hemaris (Macroglossa) bombyliformis, Esp. *Wyre Forest*, June 6, 1897, June 11, 1898; field near *Trench Woods*; one *Cowleigh Park* (W. Edwards, 1869, T.M.N.F.C. p. 177); *Broadheath* (Fletcher)
— fuciformis, L. Dry banks and woods (W. E.); rare (E. & T. p. 7).
Macroglossa stellatarum, L. 34, *Foregate Street*, August 3, 1899; common in 1899 and 1900
Deilephila porcellus, L. *Foregate Street*, June 16, July 21, 1898; *Bredon* and *St. John's* (W. H. Edwards)
— elpenor, L. *Wyre Forest*, May 24, 1896; larva, *Rushwick*, August 13, 1900; in gardens, larvæ on vines (Fletcher)
— celerio, L. Very rare (T.M.N.F.C. p. 177); *Link End House*, 1867 or 1868 (R.F.T., E. & T. p. 7); very rare (I.N.H.W. p. 140)
— lineata, F. Near *Worcester*, rare (T.M.N.F.C. p. 177); *Malvern Link Common*, 1874 (W.E., E. & T. p. 7); near *Worcester* but rare (I.N.H.W. p. 140); at rest on a garden wall at *Offenham* near *Evesham*, April 29, 1900 (L. S. Smith 'Science Gossip,' September, 1900)
— galii, Rott. (T.M.N.F.C. p. 177); one *Worfield House*, *Malvern*, 1870 (R.F.T.); larvæ, *Old Hills* (Dr. C. F. Grindrod in ' *Malvern*,' E. & T. p. 6)
Sphinx ligustri, L. *Foregate Street*, June 6, 1895, June 3, 1896, June 5, 1899; common
— convolvuli, L. *St. John's*, fourteen specimens, 1887 (W. H. Edwards); *Worcester* (Bibbs), 1899; *Malvern Pound, Wor-*

cester, September; scarce (T.M.N.F.C. p. 177); *Worcester*, 1900 (G. D. Hancock); by mothing in gardens (Fletcher)

Acherontia atropos, L. *Worcestershire*, fairly common, 1899 and 1900; larvæ in potato fields (Fletcher)

Smerinthus populi, L.
— ocellatus, L. } Common
Dilina tiliæ, L.

8. NOTODONTIDÆ

Pygæra pigra, Hufn. Seddon from pupa and one at *Malvern* (W.E., E. & T. p. 9); *Trench Woods* (Fletcher)

— curtula, L. *Monk Wood* (G. D. Hancock); *St. John's* (W. H. Edwards); among poplars in lanes, etc. (I.N.H.W. p.141); Seddon from pupæ (E. & T. p. 9)

Notodonta ziczac, L. *Foregate Street*, August 18, 1895; *Monk Wood*, July 31, 1899; *St. John's* (W. H. Edwards)

— dromedarius, L. *Foregate Street*, June 10, 1896; *Monk Wood*, 1900; *Wyre Forest* (Fletcher)

Drymonia dictæoides, Esp. *Foregate Street*, May 18, June 10, 1896; one at 'light' (Fletcher); *Wyre Forest* (J. Peed)

— tremula, Cl. *Perry Wood*, August 16, 1895; *Foregate Street*, June 2, 8, 1896; *Grimley*, near *Old Hills*, not common (W. H. Edwards)

— trepida, Esp. Scarce (T.M.N.F.C. p.180); *Cowleigh* (W.E., E. & T. p.9, I.N.H.W. p. 141)

— trimacula, Esp. *Wyre Forest*, two (W. H. Edwards, T.M.N.F.C. p. 180); of rare occurrence (E. & T. p. 9); pupa dug, *Grimley* (G. D. Hancock)

— chaonia, Hb. One pupa by digging (Fletcher)

Stauropus fagi, L. *Wyre Forest*, June, 1899, June, 1900; *Monk Wood*, uncommon (T.M.N.F.C. p. 179); *Nunnery Wood*, very rare (I.N.H.W. p. 141)

Pterostoma palpina, L. Generally distributed

Odontosia camelina, L. *Wyre Forest*, June 26, 1898; *Monk Wood*, larva, October 8, 1900; *Leigh Sinton* (W. H. Edwards)

— cuculla, Esp. *Blackmore Park* (W.E., E. & T. p. 9)

Cerura vinula, L. Common

— bifida, Hb. *Foregate Street*, May 30, 1897; *Henwick*, lamps, May 30, 1896 (T.M.N.F.C. p. 179); larvæ, *St. John's* (W. H. Edwards); one larva, *Wyre Forest* (Fletcher)

— furcula, L. (T.M.N.F.C. p. 179); very rare (E. & T. p. 8); *Bewdley Forest* (I.N.H.W. p. 141); larvæ, *St. John's*

(W. H. Edwards); two larvæ, *Peg-House Wood* (Fletcher)

Cerura bicuspis, Bkh. Pupæ cases on alder near *Malvern* (T.M.N.F.C. p. 179)

Phalera bucephala, L. Common

9. SATURNIADÆ

Saturnia pavonia, L. Larvæ, *Wyre Forest*, June 5, 1897; *Worcester*, W. Wood's garden, May, 1900; *Bilberry Hills, Broadheath*; abundant in the larva state near *Malvern*, 1869 (W. Edwards, T.M.N.F.C. p. 179); *Perry Woods* and other woods near *Worcester* (A. Edmunds, T.M.N.F.C. p. 184); *Cowleigh Park* and *Quest Hills* (E. & T. p. 12)

III. *LASIOCAMPINA*
1. DREPANIDÆ

Cilix glaucata, Sc. Common

Falcaria lacertinaria, L. *Wyre Forest*, June 13, 1898, June 10, 12, 17, 19, 26, 1899; *Monk Wood* (T.M.N.F.C. p. 179)

— falcataria, L. Common

Drepana binaria, Hufn. *Bransford*, May 11, 14, 1895; *Perry Wood*, May 21, 1895; *Monk Wood*, May 17, 1896, and *Trench Woods*

— cultraria, F. *Malvern*, not uncommon (T.M.N.F.C. p. 179, Rev. E. C. Dobrée Fox, E. & T. p. 12)

2. ENDROMIDIDÆ

Endromis versicolor, L. *Wyre Forest*, April 3, 1897, April 21, 1898, April 16, 23, 1900

3. LASIOCAMPIDÆ

Lasiocampa quercus, L. Common

Eriogaster populi, L. Generally distributed, larvæ and pupæ secured, imagos at 'light'

— lanestris, L. Larvæ in webs often observed, imago occasionally; *Bransford, Grimley, Trench Woods* and *Wyre Forest*

— rubi, L. *Hartlebury Common*, June 9, 1898; *Wyre Forest*, 1897; *Craycombe Banks*, 1898; *Bransford Bridge*, 1900; *Lathe Hill, Broadheath*

— cratægi, L. *Middleyards* (T.M.N.F.C. p. 179, I.N.H.W. p. 141); *Wyre Forest*, 1898 (W. H. Edwards); larvæ on hawthorn (Fletcher)

Clisiocampa neustria, L. } Common
Odonestis potatoria, L. }

Gastropacha quercifolia, L. Larvæ, *Worcester*, 1895; *Hartlebury Common*, July 13, 1900; *Tiddesley Wood*, fairly common; *Sinton Green* (Fletcher)

V. *PYRALIDINA*
1. PHYCITIDÆ

Salebria (Pempelia) fusca, Hw. *Wyre Forest,* 1897

— betulæ, Gz. *Ockeridge* (Fletcher)

Hypochalcia ahenella, Hb. *Bransford,* July 14, 1896

Phycita spissicella, F. *Tiddesley Wood* (Fletcher) ; *Middleyards,* July 14, 1896

Nephopteryx hostilis, Stph. *Worcester* (M. p. 371)

Ephestia kuehniella, Z. *Kidderminster,* Dec., 1900

Myelois cribrella, Hb. *Bransford,* June 3, 1896 ; *Bredon,* June 29, 1898 ; *Temple Laughern* (Fletcher)

Cryptoblabes bistriga, Hw. *Oldbury Road*

Acrobasis consociella, Hb. *Ribbesford,* June 22, 1896 ; *Hartlebury Common,* July 14, 1899

— tumidana, Schiff. *Trench Woods* (Fletcher)

2. GALLERIADÆ

Meliphora grisella, F. One at 'light,' *Temple Laughern* (Fletcher)

Melissoblaptes bipunctanus, Z. Rare (E. & T. p. 35)

Aphomia sociella, L. *Foregate Street,* June 1, 5, 1896, June 10, 1897 ; rather common (E. & T. p. 35)

Galleria mellonella, L. Rather common (E. & T. p. 35)

3. CRAMBIDÆ

Crambus pascuellus, L. Common, *Monk Wood,* etc.; rather rare (E. & T. p. 36)

— pratellus, L. Common, *Middleyards,* etc. ; common (E. & T. p. 36)

— culmellus, L. ⎫
— hortuellus, Hb. ⎬ Common

— chrysonuchellus, Sc. (Rev. E. C. Dobrée Fox, E. & T. p. 36)

— falsellus, Schiff. Common (E. & T. p. 36) ; *Dine's Green* (Fletcher)

— pinellus, L. *Middleyards,* July 28, 1899 ; *Hartlebury Common* (W. H. Edwards) ; one at 'light,' *Oldbury Road* (Fletcher)

— perlellus, Sc. *Croft Wood,* June 22, 1895 ; *Powick,* June 27, 1896 (T.W.N.C. p. 432); *Wyre Forest* (W. H. Edwards); rather common (E. & T. p. 36)

— inquinatellus, Schiff. *Hartlebury Common,* July 13, 1899

— tristellus, F. Common

Platytes cerussella, Schiff. Near *Colwall ;* rare (E. & T. p. 36)

Chilo phragmitellus, Hb. *The Rough Wood, Bransford,* July 9, 1895

4. PYRAUSTIDÆ

Schœnobius forficellus, Thnb. *Hartlebury Common,* July 20, 1898, July 13, 1899

Cataclysta lemnata, L. ⎫
Nymphula (Hydrocampa) stagnata, Don. ⎪
— stratiotata, L. ⎬ Common
Hydrocampa nymphæata, L. ⎪
Notarcha (Botys) ruralis, Sc. ⎪
Eurrhypara urticata, L. ⎭

Perinephela lancealis, Schiff. Common (E. & T. p. 35)

Phlyctænia (Ebulea) crocealis, Hb. *Wyre Forest*

— lutealis, Hb. *Bredon,* July 14, 1895 (T.M.N.F.C. p. 183) ; common (E. & T. p. 35)

— ferrugalis, Hb. *Oldbury Lane* (Fletcher)

— prunalis, Schiff. Common

— fuscalis, Schiff. Common ; rather rare (E. & T. p. 35) ; *Monk Wood* (Fletcher)

— sambucalis, Schiff. Common

Nomophila noctuella, Schiff. *Perry Wood,* September 25, 1899 ; common (E. & T. p. 35)

Psammotis (Botys) hyalinalis, Hb. *Bredon,* June 15, 1899 ; common (E. & T. p. 35)

Pyrausta octomaculata, F. *Wyre Forest,* May 23, 25, 1896, June 6, 7, 1896, June 10, 12, 1899

— nigrata, Sc. *Bredon,* June 15, 1899 ; *Holly Bush Hill* (W. H. Edwards)

— purpuralis, L. Common

— aurata, Sc. Rather rare (E. & T. p. 34)

— cespitalis, Schiff. *Wyre Forest,* July 14, 1895 ; common (E. & T. p. 34) ; *Oddingley* (Fletcher)

— olivalis, Schiff. Common

— flavalis, Schiff. *Oddingley* (Fletcher)

— stachydalis, Zk. 34, *Foregate Street,* July 15, 1898 ; common (E. & T. p. 35)

Microstega (Botys) pandalis, Hb. Common

Cynæda (Odontia) dentalis, Hb. (T.M.N.F.C. p. 183)

Scoparia cembræ, Hw. One to 'light,' *Oldbury Road* (Fletcher)

— dubitalis, Hb. ⎫
— ambigualis, Tr. ⎬ Common

Evergestis (Spilodes) straminalis, Hb. *Shrawley Wood* (St. vol. ii. p. 153 and Fletcher)

— extimalis, Sc. (T.M.N.F.C. p. 183)

Mesographe forficalis, L. Common

5. PYRALIDIDÆ

Endotricha flammealis, Schiff. Common (E. & T. p. 34)

Pyralis glaucinalis, L. *Foregate Street*, June 21, 1896, August 14, 1898
— costalis, F. Common (E. & T. p. 34)
— farinalis, L. *Tything, Worcester*, July 14, 1896 ; *Boughton* (W. H. Edwards)
Aglossa pinguinalis, L. Common

6. PTEROPHORIDÆ

Oxyptilus teucrii, Greening. *Witley, Hartlebury Common*, July 15, 1897
Platyptilia acanthodactyla, Hb. *Perry Wood*, June 6, 1898 ; *Comer Gardens* (Fletcher)
— gonodactyla, Schiff. *Bransford*, June 27, 1896 ; *Bredon*, June 15, 1899 ; rather rare (E. & T. p. 39)
Pterophorus tetradactylus, L. *Brockeridge Common*, July 14, 1898 ; *Defford Common*, July 1, 1897
— pentadactylus, L. ⎫
— galactodactylus, Hb. ⎬ Common
— spilodactylus, Curt. (M. p. 437)
Marasmarcha (Pterophorus) phæodactyla, Hb. *Middleyards*, June 27, 1896 ; *Bredon* (W. H. Edwards)
— tephradactyla, Hb. Rare (E. & T. p. 39)
— monodactyla, L. Common
— lithodactyla, Tr. *Perry Wood*, July 11, 1895 ; *Middleyards*, July 9, 1895 ; *Monk Wood* (W. H. Edwards)
Stenoptilia pterodactyla, L. *Trench Woods*, October 26, 1894 ; generally distributed (W. H. Edwards)
Orneodes (Alucita) hexadactyla, L. Common

VI. *PSYCHINA*
1. PSYCHIDÆ
2. ZEUZERIDÆ

Zeuzera pyrina, L. *Foregate Street*, June 14, 15, 1896, July 16, 1900 ; *Barbourne* and *Smith's Nurseries* (W. H. Edwards) ; *Monk Wood* (G. D. Hancock)

3. ZYGÆNIDÆ

Zygæna filipendulæ, L. ⎫
— loniceræ, Esp. ⎬ Common
— trifolii, Esp. Moist places near *Malvern Hills* (Rev. E. C. Dobrèe Fox) ; one *Monk Wood* (Fletcher) ; open places, woods, *Malvern* (W.E., E. & T. p. 6)
Procris geryon, Hb. *West Malvern*, June 10, 1895 ; *Bredon*, June 15, 1899 ; *West Malvern*, etc. ; *Storridge* (E. & T. p. 6) ; *Malvern Hills* (Fletcher)
— statices, L. *Powick Ham*, June 4, 1895 ; *Wyre Forest*, June, 1896 ; meadow near *Powick, Monk Wood*, etc., June (T.M.N.F.C. p. 177) ; *Gasworks, Malvern Link*, many years ago (W.E., E. & T. p. 5) ; *Trench Woods* (I.N.H.W. p. 139)

4. HETEROGENEIDÆ

Heterogenea asella, Schiff. One *Birchwood* (W.E.) ; very rare (E. & T. p. 12)
— limacodes, Hufn. *Monk Wood*, June 28, 1898, June 28, 1900 ; *Middleyards, Trench Woods*, scarce, June (T.M.N.F.C. p. 178) ; *Wyre Forest* (Fletcher)

VII. *TORTRICINA*
1. EPIBLEMIDÆ

Lobesia permixtana, Hb. *Eymore Woods*, May 15, 1863 (T.W.N.C. p. 79) ; *Monk Wood*, May 25, 1899 ; *Middleyards* (Fletcher)
Chrosis euphorbiana, Frr. *Worcester* (M. p. 456)
Bactra lanceolana, Hb. Bog, *West Malvern*, May 21, 1896 ; *Wyre Forest*
Exartema (Sericoris) latifasciana, Hw. *Worcester* (M. p. 457)
Eucosma (Penthina) corticana, Hb. Very common (E. & T. p. 38)
— semifasciana, Hw. *Wyre Forest* (Fletcher)
— capræana, Hb. *Monk Wood* (Fletcher)
— sororculana, Zett. Common (E. & T. p. 36)
— pruniana, Hb. Near *Waterworks, Worcester*, June 20, 1896
— oblongana, Hw. *Oddingley* (Fletcher)
— profundana, F. *Wyre Forest* (Fletcher)
— arcuella, Cl. *Wyre Forest*, June 7, 1896, June 10, 12, 1899 ; *Ribbesford*, July 17, 1899
— purpurana, Hw. *Sheriff's Lench*, July 5, 1900
— schulziana, F. Rare (E. & T. p. 39)
— urticana, Hb. *Wyre Forest*, July 9, 1897 ; common
— lacunana, Dup. *Monk Wood*, June 17, 1897
— striana, Schiff. *Worcestershire* ; common (E. & T. p. 38)
— blanderiana, L. *Worcester* (St. vol. ii. p. 261)
Pamplusia mercuriana, Hb. Rare (E. & T. p. 38)
Evetria (Retinia) buoliana, Schiff. *St. John's* (W. H. Edwards)
Enarmonia (Spilonota) simplana, F.R. *West Malvern*, May 21, 1896
— (Retinia) pinicolana, Z. Local (E. & T. p. 38)
— (Pœdisca) oppressana, Tr. *Monk Wood* (Fletcher)
Tmetocera ocellana, F. Five, *Worcestershire* ; rare (E. & T. p. 37)
Eudemis nævana, Hb. *Worcestershire*
Ancylis (Anchylopera) derasana, Hb. Between *Middleyards* and *The Rough*

Ancylis lundana, F. *Perry Wood*, May 13, 1895; *Monk Wood*, May 25, 1899; *Trench Woods* (W. H. Edwards)
— mitterbacheriana, Schiff. *Worcestershire*; common
— lactana, F. *Monk Wood*, June, 1898; *Middleyards* (Fletcher)
Gypsonoma (Spilonota) dealbana, Fröl. *Monk Wood*, July, 1899
Cydia (Grapholita) obtusana, Hw.
— ustomaculana, Curt. Rare (E. & T. p. 37)
— fractifasciana, Hw. Rare (E. & T. p. 39)
— (Catoptria) pupillana, Cl. Rare (E. & T. p. 38)
Notocelia uddmanniana, L. *Middleyards*, July 14, 1896; *Monk Wood* (Fletcher)
— (Spilonota) trimaculana, Hw. Rather rare (E. & T. p. 37)
— roborana, Tr. *Middleyards*, July 9, 1895
— (Halonota) tetragonana, Stph. *Worcestershire*
Epiblema (Pardia) tripunctana, F. *Monk Wood*, May 26, 1895; *Middleyards*, May 13, 1896; common
— (Grapholitha) nisella, Cl. Rare (E. & T. p. 37); five, *Worcestershire*
— (Phlocodes) demarniana, F.R. *Worcestershire*
— tetraquetrana, Hw. ⎫ *Worcestershire*
— tedella, Cl. ⎭
— (Halonota) similana, Hb. Common (E. & T. p. 37)
— pflugiana, Hw. *Bransford*, May 9, 13, 1896; generally distributed
— trigeminana, Stph. *Worcestershire*
— brunnichiana, Fröl. ⎫ Rare (E. & T. p. 37)
— turbidana, Tr. ⎭
— (Pœdisca) bilunana, Hw. *Worcestershire*
— ophthalmicana, Hb. *Monk Wood* (Fletcher)
— solandriana, L. *Worcestershire*; rare (E. & T. p. 37)
— semifuscana, Stph. *Worcestershire* var. piceana. Rare (E. & T. p. 37)
Hemimene (Dicrorampha) alpinana, Tr. *Worcestershire*
— petiverella, L. *Worcestershire*
— sequana, Hb. *Crown East Wood* (Fletcher)
— simpliciana, Hw. *Worcestershire*
Pammene (Stigmonota) nitidana, F. *Ribbesford*, June 17, 1897
— germarana, Hb. ⎫
— fimbriana, Hw. ⎪
— rhediella, Cl. ⎬ *Worcestershire*
— splendidulana, Gn. ⎭
— gallicolana, Z. *Worcester* (St. vol. ii. p. 241); three, *Worcestershire*
Laspeyresia servillana, Dup. *Monk Wood* (Fletcher)
— (Stigmonota) perlepidana, Hw. *Weymans Wood*, May 13, 1897

Laspeyresia compositella, Fr. *Bransford*, May 9, 1896
— nigricana, Stph. *Old Hills*, June 24, 1897
— coniferana, Rtz. ⎫ Common (E. & T. p. 38)
— ulicetana, Hw. ⎭
Carpocapsa pomonella, L. Common; *Victoria Institute* and *Boughton* (W. H. Edwards)
— splendana, Hb. Among oaks (Fletcher)
— juliana, Curt. Common (E. & T. p. 38); *Temple Laughern* (Fletcher)
Epinotia (Opadia) funebrana, Tr. Among plum trees (Fletcher)
— hypericana, Hb. *Wyre Forest* (W. H. Edwards)

2. TORTRICIDÆ

Rhacodia caudana, F. *Croft Wood*, August 11, 1898; *Nunnery Wood*, September 1, 1898, abundant; common (E. & T. p. 38)
Acalla (Peronea) hastiana, L. Common (E. & T. p. 38)
— literana, L. *St. John's* (Edwards)
— boscana, F. *Worcester* (M. p. 523)
— mixtana, Hb. *Worcestershire*
— lipsiana, Schiff. Common (E. & T. p. 38)
— variegana, Schiff. *Worcestershire*
— contaminana, Hb. Common
— shepherdana, Stph. Rather rare (E. & T. p. 37)
— aspersana, Hb. Six, *Worcestershire*; rare (E. & T. p. 38)
— holmiana, L. Common; near *Waterworks, Worcester*, June 29, 1896
Capua flavillaceana, Hb. *Eymore Wood*, May 15, 1863 (T.W.N.C. p. 79)
Cacœcia (Tortrix) podana, Sc. *Monk Wood*, June 20, 1895; *Perry Wood*, May 23, 1896; common
— cratægana, Hb. Common
— xylosteana, L. *Nunnery Wood*, August 4, 1898; common; rare (E. & T. p. 37)
— rosana, L. Common
— sorbiana, Hb. *Britannia Square*, June 9, 1896; *Trench Woods*, June 11, 1896; common; rare (E. & T. p. 37); *Bransford* (W. H. Edwards)
— costana, F. *Hartlebury Common*, July 20, 1898
— unifasciana, Dup. *Perry Wood*, July 4, 1895
— lecheana, L. *Wyre Forest*, June, 1896, common
— musculana, Hb. *Worcestershire*
Pandemis (Tortrix) corylana, F. Five, *Worcestershire*; common (E. & T. p. 37)
— ribeana, Hb. Very common (E. & T. p. 37)
— heparana, Schiff. *Perry Wood*, April 13, 1895

INSECTS

Pandemis cinnamomeana, Tr. *Middleyards,* July 14, 1896

Tortrix forskaleana, L. ⎱ *Nunnery Wood,* June
— bergmanniana, L. ⎰ 26, 1896; common

— ministrana, L. *Perry Wood,* May 21, 1900

— conwayana, F. *Trench Woods,* June 15, 1895 ; *Lord's Wood,* June 27, 1896 ; *Perry Wood,* July 10, 1896

— loeflingiana, L. *Nunnery Wood,* June 26, 1896

— viridana, L. *Perry Wood,* June 13, 1895; a common pest

— paleana, Hb. At ' light,' *St. John's* (Fletcher); very common (E. & T. p. 36)

— viburniana, F. *Worcestershire*

— forsterana, F. *Monk Wood,* July 11, 1895; *Wyre Forest, Bransford,* etc.

— (Sciaphila) virgaureana, Tr. *Worcestershire*

— octomaculana, Hw. Common (E. & T. p. 38)

— osseana, Sc. Rather common (E. & T. p. 39)

Isotrias hybridana, Hb. Common (E. & T. p. 38)

Exapate congelatella, Cl. *Dine's Green* (Fletcher)

Cheimatophila tortricella, Hb. Very common

3. PHALONIADÆ

Lozopera dilucidana, Stph. *Perry Wood* (Fletcher)

Phalonia (Argyrolepia) zephyrana, Tr. *Worcester* (M. p. 547)

— badiana, Hb. *Worcestershire*

— tesserana, Tr. *Coneybury Copse* (Fletcher)

— (Eupœcilia) nana, Hw. Rather rare (E. & T. p. 39)

Chlidonia baumanniana, Schiff. Common

Eupœcilia maculosana, Hw. *Worcestershire*

Euxanthis (Eupœcilia) angustana, Tr. Four, *Worcestershire* ; one to ' light,' *Dine's Green* (Fletcher) ; rather common (E. & T. p. 36)

— (Conchylis) straminea, Hw. *Worcester* ; one to ' light,' *Oldbury Road* (Fletcher)

— (Xanthosetia) zoegana, L. *Middleyards,* May 29, 1895 ; *Kepax Ferry,* June 12, 1898 ; *Monk Wood* (W. H. Edwards); common (E. & T. p. 39)

— hamana, L. *Monk Wood,* July 11, 1895; *Bransford,* June 3, 1896 ; common (E. & T. p. 39)

4. TRYPANIDÆ

Trypanus cossus (Cossus ligniperda), L. Larvæ, *Worcester,* 1898, 1900 ; *Old Hills* and *St. John's* (W. H. Edwards)

VIII. *TINEINA*
1. ÆGERIADÆ

Ægeria apiformis, Cl. Larvæ, *Old Hills,* May 3, 1896 ; *Powick, Hanley,* eight, not uncommon (T.M.N.F.C. p. 177); larvæ near *Spetchley,* 1899 (J. Peed)

— crabroniformis, Lew. *Bredon* and *Ockeridge* (W. H. Edwards) ; *Monk Wood,* 1898 (J. Peed)

Trochilium spheciforme, Gern. *Wyre Forest,* June 6, 1897, June 11, 18, 1899

— tipuliforme, Cl. *Dr. Clarke's garden, Worcester,* 1898 ; *Wyre Forest*

— asiliforme, Rott. *Wyre Forest,* June 6, 1897 ; *Monk Wood* and *Trench Woods* (W. H. Edwards) ; *Temple Laughern* (Fletcher) ; *Ockeridge* (J. Peed)

— myopiforme, Bkh. *Goodyear's garden, Malvern Link* (R.F.T., E. & T. p. 8); *Rose House, Worcester,* 1900 (J. Peed)

— culiciforme, L. *Wyre Forest,* June 6, 1897

— formiciforme, Esp. Osier beds near *Worcester,* 1897 (G. D. Hancock and J. Peed)

— ichneumoniforme, F. *Crown East* (Fletcher)

2. GELECHIADÆ

Epithectis mouffetela, Schiff. Five, *Worcestershire* ; *Wyre Forest* (Fletcher)

Anacampsis vorticella, Sc. *Tibberton* (Fletcher)

Xenolechia scalella, Sc. *Wyre Forest,* May 23, 1896, June 5, 7, 1897 ; *Monk Wood,* June 8, 1898, May 25, 1899

Gelechia politella, Stt. *Oddingley* ⎱ (Fletcher)
— maculea, Hw. *Ombersley* ⎰

— luculella, Hb. *Ribbesford,* July 17, 1897

— notatella, Hb. *Martley* (Fletcher)

— sororculella, Hb. Among sallows, *Middleyards* (Fletcher)

— scotinella, H.S. *Middleyards Lane* (Fletcher)

— rhombella, Schiff. *Spetchley* (Fletcher)

— lentiginosella, Z. *Worcester* (St. vol. ii. p. 331)

Brachmia rufescens, Hw. (Fletcher)

Ypsolophus marginellus, F. *The Slads,* July 24, 1899 ; *Pitmaston* (Fletcher)

— fasciellus, Hb. (M. p. 609) ; *Trench Woods* (Fletcher)

— ustulellus, F. (M. p. 609)

Chelaria huebnerella, Don. One, *Worcestershire*

3. ŒCOPHORIDÆ

Carcina quercana, F. Common ; *Lord's Wood,* June 27, 1896 ; *Dodderhill Common,* July 16, 1896, etc.

Hypercallia christiernana, L. *Wyre Forest,* July 8, 1900

Aplota palpella, Hw. *Bransford* (Fletcher)
Chimabache phryganella, Hb. ⎱
— fagella, F.   ⎰ Common
Semioscopis steinkellneriana, Schiff. *Worcester*
    (Fletcher)
Exæretia allisella, Stt. At 'light,' *Oldbury*
    Road (Fletcher)
Depressaria ocellana, F. At sallows, *Brans-*
    ford, March 19, 1896
— yeatiana, F. At 'light,' *Worcester*
    (Fletcher)
— applana, F. *Worcester*
— chærophylli, Z. *Dine's Green* (Fletcher)
— pulcherrimella, Stt. Indoors (Fletcher)
— heracliana, De Geer. *Laughern Plantation*,
    1897
Harpella geoffrella, L. *Perry Wood*, May 13,
    1896
Œcophora sulphurella, F. *Cowleigh Park*,
    May 27, 1897 ; *Stretton's Garden*, May
    22, 1898
Acompsia (Œcophora) grandis, Desv. *Bewdley*
    Forest (St. vol. ii. p. 357, M. 635)
— tripuncta, Hw. *Worcestershire*
— tinctella, Hb. *Shrawley Wood* (Fletcher)
— unitella, Hb. *Comer Lane* (Fletcher)
— panzerella, Stph. *Wyre Forest* (Fletcher)

4. ELACHISTIDÆ

Coleophora fabriciella, Vill. *Trench Woods*,
    Oddingley (Fletcher)
— frischella, L. *Himbleton* ⎫
— alcyonipennella, Koll. *Pirton* ⎬ (Fletcher)
— siccifolia, Stt. *Powick*   ⎭
— vibicella, Hb. *Trench Woods*, June, 1896
    (St. vol. ii. p. 389, Fletcher)
— albicosta, Hw. *Old Hills* (Fletcher)
Elachista albifrontella, Hb. *Perry Wood*, June
    6, 15, 1898
— gangabella, Z. *Worcestershire*
— triatomea, Hw. *Monk Wood*
— cygnipennella, Hb. *Perry Wood*, June 6,
    1898 ; *Bredon*, June 3, 1897 ; *Rock*,
    May 18, 1898
Pancalia leuwenhoekella, L. ⎱
Chrysoclista bimaculella, H. ⎰ *Worcester*
— linneella, Cl. *Cotheridge* (Fletcher)
— atra, Hw. *Bransford*, July 25, 1898
Mompha (Laverna) decorella, Stph. At 'light,'
    near *Worcester* (Fletcher)
— miscella, Schiff. *Oddingley* (Fletcher)
Heliozela resplendella, Stph. By *Laughern*
    Brook (Fletcher)
Antispila pfeifferela, Hb. One to 'light,' near
    Worcester (Fletcher)
Scythris (Butalis) fuscoænea, Hw. *Wyre*
    Forest (Fletcher)
— fuscocuprea, Hw. *Coneybury Copse*
    (Fletcher)
Endrosis lacteella, Schiff. Common

Epermenia (Chauliodus) illigerella, Hb.
    Worcester (St. vol. ii. p. 397, M. 691);
    Tibberton (Fletcher)

5. PLUTELLIDÆ

Prays curtisellus, Don. *Bransford*
Yponomeuta cognatellus, Hb. *Worcester*
— padellus, L. *Croft Bank, Broadway, Trench*
    Woods, etc.
— plumbellus, Schiff. Near *Worcester*
— vigintipunctatus, Retz. *Foregate Street*
Cerostoma caudella, L. ⎱
— xylostella, L.   ⎰ *Worcestershire*
— alpella, Schiff. *Wyre Forest* (Fletcher)
— costella, F. *Worcestershire*
— sequella, Cl. *Lovington* (Fletcher)
Plutella porrectella, L. ⎱
— cruciferarum, Z.   ⎰ *Worcestershire*
Glyphipteryx fuscoviridella, Hw. *Ombersley*
— thrasonella, Sc. *The Slads*
— oculatella, Z. *Worcester* (M. p. 704) ;
    Crown East (Fletcher)
— equitella, Sc. *Ockeridge* ; *Great Witley*
    (Fletcher)
— fischeriella, Z. *Middleyards* (Fletcher)
Simæthis fabriciana, L. *Perdiswell*, 1895;
    Middleyards, May 9, 1896, etc.

6. TINEIDÆ

Nepticula aurella, Tutt. (vol i. p. 233)
Bucculatrix nigricomella, Z. *The Grove Farm*
    (Fletcher)
— boyerella, Dup. *Dine's Green* ⎫
— ulmella, Z. *Oldbury Road*   ⎬ (Fletcher)
— cratægi, Z. *Martley Road*   ⎭
Lithocolletis amyotella, Dup. *Worcester* (M.
    p. 737)
— cramerella, F. Common
— pomifoliella, Z.   ⎫
— spinicolella, Stt.   ⎬
— corylifoliella, Hw. ⎬ *Worcestershire*
— tristrigella, Hw.   ⎭
Ornix guttea, Hw. At 'light' (Fletcher)
— betulæ, Stt. *Wyre Forest* ; by mothing
    (Fletcher)
Gracilaria alchimiella, Sc. *Trench Woods*,
    May 18, 1895 ; *Perry Wood*, May 21,
    1895 ; *Monk Wood*, July 17, 1895
— ononidis, Z. *Worcester* (M. p. 753) ; one
    indoors (Fletcher)
— hofmanniella, Schleich. (M. p. 754)
Leucoptera (Cemiostoma) spartifoliella, Hb.
    Worcestershire
Lyonetia prunifoliella, Hb. *Boughton* (Fletcher)
Bedellia somnulentella, Z. Three larvæ
    found (Fletcher)
Tischeria complanella, Hb. *Worcestershire*
— angusticollella, Z. *Worcester* (M. p. 760)
Argyresthia brockeella, Hb. *Britannia Square*,
    June 21, 1896

Argyresthia gœdartella, L. *Wyre Forest*
— pygmæella, Hb. From sallow catkins, *Middleyards*
— retinella, Z. ⎫
— conjugella, Z. ⎬ *Worcestershire*
— ephippella, F. ⎪
— nitidella, F. ⎭
Zelleria hepariella, Stt. One at *Middleyards* (Fletcher)
Swammerdamia combinella, Hb. *Crown East* (Fletcher)
Roeslerstammia erxlebella, F. *Worcestershire*
Fumea sepium, Spr. *Worcester* (M. p. 774); *Old Hills* (Fletcher)
Solenobia inconspicuella, Stt. Lichen covered palings (Fletcher)
— Douglasii, Stt. *Worcester* (M. p. 775)
Ochsenheimeria bisontella, Z. *Lathe Hill* (Fletcher)
— vacculella, F.R. *Ronkswood* (Fletcher)
Scythropia cratægella, L. ⎫
Incurvaria pectinea, Hw. ⎪
— muscalella, F. ⎬ *Worcestershire*
Lampronia luzella, Hb. ⎪
— rubiella, Bjerk. ⎭
Trichophaga (Tinea) tapetiella, L. 34, *Foregate Street*, June, 1897; *Museum, Victoria Institute, Worcester* (W. H. Edwards)
Tinea capitella, Cl. *Worcester*
— arcella, F. ⎫ *Worcestershire*
— parasitella, Hb. ⎭
— caprimulgella, H.S. *Crown East* (Fletcher)
— fuscipunctella, Hw. ⎫
— pellionella, L. ⎬ *Worcestershire*
— lapella, Hb. ⎭
— semifulvella, Hw. *Comer Lane* (Fletcher)
Nemophora swammerdammella, L. *Bransford*, May 9, 1896; *Middleyards* (Fletcher)
— schwarziella, Z. *Bransford*, May 4, 1896; *Oddingley* (Fletcher)
— metaxella, Hb. *Middleyards* (Fletcher)
Adela fibulella, Schiff. *Bransford*, May 14, 1895; *Tibberton* (Fletcher)
— crœsella, Sc. *The Slads*, June 16, 1898; *Comer Lane* (Fletcher)
— degeerella, L. *Monk Wood*, May 26, 1895; *Wyre Forest*, June 6, 7, 1896, June 12, 1899
— viridella, Sc. Common
Nemotois cupriacellus, Hb. *Oddingley* (Fletcher)

IX. *MICROPTERYGINA*

1. HEPIALIDÆ

Hepialus hectus, L. *Perry Wood*, June 19, 1895; *Monk Wood*, May 30, 1896; *Crown East* (W. H. Edwards); common
— lupulinus, L. Common

Hepialus velleda, Hb. *Farley Wood*, June 21, 1900; *Old Storridge* (W. E.); local (E. & T. p. 8)
— var. gallicus. *Nunnery Wood* (I.N.H.W. p. 140)
— sylvinus, L. *Perry Wood* (I.N.H.W. p. 140); near *Worcester* and about *Cowleigh*, August, not common (T.M.N.F.C. p. 178); rather rare (E. & T. p. 8); *Trench Woods* (W. H. Edwards); *Castle Morton*, not common (Rev. E. C. Dobrée Fox)
— humuli, L. Common

2. MICROPTERYGIDÆ

Micropteryx sparmannella, Bosc. *Worcestershire*
— purpurella, Hw. *Trench Woods*, April 19, 1899
— semipurpurella, Stph. *Worcestershire*
Eriocephala aureatella, Sc. *Eymore*, May 15, 1863 (T.W.N.C. p. 79)

The following somewhat local lepidoptera have been observed at the various places mentioned.

WYRE FOREST.—The Dark Green Fritillary (*Argynnis aglaia*), the Greasy Fritillary (*Melitæa aurinia*), the Narrow-bordered Bee Hawk (*Hemaris bombyliformis*), the White-barred Clearwing (*Trochilium spheciforme*), Yellow-belted Clearwing (*T. asiliforme*, Large Red-belted Clearwing (*T. culiciforme*), the Forester (*Procris statices*), the Least Black Arches (*Roeselia confusalis*), the Clouded Buff (*Diacrisia russula*), the Scarce Vapourer (*Orgyia gonostigma*), the Pale Eggar (*Eriogaster cratægi*), the Fox (*E. rubi*), the Kentish Glory (*Endromis versicolora*), the Emperor (*Saturnia pavonia*), the Lobster (*Stauropus fagi*), the Marbled Brown (*Drymonia trimacula*), the whole of the Polyplocidæ with the exception of the Frosted Orange (*Polyploca ridens*), the Nut-tree Tussock (*Colocasia coryli*), the Miller (*Acronycta leporina*), the Coronet (*A. ligustri*), the Reddish Arches (*Hadena sublustris*), the Birdswing (*H. scabriuscula*), the Large Nutmeg (*H. sordida*), the Dotted Rustic (*Caradrina alsines*), the Light-feathered Rustic (*Agrotis cinerea*), the Barred Chestnut (*A. dahlii*), the Northern Drab (*Monima opima*), the Powdered Quaker (*M. gracilis*), the Blossom Underwing (*M. miniosa*), the Orange Upperwing (*Orthosia croceago*), the Great Oak Beauty (*Diastictis roboraria*), the Barred Sallow (*Orthosia aurago*), the Brown Dart (*Aporophyla lutulenta*), the Silvery Arches (*Melanchra tincta*), the Pale Shining Brown (*M. advena*), the Dog's Tooth

(*M. dissimilis*), the Beautiful Brocade (*M. contigua*), the Lesser Snout (*Hypena rostralis*), the Little Thorn (*Cepphis advenaria*), the Blotched Emerald (*Euchloris pustulata*), the Waved Carpet (*Euchœca sylvata*), the Dotted Border (*Eois straminata*), the Satin Wave (*E. subsericeata*), the Seraphim (*Lobophora halterata*), the Yellow-barred Brindle (*Trichopteryx viretata*), the Argent and Sable (*Plemyria hastata*), the White Spot (*Pyrausta octomaculata*), the Dotted Grey (*Epithectis mouffetella*), the Black-spotted White (*Xenolechia scalella*), the Christiernian (*Hypercallia christiernana*), Panzers (*Acompsia panzerella*), and the Double-barred (*Cerostoma alpella*)

RIBBESFORD WOOD.—The Tortrix Moth (*Sarrothripus undulana*), the Scallop Shell (*Calocalpe undulata*), Dark Silver-striped (*Pammene nitidana*)

SHRAWLEY WOOD.—Orange Sallow (*Orthosia citrago*), Chequered Straw (*Evergestis straminalis*)

THE RAN DANS.—The Wood Tiger (*Arctia plantaginis*)

ODDINGLEY.—The Little Blue (*Chrysophanus minimus*), the Brown Argus (*C. astrarche*), the Gold China-mark (*Pyrausta flavalis*), the Narrow Long-cloak (*Eucosma oblongana*), *Gelechia politella*, *Nemotois cupriacellus*

THE TRENCH WOODS.—The Wood White (*Leucophasia sinapis*), the Clouded Yellow (*Colias edusa*), the Duke of Burgundy Fritillary (*Nemeobius lucina*), the Narrow-bordered Bee Hawk (*Hemaris bombyliformis*), the Yellow-belted Clearwing (*Trochilium asiliforme*), the Forester (*Procris statices*), the Wood Swift (*Hepialus sylvinus*), the Festoon (*Apoda limacodes*), the Dark Tussock (*Dasychira fascelina*), the Oak Hook-tip (*Drepana binaria*), the Powdered Quaker (*Monima gracilis*), the Blossom Underwing (*M. miniosa*), the Twin-spotted Quaker (*M. munda*), the Light Orange Underwing (*Brephos notha*), the Great Oak Beauty (*Diastictis roboraria*), the Silver Cloud (*Pseudopanthera punctata*), the Mallow (*Xanthorhoe cervinata*), the Warted Knot-horn (*Acrobasis tumidana*), the Long-winged (*Ypsolophus fasciellus*), *Coleophora vibicella*

HIMBLETON.—The Marbled White (*Melanargia galathea*), *Coleophora frischella*

OCKERIDGE WOOD.— The Wood White (*Leucophasia sinapis*), the Lunar Hornet (*Ægeria crabroniformis*), the Yellow-belted Clearwing (*Trochilium asiliforme*), the Large Red-belted Clearwing (*T.

culiciforme*), the Orange Footman (*Lithosia sororcula*), the Chocolate Tip (*Pygæra curtula*), the Oak Hook-tip (*Drepana binaria*), the Miller (*Acronycta leporina*), the White Letter (*Triphæna leucographa*), the Lead-coloured Drab (*Monima populeti*), the Orange Sallow (*Orthosia citrago*), the Olive (*Caradrina subtusa*), the White-spotted (*Erastria fasciana*), the Grey Birch (*Ectropis punctularia*), the White-spot (*E. luridata*), the Large Emerald (*Geometra papilionaria*), the False Mocha (*Leucophthalmia porata*) the Drab Looper (*Asthena murinata*) the Striped Twin-spot (*Xanthorhoe salicata*), the Purplish Knot-horn (*Salebria betulæ*)

MONK WOOD.—The Wood White (*Leucophasia sinapis*), the Dark Green Fritillary (*Argynnis aglaia*), the Silver-Washed Fritillary (*A. paphia*), the Marbled White (*Melanargia galathea*), the Yellow-belted Clearwing (*Trochilium asiliforme*), the Large Red-belted Clearwing (*T. culiciforme*), the Forester (*Procris statices*), the Tortrix Moth (*Sarrothripus undulana*), the Orange Footman (*Lithosia sororcula*), the Rosy Footman (*Miltochrista miniata*), the Four-dotted Footman (*Cybosia mesomella*), the Oak Hook-tip (*Drepana binaria*), the Chocolate-tip (*Pygæra curtula*), the Figure of Eighty (*Palimpsestis octogesima*), the Coronet (*Acronycta ligustri*), the Autumnal Rustic (*Agrotis glareosa*), the Twin-spotted Quaker (*Monima munda*), the Olive (*Caradrina subtusa*), the Pale Shining Brown (*Melanchra advena*), the Silver Cloud (*M. conspicillaris*), the White-spotted Marble (*Erastria fasciana*), the Orange Underwing (*Brephos parthenias*), the Light Orange Underwing (*B. notha*), the Purple Thorn (*Selenia tetralunaria*), the Blotched Emerald (*Euchloris pustulata*), the Treble Brown Spot (*Eois trigeminata*), the Plain Wave (*E. inornata*), Haworth's Carpet (*Hydriomena unifasciata*), the Seraphim (*Lobophora halterata*), *Enarmonia oppressana*, the Hooked Marble (*Ancylis lactana*), the Black Double-blotched (*Epiblema ophthalmicana*), *Laspeyresia servillana*

PERRY WOOD.—The Gold Swift (*Hepialus hectus*), the Figure of Eighty (*Palimpsestis octogesima*), the Blotched Emerald (*Euchloris pustulata*), *Lozopera dilucidana*

NUNNERY WOOD.—The Powdered Quaker (*Monima gracilis*), the Blossom Underwing (*M. miniosa*), the Dotted Chestnut (*Conistra rubiginea*)

THE CROWN EAST WOODS.—The Large Green Silver-lined (*Hylophila bicolor-

ana), the Gold Swift (*Hepialus hectus*), the Powdered Quaker (*Monima gracilis*), the Blossom Underwing (*M. miniosa*), the Twin-spotted Quaker (*M. munda*), the Lesser Snout (*Hypena rostralis*), the Blotched Emerald (*Euchloris pustulata*), *Hemimene sequana*, *Glyphipteryx oculatella*, *Tinea caprimulgella*

MIDDLEYARDS.—The Wood White (*Leucophasia sinapis*), the Pale Clouded Yellow (*Colias hyale*), the White-letter Hairstreak (*Thecla w-album*), the Large Green Silver-lined (*Hylophila bicolorana*), the Least Black Arches (*Roeselia confusalis*), the Festoon (*Apoda limacodes*), the Oak Hook-tip (*Drepana binaria*), the Coronet (*Acronycta ligustri*), the Twin-spotted Quaker (*Monima munda*), the Double Kidney (*Caradrina retusa*), the White-spotted Pinion (*C. diffinis*), the Lesser White-spotted Pinion (*C. affinis*), the Bordered Straw (*C. umbra*), the White-spotted Marbled (*Erastria fasciana*), the White-streak (*Hypenodes albistrigalis*), the Lesser Snout (*Hypena rostralis*), the Blotched Emerald (*Euchloris pustulata*), the Small Scallop (*Eois emarginata*), *Hypochalcia ahenella*, Thistle Ermine (*Myelois cribrella*), Pearl Veneer (*Crambus pinellus*), the Wainscot Veneer (*Chilo phragmitellus*), the Naked-winged (*Ancylis derasana*), *Gelechia scotinella*, *Aplota palpella*, *Chrysoclista atra*, *Nemophora metaxella*

PARK WOOD.—The Purple Emperor (*Apatura Iris*), the White Letter (*Triphæna leucographa*)

COCKSHOT HILL WOOD.—The Lunar Hornet (*Ægeria crabroniformis*)

THE CROFT WOOD.—The Clouded Yellow (*Colias edusa*), the White Admiral (*Lymenitis sibilla*), the Marbled White (*Melanargia galathea*), the Small Blue (*Chrysophanus minimus*), the Cistus Forester (*Procris geryon*), the Narrow-bordered Five-spot Burnet (*Zygæna loniceræ*), the Miller (*Acronycta leporina*), the Little Thorn (*Cepphis advenaria*), the Silver Cloud (*Pseudopanthera punctata*), the Scallop Shell (*Calocalpe undulata*)

BOW WOOD.—The Marbled White (*Melanargia galathea*)

TIDDESLEY WOOD.—The Lappet (*Gastrophaca quercifolia*), the Blotched Emerald (*Euchloris pustulata*), the Waved Carpet (*Euchœca sylvata*)

CROOME PERRY WOODS.—The Blotched Emerald (*Euchloris pustulata*)

BREDON.—The Marbled White (*Melanargia galathea*), the Brown Argus (*Chrysophanus astrarche*), the Lunar Hornet

(*Ægeria crabroniformis*), the Cistus Forester (*Procris geryon*), the Scarce Footman (*Lithosia complana*), the Wood Tiger (*Arctia plantaginis*), the Four-spotted (*Eustrotia luctuosa*), the Golden Wave (*Euchœca blomeri*), the Lace Border (*Leptomeris ornata*), the Chalk Carpet (*Hydriomena procellata*), the Small Waved Umber (*Eucrymatoge vitalbata*), the Chalk Carpet (*Xanthorhoe bipunctaria*), the Sweep (*Baptria atrata*), the Scarce Pearl (*Psammotis hyalinalis*), Wavy-barred Sable (*Pyrausta nigrata*)

GREAT FARLEY WOOD.—The Northern Swift (*Hepialus velleda*)

THE LICKEY.—The Holly Blue (*Lycæna argiolus*), the Wood Tiger (*Arctia plantaginis*), the Emperor (*Saturnia pavonia*)

THE BERROW HILL, MARTLEY.—The Duke of Burgundy Fritillary (*Nemeobius lucina*), the Chequered Skipper (*Cyclopædes palæmon*), the Swallowtail (*Papilio machaon*)

ANKERDINE HILL.—The Treble Brown Spot (*Eois trigeminata*), the Figure of Eighty (*Palimpsestis octogesima*)

BROADWAY HILL.—The Little Blue (*Chrysophanus minimus*), the Brown Argus (*C. astrarche*)

MALVERN HILLS.—The Camberwell Beauty (*Vanessa antiopa*), the Grayling (*Satyrus semele*), the Duke of Burgundy Fritillary (*Nemeobius lucina*), the Holly Blue (*Lycæna argiolus*), the Bedstraw Hawk (*Deilephila galii*), the Five-spot Burnet (*Zygæna trifolii*), the Wood Tiger (*Arctia plantaginis*), the Lunar Yellow Underwing (*Agrotis orbona*), the Mottled Grey (*Xanthorhoe multistrigaria*)

BLACKMORE PARK.—The Maple Prominent (*Odontosia cuculla*)

THE OLD HILLS.—The Bedstraw Hawk (*Deilephila galii*), the Hornet Clearwing (*Ægeria apiformis*), *Fumea sepium*

MADRESFIELD.—The Crimson-speckled Footman (*Utethesia pulchella*)

BROAD HEATH.—The Emperor (*Saturnia pavonia*), the Small Grass Emerald (*Nemoria viridata*)

POWICK HAM.—The Forester (*Procris statices*)

COTHERIDGE.—The White-letter Hair-streak (*Thecla w-album*), *Chrysoclista linneella*

SPETCHLEY PARK.—The Brindled Beauty (*Biston hirtarius*)

DINE'S GREEN AND OLDBURY ROAD.—The Pearl Veneer (*Crambus pinellus*), the Chequered Veneer (*C. falsellus*), *Exapate congelatella*, *Depressaria chærophylli*, *Bucculatrix boyerella*, *Exaeretia allisella*

OLD STORRIDGE COMMON.—The Northern Swift (*Hepialus velleda*)

MALVERN LINK.—The Greasy Fritillary (*Melitæa aurinia*), the White‑letter Hair-streak (*Thecla w-album*), the Striped Hawk (*Deilephila lineata*), Silver-striped Hawk (*D. celerio*), the Red-belted Clearwing (*Trochilium myopiforme*)

MALVERN WELLS.—The Confused (*Hadena furva*)

MATHON LODGE.—The Large Tortoiseshell (*Vanessa polychloros*)

HARTLEBURY COMMON.—The Fox (*Eriogaster rubi*), the Dotted Border (*Eois straminata*), the Large Twin‑spot Carpet (*Xanthorhoe quadrifasciaria*), the Aquatic Veneer (*Schœnobius forficellus*), Greening's Plume (*Oxyptilus teucrii*)

THE SLADS.—The Marbled White (*Melanargia galathea*), the Little Blue (*Lycæna minimus*), the Four-spotted (*Eustrotia luctuosa*), the Juniper Pug (*Tephroclystis sobrinata*), the Purple (*Eucosma purpurana*), the White-bordered (*Ypsolophus marginellus*), Sultz's (*Adela crœsella*)

OFFENHAM.—The Striped Hawk Moth (*Deilephila livornica*)

CASTLE MORTON.—The Large Tortoiseshell (*Vanessa polychloros*), the Scarce Footman (*Lithosia complana*), the Wood Swift (*Hepialus sylvinus*), the Grisette (*Acronycta strigosa*), the Small Wainscot (*Caradrina fulva*), the Hedge Rustic (*Melanchra cespitis*), the Crescent-striped Rustic (*Hadena abjecta*), the Large Nutmeg (*H. sordida*), the Dot (*Melanchra persicariæ*), the Rosy Minor (*Hadena literosa*), the Mottled Rustic (*Caradrina morpheus*), the Dotted Rustic (*C. alsines*), the Pearly Underwing (*Agrotis saucia*), the Stout Dart (*A. obscura*), the Six-striped Rustic (*A. umbrosa*), the Northern Drab (*Monima opima*), the Dismal (*Orthosia ypsilon*), the Dotted Chestnut (*Conistra rubiginea*), the Barred Sallow (*Orthosia aurago*), the Dusky Lemon Sallow (*O. gilvago*), the Centre-barred Sallow (*O. xerampelina*), the White-spotted Pinion (*Caradrina diffinis*), the Brown Dart (*Aporophyla lutulenta*), the Dog's Tooth (*Melanchra dissimilis*), the Silver Cloud (*M. conspicillaris*), the Tawny Pinion (*Polia semibrunnea*), the Chamomile Shark (*Cucullia chamomillæ*), the Bordered Straw (*Caradrina umbra*), the Pinion-spotted Pug (*Tephroclystis insigniata*), the Yellow-

barred Brindle (*Trichopteryx viretata*), the Flame (*Hydriomena rubidata*), the Broom-tip (*Eucestia rufata*)

DOWLES BROOK.—The Miller (*Acronycta leporina*)

LAUGHERN BROOK.—The Miller (*Acronycta leporina*), the Alder (*A. alni*), the Frosted Orange (*Ochria ochracea*)

NEW POOL.—The Small Wainscot (*Caradrina fulva*)

LADY POOL.—The Birdswing (*Hadena scabriuscula*)

THE SEVERN.—The Double Kidney (*Caradrina retusa*), the Miller (*Acronycta leporina*)

The following are in the larval state sometimes common pests of our orchards, hopyards, market gardens and roots :—

The Large White (*Pieris brassicæ*), the Small White (*P. rapæ*), the Green-veined White (*P. napi*), the Comma (*Vanessa c-album*), the Death's Head (*Acherontia atropos*), the Eyed Hawk (*Sphinx ocellatus*), the Currant Clearwing (*Trochilium tipuliforme*), the Red-belted Clearwing (*T. myopiforme*), the Short Cloak (*Nolla cucullatella*), the Least Black Arches (*Roeselia confusalis*), the Ghost (*Hepialus humuli*), the Black Arches (*Ocneria monacha*), the Goat (*Trypanus cossus*), the Wood Leopard (*Zeuzera pyrina*), the Pale Tussock (*Dasychira pudibunda*), the Vapourer (*Orgia antiqua*), the Lackey (*Clisiocampa neustria*), the Gold Tail (*Porthesia similis*), the Buff-tip (*Phalera bucephala*), the Dagger (*Acronycta psi*), the Cabbage Moth (*Melanchra brassicæ*), the Dark Sword-grass (*Agrotis suffusa*), the Turnip Moth (*A. segetum*), the Heart and Dart (*A. exclamationis*), the Gothic (*A. typica*), the Bright‑line (*Melanchra oleracea*), the V. Moth (*Diastictis wauaria*), the Magpie (*Abraxas grossulariata*), the Mottled Rustic (*Caradrina morpheus*), the Silver Y (*Plusia gamma*), the Figure of Eight (*Diloba cæruleocephala*), the Willow Beauty (*Selidosema gemmaria*), the Brimstone (*Opisthograptis luteolata*), the Spinach (*Eustroma associata*), the Mottled Umber (*Hybernia defoliaria*), the Winter Moth (*Operophtera brumata*), the Green Pug (*Chloroclystis rectangulata*), the Garden Carpet (*Xanthorhoe fluctuata*), the Phœnix (*Eustroma prunata*), the Garden Pebble (*Mesographe forficalis*), the Apple Tree (*Carpocapsa pomonella*)

SPIDERS

ARACHNIDA

Spiders, etc.

Scarcely any collections have been made of members of this order in the county of Worcestershire, so that very little is known of its spider-fauna. The twenty-nine species contained in the following short list were collected by Mrs. Martin of Norton, R. Innes Pocock, Esq., F.Z.S., and by Miss Vaughan of Whittington.

DRASSIDÆ

1. *Scotophæus blackwallii* (Thorell).
   Whittington (Vaughan).

CLUBIONIDÆ

2. *Clubiona pallidula* (Clerck).
   Norton (R. I. P.).
3. *Clubiona corticalis*, Walckenaer.
   Norton (R. I. P.).
4. *Clubiona brevipes*, Blackwall.
   Norton (R. I. P.).

AGELENIDÆ

5. *Tegenaria atrica*, C. L. Koch.
   Norton (R. I. P.) ; Whittington (Vaughan).
6. *Tegenaria derhami* (Scopoli).
   Norton (R. I. P.) ; Whittington (Vaughan).

ARGIOPIDÆ

7. *Araneus diadematus*, Clerck.
   Norton (R. I. P.) ; Whittington (Vaughan).
8. *Zilla* x - *notata* (Clerck).
   Whittington (Vaughan).
9. *Zilla atrica*, C. L. Koch.
   Whittington (Vaughan) ; Norton (R. I. P.).
10. *Meta segmentata* (Clerck).
    Whittington (Vaughan).
11. *Linyphia triangularis* (Clerck).
    Norton (R. I. P.).
12. *Linyphia montana*.
    Norton (R. I. P.).
13. *Linyphia peltata* (Wider).
    Norton (R. I. P.).

14. *Stemonyphantes lineatus* (Linnæus).
    Whittington (Vaughan).

THERIDIIDÆ

15. *Steatoda bipunctata* (Linnæus).
    Whittington (Vaughan).
16. *Theridion tepidariorum* (C. L. Koch).
    Whittington (Vaughan) ; Norton (R. I. P.).
17. *Theridion sisyphium* (Clerck).
    Norton (R. I. P.).
18. *Theridion ovatum* (Clerck).
    Norton (R. I. P.).
19. *Theridion varians*, Hahn.
    Norton (R. I. P.).
20. *Theridion denticulatum* (Walckenaer).
    Norton (R. I. P.).

THOMISIDÆ

21. *Philodromus aureolus* (Clerck).
    Norton (R. I. P.).

DICTYNIDÆ

22. *Amaurobius ferox* (Walckenaer).
    Norton (R. I. P.).
23. *Amaurobius similis* (Blackwall).
    Norton (R. I. P.) ; Whittington (Vaughan).
24. *Dictyna arundinacea* (Linnæus).
    Norton (R. I. P.).

LYCOSIDÆ

25. *Pardosa nigriceps* (Thorell).
    Norton (R. I. P.).
26. *Pardosa pullata* (Clerck).
    Norton (R. I. P.).

OPILIONES

27. *Phalangium parietinum*, De Geer.
    Whittington (Vaughan).
28. *Phalangium opilio*, Linnæus.
    Norton (R. I. P.).

29. *Oligolophus agrestis*, Meade.
    Norton (R. I. P.).

CRUSTACEANS

Scientific literature appears to contain scarcely any specific records relating to crustacea in Worcestershire. Nevertheless, with a view to the growing interest in questions of distribution and in the details of every local fauna, it may not be superfluous briefly to indicate what groups of crustacea will beyond question be found represented within the limits of the county, and some of the species the search for which will more or less certainly be rewarded with success.

The zoological class with which we are concerned is commonly divided into two principal branches, the Malacostraca and the Entomostraca. The former of these two has attained a position by far the higher in what may be called the scale of intellectual development, although by parasitic habits a few of its members have fallen back into a state of disgraceful degradation. Many persons are much surprised when first they hear that the unfavoured woodlouse is not only a crustacean, but belongs to the aristocratic section of the class, and is distinguished even in that section by having had the energy and enterprise to forsake an aquatic existence for life upon land. The tremendous character of the change from water-breathing to breathing air may be realized by any one who attempts to reverse the process. The woodlouse is a terrestrial isopod. An isopod is a sessile-eyed crustacean of the kind which as a rule has the breathing apparatus in the appendages of the pleon or tail-part. Of the land isopods some go wherever man goes ; some have their special provinces, districts, or isolated localities. England, without being very richly provided, has several genera and species, and some of these are so generally distributed over the country that their occurrence in this county, as in others, may be affirmed with the utmost confidence. Such are *Oniscus asellus*, Linn., ' very common throughout England, Scotland and Ireland under decaying vegetable and animal matter, not only in damp, but in the dryest localities ' ;[1] *Porcellio scaber*, Latreille, of which Bate and Westwood say that they have ' found it partial to growing vegetables, and it appears to possess a strong partiality for nearly ripe wall-fruit,' this dainty animal ' being widely distributed throughout England and Ireland ' ;[2] *Armadillidium vulgare* (Latreille), one of the ' pill-millepedes,' not to be confounded with the larger and less common *Glomeris marginata*, not a crustacean but a myriapod, with which it shares the habit of rolling itself up into a complete ball. Bate and Westwood expressly state that the *Armadillidium* is very abundant in the midland

[1] Bate and Westwood, *British Sessile-eyed Crustacea*, vol. ii. p. 471.   [2] *Loc. cit.* p. 477.

CRUSTACEANS

counties.'[1] To these may be added *Philoscia muscorum* (Scopoli), which ' prefers dry rather than damp situations, under leaves, stones and moss,' in accordance with the meaning of its name, the shade-loving tenant of mosses, a species which ' is found abundantly throughout the southern part of England.'[2]

The freshwater isopod, *Asellus aquaticus* (Linn.) and the freshwater amphipod, *Gammarus pulex* (Linn.) occupy all counties without fear or favour, the amphipod being like the isopod a sessile-eyed crustacean, that is to say, not having the eyes articulated as is the case with those organs in shrimps and lobsters. Otherwise an amphipod is very differently constructed from an isopod, having its heart in a different situation, in connection with the circumstance that its breathing apparatus is not in the tail part, but in the central compartment between head and tail.

After so far constructing a hypothetical carcinology for Worcestershire, I had the satisfaction of having it to some extent confirmed through a correspondence with the Rev. C. E. Ranken of Malvern, president of the Worcester Naturalists' Field Club. Mr. Ranken consulted the curator of the ' Hastings ' Museum, Victoria Institute, Worcester, and that gentleman, Mr. William H. Edwards, took the trouble of looking through several books and making enquiries. The conclusion Mr. Edwards came to was similar to my own, for he says, ' No one seems to have ever collected the Worcestershire crustacea, hence we have no *authentic* records.' At the same time he has begun to remove the deficiency by transmitting to me the paper which I now have the pleasure of quoting :—

' Crayfish (*Astacus fluviatilis*). We have a specimen in the museum taken in the river Severn near Worcester Bridge a few years ago ; also an old one from Dick Brook, Shrawley ; other localities for Worcestershire (as far as I know) are Crowle Brook and Dowles Brook near Bewdley.

' Freshwater Shrimp. I know nothing about the species or even genera, but what is "locally" known as the " Freshwater Shrimp " is common in the county ; but I am afraid this information is too vague to be of any value, and I cannot put my hand on specimens now.

' Woodlice. *Armadillidium vulgare* (the " Pill Woodlouse ") is common throughout the county wherever I have observed. I have seen large numbers when pupæ digging.

' *Porcellio scaber* (the " Common Woodlouse ") is only too common everywhere.

' *Oniscus asellus*. I am under the impression that I have seen this in Worcestershire, but not being a collector of crustacea, I have not observed closely enough to determine it with certainty, and though I have searched during the last few days, I have not been successful in finding specimens.'

On this welcome contribution a few remarks may be offered.

The river crayfish belongs to the genus *Potamobius*, which in various

[1] Bate and Westwood, *British Sessile-eyed Crustacea*, vol. ii. p. 495.　　　[2] *Loc. cit.* p. 451.

particulars differs from *Astacus*, the genus of the lobster. Apparently also the specific name *fluviatilis* is not the proper one for the crayfish of our English rivers, which ought rather perhaps to be called *Potamobius pallipes*. But whatever its exact designation, it has a special interest for inland counties as being the highest in rank of any crustacea that they can produce. It is not the only stalk-eyed crustacean to be found in England in fresh water, but none of the others appear to be met with far inland, and none of them approach the crayfish in size. It is only now that its distribution in our island is becoming gradually better known. For its eastward extension Mr. Walter Garstang, writing to me from the Plymouth Laboratory under date December 13th, 1900, quotes Mr. H. D. Geldart as vouching positively for its occurrence in the headwaters of the Bure, and in some other streams of the county of Norfolk, and now Mr. Edwards adds Worcestershire in the west to its domain. Huxley, discussing the absence or apparent absence of these crustaceans from localities in which they might have been expected, says: 'It is still more remarkable that, according to the best information I can obtain, they are absent in the Severn, though they are plentiful in the Thames and Severn canal.'[1]

The freshwater shrimp of which Mr. Edwards makes mention cannot well be anything but *Gammarus pulex*. The only other amphipods which the county is likely to possess are the subterranean species known as 'well-shrimps.' For their occurrence, indeed, we may claim one actual record, though whether it can strictly be called a specific record is open to question. In their interesting historical account of the genus *Niphargus*, Schiödte, Bate and Westwood include Worcestershire in the list of English localities from which specimens had been obtained. The specimens of which they are speaking are referred to the species *Niphargus aquilex*, Schiödte. The authors explain that they are found in wells surrounded by very diverse geological conditions, and append the following footnote: 'Shortly after the exhibition of the specimens from Maidenhead, at the Linnæan [Linnean] Society, Mr. Edwin Lees informed us of the discovery by himself of a specimen in water from the well of his own residence in Cedar Terrace, Henwick, Worcester. This well had been deepened in the preceding year into the red marl, which is the formation under gravel. The animal had not been previously seen, and only a single individual was observed.'[2] Since Bate and Westwood record three species of *Niphargus* and one of *Crangonyx* from English wells, since these small, pale, blind or purblind species are not so very easy even for experts to distinguish, and since the authors do not claim themselves to have seen the specimen from Cedar Terrace, it would be rash to guarantee its belonging to *Niphargus aquilex*. But the prolongation of the third uropods, which are the hindmost tail appendages, is a distinction between *Niphargus* and *Crangonyx* tolerably easy to observe, so that we may with some confidence accept the generic determination

[1] Huxley, *The Crayfish*, International Scientific Series, vol. xxviii. p. 288, ed. 3 (1881).
[2] *British Sessile-eyed Crustacea*, vol. i. p. 313.

CRUSTACEANS

as correct. Further records of these innocent and interesting animals, which from their pellucid appearance may be supposed to live on water as well as living in it, are much to be desired.

In regard to woodlice it may be observed that winter is an un-favourable season for collecting them, as they then show little or no activity and are more than ever withdrawn from view ; nor should it be supposed that only the species which have been here mentioned are likely to be found. Several others might be named as almost equally certain to occur, but they may be allowed to bide their time till con-jecture has been replaced by observation.

On turning to the Entomostraca we are confronted by possibilities indefinitely larger. If inductive philosophy can in anything be trusted, it will entitle us to affirm with supreme confidence that the waters ot Worcestershire will yield *Chydorus sphæricus* and *Daphnia pulex*, for ex-ample, among the Cladócera ; *Cyclocypris serena* among the Ostracóda ; *Cyclops viridis* among the Copépoda. Mr. J. D. Scourfield, writing in 1897, says of the Entomostraca, 'The freshwater forms hitherto re-corded may be estimated at 600, distributed as follows : Phyllopoda, 100 ; Cladocera, 200 ; Branchiura, 20 ; Ostracoda, 120 ; and Cope-poda, 160. Of these we have in the British Isles, as far as yet known, only about 190, namely Phyllopoda, 2 ; Cladocera, 75 ; Branchiura, 1 ; Ostracoda, 58 ; and Copepoda, 54.' Of the three largely represented groups several species have a more or less ubiquitous distribution. Of the two phyllopods *Apus cancriformis* seems to be at present either very rare in England or very seldom observed, whereas *Chirocephalus diaphanus*, after passing out of sight for a time, is now regaining notice. A third phyllopod, *Artemia salina*, was at one time well known as English, its habitat at Lymington in Hampshire being repeatedly mentioned in books concerned with Entomostraca. But it is no longer known at that locality, and when two or three years ago I made enquiries about it through a friend at Droitwich, this interesting brine shrimp was equally unknown there. The manager of the salt works however obligingly sent me some small beetles alive in salt, in which he said they had flourished for some weeks, having no other visible means of subsistence. It will be remembered that Dr. Baird in his account of the brine shrimps remarks that 'Their enemies, in such a fluid as the Artemia inhabits, are not numerous ; but their chief foe is a small beetle allied to the Dytiscus, which Mr. Joly observed at Montpellier, and proposes to name *Hydroporus salinus*. When it meets an Artemia it darts at it and bites it ; it then retires for a short time, but returns to the attack again and again, till it succeeds, by numerous bites, in killing the poor creature, and devouring it with astonishing avidity.'[1] Between the beetle and the shrimp our sympathy may be divided, for a diet exclu-sively of salt must have a peculiar monotony, to relieve which we may be sure that man himself would never hesitate to kill a crustacean. If the Droitwich insects be the same as those observed at Montpellier, there

[1] Baird, *British Entomostraca*, p. 60, Ray Soc. (1850).

is still a chance that where the foe exists there also the victim may be found.

Of the Branchiura the single British species, *Argulus foliaceus* (Linn.), parasitic on carp and trout and sticklebacks and some other fishes, is likely to be met with wherever its hosts are systematically searched for its discovery. It is easily recognized by its disk-like form and the pair of suckers which represent the second maxillæ.

Among parasites, which offer so rich a field for minute research, two others may be mentioned as with little doubt occurring in Worcestershire. These are the Copepoda, *Achtheres percarum*, von Nordmann, and *Lernæopoda salmonea* (Linn.). They agree in having one of their pairs of jaws, the maxillipeds, modified for attachment to the body of the fish they infest. As the specific names indicate, the former species devotes itself to the perch, while the other gives a preference to the salmon. The salmon, with its change of residence from salt water to fresh, has the interesting privilege of changing its parasites, the marine Copepoda forsaking it after it has left the sea, and giving place to the freshwater *Lernæopoda*. But I have the authority of Mr. J. W. Willis-Bund, F.L.S., of Wick Episcopi, Worcester, for including in the fauna of the county the seafaring parasite which is found on the clean-run salmon. The creature in question is named *Lepeophtheirus stromii*, Baird. It is much less abnormal than the form with which it is wont to change places, but still adaptation to life on the slippery body of a fish has made it in some respects unlike the free-swimming members of its order. It has a flattened appearance, the front division broadly oval, the tail part long and narrow, but not nearly so long as the parts which are frequently supposed to be its tail, namely, the two slender ovisacs, or egg-bearing tubes, which are three or four times as long as the body. The male is much smaller than the female. Mr. Willis-Bund has also observed parasites on trout and on some of the Cyprinidæ. Of the latter the carp is known to entertain *Ergasilus sieboldii*, von Nordmann, and other members of the family support other Copepoda of various eccentric shapes.

On the whole, then, it will be understood that if observed facts are rather meagre for a carcinological history of Worcestershire, there are very considerable natural opportunities for its future development.

FISHES

It has been the boast of Worcestershire that all the different kinds of English freshwater fish are to be found in one or other of the rivers in the county. There is more truth in this than in most of such generalizations, as the county is situate in the Severn and Trent watersheds. With one or two exceptions nearly all the different species of freshwater fish occur in the Severn and its tributaries, even if not in its Worcestershire tributaries; so it is possible, but most improbable, from their present condition that such of the English freshwater fish that are not found in the Severn watershed may be found in the Worcestershire streams that are the upper waters of some of the tributaries of the Trent.

Broadly speaking, for the purpose of the distribution of freshwater fish in England and Wales, a line representing the oolitic rocks running from Portland to the Humber divides the country into salmon rivers and coarse fish rivers; all east of the line being coarse fish, west of it salmon. It is not to be understood that no salmon are found to the east of the line, or coarse fish to the west, but that the eastern rivers are those suited for coarse fish, and were probably the original home of those fish, while the western rivers were the original home of the *Salmonidæ*, and salmon east of the line are mere survivals of a past state of things, while coarse fish west of the line are immigrants. One of the interesting points as to Worcestershire fish is the probability that originally there were no coarse fish in its rivers, but that through its tributary the Avon the immigration of coarse fish began. The date of this immigration it is perhaps impossible to fix, but it was no doubt aided and increased by the canals made during the last half of the eighteenth and the first quarter of the nineteenth centuries. In considering the Worcestershire fish the two divisions must be borne in mind, the original inhabitants and the immigrants, and these are broadly represented by the *Salmonidæ* and the *Cyprinidæ*.

Another great division of the Worcestershire fish, that is the Severn fish, is with regard to the place of breeding; several of the more important kinds are what are known as anadromous fish, that is they go up the rivers to spawn. These include the salmon (*Salmo salar*), the different forms of trout (*S. trutta*), the two species of shad, the allice (*Clupea alosa*) and the twaite (*C. finta*); and the two species of lamprey, the great sea lamprey (*Petromyzon marinus*) and the lampern (*P. fluviatilus*). The catadromous fish, those that descend from the rivers to breed in the sea, are represented only by the eel (*Anguilla vulgaris*), for although certain other forms drop down the rivers at different times of the year they do not appear to do so for breeding.

In order to keep up the stock of these two great divisions, the anadromous and catadromous, one thing is necessary: that their passage up

and down the river should be unobstructed. To intercept their passage, to catch them when migrating, all sorts of devices have been used and invented, and the statute book is one long story of the attempts of Parliament to secure a free passage for the anadromous fish. From Magna Charta to the present reign, Act after Act has been passed for this purpose, and it is not too much to say that none of them have been effectual. In Worcestershire a great change as to anadromous fish has been made in the last sixty years by the erection of weirs under the Severn Navigation Acts, which have had the effect of retarding the passage of fish up the river, partly by restricting the flow of the tide to below the county boundary, partly by preventing the free run of the fish at all times.

Another cause that has operated on the supply of the anadromous fish has been the erection of the large reservoir on the upper waters of the Verniew, one of the Welsh tributaries of the Severn. This reservoir, by impounding the rain-water, has diminished the number of spring and summer freshets, with the result that the anadromous fish have so many fewer opportunities of passing from the tidal to the fresh water, and are detained in the upper tidal water for a length of time instead of merely passing through it, and so are not only unable to come up but are caught there in greater numbers than was formerly the case.

A further cause that has tended to decrease the number of the anadromous fish is the fact that the law still allows the undiluted effluent from sewers to be discharged into a *tidal* river. The city of Gloucester discharges not only all its sewage but also all its manufacturing refuse, and after a storm, when the fish should be ascending the river, the sewers are washed out by the storm-water, and this effluent meeting the ascending fish turns them back again to the estuary.

These three causes—the obstructions, the decrease of summer freshets and the pollutions—have affected the stock of migratory fish in the Severn, causing it to decrease largely. The flounder, which used to ascend to Shrewsbury and beyond, is not now found above Worcester. Shad and twaite are only casual visitors as far as Worcester, instead of coming as formerly in cartloads. The number of lampreys is very small, and the supply of lamperns is largely reduced. As to salmon and sea trout, the same causes have diminished their numbers, but as to these fish there are special reasons for their decrease; but for the other anadromous fish the three causes above mentioned are the reasons they are rapidly ceasing to be Worcestershire fish. As to the catadromous fish, they too are largely decreasing in number, but this is not from the same causes. No doubt the cessation of summer floods has something to do with the catch being less than it used to be, for more eels were caught in a number of summer freshets than are now caught in one or two high floods. But the great cause of this falling off is the capture of the young eels when they are ascending the river in the spring. March, April and May, according to the weather, is the time for the elvers to ascend, and they then ascend in millions. To give some idea of the quantity caught, an elver would be about three inches long, and

probably at least a dozen would be required to go to an ounce—say two hundred to a pound. It is no unusual thing to take a ton of elvers in a night, that is over a million and three-quarters. It is true that this is only on the spring tides and for a few nights, but it may be said confidently that in an average season from twenty to thirty million elvers are caught. The facilities for catching have been greatly increased by the erection of the weirs, yet surprise is sometimes expressed that the supply of eels diminishes.

Passing from the division between anadromous and catadromous fish a word should be said on the changes that have been made in the Severn itself so as to render it less fit than formerly for *Salmonidæ* and better adapted for *Cyprinidæ*. Before 1842 the shoals and fords on which fish could spawn began from the point, or perhaps below the point, to which the tide regularly ascended, and continued all the way up the stream. The river was then more fitted for *Salmonidæ* than for *Cyprinidæ* ; but the improvements required for the navigation have caused all these fords to be dredged out and the river is practically turned into a canal. The result is that there are about twenty miles of canalized river between the head of the tideway and the first ford, all deep water, in no part of which could a salmonoid fish spawn, but in any part of which he could be netted. Further, across the water at intervals are placed four weirs that require a rise in the river for the fish to get over them. This water is now so well adapted for coarse fish that they increase and multiply in it to an unlimited extent, as all netting for fish other than salmon is illegal in the Severn district. The consequence is that certain kinds of fish, notably pike and chub, have greatly increased. The increase in the fish food has not been at all in proportion to the increase in numbers, the result being that the fish have largely decreased in size, and although probably in actual numbers there are more fish than there were, the average size has greatly diminished. The lack of food has driven the coarse fish into the tributaries, where they used never to be seen, with the result that they have greatly thrived, and driven the trout higher and higher up the streams so that the area of water now frequented by trout in Worcestershire is yearly decreasing, and that frequented by coarse fish increasing.

The Worcestershire fish are therefore undergoing a rapid change. Probably in the course of this century the anadromous fish will have become if not extinct at least only casual visitors, the catadromous fish will be present in lessened numbers, while the streams will be peopled mainly with *Cyprinidæ*. The occurrence of any specimen of the *Salmonidæ* will be a noteworthy event.

As far as can be made out from any existing evidence the fish that have hitherto been found in the Worcestershire rivers were very much the same as at present. A list of fish, but probably not an exhaustive one, is given in 1678 by the Statute 30 Car. II., c. 9. There it appears that the fish were salmon, trout, pike, barbel, chub and grayling. Salmon is mentioned as 'salmon, salmon marl and salmon peal.' The salmon peal is (*Salmo trutta*) the sea trout, but what the 'salmon marl' is it is impossible

to say. Since 1678 barbel, if it existed then, has become extinct in the Severn. The list is clearly not exhaustive, as no mention is made of perch, ruffe, dace, roach. The Act makes it illegal to kill elvers or young eels, a provision which was repealed and is now only partly re-enacted.

It will be seen from the following list, which represents the fishes of Worcestershire at the present time, that out of the thirty-five English freshwater forms thirty are met within the streams of the county. There is no modern record of the barbel being a Severn fish, and although common in the Trent it cannot get into the upper tributaries of that river in Worcestershire from the Birmingham pollutions; the same cause stops the burbot. The Crucian carp has never been introduced into the county. There are no lakes, so no lacustrine fish such as the char.

TELEOSTEANS

ACANTHOPTERYGII

1. Perch. *Perca fluviatilis*, Linn.

Found commonly in the Severn, Teme, Avon, Salwarp, and most of the brooks, but not nearly in such numbers as formerly. In some large pools, such as Pirton and Sharply, there are a considerable quantity, but the Perch must be regarded as one of the forms decreasing in number in the county.

2. Ruffe [Pope, Daddy Ruffe, Boar Pig]. *Acerina cernua*, Linn.

A very common, perhaps the commonest, fish in the Severn and in the lower parts of all the tributaries. It is steadily increasing in numbers.

3. Miller's Thumb [Bullhead, Cull]. *Cottus gobio*, Linn.

Although not often seen, unless specially looked for, this is a very common form in most streams. It hides under stones and roots in the day-time, and seems to feed mostly at night.

ANACANTHINI

4. Flounder. *Pleuronectes flesus*, Linn.

This fish used to ascend the Severn in considerable numbers, and to be very commonly taken by anglers using a worm, but since the erection of the navigation weirs at Tewkesbury and Gloucester, its numbers have fallen off considerably, probably because it is only able to surmount these obstacles at high tides. There are still a good many in the Teme between the mouth and Powick Weir.

HEMIBRANCHII

5. Three-spined Stickleback. *Gastrosteus aculeatus*, Linn.

Common in most of the ditches and backwaters, but not often noticed, as when in the water they are put down as minnows or young fish. Probably most of those in Worcestershire are the smooth-tailed form (*G. liwrus*, Cuv.).

6. Ten - spined Stickleback. *Gastrosteus pungitius*, Linn.

Much more local than *G. aculeatus*, but not uncommon; when it occurs in brooks it is said to be very destructive to ova and fry.

HAPLOMI

7. Pike [Jack]. *Esox lucius*, Linn.

A very common and rapidly increasing form in the Severn and all the tributaries. The prohibition of freshwater netting in the Severn a few years ago has led to an enormous increase in the number of small pike, which may now be found in almost all the streams in the county.

OSTARIOPHYSI

8. Carp. *Cyprinus carpio*, Linn.

The carp is fairly common in ponds and is occasionally found in the rivers, but it can nearly always be traced to some pond from which it has escaped.

9. Gudgeon. *Gobio fluviatilis*, Flem.

A very numerous species in the Severn and most of the tributaries, and one that seems increasing.

10. Roach. *Leuciscus rutilus*, Linn.

A very common and increasing form in all deep still waters, especially in the Avon.

11. Rudd. *Leuciscus erythrophthalmus*, Linn.

It is sometimes said that this is not a Worcestershire form ; but if the usual tests separating this fish from the roach are to be relied upon, namely (1) the position of the dorsal fin, (2) the rigid upper lip, (3) the brighter red about the eye and fins, specimens of this fish have been caught in pools in the county—for instance, from some near Ripple.

12. Dace. *Leuciscus dobula*, Linn. (*L. vulgaris*, Day).

A common form in streams on the Severn, Teme, less so on the Avon. Common in most of the brooks ; usually found below, or at the foot of, a weir or in a mill-race.

13. Chub. *Leuciscus cephalus*, Linn.

The commonest fish in the county. Found in all the rivers, and gradually pushing its way further and further up the tributaries.

14. Minnow. *Leuciscus phoxinus*, Linn.

Common in particular places in clear streams, but it has a habit of disappearing from places where it was plentiful one year, not a minnow being found there in the next ; a decreasing species.

15. Tench. *Tinca vulgaris*, Cuv.

Found in a number of the pools in different parts of the county, rarely in the rivers ; but when such is the case, the fish has escaped from some pool.

16. Bream. *Abramis brama*, Linn.

This fish is very common in the Avon, and runs to a fair size ; its range is extending. It is by no means uncommon in the Severn since the river has been deepened and dredged, and has also ascended some of the tributaries ; found in some number in the deep holes in the lower Teme.

17. White Bream, Breamflat. *Abramis blicca*, Linn.

This bream is said to be found in the Avon, and to be becoming more plentiful than formerly. It is a smaller fish than the bream, and hardly ever exceeds a pound, if it reaches that weight.

18. Bleak. *Alburnus lucidus*, Heck. & Kner.

A very common fish in the Severn and in the lower parts of most of the tributaries, but not as a rule found above the first serious obstruction in any of them.

19. Loach. *Nemachilus barbatulus*, Linn.

A common form, but not often seen, as it feeds at night and hides under stones and roots in the day-time. It is sometimes used for bait, but with that exception it is not much sought for.

20. Spinous Loach. *Cobitis tænia*, Linn.

A very local form. Although I have never met with it myself, I have seen specimens that I am informed came from the county.

MALACOPTERYGII

21. Salmon [Samlet, Smolt, Botcher, Gilling]. *Salmo salar*, Linn.

A fairly numerous fish in the Severn and certain of its tributaries ; the chief in Worcestershire being the Teme and the Dowles. In Worcestershire the number of clean run fish taken is very small, probably not averaging over 200 a year, all caught by net, but in the autumn and winter very large numbers are seen at the weirs, trying to pass up, and on the spawning beds. The young, before they are ready to migrate to the sea, are locally called 'samlets' ; when ready to migrate, and having the silver scales, 'smolts' ; on their first return from the sea, 'botchers' ; the 'grilse' of most rivers, on their second return, 'gillings' ; and after that, 'salmon' ; while a salmon that has spawned, and not since returned to the sea, is called an 'old fish' or 'a kelt.' In Worcestershire all the salmon that are legally caught are caught with a draft net.

22. Sea Trout [Sewin]. *Salmo trutta*, Linn.

For some reason this form, which is very common in the estuary, does not run up the Severn in any great numbers, and is not often taken with a bait. The mesh of the net that can lawfully be used for taking it is so large (2 inches from knot to knot) that the fish pass through it, so that probably there are more fish in the river than are observed. The marking on the form of this fish found in the Severn differs considerably to the marking on the Welsh sewin (*S. cambricus*). The Severn form rarely exceeds 3 lb., and is generally from ½ to 1½ lb. In the winter larger fish ascend and are found spawning in places where salmon cannot reach. In the Severn the sea trout go up the whole length of the river, and up the Teme as far as Powick.

23. Trout [Brown Trout]. *Salmo fario*, Linn.

Without going into the question whether *S. trutta* and *S. fario* are or are not local forms of the same species, here *S. fario* is

used to describe the fish found in the brooks in the county, and which does not as a rule migrate. So restricted, *S. fario* may be said to be a common form in some of the brooks and tributaries, but unfortunately decreasing in numbers. Few trout are now found in the Worcestershire part of the Severn itself, except sterile specimens that have turned cannibals, dropped down from some of the streams, and taken up their abode usually under one of the weirs. Originally all, or nearly all, the streams and brooks in the county held trout, and probably nothing else, but the coarse fish are yearly driving the trout higher and higher up the streams in which they still are found. In some cases hybrid forms appear as trout. Yearling trout have been obtained from a distance, turned down, and bred with the native fish, but it is doubtful if the result is satisfactory. The quality of the Worcestershire trout varies greatly ; a trout from the Teme itself is hardly ever in first-rate condition, while trout from its tributaries are at the same time in splendid order.

24. Grayling. *Thymallus vexillifer*, Linn.

The grayling is found in some numbers in the Teme and its tributaries, but is not now seen, except a chance specimen, in the Severn itself in Worcestershire. In some of the smaller streams which are suited to it the grayling does more than hold its own, and increases faster than the trout.

25. Allice Shad [Twaite, Shad]. *Clupea alosa*, Linn.

This fish, which was never very common, as only stragglers run so far up the river, has become very rare since the erection of the navigation weirs, but is still taken in some numbers in the river below Gloucester. It ascends the river at the end of April and May, but seems unable to pass up a fish ladder, and unless the tide is high enough to take the fish over the weir it now never passes up.

26. Twaite [Shad, Twaite Shad]. *Clupea finta*, Linn.

This fish used to be caught in the Severn and Teme in very large numbers every year. It ascends in small shoals to spawn in May and June. Like the shad it rarely if ever passes through a fish pass, and only comes up if there is a high tide and a freshet. The shoals hardly ever contain more than a dozen fish, but the number of these shoals used to be very large. They take a bait greedily and give most excellent sport with a rod and line.

APODES

27. Eel. *Anguilla vulgaris*, Turt.

The commonest fish in the Severn and its tributaries. The adult fish descend the river from June to Christmas on every freshet, and are caught in large numbers in fixed traps at weirs and in large nets. They run to a large size ; over 3 lb. is not uncommon, but the average would be about $\frac{3}{4}$ lb. The male eels are called 'stick eels.' The young eels, 'elvers,' ascend the rivers in March, April and May in enormous numbers, usually only on the spring tide, and in greater numbers if the wind is from one quarter—south-west.

CYCLOSTOMES

28. Lamprey [Lamprey Eel]. *Petromyzon marinus*, Linn.

This form ascends the rivers to spawn in May and June, but in decreasing numbers, probably because the localities fit for spawning are becoming fewer. The most frequented places at present are on the lower Teme, where some may be seen every year. On the Severn the fish are only taken at the weirs on their way up to the Teme. The fish work in pairs, and make a cavity in the river bed, where the spawn is deposited. The size of the stones they will remove is almost incredible. Having spawned they drop back into the deep water and are not seen again.

29. Lampern. *Petromyzon fluviatilis*, Linn.

This form ascends the rivers in very large numbers in any freshet from September to March. It is found at all the weirs on the Severn and Teme, and is taken in wicker baskets, called 'wheels,' laid on the weirs, into which they force themselves. They spawn about March. A few years ago they were taken in large numbers for bait for cod, but this trade has now fallen off.

30. Pride [Lamprey, Vamprey]. *Petromyzon branchialis*, Linn.

This form never exceeds four or five inches, and is mainly used as a bait for chub; it may be found in the rivers all the year round. In the autumn freshets numbers of so-called pride are taken in the eel nets, obviously descending to the sea, and it seems doubtful if these are not either a distinct species or the young of one of the two other species.

REPTILES
AND BATRACHIANS

Great Britain possesses seven species of reptiles and six batrachians, including the edible frog (*Rana esculenta*), which is probably an introduction from the continent. It has however 'come to stay,' and has stayed so long that it may now fairly rank as a British species. Of these thirteen species Worcestershire has eleven, five of the reptiles, and six of the batrachians. It has both the lizards (*Lacerta vivipara* and *L. agilis*) and the slow-worm (*Anguis fragilis*). But all of them seem to be decreasing in numbers, especially the slow-worm, which is now seldom seen even in places where it was formerly common.

Two of the three snakes are also resident : the ring snake (*Tropidonotus natrix*) and the adder (*Vipera berus*). There is no trustworthy record of the third, the smooth snake (*Coronella austriaca*), having ever been seen in the county, possibly because its favourite food the lizard is by no means abundant. The ring snake is fairly common ; so is the adder in certain places, especially in Wyre Forest.

Of the batrachians the common frog (*Rana temporaria*) is abundant everywhere, but *R. esculenta* has not yet been found in the county. The toad (*Bufo vulgaris*) is a common resident, but is at times more abundant than at others. There are but few records of the appearance of the natterjack toad (*Bufo calamita*) ; one was found on Dodderhill Common on August 29th, 1860.[1]

Of the newts the great crested newt (*Molge cristata*) is common, so is the common newt (*M. vulgaris*), but the palmated newt (*M. palmata*) is only locally plentiful. It is often confounded with and mistaken for the common newt, whose company it frequents.

REPTILES

LACERTILIA

1. Common or Viviparous Lizard. *Lacerta vivipara*, Jacq.

Although so abundant in the southern counties of England, the present small species is rare in Worcestershire, or at any rate very seldom observed, owing no doubt in some measure to its unattractive appearance. There is however every reason to conclude that careful search would discover it in localities where it has not yet been noticed. On the Ridgeway, which divides the counties of Worcester and Warwick, this small lizard has been found, as well as on Hartlebury Common and in Wyre Forest.

2. Sand Lizard. *Lacerta agilis*, Linn.

Pennant, in his *British Zoology* (vol. iii. p. 12, 1769) mentions a lizard which was killed at Wollescote in the parish of Old Swinford, Worcestershire, in 1721, measuring 2 feet 6 inches in length, and having a girth of 4 inches ; the forelegs were 8 inches from the head, and the hind legs 5 inches from them, and the legs themselves 2 inches in length. That statement of dimensions is wholly incredible, and doubtless Pennant was

[1] *Transactions Worcestershire Naturalists' Club*, i. p. 60.

misinformed as to the size of the creature; but there is one part of it which needs a passing notice, namely, the very small girth in relation to the length. The Rev. Mr. Shephard, who first recorded the species as British in the *Transactions of the Linnean Society* for 1802, described it as being upwards of a foot long. Professor Bell also, in his *History of British Reptiles*, mentions having seen lizards of this species approaching that length, but the Rev. Leonard Jenyns, whose accuracy is unquestionable, gives in his *Manual of British Vertebrate Animals*, 7 inches as the total length.

The sand lizard is met with in Worcestershire: Pennant gives Tenbury, as well as the places above mentioned, as a locality, and in parts of Wyre Forest and near Kidderminster it is still to be found. The present writer received one, which was taken on the Worcestershire side of the park at Ragley, the seat of the Marquis of Hertford, which measured a little over 8 inches in length, and another of smaller size, which was captured when removing some rubbish at the entrance to the excavations for gypsum at Spurnal near Alcester.

3. Slow-worm or Blind-worm. *Anguis fragilis*, Linn.

This reptile, according to Hastings, is rather less common than the snake, but whatever it was in 1834, it is certainly rarer now. It may occasionally be seen on elevated stony places, but is almost unknown in the valleys. It is still found in some numbers in parts of Wyre Forest and in Habberley Valley.

OPHIDIA

4. Common or Ringed Snake. *Tropidonotus natrix*, Linn. (*Natrix torquata*, Ray.)

Too numerous and too generally distributed to require particular notice. In spite of persecution it holds its own. It is very common in the damp osier-beds and coppices in the Teme valley.

5. Common Viper or Adder. *Vipera berus*, Linn.

A common reptile in all suitable localities, such as waste sandy and stony places. In parts of Wyre Forest it is very plentiful. Hastings mentions the Trench Woods, the neighbourhood of Malvern, and the Breedon and Abberley hills as localities where it is found, and there are many other places in the county which it frequents. At Cracomb near Fladbury Mr. H. E. Strickland discovered the variety known as the red viper, of which he contributed an account to *Lowdon's Magazine of Natural History* which appears at page 399 of vol. vi.

BATRACHIANS

ECAUDATA

1. Common Frog. *Rana temporaria*, Linn.

Common in every meadow, pool and ditch, as well as on the margins of the streams.

2. Common Toad. *Bufo vulgaris*, Laur.

Common, but not so abundant as the frog. The toad is easily tamed with gentle treatment, and will follow the hand to take flies from the fingers. Gardeners like to introduce the toad into the cucumber and melon frame, where it consumes a great quantity of insects and sometimes attains to a great size. It is far more plentiful in some years than in others.

3. Natterjack Toad. *Bufo calamita* (Laur.).

Although this toad is easily distinguished from *B. vulgaris* by the yellow line on the back, yet its appearance is very seldom reported, partly because it usually occurs in places where toads are not looked for, *e.g.* sandy commons and wastes, and partly because to most persons a toad is a toad and nothing more. A specimen was taken in August, 1860, on Dodderhill Common,[1] and doubtless other specimens would be found if looked for

[1] *Trans. Worcestershire Naturalists' Club*, i. p. 60.

in similar and suitable localities. This toad seems to live in colonies, and these colonies migrate, disappearing from a locality for a time, and then after an interval of longer or shorter duration appearing again.

CAUDATA

4. Great Crested Newt. *Molge cristata*, Laur.

Common in stagnant waters, pools, ditches and other places.

5. Common Newt. *Molge vulgaris*, Linn.

Like the last species it is found in stagnant water, but more frequently out of it, in damp cellars or other underground places. It is also sometimes found in winter in holes in banks of earth or rubbish.

6. Palmated Newt. *Molge palmata*, Schn.

Although this is the most widely distributed of all the newts, yet its recorded occurrences in Worcestershire are few, probably because it has been mistaken for *M. vulgaris*, in whose company it is often found. It can be distinguished by the absence of colour on the throat, which is of a pale flesh tint.

BIRDS

The Worcestershire birds are a subject of difficulty for two reasons. (1) The very irregular shape of the county boundary makes it hard to say what birds should or should not be included ; for instance, a bird killed in an isolated parish surrounded by another county some distance from its regular border, yet still a part of Worcestershire, and also the case of birds killed on or near the boundary, when it is either a river or a parish like Broadway jutting out into another county ; and (2) the varied conditions of the different parts of the county which make it almost impossible for any one observer to compile from his own knowledge an accurate list of all the birds. In the north-west of the county the remains of Wyre Forest give a list that is quite different from the southern district, while the woodlands of the midland part have a bird population distinct from that of the hills and open spaces on the western boundary. The Severn and its tributaries make quite unexpected additions to the list. While the increase of the population and towns in the north cause the disappearance of much of the bird life that used to be found there, the change in the cultivation, the improved farming, the increase of market gardening, have made considerable change in the different species met with in the south of the county.

Another difficulty is the old records. How far can they be relied upon ? Their account of very uncommon and unexpected specimens must be regarded with some distrust, *e.g.* the crane (*Grus communis*), especially as the heron (*Ardea cinerea*) is often locally called the crane ; but it is not safe to assert that the records, although suspicious in various cases, are necessarily incorrect, as some very unexpected visitors, *e.g.* the two-barred crossbill (*Loxia bifasciata*), have doubtless occurred.

The south of the county has been better observed than the other districts, probably the Avon valley is the only part that has been really thoroughly and satisfactorily worked, the result of which is the account of the birds given in this History. Observers in other parts have not made prolonged or systematic observations, although some very valuable notes, such as those of Mr. Howard on the mid-Worcestershire birds, have been published.[1]

The resident species of birds in the county is not a large list, and is possibly a decreasing one. Out of the 207 species of birds mentioned below as Worcestershire, the residents number but 60, and probably this list will be annually further reduced. The visitors may be divided into regular and casual, the regular containing some 45 out of the 147 are also decreas-

[1] *Zoologist*, 1899, p. 259.

ing, as the constant change in the districts makes the places they used to frequent less and less suitable for them. The casual visitors are the increasing list, partly because a number of the former regular visitors must now be placed in it, and partly because birds are at present more closely observed than formerly; so species that used not to be noticed are now recorded.

Of the residents there are none that call for special notice, except perhaps the blackcock (*Tetrao urogallus*), whose continued existence is a survival of a different state of things, and due entirely to the fact that until very recently the Crown held the Forest of Wyre. The red-legged partridge (*Caccabis rufa*) is a modern introduction, the only set off against the number of residents that have disappeared during the nineteenth century. A small heronry still exists in Shrawley Wood, so that some of the herons met with in the county are residents. Probably the snipe (*Gallinago cœlestes*) has ceased to breed in Worcestershire, against this there is evidence that the woodcock (*Scolopax rusticula*) breeds regularly but sparingly. The losses include all the hawks but the sparrow-hawk (*Accipiter nisus*) and the kestrel (*Falco tinnunculus*), all the owls but the white owl (*Strix flammea*) and the brown (*Syrnium aluco*), most of the water-birds—the wild duck (*Anas boscas*), moorhen (*Gallinulo chloropus*), coot (*Fulica atra*) and dabchick (*Podicipes fluviatilis*) being now probably the only real residents—and all the waders, if any ever bred here.

Of the two classes into which the visitors are divided, the regular and the casual, the regular seem to be decreasing chiefly from the fact of the change in the condition of things, yet it is difficult to get the regular migrants to forsake their old haunts; for instance, the Black Country near Oldbury is the last place where snipe would be sought for, yet in the autumn when they are migrating, jack snipe (*Gallinago gallinula*) are still to be met with on some of the pools in that neighbourhood, while yearly a few gulls and terns come up the Severn seeking the places they used to frequent before drainage and improvement spoilt their feeding-grounds.

The casual list is swelled by those species that formerly came regularly but now only come occasionally, such as some of the hawks, water-birds and waders. In the Severn estuary a large number of the *Anatidæ* and *Laridæ* are found regularly, these in old times, when the Severn was tidal, came up with the tide to the marshes, which afforded them shelter and food. Now the river in Worcestershire has been made non-tidal by weirs and the Longdon Marshes have been drained these birds only come occasionally. No gulls now breed in this county, those that do come usually only appear in floods. Cormorants and shags have a habit of wandering up the stream to meet the young salmon on their migration downwards. The number of young salmon that migrate from the Severn has very largely decreased, so that cormorants and shags are very seldom seen within the Worcestershire boundary. But the casual list has been largely increased, not only by regular visitants becoming casuals, but also by the fact that every rare bird is now shot and stuffed. This has resulted in various additions to the Worcestershire list. For

BIRDS

instance, the gull-billed tern (*Sterna anglica*) shot at Cofton reservoir and the curlew sandpiper (*Tringa subarquata*) shot at the same place, have both been added to the Worcestershire list by means of the common gunner and the bird stuffer.

A noteworthy feature in respect of the bird population of the county is the conversion into garden land of a large area in the southern district. The great and recent extension of the gardening industry around Evesham and Pershore, including many of the surrounding villages, and amounting to thousands of acres, has effected a considerable change among the bird inhabitants. With the exception of a few finches and starlings at all seasons, and of warblers in the spring and at the period of ripe fruit, very few birds frequent these gardens. The pretty and lively chaffinch has, however, a way of putting in an appearance on the beds of early radishes, and the linnet is sure to be seen when the various kinds of *Cruciferæ* are ripening their seeds, while the bullfinch fails not, if permitted, to pay his respects to the buds of the plum trees and gooseberry bushes all through the winter. Against such birds, and indeed all birds, the gardeners wage incessant war with the gun, so that few birds remain in the gardening district.

The Severn valley is one of the great lines of bird migration across England, the course of the Avon is another ; on two occasions the birds have been seen passing over the county in the last-named line in actual migration : once in the town of Evesham and once in the village of South Littleton. Unfortunately there is no record of the dates, but on the first occasion, the night being very still and dark, the birds were seen in countless numbers passing over Evesham in a north-easterly direction, only just clearing the chimneys, their white bellies being strongly illuminated by the street lamps. They were quite within gunshot, and were witnessed by many townspeople, who came out of doors to see what was a very remarkable sight. On the other occasion the night was very bright and moonlight, and some very small bodies, mere specks, were observed passing in front of the moon, which proved to be birds at a great height, also travelling, so far as could be determined, in a north-easterly direction.

Birds doubtless on migration have many times been heard though not seen passing over in the night. Mr. T. E. Doeg of Evesham, a good ornithologist, fixes a date in the following communication to the *Evesham Journal* of October 6th, 1899 : ' Probably some of your readers who, like myself, are often awake during the midnight hours, may have been interested during the past month in noticing the great number of migratory birds that have been passing over our district on passage from their breeding haunts in the far north to the more genial climate of the southern countries, where they spend the winter. They were particularly numerous on the very dark night of September 6th, when, from a little before twelve until after two o'clock, there was almost a constant stream of them passing over the town.' None of the birds were visible on the night mentioned.

The classification of the species as well as the nomenclature used in this article has been taken from Saunders' *Manual of British Birds*, 2nd edit., 1899.

Bearing in mind what has already been said of the nature of the county boundary and of the number of streams which pass in or out of it, which streams it should be remembered are the highways of many birds, it has been decided to introduce into the present list certain species which, though not actually killed in the county, have been so at places so near to it as to leave no reasonable doubt of their connection with it. Such species are bracketed thus [ ], and their exact locality particularized, to distinguish them from those which are strictly Worcestershire birds.

A few words on what has already been done to enumerate the birds of Worcestershire are desirable.

The earlier published lists of Worcestershire birds are extremely incomplete and not very accurate. One of the first is the *Illustrations of the Natural History of Worcestershire*, by Dr. (afterwards Sir) Charles Hastings, which appeared in 1834. It does not profess to give anything more than a selection of the most remarkable animals, but having been prepared under the auspices of a great authority on ornithology, H. E. Strickland, and contributed to by Mrs. Perrot, who at one time gathered material for a history of British birds, it is worthy of very careful consideration. It includes not only birds, but also mammals, reptiles and fish.

In Stanley's *Worcester Guide*, published about 1855, there is a list of the birds occurring round the city. It is believed it was prepared by Mr. Martin Curtler of Worcester, a gentleman whose name appears in the following pages, and who has a good collection of Worcestershire birds.

A list of the birds in the Malvern district by Edwin Lees appeared in the *Transactions of the Malvern Naturalists' Field Club* for 1870, but the record is not very satisfactory. After mentioning the goosander and the red-breasted merganser, the author speaks of the dun-diver as a distinct species in the following words : 'Dun-diver (*M. castor*, Linn.) killed on the Teme, February, 1870.' The last-named bird is however either the female goosander or the pochard (*Fuligula ferina*), which is locally called the 'dun-bird.' Again the 'yellow-legged gull (*Larus fuscus*)' is mentioned as being occasionally found on the Avon and Teme. But *L. fuscus*, although yellow-legged, is the well-known lesser black-backed gull, and appears under that name in every work on British ornithology ; while the real yellow-legged herring gull (*L. cachinnans*) has only been once met with in Great Britain. Of the *Anatidæ* Mr. Lees gives a medley of sixteen species, all of which are said to appear in the autumn and winter, but he includes the garganey or summer teal, which only appears in the spring and during the summer.

In 1889, a list of Worcestershire birds appeared in *Hardwicke's Science Gossip*, by F. G. S. A., under the title of 'Notes on Worcestershire Birds.' It enumerates 118 species.

In 1891 Mr. Willis Bund printed a tabular and systematic list of the birds which had been met with in the counties of Worcester, Here-

ford, Gloucester, Oxford, Warwick, Stafford and Shropshire. It is by far the most complete list of the birds of Worcestershire which has been compiled, but it is a list only, and supplies no details respecting the species occurring in the county. As the notices of the appearance of some of the birds were supplied by the present writer, certain of the following records are identical with some given in that list.

While fully conscious of the many imperfections of the present list of the birds of Worcestershire, the very little help which has been rendered by previous writers must not be forgotten, and may plead for the indulgence which is due to what is really the first attempt to deal with the matter systematically. That there are scattered notices of species occurring in our county which have been overlooked in it there is no doubt ; while closer observation would doubtless bring to light the occurrence of birds of which so far there is no record.

Saunders in his *Manual of British Birds* (2nd ed., 1899) gives the total number of British species as 384, an addition of 14 from 1889, when the first edition of his book was published. He thus classifies the birds : Birds that have bred in Britain in the nineteenth century, 199 ; birds that are regular winter migrants, 45 ; birds of infrequent occurrence, 66 ; birds that have occurred fewer than *six* times, 74.

The following is a comparative table of the Worcestershire birds with that of Mr. Saunders :—

Birds that have bred in British Isles in nineteenth century .	199	Birds that have bred in Worcestershire in nineteenth century	90
Winter visitors	45	Winter visitors	18
Infrequent visitors . . .	66	Infrequent visitors . . .	56
Occurred less than six times .	74	Occurred less than six times .	43
	384		207

It must not be however assumed that these last two classes at all correspond, many of the infrequent visitors to Worcestershire are included in the birds that have bred in the British Isles, *e.g.* the buzzard and the little owl, while many of those that have occurred less than six times here are fairly common birds elsewhere, *e.g.* eider duck, stormy petrel and other water-birds.

1. Missel-Thrush. *Turdus viscivorus*, Linn.[1]

This the first bird on the Worcestershire list is becoming scarcer of late years. It is one of the most harmless of our birds, while it is our earliest musician, pouring forth a sweet wild song from the very top of some tall tree almost before the frost and snow of winter have disappeared. But he is a sad thief when material for the construction of a nest is wanted, and, like Falstaff's soldiers, will not hesitate to help himself to articles put out to dry on the garden hedge. The nest of one of these birds at Cleeve Prior was found to have a yard of lace woven into its substance, while from the lining of another was taken a quantity of thick soft string, such as is sometimes used to tie sacks of corn. Deal shavings which had been swept out of a carpenters' shop were largely used in the construction of a nest, while shreds of bast matting from a garden were found to enter largely into the composition of another. But the most remarkable choice of material for a nest is the following : The dairy women in the valley of the Avon wrap their pounds of butter in small

[1] When the name of an individual following the name of a species is included in *round* brackets it indicates that the original describer of the species did not adopt the generic name now used.

pieces of white calico, a great many of which, having been washed, were laid on a cropped garden hedge to dry. A considerable number were found to be missing, but the real thief was not suspected until the pieces of calico were discovered worked with a liberal mixture of dry grass, roots and mud into a nest of a missel-thrush in an adjoining orchard.

The early-constructed nest of this bird, always in some naked tree or large bush, is seen at once by every marauding magpie who happens to come that way, discovery and destruction are with him one and the same. The magpie will perch on the side of the nest, and despite the clamour of the thrush, deliberately devour either eggs or young, or both.

2. Song-Thrush. *Turdus musicus*, Linn.

Though well known everywhere, the song-thrush is not generally suspected of being a very great consumer of snails. Yet there is no other bird which devours them wholesale as this thrush does. At all seasons when these gasteropods are obtainable the thrush smashes their hard shell on a stone to get at the contents, and being by no means a shy bird, especially where there are no guns, the breaking-up process may be readily observed. The bird takes the snail by the lip of the shell, and raising itself up to its full height, brings it down on the stone, and continues the process until the shell is so much broken that the soft mollusc can be extracted, it is then torn to pieces and swallowed. Even the large garden snail, *Helix aspersa*, is not proof against the smashing powers of the thrush, while the shells of all the smaller banded snails are easily manipulated.

3. Redwing. *Turdus iliacus*, Linn.

Arriving in this country earlier in the winter than the fieldfare, the appearance of the redwing is not so easily noted on account of its general resemblance to the song-thrush. Its mode of flying will however readily distinguish it. When put up it hurries off in a rapid and twisting flight, taking an upward direction, and very rarely near to the ground, as is observable with the song-thrush when disturbed. Whether the redwing feeds in the winter on anything more than hedge fruit and an occasional insect I am not able to say, but it has not been observed like the song-thrush and blackbird to have recourse to a special diet, nor yet to feed on turnips or other roots like the fieldfare.

4. Fieldfare. *Turdus pilaris*, Linn.

During very hard winters fieldfares suffer very severely, and even die of starvation after the fruit of the whitethorn has been consumed. At such times they frequent fields of swede turnips to feed, and attack the roots of that plant, often doing considerable mischief, for those roots which have been broken into by the bird rot off towards the spring. I have seen carrots, as well as turnips, which have thus been damaged by fieldfares.

[White's Thrush. *Turdus varius*, Pallas.

Although this rare bird has not as yet been met with in Worcestershire, one has been shot at Welford in Gloucestershire, which lies on a tongue of land running between the counties of Warwick and Worcester, and so near the boundary of the latter county that it may very properly be mentioned here. The occurrence was recorded by the present writer in one of the early volumes of the *Ibis*.]

5. Blackbird. *Turdus merula*, Linn.

Blackbirds, like song-thrushes, feed largely on snails, but instead of selecting the large ones they take the very smallest and swallow them whole. During the winter months the blackbird turns over the dead leaves lying in the bottom of woods, coppices, shrubberies and hedgerows for the small molluscs or crustaceans concealed beneath them, and if approached cautiously when so engaged, may be seen flinging the leaves alternately to the right and left while eagerly prosecuting his search.

6. Ring-Ousel. *Turdus torquatus*, Linn.

This bird is generally seen in Worcestershire as a passing visitor in the spring and autumn, sometimes remaining for a week or more on its journey. It was 'of unfrequent occurrence' when Sir Charles Hastings wrote in 1834. Lees, 1870, records it as an autumnal visitor only in the vicinity of Malvern, but Mr. W. Edwards of that place found a nest containing four eggs near there in 1877. The berries of the mountain ash appear to be a great attraction to it.

7. Wheatear. *Saxicola œnanthe* (Linn.).

Two very distinct races of wheatears visit us in the spring and autumn, but so far as I know, only temporarily : the one a small variety, and the other materially larger and more delicately coloured. Lees says that a few wheatears frequent the Malvern Hills and breed, but he gives no particulars, and indeed does not appear to have recognized the two varieties. The smaller wheatear is the less common the earlier to arrive, and is never seen except on the ground. The larger one comes two or three weeks later, and often alights on hedges, bushes, and even trees, flitting from tree to tree along a hedgerow. I

have seen the latter bird frequenting the broken stony ground on the highest point of the Cotteswold range about Cheltenham in the summer, and from the solicitude of the bird entertained no doubt of the existence of a nest somewhere near ; and as that locality is not very distant from the Malvern Hills, it is probable that it was the large wheatear which Lees observed.

8. Whinchat. *Pratincola rubetra* (Linn.).

This is during the whole of the summer one of the commonest of our migratory birds, freely nesting in the fields and meadows, the nest being very frequently mown over in the hay-making season.

9. Stonechat. *Pratincola rubicola* (Linn.).

The stonechat is much less common than the whinchat, and is resident. It frequents not only barren stony places, but also cultivated fields, and may not infrequently be seen perched on the very top sprig of a roadside hedge. The considerable difference in the plumage of the sexes enables the observer to determine at a glance when there are two together that they are a pair ; as that is often the case even in mid-winter it seems not unlikely that the stonechat pairs for life. The nest is usually so well concealed that it is most difficult to find. Generally speaking, some piece of waste land is chosen where the nest will not be laid bare by the scythe. I have found it on the Worcestershire side of the Malvern Hills, where it is said by Lees to appear as a summer visitor—but it is certainly a resident bird.

10. Redstart. *Ruticilla phœnicurus* (Linn.).

The redstart is one of the earliest of our summer migrants to visit us and is regularly distributed, nesting indiscriminately in holes of trees, walls or buildings, usually but not always so far within as not to be seen from outside, and generally discovered, if at all, by the bird flying out. The old orchards of Worcestershire are very favourite places with the redstart, and the nest is often in a hole in an aged apple tree.

11. Black Redstart. *Ruticilla titys* (Scopoli).

The occurrence of this bird in Worcestershire was for some time doubtful, resting on the statements of one having been seen at Cracombe, near Evesham. Mr. W. Edwards has, however, disposed of the doubt by the following note : 'Black Redstart found dead in the Priory Church, Malvern, in 1884.'

12. Redbreast. *Erithacus rubecula* (Linn.).

Though one of the most interesting of our resident birds, the robin is too well known to require more than a notice of him as a Worcestershire bird.

13. Nightingale. *Daulias luscinia* (Linn.).

The nightingale is plentiful in the valleys of the Severn, the Avon and the Teme, and such parts of their tributaries as run through low and fertile places ; the higher and comparatively barren regions of the county are not frequented by this unrivalled songster. But in even the most favoured spots the number of nightingales varies greatly from year to year. One year they may be heard in almost every brake and hedgerow, and in another be thinly scattered, their numbers being readily known by their song. It would not be difficult to make a census of the nightingales in a given area by counting the birds heard singing.

[Northern Nightingale. *Daulias philomela*.

About the middle of June, 1879, I heard the song of some bird, with which I was wholly unacquainted, proceeding from a thick brake of umbelliferous plants, white with blossom, in the orchard of a house in South Littleton. It was a very loud, clear and continuous song. Proceeding very cautiously I approached quite near to the bird and saw him very distinctly, and indeed watched him for some time. He was of an uniform brown colour, a little paler beneath, and the throat, swollen by song, appeared to be quite white. I have subsequently examined preserved skins of the northern nightingale and do not hesitate to identify the bird I saw with that species. The only discrepancy lies in the colour of the throat, which is not white, though light-coloured, in the skins. I may, however, observe that Temminck in his work on the birds of Europe says, ' *Gorge blanche, entourée de gres foncé*,' which agrees pretty accurately with what I saw. Herr Gätke met with the northern nightingale once only in Heligoland, and he observes, ' It would therefore appear that of the many migrants visiting this island from high northern latitudes, or the far east, few persist with such stubbornness in the north-to-south direction of their line of flight as does this species.']

14. Whitethroat. *Sylvia cinerea* (Bechstein).

The present species is so common and so well known all through the summer that it may pass with the remark that it is heard in every hedge bottom and almost every bush.

15. Lesser Whitethroat. *Sylvia curruca* (Linn.).

Although this bird is a common summer visitor it is not nearly so abundant as the last-

named, and it is not heard in the rubbish of a hedge or ditch, but more frequently from some tree or tall bush. The nest, which is extremely fragile, but nevertheless a very beautiful structure, is almost always placed at some little distance from the ground, sometimes indeed high enough to enable the observer to walk under it and see the eggs through the bottom.

16. Blackcap. *Sylvia atricapilla* (Linn.).

The blackcap is one of our early summer visitors, but as his song is not heard on his arrival his first appearance is unobserved. When however in full song his sweet wild melody proclaims his presence. Although somewhat of a mimic his music will never be taken for that of any other bird, for however much he may imitate, his finishing notes are always his own and quite unmistakable.

17. Garden-Warbler. *Sylvia hortensis* (Bechstein).

This bird is never so common as the blackcap, is more strictly a sylvan species, and certainly not, as the name implies, a frequenter of gardens. The song is a low, sweet and continuous warble, but has none of the wild music of the blackcap's.

18. Dartford Warbler. *Sylvia undata* (Boddaert).

I am unable to add anything to the statement made many years ago by Hastings of the occurrence of this bird at Springhill, near Broadway, excepting to observe that the brakes of furze which are there of considerable extent are very suitable to the habits of this species.

19. Goldcrest. *Regulus cristatus*, K. L. Koch.

We have a considerable number of goldcrests which breed with us, and the place for which preference is shown for the nest is the horizontal bough of a yew. Other evergreen trees are resorted to, such as the spruce fir, and even ivy-clad trees and bushes are sometimes selected. There is not, however, any doubt that the greater number of these small birds observed in Great Britain in the winter are autumn visitors which depart in the spring. The goldcrest is not uncommonly seen throughout the winter in the company of tits searching among the branches and sprigs of trees in woods and coppices, and uttering its small plaintive note, so unlike its merry song of the breeding season.

[Firecrest. *Regulus ignicapillus* (Brehm).

On two occasions at least this species has been met with in near proximity to the county of Worcester, once at Weston-on-Avon, and once at Dorsington, both places in the northeast corner of Gloucestershire, and by the side of the Avon. The first was seen by the present writer in a large ivy-grown hedge, and being shot proved to be a male, and the second was also seen and recognized but not shot. It is also reported to have occurred near Worcester. The motions of both more nearly resembled those of a tit than of a goldcrest.]

20. Chiffchaff. *Phylloscopus rufus* (Bechstein).

A common summer visitor, though not so abundant in Worcestershire as the willow-warbler. It is our very earliest migrant, having been heard in the vale of the Avon as soon as the last day of February. That was in 1846, when the writer both heard and saw one busily engaged in searching some hawthorn bushes for insect food.

21. Willow-Warbler. *Phylloscopus trochilus* (Linn.).
Locally, Willow-Wren.

This bird so closely resembles the chiffchaff as to be difficult to distinguish from it, yet the two are quite distinct both in their song and the coloration of the eggs.

22. Wood-Warbler. *Phylloscopus sibilatrix* (Bechstein).
Locally, Wood-Wren.

Although bearing considerable resemblance to the chiffchaff and willow-warbler the present species will not be confounded with them, being larger, and the wings relatively smaller. It is much less abundant than either of them, and appears to prefer trees in woods and coppices rather than hedges or brakes, and its song, which is a peculiar sort of trill, is often heard from some tall tree, frequently from its very top. The nest which, like those of the chiffchaff and willow-warbler, is on or near the ground and is domed, instead of being lined with feathers is lined with horse-hair.

23. Reed-Warbler. *Acrocephalus streperus* (Vieillot).

As the name imports the present noisy little bird frequents beds of reeds, and in fact a reed bed is almost a necessity to it. Occasionally it will be heard in osier aits or in beds of willow-bushes, or indeed amongst other tall plants, but only where there are no reeds. The nest is always suspended between the vertical stems of reeds, osiers, or other upright plants by the side of river or pond. Its abundance or the reverse appears almost wholly to depend on the presence or absence of reed beds.

BIRDS

24. Marsh - Warbler. *Acrocephalus palustris* (Bechstein).

A bird, which has subsequently proved to be the marsh-warbler, was known to visit the valley of the Avon in the counties of Warwick, Gloucester and Worcester, as a summer migrant more than thirty years since. The first one observed frequented some very high beans by the side of the Avon at Welford, about five miles down stream from Stratford. Others were subsequently heard and seen, but it was not until the summer of 1887 that the species was satisfactorily determined, when two were shot by the author, whose attention was called to them by their unmistakable song and by their particular movements. Since that time others have been noted. In 1888 four were heard, all in the same neighbourhood, namely, in the valley of the Avon, near Littleton. After that date others were noted, and in the middle of June, 1892, a pair were seen by the author in some rank herbage in the bottom of a deserted stone quarry, when on search being made a nest was found suspended between the stems of some nettles. But an animal of some kind had apparently rushed through the nettles and pushed the nest aside so that it could no longer be made use of. It contained one egg. Another nest was speedily constructed near the spot, and was found to be suspended between the stems of some umbelliferous plants. The pair of birds were watched going to and from the nest until four eggs were laid, which with the one in the first nest made up the full number, and after an interval of a few days, during which no more eggs were laid, both nests with the eggs were taken.

Since the date above mentioned, the marsh-warbler has been repeatedly heard in the same neighbourhood, and no doubt remains that it is a regular summer visitor with us, though not in any considerable numbers. It is a thorough mimic and has been heard to imitate the notes of the skylark, swallow, sparrow, chaffinch, blackbird, thrush, starling, partridge, and some others, which are mixed and blended with its own notes into a low but very sweet song. The precise spots chosen by the marsh-warbler are such as are frequented by the common whitethroat and the sedge-warbler, but it has not been heard in the reed beds of the Avon.

25. Sedge-Warbler. *Acrocephalus phragmitis* (Bechstein).

A common bird all through the summer, and its chattering song may be heard in every hedge, and almost every bush. The place chosen for the nest corresponds with that selected by the whitethroat.

26. Grasshopper-Warbler. *Locustella nævia* (Boddaert).

Although the grasshopper-warbler cannot be said to be a rare bird in Worcestershire, it is by no means abundant, and is very local, being more frequently heard in the western part of the county than in the north or the eastern side. It occasionally haunts corn, more especially barley-fields, in which there is little doubt it sometimes breeds. The few nests the writer has seen were all placed directly on the ground; one of them on a steep grassy hedge bank, and three others in a field of Italian rye-grass. The latter were all exposed at the same time by the scythe in a field near the Avon. By approaching cautiously the parent bird could be seen upon the nest, which had then nothing to hide it, and would creep off out of sight, having more the appearance of a mouse than a bird. All the three nests were made of the withered leaves of the rye-grass, and the lining was of the same but of finer leaves.

[**Savi's Warbler.** *Locustella luscinioides* (Savi).

The present species is included by Mr. Willis Bund in his list of Worcestershire birds, and also in the list of the county of Salop. A small bird having the size and colour of Savi's warbler has been seen several times during the summer in an osier bed in the Avon, a few miles up stream from Evesham. On the first occasion it was seen both by the author and his brother, and in the following year by his brother, near the same spot. The habit of these birds was to creep up an osier quite to the top, and then take a short flutter upwards and float down on open wings somewhat as a tree-pipit does from the top of a bush or tree. The short flights were often repeated, but there was no song of any kind.]

27. Hedge - Sparrow. *Accentor modularis* (Linn.).

It is unnecessary to dwell upon this very common resident which may be seen every day about our dwellings.

28. Alpine Accentor. *Accentor collaris* (Scopoli).

An alpine accentor was shot several years since near the village of Ettington, a few miles from Stratford-on-Avon, and is still preserved in a case of local birds. As Ettington lies almost on the line of division between the counties of Warwick and Worcester, the bird

may with equal probability have been killed in either county. An enquiry made with a view to determine the point only proved that it was shot near the village.

The present species has been reported to have visited the Malvern Hills, but there is no mention of it in the list compiled by Lees.

29. Dipper. *Cinclus aquaticus*, Bechstein.

So long ago as 1834 Sir Charles Hastings wrote of the dipper as 'of unfrequent occurrence' in the county; and Lees, in 1870, reports it as 'becoming rare' in the neighbourhood of Malvern. It is still by no means scarce on the tributaries of the Severn and Teme on the Herefordshire side of Worcestershire, on some of which it nests annually. In 1896 there was a nest on the Teme within two miles of Worcester. In other parts of the county it is much less common. Occasionally, but only very occasionally, one is shot on one or other of the small streams which feed the Avon, and some have been seen in very immature plumage on the Avon, leaving no doubt that they were bred there.

[Bearded Reedling. *Panurus biarmicus* (Linn.).

Locally, Bearded Tit.

This bird can only be mentioned as a probable former inhabitant of Worcestershire, and the ground for the belief that it did at one time frequent some parts of the county may be briefly stated as follows : It has been traced up the Thames into Gloucestershire and the upper reaches of the river are fed by streamlets which pass through parts of Worcestershire, in which, where reeds grow, the bird would find suitable haunts. In the second edition of Pennant's *British Zoology*, the author relates having seen the bearded tit near Gloucester, and it is more than merely probable, therefore, that the reed beds of the Severn and its tributaries would be frequented by it.]

30. Long-tailed Tit. *Acredula caudata* (Linn.).

This is one of the numerous birds found in our county, which, though hardly to be styled rare, is nevertheless not often seen in places where years ago it was common. Its beautiful nest is so conspicuous that, except in very little-frequented districts it stands no chance of escaping notice and destruction. The nests are still brought into the Worcester market for sale as curiosities, in spite of the Wild Bird Acts.

31. Great Tit. *Parus major*, Linn.

The great tit is a bird which can well take care of himself, and there is no danger of the species becoming a rarity. No food is more to his taste than the seeds of the sunflower. Years ago that handsome plant might be seen in almost every garden, and this bird, as well as the blue tit, fed freely on its ripened seeds, but for a long period the sunflower was but rarely grown. Quite recently, however, it has again made its appearance, though not so abundantly as formerly, and the tits are again busy in the autumn with the great disc-shaped heads. Nuts also at that season are much relished by the great tit, but their kernels are difficult of access. The heads of the garden poppy are often broken into by this bird, not however to reach the seed, but for the earwigs which are always concealed in them. The rough stone walls around the village of South Littleton furnish very favourite nesting-places for this tit, where however their eggs or young are not infrequently destroyed by mice.

32. Coal-Tit. *Parus ater*, Linn.

Of all our tits, excepting the long-tailed tit, the present species is the least common in Worcestershire; and from the circumstance that the nest is very rarely if ever found in the county, it seems probable that it is only a winter visitor to us. In the southern counties it is far more abundant at all seasons. It is a shy bird, having but little if any of the impudence which is so conspicuous in some of the tits, giving way to all the other species when food is put out for their use in the winter. The coal-tit is not infrequently seen in the company of the goldcrest searching the tops of coppice trees and overgrown hedgerows.

33. Marsh-Tit. *Parus palustris*, Linn.

Second in degree of infrequency in the county is the marsh-tit, and it is most commonly seen in small companies in woods, coppices and brakes, and not often near houses and homesteads. A nest of which I made a particular examination, was in the soft touchwood of a pollard withy tree; the hole which contained it having been excavated by the pair of birds, which I watched bringing out the fragments of decayed wood.

34. Blue Tit. *Parus cæruleus*, Linn.

This is one of the birds which can adapt itself to such varying conditions that there is no probability of its becoming rare, or even fewer in number, besides which it appears to be a prolific species. A pair of these birds took possession of the letter-box at the house where the present writer at one time dwelt, and having constructed a nest in it an egg was laid. The nest and egg were removed

on account of the birds doing damage to the letters, but still eggs were laid, and had to be taken out every day until sixteen was reached, when the place was abandoned by the birds.

35. Nuthatch. *Sitta cæsia*, Wolf.

The nuthatch is a fairly common bird in the county, and its grating 'gurra gurra' may be often heard. Although the nuthatch does not excavate for itself, its well-known habit of closing with mud the entrance to the place in which the nest is placed to the size required for the ingress and egress of the bird, is a very great protection against the interference of birds larger than itself. In an old ash tree in the South Littleton churchyard was a hole of which a pair of nuthatches took possession and narrowed the entrance to keep out a pair of starlings which had inhabited it for several years. The mud used was from a road maintained with lias stone, which when dry was almost as hard as stone itself, and most effectually kept the starlings from entering. The entrance to the hole in which the nest of the nuthatch is placed is not always narrowed. A pair of these birds reared their young in an old wall on the premises of the writer, and the entrance was not in any way contracted.

36. Wren. *Troglodytes parvulus*, Koch.

Locally, 'Jenny Wren.'

The wren is without exception the most prying little bird we have, and its food appears to consist of very small insects or eggs, which are procured by unceasing and close search in everything that comes in its way either on the ground or near to it, for the wren, unlike the tits and the goldcrests, is never seen feeding in the tops of trees. The inquisitiveness of the bird when on the banks of the Avon sometimes leads to a rather curious ending. Eels are taken in the summer by means of wicker traps, large baskets locally 'putcheons,' which are taken out of the water in the autumn and laid by to dry previously to being stored away for the winter. These are found almost invariably to contain wrens which have entered the aperture for the eels, and have failed to find the way out.

A very extraordinary choice of a place for its nest is sometimes made by this little bird. A pair of trousers, belonging to a man who had been engaged in the village of South Littleton, had been hung up to dry on a line and left there some time. When they were taken off the line a small bird flew out, which proved to be a wren which had constructed a nest in them. The garments were immediately replaced on the line and from the nest a brood

of wrens was successfully reared and took flight.

37. Tree-Creeper. *Certhia familiaris*, Linn.

Although the tree-creeper is not rare it is far from numerous, and its nest is but seldom seen. Three nests examined by the author were in very dissimilar places. One was in a crack in an old mud wall forming the back of a cowshed in the corner of a pasture field, and was composed principally of red cow-hair. The second was placed in the fork of a large pear tree, just where two large vertical arms separated a little, and then united above leaving a slit below. The third one was attached to the inside of a piece of loose bark on a pollard withy by the side of the Avon near Cleeve Prior. It was discovered by the bird flying out. Some weeks afterwards the piece of bark was torn down, when the young had evidently flown. The nest was found snugly occupying a recess inside the bark, and was formed principally of what appeared to be bits of stick, which proved on examination to be the dead and dried up succulent points of climbing ivy, which, by exposure, had become extremely light and fragile. It was lined with fine fibre and rabbit's fur.

38. Pied Wagtail. *Motacilla lugubris*, Temminck.

The pied wagtail though a common, can hardly be called an abundant bird with us, and appears to breed less frequently than formerly. Early in the autumn, however, flights consisting chiefly of immature birds retire in the evening to the osier beds on our streams to roost, though certainly not in such numbers as in past years. Later in the autumn, or at the approach of winter, small companies of this wagtail, apparently on migration, appear, as they are only observed for a short time.

[White Wagtail. *Motacilla alba*, Linn.

I can only say of this species that I have seen it by the side of the Avon near Stratford, and do not doubt its occasional appearance in Worcestershire. Mr. Whitlock has discovered that it is a regular visitor to the Trent valley, though in quite limited numbers ; and its occurrence by the side of the Severn and its tributaries may be confidently predicted.]

39. Grey Wagtail. *Motacilla melanope*, Pallas.

This, the most elegant in form and most interesting in its movement of all our wagtails, is usually an autumn visitor to our county, but has never, to my knowledge, been known to breed. In only one instance, in a wide district in the midland counties, has this bird been seen in breeding plumage, namely, in the

early part of the summer of 1898, at Loxley near Stratford-on-Avon.

The margins of our streams and pools are the almost exclusive haunts of this prettily coloured and active little bird, where it may be seen singly or in pairs, but no doubt on migration, as it is obviously a come-and-go visitor, and is not observed continuously at the same place. In the spring one occasionally appears, though but rarely. Lees says it is 'not common' near Malvern.

[Blue-headed Yellow Wagtail. *Motacilla flava*, Linn.

The present species has been met with at least three times near Welford-on-Avon in Gloucestershire, which lies between two parts of Worcestershire ; but there is no direct evidence of its having occurred in the latter county, though it is more than probable that it has done so.

The male may be readily recognized by the bluish-grey of the top of the head, and both male and female by the presence of white on the *three* outer tail feathers on each side. In the common yellow wagtail *two* outer tail feathers on each side are so marked. One of the Welford specimens, shot by Mr. W. H. Baylies, and now in the author's collection, is a female, but shows the white of the tail feathers as above stated very distinctly. The yellow of the under parts is also of a deeper hue than in the common species, and is more conspicuous when the bird is on the ground or flitting before the observer.]

40. Yellow Wagtail. *Motacilla raii* (Bonaparte).

A very common summer visitor, frequenting ploughed fields and meadows, and nesting in both those situations, the nests being always on the ground.

41. Tree-Pipit. *Anthus trivialis* (Linn.).

An abundant summer visitor with us, breeding in numbers, seeming to prefer meadows and waste land for nesting-places to ploughed and cultivated fields.

42. Meadow-Pipit. *Anthus pratensis* (Linn.).

This pipit, which is a common resident and breeds with us, frequents sheep pens in the winter, where it sometimes suffers very severely from the effects of wool becoming tightly wound round the toes, which get loaded with mud. This hardens in the spring, and the toes are so much constricted as to be not infrequently lost. The pied wagtail, also frequenting the same places, sometimes suffers similarly.

[Richard's Pipit. *Anthus richardi*, Vieillot.

Hastings says of this species : 'The *Anthus richardi* is reported to have been killed in the low meadows at Fladbury.' I assume that the Avon meadows are here meant. There is very great reason to believe that Richard's pipit has been seen feeding on a patch of shingle and mud in the Avon at Welford. Mr. W. H. Baylies, residing at that place, a most accurate observer of wild birds, describes the bird in question as having somewhat of the elongated form of a wagtail, with the long dark markings about the face well defined and conspicuous. He was quite sure the bird he saw was neither a tree, meadow or rock pipit, with all of which he was well acquainted. It is however possible it was the tawny pipit (*A. campestris*), for which it is not difficult to mistake Richard's pipit.]

43. Rock-Pipit. *Anthus obscurus* (Latham).

All I can say of the rock-pipit is that it sometimes appears by the side of the Avon during the winter, and that one year a considerable number were shot at different localities in its course, some of them as high up as Warwick. The impression at the time was that they had proceeded up stream from the Severn as a migratory flight.

44. Golden Oriole. *Oriolus galbula*, Linn.

Of this handsome bird Lees says : 'Seen by the late Colonel Patrick near Whitehall St. John's'; and Mr. W. Edwards, of Malvern, records the appearance of one at Malvern Wells in 1869. I have the following note which I made on the occasion of a golden oriole visiting South Littleton in 1892 : 'A golden oriole was seen feeding with some starlings on ripe pears in the orchard here in the forenoon of the 12th of October, 1892, which, from the brilliancy of the plumage, must have been a male. Being scared away, he did not return to the same spot, but was seen a week later in the vicarage garden, which adjoins the orchard above mentioned. After an interval of a few days, he was again observed in the same garden ; and between then and the end of the month he was watched feeding on the ground, after the manner of a blackbird, under an apple tree in a close near to the same place. On each occasion he was seen it was noticed that when disturbed he flew right off and out of sight.'

About the same time a golden oriole was seen by the Rev. C. W. Simons, rector of Saintbury in the parish of Willersey, which adjoins Saintbury, and also Broadway, Worcestershire, and is about six miles distant from Littleton.

45. Great Grey Shrike. *Lanius excubitor*, Linn.

The great grey shrike, though a comparatively rare visitor to us, has nevertheless so often been seen that an enumeration of the dates of its occurrence at several places in the county seems scarcely necessary. I have notes of its appearance in the valley of the Avon, and Lees gives Blackmoor Park as a place which it visited in 1867, while Mr. W. Edwards says that one was several times seen in the Malvern Cemetery in 1897.

46. Red-backed Shrike. *Lanius collurio*, Linn.

This is a regular summer migrant, and breeds in the Teme valley and in many places in the county. Its habit of impaling food on thorns is too well known to require confirmation. A more or less vertical thorn, and one which grows out of a strong branch of a hawthorn bush, generally so near the middle as to be out of sight, is selected, and unless close search is made it escapes observation. The following articles of food have been seen by the author impaled on thorns by this shrike, namely, mice, shrews, voles, young birds, including a young partridge, blackbeetles, humblebees, bluebottle flies and large-bodied moths.

[Woodchat Shrike. *Lanius pomeranus*, Sparrman.

'Stated by Mrs. Perrott to appear in the neighbourhood of Evesham' (*Hastings*, p. 65, 1834).]

47. Waxwing. *Ampelis garrulus*, Linn.

The waxwing has occurred in the county several times, perhaps not very infrequently. A fine male was shot at Atch Lench in the winter of 1859–60, and soon after came into the hands of the writer. In February, 1893, one which had been shot near Worcester was brought to Mr. Holloway of that city for preservation. During that winter a considerable number of waxwings visited England.

The waxwing is stated by Hastings to be of 'infrequent occurrence' in the county, and Lees reports that specimens have occurred near Malvern, but he supplies no particulars. Mr. W. Edwards, however, writing from Malvern, says: '1896, three specimens were killed, two at Welland and one at Malvern Wells. I saw a pair feeding on the lawn at Holly Mount.'

48. Pied Flycatcher. *Muscicapa atricapilla*, Linn.

'An inhabitant of the woods near Eardiston' (*Hastings*, p. 65).
To the above I can add several other localities in the county, namely, near to the city of Worcester, Spetchley and Malvern. Lees speaks of it as a Malvern bird, 'Rare, but occasionally seen'; and Mr. W. Edwards says, 'One at the Rhydd, near Hanley Castle.' This bird has also been seen at Powick. In the near parts of the counties of Warwick and Gloucester several specimens have been recorded.

49. Spotted Flycatcher. *Muscicapa grisola*, Linn.

This is a regular summer migrant, and one of the latest, seldom making its appearance before the end of May. The apple orchards of Worcestershire are peculiarly suited to the habits of the flycatcher, and pairs may be noted in such places all through the summer, taking their station on some low bough or the top of a stake and capturing insects on the wing under the tree. In old orchards there is abundance of places on the crooked and moss-grown trees which are convenient for the lodgment of a nest, and they may be seen stuck about in the quaintest manner. I believe that only one brood is raised, for as well as arriving late in the spring, the flycatcher is one of the earliest to depart in the autumn.

50. Swallow. *Hirundo rustica*, Linn.

It is with the greatest regret that I am obliged to relate that in Worcestershire, as in other counties, the swallow has within the last few years become a comparatively rare bird, and the following will, I believe, give a tolerably exact idea of the decrease in its numbers. The premises where I now live used a few years ago to afford convenience for as many as seven nests; but by a gradual decrease they were reduced to one in 1898, and in the summer of 1899, not a single pair nested here. The accommodation remains, and the old nests are still in place, but the birds have gone. That this is not a merely local record will, I think, be evident if a census of the swallows is made at their roosting-places in the osier beds in our streams, where the decrease in their number is so remarkable that I shall not be exaggerating if I say that where there are now scores there were formerly thousands.

51. House-Martin. *Chelidon urbica* (Linn.).

Like the swallow, the martin now appears in decreased numbers, but in not nearly so great a degree. There never was a time when it was as abundant as the swallow, and I cannot call to mind its roosting in clouds like that bird.

52. Sand-Martin. *Cotile riparia* (Linn.).

There does not seem to be any diminution in the number of sand-martins, though, as the

species is local on account of the requirements of a suitable place for a nest, it may really be less abundant than it appears to be. Nevertheless, where there are good breeding-places its numbers are as great as formerly.

53. Greenfinch. *Ligurinus chloris* (Linn.).

The greenfinch was at one time more abundant than it is now, and might be seen in considerable flocks in rickyards in the winter, where it fed chiefly on the corns of barley; and I have observed quite large flights clinging to the sides of ricks of that grain. There are few of our small birds which have bills strong enough to break up a barleycorn, but the greenfinch can do it quite easily. The husk containing the seeds of the mangel-wurzel, when ripe, is exceedingly rough and hard, and is proof against the attacks of nearly all our seed-eating birds; but the greenfinch can crush it, and will certainly do so if not kept off when the seeds are ripening.

54. Hawfinch. *Coccothraustes vulgaris*, Pallas.

This is one of the very few birds which have become more abundant within the last twenty or thirty years. Hastings, writing in 1834, reported it as infrequent in the county. Lees speaks of it as a rare bird around Malvern, but sometimes breeds. Some time in the 'thirties' a hawfinch was shot in the valley of the Avon, which was thought to be so remarkable a bird that a great many people visited the house where it was to examine it. Of late years it has become comparatively common in the county, where it breeds annually.

55. Goldfinch. *Carduelis elegans*, Stephens.

Mr. Aplin, in his work on the Birds of Oxfordshire, mentions two distinct varieties of the goldfinch; the one large, light in colour and brilliant, which is a summer migrant, and the other small, dark-coloured and resident. Both varieties occur in Worcestershire, but the larger and brighter one certainly remains with us until at least mid-winter, and I have specimens which were shot in the alder trees of the Avon in the middle of December, 1896. We have a fair number of goldfinches breeding with us, due in some measure to the preference shown to the pear tree as a nesting-place, and the pear is essentially a Worcestershire tree. When our pear trees have lost their leaves the nests of the goldfinch may be seen on the very ends of the branches, looking like small round balls. The seeds of all kinds of thistles, as well as of the teazel and burdock, afford food for the goldfinch, and in mid-winter the alder and ash are visited and

the seeds eaten, but it is only the germ of the latter which is consumed.

56. Siskin. *Carduelis spinus* (Linn.).

The siskin is an irregular winter visitor, occasionally appearing in considerable numbers, though whole seasons may pass and none or only a few stragglers be seen. The Rev. F. O. Morris, in his work on British Birds, has the following : ' When at school at Bromsgrove, in Worcestershire, I and my schoolfellows used to shoot several of these birds out of pretty considerable flocks, which used occasionally to frequent the gardens near the town, and more generally the alder trees by the side of Charford brook.' He also speaks of their being at Stoke Prior, a little lower down the same stream, in 1852. The alder trees by the side of our streams are the chief resorts of the siskin in the years when it visits us, which was the case in the winter of 1889–90. Their stay, however, was very brief; they were here to-day and gone to-morrow.

57. House-Sparrow. *Passer domesticus* (Linn.).

The sparrow it need hardly be said is only too abundant, and is a scourge to other birds of his own size.

58. Tree-Sparrow. *Passer montanus* (Linn.).

This species is very much less abundant than the house-sparrow, and though frequenting open fields and small enclosures is very seldom seen near houses. The nest is often placed in a hole of a pollard withy or apple tree, or in the thatch of a cattle shed, but is always outside, and seldom, if ever, inside the building.

59. Chaffinch. *Fringilla cœlebs*, Linn.

The chaffinch is a common and well-known bird, though by no means a favourite with the growers of radishes. The nest, the beauty of which is unrivalled, is usually placed in the fork of a bush or tree, but occasionally a departure from the general habit has been noticed. A nest was seen by the writer in a recess or niche in the upright bole of an aged and lichen-covered pear tree, and so much resembled the bark of the tree that had not the bird flown out it would have escaped notice. Another was placed in the crooked and tangled roots of an ash tree in the vertical bank of a brook, only a foot above the water, and a third was in a still more unlikely place, namely in the side of a wheat rick in a rickyard. The last-named one was described by a labourer who found it as being ' like a ball of worsted ' stuck in the side of the rick. He might have said of grey worsted, for that was what it considerably resembled when seen

from a little distance, no attempt having been made by the bird to approximate the colour of the nest to its surroundings.

60. Brambling. *Fringilla montifringilla*, Linn.

This is an uncertain visitor, appearing in winter, and mixing with flights of finches and linnets, but not with sparrows. It is noticeable from the white patch over the tail, which is very conspicuous when the bird is flying away from the observer. An unusual number visited the valley of the Avon in the winter of 1899–1900, and a considerable flight appeared in February of the latter year in company with linnets, and fed on seeds which had been thrown out from the great tithe barn built by the Abbots of Evesham at Middle Littleton. Nearly twenty were shot by an inhabitant of the village, which being subjected to examination were observed to be males and females in about equal proportion. Although the males had generally the usual rufous breast and throat, three of them had more or less dark-coloured throats. That peculiarity is worthy of particular mention, as it is not mentioned by Yarrell, Macgillivray, Howard Saunders nor Temminck, though Degland says that the upper part of the neck (presumably all round) is dark in colour in summer. From the circumstance of some of the dark throats being more or less mottled by light rufous feathers, it seems probable that the dark colour is a seasonal as well as a sexual peculiarity. Mr. Aplin, in his work on the birds of Oxfordshire, speaks of the occasional dark-coloured throats in this bird as a variety only, and he further says that part is sometimes white instead of black.

61. Linnet. *Linota cannabina* (Linn.).

There is no diminution in the numbers of the present species, all that is necessary for a full show of linnets being a weedy stubble after harvest, where a good quantity of charlock seed has been scattered. The favourite place for the nest is a brake of furze, but any close bush will do, and when there is no such accommodation in a state of nature, a cropped hawthorn hedge is chosen and freely used.

62. Lesser Redpoll. *Linota rufescens* (Vieillot).

The lesser redpoll is a winter visitor, and frequents the sides of streams, especially if there are alder trees and bushes, on the seeds of which it feeds, and sometimes on the seeds of the willow herb. Mr. Howard Saunders, in his *Manual of British Birds*, speaks of this bird as occasionally breeding in Worcestershire, but I have never been fortunate enough to find a nest in the county, though I have seen one at Alcester, Warwickshire, which is but a little way from the boundary.

63. Twite. *Linota flavirostris* (Linn.).

The twite is a rare straggler with us, and only seen in severe weather, when its monotonous note declares its presence.

64. Bullfinch. *Pyrrhula europæa*, Vieillot.

In those parts of the county where there is much market gardening the bullfinch is not a favourite, and certainly the fruit-growers have no great reason to like him. Whatever may be said in his favour, the damage he does to fruit trees and gooseberry bushes is too serious to be overlooked. Commencing on a branch of a gooseberry bush, the bullfinch will climb along it and consume every bud, leaving the ground beneath littered with the chaff made in getting at the inner part, which is eaten. The seed of the ash is also consumed by this bird. Unlike the goldfinch, which picks out the germ only, the bullfinch feeds on the whole of the seed, commencing at one end and biting bits off until all is eaten.

[Pine-Grosbeak. *Pyrrhula enucleator* (Linn.).

I include this bird in the list of Worcestershire birds on the authority of Hastings. Its occurrence is most doubtful.]

65. Crossbill. *Loxia curvirostra*, Linn.

The crossbill is one of the birds reported by Hastings as of infrequent occurrence in Worcestershire sixty years ago; but Lees, writing in 1870, says that it is now seen occasionally, but formerly it would seem that its visits were more frequent, as in an old *History of Birds* published in the last century it is said that crossbills visit the orchards of Worcestershire and Herefordshire in great numbers, destroying the apples for the sake of their enclosed kernels.' He also quotes Mr. Edwards as an authority for stating that crossbills were abundant in the neighbourhood of Malvern in 1869. Subsequently however Mr. Edwards has made the statement that this bird 'frequents the Hill every year near the Wells.' This is most likely due to the confusion between this bird and the hawfinch. A local name of the hawfinch is ' grossbeak,' and this is confused with ' crossbeak.' Certainly is not an annual visitor.

In the very early spring of 1870 (the spring following the winter when so many were seen at Malvern), a flight alighted on a spruce fir on the lawn at the Vicarage, South Littleton, and two were shot. Shortly afterwards several appeared in an ancient oriental cyprus on the lawn of the house in which the writer now

lives in South Littleton. They were busily engaged in feeding on the seeds in the close hard cones which would have defied even the specially adapted mandibles of the crossbill to open had they not been operated on by the vicissitudes of the previous winter. That flight remained two days until the supply of cones was exhausted.

66. **Two-barred Crossbill.** *Loxia bifasciata* (Brehm).

I am unable to report a second occurrence of this bird in the county. Mr. Strickland's specimen, long ago noticed, is still preserved in the Cambridge Museum.

67. **Corn-Bunting.** *Emberiza miliaria*, Linn.

This is one of those birds which, though not uncommon, is not by any means abundant. In the valley of the Avon (taking in parts of the counties of Warwick, Gloucester and Worcester), this bunting breeds by preference in fields of vetches, and the nests are often destroyed when the vetches are consumed by horses and sheep.

68. **Yellow Hammer.** *Emberiza citrinella*, Linn.

This is one of our most abundant resident birds, and the nest is to be found in the bottom of every hedge and brake as well as in the open fields. The song is said by the country people to be as follows :

'A little bit, a bit, a bit of bread and no cheese.'

The 'no' is strongly accented and the last word drawn out. Another version of the same is—

'A dish, a dish, a dish of green p–e–a–s.'

The last word, ' peas,' being much drawn out.

69. **Cirl Bunting.** *Emberiza cirlus*, Linn.

The cirl bunting is not a rare though a very local bird in Worcestershire, and is observed to frequent the same spot in limited numbers from year to year ; the favoured locality being in the clay districts rather than in the alluvial or sandy ones. It is a shy, retiring bird, and frequents trees much more than does the yellow hammer, the male often choosing a tall elm for his place of song, from near the top of which you will hear him, but will not easily discover his whereabouts. His song bears considerable resemblance to that of the yellow hammer, but has not the long terminal note.

70. **Reed-Bunting.** *Emberiza schœniclus*, Linn.

The reed-bunting, or, as it is often called, the reed-sparrow, is a resident, and found by the side of all our streams and some of our pools.

71. **Snow - Bunting.** *Plectorophenax nivalis* (Linn.).

It is only in severe winters that the present species make its appearance with us, and then only in small numbers, generally singly. Lees records one instance of its occurrence near Malvern, on the hills, in February, 1856. Mr. W. Edwards mentions having seen on two occasions flocks on the Malvern Hills in severe winters. A specimen in the collection of the present writer was shot in the rickyard at the Manor House, Cleeve Prior, on November 27th, 1849, when it was feeding in company with sparrows and other small birds.

72. **Starling.** *Sturnus vulgaris*, Linn.

The starling is one of the few birds which, in face of all opposition and in a country in which there is a dense and increasing population, not merely holds its own but actually increases in numbers. The flocks which accumulate in the autumn to visit some common roosting-place are almost incredible in respect of numbers. The reason of their increase may be found in the readiness with which the starling adapts itself to changes of surroundings, especially at nesting time. Take the following as an instance. For several years a pair bred in a woodpecker's hole in a large elm in close proximity to the writer's residence, but the tree being blown down it might have been supposed that the starlings would have abandoned the hole, which in the prostrate tree was only a few inches from the ground. It was not so, however, for they entered it and successfully reared a brood in it.

73. **Rose-coloured Pastor.** *Pastor roseus* (Linn.).

Lees in his list of the birds of the Malvern district reports that a female of this species was shot in the vicinity of Powick in August, 1855, and to that record I can add the following :—

A few years since a bird supposed to be a young starling, which had been shot near Worcester, was brought to Mr. H. Holloway of that city for preservation, and remained unnoticed in his hands until the year 1899, when it was seen and identified by the present writer as an immature rose-coloured pastor. All that could be learned about it was that it was brought when freshly killed by the man who shot it, and that it was in the company of young starlings near to the city at the time.

74. **Chough.** *Pyrrhocorax graculus* (Linn.).

This bird was killed at Lindridge in November, 1826. It was perched on the summit of a building adjacent to Sir C. Smith's,

where it was probably resting after a long flight (*Hastings*, p. 66). Its nearest locality to Worcestershire is in some of the Welsh cliffs.

[Alpine Chough. *Pyrrhocorax alpinus*, Koch.

On the authority of a very careful observer, Mr. J. Hiam, who saw a bird of this species near his residence at Astwood Bank, Worcestershire, I introduce it into the present list, though with great doubts as to it being anything more than an escaped bird. At the same time, as it was met with on four different occasions in Heligoland by Herr Gätke, there is no reason why truly wild birds of this species should not appear in Great Britain (see *Saunders*, p. 232).]

75. Jay. *Garrulus glandarius* (Linn.).

The jay was a common resident in Worcestershire, and is still found in decreasing numbers wherever there are woods and coppices suitable to its habits.

76. Magpie. *Pica rustica* (Scopoli).

In all the most highly cultivated parts of the county, as well as where game is preserved, this bird has sensibly decreased in numbers.

A tame magpie which was kept some years ago by a woman having the care of a crossing on the Great Western Railway, three or four miles from Evesham, built a great domed nest in what is locally known as a washing pan, which stood at the door of her hut, and laid in it a full complement of eggs. These were taken out and replaced by other magpie's eggs, but the cheat was at once discovered by the bird, and every one of them was speedily broken by her.

77. Jackdaw. *Corvus monedula*, Linn.

The daw is one of those birds which can bend to circumstance in the battle of life, and so holds its own. Accordingly it is a common resident.

78. Raven. *Corvus corax*, Linn.

When Hastings wrote, in 1834, the raven had become a rare Worcestershire bird. However, late in the 'forties,' it was still breeding at Stanford Court, the seat of the Winington family, as I was informed by the Rev. W. Rufford, Vicar of Sapey, in a communication from him in July, 1849. Lees says that in 1870, when he wrote, the raven might be occasionally seen passing over the Malvern district, and relates that many years before that date he saw a nest with young just fledged at Sarn Hill, Bushley. If it ever appears now in the county it is as a casual wanderer from Wales.

79. Carrion-Crow. *Corvus corone*, Linn.

We still have the carrion-crow, or as it is often called provincially the gor crow, and in some localities it is pretty common ; yet, taking the county through, its numbers have greatly diminished within the last four or five decades.

80. Grey or Hooded Crow. *Corvus cornix*, Linn.

The hooded crow is mentioned by Mr. Willis Bund as a resident, but no instance of its breeding in the county has come to my knowledge. It has not very infrequently occurred, but always, so far as I know, as a straggler, and bearing in mind the great number which annually pass Heligoland and reach our eastern coast, it does not seem improbable that some of them may stray into our county.

I have known the hooded crow frequent the sides of the Avon and feed on the mussels which became accessible when the water ran low by the action of the locks. It is also sometimes seen in our pastures accompanying the herds of cattle. Lees mentions one instance only of the occurrence of the hooded crow at Malvern.

81. Rook. *Corvus frugilegus*, Linn.

There is no diminution in the number of our rookeries, nor yet in the number of the nests. It sometimes happens that a carrion-crow will visit a rookery to feed on the rooks' eggs. The crow will perch on the edge of a nest, and in spite of the attempt of the rooks to drive him off, will deliberately consume the eggs. The owner of the rookery, though fully aware that there is something wrong with the rooks, does not easily discover what is the matter ; the colour of the crow so nearly resembling that of the rooks as to render detection difficult. I have known a rookery almost destroyed by such a marauder, or perhaps by a pair of them.

82. Sky-Lark. *Alauda arvensis*, Linn.

The sky-lark is, I am happy to say, a common and resident bird in our county, and we still have his music in our fields and meadows all through the summer.

In the afternoon of December 28th, 1899, a bird flew past my brother, W. B. Tomes, and myself, near the Avon, in the parish of North Littleton, which from some resemblance about the head and beak to a hawfinch attracted our attention. But the flight was decidedly that of a lark. It alighted in an adjacent field, and in the act of doing so exhibited some white in the middle of each

wing, which became apparent when relieved against the dark ground. I entertain but little doubt that it was a white-winged lark (*Alauda siberica*). A supposed sky-lark, having white in each wing, was seen by my brother and a friend in September, 1898, when partridge shooting near Littleton, which may have also been a bird of that species, though of course the probability would be in favour of its being only a pied sky-lark.

83. Wood-Lark. *Alauda arborea*, Linn.

In the valley of the Avon, as well as in other parts of the county, the wood-lark is rare, but its peculiar but cheery song may frequently be heard in the valley of the Teme.

84. Swift. *Cypselus apus* (Linn.).

While the swallows and martins have so seriously diminished in numbers, the swift is quite as plentiful as it ever was. It is so emphatically a bird of the air that the common people say it ascends into the higher regions of the atmosphere to roost ! That the intercourse between the sexes takes place high up in the air, as observed by Gilbert White at Selborne, the present writer can from personal observation confirm.

Whether the alpine swift, *Cypselus melba* (Linn.) can be claimed as a Worcestershire bird, or even as a Gloucestershire species, is open to question, but a swift of great size and having a white under part passed over the present writer near the village of Weston-on-Avon, within gun-shot, in the first week in July, 1876, flying in a south-west direction. There can be no doubt that it was either an alpine swift, or the still rarer needle-tailed swift, *Acanthyllis caudacuta* (Latham).

85. Nightjar. *Caprimulgus europæus*, Linn.

The nightjar, or goatsucker, cannot be called at all abundant in the county ; but is met with in such localities as are congenial to its habits, which may indeed be said of its appearance in other counties. Its abundance or the reverse appears to be dependent rather on the nature of the locality than its latitude. Hastings is silent about the goatsucker. It is still fairly plentiful in Wyre Forest. In the Malvern district it is said by both Lees and Edwards to be not uncommon, and the latter gentleman has met with the nest and eggs. It has also bred at Cracomb near Evesham.

86. Wryneck. *Iÿnx torquilla*, Linn.

The wryneck, though not rare, is much less frequently heard or seen than formerly, and from enquiry it appears to be seldom brought to the bird stuffers for preservation. The

falling off in numbers may be attributed to the want of proper habitats, as the old orchards of Worcestershire were everything that could be desired, affording at once abundance of insect food as well as suitable building places ; but the more modern orchards afford neither.

87. Green Woodpecker. *Gecinus viridis* (Linn.).

Locally, Iccle (? Hickwall).

This bird is one which, notwithstanding the diminution in the quantity of timber, still remains as common as heretofore, and may be seen and heard in suitable localities at all seasons.

88. Great Spotted Woodpecker. *Dendrocopus major* (Linn.).

Hastings says nothing of this woodpecker by which we can learn anything of its frequency, only that it is less common than the green woodpecker. Lees gives it as occurring near Malvern, where it is 'rather uncommon.' It appears to be more common in that part of the county adjoining Herefordshire than elsewhere, from which locality a considerable number of species are annually brought into Worcester for preservation.

89. Lesser Spotted Woodpecker. *Dendrocopus minor* (Linn.).

More frequent in the county than the last, this little bird is also more generally distributed, and is partial to orchards, in which in the early spring it makes its presence known by its loud jarring noise, said to be occasioned by the rapid action of the bill on a decayed branch. It has a habit at that season of climbing up to the very top sprig of a tall tree, and from that conspicuous place uttering its note, which somewhat resembles that of the wryneck, but is keener and louder. The nest is in a hole made by the bird in a dead branch high up in an apple, plum, or cherry tree, in an orchard or garden. The statement that the young will issue from the hole and climb about the tree is, so far as the observation of the writer has gone, entirely erroneous. On the contrary they sometimes issue from the hole and fall to the ground, as he can affirm from personal observation.

90. Kingfisher. *Alcedo ispida*, Linn.

A good deal has been said of late about the scarcity of the kingfisher, and the wanton destruction of the bird on account of the beauty of its plumage has been mentioned as the sole cause. That the blue plumage has exercised great influence in the reduction of the number of this the most brilliantly-coloured British bird there can be no doubt. Only quite recently

the writer was shown in the hands of a local bird stuffer a box full of kingfishers (more than twenty in number) mounted for the decoration of ladies' hats. Fortunately however the demand had fallen off, and the specimens were no longer required by the hat maker. But we must not credit the destruction of kingfishers for such a purpose as the sole cause of their rarity. Spring floods such as the disastrous floods of 1887, when all the low-lying meadows were under water, destroyed the nests of the kingfisher wholesale, and from that date there was a very obvious falling off in its numbers. The bird still is found in some numbers on the rivers and brooks in the county.

[Bee-Eater. *Merops apiaster*, Linn.

I can record the appearance of one which was shot not far from the boundary of the county, at Redhill near Alcester, on May 29th, 1886. It proved on dissection to be a female containing five or six eggs, and as it was in the company of a second, would probably have bred. Another, some years ago, was shot near Longdon.]

91. Hoopoe. *Upupa epops*, Linn.

The hoopoe is mentioned by Hastings as of infrequent occurrence in Worcestershire. A specimen preserved in the Worcester Museum was killed at the Yew Tree, Ombersley, and recorded in the *Zoologist* in 1862 by Mr. A. Edwards, who also referred to one which occurred about twenty years previously near the Trench Woods, about seven miles from Worcester. He also secured a third which was shot about the same distance from the city between that time and 1862, the date of his communication. A hoopoe was shot by the late Mr. W. H. Ashwin at Bretforton on the 4th of May, 1875. The latest instance of the appearance of the hoopoe in the county, of which I have any knowledge, is of one shot near Shipston-on-Stour, but I am in ignorance of the precise date.

92. Cuckoo. *Cuculus canorus*, Linn.

This well-known summer visitor is fairly common all over the county. For many years past I have had a very decided opinion that the female cuckoo conveys her eggs into the nests of other birds by means of her beak, and I arrived at that conclusion from having found both eggs and young in nests so placed that it would have been impossible for her to have laid her eggs there in the manner of other birds. Once I saw a young cuckoo in the nest of a wren, which was overhead in the thatch in the inside of a cattle shed. The young bird had its head out at the hole of the domed nest, and was being fed by the wrens. It would have been impossible for the female cuckoo to have laid the egg in that nest. The above particulars were given by me to Mr. Gould at the time he was engaged with his great work on British birds. On another occasion I found a cuckoo's egg in the nest of a redbreast in some ivy against a wall, and the nest was so close to the wall that the latter really formed one side of the nest. Moreover, the nest was closely overhung by large leathery ivy leaves, and a bird of the size of a cuckoo could not possibly have sat upon it. The nest of the reed-warbler is always suspended between three or four upright stems, generally those of reeds, and nests so placed are often found to contain the egg or young of the cuckoo, and it may be safely asserted that a cuckoo could not lay an egg in such a nest.

I have great reason for suspecting that I have more than once disturbed a female cuckoo when laying her egg. It is not unusual in the breeding season to see a silent cuckoo rise from some bare place, such as an unfrequented road, and alight again after a short flight, as if reluctant to leave the spot. After two or three such short flights, a longer one will bring the bird back to the place where it was first seen—doubtless if, as is now generally thought, the cuckoo takes her egg in her beak, it would be laid on some spot from which it could easily and safely be taken up, and that would not be amongst herbage of any kind, not even the grass of a pasture, but on some bare place. Cuckoos flitting before one in the way I have mentioned are not unusual, and are always single and always silent.

93. White or Barn Owl. *Strix flammea*, Linn.

It is with the greatest regret that I am obliged to record the very great decrease in the number of this handsome, interesting and useful bird in our county, but year by year it becomes less frequent, and the time is not far distant when it will be spoken of as formerly known in Worcestershire. A very remarkable variety was killed at the Limekiln Farm, Martley, Worcester, early in the month of June, 1897, which came into the hands of the writer shortly after that date. The whole of the under surface is of a deep yellowish salmon colour. Around the eyes there is a considerable extent of bright chestnut, and the upper parts of the body are darker in colour than is usually seen in the ordinary specimens of the barn-owl. In size it rather exceeds the usual individuals. This variety

is known to ornithologists as the 'western owl,' and a figure of it will be found in Dresser's *Birds of Europe*. I am happy to have been able to introduce it into the Worcestershire list.

94. Long-eared Owl. *Asio otus* (Linn.).

A resident bird, which may be said to be uncommon rather than rare; the long-eared owl has however never been mentioned as breeding in Worcestershire. It is to a great extent a woodland species, and is partial to plantations in which there are many evergreens, such as pines and spruce firs.

95. Short-eared Owl. *Asio accipitrinus* (Pallas).

Of this species Mr. Willis Bund says: 'Mostly autumn migrants; a few reside,' which applies to Great Britain and not exclusively to Worcestershire. Lees speaks of it as of a rare occurrence in the Malvern districts. So far as I can learn there is no record of this species having ever bred in Worcestershire, but it is not uncommon in some parts of the county as an autumn visitor. On the Cotteswold Hills it is not at all infrequent, and seems to prefer turnip fields.

96. Tawny or Brown Owl. *Syrnium aluco* (Linn.).

This owl must be considered as the commonest owl in Worcestershire. It has a much better idea of taking care of itself than the barn-owl, and will sometimes take up its quarters very near our dwellings and observe so much caution that its presence would remain unknown were it not for its droppings which betray it.

97. Little Owl. *Athene noctua* (Scopoli).

There are two undoubted Worcestershire specimens of this species, one in the Museum at Worcester and the other in the collection of the writer. The first was taken at Eardiston, the residence of Sir C. S. Smith, but there is no record of the date, and the second was shot in the spring of 1897 at Lulsley, near Knightwick, in this county. It was first seen on the roof of some farm buildings, and was subsequently shot from there.

98. Scops-Owl. *Scops giu* (Scopoli).

Besides the recorded specimen mentioned by Hastings, I have heard of one which was brought to the late veteran taxidermist of Worcester, Mr. H. Holloway, for preservation. It came into his hands between thirty and forty years ago, when freshly killed, but I have failed to gather any particulars concerning it.

99. Marsh-Harrier. *Circus æruginosus* (Linn.).

About thirty years since a bird of this species was shot at Witley Court. I know of no other occurrence of this harrier in Worcestershire, and this solitary specimen is in immature plumage.

100. Hen-Harrier. *Circus cyaneus* (Linn.).

The hen-harrier must now I think be mentioned as having formerly occurred in Worcestershire, not a straggler having appeared for some years. A female in the Worcester Museum was taken at Eardiston, but the date is not known. The latest occurrence in the county of which I have any knowledge is that of a female which was shot near Shipston-on-Stour in 1877, and brought to Mr. Quartermain, of Stratford-on-Avon, for preservation, where I saw and examined it.

[Montagu's Harrier. *Circus cineraceus* (Montagu).

I possess an adult male which was shot a good many years ago at Sutton Coldfield in Warwickshire, not very distant from our county boundary.]

101. Buzzard. *Buteo vulgaris*, Leach.

Of late years the buzzard has become a rare bird in all the midland counties, its appearance being confined to stragglers, few in number and far between. Only one specimen of local occurrence is in the Worcester Museum, and that was taken at Croome Park. The latest Worcestershire specimen which I have heard of was killed at Witley Court in the early part of 1892, and brought to the late Mr. H. Holloway, of Worcester, for preservation. The buzzard was considered to be rare in the Malvern district so long ago as 1870, and Mr. W. Edwards regarded the occurrence of one at Eastnor in 1869 as worthy of record. It still breeds in Wales at no very great distance from the Worcestershire boundary.

102. Sparrow-Hawk. *Accipiter nisus* (Linn.).

Like all the birds of prey the sparrow-hawk is less frequently seen in the midland counties than it used to be; though it cannot now be said to be otherwise than common, and it is certainly a resident bird, breeding for the most part in woods and coppices where it is least likely to be observed. The eggs are always, to the best of my knowledge, laid in an old nest of some other bird, as that of a crow or a magpie, often one that has been reduced by the wear of more than one winter to a lump of decayed sticks. The mere platform made by the ringdove has been known to serve the turn of the sparrow-hawk, but whatever is its

selection there is always a kind of super-structure of its own, which in one nest examined by the writer was composed wholly of dead couch grass, locally known as 'squitch.' It is very rarely that the nest is at any great height from the ground.

103. Kite. *Milvus ictinus*, Savigny.

It would seem that when Hastings wrote in 1834, the kite, though very rare, was not extinct in Worcestershire. His words are, 'The Kite, *Milvus vulgaris*, and Osprey, *Balbucardus haliaëtus*, but very rarely occur.' Lees mentions the middle of the last century as the date when the kite was well known on the Malvern Hills, but was no longer there in 1870. Yet he makes the following remarkable statement : 'Curiously enough about twenty years ago the Grimsend estate was unoccupied for a considerable time ; the kites returned to their old haunts, and remained till the Grimsend again secured a tenant.' He records one as having been shot in Croome Park in the winter of 1869–70. I have a note of one having been killed there which is now in the collection of Mr. Martin Curtler, and which may be the bird mentioned by Lees.

104. Honey - Buzzard. *Pernis apivorus* (Linn.).

I can record two instances only of the occurrence of this bird in Worcestershire. One was killed at Eardiston, and is now in the Worcester Museum, and the other was taken at Witley Court about thirty years since, and is now in the collection of the present writer. It is probable that there are other Worcestershire specimens in private collections, for Hastings wrote, ' not of uncommon occurrence.' The latest appearance of this fine bird which I can record was about the middle of May, 1894, when one was taken in a jay trap at Ragley Park, on that side of the estate nearest the Ridgeway, which divides the counties of Warwick and Worcester. Although therefore it was probably not killed in Worcestershire it must have been in very near proximity to it.

[Iceland Falcon. *Falco islandus*, Gmelin.

In one instance only have I known the Iceland falcon to occur in the midland counties. One was shot by Mr. John Hyatt on his estate at Quinton in Gloucestershire, in very close proximity to the boundary of Worcestershire, in the autumn or early part of winter of 1852. It was seen and examined by me when freshly killed, and the species determined.]

105. Peregrine Falcon. *Falco peregrinus*, Tunstall.

The peregrine is a regular visitor to our county, no winter passing when a certain number of them are not seen. The vicinity of rivers appears to be the most favoured locality for them, as they prey on teal and moorhens. But peewits, wood-pigeons, and partridges also form part of their diet, and the feathers of these birds are left in the meadows showing what has been their bill of fare. But besides the feathers of the birds on which they have fed, they cast some of their own, which on examination not only determine the age of the traveller but also the sex. Lees appears to have regarded the peregrine as a rare bird, and mentions one killed at Croome Park, 'some years ago,' and Mr. W. Edwards records one shot at Cradley in 1872, and another at Evesham in 1878. This falcon builds in Wales not a very great distance from the county boundary.

106. Hobby. *Falco subbuteo*, Linn.

The hobby was formerly a comparatively common summer visitor to the vale of the Avon, when the swallow was an abundant bird, but has now become rare. Several nests have come to the knowledge of the writer in the Avon valley, though only one which was within the boundary of the county. It was found at a place called Porter's Coppice near Evesham, and full-fledged young were taken from it, one of which was seen and examined by the writer. Another nest was discovered near the village of Willersey, Gloucestershire, half a mile from Broadway in Worcestershire.

The time to see and note the hobby in former years was in the autumn when the swallows were gathered in countless numbers in the evening to roost in the osier and reed beds of the Avon. On the evening of the 30th of July, 1847, the writer and two friends took their station near some osier beds at Welford-on-Avon, with the intention of looking after the hobbies which were known to come there to feed on the swallows. The air was literally filled with the latter birds for a distance of a quarter of a mile up and down stream. At first one hobby appeared and passed on rapid wing through and through the cloud of swallows, occasionally making a dash at one. Soon afterwards a second came, followed at intervals by two others, making up four which were in sight at the same time, and were passing backward and forward through the swallows just where they were thickest. One hobby being shot, the others left

the spot. On other occasions hobbies have been observed where the swallows gathered in the evening, but at no other time were so many seen at once. More frequently, only one, or perhaps two, have put in an appearance. What always seemed remarkable was that with so great a number of swallows captures were very infrequent. The latest note I have of the hobby waiting on the swallows is dated the 7th of September, 1893, when one appeared near the mill on the Avon at Harvington, where a small flight of swallows had gathered. Now, however, the latter bird has become too rare to attract the hobby. Lees records, on the authority of Mr. Edwards, a nest of a hobby at Mathon in 1868, and the latter gentleman favours me with a note recording that a nest with young was found at Eastnor in 1897.

107. Merlin. *Falco æsalon*, Tunstall.

The merlin is, strictly speaking, migratory with us, appearing in the autumn, winter, or very early spring. Years ago when the swallow was abundant the merlin as well as the hobby frequented the roosting places of that bird in the osier and reed beds. But the merlin did so very occasionally, being indeed but rarely seen so early in the autumn. November is the month when we most frequently see the merlin, about the time when the redwings make their appearance. Larks appear to be a favourite food of this little falcon, especially on the slopes of the hills.

108. Red-footed Falcon. *Falco vespertinus*, Linn.

A bird of this species, which from its uniformly dark colour was certainly an adult male, was seen and closely watched for some time by Mr. W. H. Baylies while busily engaged in hawking for cockchaffers in some large elms near his house in June, 1870. As Mr. Baylies is intimately acquainted with the hobby and the merlin, he can certainly assert that the bird he saw was not either of those birds, but, indeed, there can be no doubt from the colour as to the species.

109. Kestrel. *Falco tinnunculus*, Linn.

A common and resident bird, locally known as the mouse-hawk, nesting generally in an old nest of a crow or magpie. During winter the kestrel usually retires to the same places to roost for some time, which is very often on some small branch growing out on the sheltered side of a large tree, quite close to the bole, beneath which the castings may be found in great quantity. They become disintegrated by the rains of winter, and all are

then seen to be made up of the bones and fur of small mammals, with now and then the bones and feathers of a small bird, and the elytra of beetles.

110. Osprey. *Pandion haliaëtus* (Linn.).

According to Hastings, the osprey was, when he wrote, in 1834, one of the birds which were known to 'but very rarely occur,' and in a note he records it as 'once seen flying over the River Teme.' I am unable to add anything to its history as a Worcestershire bird, but I have a specimen which was shot in January, 1864, in the Avon, between the counties of Warwick and Gloucester, and only a short distance from the point where the stream comes into Worcestershire. I have the record of several which have been taken in the neighbouring county of Warwick.

111. Cormorant. *Phalacrocorax carbo* (Linn.).

Hastings says : 'The cormorant, *Phalacrocorax carbo*, in time of floods often visits the interior of the country.' I can endorse that statement. It is also sometimes driven inland by storms and high winds ; all the specimens which I have seen have been in immature or in winter plumage. A few years ago one was found after a storm in the head of a pollard withy tree by the side of the Avon.

112. Shag or Green Cormorant. *Phalacrocorax graculus* (Linn.).

Like the last species, and indeed like so many other sea birds, this is now usually a a storm-scattered wanderer, and seldom seen unless driven by wind and storm out of its proper habitats, or during a succession of floods ; but specimens are not very infrequently found in a state of exhaustion.

113. Gannet or Solan Goose. *Sula bassana* (Linn.).

'This singular straggler was met with flying over an arable field at Alfrick, in this county, in the winter of 1833, and is now in our museum' (*Hastings*, p. 70). A specimen in the Worcester Museum, which is in adult plumage, was taken at Norton, and an immature one in the same collection at Cleveload-on-the-Severn, in the county of Worcester. On several occasions gannets have been found in a state of exhaustion in the neighbouring counties of Oxford, Gloucester and Warwick. Lundy Island is their nearest residence.

A tropic bird, *Phæton aethereus*, it is said was picked up dead near Malvern in the fifties. It is believed on the Herefordshire side of the hill at Cradley.

114. Common Heron. *Ardea cinerea*, Linn.

'The Heron, *Ardea cinerea*, is of frequent occurrence, although no heronry now exists in the county, and the nearest is in the park adjacent to Warwick Castle.' So wrote Hastings in 1834, but since that date there has been a heronry in the park at Ragley, and a few breed there at the present time. In Worcestershire the only heronry now (1901) is in Shrawley Wood. The authority above quoted adds in a note : 'A heronry existed some years ago at Croome, but the birds being troublesome, and making too free with the fish of the ponds, it was destroyed.'

115. Night-Heron. *Nycticorax griseus* (Linn.).

Mr. Willis Bund includes the night-heron in his list of Worcestershire birds, referring to the following instance of its occurrence. A few years since an adult night-heron was flushed from amongst the aquatic herbage of a small pool at Bradley Green, near Feckenham, and was shot. It was afterwards brought to Alcester for preservation, where it was seen by the writer.

116. Little Bittern. *Ardetta minuta* (Linn.).

An adult little bittern was shot more than thirty years since on a brook between the villages of Aldington and Badsey, and in close proximity to the latter place. I have no knowledge of any other specimen having been met with in Worcestershire, but an immature one was shot in Warwickshire, and brought to Stratford-on-Avon for preservation.

117. Bittern. *Botaurus stellaris* (Linn.).

Hastings records the bittern as having been often shot on the banks of the Severn. Mr. Willis Bund, including it in his Worcestershire list, adds : 'Formerly resident, now only a straggler,' which applies to it as a British as well as a Worcestershire bird. I can now only speak of it as a rare species in this county. Lees says that one was shot on the pool before Hopton Court in the parish of Leigh ; and Mr. W. Edwards, of Malvern, records one shot at Eastnor in 1876. A few years since a bittern was shot on the Avon near Pershore, and the occurrence recorded in the *Field* newspaper.

118. White Stork. *Ciconia alba*, Bechstein.

Sir Charles Hastings, on page 68 of his *Illustrations*, mentions the occurrence of this bird near Fladbury, and adds the following note : 'Mrs. Charles L. E. Perrott, on whose authority this information is given, says that "the crane and *Ciconia* were both shot by the late Mr. Perrott's keeper, but I should be inclined to think that they had escaped from some private collection."' Lees records one which was shot on the Severn near Tewkesbury many years since. Most likely it was the same bird to which Mrs. Perrott alluded.

119. Spoonbill. *Platalea leucorodia*, Linn.

The spoonbill has been shot from the large sheet of water in the park at Westwood on two occasions, but I have not the date, and the specimens are preserved in the collection of British birds of Mr. Martin Curtler, of Worcester. A spoonbill is recorded by Lees as having been shot on the Avon near Tewkesbury several years previously to 1870 (the date of his list of Malvern birds), which was at that time in the Worcester Museum.

120. Grey Lag-Goose. *Anser cinereus*, Meyer.

The present species is recorded by Hastings as being 'of frequent occurrence in the winter season in our various rivers and pools.' It is the *Anser palustris* of which he was then speaking, which is one of the names of the grey lag-goose ; and that that species did in former years pass over our county, and sometimes remain to rest, there is no doubt. The larger size and lighter colour were quite sufficient to distinguish this from the other species of grey goose, even at a considerable distance when passing over head.

121. White-fronted Goose. *Anser albifrons* (Scopoli).

As with the bean and pink-footed geese, the present species travelled in considerable numbers to and from the west in the autumn, and an occasional one out of a gaggle, which had stayed to rest, was shot, and the species determined. On one occasion an adult in full plumage was taken near the village of Offenham, and was preserved by the well-known ornithologist, Mr. H. Doubleday of Epping, who happened to be there at that time, and was placed in his fine collection of British birds. It still is found in considerable numbers in the Severn estuary, especially near Berkeley, and specimens occasionally in hard weather make their way further up the Severn to Worcestershire borders.

122. Bean-Goose. *Anser segetum* (Gmelin).

The late Mr. John Cordeaux in a history of British Anseres, which appeared in a recently published *History of British Birds*, gives a very interesting account of the bean-goose, and explains the reason of its present scarcity, which is undoubtedly due to the enclosure of open lands in the marsh districts of Lincoln-

shire, and the abandonment of the extensive growth of beans on which the geese fed, and which gave the name to the present species. It was to and from that locality that the several kinds of grey geese made their annual autumn migration to and from the low-lying lands near the mouth of the Severn, as mentioned by Yarrell. The present writer well remembers the large flights of geese of more than one species which annually passed over on their way westward or on their return eastward ; and an old inhabitant of South Littleton, whose diary contains many curious and interesting entries, made the following record relating to wild geese :—

'1839, Nov. 9th. A flock of 200 wild geese fled over Littleton in a north-east direction in 4 separate flocks about 20 yards apart : this was the biggest lot together I ever saw ; there had been many small flocks seen flying that way a few weeks before at different times.'

To that the writer added the following :—

'Additional note. The 3 Geese seen on the 16th of December were flying westward instead of towards the north-east as stated above.'

Gaggles of geese are now very rarely seen travelling, but on December 15th, 1898, about fifty grey geese passed over Littleton in a north-east direction, and on the following day three similar birds were seen pursuing the same line.

123. Pink-footed Goose. *Anser brachyrhynchus*, Baillon.

Like the last species, the pink-footed goose was formerly fairly common in the Severn district. The large gaggles of wild geese which were seen journeying westward about Michaelmas were either of this species, the bean-goose, or the white-fronted goose. The writer has examined individuals of all three which have been shot, and has satisfactorily determined the species.

124. Barnacle - Goose. *Bernicla leucopsis* (Bechstein).

The barnacle is included by Hastings in his list of Worcestershire birds, but he does not give any indication of its frequency or locality. That it has, however, occasionally frequented the Avon the writer can from personal observation affirm. It must, however, be regarded as a rare bird in the county.

125. Brent Goose. *Bernicla brenta* (Pallas).

This can only be mentioned as another irregular visitor to Worcestershire. It has never, like the grey geese, made periodical moves in large flights, but has appeared in an erratic manner, and generally singly, during the winter.

126. Whooper Swan. *Cygnus musicus*, Bechstein.

According to Sir Charles Hastings, the whooper has occurred in Worcestershire on several occasions, chiefly in the Severn and Teme, namely, at Powick Weir on the Teme in February, 1830 ; one in the Severn between Severn Stoke Church and the Rhydd in the same month of that year ; and another at Diglis, also in the Severn, on February 11, but the year not mentioned. Lees says that it appears, though rarely in severe winters, in the Severn and Teme. The present writer has known a small flight of these fine birds frequent the Avon near Harvington for several days. That was in the winter of 1894–95. It does not seem that any attempt has ever been made to distinguish the swans that have been killed, they have all been assumed to be *C. musicus* although it is quite probable some were *C. bewicki*.

127. Common Sheld-Duck. *Tadorna cornuta* (S. G. Gmelin).

The present species is essentially a coast or estuarine bird, and appears in our inland streams only occasionally. It breeds in considerable numbers in the Severn estuary where it is known as the 'Borrow duck.' All the Worcestershire specimens I have seen have been immature. It is mentioned by Hastings as a straggler.

128. Mallard or Wild Duck. *Anas boscas*, Linn.

A resident bird which breeds wherever there are suitable and protected places. The head of a pollard withy tree is not infrequently chosen as a nesting-place.

129. Shoveler. *Spatula clypeata* (Linn.).

A winter visitor, appearing on our streams very occasionally. I do not find any mention of it as a Worcestershire bird in *Hastings*, but Willis Bund includes it in the list of birds of our county, and Lees mentions one which was shot at Rosebery Rock on the Teme. It appears occasionally in the Avon.

130. Pintail. *Dafila acuta* (Linn.).

This duck is mentioned by Hastings as of 'frequent occurrence in the winter season in our various rivers and pools,' a statement that does not by any means accord with my knowledge of the species. I have found it to be of unusual appearance in our rivers.

BIRDS

131. Teal. *Nettion crecca* (Linn.).

An autumnal and winter visitor to our streams, sometimes coming in considerable flights ; but it does not generally remain long in one place, and is now unknown in summer, although it is probable that formerly it bred in the county.

132. Garganey. *Querquedula circia* (Linn.).

A rare spring visitor to the Severn, Avon and Teme. Seen only in passage.

133. Wigeon. *Mareca penelope* (Linn.).

A winter visitor which is found in most of our streams, and appearing either singly or in small companies.

134. Pochard. *Fuligula ferina* (Linn.).

This also is a winter visitor, but sometimes common. There is no record of its ever having been seen except in winter.

135. Tufted Duck. *Fuligula cristata* (Leach).

Occurs not unfrequently in the winter. Most of those I have had the opportunity of examining have been immature examples.

136. Scaup-Duck. *Fuligula marila* (Linn.).

The present species appears inland much less frequently than the tufted duck, and indeed is very rarely seen in the rivers of the county except in very severe weather, and even then it is only a straggler. Immature birds are, however, more frequently seen than adults of either sex.

137. Goldeneye. *Clangula glaucion* (Linn.).

The goldeneye is not rare in our rivers and ponds in the winter, but nearly all the specimens met with are immature. Occasionally, but very occasionally, an adult bird occurs in the spring, apparently a passage bird.

138. Long-tailed Duck. *Harelda glacialis* (Linn.).

According to Hastings it has appeared in Worcestershire as a straggler.

139. Common Eider Duck. *Somateria mollissima* (Linn.).

On the authority of Mrs. Perrott, quoted by Hastings (p. 70), an eider duck is supposed to have been killed near Evesham.

140. Common Scoter. *Œdemia nigra* (Linn.).

A coast bird, which but rarely appears on our inland waters, and then only as a straggler.

141. Velvet-Scoter. *Œdemia fusca* (Linn.).

Admitted into the lists of the Worcestershire birds solely on the authority of Sir Charles Hastings who, however, does not give either time or place of its occurrence.

[Surf-Scoter. *Œdemia perspicillata* (Linn.).

Although I cannot strictly include the rare surf-scoter in the list of Worcestershire birds, I can record the occurrence of one on the Avon, only a little way from the boundary of our county, which I saw and examined in Stratford, where it was brought for preservation.]

142. Goosander. *Mergus merganser*, Linn.

The present bird is recorded by Hastings as of ' frequent occurrence ' in Worcestershire, but no locality is mentioned, and although it cannot now be said to be frequent, it is not very rare in the winter on the principal rivers.

143. Red-breasted Merganser. *Mergus serrator*, Linn.

This is another species which is given by Hastings as frequent, but which is certainly rare in Worcestershire, if indeed there is any record of its occurrence. Mr. Willis Bund does not include it, though Lees speaks of it as making an occasional visit to the county. The writer has not met with a Worcestershire specimen, though he has one shot on the Avon a few miles from the boundary.

144. Smew. *Mergus albellus*, Linn.

Two instances only of the appearance of the smew in Worcestershire have come to the knowledge of the writer. Lees mentions one which was killed in the Severn above Worcester in the spring of 1855 ; and another which was shot at Ombersley in January, 1891, was brought by Mrs. Croft of that place to Mr. Jones, of Worcester, for preservation.

145. Ring-Dove or Wood-Pigeon. *Columba palumbus*, Linn.
Locally, Quice.

A common resident and yearly increasing in numbers. Towards the spring, when the usual food of the quice has become scarce, the osier beds of the Avon are frequented by it for the sake of the bulbous roots of the pilewort (*ranunculus*), which have been laid bare by the winter floods, and on which it feeds. So long however as the more ordinary food can be found the quice will not be seen amongst the osiers, nor indeed on the river bank.

146. Stock-Dove. *Columba œnas*, Linn.

Though a common bird the stock-dove is by no means so abundant as the ring-dove. Besides the holes of trees, the head of a pollard ash or withy is sometimes chosen as a nesting-place, and on the Cotteswold range the face of an abandoned quarry affords suitable accommodation for the nests.

147. Turtle-Dove. *Turtur communis*, Selby.

This is now a common summer visitor to Worcestershire, and distributed all over the county, but seems to prefer the alluvial tracts bordering the streams to the clay districts. Half a century ago it was by no means common, and was not mentioned as a Worcestershire bird by Hastings in 1834, and several years subsequently to the date the author remembers one being shot in the vale of the Avon, which was regarded as a great curiosity. It was found by a sportsman in a stubble field, and as the tail was spread when the bird rose, the white band at the end was conspicuous, and in default of a more accurate name the bird was designated a 'ringtail.' The increase in numbers took place gradually, and not by the influx of flights, or by a sudden addition to the number of pairs.

148. Pallas's Sand-Grouse. *Syrrhaptes paradoxus* (Pallas).

Mr. Willis Bund inserts this bird in the Worcestershire list from one, and one only, having been seen by the present writer and his brother at Littleton, on May 18th, 1888. I transcribe the note I made at the time, verbatim : ' A sand-grouse flew past my brother, W. B. Tomes, and myself, as we were walking along the line of the Liassic escarpment, near North Littleton, and so near that we could readily determine the sex to be a male. The flight was remarkably straight and swift, and in a south-easterly direction, directly towards the Cotteswold Hills. The pointed tail was very conspicuous, and a short, sharp monosyllabic note, something resembling " *check, check, check* " was uttered the whole time the bird was within hearing.' There does not appear to be any other notice of the appearance of the sand-grouse in Worcestershire.

149. Black Grouse. *Tetrao tetrix*, Linn.

' Wyre Forest, near Bewdley,' and ' is also found on the Clee Hills, and in the woods upon the banks of the Teme, near Eastham ' (*Hastings*, p. 64). It is still found in some numbers in the Forest.

150. Red Grouse. *Lagopus scoticus* (Latham).

' Inhabits Wyre Forest, near Bewdley ' (*Hastings*, p. 63). This is most doubtful. The Brown Clee in Shropshire is the nearest place where it regularly occurs, but an occasional straggler may be found in the north-west corner of the county.

151. Pheasant. *Phasianus colchicus*, Linn.

Plentiful in preserves but its continued existence as a Worcestershire bird depends mainly upon its preservation for sporting purposes.

152. Partridge. *Perdix cinerea*, Latham.

Is plentiful or the reverse according as it is protected.

153. Red-legged Partridge. *Caccabis rufa* (Linn.).

The same may be said of this as the two preceding birds. So far as I have been able to observe the present species continues to hold about the same numerical proportion to the common partridge as for some years past. It is more common in the south than in the other parts of the county, but it is nowhere very numerous.

154. Quail. *Coturnix communis*, Bonnaterre.

Hastings says that a few quails are met with at Spring Hill. It may however be said to occur over the greater part of the county, though perhaps irregularly. It is not however known except as a summer visitor ; instances of its having bred in Worcestershire are recorded. The writer has met with a nest at Littleton, and Lees mentions it as breeding at Malvern.

155. Corn-Crake or Landrail. *Crex pratensis*, Bechstein.

The abundance, or the reverse, of this bird is easily determined by its loud raking note, which there is no danger of confounding with that of any other bird. There can be no doubt that it is much less numerous than formerly, for where one might at one time have found several, one does not now hear more than one or two, or perhaps none at all. The people in the villages where the Cotteswolds break into the vale of the Severn and Avon, believe that as they hear the corn-crake on the hill or in the vale, so they will have wet or dry weather : if on the hills, wet ; if in the vale, dry. In the disastrous season of 1879, when the lowlands were in a more or less condition of flood through the whole summer, the corn-crakes were heard only on the higher ground.

156. Spotted Crake. *Porzana maruetta* (Leach).

This can hardly be mentioned as being rare, though it is only occasionally met with, and generally in the summer. Mr. Willis Bund speaks of it as becoming scarcer. Lees mentions it as occasionally appearing around Malvern. I have seen and examined several specimens which were killed in the county, and one which was shot by the side of the Avon, near to the county boundary, at the very unusual time of mid-winter.

BIRDS

157. Water-Rail. *Rallus aquaticus,* Linn.

Although the water-rail is a resident bird in Great Britain, it is certainly to a considerable extent migratory in Worcestershire, there being a great addition to its numbers late in the autumn, mostly in November. Indeed, as there is not up to the present time any recorded instance of its breeding in the county, the question is whether it is not wholly migratory with us.

158. Moor-Hen. *Gallinula chloropus* (Linn.).

A common and resident bird, found in all our streams and ponds, where it breeds. It is not generally known that the moor-hen will feed freely on apples. A brook which passes near South Littleton, and has orcharding on its banks, is frequented by moor-hens, where the writer has repeatedly seen them feeding on the fallen fruit. Sometimes nearly a dozen have been seen so engaged at one place.

159. Coot. *Fulica atra,* Linn.

The coot is common, but seems to need some protection, being found in great numbers on ornamental water, rather than on rivers on which there are pleasure boats, while it is rarely seen on streams having a public navigation.

160. Crane. *Grus communis,* Bechstein.

The admission of the crane into this list rests solely on a statement made by Mrs. Perrott, which is quoted by Hastings (p. 68), and given verbatim when speaking of the white stork. The heron (*A. cinerea*) is locally called the crane, and this probably gave rise to the occurrence of the crane as a Worcestershire bird.

161. Great Bustard. *Otis tarda,* Linn.

'A straggler of the great bustard, *Otis tarda*, was killed near Worcester a few years ago' (*Hastings,* p. 70).

162. Stone-Curlew. *Œdicnemus scolopax* (S. G. Gmelin).

This bird is stated by Sir Charles Hastings to extend 'its range just within the southern limits of our county, a few breeding among the stony barren parts of the Broadway and Bredon Hills.' In a note he adds : 'A young bird of this species was caught alive in the summer of 1832, near Twining, and brought to Worcester, where it was identified by the curator of our museum.' The Worcester Museum contains two specimens of the stone-curlew which were killed at Eardiston. In the near part of Warwickshire, in the vale of the Avon, two specimens have been shot, both of which came into the hands of the present writer when freshly killed.

163. Dotterel. *Eudromias morinellus* (Linn.).

The dotterel is so rare in Worcestershire that its occurrence is confined to a single instance. A female or immature male was killed at Welland, and presented to the Worcester Museum by Mr. Turner, on September 6th, 1861. A male in mature plumage was shot some years since in the Avon valley, in the near part of Gloucestershire, which came into the hands of the writer.

164. Ringed Plover. *Ægialitis hiaticula* (Linn.).

It is very seldom that this bird is seen inland, and is certainly rare in Worcestershire. Neither Hastings nor Lees mentions it, but the writer has seen one which was shot by the side of the Avon at Offenham, and several others on the same river in the near parts of Gloucestershire.

165. Golden Plover. *Charadrius pluvialis,* Linn.

No single instance of the breeding of the golden plover in Worcestershire has come to the knowledge of the writer, but there is a male which has partially assumed the black breast of summer in the Worcester Museum, which was killed near Droitwich. It appears not uncommonly during the winter in flights, generally associating with lapwings.

166. Lapwing. *Vanellus vulgaris,* Bechstein.

A common and indeed an abundant resident, though not breeding very numerously. After the disastrous floods on the Avon in 1879, which carried away so much of the hay from the low-lying meadows and left them in the condition of mud-flats, vast numbers of lapwings came upon them to feed, and a perfect babble of their voices could be heard all through the night. Towards morning they left the meadows and rested for the day in the open fields.

167. Oyster-Catcher. *Hæmatopus ostralegus,* Linn.

Hastings did not include the oyster-catcher in his list of Worcestershire birds, but observed that it had been shot on the Teme, near Ludlow. It has, however, been killed more than once since that date (1834), at several places in the county, but it can only be recorded as a very occasional straggler. According to Lees it has been shot on the Teme, and was seen flying about the Severn in January, 1860. I have seen several which were shot in the vale of the Avon, though not in the county.

168. Avocet. *Recurvirostra avocetta*, Linn.

Hastings gave the following, in 1832, respecting this bird : 'The avocet, *Recurvirostra avocetta*, was shot a few years ago close to Worcester bridge.' Another avocet (unless it was the one above mentioned) was shot near Worcester a good many years ago, and when mounted by Mr. H. Holloway of that city, went into the collection of the late Mr. R. Berkeley, of Spetchley Park. Pennant (*British Zoology*, p. 400) gives as a locality for the occurrence of the avocet, the Severn's mouth, and he also says that it is found 'sometimes on the lakes of Shropshire.' It was probably not very rare at one time on the Severn.

169. Grey Phalarope. *Phalaropus fulicarius* (Linn.).

This is an occasional visitor to our county in considerable numbers in certain seasons, but only occasionally, years passing without the occurrence of a solitary one. The most recent dates of its appearance are 1891 and 1896, when a considerable number were observed, as I learn from Mr. Edwards, the curator of the Worcester Museum. He informed me that they frequented the meadows near Powick.

170. Woodcock. *Scolopax rusticula*, Linn.

The woodcock is common as an autumn visitor, and is generally distributed in the county, though not anywhere very abundant. It requires places suited to its particular habits, which do not correspond with those of other *Scolopacidæ*. Old sportsmen assert that the woodcock, besides frequenting wet places, is partial to dry bottoms in woods where there is underwood, and where the leaves in winter lie thick. These the woodcock is reported to turn over in the search for food, which is said to be insects ; and, furthermore, they say that they can determine whether it was a woodcock or a blackbird which had been feeding. The latter bird, we know, flings the leaves off right and left, and leaves them scattered about ; but the woodcock, we are informed, merely turns them over. The woodcock breeds sparingly in Wyre Forest, and it is believed in some other of the large woods in Worcestershire ; Lees mentions Martley, Acton Beauchamp and Lulsley as localities where it has nested, and other localities could be given.

171. Great Snipe. *Gallinago major* (Gmelin).

I include this in the Worcestershire list wholly on the authority of Sir Charles Hastings ; but at most it is only a very casual straggler on the autumn migration.

172. Common Snipe. *Gallinago cœlestis* (Frenzel).

It would be useless to say that the snipe is not much less abundant than formerly. Many places at one time suitable to its habits have been drained, and are no longer frequented. The snipe is very rarely seen with us in the summer, and I have never heard of a nest having been discovered. Occasionally, however, one appears in the end of the summer or the early autumn.

In July, 1849, my brother, W. B. Tomes, flushed a snipe on several consecutive days from the dry and shingly bed of a brook in connection with the Avon, and, as the date as well as the spot was remarkable, he shot the bird on the 29th of that month. It came into my hands the same day, and when proceeding to preserve it, I observed what had the appearance of a flesh maggot in its mouth ; and such it proved to be. An examination of the spot revealed the presence in an overhanging withy tree of some parts of a dead sheep, which had been hung there by a shepherd, and from which had fallen the unusual food above mentioned, and on which the snipe had doubtless been feeding for several days. It was probably a distant straggler, and certainly a very remarkable one, all the upper parts being very richly and thickly pencilled with bright rufous, the usual light-coloured longitudinal markings being reduced to little more than mere lines. In the nature of the markings on the back this bird bore some resemblance to Sabine's snipe, though not in colour.

173. Jack Snipe. *Gallinago gallinula* (Linn.).

This is essentially a solitary species, more than one being very seldom seen at the same spot except on migration. It is a skulking little bird, requiring more cover than the common snipe, but nevertheless is easily accommodated ; almost any dirty puddle by the side of a stream will do, but there must be some herbage amongst which it can hide, for it seldom appears on an open mud flat. About the middle of October is the date when we expect to notice some evidences of its first appearance.

174. Dunlin. *Tringa alpina*, Linn.

Although so abundant on the coast, it is remarkable how seldom the dunlin is seen inland. It can indeed be mentioned only as a rare straggler. Lees says it is a wanderer from the coast, not more than four specimens have come within the observation of the writer during a period of half a century, one of which was killed by flying against the telegraph wires of the railway near Evesham, and

the others were shot in the valley of the Avon in Gloucestershire.

175. Curlew-Sandpiper. *Tringa subarquata* (Güldenstädt).

A flight of curlew-sandpipers appeared on the Cofton reservoir in September, 1885, some of which were shot, and, having been taken into Birmingham to be mounted, came into the hands of the present writer. This appears to be the only record of the occurrence of this bird in the county.

176. Sanderling. *Calidris arenaria* (Linn.).

Hastings mentions the sanderling as having been shot on the Teme in December, 1826; and Lees gives Longdon Marsh as a locality where it has been seen. A specimen in the Worcester Museum is labelled 'Salwarp'; and that is all the information to hand of the sanderling as a Worcestershire bird.

177. Common Sandpiper. *Totanus hypoleucus* (Linn.).

This is a very regular spring visitor to our streams, but only as a passage bird on its way to its breeding places on the moors in the western country. About the first week in May it appears, but soon departs, coming again in the early part of September, at which time the greater number are young birds.

178. Green Sandpiper. *Totanus ochropus* (Linn.).

The green sandpiper can only be mentioned as an irregular and rare visitor to our county, appearing in spring and autumn, and never nesting with us. It is usually, perhaps always, found singly, and not unfrequently in some quiet pool or brook, and more rarely in the larger rivers. I remember on one occasion seeing a bird of this species resting in a very upright posture on a dead branch projecting from the stagnant water of a pool by the side of the Midland Railway between Evesham and Ashchurch, as I was passing in the train. That was in the autumn of 1880. Nearly all the specimens which have come into my hands have been shot from pools in little-frequented pasture fields.

179. Spotted Redshank. *Totanus fuscus* (Linn.).

Only once have I met with the present species in Worcestershire. In the village of Cleeve Prior there was originally a village green, now enclosed and converted into gardens, in the middle of which was a considerable sized horsepond, and in that pond a spotted redshank was shot on August 15th, 1848, which at once came into my hands, and is now in my collection.

180. Greenshank. *Totanus canescens* (Gmelin).

As a Worcestershire bird, this rests on the authority of Hastings and on Lees, who state that one was shot on the Teme as long ago as 1826. I have a specimen which was shot out of a flight in the adjoining part of Gloucestershire, but it is a not unlikely bird to be met with on migration.

181. Common Curlew. *Numenius arquata* (Linn.).

The curlew can only be mentioned as an occasional visitor to Worcestershire, and indeed is more frequently seen passing over, or resting for a time on some hill-top on its way. The well-known whistle is often heard in the night; and as the barred quills are sometimes picked up and mistaken for those of falcons, it is not unlikely that our fields and meadows are more often frequented by the curlew than is supposed. Lees says that it appears occasionally on the Severn and the Teme.

[**Whimbrel.** *Numenius phæopus* (Linn.).

Hastings says that the whimbrel has been met with on the Severn and Teme, but the writer has seen no Worcestershire specimen, nor any confirmatory record of its appearance in the county.]

182. Black Tern. *Hydrochelidon nigra* (Linn.).

An occasional black tern appears on our rivers in the spring, that is in April or early in May, but only at long intervals. As the species is becoming scarce in Great Britain, it may not be amiss to note a few instances of its occurrences in Worcestershire. Lees mentions one killed in 1855, but gives no locality, and he also speaks of its appearing on the Severn. An adult male was shot on the Avon, where it divides the counties of Worcester and Warwick, on April 5th, 1853. Another was seen on the Avon on May 9th, 1884, near Harvington; and an adult female was shot on the same stream, and very near the same place, on April 24th, 1891. Others have been seen of which I have heard, but of which I have no note; and an occasional immature bird of this species has appeared in the autumn.

[**White-winged Black Tern.** *Hydrochelidon leucoptera* (Schinz).

There is no record of this rare and remarkable-looking bird having been certainly seen in Worcestershire, though there is no reasonable doubt that one shot on the Avon at Welford, on May 8th, 1884, had passed through the county on its course up the Avon. And that it did pass up the Avon to the place where it was shot is well known,

as it was observed doing so. Arrived at Welford, it was seen and shot by Mr. W. H. Baylies on the day above mentioned, and is now in the writer's collection. The plumage is that of an adult, but the sex could not be determined, as the internal parts were destroyed by shot.]

183. Gull-billed Tern. *Sterna anglica*, Montagu.

I can only record a single undoubted occurrence of the gull-billed tern in Worcestershire, and I have no note either of the date of appearance or sex. It was shot while flying over the reservoir at Cofton, near Barnt Green, Bromsgrove, and taken to Birmingham for preservation. A specimen has also been met with in Warwickshire, quite near to the boundary of Worcestershire.

184. Common Tern. *Sterna fluviatilis*, Naumann.

So far as I know, the common tern is a rare bird in the county, and indeed in the valleys of the Severn and Avon ; at any rate, I have seen but few specimens either in the hands of local bird stuffers or in collections. Specimens of terns, both adult and immature, supposed to be of this species, have nearly always proved on examination to be Arctic terns. A pair, however, of common terns were shot while flying over the Avon on August 18th, 1841, which proved on examination to be male and female in full plumage. The date is rather early in the autumn for the appearance of any species of tern in passage.

185. Arctic Tern. *Sterna macrura*, Naumann.

This is by far the most common tern seen in our inland county, and has been known to appear in extraordinary numbers during the spring migration. In 1842 an immense flight came ' in and about the estuary of the Severn, and up the line of its course.' So wrote Yarrell in his *History of British Birds*. He might have added that their flight extended up the tributaries of the Severn. A full account of that remarkable appearance of Arctic terns was published in the *Annals and Magazine of Natural History*, by Mr. H. E. Strickland, then residing at Cracombe near Evesham. As many as forty which had been shot on the 8th and 9th of May of the year above mentioned, were taken, as we learn from that account, to one bird stuffer in that town. The present writer well remembers that flight of unusual birds appearing over and about the Avon. Every man who could command a gun of any description, large or small, sallied forth intent on slaughter ; and there was no need to wait long for the chances of a shot,

for the birds were by no means wary, but came freely within range. From any station by the side of the stream twenty or thirty could be seen at once. Since that date a few have appeared taking the same course up stream, but only as single stragglers. Immature specimens are common in local collections, all of which have been taken at the time of the autumn migration.

186. Little Tern. *Sterna minuta*, Linn.

A rare straggler, but has appeared on the Severn and the Avon. Hastings records it as a Worcestershire bird, on the authority of Mrs. Perrott, it having been observed, according to that lady, on the Avon. Lees says that the one mentioned by her was seen a little above Tewkesbury. The present writer has specimens which were shot on the Avon.

187. Little Gull. *Larus minutus*, Pallas.

According to Lees, one was shot at Upton-on-Severn ; and I saw one some years ago which was shot on the Avon and taken to Stratford to be stuffed. On enquiry I was told that it had been killed a little lower down the stream than Bidford, and probably therefore in the county of Worcester, or, if not, in very close contiguity to it.

188. Black-headed Gull. *Larus ridibundus*, Linn.

Like all other gulls which have been met with in Worcestershire, this species is only a straggler, though it cannot be said to be rare. There is a large breeding colony in Staffordshire.

189. Common Gull. *Larus canus*, Linn.

An occasional individual of this species appears in our cultivated fields, and stays for awhile, taking up its quarters in the large open parts, and feeding on worms and insects. I have known one frequent a ploughed field for more than a week, following the plough, always however at a respectful distance, and devouring the worms which were brought up.

190. Herring-Gull. *Larus argentatus*, Gmelin.

An occasional bird of this species may be noted in Worcestershire, most frequently in mottled immature plumage. It cannot, however, at any age be considered as any other than a waif and stray, and is really much more often seen passing over the county than actually frequenting it.

191. Great Black-backed Gull. *Larus marinus*, Linn.

Hastings mentions the appearance of this gull in Worcestershire on several occasions, and gives the following in a note on page 71 :

'Mr. Flinn, of Worcester, killed a very fine specimen, after a desperate resistance, in a field near the Dog and Duck, at Henwick, where it had flown out of the Severn, in January, 1833. This specimen is now in the Society's Museum.' The same authority mentions the Teme and the Avon as rivers on which the bird has been met with. Nothing additional is given by Lees, though it is included by him in the Malvern list. My own knowledge of this as a Worcestershire bird is confined to such as I have seen pass over. It regularly frequents Lundy Island, and may generally be seen in the Severn estuary where it is known as the salmon gull.

192. Lesser Black-backed Gull. *Larus fuscus,* Linn.

In the winter when the low-lying lands adjoining the Severn are flooded, small flocks of gulls generally come up from the Severn estuary. Among them are often specimens of this gull. Mr. Willis Bund informs me he has on one or two occasions shot examples.

193. Kittiwake. *Rissa tridactyla* (Linn.).

The kittiwake is an occasional visitor to our county, frequenting our rivers or other waters, and never, so far as my observation has gone, having recourse to the open fields.

194. Arctic or Richardson's Skua. *Stercorarius crepidatus* (Gmelin).

Three instances of the occurrence of this bird in Worcestershire may be mentioned. Morris, in his work on British birds, records one which was met with on the Severn, near Worcester, early in November, 1846; and I have seen and examined a preserved specimen of one shot while resting in the middle of a field at a place called Hoden, in the parish of Cleeve Prior, during the partridge shooting some years since. The third was killed on September 28th, 1899, at Hampton, near Evesham, as I am informed by Mr. T. E. Doeg of Evesham, to whom the specimen was brought when killed. It was an immature bird, as was also the one shot near Cleeve Prior.

195. Little Auk. *Mergulus alle* (Linn.).

This small sea bird has not unfrequently been taken up in Worcestershire and the adjoining counties in a state of exhaustion or dead, chiefly after heavy gales from the southwest. All the specimens examined have been in winter plumage, excepting one in breeding plumage taken up dead at Great Alne near Alcester, Warwickshire, of which I have not the date.

196. Puffin. *Fratercula arctica* (Linn.).

Like the last species the puffin appears only as a storm-driven victim, and is rarely found in Worcestershire excepting dead or exhausted. All those which I have had the opportunity of examining have been in immature plumage, and with the beak not fully developed. It breeds in numbers on Lundy Island.

197. Great Northern Diver. *Colymbus glacialis,* Linn.

Hastings records two occurrences of this fine bird in the county of Worcester, namely, one on the large sheet of water in Westwood Park in 1821, and another which was shot on the Severn in December, 1827. There is a specimen in the Worcester Museum which is labelled as having been killed on the Severn in close proximity to that city, which may be the one killed in 1827. I have known one shot on the Avon near Stratford.

198. Red-throated Diver. *Colymbus septentrionalis,* Linn.

This species has occurred in Worcestershire too frequently to require a detailed statement of each appearance. In nearly every instance it has been a visitor to the Severn or its tributaries, and in immature plumage. Once only has it been known to occur in adult dress in the valley of the Avon, namely, in November, 1858, when one was found in a state of exhaustion by the side of the road between Stratford-on-Avon and the village of Loxley.

199. Great-crested Grebe. *Podicipes cristatus* (Linn.).

There are but few recorded instances of the appearance of this bird in the county. A specimen in full summer plumage in the Worcester Museum is recorded as having been taken at the Camp, near Worcester; and another in the same collection, also in summer plumage, was shot at Woodhampton. A third, in similar plumage, was killed on the Severn at Kempsey, and is now in the writer's collection. About 1870 an immature bird of this species was taken on the Cofton reservoir, near Barnt Green.

200. Red-necked Grebe. *Podicipes griseigena* (Boddaert).

Hastings records two specimens of the red-necked grebe, on the authority of Mrs. Perrott, one being shot on the Severn, and the other on the Avon. Both were in the collection of H. E. Strickland, Esq., then living at Cracombe, near Fladbury. A bird of this species was shot on the Severn, at the Pitchcroft, Worcester, in the winter of 1886–87 or 1887–88, and was brought to Mr. Holloway

of that city, for preservation. It is now in the collection of the writer. Several other occurrences of this grebe on the Avon are on record, all of which are in winter plumage.

201. Slavonian Grebe. *Podicipes auritus* (Linn.).

This, as an autumn and winter visitor to our streams, is rather more frequent than either the crested or red-necked grebe. I have seen and examined specimens in winter plumage from the Severn, the Avon and the Arrow; but it is not mentioned by Hastings.

In its highly-ornamental and richly-coloured summer dress it is very rare, but two, male and female, in perfect breeding plumage, were ruthlessly shot at Wootton Warren some years ago, after they had commenced building a nest. They were sent for preservation to John Spicer of Warwick, where I saw them. Wootton Warren I would observe, though in Warwickshire, is only a mile from Oldberrow in Worcestershire.

202. Eared Grebe. *Podicipes nigricollis* (Brehm).

A few instances of the occurrences of this grebe on the Avon in winter plumage have come to my knowledge; and a most beautiful specimen in full summer dress was killed some years since at Wootton Warren, and sent to John Spicer of Warwick to be stuffed, in whose hands I saw it.

203. Little Grebe or Dabchick. *Podicipes fluviatilis* (Tunstall).

From the frequent appearance of this almost everywhere common bird in the Worcestershire streams and other waters, it might be expected that the nest would be often seen. Yet it is not so, for indeed it is but rarely found. I have never seen or heard of a nest on the Avon or its feeders, though I have an immature but full-grown young one which was taken in a net on the Arrow near Alcester. Mr. W. Edwards, of Malvern, has been more fortunate, and reports of the little grebe that it is 'common on New Pool, where it breeds.'

204. Storm-Petrel. *Procellaria pelagica*, Linn.

This is another storm-driven straggler with us, and is of very rare occurrence. Three times only has it come within the knowledge of the writer during a period of more than fifty years. One was taken in the streets of Worcester, where it appeared on the wing. Another near Alcester, Warwickshire, also on the wing; and the third was in the same county at Wormleighton, where it was first observed flying about. In no instance has it been found dead.

205. Leach's Fork-tailed Petrel. *Oceanodroma leucorrhoa* (Vieillot).

Unlike the last-named species, the present bird has occurred not very infrequently in Worcestershire and in the adjoining counties, and in every instance has been found dead, generally after heavy gales from the south-west. I have the records of more than a dozen specimens which have been picked up dead in or near the valley of the Avon. The latest county record is of one at Alfrick in November, 1899.

206. Manx Shearwater. *Puffinus anglorum* (Temminck).

This is one of the storm-driven castaways which are sometimes picked up exhausted after high winds in the autumn. Several are on record in the valley of the Avon. One was taken alive and unhurt in a field of wheat which was in stook (locally 'shuck') at Littleton, on August 27th, 1891. Another had been similarly taken, also in a field of wheat in shuck, in the same month, August, 1888, near Stratford-on-Avon. It was supposed that in both these instances the birds had been driven forcibly against the shucks of wheat, and had fallen to the ground. Some other occurrences of this seafaring bird having been found exhausted either in or near our county are on record.

207. Fulmar. *Fulmarus glacialis* (Linn.)

Hastings in a note gives the following respecting the fulmar: 'The fulmar,' says Mrs. Perrott, in a communication to our society, 'was found near the village of Hill, much exhausted, but from the kindness of a neighbour was kept alive to be forwarded to me. Unfortunately, the lad to whom it was entrusted, on receiving a bite from the bird, killed it. I however made a sketch.'

MAMMALS

As the mammals indigenous to the British Islands are neither numerous as species nor yet of very varied natural affinities, and as a certain percentage of these are marine forms, which are only most casual visitors to the non-tidal parts of the Severn, it follows that Worcestershire has but a short list of indigenous species. The number and description of the mammals of a county, unlike the birds, depend to a large extent on its climate or, in other words, its geographical position. For example, the greater horse-shoe bat, the serotine bat, and the dormouse, which frequent the southern counties, are very rarely met with so far north as Worcestershire.

The *Cervidæ*, or deer, have become extinct in the county since the seventeenth century. The disafforestation of Malvern Chase and Feckenham Forest under Charles I. must have largely reduced their number. The Session's records contain evidence, an indictment for killing them, of the existence of wild deer in Malvern Chase in 1614. These were most likely red deer (*Cervus elaphus*) ; probably the Civil War led to their practical extermination here, they continued for some time longer in Wyre Forest. The deer remained in the Gloucestershire Forest of Dean until living memory, and an occasional straggler found its way into the old limits of Malvern Chase in Worcestershire. But practically the wild red deer became extinct in the county about the middle of the seventeenth century. From that date the only deer have been the fallow deer (*Cervus dama*) in the different parks.

Worcestershire has not like its neighbour Staffordshire been fortunate in retaining the British wild cattle (*Bos taurus*) on its list. No doubt these animals at one time, up to what date is uncertain, wandered over Cannock Chase, Pensnett Chase, and the north of the county, but the development of the minerals in north Worcestershire must have been fatal to the wild cattle, and the county was not sufficiently lucky to possess such a park as Chartley to shelter and protect them. The modern improvements that have in the last sixty years been made in the Severn have effectively prevented any of the marine mammals from now visiting the county, even if the reason which brought them to it was not disappearing. It is well known that both seals and porpoises are much addicted to salmon and if salmon are numerous will follow that fish some way up a river. The appearance of a seal, probably the common seal (*Phoca vitulina*), has been recorded on one or two occasions in the early part of the nineteenth century, while a casual porpoise (*Phocæna communis*) has been recorded within living memory as appearing in the Severn within the county. The theory of the fishermen that when a shoal of

salmon are ascending a stream the porpoises try to get between them and the narrow part of the river if true would account for this, even if the more obvious reason, the porpoises following the salmon as far as they could up the river, did not do so. Since the erection of the Navigation Weirs at Gloucester and Tewkesbury the appearance of a porpoise in Worcestershire is almost unknown. The result is that the ordinary Worcestershire mammals are confined to the bats (*Cheiroptera*), insect eaters (*Insectivora*) moles and shrews, the small carnivora and the rodents, which give a total of thirty-two.

The only list of the county mammals which has yet been published was that in 1834 by Sir Charles Hastings in his *Illustrations of the Natural History of Worcestershire*, which is not and did not claim to be exhaustive and was in some cases compiled on insufficient observations. It is believed that the present is the first attempt that has been made to give a complete list. From the varied nature of different parts of the county it is quite possible that some species with a very local range may be omitted, but it is believed all are included. Those mentioned have been strictly verified, while some, like the greater horse-shoe bat (*Rhinolophus ferrum-equinum*) which Sir Charles Hastings mentions as having been found in Worcestershire, but of which no verified recorded appearance exists, and is not usually found so far north, are omitted.

CHEIROPTERA

1. Lesser Horse-shoe Bat. *Rhinolophus hipposiderus*, Bechstein.

The lesser horse-shoe bat is by no means rare in this county as well as in the adjoining ones. It is generally found singly, though sometimes in considerable numbers. Many years ago it frequented the roof of Ragley Hall, the seat of the Marquis of Hertford, from which place the author took a considerable number, some of which were kept alive for two or three weeks. They were remarkably shy and retiring in their habits, but particularly quiet and gentle. In the large open space in the roof of the mansion some of these small bats might be seen flitting about in the gloom at any time of the day, but they shunned observation, and retreated to some cranny or joint in the timber when approached. Although numerous there, they were always found hidden away singly. Of the flight of this bat or of its habits when abroad in the night I can say nothing, not a single example having ever in my experience been obtained by the use of the gun.

2. Long-eared Bat. *Plecotus auritus*, Linn.

The comparatively enormous size of the ears of this bat will at once distinguish it from all other British species. Each ear is almost as long as the body and head of the animal. If you could imagine a horse with ears five or six feet long, you would have some idea of the relative size of those parts in this remarkable species. Though not by any means abundant, the long-eared bat is not local in Worcestershire, but inhabits the whole of the county. Old buildings and churches are its favourite places of retirement, but so far as has at present been observed, preference is shown to certain spots, where they congregate, though they are not properly speaking gregarious.

3. Barbastelle. *Barbastella barbastellus*, Schreber.

Bell—*Barbastellus daubentonii*.

This is a very solitary species, and by no means common in the county. All sorts of odd places are chosen by the barbastelle in which to repose during the day. Any crevice will serve its turn, and it would seem that the same place is not frequented on consecutive days, as bats of this species have more than once been found in places which could only be temporary. I remember to have seen one taken from a stack of boards in a timber yard at Arrow near Alcester, which stack had only been put there the day

before. Another one was taken from behind the shutter of a cottage window in the village of Weston-on-Avon, which shutter was daily opened and shut. On the wing the barbastelle is readily distinguished from every other British bat by its dark colour, broad wings, and by its slow, irregular and owl-like flight, which is sometimes quite close to the observer, perhaps only three or four feet from his face. But as it comes abroad quite late in the evening, it can only be observed for a very short time. No particular situation is chosen for its nocturnal flight, which may be among buildings or in the open fields; but wherever it may be, when once seen it is speedily lost sight of.

4. Great or White's Bat (Noctule). *Pipistrellus noctula*, Schreber.

Bell—*Scotophilus noctula*.

This, the largest bat inhabiting Worcestershire, is pretty generally distributed, and may be recognized on the wing by its high, straight and rapid flight, which is frequently over some stream. It was the high and vigorous flight of this species which induced Gilbert White, in the *History of Selborne*, to designate it *Vespertilio altivolans*, the high-flying bat. It retires to rest during the day, and to hibernate through the winter to holes in trees, but very rarely if ever to buildings. The hole made by the green woodpecker in an aged elm has been found to be literally filled by these bats.

5. The Hairy-armed Bat. *Pipistrellus leisleri*, Kuhl.

Bell—*Scotophilus leisleri*.

Not very inferior in size to the last species, the hairy-armed bat is rare in all parts of England, not many instances of its occurrence having been recorded. One was shot while on the wing in the vicinity of the ancient manor house at Cleeve Prior early in the summer of 1853, when two were observed. Afterwards one was shot (by a party of rook-shooters; probably therefore about the middle of May) the other took flight and did not return. Since that time others have been seen, but only very occasionally, whole summers passing without one being observed. It may be easily recognized by its exceedingly erratic and zig-zag flight, which may be high or low, in the open fields or in sheltered places. Instead of pursuing a pretty regular beat, as does the noctule, the present bat is here and there, and almost as soon as you see it, it is gone, and does not reappear. Of the diurnal retreat of this species I can say nothing.

6. Pipistrelle. *Pipistrellus pipistrellus*, Schreber.

Bell—*Scotophilus pipistrellus*.

This bat is common and distributed all over the county, and may be found reposing singly during the day in all sorts of places—holes in trees, crannies in old walls or buildings—and the author remembers once taking one out of a mortise-hole in a gatepost. It is equally general in its choice of feeding ground, being observable either singly or in pairs in some sheltered corner between buildings or amongst the stems of trees, almost always low down, and taking the same short beats, backward and forward. When Shakespeare spoke of the cloistered flight of the bat, he probably referred to this bat as it describes that of the pipistrelle with great accuracy, and this bat is common in the Avon valley and round Stratford.

7. Natterer's Bat. *Myotis nattereri*, Kuhl.

Bell—*Vespertilio nattereri*.

This is of somewhat greater size than the little bat which is most commonly observed, and is lighter in colour than any other Worcestershire species, excepting the lesser horseshoe bat before mentioned. In its place of retreat it is strictly gregarious, crowding together in masses of sometimes hundreds. Yet it is not of frequent occurrence, and of its habits during the hours of the night very little is known, but there is reason to believe that it feeds in companies. There was formerly quite a colony of Natterer's bats in the roof of Arrow Church near Alcester, between the ceiling and the tiles, which was visited on more than one occasion many years since by the late Sir W. H. Flower and the present writer. Some of the bats captured there on one occasion were taken home by the author and turned loose in a room, and the window opened to allow them to depart. At first one or two passed through the window, but would not leave without their companions, returning into the room again, and this was repeated until all became aware of the open window, when they departed in a body. They proved when taken in hand to be very gentle creatures, evincing no disposition to bite, and their gregarious or sociable nature was well shown by their refusal to escape except in company.

8. Daubenton's Bat. *Myotis daubentoni*, Leisler.

Bell—*Vespertilio daubentonii*.

This might almost be designated an aquatic bat, so much does it affect streams and

ponds, appearing to feed by preference on insects close over still water. It comes abroad quite late in the evening, some time after the pipistrelle has made its appearance, and may then be seen so close to the surface of the water of some pond or still reach of the river Avon that the reflection is undistinguishable from the creature itself. The diurnal place of retirement is some old building, holes in trees so far as I know never being chosen. The belfry of the church at Stratford-on-Avon was formerly much frequented by this bat, and the late Sir W. H. Flower and the present writer obtained specimens there by swinging the bell ropes about just when the bats came out of crevices and were flying round the belfry. They were struck by the ropes and came to the floor. Daubenton's bat may be distinguished from its allies, Natterer's bat and the whiskered bat, by its having the feet less fully enclosed in the wing-membrane.

9. **Whiskered Bat.** *Myotis mystacinus*, Leisler.
Bell—*Vespertilio mystacinus*.

There is no English bat which can more properly be styled an arboreal species than the present one, notwithstanding that it reposes during the day in buildings. At the present moment there is quite a large colony of whiskered bats in the roof of the house of the writer at Littleton, from which place more than a hundred were seen to emerge one evening in July, 1899. They dropped out of a hole under the slates either singly or in twos or threes, and lost no time in getting into the top of a large walnut tree, through which they passed, and scattered off to other trees to feed amongst the branches. The flight of this bat may be described as quivering through and through the branches and amongst the leaves. You rarely, perhaps never, see a whiskered bat taking a backward and forward beat in a sheltered corner, like the pipistrelle, the flight being almost always in trees and generally high up.

INSECTIVORA

10. Hedgehog. *Erinaceus europæus*, Linn.

The hedgehog is so well known in the county as to demand little notice. It is however becoming scarce in some parts of the county, partly because it is killed wherever it is met with, by labourers because it is supposed to suck cows, by keepers because it is known to suck eggs, and partly because under the conditions of modern farming the old wide hedges that used to furnish it with shelter are being swept away. It has its regular hunting ground and may be seen night after night to go out along a particular track, occasionally it travels a considerable distance.

11. Mole. *Talpa europæa*, Linn.

The abundance or the reverse of the mole in any district depends entirely on the assiduity of the mole-catcher, for when trapping is carried on industriously the creature is soon quickly reduced in numbers. It is the custom in some places in Worcestershire to pay the mole-catcher a specified sum per acre for its destruction. In the neighbourhood of Bengworth two varieties of this animal were at one time not infrequent, one of a pale cream colour and the other, which was much the rarer, of a dark ash colour. In the Victoria Museum, Worcester, are specimens of moles of various colours which have from time to time been caught in different parts of the county.

12. Common Shrew. *Sorex araneus*, Linn.

A common and regularly distributed species over the whole of the county.

13. Pigmy Shrew. *Sorex minutus*, Pallas.
Bell—*Sorex pygmæus*.

This very small creature is much less abundant than the common shrew, to which it bears considerable resemblance except in size. It would be correct to say that for one instance of its occurrence twenty of the common shrew would be seen. It is found in the same sort of situations which are frequented by the common shrew.

14. Water Shrew. *Neomys fodiens*, Pallas.
Bell—*Crossopus fodiens*.

As its name implies, this is an aquatic creature, and is almost always found in the vicinity of water. The low-lying meadows by the side of the Avon, Severn and Teme are much frequented by the water shrew, and they are sometimes discovered when the scythe comes into use. Shallow rippling ditches and rills as well as brooks are favourite haunts, more especially such as have a gravelly bottom. It is said, and with truth, to eat the spawn of fish that it finds in such places, but it also finds beneath the stones the small crustacean *Gammarus pulex*, and the water shrew makes use of its long snout to turn over the stones and capture it. But such small creatures are not the exclusive diet of the water shrew, the present writer having once seen one escape from the dried-up body of a barn-door fowl lying in an outhouse. The shrew had eaten its way into the interior through the abdomen. On another occasion a common rat which had been caught and killed by the jaws of a

steel trap was attacked by a water shrew, which was discovered making violent attempts to get a hole through the tough skin of the rat.

The so-called oared shrew, *Sorex ciliatus*, is nothing more than a dark-coloured variety of the water shrew, which is not infrequently met with in the summer.

CARNIVORA

15. Fox. *Vulpes vulpes*, Linn.

Bell—*Vulpes vulgaris*.

An animal wholly dependent for existence in our county upon the sport which he affords. Were foxhunting to go out the fox would speedily go out with it.

16. Pine Marten. *Mustela martes*, Linn.

Bell—*Martes abietum*.

'Rarely to be found even in places formerly known as his usual haunts,' were the words made use of in 1834 by Sir Charles Hastings, but whether they were intended to apply to the yellow-breasted or white-breasted marten as a Worcestershire mammal I am unable to determine. It is doubtful if the white-breasted marten has been found in the county for many years if at all, no record of it exists; but I can however speak of the yellow-breasted as having been killed more than half a century since at Falke Mill near Evesham. The animal was taken to a bird stuffer in that town, and when preserved remained for many years in the possession of the party who killed it; but finally, when faded, dirty and dilapidated, it came into the hands of the present writer. That is the latest recorded occurrence of this marten in Worcestershire, but it may possibly still exist in some of the large woods.

17. Polecat. *Putorius putorius*, Linn.

Bell—*Mustela putorius*.

Formerly not rare in Worcestershire, but now only known in a few favoured localities, in the large woodlands and remote wooded districts, but it is nearly if not quite extinct in the county.

18. Stoat. *Putorius ermineus*, Linn.

Bell—*Mustela erminea*.

Like the weasel the stoat is distributed over the whole of the county. It is a wild and fearless animal, and not easy of observation, but the occasional assumption of the white or ermine fur in the winter renders it a conspicuous object, and as it may be seen at a considerable distance, some idea of the range of its operations may be arrived at. One which the author repeatedly observed had a beat of fully two miles in extent—rather a wide manor for so small an animal. Another stoat, also white, was seen by the author to hurry into a hedge, where it might have been expected to conceal itself; but it passed straight through, across a lane, into a coppice of several acres in extent on a steep slope, up which it took a straight course and out at the top, without so much as a check. The distance traversed in a nearly straight line was fully a quarter of a mile in what might be termed a cross-country run, and how much further could not be ascertained. It is the habit of the stoat to get clear away, and not to skulk, when there is danger.

19. Weasel. *Putorius nivalis*, Linn.

Bell—*Mustela vulgaris*.

This animal is too generally distributed and too well known to need more than a brief notice and to observe that its food appears to consist chiefly of field mice and field voles. A family of three-fourths grown weasels which the author had the opportunity of observing were wholly fed by the parent on these small rodents. Nothing could exceed the restless activity and playfulness of the young ones, clinging to each other and rolling over and over like a family of kittens, but much quicker, and they seemed never to tire of the amusement. The weasel seems to take a regular and circumscribed beat, if we may judge from the habits of one which frequented the hut of an old crossing-keeper on the Great Western Railway near Bretforton, where it was daily seen by the old man, who never molested it, as it destroyed the mice, which before its appearance were in considerable abundance.

20. Badger. *Meles meles*, Linn.

Bell—*Meles taxus*.

The badger is a creature whose very existence is due to its fossorial capabilities, for were it not a skilful excavator and able to make a safe retreat for itself, its size and consequent inability to escape observation would most surely lead to its extinction. The badger still remains in some of the wooded localities in Worcestershire and if not in increased certainly not in reduced numbers. It is frequent in some of the detached parts of the county, as at Blockley and Daylsford, and it is by no

means rare on the near parts of the Cotteswolds, where it finds safe harbourage in the fissures in the oolite quarries, of which there are many, as well as in the adjoining parts of Oxfordshire.

21. Otter. *Lutra lutra*, Linn.

Bell—*Lutra vulgaris.*

In 1834 Sir Charles Hastings mentioned the otter as occurring in the Teme and some other small streams in Worcestershire, but not in the Severn. It still haunts the Teme and its tributaries, probably in increased numbers, and since the Avon has ceased to be a navigable river has become comparatively common in that stream. In streams of the size and depth of the Avon otter hunting is not practicable, and it is not likely therefore that the animal will be exterminated, or indeed much reduced in numbers. In the tributaries, where the otter is not rare, there would be a much greater chance of successful pursuit. One of these feeders of the Avon, the Stour, falling into that stream near Stratford, passes through the outlying part of Worcestershire at Shipston, where it is frequented by the otter. The otter by no means confines itself to fish and has been on several occasions killed when it has left the river and sought out poultry. It is said that a favourite article of its diet are eels, but while it doubtless takes them when it can catch them it seems to be generally carnivorous.

RODENTIA

22. Squirrel. *Sciurus leucourus*, Kerr.

Bell—*Sciurus vulgaris.*

Of this pretty denizen of the woods and coppices I need only say that it is still common.

23. Brown Rat. *Mus decumanus*, Pallas.

Nothing more need be said of this omnivorous and cannibal species than to observe that it is only too plentiful, is a thorough pest and appears to be increasing.

24. Black Rat. *Mus rattus*, Linn.

Some years since a number of rats of this species were taken at several places more or less near to the Worcestershire Avon at a time when that stream was navigable ; the supposition being that they were brought from the docks in Gloucester in barges laden with corn. That supposition gains support by the disappearance of the black rat from the same places since the navigation of the Avon has ceased. Sir Charles Hastings mentions this animal as occurring at Wick near Worcester and a few farmhouses in the county. It however seems of recent years to be almost if not quite exterminated by the brown rat, no specimens having been taken at Upper Wick for some years.

25. House Mouse. *Mus musculus*, Linn.

Too troublesome as well as too abundant to be dwelt upon.

26. Wood Mouse or Long-tailed Field Mouse. *Mus sylvaticus*, Linn.

A very pretty creature with large black eyes, large rounded ears and a long tail. It is common in the fields and gardens, sometimes doing in the latter place considerable damage by consuming the early planted peas. Occasionally this mouse will enter buildings and even dwellings, and has been captured in the cellar of a farmhouse, where it had eaten nearly the whole of the inside of a cheese. The nest for the reception of the young, as well as for winter quarters, is usually a burrow of its own construction, and as it is by no means infrequently turned up by the plough, it may probably be the mouse which has been immortalized by Burns, if indeed it is an Ayrshire creature. The present species is very easily tamed, and when kept in confinement is very gentle, evincing no disposition to bite when handled, as I can affirm from personal observation.

27. Harvest Mouse. *Mus minutus*, Pallas.

Formerly more abundant in the valley of the Worcestershire Avon than at present. It is most commonly found in cornfields, more especially wheatfields, in which its symmetrical and beautiful nest is occasionally seen suspended amongst the stems of wheat. When reaping machines were unknown, the long stubble after harvest was cut by the scythe and put into small heaps called cocks, and beneath them the little harvest mouse was often found, as well as sundry shrews, long-tailed field mice and voles. A harvest-mouse which was kept in captivity for some time by the author and fed principally on hempseed, changed from the usual yellow to a deep rich chestnut colour.

28. Water Vole. *Microtus amphibius*, Linn.

Bell—*Arvicola amphibius.*

It is common in all our streams, streamlets

and ponds, feeding freely on water plants, the bulrush and duckweed being preferred, and sometimes doing considerable damage to the former of these two plants. In the winter and during floods it is driven to consume the bark of young trees and bushes, the maple and osier being most frequently selected, and I have seen whole bushes of maple with the branches completely barked by the water vole when hard driven for food.

29. Field Vole. *Microtus agrestis*, Linn.
Bell—*Arvicola agrestis*.

A common obese and stupid-looking creature, having small eyes almost hidden in the long fur, and with a very short tail. When low-lying meadows are mown the nest of this vole is often discovered, and so far as my observation has gone, is always in some depression and not in a burrow. In confinement it is stupid and uninteresting, but soon becomes tame. It is becoming scarcer on account of its nests and young being constantly destroyed by the mowing machine.

30. Bank Vole. *Evotomys glareolus*, Schreber.
Bell—*Arvicola glareolus*.

Though not uncommon the present is less abundant than the last species, from which it may readily be distinguished by its less obese form, longer tail and more rufous upper parts. In habits it does not differ from the last species.

31. Common Hare. *Lepus europæus*, Pallas.
Bell—*Lepus timidus*.

It is unnecessary that I should further remark of the hare than that except for preservation it would speedily become extinct. Under the operation of the Ground Game Act it is even questionable whether preservation will prevent its extinction.

32. Rabbit. *Lepus cuniculus*, Linn.

The great fertility of the rabbit, added to its burrowing habits, operate to prevent its becoming scarce.

EARLY MAN

THE imagined paucity of material is probably the reason why so far no one has thought it worth while attempting to work out the history of Prehistoric man in the county. All that has yet been done is to chronicle the finds of certain implements and weapons. The accounts of these finds are scattered through various books and the proceedings of various societies. No attempt has been made to utilize the evidence which they furnish as to the presence of the successive races, or the struggles among the primitive peoples who occupied the tract of forest which now forms Worcestershire. It is unfortunate that this should be so, as the county has a story of its own, quite distinct from its neighbours. Its southern border, the Avon valley, was the route that invaders from central England would naturally follow on their way to the west, while the valley of the Severn was a frontier, possibly the frontier of the Iberians against the Goidels and of the Goidels against the Brythons, as in historic times it became the frontier between the English and Welsh. It is not without interest to note that most of the finds in the county are either in these river valleys or on the hills overlooking them. The northern and eastern parts of the county have so far yielded practically nothing towards its early history. Everything that has been found comes from the part south and south-west of the Lickey Hills.

It is proposed here (*a*) to give some account of the earliest history of the county as evidenced by the finds, and (*b*) a list of the finds and other traces of pre-Roman times which have occurred within the county. In dealing with the first point the general proposition will have to be stated and the finds utilized to apply it to Worcestershire. Much is and must of necessity remain matter of inference. As the area of the county is but small all that can be done is to state what was presumably taking place within it, and to rely upon the presumptive evidence which the presence of weapons and implements affords to show that the races of men who used those weapons and had those implements inhabited the county. In the present condition of things it is impossible to do more. At the outset it may be stated that so far no trace of Palæolithic man has been found in the county, possibly because a thorough scientific search has never been made for such traces.

The Prehistoric period as defined by Professor Boyd Dawkins comprises 'the period which covers all the events which took place between the Pleistocene age on the one hand and the beginning of the Historic

on the other.'[1]   It commences with the time when by a great submergence Britain was separated from the continent on the east and from Ireland on the west—when this subsidence of the land made the large estuaries of the Severn and Avon.   This subsidence and its results must have produced a profound change in the general conditions of the country. It was no longer part of the regular continental system.   It had become an isolated sea-girt region; the great beasts, being no longer recruited by wanderers from the continent, soon became extinct.   The inhabitants were no longer nomadic tribes, having the whole continent of Europe to wander over; they were confined to a narrow locality, and this confinement must have deeply affected their modes of life, especially when in all probability it was accompanied by considerable climatic changes, necessitating an alteration in the people's habits.   It is impossible to fix the period during which these great changes were brought about, or to give anything like dates for their beginning or their end.   All that can be said is that the Prehistoric period extends from the time of the separation of Britain from the continent to the time of Cæsar's invasion.   Between these two limits the inhabitants of these islands passed from the stage of the Palæolithic man to the civilization which they possessed when the earliest historic record of them is reached.   During this interval their development was enormous and must have occupied long series of years, how many it is impossible to say.   A modern writer puts it at somewhere about 270,000 years,[2] this, it is needless to say, is only his guess.

The interval between the separation from the continent and historic times is divisible into three distinct periods, called either after the weapons (a) Neolithic, (b) Bronze and (c) Iron, or after the people using those weapons (a) Iberian, (b) Goidelic and (c) Brythonic.

Traces of each of these periods, mostly consisting of finds of the weapons, have been discovered in the southern and western parts of Worcestershire, but so far in the north and east of the county nothing has been found.

The present height of the Severn at Worcester and of the Avon at Evesham, under 100 feet above sea-level, proves that one great feature in the history of the county since the subsidence has been the silting up of the estuaries.   In this silt remains have been found which can be ascribed to each of the three periods of the Prehistoric age.

The men of the Neolithic times, so far as our present evidence goes, were mostly herdsmen and flockmasters.   When they advanced into Worcestershire, they settled on the highlands which overlook the rich pastures of the river valleys.   In Worcestershire these highlands were (a) the Lickey Hills, that ridge of hills running across the county from Alvechurch to Stourbridge; (b) the Malvern Hills, the ridge running north and south and forming the western county boundary; and (c) Bredon Hill, the great detached outlier of the Cotswolds on the south.   Each of these three groups of hills has furnished evidence of the presence of Neolithic settlers in the shape of weapons and implements.

---

[1] *Early Man*, p. 247.   [2] Hackel, *The Last Link*, 149.

EARLY MAN

On the Lickey Hills, at Tutnall near Tardebigge, on the east side of the range on the highlands overlooking the Avon and Severn, considerable numbers of flint implements have from time to time been found, mostly on some fields there known as 'Nine Lands,' 'Orgates,' 'Long Close' and 'Lone Fields.' A collection of these implements was exhibited to the Society of Antiquaries in March, 1897. It consisted of 'a rough axehead, a bored water-worn pebble, two spindle wheels, part of a whetstone, a rubber, a sling-stone, a fragment of a broken axehead with partly bored hole for its reverse, and a number of flake-borers, scrapers and arrowheads, all of flint.'[1] On the opposite side of the Severn estuary, on the Malvern Hills, but the precise spots are not known, a number of flakes have been found. These are now in the Victoria Museum at Worcester. In the south, on Bredon Hill, flint flakes have also occurred from time to time, but here again unfortunately the precise localities are unknown. These flakes also are in the Worcester Museum.

The highlands, overlooking the rich pastures of the plains, are the places where most probably the Neolithic men settled. Had the finds been only at one of the places they would not have possessed any great importance, but occurring as they do all round the estuary they strongly support the view that the south part of the county was settled by Neolithic men. Taken separately the implements prove little or nothing ; indeed it may be doubted whether some of them do not belong to a later period, which might prove that the same localities were occupied by successive races. But taken in conjunction with all the places where they have been found, and the fact that in the low ground below other Neolithic implements have been discovered, they go far to establish even if they do not prove the presence of Neolithic man in Worcestershire. In the Avon valley a stone axe was unearthed, and other Neolithic implements have been found on Bevington Waste, on the borders of Worcestershire and Warwickshire, and lower down the Avon valley at Offenham, Sedgeberrow and Defford. In the Severn valley a basalt double-edged celt was found in the drift near Bewdley, and in the Teme valley stone implements have been found at Lindridge and at Broadwas.

The cumulative testimony of these finds therefore tends to prove that on the highlands there were settlements, that the lowlands were traversed by the settlers, who one and all, whether on the highlands or in the valleys, used stone implements. These stone implements are recognized as belonging to the Neolithic period. Therefore it seems to be established that Worcestershire during the whole or some part of the Neolithic period was a district inhabited by Neolithic men.

This is all that can be said with any certainty. To what extent the county was populated, for what period, whether permanently or only temporarily, as the tribes wandered from district to district, on these points there is no evidence. It is quite possible that further research may

---

[1] *Proceedings Society of Antiquaries,* xvi. 319.

throw more light on the state of the county at this time. In other counties, in addition to finds of axes, adzes and flakes such as have been found in Worcestershire, a systematic search has been rewarded by the finding of bone instruments, rude fragments of pottery and the remains of domestic animals. In some counties traces of the clusters of huts which formed the tribal dwellings have also been discovered, in others remains of the mounds which formed the places of interment of the Neolithic men. None of these details have as yet been found in Worcestershire, possibly because they have not been properly looked for. After an exhaustive search has been made it may be possible for some future writer to do more than merely state the fact of the existence of Neolithic man in the county.

Fig. A gives a rough sketch of the county showing the places where the Neolithic remains have up till now been found. A glance at it shows the position of the hills and the river valleys where the traces of this race of men have been discovered in the county.

THE BRONZE AGE

The Neolithic dwellers in Britain devoted their attention to agriculture. They were rudely disturbed in their occupation of the island by a race of invaders who having the advantage of better weapons succeeded in dispossessing the inhabitants from their English settlements and driving them first to the west of the Severn and afterwards to remote corners of Wales.

It is in this period that the importance of Worcestershire commences, for in it probably began that series of conflicts that was continuous until Wales became part of England. Successive invaders drove the previous occupants of the county to the districts west of the Severn. The row of forts on the western boundaries of Worcestershire bears evidence to this fact. The forts on this line mark either the limits of the invasion, or the advance line of defence of the old inhabitants against further aggression, or the advance line of the invaders' outposts to prevent raids from the old inhabitants of the district from which they had been dispossessed. This feature remains to the present day along the hills to the west of the Severn from Abberley to Malvern, and from Malvern to Redmarley. Most of the hills that command any of the passes to the west show traces of earthworks, such as Woodbury and the Berrow at Martley, which command the passes into the Teme valley; on the Malvern Hills the Camp Hill and Midsummer Hill command the roads over these hills. Probably all these camps in their present form have few if any remains of the work of the early invaders or defenders of the country; but other traces of earthworks remain to point out the then state of things—the invaders pushing on, the dwellers in the county resisting the invasion.

There is considerable evidence of the occupation of Worcestershire by the Goidels, as the invaders who dispossessed the Neolithic men are called. Here the evidence does not only consist of finding weapons and

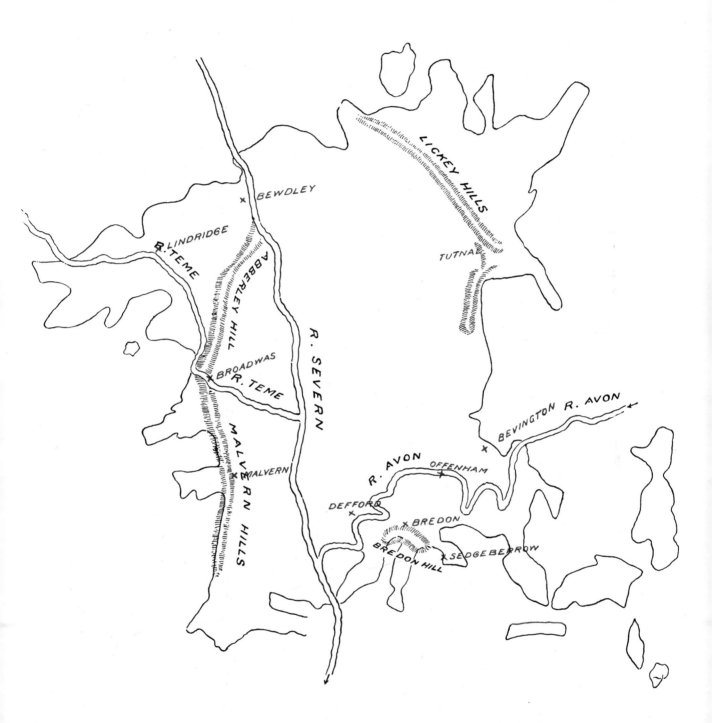

FIG. A.

To face page 182.

implements, but is of a twofold character. There is evidence (1) as to their weapons and implements, (2) and also as to their customs.

(1) The finds of weapons indicate that the Goidel invaders followed the line of the Avon from Warwickshire to the Severn. All along its course from where it enters the county to about the middle of its passage through Worcestershire traces of the Goidels have been found. From Harvington comes a bronze celt, from Church Lench a bronze palstave, from Aldington a stone bracer, from Evesham, Sedgeberrow, Cropthorne and Defford bronze celts. All these places are on or near the Avon, and show that the Goidels occupied the upper part of the Avon valley. In the Severn valley implements of the Bronze age have been found at various places, mostly at spots near where some of the old tracks are supposed to have crossed the river. At Dowles above Bewdley a bronze axe was found in 1899 when excavating the river drift for the Birmingham waterworks. Other finds are at Bewdley, three looped bronze palstaves and a socketed bronze gouge. At Astley a bronze looped palstave. At Holt a looped bronze celt. At Ombersley a ringed palstave. At Worcester a socketed and looped celt; a bronze spearhead at Kempsey. Another spearhead near the old ford at Pixham. It is curious that nothing so far as is known has been found in the Severn below Pixham, but it may be because the tracks that crossed the river lower down were fewer and less frequented than those that crossed higher up; at all events further evidence is required on the point how it is that all the implements that had been found both in the Avon and the Severn have been discovered in the upper and middle parts of the courses of those rivers and not in the lower portions. It may possibly be that at this date the lower portion had not silted up, but remained large tidal streams practically unfordable. So far as the Severn goes it might have been expected that more things would have been found in the lower reaches of the river because they have been dredged out to a uniform depth for navigation purposes in recent years.

(2) When the Goidels invaded the country they had reached that stage of civilization at which their dead were disposed of by burning. After burning, the charred bones were placed in an urn or vessel which was buried, sometimes with and sometimes without other articles. Two interments said to be of the Bronze age have been found in the county, one in the Avon valley in a gravel pit at Charlton near Cropthorne, where an urn containing charred bones was found some 6 feet below the surface. A bronze celt is said to have been found near it. The other on the summit of the Worcestershire Beacon, the highest point of the Malvern range, where in 1849 the engineers engaged on the ordnance survey found in the ground an urn containing half-charred bones. This would probably be the grave of some great chief placed in a spot from which it was believed he could watch the movements of his inveterate foes.

The inferences from the finds confirm the evidence derived from the interments, that for some time a portion of the county certainly was

occupied by Goidels. There is however so far nothing to show either the extent or the duration of that occupation. Fig. B shows how large an area of the county has as yet given no sign of Goidel occupation, as well as how closely the Goidel followed in the lines of the Neolithic settlement.

THE IRON AGE

The Goidels in their turn were displaced and driven over the Severn by a new set of invaders. As the Goidels expelled the Neolithic men, so the Brythons, as the new comers were called, expelled the Goidels. They had the advantage over the Goidels that they used iron for their implements and weapons, and it was probably due to this superiority of their weapons that they drove out the Goidels, as the latter by their better weapons had driven out their predecessors. The Brythons have left very clear traces of their occupation of the county, which, whatever may have been the date of its commencement, lasted to the time of the Roman Conquest. They were probably a far more civilized race than any of those who preceded them ; not only had they weapons and implements, but also personal ornaments. One of these, a bronze torque, was found at a depth of about 2 feet in a gravel pit at Perdeswell near Worcester. 'It is curved, forming nearly a semicircle, and composed of twenty small pieces of bronze curiously twisted and tooled, each alternating with pieces finished like a small pulley strung upon a small iron wire ; the whole strongly encrusted with highly polished patina.'[1] Another ornament, an armlet, said to be of this period, was found at Stoke Prior, which is of interest as showing that the finds of this age are not confined to the river valleys and the overlooking hills. Stoke Prior being in the centre of the county. Broadway, almost in Gloucestershire, also supplies a sword of this period ; in fact in this age the finds become of less importance for the occupation of the district is better evidenced by the earthworks (see fig. c).

EARTHWORKS

The earthworks are not numerous, the majority being camps or forts. There is considerable doubt as to the precise period to which they belong. None of them has ever, as far as is known, been properly investigated, nor have discoveries of weapons or implements furnishing evidence of the time of their construction been found in connection with them. The following accounts must therefore be taken as only provisional.

(1) Wychbury (fig. 1), in the north of the county on an outlying hill above Pedmore and Hagley, overlooking the Stour valley and what was afterwards Pensett Chase, is a large fort, heart shaped in outline, with a double rampart on the south and an entrance to the south-east. It has been called a Danish camp and a Roman camp, but it seems more probable that it was originally of the British period. Except Bredon, Wychbury is the only camp now known to the east of the Severn ; it

---

[1] *Archæologia*, xxx. 554.

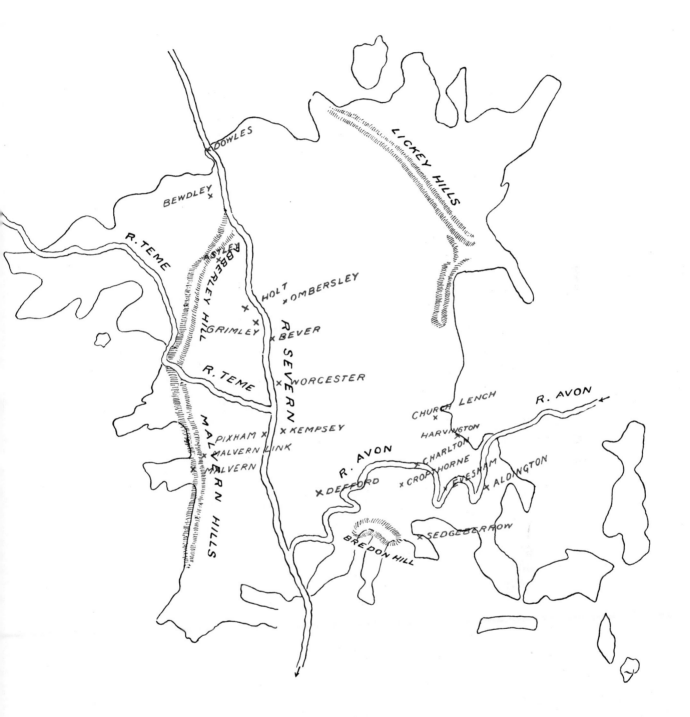

FIG. B.

To face page 184.

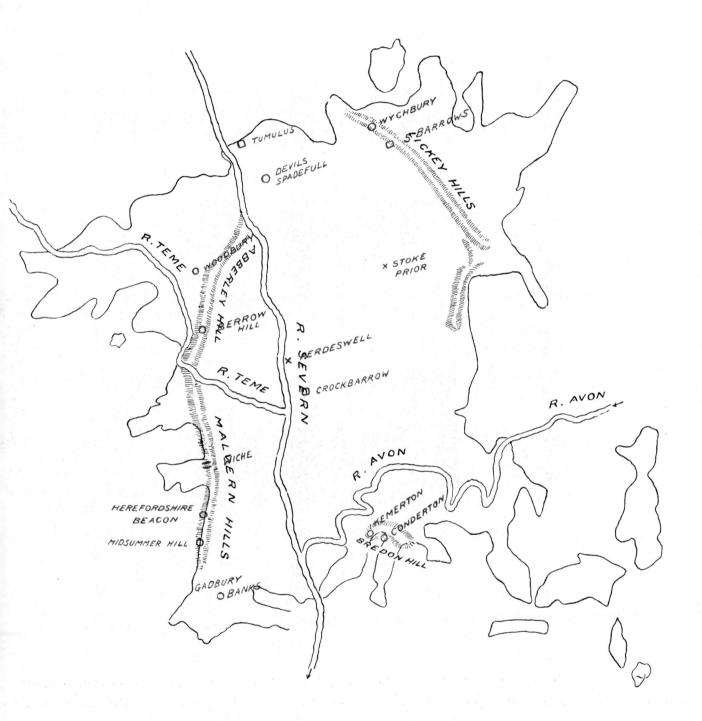

TUMULUS

DEVILS
SPADEFULL

WYCHBURY

5-BARROWS

STICKEY HILLS

R. TEME

ABBERLEY HILL

BERROW
HILL

STOKE
PRIOR

R. SEVERN

R. TEME

R. SERDESWELL

CROCKBARROW

R. AVON

R. AVON

MALVERN HILLS

WICHE

HEREFORDSHIRE
BEACON

R. AVON

MIDSUMMER HILL

KEMERTON

CONDERTON

BREDON HILL

GADBURY
BANKS

Fig. C.

To face page 184.

forms the north-western end of the Lickey range, here called the Clent Hills, of which Tutnall, where the Neolithic implements were found, is the south-western end. This range of hills is the dividing line between the watersheds of the Trent and the Severn, and probably therefore research would show traces of forts on some of them, as they must have formed the eastern line of defence to the Severn valley.

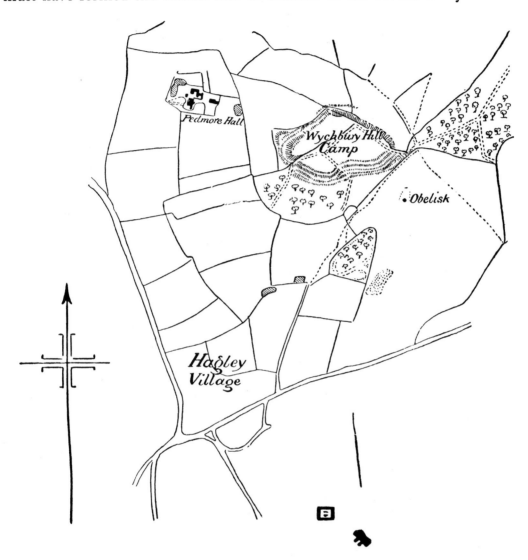

— *Scale 6 Inches to a Statute Mile* —

FIG. 1.

Crossing to the west bank of the Severn, earthworks become more numerous. It is probable that some traces might be found on the hills above Ribbesford and on the Abberley range, but there can be no doubt as to the entrenchment of the height above Witley which overlooks not only the west bank of the Severn valley but also guards the entrance into the Teme valley.

(2) On this height, known as Woodbury Hill (fig. 2), is an extensive camp of an irregular oval shape with a single rampart enclosing a space of some 30 acres. No relics of any kind are recorded as having been found here. To what period the original camp belonged is most difficult to say, for this hill has been occupied so often, and its position rendered its occupation so necessary whenever any military movements were going on in the district, that probably it has been a camp in every contest in the Severn valley. It was according to local tradition occupied by Owen Glendower in 1405, and by the duke of Buckingham in his ill-starred expedition of 1483 ; but it is obviously of a far remoter antiquity, and in all probability the original camp was made by one of

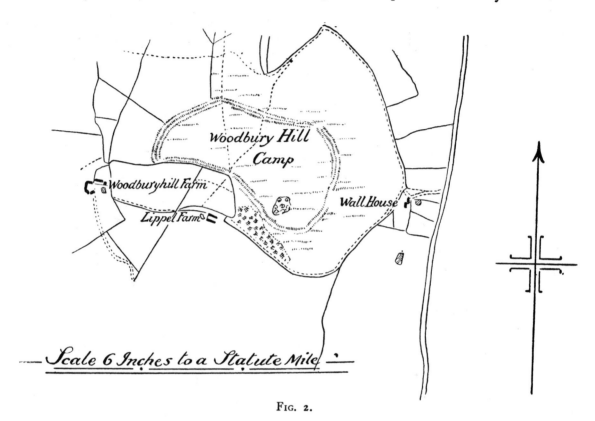

Fig. 2.

the occupying races in the Severn valley who were being pressed westward by some one of the different bands of invaders.

(3) Following the range of hills to the west, traces of earthworks are to be found on an isolated hill above Martley known as the Berrow. Its western base adjoins the river Teme, and on its eastern side it is crossed by the road into Herefordshire from Worcester. This post would guard the passage of the river and the way from Worcestershire to Herefordshire. The traces of earthworks are plain, but it is not easy to determine what they were ; so far no relics of any kind are recorded as having been found on or near it.

A little beyond the Berrow to the west, the Teme passes through this range of hills. On most of the hilltops traces of what are probably

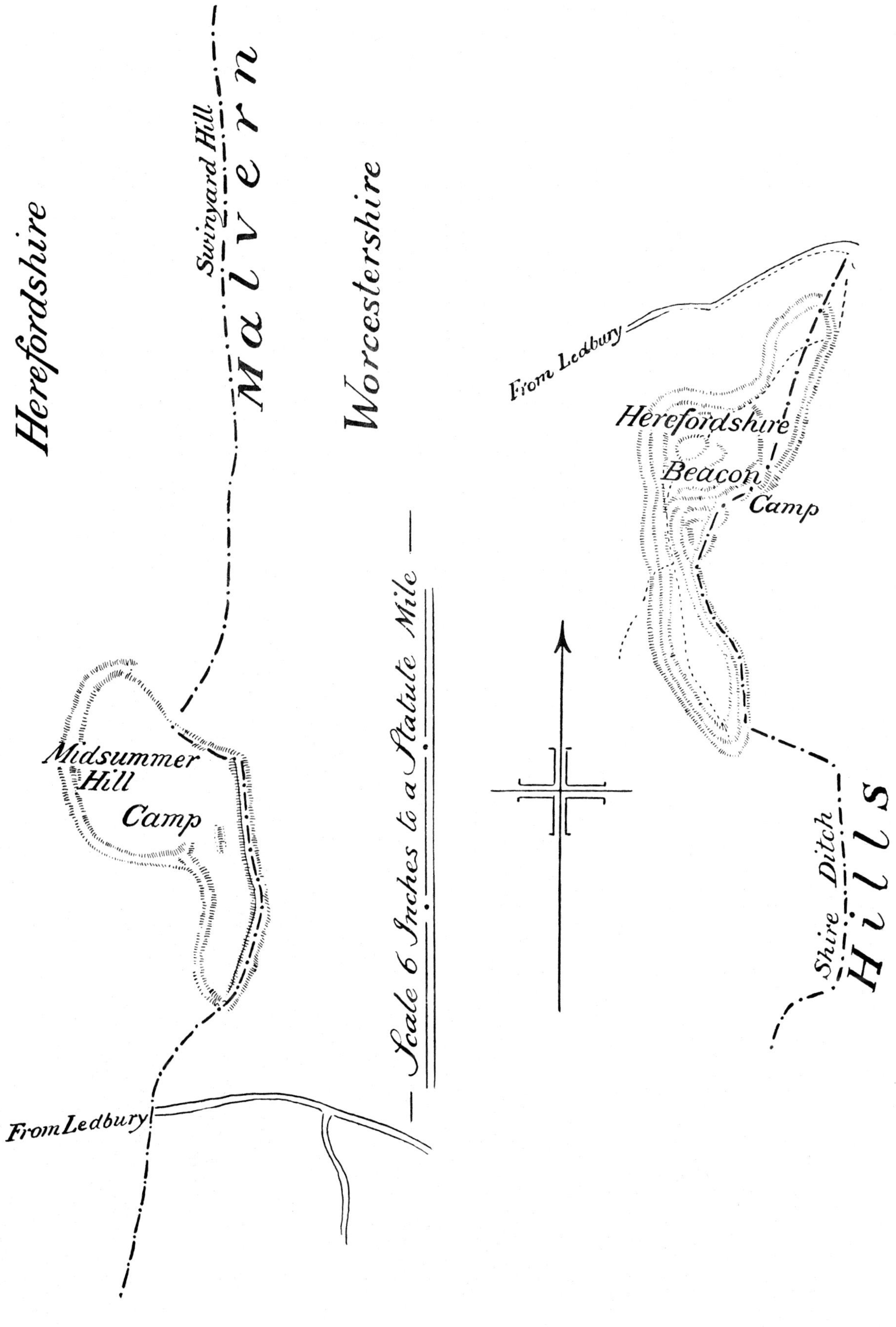

Herefordshire

Swinyard Hill

Malvern

Worcestershire

Midsummer
Hill
Camp

From Ledbury

Scale 6 Inches to a Statute Mile

From Ledbury

Herefordshire
Beacon
Camp

Shire Ditch

Hills

FIG. 3.

To face page 186.

remains of forts erected to guard the passage of the river are to be found. It is however quite possible that these traces of what on a cursory examination look like remains of entrenchments may only be the survivals of the ancient common cultivation that occur so often on the Welsh hills. Their presence is only another reason for a thorough and searching examination of all the hills not only along this range, but also of the range of hills from Clifton-on-Teme to Tenbury, for until this is done it will be impossible to say with any accuracy what are the camps or other earthworks in this part of the county.

This range of hills joins the Malverns near Cradley; the Malvern range runs nearly north and south. The first recognized work on the Malvern Hills is the cutting in the rock at the Wych, which is said to have been made by the Romans. As it does not appear to have been on the line of any Roman road it is difficult to see why it should have been then made; possibly it is of earlier date. Further to the south the first of the Malvern camps occurs.

(4) There are two great camps (fig. 3) on the Malvern Hills, one above Little Malvern, known as the Herefordshire Beacon, on one side of which the road leading into Herefordshire from Worcestershire passes. Although it has been the subject of a good deal of literature it has never yet been really or properly explored. It consists of a triple entrenchment enclosing altogether a considerable area, though that of the citadel or central portion is quite small. Its form will be better understood from the following rough plan than from a verbal description.

The origin of this camp has been ascribed to Caractacus, Dr. Card a former vicar of Malvern in 1822 published a book to prove this.[1] But the connection of Caractacus with the camp is pure conjecture, there is absolutely no evidence whatever to support it. Two rather remarkable finds have been made near it: one in 1647, when an urn containing some 300 Roman coins was discovered near the camp; the other in 1650 of a gold armlet set with precious stones, which was broken up and the stones sold separately.

(5) Following the line of the hills, about two miles to the south is another camp; the boundary between the counties of Hereford and Worcester passes through it. The hill on which it is situated is known as Midsummer Hill, it has two peaks, both of which are included in the works which form the camp. There is a double line of entrenchments, a double fosse and vallum. No relics are recorded as having been found at or near this camp. It must have been a strong position, and guarded the road which led from the hill to the camp next described, which is situated in the vale. This road crossed the hills near this point. The camp is almost at the end of the Malvern range, with it the western forts of the county terminate.

To complete the defence of the district there are two isolated hills in the plain that lies between the Malvern Hills and the Cotswolds,

[1] *A Dissertation on the Worcestershire Beacon*, by the Rev. H. Card.

both of them are fortified. The first is of such low elevation as hardly to deserve the name of a hill—it is rather a tump ; the second is the great outlying detached hill of the Cotswolds—Bredon.

(6) The tump or hill is called Gadbury Bank near Eldersfield (fig. 4). Although of a very low elevation, only some 186 feet, yet as it is the only spot rising above the dead level of the river, from its isolated position really occupies a commanding situation, and there is a very extensive view from its summit. The earthworks are an irregular oval,

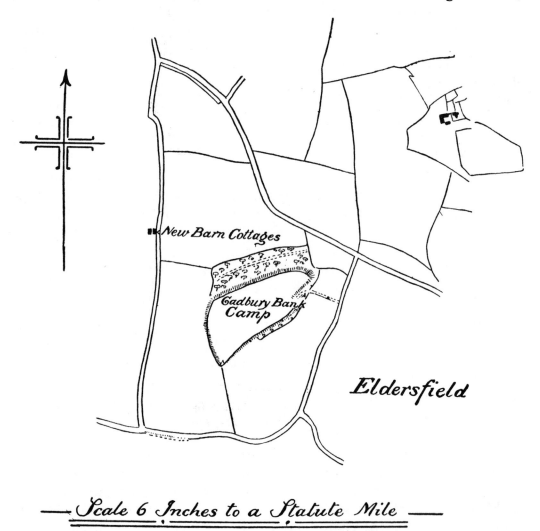

New Barn Cottages

Gadbury Bank
Camp

Eldersfield

— Scale 6 Inches to a Statute Mile —

Fig. 4.

following the shape of the summit of the hill which it encloses. There is an oblique entrance on the north-east side, and another but smaller one on the north-west corner. Its greatest length is said to be 390 yards and its width across the centre 112 yards. No objects are mentioned as having been found here, nor is there any record or tradition regarding it. From its position it would seem that advantage was taken of the only suitable place for a fort in the river valley between Malvern and Bredon. Formerly it must have been a very strong position, as it was in the

midst of marshes which were barely passable and were on the banks of a tidal river. The tide was blocked out and the marshes only drained within the last half-century.

Bredon Hill, the next elevation to the east, was the great defensive post in the south of the county, it commanded both the Severn and Avon valleys and probably was more or less fortified from the earliest times. The division of the counties of Worcester and Gloucester passes across the hill, so it is not always easy to say which earthworks are in which. They all however formed part of one defensive system. The two most important are the camps of Conderton and Kemerton.

(7) Conderton is an irregular oval entrenchment measuring 163 by 71 yards with a single rampart. The entrance is from the north-east. This has been called a Danish camp—why it is not easy to say, except that pirates usually called Danes came up the estuary on various occasions. Some Roman coins are said to have been found in the neighbourhood. It is probable that this camp or fort is but a part of the series of forts on this hill.

(8) Kemerton is in Gloucestershire (fig. 5). It is an entrenchment of a triangular shape well defended on the north and western sides by the very steep escarpment of the hill. On the south and east the line of entrenchment is double. Nash, writing at the end of the eighteenth century, states that ' it was ploughed two or three years ago, and several iron weapons found of so rude and bad workmanship as bespoke them rather Danish or Saxon than Roman.' No description of these weapons exists. A landslip occurred early in the nineteenth century, when a quantity of wheat of a burnt appearance was found in this camp. These grains were black or nearly so ; a slight pressure between the fingers reduced them to powder. As the chasm caused by the landslip opened, it exposed a vein of black earth about 4 or 5 inches thick immediately under the soil, which in some places was not more than 6 inches deep, but varied to 18 inches or 2 feet. Quantities of perfect grains of wheat were found in it ; there was no appearance of straw or ears of corn.

In this camp is a remarkable mass of rock. It is formed of the oolite of which the hill is composed, and has been made by excavating all round the mass. It is near the side of the camp facing Malvern and not far from the edge of the escarpment. It is locally called the Bambury Stone.

Bredon completes the list of camps in the district at present known. A glance at the map will show that they form a defensive line on the west and south of the county, while the east is entirely unprotected ; that at the south-eastern corner there was a strong fort guarding both the Avon and Severn, which was connected with the Malvern line by Eldersfield. The absence of forts on the east and north, assuming that after careful search none are found, would seem to indicate that it was not from those quarters the dwellers in the county apprehended danger. It was down the Avon valley the invaders came, and Bredon was fortified to close that line of approach. This may seem to explain why it is no finds have been

made in the lower parts of the Severn and Avon valleys. Bredon did the work for which it was designed and turned the invaders from the lower Avon valley across the county. It is however impossible to do more than conjecture until a thorough examination has been made, and it is seen whether or not there is anything to be taken into account which will tend to modify the story that on the existing evidence is told by the forts, of the early county history.

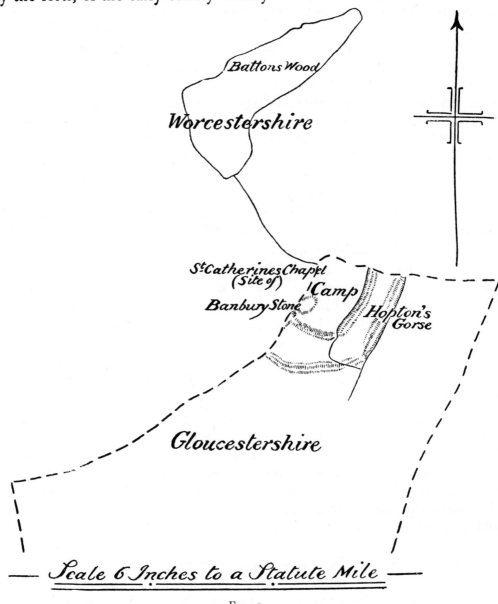

FIG. 5.

Of earthworks other than camps there are but few in Worcestershire.

(1) Crookbarrow or Cruckbarrow Hill is an elevation almost adjoining the Norton Barracks at Worcester. A portion of the lower part is clearly natural, while the top part, it is believed, is partly artificial. Like everything else it is said to be Roman, and Roman coins are said

to have been found near it. In shape it is elliptical, and at the base is 512 yards in circumference. It has been said to be a British broad barrow, but there is no evidence of any kind that the mound is sepulchral or as to its character in any way.

(2) In the parish of Kidderminster Foreign near the Severn, a little above the place where the Birmingham aqueduct crosses the river, is a small tumulus, but there is not even a tradition as to it or what it is. From its situation and size it is probably sepulchral, but there is nothing to furnish any clue as to it.

(3) The Devil's Spadeful. Adjoining the railway from Kidderminster to Bewdley on the sandy ground near Spring Grove, is a tumulus called by the above name. It is said the devil was going to dam up the Severn, and carried the earth forming this tumulus on his spade for the purpose, but losing his way he dropped it down here. There is no record of any examination having ever been made of it. Probably it is sepulchral.

(4) Towards the end of the last century there was a group of five barrows on the Clent Hills ; these were opened and examined by Nash. All contained remains of burnt bones and charred wood. In one was an urn which was broken by the spade of the workman who was excavating the mound ; it appeared to be of very ill-burnt clay. Probably they were a group of British barrows.

This account of the earthworks in the county is meagre in the extreme, and it is much to be regretted that a better list cannot be furnished. It however comprises all the known earthworks that have up till now been recorded.

TRACKWAYS

No account of Prehistoric Worcestershire should omit some allusion to the ancient roads or trackways in the county. Some writers have recognized a large number of these leading from the different camps to other places in the county ; the existence of most of them has however to be proved. That there were tracks crossing the Severn at different places seems clear, the survival of the name ' Rhydd ' as a place on the Severn would seem to locate a ford where one of these tracks crossed the river. There were probably others that crossed at Worcester and at Bewdley, while the names of Bransford, Knightsford and Stanford on the Teme point to tracks crossing that river at those places. The tracks seem to have been of two kinds :—

(a) The ordinary trackway from camp to camp or from place to place. These often kept the high ground and ran along the ridge of the hills.

(b) The trackways leading to the saltsprings at Droitwich.

Of the first kind there seem to have been at least three :—

(1) A track from the Midsummer Hill camp on the Malvern Hills to the east, crossing the Severn at the Rhydd, and then probably turning to the left and running parallel to the Severn to Worcester and on to Droitwich, and thence to the Staffordshire border.

(2) A track starting also from Midsummer Hill camp went north to the camp at the Herefordshire Beacon, thence along the ridge of the hills to Storridge, thence turning to the right went across the Teme at Knightsford and along the ridge past Martley to Woodbury.

(3) A third track appears to have run from Worcester to the Hundred House and Stanford, where it crossed the Teme ; then mounting the high ground near Clifton ran along the hilltops till it reached Kyre, thence downhill into Tenbury.

(*b*) The tracks leading to and from the saltsprings at Droitwich.

It is often stated that there were two saltways running from Droitwich—the upper and the lower. The upper is said to be easily traced from Birmingham over the Lickey to Droitwich, but although there may have been such a road it certainly cannot be easily traced and no one in the locality is able to point it out. It is however most likely that some such track existed.

The lower saltway would probably be the track already mentioned that passes from the Rhydd to Worcester and so on to Droitwich, running parallel to the Severn. As regards both these saltways the evidence is most uncertain, or rather there is no evidence only tradition that they existed.

The accompanying map (fig. D) indicates the course of the tracks that have been mentioned.

All these trackways however are most difficult to trace with any accuracy or authority ; they rest far more on conjecture than on evidence. It is assumed and possibly rightly that there must have been tracks across the forest between the camps and between the different settlements. Acting on this assumption, by the aid of field names and conjecture the route where it is supposed the track ought to have gone has been laid out. This process gives rise to two difficulties. While it is quite possible that the route marked out might be a trackway, was it one in fact ? and even if it is proved to have been in fact a trackway, was it a pre-Roman one ? It is difficult to get a satisfactory answer to either of the questions, hardly possible to get one to both.

It is much to be regretted that a fuller account cannot be given of Prehistoric Worcestershire. But until the various localities in the county are fully explored by competent persons it is quite impossible to do this. Without a proper examination the earthworks cannot be dealt with, and until this is done no real progress can be made. All that is at present possible is to do what has been attempted here. It is believed it is the first attempt to arrange such evidence as there is in something like order and let it speak for itself. It is hoped it may be the means by indicating what is required to be done to induce some one to undertake the task.

The above remarks relating to earthworks and trackways have been prepared by Professor Windle, F.R.S., who has made out the following list of Worcestershire finds, which will be of the greatest

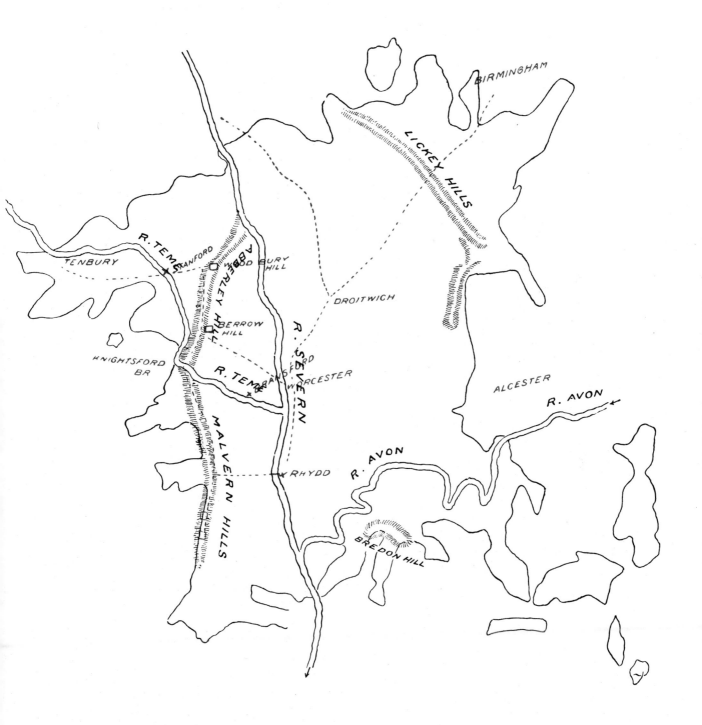

Fig. D.

To face page 192.

service to any one who undertakes the business of a thorough examination of Prehistoric Worcestershire.

The finds of Prehistoric implements and weapons that have been recorded are here grouped under the localities in which they have been found. No attempt is made to distinguish between the ages Neolithic, Bronze and Iron to which the articles belong. The localities are divided into four groups :—

(*a*) Avon Valley.
(*b*) Severn Valley.
(*c*) Teme Valley.
(*d*) Mid-Worcestershire.

(*a*) AVON VALLEY.

i. *Bevington Waste.* A rough stone axe was found here by a workman and placed on a rockery in his garden, from whence it was obtained by the late Canon Winington Ingram. It is now in the Victoria Museum, Worcester.

ii. *Harvington.* A bronze celt, socketed, ringed and reeded, evidently cast in a mould consisting of two halves, for the mark where the two parts met is very clearly shown on the implement, was found in a deep watery ditch between Harvington and Salford, this ditch forms the boundary between the counties of Worcester and Warwick. It has a total length of $4\frac{1}{2}$ inches and was in the possession of the late Mr. E. Bomford of Spring Hill, Fladbury.

iii. *Church Lench.* A bronze palstave found at Church Lench forms part of the Winington Ingram collection in the Victoria Museum, Worcester.

iv. *Offenham.* A celt of black stone was dug up in a ditch in this parish and is now in the possession of the Rev. F. S. Taylor. It is 3 inches in length, 2 inches in width at one end, $1\frac{5}{8}$ inches at the other, and has been sharpened at both ends.

v. *Aldington.* A rectangular piece of chlorite slate $5\frac{3}{8}$ inches long, $1\frac{3}{4}$ inches broad, and $\frac{1}{4}$ of an inch thick, slightly convex on one surface and with a corresponding concavity on the other was found in a gravel pit at Aldington. It has four holes through it, one at each corner, just low enough on the convex face for a small cord to pass through it. The hole is countersunk on the concave face. This implement has been described as a bracer (Evans, p. 381 ; *Wilts Arch. Mag.*, vol. x. (1867), pl. vi.).

vi. *Evesham.* A bronze palstave found near Evesham, now in the possession of Mr. R. F. Tomes of Littleton.

vii. *Sedgeberrow.* In deepening the channel of the brook at this place the sharpened half of a basalt celt was found, together with the portion of another (May's *History of Evesham*, ed. 2, p. 365 ; Allies, *Antiquities*, p. 85).

viii. At the same time, about 1827, and in the same place, while deepening the brook two oval-shaped spearheads of bronze of

most perfect workmanship with portions of their staves attached were found stuck into the bank at a depth of several feet ; pieces of defensive armour were likewise found, and part of a steel band, apparently for the shoulder retaining the bronze rivets that attached it to the cuirass. Several very large antlers were dug up at the same time (May's *History of Evesham*, ed. 2, p. 365).

ix. *Cropthorne.* A bronze celt of early type was found in a gravel pit here, it is now in the Victoria Museum, Worcester.

x. *Charlton.* An urn now in the Victoria Museum was found here in 1863 in a gravel pit 6 feet below the surface at the ballast hole. The gravel had been moved to let it in. It contained burnt bones. A bronze celt was found near it.

xi. *Defford.* A stone celt was found here near the Avon while excavations were being made for railway purposes. It measured $6\frac{1}{2}$ inches by $2\frac{1}{2}$ by $1\frac{1}{2}$ inches. A portion of a human skeleton was discovered near it and most unfortunately destroyed before being examined by any competent person. This celt has been removed from the county by the contractor for the works.

This completes the list of finds in the Avon valley itself.

xii. On *Bredon Hill* overlooking the valley there have been found from time to time various flint flakes. These are now in the Worcester Museum, there is nothing known as to or what precise part of the hill or under what circumstances they were found.

xiii. *Broadway.* A bronze sword was found on Broadway Hill near the tower, and therefore near the line of the so-called old trackway—the Buckle Street. It is $24\frac{1}{2}$ inches in length ; it has nine rivet holes, three in the tang and three in each of the wings (Evans, p. 280).

(*b*) SEVERN VALLEY.

i. *Dowles.* A bronze celt was found in the gravel in the Severn in 1899 while excavating for the aqueduct of the Birmingham Corporation. It was exhibited to the Society of Antiquaries, December, 1900. It is now in the possession of Mrs. Robert Woodward of Arley Castle.

ii. *Bewdley.* A double-edged celt of basalt was found in the river gravel at Bewdley (*Proceedings of the Worcestershire Naturalists' Club*, i. 194).

iii. Three looped bronze palstaves were found near Bewdley.

iv. A socketed bronze gouge was also found near Bewdley.

v. *Ribbesford.* A holed celt of greenish stone found at Ribbesford in the bed of the Severn while digging for gravel. It weighs 16 ounces, is 5 inches long, $2\frac{1}{2}$ inches broad, 2 inches wide at one end and $1\frac{1}{2}$ inches at the other. One end is sharp, the other blunt. It is now in the Museum of the Society of Antiquaries (Evans, p. 188 ; Allies, p. 146, pl. iv. fig. 5 ; Wright's *Celt, Roman and Saxon*, p. 70, fig. 2).

vi. *Astley.* In the year 1843 a bronze palstave was found in the

cleft of a rock 21 feet 6 inches below the alluvium and about 45 yards from the bank of the river Severn at Lincombe in Astley parish. It weighed nearly $1\frac{1}{4}$ pounds, was about 6 inches long, 3 inches broad at one end and 1 inch at the other (Allies, p. 112, pl. iv. ; Evans, p. 81).

vii. *Holt.* A looped bronze celt was found in the year 1844 in the middle of the bed of the river Severn near Holt, about 3 feet 6 inches under the gravel, as the workmen were dredging midway between the bridge and the entrance of the cutting from the lock for the purpose of the Severn navigation improvements. This celt was $4\frac{1}{4}$ inches in length (Allies, p. 149, pl. iv. No. 6; Evans, p. 129).

viii. A bronze pin $4\frac{1}{2}$ inches in length found about 18 feet below the surface and about 200 feet distant from the Severn in the cutting outside the south gates of the lock near Holt. It has a small cross formed of five knobs attached to the front of the ring. Sir John Evans says it belongs to quite the close of the Bronze period if not to the late Celtic (Allies, p. 149, pl. iv. No. 7; Evans, p. 381).

ix. *Ombersley.* A glass ball alternately deep amber colour and white, an oblate spheroid in shape and measuring a little over $1\frac{1}{2}$ inches by little more than 1 inch, found at Chatley near Ombersley, and is now in the Victoria Museum, Worcester.

x. *Ombersley.* A ringed palstave $6\frac{1}{4}$ inches long, weighing $17\frac{1}{2}$ ounces, was dug up in a field about 9 inches below the surface which was formerly part of Lynal (Linnal or Lyneholt) Common by Boreley in Ombersley. It is in the Worcester Museum.

xi. *Grimley Ham.* A holed celt of basalt found 14 feet deep in the alluvial soil at a distance of about 127 yards from the Severn. It weighed 8 pounds $5\frac{1}{2}$ ounces, was 9 inches long, 3 inches broad, 4 inches thick at the blunt end and $3\frac{1}{2}$ inches broad at the sharp end. The hole for the handle was $1\frac{3}{4}$ inches in diameter (Evans, *Ancient Stone Implements*, p. 180; Allies, p. 150).

xii. *Grimley.* A holed celt found at Ball Mill in a gravel bed several feet beneath the surface. The bed where it was found lay on some rather elevated ground on the western side of the Severn nearly opposite to Bevere Island and within a short distance of it. This celt was 5 inches long, 2 inches broad at one end, $1\frac{3}{4}$ inches at the other, $1\frac{1}{8}$ inches broad and $1\frac{3}{4}$ inches thick in the middle. It weighed $9\frac{1}{2}$ ounces, was edged at both ends, but the one end had been rather blunted and lessened by use (Evans, p. 166; Allies, p. 150).

xiii. *Bevere.* At this place on the opposite bank of the Severn to Grimley about the year 1809 a bronze celt was dug up in the island between it and Grimley. It was $4\frac{1}{8}$ inches long, $2\frac{3}{8}$ inches broad at the widest end, $1\frac{3}{8}$ inches at the middle, $\frac{3}{4}$ of an inch broad at the narrowest, $\frac{1}{4}$ of an inch thick in the centre. It weighed $6\frac{3}{4}$ ounces, and was rather sharp at both ends, but most so at the smaller (Allies, p. 151, pl. iv. No. 11; Evans p. 42).

xiv. *Worcester.* A socketed and looped celt was found in the black soil within the base of the Earth Hill, Worcester, when it was being excavated. A great part of the socket and ring is broken away from the specimen, which is in the Victoria Museum at Worcester. It has four parallel indented tapering grooves on each side (Allies, p. 18, pl. i. No. 1 ; Evans, p. 120).

xv. *Worcester.* A bronze spearhead found at Diglis near Worcester and thus described by Allies :—

In the year 1844 about 1½ miles below Worcester and ½ a mile below the Diglis Lock a bronze spearhead of very unusual shape was dredged up by some workmen employed in the improvement of the navigation of the Severn. It is 10½ inches long, 2¾ inches broad and weighs 8 ounces.

It is figured in *Archæological Journal*, ii. p. 87 (*Proceedings of the Archæological Institute at York*, 1846, p. 39, pl. v. fig. 4, and noticed in p. 34 of that work). It was also exhibited at a meeting of the Society of Antiquaries of London, May 29, 1851, when a paper was read by Mr. Akerman 'On some of the Weapons of the Celtic and Teutonic Races.'

xvi. *Worcester.* A fragment of a torque was found in 1840 at Perdeswell, about 2 miles from Worcester, in a gravel pit about 2 feet deep. It was rather more than a third of a circle, 8 inches long in the curve, and weighed ½ a pound. An iron rod ran through its centre connecting the bronze pieces or vertebræ, which are twenty in number and are curiously twisted and tooled. Between each piece there is a thick ring shaped like a pulley and the whole is fitted close together. The circumference of the perfect torque must have been about 18 inches. At the date of the publication of his book, 1852, this torque was in the possession of Mr. Allies. It is figured in *Archæologia*, xxx. p. 564 ; *The Archæological Journal*, iii. p. 34 ; and in Allies, p. 230, pl. vi. ; Evans, p. 381.

xvii. *Kempsey.* A spearhead with loops at the base of the blade which connect it with the socket was dredged out of the Severn between Kempsey and Pixham Ferry by some workmen employed in the navigation works. It measures 10½ inches in length. There were also found at the same spot in the bed on the west, the Powick side of the river, the remains of oak piles and of planking which had been fastened to the piles. These extended about half way across the river (Allies, p. 60 ; Evans, p. 330 ; *Journal Archæological Institute*, iii. p. 354).

xviii. *Malvern Link.* It is stated in Nash's *Worcestershire* (circa 1781), vol. ii. p. 139 : 'In the Link in the parish of Malvern was lately found, many feet underground, a celt weighing 10 ounces, about 5½ inches long, of a mixed metal between brass and copper, with a small ring or loop. It has a beautiful patina upon it.' Nothing further is known of this except that Allies, at p. 167, reproduced the account with a figure.

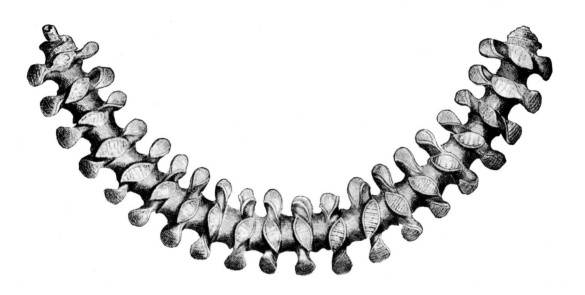

FRAGMENT OF A TORQUE FOUND AT PERDESWELL.

To face page 196.

xix. *Malvern*. Some flakes are in the Victoria Museum, Worcester, which are said to have been found upon the Malvern Hills, but neither the place of finding nor the date at which any of them were found seems to be known.

xx. *Malvern*. Further flakes have recently been found on this range and are in private hands.

xxi. *Malvern*. On the summit of the highest point of the Malvern range—the Worcestershire Beacon, 1,390 feet—in November, 1849, the late Mr. Edwin Lees met with some of the Royal Engineers who were engaged on the ordnance survey. They showed him part of a human skull found three days before in excavating on the summit of the Beacon to find the marks made as a datum during the former survey. On uncovering the rock about 9 inches below the surface, on the outer edge towards the south of the pile of loose stones, a small urn was found in a cavity of the rock with some bones and ashes. The urn was placed in an inverted position covering part of the ashes, and the half-burnt bones lay near and around it. Its height is $2\frac{1}{2}$ inches, breadth at the top 3 inches. The bottom is nearly $\frac{3}{4}$ of an inch in thickness. The impressed markings are very deficient in regularity. They consist of a zigzag corded line both externally and within the lip impressed on the surface. The urn is figured by Allies, p. 165. On the north side of the same heap of stones another deposit of bones was found, but no pottery. Both the bones in the urn and the other deposit were examined with a microscope and found to be adult human bones which had been partly burnt.

(c) TEME VALLEY.

i. *Lindridge*. A greenish-coloured stone about $4\frac{3}{4}$ inches in length by 1 inch in width and $\frac{1}{4}$ of an inch thick, perforated at one end only with countersunk holes at each of the two corners, a third hole between them being only partly drilled. The other end is sharper and undrilled. Was found in a gravel pit at Lindridge. It is now in the Victoria Museum, Worcester.

ii. *Broadwas*. A holed celt is reported in the *Proceedings of the Worcestershire Naturalists' Club*, i. p. 194, to have been found at the Devil's Leap near Broadwas.

(d) MID-WORCESTERSHIRE.

i. *Stoke Prior*. Two armlets—one of large diameter with flat broad ends and ornamented with punctured markings, the other with a smaller diameter but more massive, broader and plain—were found with the remains of a skeleton near Stoke Prior. The larger one is now in the British Museum (Evans, p. 383, fig. 476).

ii. *Tutnall*.

(a) An early celt of felsite roughly shaped measuring $4\frac{3}{4}$ inches in length, 2 inches in breadth at its wider end and $1\frac{3}{4}$ inches at its narrower. It is $\frac{3}{4}$ of an inch thick.

(b) A holed stone hammer formed of a brownish water-

worn quartzite pebble $4\frac{1}{2}$ inches in length and $3\frac{3}{4}$ inches in breadth. It has had a large piece chipped off one end, and has since it was found been broken across and mended.

(c) A piece of grit with a cavity of about $\frac{3}{4}$ of an inch deep in it. Probably half a stone hammerhead which has been broken in two. A fresh hole has been begun to be bored in the larger half.

(d) Two stone spindle wheels.

(e) A small sub-cylindrical piece of the local new red sandstone about $1\frac{1}{2}$ inches in length and $\frac{3}{4}$ of an inch in diameter.

(f) A small ball of limestone about 1 inch in diameter.

(g) Arrowheads of different kinds.

    i. Leaf-shaped. One of them is worked in white flint, another of a quartzite stone, one side with a smooth rounded surface, the other with a rough fractured surface.

    ii. Triangular.

    iii. Tanged.

    iv. Tanged and barbed.

    v. Single-barbed.

(h) Borers or awls.

(i) Scrapers, both of the varieties known as thumb and finger flints.

(k) Flakes of various shapes and sizes.

All these have been collected on his farm there by Mr. John Moore of Tutnall, Tardebigge, at various times and are now in his possession. They have been described and figured in the *Proceedings of the Birmingham Archæological Association*, 1896, and in *Proc. Soc. Antiq.*, March, 1897.

This completes the Worcestershire list of Prehistoric implements so far as is known. There are doubtless more which have not been recorded ; perhaps the publication of this list may bring some of them to light. Should this be the case, as individual specimens have little if any value to the possessor, while their collective value as part of a series is considerable, it may be hoped that the owners will at least deposit them for a time in the Victoria Museum at Worcester, so that the list of county implements may be made as complete as possible.

At present it stands as follows :—

Avon Valley .	13
Severn Valley	20
Teme Valley	2
Mid-Worcestershire	11
	46

Of these only 11 are available for study—9 in the Victoria Museum at Worcester, 1 in the British Museum and 1 in the Museum of the Society of Antiquaries. Of the remainder 15 are known to be in the possession of individuals, while the localities of the remaining 20 are unknown.

ROMANO-BRITISH WORCESTERSHIRE[1]

1. INTRODUCTORY SKETCH

THE expression Romano-British Worcestershire is, speaking strictly, a contradiction in terms. When the Romans ruled our island, neither Worcestershire nor any other of our counties was yet in existence, nor was the province of Britain divided up into any districts geographically coinciding with them. Neither the boundaries of the Celtic tribes nor those of the Roman administrative areas, so far as we know them, agree with our existing county boundaries, and students of the Roman remains found in any one county have to deal with a division of land which for their purposes is accidental and arbitrary. Worcestershire therefore, to the archæologist concerned with the Roman period, is merely a meaningless area devoid of unity. He can describe it but he must not attempt, and he is not able to write anything like a real history of it. This fact makes it desirable in the following paragraphs to diverge a little from the plan followed by most county historians in dealing with the Roman antiquities of the county described. Hitherto it has been customary to give a narrative of the chief events recorded by ancient writers as having occurred in Britain, and to point out which of these events took place, or may be imagined to have taken place, within the county. The result is always to give an impression that somehow the county had in Roman times some sort of local individuality and local history. We shall here adopt a different plan, suggested by the recent developments of topographical research. Utilizing the abundant archæological evidence, which is now far better known and appreciated than it was a hundred years ago, we shall try first to sketch briefly the general character of the Roman province in Britain, its military, social and economic features. We shall then point out in some detail how far the

---

[1] For the following article I have searched most of the literature and, so far as I could, have visited the chief museums and sites. I am especially indebted to a volume on the *Antiquities of Worcestershire*, by Mr. Jabez Allies (ed. 2, 1852) though I cannot invariably accept his conclusions. I have also to thank various helpers : Mr. W. H. Stevenson, Mr. R. P. L. Booker, Mr. John Amphlett of Clent, Mr. R. F. Tomes, the Rev. J. H. Bloom of Whitchurch, Dr. Cuthbertson of Droitwich, Mr. W. H. Edwards of Worcester Museum, Mr. J. W. Willis-Bund, and others named below. I have further consulted Prattinton's MSS. preserved by the Society of Antiquaries in London, but without much profit

antiquities of Worcestershire illustrate this general sketch; that is how far the district now called Worcestershire was an ordinary and average bit of Roman Britain.

The Roman occupation was undertaken by the Emperor Claudius and commenced in A.D. 43. At first its progress was rapid. Within three or four years the Romans overran all the south and midlands as far as Exeter, Shrewsbury and Lincoln : part was annexed, part left to 'protected' native princes. Then came a pause : some thirty years were spent in reducing the hill tribes of Wales and Yorkshire, and during this period the 'protected' principalities were gradually absorbed. About A.D. 80 the advance into Scotland was attempted : in 124 Hadrian built his Wall from Newcastle to Carlisle, and thereafter the Roman frontier was sometimes to the north, never to the south of this line. The 'province' thus gained fell practically though not officially into two marked divisions, which coincide roughly with the lowlands occupied in the first years of the conquest and the hills which were tamed later. The former were the regions of settled civil life, and among these we have to include the district now called Worcestershire. The troops appear to have been very soon withdrawn from them, and with a few definite exceptions there was probably not a fort or fortress or military post throughout this part of our island. On the other hand the Welsh and northern hills formed a purely military district, with forts and fortresses and roads, but with no towns or ordinary civilian life. It was the Roman practice, at least in the European provinces of the Empire, to mass the troops almost exclusively along the frontiers, and Britain was no exception. The army which garrisoned this military district was perhaps forty thousand men. It ranked as one of the chief among provincial armies, and constituted the most important element in Roman Britain. With the military district however we are not now concerned. For our present purpose it suffices to note its existence, in order to explain why traces of military occupation are absent in Worcestershire. But we may pause to examine the chief features of the non-military districts within which Worcestershire is included. These features are not sensational. Britain was a small province, remote from Rome and by no means wealthy. It did not reach the higher developments of city life, of culture or of commerce, which we meet in more favoured lands—Gaul or Spain or Africa. Nevertheless it had a character of its own.

In the first place, Britain like all the provinces of the Western Empire became Romanized. Perhaps it became Romanized later and less perfectly than these, but in the end the Britons adopted generally the Roman speech and civilization, and in our island, as in all western Europe, the difference between Roman and provincial practically vanished. When the Roman rule in Britain ended (about A.D. 410), the so-called departure of the Romans did not mean what the end of English rule in India or French rule in Algeria would mean. It was not an emigration of alien officials, soldiers and traders ; it was more administrative than

racial. Probably the country folk in the remoter parts of Britain continued to speak Celtic during the Roman period : thus much we may infer from various continental analogies and from the revival of the Celtic language in the sixth century. But the townspeople and the educated seem to have used Latin, and on the side of material civilization the Roman element reigns supreme. Before the Roman period there was a Late Celtic art of considerable merit, best known for its metal work and earthenware, and distinguished for its fantastic use of plant and animal forms, its employment of the 'returning spiral' (fig. 1), and its enamelling. This art and the culture which went with it vanished before the Roman. In a few places, as in the New Forest, its products survived as local curiosities ; in general it met the fate of every picturesque but semi-civilized art when confronted by an organized coherent culture. Almost every feature in Romano-British life was Roman. The commonest good pottery, the so-called Samian or Terra Sigillata, was copied directly from an Italian original and shows no trace of native influences ; it was indeed principally imported from abroad. The mosaic pavements and painted stuccoes which adorned the houses, the hypocausts which warmed them, and the bathrooms which increased their luxury, were equally borrowed from Italy. Nor were these features confined to the mansions of the wealthy. Samian bowls and coarsely coloured plaster and makeshift hypocausts occur even in outlying hamlets. The material civilization of Roman Britain comprised few elements of splendour but it was definitely Roman.

FIG. 1. LATE CELTIC ORNAMENT ILLUSTRATING THE RETURNING SPIRAL.

Agreeably to this general character of the province we find town life in it, but not much town life. The highest form of town life known to the Romans is naturally rare. The *coloniæ* and *municipia*, the privileged municipalities with constitutions on the Italian model which mark the supreme development of Roman political civilization in the provinces, were not common in Britain. We know only of five. Colchester, Lincoln, Gloucester and York were *coloniæ*, Verulam probably a *municipium*, and despite their legal rank none of these could count among the greater cities of the Empire. Four of them indeed probably owe their existence, not to any development of Britain, but to the need of providing for time-expired soldiers. On the other hand many smaller towns reached some degree of municipal life, of which we cannot precisely specify the character. Originally (as it seems) Celtic tribal centres, they grew into towns just as the tribal centres of northern Gaul grew into towns, under the influence of Roman civilization. They were often small, but their sizes varied widely—from hardly twenty to more than two hundred acres. Strong walls protected them from external assault ; inside, at least in the larger towns a forum built on a Roman plan provided accommodation for magistrates, traders and idlers. Instances of such towns are Silchester and Winchester in Hampshire ; Canterbury

and Rochester in Kent ; Dorchester and Exeter, Cirencester, Leicester, and far in the north Aldborough in the Vale of York.

Outside these towns the country seems to have been principally divided up into estates usually called ' villas,' and in this respect again Britain resembled northern Gaul. The ' villa' was the property of a large landowner who lived in the ' great house' if there was one, cultivated the land immediately round it (the demesne) by his slaves and let the rest to half-serf *coloni*. The estates formed for the most part sheep runs and corn land, and supplied the cloth and wheat which are occasionally mentioned by ancient writers as products of the province during the later Imperial period. The landowners may have been to some extent immigrant Italians, but it can hardly be doubted that, as in Gaul, they were mostly the Romanized upper classes of the natives. The common assertion that they were Roman officers or officials may be set aside as rarely if ever correct. The peasantry who worked on these estates or were otherwise occupied in the country lived in rude hamlets, sometimes in pit-dwellings, sometimes in huts, with few circumstances of comfort or pleasure. Their civilization however, as we have said, was Roman in all such matters as the better objects in common use or the warming and decoration of the houses.

One feature, not a prominent one, remains to be noticed—trade and industry. We should perhaps place first the agricultural industry, which produced wheat and wool. Both were exported in the fourth century, and the export of wheat to the towns of the lower Rhine is mentioned by an ancient writer as considerable. Unfortunately the details of this agriculture are almost unknown : perhaps we shall be able to estimate it better when the Romano-British ' villas' have been better explored. Rather more traces have survived of the lead mining and iron mining, which at least during the first two centuries of our era was carried on with some vigour in half a dozen districts—lead on Mendip, in Shropshire, Flintshire and Derbyshire ; iron in the Weald and the Forest of Dean. Other minerals were less important. The gold mentioned by Tacitus proved very scanty, and the far-famed Cornish tin seems (according to present evidence) to have been worked comparatively little and late in the Roman occupation. The chief commercial town was from the earliest times Londinium (London), a place of some size and wealth, and perhaps the residence of the chief authorities who controlled taxes and customs dues.

Finally let us sketch the roads. We may distinguish four groups all commencing from one centre, London. One road ran south-east to Canterbury and the Kentish ports. A second ran west and south-west from London to Silchester, and thence by ramifications to Winchester, Dorchester and Exeter, Bath, Gloucester and South Wales. A third, Watling Street, ran north-west across the Midlands to Wroxeter, and thence to the military districts of the north-west ; it also gave access to Leicester and the north. A fourth ran to Colchester and the eastern counties, and also to Lincoln and York and the military districts of the

north-east. To these must be added a long single road, the only important one which had no connection with London. This is the Foss, which cuts obliquely across the island from north-east to south-west, joining Lincoln, Leicester, Bath and Exeter. These roads must be understood as being only the main roads, divested for the sake of clearness of many branches and intricacies ; and understood as such they may be taken to represent a reasonable supply of internal communications for the province. After the Roman occupation had ceased, they were largely utilized by the English, but they do not resemble the roads of medieval England in their grouping and economic significance. One might rather compare them to the railways of to-day, which radiate similarly from London. In Worcestershire we shall be concerned principally with branches and routes of lesser importance, but the preceding sketch seemed desirable in order to fit these lesser routes into their proper places.

Such in the main was that large part of Roman Britain in which ordinary non-military civilized life prevailed. To that part Worcestershire belongs, and when we pass on to survey in detail the Roman remains discovered in the county, we might expect to meet the features which we have sketched in the preceding paragraphs. To a certain extent our expectation will not be disappointed. There undoubtedly existed in Worcestershire a Romano-British civilization of the normal type, with town and villa and road. But though normal in type, that civilization was by no means normal in amount. Towns and villas and roads were very scarce ; industries were wholly or almost wholly absent, and in general the remains with which we have to deal are few and comparatively unimportant. Much of the county was doubtless forest ; much must have needed draining, and the whole valley of the Severn from Bewdley to Tewkesbury contained probably a small population. It is not merely that Worcestershire possesses fewer Roman remains than its southern neighbour of Gloucester, with its two great towns and its crowd of villas large and small, and its numerous and important roads : even Herefordshire in this respect excels Worcestershire. Some allowance must perhaps be made for the absence of exploration, for Worcestershire is almost unique among the English counties in this, that no single Roman remain within its borders has ever been excavated of set purpose. But even so we must admit that the county is to be classed as one of the thinner spaces (if we may use the phrase) in Roman Britain.

2. PLACES OF SETTLED OCCUPATION : WORCESTER.

Worcestershire, so far as it is at present known to us, contains no site which can be described as being demonstrably the site of a large Romano-British town. It has no Gloucester or Cirencester. But the various remains found at Worcester, though they include no definite traces of houses or other buildings, may nevertheless be accepted as evidence of some little town or settlement.

A HISTORY OF WORCESTERSHIRE

The Romano-British name of the place is not known nor has any probable conjecture ever been suggested concerning it. The earliest forms of the English name as preserved in Saxon charters are Wigeran (or Wiogeran) Ceaster, and the first half of this, Wigeran or Wiogeran, which has certainly nothing to do with the Hwicii, and probably is not English at all, may conceivably contain some vestige of a British name. But no name occurs in the Itinerary of Antonine or in any other Roman document about Britain which can be identified with Worcester. Some sixteenth-century writers suggested the Bravonium of the Itinerary, a station on the road from Viroconium (Wroxeter) to Isca (Caerleon), and in sixteenth century fashion went so far as to dub old Senatus, prior of Worcester in 1189 A.D., Senatus Bravonius.[1] But the route from Wroxeter to Caerleon unquestionably ran through Herefordshire, not through Worcestershire, and Bravonium is probably Leintwardine. Others identified Worcester with Brannogenium, which Ptolemy names as chief town of the Ordovices. But this guess must also be rejected, for the Ordovices lived in North Wales. We must be content not to know the Roman name of the place.

Another ancient name has often been given to Worcester. This professes to be a British and not a Roman name, and it is undoubtedly not authentic, but its history is curious and worth a glance. It begins in or about the seventh century when an unknown author compiled a list of twenty-eight cities in Britain. The names of these cities are Celtic with Caer prefixed ; most of them are entirely unknown and the value of the whole list is extremely slight. However it contains a Caer Guiragon, or perhaps Guoeirangon or Guoranegon (the manuscripts vary), and with this name we are concerned. The list came into the hands of a twelfth-century historian and antiquary, Henry of Huntingdon, who altered it to his taste, inserted identifications apparently of his own devising, and incorporated the result in his book. Among the identifications we find Caer Gorangon (so Henry spells it) equated with Wigornia, that is Worcester. No reason is given ; and so far as one can see no reason existed, beyond the obvious fact that Wigornia and Gorangon each contains the letters *gor* and *n*. In this item, as indeed throughout the list, Henry appears to have guessed in a manner which we should now call most arbitrary, and no real value can be attached to his identifications. Unfortunately, having once been made they stuck. Medieval chroniclers and modern antiquaries alike repeated them, connected other names with them, and piled up spacious but baseless hypotheses. In the case of Worcester, Caer Gorangon (respelt Caer Wrangon) was put beside Bravonium and Brannogenium by sixteenth-century writers ; Bravonium was rechristened Branonium and the three names fused into

---

[1] Leland *De Scriptoribus Britann.* (ed. Hall) and *Genethliacon Edwardi* (ed. Hearne in the *Itinerary*, ix. p. xxviii.). Valentine Green in his *Survey* (1764) and *History of Worcester* (1796) states that Senatus called himself Bravonius, but this is wrong : the epithet does not occur till the sixteenth century. Its earlier occurrence would indeed be very remarkable, since the name Bravonium is preserved solely in the *Itinerary*, and that work was unknown till about 1500 A.D.

one—Branogena or Brangonia, which Humphrey Lhuyd and Leland and many subsequent topographers have proclaimed to be the Roman name of Worcester.[1] It is one long juggle with names—interesting as characteristic of earlier antiquarian methods but wholly devoid of scientific value. In dealing with ancient Worcester we shall do well to leave alone Caer Guiragon or Gorangon and all names constructed out of it.

The Romano-British settlement at Worcester appears to have occupied much the same site as the modern town, a long strip of high land above the eastern bank of the Severn. But the recorded remains give no real indication of its size or character. Roman coins have been found at many points from Barbourne on the north to Diglis on the south, and they comprise not only the usual third and fourth-century issues down to the end of the Roman period, but also a considerable proportion of first and second-century coins—one of Augustus, two of Tiberius, many of Claudius and his successors.[2] Other objects have been found rather less frequently over the same area. The following paragraphs contain the principal discoveries and alleged discoveries arranged from north to south.

(1) At the White Ladies, the site of a medieval nunnery in the Tything, somewhat north of St. Oswald's Hospital, many coins, mostly but not wholly of the third and fourth centuries, were found in and before 1842, and with them were associated a number of Greek coins, some of pre-Roman date.[3] But these, both Greek and Roman, as Mr. Willis-Bund informs me, were purposely buried by a lady who afterwards admitted the act.

(2) A little west of this, under the house in the centre of Britannia Square, some discoveries were made in 1829—a circular foundation of sandstone 30 feet in diameter, general débris and coins of the late third and the fourth century. The foundations were explained as a fort built by Ostorius Scapula about A.D. 50, but they are much too small for a fort and their connection with Ostorius is a gratuitous fiction for which no shred of evidence exists; they do not seem indeed to have been examined by any competent archæologists, and we possess no actual proof that they are of Roman date at all.[4]

(3) West of Britannia Square in the low riverside area called Pitchcroft, now occupied by the racecourse, a great quantity of *scoriæ* as from iron-smeltings, and among them some pottery which was taken to be Roman, were found in the eighteenth century. It was probably here that the seventeenth-century engineer, Andrew Yarranton, noted 'the hearth of a Roman footblast' and a peck of Roman coins in an urn near it, and *scoriæ* enough for him and his friends (as one of them asserts) to take 'many thousand tons or loads' up the Severn to their iron-furnaces to be resmelted. That these *scoriæ* date from the Roman period is a common

---

[1] Lhuyd, *Commentarioli fragmentum* ; Leland, reff. of preceding note.

[2] Allies, *Antiquities of Worcestershire*, ed. 2, 1852, pp. 1–32 ; Val. Green, *Hist. of Worcester*, i. 108 ; *Worcestershire 1882 Exhibition Catalogue*, p. 50, mentions two coins (Vespasian and Constantine) found in Barbourne. Coins are so easily shifted amidst rubbish or even found and lost again elsewhere, that it is no use here to catalogue all the precise localities where individual specimens have been noted.

[3] Allies, pp. 5–8.   [4] Allies, pp. 1–3.   Forty-nine of the coins are in the Worcester Museum.

view.[1] But the coins and alleged pottery are hardly conclusive evidence, and Mr. Willis-Bund informs me that iron ore was largely brought down the river to be smelted with wood in the sixteenth century : similar *scoriæ*, which can be dated by documents, appear to exist at Powick. A gold coin of Tiberius (Cohen, No. 15) was lately found in the Severn near Pitchcroft.

(4) Another object found in the northern part of the town is a small and not ungraceful bronze vase from Sansome Fields, now in the Worcester Museum.

(5) The centre of the town has yielded fewer remains. Drain-laying in Broad Street in 1797 and in High Street in 1853 and 1896 revealed more *scoriæ*, apparently concreted with pebbles to form what was considered by the discoverers a roadway running north and south, but again we have no clear proof of Roman origin. Some walling and tiles thought to be Roman have been found in Swithin Street, but their age is doubtful.[2] A fibula was dug up in Copenhagen Street in 1857.

(6) An unquestionably Roman object from this quarter was found in 1844, at a depth of 18 feet, under 12 High Street. It is a little bronze  statuette (fig. 2) $2\frac{3}{4}$ inches long, of an undraped female figure, with one hand on her lips, the other behind her and her feet crossed. Several more or less similar figures are known to archæologists. They were formerly explained as representations of an obscure Roman goddess of silence, Angerona, but this view has long been abandoned and they are now recognized to be amulets against the evil eye, the hand being placed on the lips to prevent evil influences entering thereby. Some specimens have a small loop or hole by which they could be suspended.[3]

(7) Roman remains are commonest at the south end of the modern town. Noteworthy discoveries were made about 1833 during the removal of the Castle Mound, which used to occupy a site immediately south-west of the Cathedral, near the river. This mound was of Saxon or Norman origin, and at its base the labourers found some eighty or ninety coins, including several of the first century (seven of Claudius for instance), fibulæ, bronze bells and pottery, including Samian, and among the Samian one piece which might

FIG. 2. ROMAN CHARM OR AMULET.

---

[1] Treadway Nash, *Collections for the Hist. of Worcestershire*, Supplement (issued 1799), p. 97; Andrew Yarranton, *England's Improvement by Sea and Land*, ii. (1698) p. 162, cited by Nash, ii. p. cviii. ; Val. Green, *Hist. of Worcester*, i. 10 note. The 1698 issue of Yarranton's work, published posthumously, is not in any library accessible to me, and I have cited it after Nash. The 'many thousand tons' sounds an exaggeration.

[2] Nash, Supplement, p. 97 ; Allies, p. 2 ; Bozward, in Berrow's *Worcester Journal*, Oct. Nov. 1889 ; piece of concrete in Worcester Museum ; information from Mr. Willis-Bund.

[3] Allies, p. 13, with figure ; brief mentions, *Archæological Journal*, ii. 74 ; *Journal of the British Archæol. Assoc.*, ii. 48. For the whole class of figures see Otto Jahn's paper *Ueber den Aberglauben des bösen Blickes bei den Alten*, in the *Berichte über den Abh. des kön. sächsischen Gesellschaft der Wissenschaften zu Leipzig*, vii. (1855) 47–49 ; and Wissowa, in Roscher's *Lexikon der Mythologie*, s.v. Angerona ; compare Frazer's *Golden Bough* (ed. 2, 1901) i. 313.

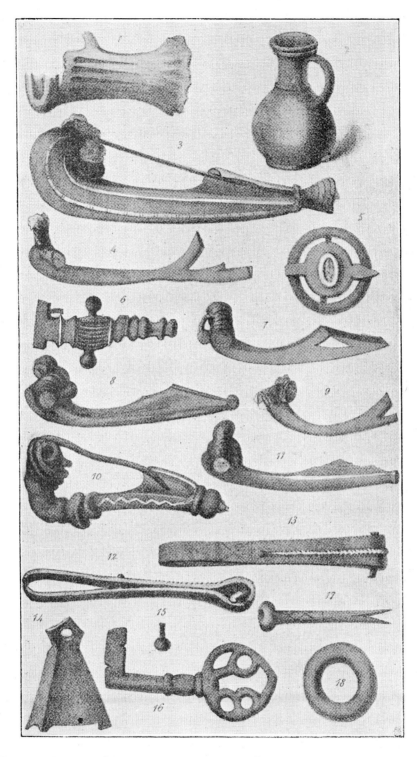

Fig. 3. Fibulæ and other Objects found beneath the Castle Mound, Worcester (pp. 206, 207).

well belong to the first century. There were also some foundations and a quoined well which, being beneath the mound, may be of Roman date. A few Roman objects seem also to have occurred in the earth of the mound itself, and were doubtless scraped up with that earth when the mound was built.[1] The accompanying illustration (fig. 3) shows some of the remains.

(8) South of this but near it, 200 yards west of the Porcelain Works and near the Severn bank in Diglis, Samian and other coarser pottery, two bronze coins of Domitian, a bronze armilla, fluetiles, a structure taken to be a kiln, and some burnt bones which were thought not to be human, were found in 1860. At the same date Samian and other sherds, amphoræ, pelves and the like, and some bits of glass were noted in the course of some repairs at the Cathedral south of the Lady chapel. Samian and other fragments have also been found at St. Alban's Home in the same vicinity.[2] Mr. Allies also mentions an urn with thirty coins of Carausius as found near this in Upper Deal.

(9) A little further south, Roman pottery, a coin of Marcus and animals' bones were discovered at a depth of 30 feet, when the Severn Navigation Canal lock was constructed at Diglis in 1843. Presumably the spot had in Roman days been water or soft marsh and had since silted up.[3]

(10) Finally a puzzling find was made on the south-east side of the town, beside the London road and opposite Fort Royal, in 1843. This was an underground chamber, roughly 10 feet square, dug out of solid marl, faced or walled with bricks and tiles in alternate courses, and paved with brick. The covering of the structure had fallen in long before it was unearthed, and the interior was filled with tile and brick débris. The walls and floor show distinct marks of heat and smoke, and the whole was taken to be a hypocaust, but if one may judge from the accounts which have been preserved, neither the age nor the character of the remains is quite clear. A little way off a few coins of the third century were found at the same time (Severus Alexander—Tetricus), and near by though quite distinct a bronze coin of Domitian was found at Lark Hill Crescent.[4]

This is not altogether a satisfactory list. We cannot feel sure that all its items date from the Roman period, and even if we assume that, we cannot point out in it one single recognizable trace of any definite kind of building public or private. Still the number and character of the certain and probable items is significant, and we seem to be justified in assuming that some small country town or village occupied the site of Worcester in Roman times. The comparative frequency of first and second-century coins suggests further that this town or village was

---

[1] Allies, p. 15 ; *Gentleman's Magazine*, 1834, i. 96 ; Dunkin's *Report of the British Archæol. Assoc. Meeting at Worcester*, p. 35 ; remains in Worcester Museum.

[2] R. W. Binns, *Proceedings of the Society of Antiquaries of London*, i. (1860) 148, and *A Century of Potting in Worcester*, p. 184 ; remains in the Porcelain Works Museum and from St. Alban's Home in the Worcester Museum ; Catalogue of the Museum, Archæol. Institute Meeting at Worcester, 1862, p. 7.

[3] Allies, p. 28.   [4] Allies, p. 23, and for the coin of Domitian, p. 5.

already in existence in the early part of the Roman occupation. If we accept the Pitchcroft *scoriæ* as Roman, we could add to our conception of Roman Worcester the notion of iron-smelting, though we should be unable to explain why such an industry arose at a place then so unimportant.

But we cannot claim for ancient Worcester any reputation as a centre of a potting industry. The kiln found in Diglis testifies only to homely wares produced for casual local needs, such as we meet at hundreds of other sites in Roman Britain, and, as no good potter's clay exists in the neighbourhood of Worcester, we could expect nothing else. The natural earthenware of the district is seen, for instance, in a reddish ware, which is somewhat like modern flowerpot ware. Specimens have been found freely at Diglis, Kempsey and elsewhere, both in and beyond the bounds of Worcestershire.

3. PLACES OF SETTLED OCCUPATION : DROITWICH, ETC.

To this small town or village at Worcester we have to add a few other instances of what we may suppose to be permanent civilian occupation, although our knowledge is in no single case adequate to a proper description.

(1) Droitwich. The Roman remains at Droitwich appear to lie mostly on the north-western side of the town, near but on the north side of the little river Salwarp, and close to the canal and the railway to Stoke Prior ; they have indeed been found principally in the construction of either canal or railway (fig. 4). In 1847 when the railway was made, definite traces of a dwelling-house were found in Bay's Meadow, close to Bury Hill Farm and the junction of the Stoke Prior line with the Oxford, Worcester and Wolverhampton line, and on the north limb of the former, now disused. These traces comprised two tessellated pavements, foundations in red sandstone, tiles, pottery (including Samian), fibulæ and other bronze objects, iron nails, coins and so forth. Both mosaics were much damaged, but a piece of one was secured for the Worcester Museum and shows a geometrical pattern in red, white and bluish grey (fig. 5). East of this site, at Ellin's Saltworks in the Vines, pottery has been found. Coins have occurred at various places along the Stoke Prior railway : they include a few of the first and second centuries, more of the late third and fourth, and range from Vespasian to Gratian.[1] Coins of Claudius, Nero, Galba, Hadrian and others, are said to have been found in High Street during the drainage works of 1878 ; and I have seen a gold coin of Galba, and a 'first brass' of Claudius from these finds.[2] It is also said that vases, coins and tiles were found in making the canal, and that remains of Roman baths have been unearthed with conduits for the supply of water;[3] but I am told that

---

[1] Allies, *Archæological Journal*, iv. 73, 146 ; vi. 404 ; and *Antiquities of Worcestershire*, pp. 98, 101 ; *Journal of the British Archæological Association*, iii. 119 ; vi. 150 ; Wollaston Collection of Drawings of Mosaics (South Kensington Museum), No. 72 ; *Transactions of the Worc. Naturalists' Club*, i. 97.

[2] *Transactions of the Worc. Naturalists' Club*, i. 282 ; Kelly's Directory. The coin of Galba is Cohen, 286.

[3] Bainbrigge, *Droitwich Salt Springs* (Worcester, 1873), pp. 45, 46.

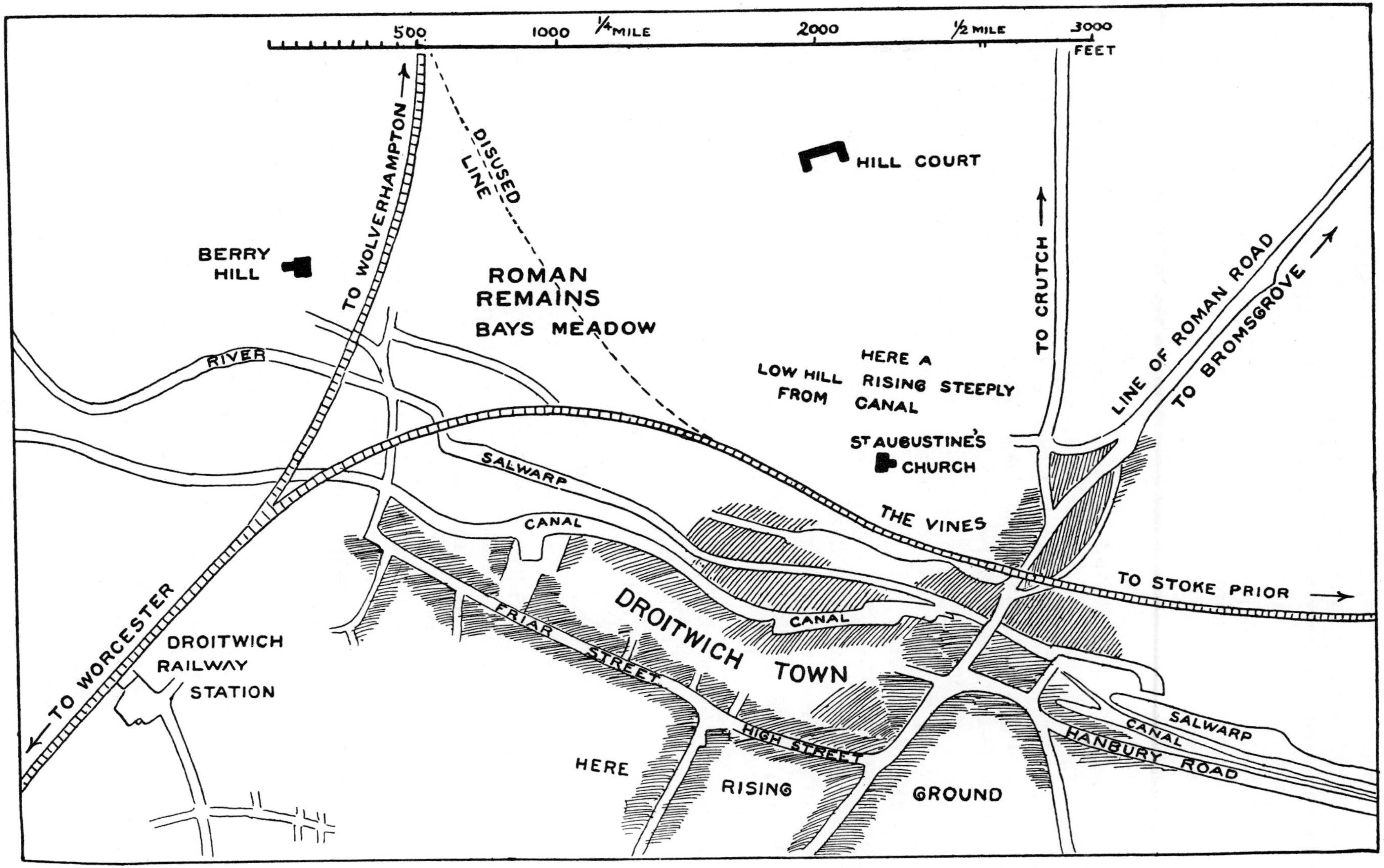

FIG. 4. SKETCH MAP OF DROITWICH, SHOWING SITES WHERE ROMAN REMAINS HAVE BEEN FOUND.

TO WORCESTER

DROITWICH RAILWAY STATION

BERRY HILL

RIVER

TO WOLVERHAMPTON

DISUSED LINE

ROMAN REMAINS
BAYS MEADOW

CANAL

SALWARP

FRIAR STREET

HERE

DROITWICH TOWN

RISING

HIGH STREET

CANAL

LOW HILL RISING STEEPLY FROM CANAL

HERE A

ST AUGUSTINE'S CHURCH

HILL COURT

GROUND

THE VINES

TO CRUTCH

HANBURY ROAD

CANAL

SALWARP

TO STOKE PRIOR

LINE OF ROMAN ROAD

TO BROMSGROVE

500   1000   ¼ MILE   2000   ½ MILE   3000
FEET

209

these statements are probably incorrect. On the whole the finds indicate a 'villa' rather than a town or village. We may suppose that some wealthy Romano-Briton pitched here his dwelling in a sheltered place, and it may be that he used the salt springs for which Droitwich has long been famous. Or we might imagine instead a little spa, and perhaps the existence of Roman roads which seem to lead towards Worcester and Alcester and Birmingham,[1] might make the latter hypothesis the more probable. But it is idle to guess.

(2) Kempsey. Here, 4½ miles south of Worcester, various antiquities have been discovered between the village and the river, near the church or a little north of it. The most striking of these is an inscription found some years before 1818, lying in two pieces with other stones 4 feet deep in the west wall of the kitchen garden of the parsonage farm, north-west of the church. Many of the other stones were cemented together and formed some kind of ancient foundation ; whether the inscription was one of these, is not recorded. It is itself a flat slab of freestone, 33 inches high by 20 inches wide, and is now in the Worcester Museum where I have examined it. It reads as follows :—

VA_CoNST
ANT.No
PE IN
VICTO
AVG

Val(erio) Constantino P(io) fe(lici) invicto Aug(usto)
'To the Emperor Valerius Constantinus, pious, fortunate, unconquerable, Augustus.'

Probably the commencement of the inscription is lost ; it may have begun IMP. CAES. FL. *Imp(eratori) Cæs(ari) Fl(avio)*. Flavius Valerius Constantinus was Constantine the Great, and this stone was presumably set up in his reign (A.D. 308–337). It appears to be a milestone, or rather a road-stone, of the type common in the fourth century, in which the mileage was often omitted—though here it might have been broken off. But it might conceivably be no more than an honorary slab (see p. 213). Near it were found Roman tiles indicating some building. A little north, in a field called the Moors, gravel-diggers in 1835–9 found a number of small pits containing ashes, the burnt bones and teeth of a horse, a few fibulæ, a coin of Nero and many potsherds of various kinds, including Samian and the 'red-earth' ware noticed above (p. 208). Mr. Allies, the chronicler of the finds, calls the pits cists or graves, but no human remains seem to have been found, and the pits themselves which measured 6 feet by 6 feet or 6 feet by 8 feet, are not shaped sepulchrally. We may rather regard them as the rubbish-pits which regularly occur near dwelling-houses. A 'camp,' now for the most part obliterated, is stated to have been formerly traceable at this place, the church being close to its southern end. According to the best measurements available, those made by Mr. Allies fifty years ago, its east and west sides were each 200 yards long, its north side 180 yards, its south side 90 yards, so that it formed an irregular quadrilateral of about 4 acres. It has usually been

---

[1] There is also a curiously straight road due north to Crutch Hill.

RESTORATION OF A MOSAIC PAVEMENT FOUND AT DROITWICH.

FROM A DRAWING MADE FOR DR. WOLLASTON.

This Restoration differs from that adopted in the treatment of the original fragments, now preserved in a restored form in Worcester Museum.

Fɪɢ. 5*a*.   Fʀᴀɢᴍᴇɴᴛ ᴏꜰ Mᴏꜱᴀɪᴄ ꜰᴏᴜɴᴅ ᴀᴛ Dʀᴏɪᴛᴡɪᴄʜ, ɴᴏᴡ ɪɴ Wᴏʀᴄᴇꜱᴛᴇʀ Mᴜꜱᴇᴜᴍ (Rᴇꜱᴛᴏʀᴇᴅ).

Nᴏᴛᴇ.—It is well attested that the mosaic, as now preserved in Worcester Museum, has been restored.   An old drawing shown me by Mr. W. H. Edwards, makes me suspect that only the central device and circle round it are original ; and that all the rest, both here and in fig. 5*b*, is conjectural restoration of fragments found in broken and detached disorder.

To face page 210

styled a Roman camp, but its shape is not that of an ordinary Roman fort or encampment, and no definite evidence really exists to assign it to any age. The unquestionably Roman remains of Kempsey indicate a dwelling or a village, and the earthwork, if Roman at all, may be the enclosure round the one or the other.[1]

(3) Eckington. Here at a spot some 200 yards north of the village and three-quarters of a mile from the river Avon, the railway constructors met with foundations of buildings in stone, bricks, drains, three quoined wells or pits, many bones of men and animals, and much Roman pottery, including a *pelvis* (or *mortarium*) now in the Worcester Museum (fig. 6), and pieces of the red-earth ware noticed above. These remains seem to indicate a dwelling-house or 'villa' of some sort.

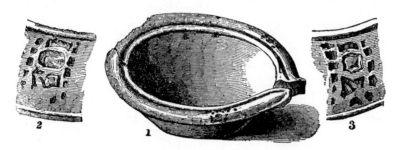

FIG. 6. PELVIS FOUND AT ECKINGTON.

To this brief list we may perhaps add some fainter traces of habitation in the parishes of Aldington, Badsey and Littleton, a little east-north-east of Evesham. Here Roman pottery and coins may still be noticed in comparative abundance. The pottery is mostly very plain; the coins are late 'third brass'; foundations and traces of buildings seem wholly unknown, and it would be rash to conjecture the existence of anything so elaborate as a 'villa.' But it is at least noteworthy that we meet in this district more distinct signs of Romano-British man than in most parts of Worcestershire, and the comparative abundance of his remains suggests that further search might not be unprofitable.[2] The same may possibly be true of the south slopes of Bredon Hill.

There is lastly one settlement which we shall not seek in Worcestershire nor indeed anywhere at all. 'Richard of Cirencester' mentions a station 'Ad Antonam,' as fifteen miles from Gloucester and fifteen from Alauna. Various sites have been selected for it in Worcestershire—Eckington, Evesham, Blackbank near Aldington, Overbury, Bengeworth and so forth. But it is now well recognized that the treatise ascribed to Richard of Cirencester is really an eighteenth-century forgery by one

[1] Allies, pp. 54–59 ; Dunkin's *Report of the British Archæol. Association Meeting at Worcester*, p. 261; E. M. Rudd, *British Archæological Association Journal*, iv. 312 ; *Corpus Inscriptionum Latinarum*, vii. 1157 ; inscription and pottery in Worcester Museum. Mr. H. H. Lines (Berrow's *Worcester Journal*, Oct. 25, 1890) challenges Mr. Allies' measurements, but his own do not inspire confidence. As a matter of fact the earthworks seem to have been faint as long ago as Aubrey's day (MS. 14, p. 180, in the Bodleian). At present little is visible, except perhaps the north-east corner in an orchard north of the church, and that is practically all that Prattinton saw (MS. vol. xxi.)

[2] References in the Index : information from Mr. R. F. Tomes and the Rev. F. S. Taylor, who were kind enough to show me the chief sites.

Bertram of Copenhagen. Alauna is Bertram's guess for Alcester, and Ad Antonam a name which he invented from a misreading of Tacitus. It occurs nowhere else, and we may dismiss it from further consideration.

4. THE ROADS

In a district such as we have hitherto described, where towns were very few and small and country houses very rare, we should expect roads also to be infrequent, and as a fact we can trace few Roman roads within the bounds of Worcestershire. Even the evidence for determining Roman roads is scantier in Worcestershire than elsewhere. We possess of course the usual archæological evidence. We can point occasionally to ancient metalling along a line where we might look reasonably for a Roman road, but the Worcestershire instances of such metalling are few and unsatisfactory. We can point also to still-existing tracks running with persistent straightness from one Roman site to another, and in this point we are a little better provided. But our written evidence is very scanty. A few charters and place names[1] and boundaries help us, but we can make no use of what is in other counties our chief aid, the *Itinerarium Antonini*, since no route described in that document passes through any part of Worcestershire.

The Roman roads of our county fall into two sections. There are in the first place two local roads (as they seem to be) which serve Worcester and Droitwich and one or two other sites, along with which we must notice some conjectured but uncertain roads. And in the second place there are in the extreme east of the county some traceable portions of two more important roads, the so-called Rycknield Street and the Fossway. These do not really belong to the area of the county : they graze it as it were accidentally, but it may be none the less convenient to speak of them.

(1) Worcester, Droitwich, Birmingham. A road running almost invariably straight for over twenty miles can be traced along the existing roads from Worcester to Selly Oak outside Birmingham. The road leaves Worcester by Rainbow Hill, and for a little while is represented only by a part of the boundary between North Claines and Hindlip parishes. From Martin Hussingtree onwards there is still a direct highway through Droitwich and Bromsgrove, swerving slightly to ascend the Lickey, and thence running direct to Selly Oak and coming into the line of Rycknield Street. The straightness of this road and its connection with Roman sites at the two ends and at Droitwich, mark it out as in all probability a Roman road. It was recognized as such by Bishop Lyttelton and is often called the Upper Saltway, though there does not seem to be ancient authority for this term as applied to this road.[2] Possibly it was known as an old road in the fourteenth century (p. 215).

(2) Droitwich, Alcester, Stratford-on-Avon. Here again we depend

---

[1] It is necessary to add a caution that ' Port Way ' does not denote a Roman road. The term ' Street ' also, except in early pre-conquest documents, has often no special significance.

[2] Nash, ii. p. cvii. ; Ordnance Maps, xxii., xv., xvi., x. At Northfield there is a Street Farm.

on the line of the existing highway, and that line it must be confessed is less clear than it is in the case of the Droitwich and Bromsgrove route. It appears however not to be improbable ; and as Alcester is a well ascertained Roman country town, we may accept it at least provisionally. It is often called the Lower Saltway, but again there seems to be no ancient authority for the appellation.

(3) Worcester to the north, up the Severn valley. Antiquaries have generally agreed to trace a road from Worcester into Staffordshire, either by Over Arley on the Severn, or by Clent, Hagley and Stourbridge. The evidence for the former consists of a 'street' mentioned in a late charter at Over Arley; for the second, a road-name, Kings Headland, near Hagley and Clent.[1] Neither can be called adequate. Likely as it may seem that there should have been a direct road along or near the Severn from the large town of Glevum (Gloucester) to the large town of Viroconium (Wroxeter), we must admit that it is as yet a mere supposition.

(4) Worcester to the west, Herefordshire and the Romano-British town at Kenchester. An unquestionable Roman road can be traced from Kenchester twelve miles eastward to Stretton Grandison, and it has often been conjectured to have gone on, through the Wyche Pass in the Malvern Hills, to Worcester. No trace however of this continuation exists. It is probable that, if the road was continued from Stretton Grandison, it ran south-east by Newent to Gloucester, and there are some faint indications of it as far as Newent.

(5) Worcester to the south, Kempsey, Tewkesbury and Gloucester. An ancient paved way, described as 'generally four feet wide, and made of blocks of lias stone set edgewise against each other,' has been traced, and is said to be still traceable, between Ripple and Tewkesbury, and this, combined with the Kempsey inscription (p. 210), and some theories such as Stukeley's idea that Upton was a Romano-British town Ypocessa, produced the suggestion of a Roman road along this line. But Stukeley's idea is a wild fancy, and the paved way, so far as one may judge by the description, resembles far more a medieval path to Tewkesbury Abbey than a Roman road. If we are to look for a Roman road in this part of the county, I would suggest excavation along the line traceable from Worcester by St. Peter's, Timberdine Farm (footpath and hedge), Napleton near Kempsey, Earl's Croome, Green Street and Stratford Bridge. But this must be sought by the spade, or otherwise proved by fresh evidence. On our present knowledge we can only say that the Kempsey inscription suggests, though it does not absolutely prove, the presence of a road near that village.[2]

From these real or supposed roads of local communications we turn

---

[1] Lyttelton, quoted by Nash ; Amphlett and Duignan *Midland Antiquary*, ii. 53, 101. The charter mentioning the Over Arley 'street,' is the well-known Wolverhampton charter (Dugdale's *Monasticon*, vi. 1443), which, though professing to date from A.D. 916, is in reality quite late. A charter mentioning a 'mickle street' at Wolverley (*Cartularium Sax.*, 513) is also quite late. Both belong to an age when the word 'street' had ceased to denote especially Roman roads.

[2] For the localities see the Ordnance Maps of Worcestershire (6-inch), xxxiii., xl., xlvii., xlviii. ; for the probably medieval paving, Allies, pp. 63–67.

to the two unquestionably Roman roads which, as we mentioned above, graze the eastern edges of the county. These are the so-called Rycknield Street and the Foss Way, the former the more important for a Worcestershire topographer, the latter barely entering the county, but by far the more important as a road of Roman Britain. Both roads have one interesting feature, in that they are almost the only two Roman roads in the Midlands which do not run towards London. And first, Rycknield Street.

(6) By Rycknield Street we mean a road from the Roman 'station' outside Derby to Wall, the Romano-British Letocetum near Lichfield; and thence past Birmingham to Alcester, also a Romano-British town or village ; and finally to the Foss Way at Bourton-on-the-Water. This road is easily traceable, and indeed largely still in use ; and its unswerving straightness and connection with Roman sites justify us in calling it a Roman road. Its course needs no long discussion. Entering Worcestershire close to Birmingham, where it seems to meet a Roman road from Worcester and Droitwich (No. 1), it runs as a road in present use past Stirchley Street, Weatheroak Hill near Alvechurch, and Beoley ; then it enters Warwickshire, and passes Studley, Alcester, Bidford and the two Honeybournes ; at Bidford it begins to be called Buckle Street. A little further south, at Weston Subedge, it mounts the range of Broadway Down, and its course is less clear. The map-makers—on what authority I do not know—give the name of Buckle Street to a ridgeway which runs along the hill-top above Cutsdean and Temple Guiting, and descends ultimately to Bourton. This may represent the Roman line, which in that case diverged from its hitherto straightness and made a westward curve. But it may instead have continued nearly straight, and we may think to see its traces in the parish boundary between Weston and Saintbury and in the Worcestershire county boundary, which forms the eastern limit of Broadway parish. A road following this line would, if produced straight on, coincide with the four miles of absolutely straight road called Condicote Lane, and thus reach Bourton by a route which would be a direct continuation of the northern part of the road between Birmingham and Weston Subedge. In either case it will be observed the road runs into the Foss Way at Bourton.[1]

Unfortunately the name of the road is much more obscure than its course. We have called it Rycknield Street, but we have done so simply for convenience, because that name is now usually applied to the road, and for the same reason we have adopted the usual spelling of a variously written word. But in reality the name is an old and famous puzzle, and deserves some notice here. The story appears to start with the Icknield Street. That road, under the title Icenhylt or Icenhilde Street, is a trackway through Berkshire and Oxfordshire, of which the course is still traceable and the name attested by Anglo-Saxon documents earlier than the Conquest : it is not a Roman but possibly a British road, and so far we

[1] Ordnance Survey Maps (6-inch): Worcestershire, v., x., xvi., xxiii., xxiv., xliii., lvii. ; Warwick, xxxi., xlix. ; Gloucestershire, xii., vii., xiv.

have no concern with it. But antiquaries of the twelfth and following centuries, Henry of Huntingdon (p. 204), Ranulf Higden of Chester and others, got hold of the name and made use of it, obviously without knowing exactly what it meant. Hence one of them said that Icknield Street ran from east to west—which is the truth, somewhat exaggerated —and another that it ran from north to south. The views of the antiquaries spread, and two Icknield Streets arose into use as names, the one for the real Berkshire and Oxfordshire street somewhat extended, and the other for the road which we have been describing from Derby to Wall, Alcester and the Foss Way. Hence we meet, in a deed dating from Henry III., a Henry de Ikenyld Street, and in another deed, dating from Henry VIII., an Ikneld Street, both at or near Alvechurch, close to which our road runs.[1]

Now it is precisely this intrusion of Icknield Street into the west that is in all probability responsible for the name Rycknield Street. For the conjecture of old Thorpe is by no means unlikely, that Rycknield is merely a misreading of Icknield, spelt as it sometimes is with a prefixed H. The name Rycknield does not appear in any form till the fourteenth century, while Icknield Street, as we have just seen, is attested near Alvechurch in the thirteenth century. The first mention of Rycknield seems to be in the works of Ranulf Higden of Chester, who, like most medieval chroniclers, mentions the ' four great roads ' of Britain. These roads are, he says, the Foss Way, Watling Street, Ermine Street and ' Rykeneld Strete '; and it will be noticed that ' Rykeneld Strete ' here occupies the place which is given to Icknield Street by all Higden's predecessors, and indeed by very many subsequent writers. It is difficult not to suppose that Rykeneld is not a mere clerical misreading of Hikeneld, that is Icknield. But the matter does not altogether end here. Higden describes the course of ' Rykeneld Strete ' as running from Mavonia (St. David's) through Worcester, Wich (that is Droitwich) and Birmingham to Lichfield, Derby and beyond. Whether he knew anything of the route which we have noticed as No. 1 in our list must remain doubtful, and does not much matter : his remarks were interpreted to refer to the road which we have described, and which before him was called Icknield, the road w. ch runs through Alcester. Gradually, as the medieval writers became more clear and critical, they recognized the inconsistency of two Icknield Streets, one of which was apparently Rycknield also, and they called the Worcestershire road Rycknield Street alone, though traces of the other name survived in some abundance in local names and deeds. And later writers of the seventeenth and eighteenth centuries, influenced by Higden in another way, tried to trace Rycknield Street turning towards Wales. Somewhat perversely neglecting the Worcester and Droitwich road (No. 1 above), they imagined various other routes. Such is, for instance, a road turning off from the real Roman road at Bidford and running south-west along the terrace of Cleeve Hill, for

---

[1] Allies, pp. 332, 339.

which, as a Roman road, there seems to be no proper evidence. The conclusion of the whole matter is that the road by Birmingham and Alcester to Bourton and the Foss is a genuine Roman road, but that its titles Icknield or Rycknield Street are in all probability the invention of medieval antiquaries.[1]

Part of the road had however a genuine Anglo-Saxon name, Buggilde Straet or Bucgan Straet, which appears to be older than the Norman Conquest. This name was used between Bidford and Weston Subedge, and seems to be derived from an English personal name of the feminine gender.[2] It is of course English, and concerns us merely as showing that the road was recognized as an old one very early in English history. It is still in use, as I am assured, between Bidford and Weston, in the form of 'Buckle Street.'

(7) It remains briefly to notice the Foss Way. This traverses only two outlying portions of south-eastern Worcestershire, the parishes of Tredington near Shipston-on-Stour and of Blockley. It forms a modern high-road and its course its unmistakable. At Dorn, in Blockley, some noteworthy remains have been found close to its course (see Index).

5. MISCELLANEOUS

Towns, villas, roads indicate some form or other of settled occupation. We pass on to notice scattered finds, coins, pottery and the like, which we cannot refer to any definite place in the civilization of Roman Worcestershire. Some of these probably are so imperfectly known to us that we fail to catch their significance ; others certainly seem to be due to chance, and neither class can be used to assist materially our ideas of the Romano-British life in our county. We shall therefore summarize such sporadic discoveries in the alphabetical list with which our article concludes, without wasting words in what must be idle speculation. There is however one of these scattered finds which, though most inadequately recorded, nevertheless deserves the compliment of a special mention. This is the large hoard of gold and silver coins, principally of the late fourth century, which was found at Cleeve Prior in 1811.

In October, 1811, a workman named Thomas Sheppey, while digging stone in a quarry, found two urns of 'red earthenware' which had been carefully buried in a stratum of clay and protected by stones laid above and below them. One of these urns contained gold coins and the other silver coins. Unfortunately the hoard was rapidly dispersed. The finder utilized some of the coins as current money, and sold the rest or most of the rest in small parcels to residents in the neighbourhood and others, and the coins were thus scattered among many owners. Some details have however been preserved concerning them. The bulk of

---

[1] See the references in Allies, pp. 340-53 ; Guest, *Origines Celticæ*, ii. 220. The Rykeneld Street which Gale, Allies and others find in a deed of A.D. 1223 near Stoke-upon-Trent seems, according to Guest, to be due to a misreading. Guest tries to defend the antiquity of the name Rycknield against Thorpe, but without meeting the real points of the case.

[2] A. S. Napier and W. H. Stevenson, *Crawford Charters* (Oxford, 1895), p. 56.

them belonged to the close of the fourth century, about which time the hoard was obviously deposited in its hiding-place. The gold coins included issues of Valentinian I and II, Valens, Gratian, Theodosius and Arcadius. The finder declared that in total they weighed 6 lb., and, if we assume they resembled the ordinary gold coins of the period, they must have numbered between 550 and 600 if the man reckoned by avoirdupois, as a labourer would probably do, or between 450 and 500 if he reckoned by the troy weight usually employed for precious metals. Canon Digby of Offenham gave Mr. Allies an account of 255 of these, but it has not survived. The gold coins are said to have been in singularly good preservation and for the most part to have consisted of very pure gold, but some were only plated copper. This last statement may however be an error, for the gold coinage of the fourth century was almost uniformly pure, and as its value depended largely on its weight, forgeries were necessarily difficult. The silver coins of the hoard included issues of Constantius II, Julian, Valens, Valentinian I, Gratian, Magnus Maximus, Theodosius, and Honorius, with, according to Mr. Allies, one coin of Vespasian. They were stated by the finder to number about 3,000 ; of 832 Canon Digby gave Mr. Allies an account. The silver coins were, it is said, much more worn than the gold, as indeed one might expect. Mr. Allies and Mr. May add that the hoard also comprised coins of Gordian, Valerian, Constantine, Valens and Flavius Victor, but they do not mention the metals.[1] Let me further point out that at the Worcestershire Exhibition of 1882 the late Canon A. H. Winnington Ingram, rector of Harvington near Cleeve Prior, exhibited coins from the hoard and an object described in the 'Catalogue' (p. 53) as 'a Roman lady's bronze chatelaine found at Cleeve Prior.' I do not know whether this had anything to do with the hoard, nor can I discover what has since become either of the coins or the 'chatelaine.'

It would be unwise to speculate either on the former owner of these coins or the cause of their burial. I will say only that it does not seem to me absolutely necessary to refer even so large a hoard as this to a lost public treasure or army chest. For the rest, the troubles which fell upon Britain at the end of the fourth and beginning of the fifth century afford not one but several possible reasons for the burial and loss of hoards. To the numismatist, as distinct from the historian, the interest of this hoard lies rather in its silver than its gold. Hoards of the silver coins minted in the last half of the fourth century are by no means common : only two or three instances are known in Britain and hardly any on the continent. And if with these *siliquæ* (as they were called) of the late fourth century there were combined silver coins of Vespasian and perhaps of Gordian and Valerian (if such

---

[1] Berrow's *Worc. Journal*, Oct. 31, 1811 ; *Archæologia*, xviii. 329 ; *Gentleman's Magazine*, 1811 (ii.), 506 ; G. May, *Hist. of Evesham* (ed. 2), p. 244 ; Allies, p. 91 ; R. F. Tomes, Berrow's *Worc. Journal*, June 27, 1891 ; Prattinton's MS. (vol. vii.) contains notes of fifty silver coins. I have made extensive private inquiries, with little result. The site of the find is duly marked in the 6-inch Ordnance Map (xliii. N.W.) half a mile due west of the village.

can be called silver), the interest and perhaps also the problems of the hoard increase.[1]   In any case it is one of the most striking, and in bullion value one of the most precious, of the hoards yet found in the Roman provinces of western Europe, and one can only regret that the neglect of antiquaries has suffered it to remain so little known.

6. INDEX

The following is an alphabetical list of the principal places where Roman remains have been found in Worcestershire.   For discoveries noticed in the preceding pages I have simply referred to the descriptions there given; for the others I have briefly indicated the nature of the discoveries and the chief printed or other authorities.

ALDERMINSTER . . At Goldicote, fibula [J. H. Bloom].

ALDINGTON . . . Small Roman coins dug up in front of the manor house; coins, etc. 'in a field on the left as you ascend the road from the bridge over the brook towards the railway,' on the route from South Littleton to Bengeworth [R. F. Tomes, Berrow's *Worc. Journal*, June 20, 1891].

Remains at Blackbanks, near Blackminster Farm, west of road from South Littleton to Badsey and south of the brook; fragments of pottery (including Samian), a fibula, spindlewhorl, coins mostly of the fourth century [R. F. Tomes, Berrow's *Worc. Journal*, June 20, 1891]; information from Mr. Tomes and Mr. A. H. Savory.

BADSEY . . . . Rude pottery, human and animal bones, slabs of stone marked by fire, 'third brass' of Constantine, at Foxhill, a mile east of Badsey church [G. May, *Hist. of Evesham* (ed. 2), p. 244 ; Allies, p. 88].

BELBROUGHTON . Urn with over 100 coins of Hadrian, Marcus, Pius, Gordian, Philip and others, found 1833 near Farfield [Allies, p. 135].

BEVERE ISLAND . . Coins, but doubtful [Allies, p. 151].

BLOCKLEY . . . See Appendix II.

BREDICOT . . . Urn of red earthenware with 140 'third brass.'   Among 62 examined there were 7 Gallienus, 1 Salonina, 1 Postumus, 9 Victorinus, 24 Tetricus, 11 Claudius Gothicus, 1 Probus, 4 Carausius.   Found 1839 in making Gloucester and Birmingham railway [Allies, p. 95].   Some of the coins are in the Worcester Museum.

BREDON HILL . . Silver earring, coins of Quintillus, Allectus, Constans, fibula found in 'Nettlebed' on south slope of Bredon Hill.   Coins of Vespasian, Severus, Gallienus, Constantine found sporadically in ploughing [*Archæological Journal*, iii. 267 ; May, *Evesham*, p. 365 ; Allies, p. 83].   Fragments of pottery and coins of Victorinus, Tetricus, Claudius II, Maxentius, Constantine I and II, Valens, picked up during a number of years on the arable fields near Conderton and Overbury, on the south side of Bredon Hill, are in possession of Mr. W. Bruton [W. H. Edwards]. Mr. Bloom tells me of Samian and other potsherds, three circular fibulæ and coins (one Hadrian, others third and fourth century), found partly in and partly near Overbury camp. There may have been a dwelling of some sort hereabouts.

BROADWAY . . . A few coins on Middle Hill [J. H. Bloom].

BROMSGROVE LICKEY At north end, Pigeonhouse Hill, 17 coins of Claudius Gothicus, Diocletian, Maximian, Constantius, Constantine, etc. [Allies, pp. 102, 312].

---

[1] Mommsen-Blacas, *Histoire de la Monnaie Romaine*, iii. pp. 68 note, 133.

BUSHLEY . . . . Coin of Constantine I dug up in churchyard, and fibula [*Associated Architectural Societies' Reports*, xxiv. 214].

CLEEVE PRIOR . . Hoard : p. 216.

CLENT . . . . Jar with gold coins found 1790 on Clent Heath ; silver coins found 1792 at Old Mill ; jar of gold and jar of silver found in a meadow east of Old Mill [Allies, pp. 135, 136, on the authority of William Timings, resident at Clent and author of a rather uncritical *Guide to the Clent Hills* (ed. 2, Halesowen 1826). But Timings only vaguely mentions 'jars containing coins of the Roman Emperors,' found on Clent Heath (p. 87), and there may be some mistake].

COMBERTON (LITTLE) ... Glass bottle found in a pond, 1893 [*Worcestershire Chronicle*, February 24th, 1894]. Late coins, including Julian, and pottery in the churchyard [Kelly's Directory].

CONDERTON . . See Bredon Hill.

CRUCKBARROW HILL ... Earthwork, doubtless pre-Roman ; Roman coins alleged [Allies, p. 216].

DROITWICH . . . Villa or spa : p. 208.

ECKINGTON . . . Perhaps a villa : p. 211.

ELDERSFIELD . . Roman coins vaguely asserted at Gadbury Camp [*Archæological Journal*, xxviii. 237].

HAGLEY . . . . Urn full of coins of the Lower Empire, in fields near Wichbury, found in the eighteenth century : perhaps other coins [Nash, i. 485 (hence Gough, *Add. to Camden*, ii. 501 ; Brewer, *Beauties of England*, xv. ; Timings, p. 86 ; Allies, p. 137)].

HANBURY . . . Coins alleged, but very doubtful [Nash, i. 547 ; Allies, p. 320].

HARTLEBURY . . Bronze coin of Alex. Severus, at Lincomb [Allies, p. 113].

HIMBLETON . . . Pottery, including Samian, horns of deer, etc. [*Transactions of the Worc. Naturalists' Club*, i. 97].

HINDLIP . . . . Bronze coin, in rectory grounds, 1840 [Allies, p. 295].

INKBERROW . . . Coin (bronze medallion) of Hadrian, found about 1810, in possession of Mr. G. L. Eades of Evesham.

KEMPSEY . . . Dwellings : p. 210.

LITTLETON (NORTH) ... Pottery and coins strewn about the fields on Cleeve Hill, on north side of the road from North Littleton to the Fish and Anchor Inn ; the coins third and fourth century 'third brass' [R. F. Tomes, Berrow's *Worc. Journal*, June 20, 1891 ; information from him and the Rev. F. S. Taylor].

MALVERN . . . Coin of Vespasian, near St. Ann's Well [Allies, p. 62].

MALVERN LINK . Rude pottery, found by Malvern Crystal Ice Co. [Worcester Museum]. Also much mostly rude pottery, thought to indicate a kiln, found in 1887 in the Knapfield, Howsell, north of Malvern Link ; and in 1899 in the same locality [Malvern and Worcester Museums].

MALVERN (LITTLE) Hoard found 1847 on the west side of the Ledbury Road, opposite Little Malvern Grove and half a mile from the foot of the Herefordshire Beacon: urn, about 300 coins (some inside, some apparently loose), 'second brass,' well preserved, of Maximian, Diocletian, Chlorus, Galerius Max. and Maximinus Daza (A.D. 286–311) [*Gentleman's Magazine*, 1848, i. 526 ; Vaux, *Numismatic Chronicle*, xi. (1849), 32 ; Allies, *Archæological Journal*, iv. 356, and *Antiq. of Worc.*, p. 160 ; Mommsen-Blacas, iii. 137].

MAMBLE . . . See Soddington.

OFFENHAM . . . Coin of Faustina junior at Court Farm House [Allies, p. 90].
Coins, etc., at Faulke Mill [R. F. Tomes, Berrow's *Worc. Journal*, June 20, 1891].
Coins of Tetricus, Licinius, Constantine I, Constantius II, one each [J. H. Bloom].

OMBERSLEY . . . On Hadley Heath Common in levelling two mounds in 1815, 'red earth' ware and Samian [Allies, p. 106].

OVERBURY . . . See Bredon.

POWICK . . . . Two sepulchral urns found 1832 between junction of Upton and Malvern roads ; two more found 1833 west of village : coin of Claudius Gothius, coin of Constantine junior [Worcester Museum ; Allies, p. 73].

RIBBESFORD . . . Gold coin of Tiberius found in Wyre Forest about 1770, according to Nash (ii. 277; followed by Gough, *Add. to Camden*, ii. 476; Allies, p. 146). I suspect this must be the same as the gold coin of Tiberius (**PONTIF MAXIMVS**, seated figure with spear and olive = Cohen, 15) said by J. R. Burton, *History of Bewdley*, p. xlix. (London, 1883), to have been found '100 years ago' at Button Oak. But that is over the Shropshire border in the north of the Forest.

RIPPLE . . . . Pottery, stratum of black ashes, at Bow Farm, near the Severn [Allies, pp. 62–68]. For the supposed road see p. 213.

SEVERN STOKE . . Coin of Magnentius [Allies, p. 291]. Fibula [Bozward, *Worc. Journal*, 1889].

SODDINGTON-IN-MAMBLE   In 1807, when the old mansion of the Blounts was demolished, there was found below it a pavement of thin bricks and many earthenware tubes as if for an aqueduct, and a quarter of a mile away a buried brick-kiln with 10,000 unused bricks in it [*Gentleman's Magazine*, 1807, ii. 1009 ; Allies, p. 147]. But no pottery or coins or other Roman objects are recorded ; the bricks and tubes were not seen by any competent authority, and Allies and others are perhaps rash in calling this the remains of a Roman villa.

TREDINGTON . . At Talton 5 coins, Julian (2), Valentinian I, Flavius Victor, Valentinian III (votis. xxx. mult. xxxx.) found 1861 [J. H. Bloom].

At Newbold-on-Stour, pottery and horns of red deer, found 1838 [Way, *Catalogue of Gloucester Museum, Archæol. Institute Meeting*, 1860, p. 12].

UPTON-ON-SEVERN . Coins, vaguely recorded [Gough, *Camden*, ii. 471 ; hence Allies, p. 60, and others]. Stukeley, *Itinerarium Curiosum*, p. 69, put Ypocessa here, a place named in the list of the *Ravenna Geographen*. But he had no better reason than that one name begins with Up and the other with Yp. The name Ypocessa itself is probably misspelt, and the situation of the place wholly unknown.

A fibula found here is in the Malvern Museum [*Catalogue of Archæol. Institute Museum at Worcester*, 1862, p. 9 ; private information].

WICHENFORD . . Two coins (Victorinus, Constans) [Allies, p. 149].

WORCESTER . . . Town : p. 203.

„   NEAR . Coin said to be of Julia, dau. of Augustus [*Shrewsbury Chronicle*, April, 1815].

APPENDIX I : THE WORCESTERSHIRE CAMPS

I have said nothing in the preceding pages about the earthen camps in Worcestershire. A good deal has been written about these camps, notably by the late Mr. H. H. Lines in the *Birmingham and Midland Institute* (Archæological Section), 1877, pp. 11–22, in Berrow's *Worcester Journal*, October, 1890–January, 1891, and elsewhere, and attempts have been made to connect them with the operations of Ostorius Scapula against Caratacus about A.D. 50. But no kind of remains appears ever to have been found such as would justify these and similar speculations, and until remains are found the student of Roman Worcestershire must leave the camps alone. It is however extremely probable that they are for the most part far older than either Caratacus or the Romans.

APPENDIX II: DORN

Dorn is a hamlet of Blockley, situated on the west side of the Foss Way, in one of those detached south-eastern fragments of Worcestershire which belong geographically rather to Gloucestershire or Warwickshire. As it thus lies apart from the bulk of the county, I have preferred to describe its Roman remains in an appendix which is itself somewhat of a detached fragment. These remains are of some interest and extent, and appear to denote a village, or 'villa,' or some other form of permanent occupation close to the Roman road now represented by the Foss Way. The site has long been recognized as Roman. Nash, writing in the eighteenth century, was able to mention ancient foundations of uncertain age and Roman coins of the third and fourth centuries : Severus (silver), Etruscilla, Carausius, Allectus, Crispus (bronze). Much more has been left unpublished. The present farmer of Dorn Farm tells me that he has noticed evidences of stone foundations about 300 yards south-east of his house, in a large arable field lying between that and the Foss Way, and the spot, which he pointed out to me, is still strewn with fragments of Roman pottery (including Samian), stones showing the action of fire, a few bits of tile, and so forth ; coins have also been picked up here—mostly third and fourth century—and the soil is richer and blacker than elsewhere in the field. West of this, on the line of the Great Western Railway, various Roman remains were found in the construction of a deep cutting : in particular, a number of wells or rubbish-pits, traditionally given as eighteen or nineteen, and two very similar sculptured stones which are now preserved at Dorn Farm, where I have been able to examine them. They are altar-shaped, except at the top, with a sunk panel on the face and in it a small figure in relief. One of them measures 44 inches in height, and 15–18 inches in width : the figure on it is that of a Genius, draped with a pallium wrapped round the waist and falling to the knees, booted with *cothurni* and covered on the head in some not now distinguishable fashion ; the left hand holds a patera over a low altar, the right arm uplifts a Horn of Plenty. The other stone is slightly smaller (42 inches high) ; the figure on it seems to resemble that just described, but is much worn and indistinct. West of the railway again pottery can still be picked up in an arable field. Numerous coins have been found at one spot or another. At Dorn Farm I was shown about 170—three silver, of Nerva, Julia Maesa, Septimius Severus ; two 'second brass' of Pius, and many 'third brass' and minims. I am informed that Mr. T. S. Potter has over 100 coins, ranging from A.D. 250–400, and the Rev. J. H. Bloom has a few 'third brass' of the same period. Without excavation we can hardly decide whether a villa with outbuildings stood here or some wayside village connected with the Foss.[1]

[1] Nash i. p. 101, ii. postscript p. 20 ; hence Gough's *Additions to Camden*, ii. 489, and Allies, p. 87. I am especially indebted to the Rev. J. H. Bloom for help with this site.

ANGLO-SAXON REMAINS

THOUGH poor in relics of the earliest Teutonic settlers, the county of Worcester has yet a history that can be traced in outline throughout the Anglo-Saxon period, for there are notices that throw some light upon the early pagan times which in so many districts are a blank or else are filled with fabulous events. To raise the veil that still obscures the county's past before the era of St. Augustine, discoveries in three localities would not in any case suffice, and that is perhaps the total number recorded in Worcestershire. Even these excavations were prosecuted with insufficient care and not recorded in enough detail to give them more than average importance ; but on the other hand the scarcity of finds is itself a factor in determining the probable course of events before written history begins, and Bede in his *Ecclesiastical History*[1] has given us historic facts with which to co-ordinate the results of archæology.

A people called the Hwiccii or Hwiccans are known to have occupied a region in the west of England which included the vales of Berkeley and Evesham, and appear to have maintained their boundaries as a political unit for the space of two and a half centuries, while greater states around them rose and fell in turn. The old pre-Reformation diocese of Worcester roughly marks the bounds of their dominion, of which the county town was throughout the recognized metropolis.[2] It was about the year 679 that Theodore, archbishop of Canterbury, consecrated Bosel the first English bishop of the Hwiccans ; and it may be reasonably inferred, from the extent of the diocese, that the kingdom or sub-kingdom comprised the whole of Worcestershire with the exception of the north-west corner beyond the Abberley Hills, all Gloucestershire east of the Severn, the township of Bristol and the southern half of Warwickshire. At some period it seems to have further included part of the lower Severn valley west of the river, and the township of Bath. These limits were not fortuitous, but were set by nature and by conquest in such a way that the part played by each can be suggested with some degree of probability.

The first mention of events in this part of the country is in the *Anglo-Saxon Chronicle* under the year 577, when 'Cuthwine and Ceawlin

---

[1] Bk. ii. chap. 2 ; bk. iv. chaps. 13, 23.   [2] Kemble, *Codex Diplomaticus*, No. xci.

fought against the Britons and slew three kings at Deorham.' The site of the battle is generally allowed to be Dyrham, a village on the turnpike road between Bath and Gloucester ; and the victory of the West Saxons naturally led to the reduction of these two towns as well as of Cirencester. These important stations of the Roman province dominated the lower valley of the Severn as well as the head waters of the Thames ; and the fall of Corinium especially must have been of primary importance to the victors, as the town lay at the junction of British and Roman highways to the north, to Gloucester and the Mendip Hills, to Speen and Winchester, and across to the eastern counties. That such a position was willingly surrendered is most improbable, but later events go to show that the prize was not long in the hands of Wessex. The historical records of the time are meagre, but have been amplified by conjectures that lay bare the hidden springs of diplomacy in those remote times. After the death of Cutha at Feathanleah, the Hwiccans are supposed[1] to have chosen Ceol or Ceolric, Ceawlin's nephew, as their king ; and the few words of Florence of Worcester under the year 597 have been interpreted[2] as recording a rebellion raised against Ceawlin by his successor at the instigation of Æthelbert of Kent, who was the next 'bretwalda.' William of Malmesbury,[3] who may certainly have perpetuated a local tradition of the fight, but wrote five centuries after the event, is quoted as the authority for an alliance between Britons and Angles (presumably Hwiccans) against the West Saxon conqueror, who had incurred the odium of his own kinsmen by unheard-of enormities. This explanation of the events that led to a separate West Saxon kingdom in the Severn valley is supposed to receive support from a passage in a monkish compilation of the fourteenth century[4] which associates the Scots in the victory over Ceawlin at Woddesbeorg in 591. This evidence is however rejected by the latest editor of the *Anglo-Saxon Chronicle*,[5] and the only hope of showing the survival of British influence within the Hwiccan kingdom lies in archæological investigation.

Whether the overthrow of Ceawlin was effected by Hwiccan or British arms, it is almost certain that the key of the west was put into Mercian hands by the understanding with Penda in 628, and that the supremacy of Wessex in the Severn valley lasted no more than half a century.

While Worcester was the centre, Cirencester was in the south of the Hwiccan territory;[6] and in order to facilitate comparison of Anglo-Saxon relics in these parts, we may here inquire what were the natural boundaries of the kingdom of the Hwiccans; for in early times dominion and intercourse were to a great extent limited by the physical features of the country. The Bristol Avon no doubt marks the southern limit of their dominion, while the Severn must have been a substantial barrier

---

[1] J. R. Green, *Making of England* (1897), i. 236.   [2] Thorpe's edition, p. 9 note.
[3] *Gesta Regum*, i. 17.
[4] Fordun's *Scotichronicon*, translation by W. F. Skene, bk. iii. p. 106.
[5] Plummer, *Two Chronicles Parallel*, ii. 17.   [6] Florence of Worcester, under 879.

between Hwiccia and the unsubdued marauding Britons of what is now alone called Wales. From the neighbourhood of Bath as far as Cirencester, the diocesan boundary in some parts follows the Fosse Way, though it is generally rather to the west of the line. After passing the important junction of Cirencester it ran eastward, and no doubt bore some close relation to the present border between Gloucestershire and Oxfordshire, though there is no conspicuous natural feature to mark its course. An important point for the purposes of archæology is that Fairford would thus be included in the Hwiccan kingdom, and the extensive remains discovered there may throw some light on the scanty relics of the pagan period in Worcestershire itself.

The escarpment of the Cotswolds, along which are yet to be seen remains of many prehistoric strongholds, apparently had nothing to do with the limits of Hwiccia ; and in the absence of any other obvious line of demarcation, the Fosse Way was in all probability utilized as such by the early Teutonic settlers of these parts. There are some indications in Northamptonshire that the Roman roads which crossed that county served to mark out the territories of tribes which roughly correspond to the dialects ; and this view has also been put forward with regard to the Fosse Way by the author of a paper on ancient roads on the Cotswolds.[1] From a consideration of the diocesan boundary, which extends far into Warwickshire, it seems likely that all between the Fosse Way and the forest of Arden was included in the Hwiccan kingdom ; and if this can be established, the relics of Worcestershire can be further illustrated by discoveries in the Avon valley, as at Longbridge, near Warwick, and Bidford, 4 miles south of Alcester. Interments of the pagan period have come to light near Evesham, and it seems hard to resist the conclusion that those further up the river belonged to the same tribe, for the valley of the Avon would have been the natural and almost the only practicable opening at the time for the increasing population of the lower Severn valley.

What is now Oxfordshire was certainly one of the principal seats of the West Saxons, and was therefore not available for occupation by the Hwiccans. The Britons to the south and west forbade expansion in those directions and the forest belt at the north checked advance long enough to leave a trace in the dialects of the adjoining settlers. The north-east alone remained, and here were no natural impediments.

A writer with considerable local knowledge states[2] his belief that ' the district afterwards known civilly as the Hwiccan realm, and ecclesiastically as the diocese of Worcester, represented the extent of Ceawlin's conquest after the battles of Dyrham and Fethanleah, and that if ever the site of Fethanleah is fixed, it will be found to lie in the northern part of this district,' and not at Faddiley in Cheshire nor Fretherne in Gloucestershire. Mr. Taylor goes on to suggest that the conflict probably took place near Stratford-on-Avon, in the neighbourhood of which was a

---

[1] Mr. John Sawyer, *Transactions of Bristol and Gloucs. Archæological Society*, 1896–7, p. 254.
[2] Rev. C. S. Taylor, *op. cit.* p. 270.

place called Fæhhaleah in king Offa's time, and that the many towns which the victors spoiled were located between the Avon and the forests of Wyre and Arden.

The bounds of Bosel's diocese may or may not have coincided with those which survived till the Reformation, but it is necessarily with an earlier period than his that the present chapter principally deals. The advent of the Christian missionary tended to restrict and transform the funeral rites of paganism, and the scanty remains from Anglo-Saxon graves in the county must belong to a time when the heathen custom of burying the dead in full dress, with arms, utensils and ornaments, had not died out under the influence of the Church. From the date of the first bishop's consecration and from a comparison with the other kingdoms of Saxons, Jutes or Angles, the time of whose conversion is recorded, it may be reasonably inferred that Christianity became a living force along the lower Severn valley in the third quarter of the seventh century. It is therefore allowable to fix this as the latest probable date for the interments that have come to light, though it is not by any means certain that various objects were not interred with the dead up to the time when the pagan tombs were abandoned in favour of the consecrated churchyard about the middle of the eighth century. That pagan practices were easily and quickly stamped out is in itself improbable. Proofs are not wanting of heathen survivals in late burials that have come to light in England, but perhaps the most striking instance is the discovery at Worms, on the Rhine, of a bronze bowl filled with hazel nuts in a grave marked by a Christian tombstone. Inscribed memorial stones of this period occur for the most part within a limited area on the continent, but a bowl of the same kind also filled with nuts is preserved in the national collection and was found in a Kentish grave, which differed in no other way from many others in that part of England.

Again, if credence be given to the annal of 577, it is possible to limit the date of the Worcestershire burials in the other direction, and thus to confine them within about a century and a half. Their scarcity alone would point to some such conclusion, though it would be unwise in such a case as this to argue from mere numbers, for narrow limits can also be assigned to the area in which such finds are to be expected. In fact it is only about one-fifth of the county that is here concerned, and if the remainder had yielded relics in the same proportion, Worcestershire would indeed be well represented for purposes of archæology. As it is, the spade has revealed what history would lead us to expect, and that in the only part of the county where the population can have been at all concentrated in the early pagan days. In the absence of systematic drainage the natural moisture of our climate would render a forest tract no small impediment to progress by producing a thick and tangled undergrowth [1] that would fail to attract any but the fugitive and outlaw. It is true that Roman engineers cut a road through the heart of Arden and the Sussex Weald, but their successors preferred an isolated life amid

[1] Pitt-Rivers, *Excavations in Bokerly*, etc. iii. 9.

the natural riches of the river-bottoms, where the alluvial soil responded even to the most primitive methods of husbandry. The neighbourhood of the Severn however was exposed to forays by the Welsh, who were not thrown back far beyond the river even by the victorious Offa, if the famous earthwork may really be assigned to him.

In any case the Avon valley would prove more inviting to the early settlers than the woodland beyond the Severn known as Malvern Chase, which occupied the whole of the south-west portion of the county. Above this lay the forest of Wyre, which was the western continuation of Feckenham and of the greater Arden which stretched across Warwickshire. From the county town eastward to the border ran the southern limit of Feckenham Forest, and Upton Snodsbury thus marks perhaps the most northern settlement of the Hwiccans in the sixth and seventh centuries. Between this and the two remaining sites, Bredon's Norton and Little Hampton in the south-eastern angle of the county, we may thus look for the chief and perhaps the only relics of the tribe within the present county borders. Other traces of their occupation may no doubt be detected in place names and traditions; and though local etymology has its pitfalls, it is hard to abstain from connecting some names with that of the tribe which bestowed them. Thus there appears to be no warrant in philology for the historian's conception[1] of the county town in a literal sense as the 'stronghold of the Hwiccans,' the name occurring in charters under the forms of Wigernaceaster, Wigarceaster, Wigraceaster, and in Latin, Wigornia. But an instance that seems to carry conviction with it is Wychwood Forest in Oxfordshire, which appears in a charter dated 841 as Hwiccewudu.[2] Though included in the neighbouring county, this woodland may well have served as a neutral zone between the West Saxons proper of the upper Thames valley and their kinsmen on the Severn. According to a perambulation[3] made in 1300 the forest stretched as far west as Tainton, which is virtually on the present border of Gloucestershire, in the neighbourhood of Burford; and possibly included Daylesford, which is still in an outlying portion of Worcestershire between Stow-on-the-Wold and Chipping Norton.

If the year 577 be accepted as the earliest date for West Saxon burials in Worcestershire and other Hwiccan districts, it may be allowable to use the same authority for the subsequent period and to put a limit of date to West Saxon dominion in these parts. It is possible to see in the treaty of Cirencester the formal acknowledgment by Cynegils and Cwichelm of Penda's sovereignty;[4] and it was either at that time or in 645, when Cenwealh was driven out for repudiating his Mercian wife, that Hwiccia ceased to belong to Wessex and became a province of the midland kingdom.

A change of rulers would not necessarily imply any modification of

[1] Dr. Stubbs in *Dictionary of Christian Biography*, iii. 181–2.
[2] Prof. Earle, *Journal of Archæological Institute*, xix. 52.
[3] A map and details are given in *Archæologia*, xxxvii. 425.
[4] J. R. Green, *Making of England* (1897), ii. 19 ; Freeman, *Norman Conquest*, i. 37.

funeral customs, and it would be unwise to assign all distinctly West Saxon burials in Hwiccia to the period before its conquest by Penda. But on the other hand there are sufficient grounds for classing all burials that display a Mercian or Anglian influence as belonging at the earliest to the second half of the seventh century; for as communication with Wessex ceased, closer contact with the midlands would lead to the introduction of foreign elements which would to some extent be represented in the contents of the graves.

If Worcestershire were rich enough in relics to make a thorough classification possible, we might expect to find the earliest graves exclusively West Saxon, perhaps with traces of the earlier British civilization; while a mixture of West Saxon and Anglian ornaments, or the latter occurring alone, would betoken a burial subsequent to the middle of the seventh century. So far as the discoveries go historical evidence is supported by archæological results, but it would be idle to assert that a complete vindication of the records is as yet possible on these lines, for the value of the few excavations already made is much impaired by defective observation and description.

To pass to an enumeration of the relics recovered from pagan or semi-pagan burials in the county, the first site that claims notice is Upton Snodsbury, which lies about six miles east of the county town. Here was apparently a cemetery, from which some objects were exhibited to the Society of Antiquaries[1] in 1866, but a fuller and more accurate account of the find was communicated to the Archæological Institute[2] in the following year by Mr. Ponting of Worcester. To borrow from his paper, it appears that the local field club had rejected two crystal 'spindle-whorls' (figs. 4, 5) as modern before any archæological examination of the site had been undertaken, and many interesting relics were no doubt lost in the interval. In digging gravel labourers had come upon iron spearheads and numerous amber beads (fig. 3), many of which were subsequently recovered from cottagers in the vicinity. A broad, two-edged iron sword, 3 feet long and evidently of the usual pattern, was discovered, as well as 'three bronze brooches of cruciform type (figs. 6, 7, 8) and a pair of scyphate or saucer form (fig. 9) ornamented with concentric circles.' A trench about 30 feet in length, 6 feet deep and 3 to 4 feet wide was noticed and yielded many objects which were thrown aside as of no value and irrecoverably lost. The brooches and amber necklaces just mentioned were however found, not in the trench, but lying apart at a short distance, and the site was on a bank with a warm south-western aspect and a brook flowing below. All the objects figured are preserved in the Victoria Institute at Worcester, and have been specially drawn for the present chapter by kind permission of the committee.

In the critical remarks that follow the account, the Anglo-Saxon character of these remains is regarded as obvious. The spindle-whorls

[1] *Proceedings*, new series, iii. 342; Llewellynn Jewitt's *Reliquary*, April, 1873, xiii. 206.
[2] *Journal*, xxiv. 351.

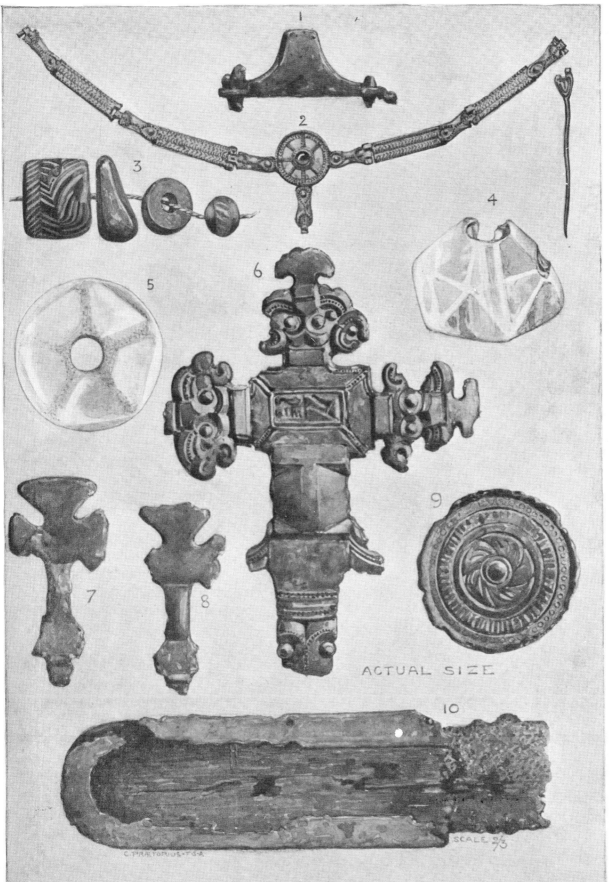

1

2

3

4

5

6

7   8

9

ACTUAL SIZE

10

C. PRÆTORIUS. F.S.A.

SCALE ⅔

ANGLO-SAXON REMAINS. WORCESTERSHIRE

of quartz crystal are compared with a particularly fine specimen found at Myton,[1] in a part of Warwickshire that was probably included in Hwiccia. Several other specimens are figured in Neville's *Saxon Obsequies* from the cemetery at Wilbraham, Cambs. The spearheads vary in size, but all present the Anglo-Saxon characteristic, their sockets being open along one side. Some glass beads (fig. 3) are also mentioned, and the largest of the cruciform brooches retained traces of gilding.

The brooches as usual are the most interesting and instructive part of the find, and the discovery of the peculiar saucer-shaped variety stamps the cemetery at once as West Saxon, for they occur only in England and are confined to a very definite area, where the West Saxons are known to have been located in the pagan period. But the case is different with the cruciform brooches found at Upton Snodsbury. In the first place the term has often been used to include what are better described as square-headed, and in the present case does not apply equally well to all three specimens. The term 'cruciform' has not only been applied to the large gilt Anglian specimens, as those from Sleaford, Lincs, in the national collection, but also to a quite different variety[2] from Long Wittenham, Berks, only about 3 inches long, with none of the Anglian characteristics. The large brooch (fig. 6) is incomplete at the foot, and belongs to an Anglian type, closely resembling one from Sleaford; while the smaller pair (figs. 7, 8), without being characteristic, are more akin perhaps to some from the upper Thames valley.

The brooches and ornaments already referred to are however surpassed in value if not in interest by a remarkable gold ornament for which the term 'union-pin' has been suggested. This was discovered about forty years since near Little Hampton with a skeleton, together with an Anglo-Saxon sword, which was presented to the Society of Antiquaries. The exact site of the discovery is somewhat uncertain, but according to the original account it was on the right bank of the Avon, between Little Hampton and the Birmingham and Gloucestershire railway as it runs into Evesham. Great and Little Hampton both lie on the southern bank of the river, and the interment must have therefore been in the bend of the Avon a little to the south-west of Evesham.

The coloured drawing (fig. 2) will convey an accurate idea of the jewel, which has been described by the late Sir Wollaston Franks.[3] It consists of four oblong pieces of fine gold filigree linked together by shorter pieces, which are hollow and rounded. In the middle is a disc of gold, with a circular slab of garnet in the centre, from which radiate applied gold wires forming a wheel of eight spokes. Attached to the disc is a short hollow link intended to connect a pendant. Of the two gold pins found at the ends of the chain one only remains, but is an important factor in determining the use and character of the relic. The

---

[1] Figured in *Journal of Archæological Institute*, ix. 179.
[2] Two examples are figured in *Archæologia*, xxxix. 142, pl. xi. figs. 8, 9.
[3] Society of Antiquaries, *Proceedings*, ser. 2, iii. 27.

closest parallel is afforded by a more complete specimen discovered in an interment on Roundway Down, to the north of Devizes. There is a coloured drawing of it on the first plate of Akerman's *Pagan Saxondom*; the original lay on the breast of a supposed female skeleton, at the feet of which had been deposited a bronze-mounted bucket, such as have come to light in many parts of England and the continent. It is possible that the Romanized Britons, who seem to have survived the Anglo-Saxon invasion in this part of the country, may have left a trace of their handiwork in this piece of jewellery.

Pairs of bronze pins connected in the same way by a simple bronze chain have been found in association with remains of the Anglo-Saxon period at Breach Down, Kent,[1] and at Long Wittenham, Berks; while a third, in the Bateman collection,[2] was probably found in Derbyshire. There seems no doubt that they were worn on the breast, perhaps originally serving to fasten the outer garment near the shoulders. This was evidently the purpose of somewhat similar fastenings that sometimes occur in Gaulish graves on the continent, and specimens are published from Caranda (Dept. of the Aisne)[3] and the Department of the Marne.[4] That the Anglo-Saxon examples were lineally descended from the Gaulish type is more than probable, and it is interesting in this connection to note that while the Kentish specimens were no doubt imported from France, the workmanship of the Little Hampton jewel shows Roman rather than Teutonic influence, and may point to a survival of Roman handicraft in a part of Britain remote from the main centres of Teutonic occupation. The minute plaited strands of gold that are applied lengthwise to the larger links of the chain bear a very close analogy to the Roman bracelet recently discovered at Rhayader in Radnorshire with other pieces of jewellery dating from about the third century. And though the garnet setting points to a post-Roman date and connects the work with Kentish and other jewellery of succeeding centuries, the design of the centre seems obviously akin to the wheel ornaments commonly found attached as pendants to neck-chains of the Roman period in Britain. On specimens from Wales and Northumberland, now in the British Museum, the number of spokes is the same as on the Worcestershire jewel; and it is just possible that this design was popular as perpetuating the form in which money seems to have been current among the Gaulish tribes by whom parts of Britain had been occupied before Cæsar's landing on the island.

Further south, in the chapelry of Norton-in-Bredon, have been found various Anglo-Saxon relics, consisting of iron shield-bosses and spearheads, a knife and fragments of a sword, with part of the scabbard mounted in bronze, and a blue and reddish-yellow bead. The discovery was made during excavations at Norton Pitch near Bredon Hill; and

[1] British Museum, from the Londesborough Collection.
[2] Figured in his *Catalogue of Antiquities*, p. 157 ; and *Journal of British Archæological Association*, ii. 237.
[3] *Album Caranda* (F. Moreau), vol. 3, pll. 56, 94. Nouvelle Série.
[4] *La Champagne Souterraine* (Morel Collection), pll. 13, 29, 40.

the objects were presented to the museum of the Worcestershire Natural History Society in 1838 by one of the engineers employed in making the Birmingham and Gloucester railway. These are figured on a small scale in Allies' *Antiquities and Folk-lore* of the county, plate iii. One of the shield-bosses still retains a rivet which fastened it to the wooden shield ; and on more than one occasion similar rivets have been found in the graves, still retaining their original tin or silver coating. Specimens may be seen in the national collection from White Horse Hill and Long Wittenham, Berks, from Kempston, Beds, and the Isle of Wight, and they were evidently not confined to any one tribe or locality. The same may perhaps be said of the bronze chape (fig. 10), such as still remains attached by rust to the sword[1] found at Norton. Roach Smith, in describing the important discovery at Fairford, remarked[2] that the protection of the scabbard with a bronze rim at the top and bottom was a peculiarity he had noticed in other examples found in Gloucestershire and Worcestershire. His observation would have carried more weight in the present case if he had pointed to drawings or descriptions of other specimens in the Hwiccan district ; and two instances will suffice to show that such examples are not confined to the district in question. A remarkably well-preserved chape from Brighthampton, Oxon,[3] has the same peculiarity, and the bronze binding is ornamented with figures of lions with the head turned round over the back, a design that seems also to have been a favourite one with the Anglo-Saxon craftsmen of the Christian period. Another found near Burford, Oxon, is in the British Museum.

But archæology cannot at present be said to have shown any essential difference between burials in Hwiccia and in the original kingdom of the West Saxons. In addition to the objects already mentioned as showing connection with the occupants of the upper Thames valley, there are preserved in the museum at Worcester some of the antiquities collected by the late Canon Winnington Ingram of Harvington. Some of these were doubtless found in his own neighbourhood along the Avon valley in the south-eastern angle of the county ; and an exceptionally fine pair of saucer brooches, of the type discovered at Upton Snodsbury, are known to have come from Bidford, just across the county border in Warwickshire. Six miles to the north-east of this place have been found similar specimens at Aston Cantlow,[4] and further up the Avon at Long-bridge near Warwick.[5] This series of discoveries goes some way towards proving that the same tribe had settlements along the river above and below the present border of Worcestershire ; and lends support to the view that the conquests of Ceawlin took this direction, stopping short only at the early Mercian frontier about Rugby. The blending of races in this vicinity is strikingly suggested by the discovery of the West-Saxon

---

[1] Part of a pommel (fig. 1), found in the county, belonged to such a sword. Akerman, *Pagan Saxondom*, pl. xxiv. gives details.

[2] *Archæologia*, xxxiv. 81, pl. x. fig. 3.   [3] Figured in *Archæologia*, xxxviii. 96, pl. ii.

[4] Society of Antiquaries, *Proceedings*, 2nd series, iii. 424.   [5] British Museum.

brooch with human remains cremated in the Anglian manner at Marton,[1] where the Fosse Way crosses the Leam.

'It is hard to believe, however,' says a recent writer,[2] 'that the title of Hwiccans did not mark some slight difference beside that of place between them and their brethren to the south of them. At all events, separated politically if not ethnologically from the other West Saxons, it was but right that they should possess a bishop for themselves, and his title proves him to have been a tribal bishop, with his see in the chief town of the tribe.'

Allusions to British interference in West Saxon politics have already been noticed, but perhaps safer indications are afforded by the geography of the district concerned. Hwiccia was a buffer state between Saxons and Welsh, and it is possible that within its borders the two races may have effected a compromise to their mutual advantage. Such an understanding with the indigenous population would not be unparalleled in Anglo-Saxon history, for Penda joined Cædwalla of the north against Oswald of Northumbria ; and the vitality of the Hwiccan kingdom may have been due in part to a judicious blending of native and foreign elements.

It might be expected that the dwellers on the Severn would be more 'Celtic' than, for example, their contemporaries on the eastern coast ; and in accordance with this principle traces of Romano-British civilization would be more plentiful in south Worcestershire than in a locality like Frilford, Berks,[3] that lay nearly in the centre of Wessex.

With regard to the affinities of the population in the Avon and lower Severn valleys at the period now under discussion, Dr. Beddoe has some interesting remarks.[4] The Saxon dialect prevails in east Worcestershire, though the county became Mercian very early. It has a lower index of nigrescence than the district further to the east ; that is, the Hwiccans of Worcestershire exhibit black eyes and hair with dark complexion more frequently than the purer Saxons of the Thames and Cherwell valleys. They are perhaps a mixture of Saxon and Iberian, these races being very similar from the physical point of view except as to colour ; and the dark strain in Worcestershire may be accounted for by the fact that the native Britons of Wales were always in a majority in the hills west of the Severn.

An interesting relic of the later Anglo-Saxon period has been variously described and poorly figured in the *Gentleman's Magazine*.[5] From comparison with a similar though later object in the British Museum and another recently found at Canterbury, it may be concluded that this subject of many curious speculations in the eighteenth century was the upper part of a censer. It is a four-sided cover of bronze 4 inches

---

[1] *Associated Architectural Societies* (1850–1), *Northants*, p. 231.
[2] Rev. Geoffry Hill, *The English Dioceses*, p. 127.
[3] For Romano-British and Anglo-Saxon remains here see *Archæologia*, xlii. 417.
[4] *Races of Britain*, p. 255.
[5] 1779, p. 536 (figured) ; 1780, pp. 75, 128. The passages are collected in Gomme's Gentleman's Magazine Library, *Archæology*, part 2, pp. 246–7.

high, vaulted at the top, with open-work between ribs representing birds and fishes among scrolls. At the base of each side, which measures $2\frac{1}{4}$ inches, are three round arches surmounted by a tympanum filled with a scale pattern, below which on one face is the inscription THODRIC ME WORH[TE] : *Th(e)odric made me.* From various points project heads of a grotesque character, while at each corner of the base are pierced lugs for the rods that connected the cover with the body of the censer. In the opinion of Mr. W. H. Stevenson there is practically nothing to go upon in determining the date from the lettering, beyond the fact that the pronoun is *me* and not *mec.* The latter form occurs on the jewel of Alfred, but *me* was also in use during his reign. Prof. Earle in a recently published work [1] states that *mec* was already an archaic form in the ninth century and is never found in the prose of the tenth. But considering that the *mec* form was naturally retained before a vowel, there was probably little difference in date between the famous AELFRED MEC HEHT GEWYRCAN : *Alfred ordered me to be made*; the inscription on a gold ring in the British Museum, AETHRED MEC AH EANRED MEC AGROF : *Aethred owns me, Eanred engraved me*; and the Pershore example, which is of the same character. Further, to judge from the arcading round the censer, the tenth century would be a likely date. Though there is nothing in the ornament to show a religious use, it is not an unreasonable supposition that this interesting relic of antiquity, which was found in a mass of gravel during excavations for a cellar near the middle of the town, once belonged to Pershore abbey, and may well have been lost at the destruction of that house by Ælfhere about the year 976. [2]

[1] *The Alfred Jewel*, pp. 17, 154.   [2] *Journal of Archæological Institute*, xix. 238, note 9.

DOMESDAY SURVEY

THE survey of Worcestershire in Domesday Book presents so many features of interest and historical importance that it is not easy to do them justice within the compass of a single paper. 'There is no shire,' in Mr. Freeman's words, 'of whose condition during the Conqueror's reign we are able to put together a more vivid picture from the combined evidence of the Survey and of local records.'[1] Devoting a special appendix to 'The condition of Worcestershire under William,'[2] he observed with truth that 'our accounts of the state of Worcestershire during the reign of William deserve special examination; Domesday is remarkably rich in this shire, and we draw much help from the cartulary put together by Heming, a monk of the cathedral monastery.' A more recent writer, Professor Maitland, has devoted, in his work on Domesday,[3] great attention to Worcestershire, and has claimed for the documents in Heming's Cartulary that 'among the charters that have come down to us there is no series that is longer, there is hardly a long series which is of better repute, than the line of the land-books which belonged to the church of Worcester.'[4]

Problems of assessment, problems of jurisdiction, problems connected with the tenure of land, are in turn raised and partly solved by the evidence that Worcestershire affords; the growth of a feudal system has been detected on its church lands; the whole hierarchy of rural life, from the great thegn and the free tenant to the swineherd, the bond-woman and the serf, receives illustration from its survey. For Worcestershire, alone in England, are preserved the names of the Domesday commissioners, in whose presence bishop and abbot, baron and rapacious sheriff, clamoured and wrangled alike, whether as spoilers or despoiled. Indeed, the personal touches revealed here by the records constitute, doubtless, for most readers, their greatest attraction and value. It is, however, to the information that the Domesday of the shire can be made to yield on such subjects as the financial system, the here important salt industry, and the effect of the Norman Conquest on the landed possessions of the church, that the serious student of history will the most eagerly turn.

It would seem desirable, at the outset, to name the subsidiary sources available, in this county, for use by the side of Domesday. Foremost among these is the cartulary mentioned above, 'compiled not long after

---

[1] *History of the Norman Conquest* (1871), IV. 173. [2] *Ibid.* (1876), V. 759-766.
[3] *Domesday Book and Beyond* (1897). [4] *Ibid.* p. 227.

the Conquest by the monk Heming at the instance of bishop Wulfstan.'[1]
Broadly speaking, its contents consist of three divisions : first, in
order of date, are the charters before the Conquest ; next are the documents and narrative relating to the period of the Conquest ; thirdly
comes a brief survey of the lands held by the monastery of Worcester,
which I assign to the reign of Henry I., and which is of some importance
for collation with the Domesday text.[2] For the rival monastery of
Evesham we have its local chronicle in print[3] and its MS. cartularies.[4]
In one of the latter there is found a valuable survey of Droitwich, of
which I shall speak below, and in another a fragment of a survey belonging to the reign of Stephen.[5] Lastly, we have, in the *Testa de Nevill*
(pp. 43–4), and in the *Red Book of the Exchequer*, (pp. 566–7), a
part of the returns to the great Inquest of 1212, which was not
unworthy of comparison with the Domesday Survey itself. And to these
must be added a remarkable return for the bishop of Worcester's fief,[6]
which I assign with certainty, from internal evidence, to the reign of
John. Neither its importance nor its early date has hitherto, it seems,
been realized. Some assistance may also be derived, for the rural
economy of Domesday, from a study of the 13th century survey of the
manors belonging to the monastery of Worcester, which was printed
by archdeacon Hale.[7]

The main object of Domesday Book,—it is now recognised by
scholars,—was the record of the liability of the land to the tax known as
Danegeld, or, as Domesday styles it, ' geld.' ' One great purpose,' as
Professor Maitland has observed, ' seems to mould both its form and its
substance ; it is a geld-book.'[8] The first subject, therefore, to be discussed in the survey of Worcestershire is the principle on which the
county was assessed. Down to very recent years it had been generally
assumed that the ' hide ' of Domesday was a measure of land, although there
was no agreement as to the area it represented. But we now know that
this term, so prominent on the pages of Domesday, denoted only a unit
of assessment irrespective of area or value.[9] By a purely artificial arrangement, counties, hundreds, and ' vills ' (or, to speak loosely, villages), were
respectively assessed in lump sums, based, it is essential to remember, on
a ' five-hide unit.' Thus, for instance, Cropthorne with Netherton was
assessed at 50 hides, Fladbury at 40, Broadway and Bromsgrove at 30
each, Chaddesley (Corbett) at 25, Kidderminster at 20, Worcester at 15,
Droitwich (we shall find) at 10, and Rushock at 5. In one instance, that

---

[1] *Domesday Book and Beyond*, p. 227. It was printed by Hearne in 1723. Professor
Maitland holds that ' where Heming's work can be tested, it generally gains credit ' (*Ibid.*).

[2] See my paper on 'The Worcestershire Survey' in *Feudal England*, pp. 169–180, and
the paper below on 'Some Early Worcestershire Surveys.'

[3] It is Vol. 29 of the Rolls Series.

[4] MS. Cott. Vesp. B. XXIV. and MS. Harl. 3,763.

[5] For both of these see *Feudal England*, pp. 177–8 and pp. 327–331 below.

[6] *Testa de Nevill*, pp. 41–2.

[7] *Registrum Prioratus Beatæ Mariæ Wigorniensis* (Camden Society).

[8] *Domesday Book and Beyond*, p. 3.

[9] See my *Feudal England*, pp. 44–49, and *Domesday Book and Beyond*, pp. 450 *et seq.*

of Ombersley, Domesday tells us that, under the Confessor, it was reckoned as (*fuit numerata pro*) 15 hides, but only taxed on 12, as 3 were exempt (fo. 175*b*); in another, that of a Warwickshire manor held by the bishop of Worcester (fo. 238*b*), Domesday says that 'there are there 15 hides,' and bishop Wulfstan spoke of it as 'terram xv. hidarum'; but Henry I., on a visit to Worcester, quitclaimed to the prior and monks all his dues on '5 hides' out of these,[1] which had the effect of reducing its assessment to 10 hides. On the same occasion he freed the 4 hides at Fepston from all his dues similarly.[2]

But although this system of assessment can be widely traced in Domesday, it is hardly ever that we can trace its application to the Hundreds, and indeed to the county as a whole, so clearly as we can in Worcestershire. Its case, therefore, has been specially selected, as an illustration, by Professor Maitland, who observes that 'In Worcestershire we have strong evidence of a neat arrangement of a whole county.'[3] This arrangement, he suggests, can be carried back as far as the days of Edward the Elder (Alfred's son), when the document he styles 'the Burghal Hidage' assigns 1,200 hides, in his opinion, to 'Worcester.'[4] In the 'County Hidage,' a document which, he holds, 'speaks to us from the earlier part of (Edward) the Confessor's reign or from some yet older time,' Worcestershire is assigned exactly 1,200 hides.[5] That the Domesday assessments, when added up, produce, for the whole county, a total almost identical, is less noteworthy than the fact, on which the Professor insists, that the county seems to have contained twelve territorial Hundreds, which brings this local division into closer connection than usual with the sum of a hundred hides. Analyzing from this standpoint the assessments recorded in Domesday, Professor Maitland shows that the 'triple Hundred of Oswaldslaw' contained exactly 300 hides; that the church of Westminster is assigned 199, and credited with 200; that the manors of the church of Pershore contained just 100, and that those of the church of Evesham had been made up, by special additions, to the same figure. As Domesday explicitly states that there were twelve Hundreds in the county,[6] the Professor, at the close of his calculations, arrives at the striking conclusion which must be given in his own words.

> We thus bring out a grand total of 1204 hides. Perhaps the true total should be exactly 1200; but at any rate it stands close to that beautiful figure. And now we remember how we were told that there were 'twelve hundreds' in Worcestershire from seven of which the sheriff got nothing. Of these twelve the church of Worcester had three in its Hundred of Oswaldslaw, the church of Westminster two, the church of Pershore one, and the church of Evesham one. But the Evesham or Fissesberge Hundred was not perfect; it required making up by means of 15 hides in the city of Worcester and 20 in the hundred of Dodingtree. Thus five hundreds remain to be accounted for, and in its rubrics Domesday Book names just five, namely, Came, Clent, Cresselaw, Dodingtree, and Esch. We cannot allot to each of these its consti-

---

[1] Hale's *Registrum Prioratus Beatæ Mariæ Wigorniensis*, pp. 84*a*–85*a*.
[2] *Ibid.* p. 58*b*.
[3] *Domesday Book and Beyond*, p. 451.   [4] *Ibid.* p. 504.   [5] *Ibid.* pp. 456, 458.
[6] 'In ipso comitatu sunt xii hund[reta]' (fo. 172).

tuent hides, for we never can rely on Domesday Book giving all the 'hundredal rubrics' that it ought to give, and the Worcestershire hundreds were subjected to rearrangement before the day of maps had dawned. An intimate knowledge of the county might achieve the reconstruction of the old hundreds. But, as it is, we seem to see enough. We seem to see pretty plainly that Worcestershire has been divided into twelve districts known as hundreds each of which has contained 100 hides." [1]

The History of the Worcestershire Hundreds is one of much obscurity; [2] but when they emerge into the light of day in the 13th century, we find the Bishop's triple Hundred of Oswaldslaw still in existence; the 300 hides belonging to Westminster and Pershore represented by the Hundred of Pershore; [3] Evesham's Hundred of Fishborough converted into that of Blakenhurst; and the four Domesday Hundreds of Came, Clent, Cresselau, and Esch amalgamated in that of Halfshire, while that of Dodintree retains its name. As there are sometimes found parishes of which the outlying portions are accounted for by their representing the former possessions of some religious house, so was it even with some Hundreds. More than half of Worcestershire had, under the English kings, been divided into Hundreds consisting not of geographical areas, but of the scattered possessions of certain religious houses. And, stranger still, these possessions were older not only, as we see, than the Hundreds, to which they thus gave shape, but even than the county, as it stands, itself. A glance at the Domesday map will show that its outlying portions consist mainly of lands bestowed upon the church of Worcester, and that parts of Gloucestershire or Warwickshire may find themselves in Worcestershire to-day as the direct consequence of some gift made to the monks of Worcester a thousand years ago.

But even private lords could change, or procure the change, of the boundaries of a county. All Halesowen was in Worcestershire at the time of the Norman Conquest; but the mighty earl of Shrewsbury, who secured its chief manor, succeeded in throwing his part of it into Shropshire, at a period subsequent to Domesday, and this has only been restored to Worcestershire in modern times. I cannot but suspect that Forthampton, at the other end of the county, may have originally belonged to Worcestershire, by which it is almost surrounded, and have owed its inclusion in Gloucestershire to the fact of its forming part of the great Tewkesbury lordship of Brihtric the son of Ælfgar.

Domesday throws some light on a loss that was certainly suffered, for a long while, by the county. The story told by the monks of Worcester, to account for the sheriff of Staffordshire 'farming' Tardebigg and Clent in Worcestershire with Swinford in Staffordshire, was that, according to St. Wulfstan's statement, a certain 'dean' there, Æthelsige by name, prudent, wise, and enjoying high favour at court, bought these three vills from king Æthelred for 200 pounds of silver,

---

[1] *Domesday Book and Beyond*, p. 455.

[2] A valuable list of them, giving the vills (with the number of hides in each) in the Norman period, will be found in the opening fos. of Vesp. B. XXIV.

[3] There is reason to believe that Pershore Abbey, long before that of Westminster Abbey was founded, had certain rights over this triple Hundred (see Domesday, fo. 175*b*).

as a possession for the monastery at Worcester, reserving to himself a life-interest. On his dying in the midst of the struggle for the crown between Cnut and Eadmund 'Ironside' (*circ.* 1016), these vills were seized, they said, by 'Ævic' (or 'Eirc') then sheriff of Staffordshire, in the hands of whose successors they remained to the wrong of the monastery.[1] Mr. Eyton, without alluding to this story, observed that the connection of the sheriff of Staffordshire with these manors was probably the cause 'that led to Tarbeck, Clent, and Brome[2] being subsequently annexed to Staffordshire. . . . These estates are now 're- mised' into Worcestershire.'[3]

We have seen, by this time, how needful it is, in dealing with the Domesday Survey, to bear in mind the fluctuation, at various times, of the area of the shire. But there was another disturbing element, which, although it did not affect the actual county boundaries, had a very important influence on its survey in Domesday Book. It appears to have been overlooked by students of the Worcestershire Domesday, whether in the past or in the present, whether general or local, that the surveys of several manors in the county are found in quite another part of Domesday Book.[4] In the midst of the King's lands in Herefordshire (fo. 180*b*) we find surveys of Martley, Feckenham, Holloway,[5] Hanley (Castle), Bushley [6] with Pull (Court), Queenhill (Chapel), Eldersfield, and Suckley. Moreover, under Gloucestershire (fo. 163*b*) we find another and independent survey of Hanley (Castle), of which place Domesday was supposed to contain no mention. On the one hand, these entries constitute an important addition to the survey of the shire, of which they affect the manorial history and the reckoning of the population in 1086 ; on the other, they possess, for the Domesday student, a quite peculiar value in so far as they preserve independent surveys of the same estate. One alone of the places affected, namely Hanley (Castle), is described by Domesday as 'in Gloucestershire' (fo. 180*b*). The explanation of this description is found under Gloucestershire (fo. 163*b*), where we learn that, with Forthampton, it belonged to that great lordship of Tewkesbury, which had been held before the Conquest by Brihtric son of Ælfgar,[7] and 'the members' of which paid their geld at

---

[1] Heming's Cartulary, pp. 276–7.
[2] Probably included in the Domesday Survey of Clent.   [3] *Staffordshire Domesday*, p. 8.
[4] See, for instance, Nash's *Worcestershire*, Ellis' *Introduction to Domesday*, II. 507, Maitland's *Domesday Book and Beyond*, p. 454, and *Proceedings of the Worcester Architectural and Archæological Society* (1892), p. 264.   [5] Adjoining Feckenham.
[6] Confused, not unnaturally, with Bisley (in Gloucestershire) by Professor Freeman (*Norman Conquest*, IV. 762), and in *The Red Book of the Exchequer* (pp. 568, 656, 662, 689, 704).
[7] The story of this great thegn should come under Gloucestershire, but in his appendix on 'Brihtric and Matilda' (*Norm. Conq.* [1871], IV. 761–4), Professor Freeman pointed out that the legend connecting their names is 'slightly' supported by its placing his arrest at Hanley, 'which we see from Domesday was really one of his lordships.' He spoke of it, indeed, as a 'Gloucestershire' entry (p. 762), but the place is Hanley (Castle), Worcestershire. The words of the rhyming story are :
> 'Pris fu a Haneleye a son maner,
> Le ior ke Saint Wlstan li ber
> Sa chapele auoit dedie.'

Tewkesbury itself. But Martley and Suckley, as we are reminded by the note at the end of the Worcestershire Domesday, paid their geld in the Hundred in which they were locally situate, while Feckenham with Holloway similarly belonged to their own Worcestershire Hundred. The note which thus records these facts is a fitting introduction to the surveys of these manors under Herefordshire, which will accordingly be given after it in the Domesday text below.

The cause of these manors receiving this exceptional treatment is to be found in one of the phenomena of the Conquest, the brief but eventful career of William Fitz Osbern as reigning earl of Herefordshire (1067–1070). What was his official position in Worcestershire it is not easy to decide, but a writ addressed to archbishop Ealdred, bishop Wulfstan, earl William (Fitz Osbern), and all the thegns in Gloucestershire and Worcestershire,[1] suggests that he exercised power of some kind over the shire. In any case he annexed the lands that he held within its borders to Hereford, the seat of his power, so far that they were surveyed, we have seen, under Herefordshire, although they seem to have been only members of his great lordship of Hereford in the sense of paying their rents as part of its collective revenue. He left, however, on Worcestershire a more permanent impress by those benefactions to the abbeys he had founded at Cormeilles and La Vieille Lyre, which enable us, here as elsewhere, to trace his hand. The charters of confirmation granted to these abbeys by Henry II., early in his reign, read in conjunction with Domesday Book, place it in our power to detect the endowments bestowed on them by their great benefactor. The monks of La Vieille Lyre obtained the church of Hanley (Castle), with its appurtenances, and ' the tithe(s) of the forest of Malvern, save the (proceeds of the) chase ' ; the tithe(s) of the whole demesnes of Queenhill (chapel) and Bushley, with small holdings of land in each ; the tithe(s) of the whole demesne of Eldersfield and Feckenham, with a small holding at the former, and the church and a ploughland at the latter.[2] To the monks of Cormeilles were given the churches of Suckley and of Martley, with all their chapels, tithes and appurtenances, together with some small holdings and with the tithes of Holloway, and land at Tenbury.[3]

---

[1] *Monasticon Anglicanum*, I. 301.

[2] 'In episcopatu Wigorniæ ecclesiam de Hanlega cum appendiciis suis, et decimam forestæ de Malverniæ, præter venationem. Decimam totius dominii de Cohella (*sic*), et decimam totius dominii de Brisseleia (*sic*), et unum hominem et decimam totius dominii de Fortelmetona, et unum hominem et decimam totius dominii de Eldresfeld, et unum hominem et decimam totius dominii de Fecheham cum appendiciis, et unam carucatam terræ ' (*Monasticon Anglicanum*, VI. 1092). In 1160 we find on the Pipe Roll the abbey of Lyre receiving the bulk of the tithes of Hanley (the monks of Malvern receiving the rest), while an annual payment of 30 shillings represented a commutation for their other tithes from the King's manors.

[3] 'Ecclesiam de Sukeleia, cum omnibus capellis, et decimis, et pertinentiis suis ; et totam decimam de dominio, et unam virgatam terræ ; et ecclesiam de Merleia cum omnibus capellis et decimis et pertinentiis suis ; et tres virgatas terræ et totam decimam de dominio. Ad Wich rectum suum in salinis. Ad Holewei totam decimam de dominio, et unam virgatam terræ . . . et de decima de Sukeleia et de Merleia sexaginta et quindecim solidos ' (*Ibid.* VI.

When the forfeiture of the earl's son and successor (1074) placed all his lands at the disposition of the Crown, it confirmed his endowments to his two abbeys, and commuted the tithes of Martley and Suckley for seventy-five shillings a year (as stated in the charter cited in the footnote), which sum, accordingly, is found on the 12th century Pipe Rolls, allowed year by year to the sheriff of Worcestershire. And even in 'the hundred years' war' we find the Crown impounding, as held for the benefit of aliens, endowments originally bestowed by earl William Fitz Osbern.[1]

This is hardly the place to discuss the Earl's aggressions on the manors belonging to the monks of Worcester or those that were laid to the charge of his satellites, Gilbert Fitz Turold and Ralf de Bernai,[2] but attention may be drawn to the fact that his lands were mostly near the Herefordshire border.[3] His possession, however, of Feckenham as well as Hanley (Castle) suggests that he had an eye to the hunting in Feckenham Forest as in Malvern Chase.

We have now examined some of the causes which either modified the limits of the shire or accounted for the survey of part of it under another county. In spite, however, of these influences, and of the fact that, as we shall see below, he miscalculated altogether the assessment of Droitwich, Professor Maitland's remarkable conclusions are not materially affected, and Worcestershire remains, in the light of his results, one of the most instructive counties in England for the study of assessment and taxation in Anglo-Saxon times.

It was chiefly, we saw at the outset, as a record of assessment for taxation that Domesday Book was compiled. But of great importance also to the Crown was the evidence it afforded on the pecuniary rights, apart from taxation, to which the King was entitled. In the rural districts these were derived from the profits of jurisdiction and from his own lands ; in the towns their sources were more complex. The system of composition under which these rights were ' farmed ' was obviously one that needed enquiry, with a view to revision, from time to time. The importance of the Worcestershire evidence, on this subject, in Domesday is that it enables us to trace, on the one hand, the beginnings of that composition for the royal rights in a county which was known as the *firma comitatus*, and that it indicates, on the other, the sources of certain payments which are found elsewhere in the Survey with no clue to their origin. Taking these points in order, we learn that the sheriff, at the time of Domesday, was paying annually a lump sum of £123 4s. ' by weight' (*ad pensum*) ' from the demesne manors of the King.' This sum was the nucleus of that *firma comitatus* which seems, in 1160 (6

1,077). Allusions to these endowments, and those of Lyre, will be found in the Domesday text below, under the several localities.
    [1] The monks of Cormeilles sold their tithes at Holloway to Bordesley Abbey for six and eightpence a year (Madox's *Formulare*, p. 300).
    [2] Sheriff of Herefordshire under the Earl.
    Martley, Suckley, Eldersfield, and Hanley (Castle).

Hen. II.), to have been over £200, but which clearly included, at that date, royal manors which, at the time of Domesday, were 'farmed' under Herefordshire together with the revenue from Worcester itself. This last revenue consisted, at the time of Domesday, of £23 5s. 'by weight' annually, for which the sheriff was responsible. Part of this sum had accrued on the forfeiture of Eadwine, who, as the local Earl, had drawn from the city £8 a year under the Confessor, the Crown at that time receiving only £10 'beyond the rent (*censum*) of the houses.'[1] A curious complication is introduced in the case of Worcester by the special rights of the Bishop, who was there entitled, like the Earl, to his 'third penny,' and who received, in right of it, £6 under the Confessor and £8 under the Conqueror, in addition to holding a number of houses as appurtenant to one of his manors (fo. 173*b*). His rights appear to be traceable to a most remarkable endowment, in the time of king Alfred, which Professor Maitland paraphrases thus :

> Æthelred and Æthelflæd, the ealdorman and lady of the Mercians, have, at the request of the bishop, built a *burh* at Worcester, and they declare that of all the rights that appertain to their lordship both in market (*ceapstowe*) and in street, within the borough and without, they have given half to God and St. Peter,[2] with the witness of king Alfred and all the wise of Mercia. The lord of the church is to have half of all, be it land-fee, or fiht-wite, stealing, wohceapung (fines for buying or selling contrary to the rules of the market), or borough-wall-scotting.[3]

Kemble, who printed in full a translation of the actual charter, spoke of it as 'a valuable instrument and one which supplies matter for reflection in various ways.'[4] The charter twice mentions the market, and also confirms the Bishop's rights 'without the market-place,' as enjoyed by his predecessors. I think, therefore, that we might connect the *ceapstowe* of this document with that *forum* (market-place) of Worcester in which, says Domesday, the Bishop had 25 houses in addition to the other houses that he held in the city.

Returning to the payments made by the sheriff, as recorded in Domesday, the most interesting, perhaps, and most instructive are the sums which represented a commutation for the profits of jurisdiction in the courts of the shire and of the several Hundreds. In Worcestershire, as in Wiltshire, Warwickshire, Northamptonshire, and Oxfordshire, the King was entitled to receive annually £10 for a hawk and twenty shillings for a sumpter-horse, while the Queen was entitled to £5 in each of these counties except Wiltshire. But in Worcestershire it is specially recorded that the hawk is a Norway (*norresc*) hawk ; in Worcestershire the sheriff

---

[1] We are, unfortunately, not given, as we are under some towns, any details of these houses, but Heming's Cartulary (Ed. Hearne) preserves a list (pp. 290–1) of twelve 'mansiones' held by the monks of Worcester 'in burgo regis,' and paying him a penny or twopence a year each (with 'service' once a year), except one which paid him 7½*d.*, and another 15*d.*

[2] Then the patron saint of the church of Worcester.

[3] *Domesday Book and Beyond*, p. 194.

[4] *Saxons in England*, II. 328–331. The charter excludes from the rights granted to the Bishop the wain-shilling and load-penny from Saltwic (*i.e.* Droitwich). These terms remind us of the *caretedes* and *summæ* of Domesday.

is found paying, independently of his *firma*, £13 (not £11), 'for hawk and sumpter-horse' under Henry II.; and in this county alone is the source of these payments explained. Domesday having recorded that the sheriff pays £17 'by weight' for (*de*) the county, and £16 in the form of the above three payments, goes on to tell us that 'Hæ xvii libræ ad pensum et xvi libræ ad numerum sunt de placitis comitatus et Hundretis' (fo. 172).[1] The 'county,' therefore, for which he paid the £17 means the county court, that is, the profits arising from the pleas there held, while the £16 represented the profits derived from the Hundreds. On these latter profits the best evidence is found in some curious calculations of the time of Henry II., printed in *The Red Book of the Exchequer*.[2] These, unfortunately, do not include Worcestershire, where the total sum given in Domesday (£16) strikes one as very small. But, as will be seen in the text, the sheriff records his protest against even this amount being exacted from him when seven out of the twelve Hundreds were so completely in the hands of the Church that he did not receive from them anything at all. The highly favoured Abbey of Westminster seems to have obtained a further exemption, for Domesday records that it was alleged to have been given by king Edward the profits even of his special pleas.

Evidence on quite another subject can be obtained from the above passage dealing with the Worcestershire Hundreds. It will have been observed that some of the money, such as that which was derived from the profits of the 'county,' was payable 'by weight,'[3] that is, in silver pennies (the coin actually in use), which the scales had proved to be of full weight. But occasionally, as with the profits of the Hundreds, a different reckoning is used; the money is payable 'by tale' only without being weighed. Now we can, in this case, obtain a useful piece of information by setting out the compound addition that Domesday records.

> x libras denariorum de xx in ora
> c solidos reginæ ad numerum
> xx[ti] solidi de xx[ti] in ora
> _____
> [Total] xvi libræ ad numerum

This sum, as it seems to me, proves the absolute identity, in the minds of the compilers of Domesday, between pounds 'by tale' and pounds reckoned 'at 20 pence to the ounce.' We have become so accustomed to think of the 'pound' as a coin that it almost requires an effort to realize that it then possessed its original meaning of a pound in weight (of silver). This pound, in Worcestershire at the time, was divided into twelve ounces, and we consequently find payments, at various places in the

[1] See Domesday text below for translation.
[2] Ed. Rolls Series, pp. 774–778.
[3] The Worcestershire Domesday sometimes uses an alternative form 'ad peis' for the customary 'ad pondus.'

county, reckoned in ounces (of silver).[1] To say that money was payable 'at 20 pence to the ounce' means that a payment 'by tale' of 20 silver pennies discharged, irrespective of their weight, the liability to pay an ounce of silver. Similarly, a pound paid 'by tale' meant that the payment could be made in the form of 240 pennies. As I have shown in *Feudal England*, the Domesday scribes delighted in using alternative phrases for the same thing; but, although we might have suspected the identity of the two formulas employed above, there is no other passage in Domesday, I believe, that proves that identity, which might otherwise have been questioned.[2]

While on the subject of the coin, something ought to be said about the moneyers of Worcester. For a further source of royal revenue is found in their customary payments. At Worcester, however, Domesday tells us only that each moneyer used to pay 20 shillings, on a change of coinage, when he 'received the (fresh) dies at London.' The same payment was due from the moneyers of Dorchester and Bridport and of Lewes; but although we gather under Hereford that the moneyers had to go somewhere to receive their new dies, it seems to be only under Worcester that the place is stated to be London.

There was one source of royal revenue which is not here mentioned, although it must have existed. This was the proceeds of the forests. When the records of the revenue emerge, half a century after Domesday, we find the *census* of the royal forests kept distinct from the *firma* of the shire. Under Henry II., we learn from the Pipe Rolls, there was paid for the forest of Feckenham £20 a year and £3 for Malvern chase. The extent of forest shown in Domesday as then existing in the county must have produced, at the date of the Survey, some revenue for the Crown.[3]

Although we have had to deal first, as Domesday does, with the Crown and its rights, the interests of the Church in this county were infinitely greater than those of the Crown. Not only was the sheriff, the King's officer, excluded, by the privileges of the Church, from seven out of twelve hundreds; as tenants-in-chief, the four houses of Worcester, Westminster, Evesham, and Pershore held between them more than half of the assessed value of the county.[4] The largest share by far was that of 'the Church of Worcester.' In addition to its great Hundred of Oswaldslow, reckoned at 300 hides, it possessed 94 hides, outside it, in the county, which the Henry I. Survey speaks of as 'in Kinefolka.'[5] Next to Worcester came Westminster with its 200 hides; then the 100

---

[1] See the Domesday text, *passim*.

[2] For in at least two passages (fos. 34, 38b) 'libræ ad numerum de xx[ti] in ora' are found, as if the two formulas had independent meanings.

[3] See further, for the forests, p. 270 below.

[4] *i.e.* of the 'hides' recorded in Domesday. The hide, as explained above, was not an areal measure, but only a unit of assessment.

[5] See *Feudal England*, p. 174. This curious word should, perhaps, be compared with that 'Haliwerfolc,' which, as Mr. Lapsley has explained in his learned monograph on *The County Palatine of Durham*, was employed, in the 12th century, 'to indicate the territorial soke or franchise of the Bishop' of Durham.

hides of Pershore ; and lastly, the 65 hides, in Fishborough Hundred, of Evesham. This gives us a grand total of 759 hides as held by the Church out of the 1,200 hides at which the county was assessed.

Taking first the possessions of ' St. Peter,' the patron saint of the Church of Worcester in Old English days, we find its whole fief in the shire (fos. 172*b*–174) entered under the heading, 'the land of the Church of Worcester.' As this heading has given rise to some misunderstanding, it would seem desirable to explain that ' the Church ' means the Bishop and monks between them. In the adjoining county of Hereford we similarly find the heading, ' the land of the Church of Hereford ' (fo. 181*b*), but the corresponding entry in the schedule of names (fo. 179) is ' the bishop of Hereford.' In this, as in many other matters, the practice of Domesday was not uniform. Sometimes it spoke of the fief as the Bishop's, and sometimes as that of his church ; in one case it would group together the manors of the Bishop and monks, and in another it would treat them as distinct, and survey them, accordingly, apart. In Worcestershire the peculiar privileges attached to the triple Hundred of Oswaldslow belonged to the Bishop, as its lord, alone ; but, in the words of archdeacon Hale, ' the beneficial occupation, if we might so speak, was shared between the Bishop and the monastery.'[1] The learned writer reckoned that, of its 300 hides, 82 were assigned to the monks, while the Bishop retained the rest.[2] If the Domesday text be studied carefully, it will be found that, within Oswaldslow, the manors in the Bishop's hands come first as usual, and are followed by those held by the monks, beginning with Overbury. Outside the Hundred of Oswaldslow, Domesday does not enable us to distinguish the manors of the Bishop from those of the monks, except in one instance. The Henry I. Survey, however, does enable us to do this, and shows them holding in those manors an equal number of hides.[3]

The great fief of the Church of Worcester, comprising, as we have seen, in hides, nearly a third of the county,[4] is headed by a formal record of the Bishop's special privileges in the triple Hundred of Oswaldslow (fo. 172*b*), as deposed to (Domesday tells us) by the whole county (court).[5] Heming's Cartulary contains (pp. 287–8) a version of this return, with some slight variations, which is followed by a statement of the highest importance for students of the Domesday Survey. We are there told that the county (court) made this return on oath, exhorted

---

[1] *Registrum Prioratus Beatæ Mariæ Wigorniensis* (Camden Society), p. iv.

[2] 'Of the fifteen manors of which the Hundred consisted, eight were held by the Bishop and seven by the Monks. The division, however, was not so equal as at first sight appears ; the eight Episcopal Manors contained . . . 225 hides ; whereas the seven which were in the hands of the Monastery or church contained only seventy-five. . . . The Monastery also held of the Bishop as " De Victu Monachorum," parts of three Episcopal Manors, amounting to seven hides ' (*Ibid.*).

[3] *Feudal England*, p. 174, and p. 326 below.

[4] The monks claimed other manors as having formerly belonged to it. See, for instance, pp. 238–239 above.

[5] See translation of Domesday text below.

thereto by bishop Wulfstan, 'in the presence of king William's magnates (*principibus*), namely, Remigius bishop of Lincoln, earl Walter Giffard, Henry de Ferrers, and Adam brother of Eudo the King's *dapifer*, who were appointed by that King to enquire (into) and survey the possessions and customary rights both of the King and of his magnates, in this province and several others, at the time when he caused all England to be surveyed.' Again, in its transcript of the documents relating to the Worcester and Evesham dispute concerning Hampton and Bengeworth, Heming's Cartulary gives us (pp. 75, 77) the names of those 'officers (*principibus*) of the King who had come to make enquiry concerning the lands of the county,' namely, bishop Remigius, Henry de Ferrers, Walter Giffard, and 'Adam.' These are believed to be the only places in which the names of Domesday commissioners are given, and it should be observed that none of these was a holder of land in Worcestershire. It was doubtless William's plan to select for each district commissioners unconnected with it by tenure of land.

On the next page of Heming's Cartulary (fo. 133*b*) we find an interesting list of 'those who swore on the Bishop's behalf' and 'on the prior's behalf' as to the Hundred of 'Oswaldes Lawe,' together with the witnesses. Sir Henry Ellis, unfortunately, took this to be a list of the jurors at the Domesday Inquest;[1] an error in which, naturally enough, he has been followed by others. As a matter of fact, this interesting list dates itself as of the time of bishop John (1151–1157),[2] and, as is duly noted by Hearne, is entered in another (and a later) hand. The Domesday documents, in Heming's Cartulary, which I have spoken of above, supply no names of jurors, but the first tells us that the King's commissioners, having taken the sworn testimony, set the return on record in a *cartula*, 'which is preserved in the royal treasury with the rest of the survey of England' (*cum totius Angliæ descriptionibus*).

This return, as given in Domesday, has to be compared with the famous charter attributed to king Edgar, 'perhaps the most celebrated of all land-books.'[3] The monks of Worcester entered it on their Register[4] as their title-deed to the Hundred of Oswaldslow, and dated it 964. To Hickes belonged the credit of showing, in his *Dissertatio Epistolaris* (1703), that what passed for the original charter[5] was in truth a document written about 1200, while the date of the copy in the Register is about half a century later. As Professor Maitland has observed, we cannot accept 'the would-be charter as genuine,' or 'even accept it as a true copy of a genuine book,' but he thinks that it 'tells a story that in the main is true.' This he deems 'the easiest answer' to the question, 'Why was a charter of Edgar produced, perhaps rewritten and revised, perhaps concocted?' As the matter is one of considerable im-

---

[1] *Introduction to Domesday*, I. 19.
[2] See *Feudal England*, p. 169.
[3] Maitland's *Domesday Book and Beyond*, p. 268.
[4] Hale's *Registrum Beatæ Mariæ Wigorniensis*, pp. xxx.–xxxiv., 21*b*–24*b*.
[5] Harl. MS. 7,513. Hickes gave a facsimile.

THE DOMESDAY SURVEY

portance in the early history of Worcestershire, it is impossible to pass it by without some discussion. Professor Maitland bases his conclusion on the fact that 'In 1086 the church of Worcester had to all appearance just those rights which the *Altitonantis*[1] professed to grant to her; already they were associated with the name of Oswald; already they were regarded as ancient privileges.' Urging with much force that 'kings and sheriffs did not permit themselves to be cheated wholesale out of valuable rights,' he accepts the witness of Domesday to the antiquity of the church's rights and connects it with the story that they had been granted to St. Oswald, when bishop, by Edgar.[2]

That the charter in its present form cannot possibly be genuine is, one must repeat, admitted. But does it, as in some similar instances, 'tell a story that in the main is true'? On the whole, there does not seem to be sufficient cause for rejecting this conclusion. The stress laid by the alleged charter on the monks' exclusive rights over one of the three hundreds of which Oswaldslow was composed is, no doubt, somewhat suspicious in the light of the Domesday entry; and if the document were strictly interpreted, its wording would certainly exempt from Danegeld the whole 300 hides, although we do not find them so exempt in Domesday. But there might well be alterations. It is, however, a singular fact, revealed on close scrutiny, that the lands which Edgar is represented as adding to the 50 hides at Cropthorne in order to make 'a perfect hundred' out of the monks' estates, do not, as Professor Maitland imagined, amount to just 50 hides,[3] but comprise 20 hides more, as we learn from other sources.[4] But, although the calculation works out wrong in detail, the broad fact remains that the triple Hundred of Oswaldslow did contain exactly 300 hides; and, remembering that the monastery had other manors up and down the county, I consider the existence of such a 'Hundred' proof that some king did erect a triple Hundred out of its Worcestershire manors by taking for the purpose as many as amounted, in assessed totals, to 300 hides, and leaving the rest outside it. I cannot quite agree with Mr. Maitland that 'this triple Hundred of Oswaldslow was made up,' according to the charter, 'of three old Hundreds, called Cuthbertslaw, Wulfhereslaw, and Wimborntree';[5] for, as I read it, what was done was rather to rearrange the Hundreds—just as Domesday shows us the Hundred of Fishborough [6] rearranged—so as to assign to the monastery the above

[1] The opening word of Edgar's charter is here used as its title.
[2] *Domesday Book and Beyond*, p. 269.
[3] *Ibid.* p. 452.
[4] At Teddington 3, Mitton 1, Blackwell 2, Icomb 1, these 7 hides being theirs still in 1086; at Daylesford 3, and Evenlode 5, these 8 hides being entered as formerly theirs in Domesday; and at Dorne in Blockley (as we gather from Heming's Cartulary, p. 304) 5. The total, therefore, with these 20 hides added, would be, not 50, but 70 hides.
[5] *Domesday Book and Beyond*, pp. 268, 452.
[6] 'In Fissesberge Hundret habet æcclesia de Evesham lxv hidas. . . . In illo Hundret jacent xx hidæ de Dodentreu, et xv hidæ de Wirecestre perficiunt hundret.' The

247

three Hundred-courts, and at the same time to form for them scattered and artificial Hundreds out of the 300 hides selected for the purpose from the monastery's lands. The whole then formed the privileged district of Oswaldslow.

What the privileges were that the Bishop claimed within this district is not absolutely clear. It is certain, from Domesday, that the King's sheriff was excluded from exercising any jurisdiction within it, and that all the profits of the local courts and other royal rights in the district went to the Bishop. But much obscurity surrounds his rights with regard to the Danegeld within the district and to its quota of military service known before the Conquest as ' expeditio ' or ' fyrd.' As to the former, the Bishop, I hold, did not enjoy, like St. Petroc in the west, or St. Edmund in the east, the special privilege of retaining for himself the money paid as Danegeld,[1] but was entitled to collect it through his own officers and to receive the penalties, if any, incurred by its non-payment. As to the duty of military service, the Bishop's Hundred of Oswaldslow was, similarly, not exempt from it ;[2] but its quota was led by his own officers, instead of being under the sheriff, and any fines for neglect of the duty (*fyrdwite*) would be collected through his courts.

Military service was due to the King not only by land but by sea; there was *scipfyrd* as well as *landfyrd*.[3] This is a point of much importance in connection with the Hundred of Oswaldslow, for the disputed charter speaks of ' naumachiæ expeditionem, quæ ex tota Anglia regi invenitur,' and constitutes the triple Hundred in order that the Bishop, with his monks, may have a separate ' naucupletionem quod Anglice " Scypfylled " vocatur.'[4] Recent research has favoured the view that there was some arrangement of Hundreds in threes with a liability on each group to provide a ship's crew.[5] And even the term ' Scipsocne,' which is applied, in the same charter, to Oswaldslow, is paralleled by the application of ' Sipe Socha ' to each of three Warwickshire Hundreds in 1170.[6] But what is most noteworthy is that we have actual mention of ' Eadric who was, in the time of king Edward, steersman of the bishop's ship and leader of the bishop's force (*exercitus*) in the King's service,' as present at the great trial between the houses of Worcester

---

composition of this Hundred receives some further illustration from a survey of the Evesham Abbey manors in Cott. MS. Vesp. B. XXIV. fos. 49*d*, 53. A marginal note describes as ' T.R.E.' the hidation which is there given, and which seems to be occasionally in excess of that recorded in Domesday.

[1] See, for this privilege, my paper in *Domesday Studies*, I. 126–8, and *Feudal England*, p. 101.

[2] Compare Hale's *Registrum Beatæ Mariæ Wigorniensis*, p. xxxiii.

[3] The duty of ' expeditio ' by sea is referred to, in Domesday, at Exeter, Malmesbury, Warwick, Leicester, Stamford, etc.

[4] Hale's *Registrum*, p. 23*b*.

[5] *Ibid.* p. xxxiii. ; Stubbs' *Const. Hist.* (1874), I. 105–6 ; Earle, cited by Freeman in *Norman Conquest* (1870), I. 647 ; Vigfusson, citing Steenstrup in *Eng. Hist. Review*, III. 500 ; Canon Taylor in *Domesday Studies* (1888), pp. 75–6).

[6] Pipe Roll, 16 Henry II. pp. 90–91. Compare Stubbs as above, p. 106 *note*.

and Evesham,[1] while we can not only identify this officer in Domesday (fo. 173*b*), where 'Edric Stirman' is entered as having held 5 hides at Hindlip, but can recognise him in 'Edric de Hindelep' at the final settlement before the Domesday Commissioners between bishop Wulfstan and abbot Walter.[2] That the duty of this naval service was fully recognised down to the Conquest is seen in the mention of 'navigia' as having been due from the 10 hides at Bishampton.[3] One is tempted, were it not rash, to suggest that if the service were due at the rate of one man from 5 hides,[4] the complement of 'the bishop's ship' would be just sixty men, which seems to have been the number of the crew in the great war-galley introduced by Alfred.[5]

When we turn from the sea to the land service our chief difficulties begin. For beyond the entry, under Bishampton, of 'expeditiones' being due, Domesday is silent on the fyrd save for the passage on the liability to military service at the opening of the county survey. Heming's Cartulary, however, is more explicit on the matter. In addition to the above mention of Eadric as leader of the Bishop's 'exercitus,' its report of the great trial between Worcester and Evesham represents the Bishop as claiming 'geldum regis et servitium et expeditiones in terra et in mari' from the abbot in respect of the 15 hides at Hampton (by Evesham),[6] while William's writ, which follows, asserts the Bishop's right there to 'geldum et expeditionem et cetera mea servitia.'[7] The writ of the bishop of Coutances, before whom the case was tried, certifies that the 15 hides at Hampton 'debent placitare et geldum et expeditionem et cetera legis servitia . . . persolvere' in the Bishop's Hundred of Oswaldslow.[8] This decision is referred to no less than three times in Professor Maitland's learned work on *Domesday Book and Beyond*.[9] The one conclusion that can, I think, be safely drawn from the evidence before us is that the Bishop's Hundred of Oswaldslow had to provide a fixed quota of men to the King's *fyrd*, irrespective of its population. It is only on this hypothesis that we can explain the bishop's anxiety to assert the liability of each estate to provide its proportionate contingent. I have elsewhere shown that this system, in force before the

---

[1] Heming's Cartulary, I. 80.

[2] *Ibid.* pp. 76, 297. Another steersman (the recognised chief officer of a galley) is found in Worcestershire at Pershore, where Domesday (fo. 174*b*) shows us 'Turchil stirmannus regis Edwardi' holding land in the time of that King, to whom Pershore had belonged.

[3] Domesday, fo. 173. The somewhat difficult phrase in William's writ commanding the trial between Worcester and Evesham refers the judges to the day 'qua novissime, tempore regis Edwardi, geldum acceptum fuit ad navigium faciendum' (Heming's Cartulary, I. 78), as if the service were commuted for money.

[4] See *Feudal England*, pp. 45, 67–9, 232–4, and *Domesday Book and Beyond*, pp. 156–9.

[5] 'Some had sixty oars, some more' (Anglo-Saxon Chron., II. 74). I agree with Sir James Ramsey (*Foundations of England*) that the oarsmen were also the fighting crew.

[6] Heming's Cartulary, I. 80.   [7] *Ibid.* 78, 83.   [8] *Ibid.* 77.

[9] pp. 85, 159, 308. I can hardly agree with his paraphrase that 'the men of two villages, Hamton and Bengeworth, were bound to pay geld and to fight along with the bishop's men' (p. 308), for the duty seems, as he had pointed out just before, to have been incumbent on the hides rather than the men, and to have been discharged by a few individuals.

Conquest, must on no account be confused, as it has been by Professor Maitland, with the liability of the Bishop, under the system introduced by the Normans, to provide 60 knights (or, as he maintained, 50) in respect of his entire fief extending over three counties.[1] If he had to send 60 men—and this total is only a conjecture—to the King's *fyrd* before the Conquest, in respect of his Hundred of Oswaldslow, that total was wholly unconnected with the quota of knight-service due, after the Conquest, in respect of his entire fief.[2]

Dealing, however, with what he terms 'Feudalism in Oswaldslaw,'[3] Professor Maitland attaches very great importance to bishop Oswald's letter to king Edgar[4] recording the terms of his land loans, which ' is for our purposes the most important of all the documents that have come down to us from the age before the Conquest.' But if we cannot accept as genuine, in its present form, Edgar's charter constituting the Hundred of Oswaldslow, we must also, I think, view critically ' this unique document.'[5] For its only existing version is at least later than the Conquest, and it seems to me to proceed clearly from the same mint as ' Altitonantis.'[6] The clause on which Professor Maitland would specially insist is the condition enforced on those to whom the lands were granted ' ut omnis equitandi lex ab eis impleatur quæ ad equites pertinet.' They are, ' above all,' riding-men, and must fulfil ' the law of riding.' The importance of this, for the Domesday student, is that the Professor finds in ' Oswald's riding men' the predecessors of 'the *radchenistres* and *radmanni* of Domesday Book, the *rodknights* of Bracton's text.' The class entered in Domesday under this mysterious name is almost wholly confined to the counties near the Welsh border from Gloucestershire on the south to the modern South Lancashire on the north, and is well represented in Worcestershire. The entry, perhaps, which most favours the view that riding was the essence of the service due from these tenants is that, under Bredons Norton, of Leofwine having held 2 hides, ' et inde radman episcopi fuit' (fo. 173). But the actual charters of bishop Oswald granting lands for three lives make no mention of this service;[7] and on Westminster Abbey's Deerhurst manor, just over the Gloucestershire border, we find several small estates, from half a hide to two hides, held

[1] This is particularly well seen in the return, *temp.* John, of the 'Servicium debitum domino Regi de episcopatu Wigornie' (*Testa de Nevill*, pp. 41–2).

[2] See my paper on 'Military Service before the Conquest,' in *English Historical Review* (1897), XII. 492–4. The point is of much institutional importance.

[3] *Domesday Book and Beyond*, pp. 303–313. The Professor seems to have based his argument on the belief that Oswald's letter applies only to his grants within Oswaldslow, but it covers his grants in other places, such as the Gloucestershire Compton, so that the terms of his grants must have been unconnected with his special position within Oswaldslow.

[4] Codex Diplomaticus, I. xxxv.; VI. 124. Heming's Cartulary, I. 292–6.

[5] *Domesday Book and Beyond*, p. 312.

[6] For instance, the 'Dunstanum archiepiscopum et venerandum Athelwoldum Wintonie episcopum et virum magnificum Brihtnothum comitem' of Oswald's letter echoes the 'Dunstanum archiepiscopum et Athelwoldum Wintoniensem episcopum et virum magnificum Brightnodum comitem' of Edgar's charter. It should further be observed that Oswald's grants range down, as the Professor observed, to 992. But Edgar died in 975.

[7] Heming's Cartulary, *passim*.

by 'Radchen[istres], id est liberi homines T.R.E.' (fo. 166). This suggestive entry proves to be in perfect harmony with the survey of that abbey's Worcestershire manors (fos. 174*b*–175). For we there find a number of similar estates entered as having been held T.R.E., sometimes by 'liberi homines,' sometimes by riding-men. At Longdon[1] there were 'nine free men (who) held 18 hides, and mowed for one day in the meadows of their lord, and did such service as they were bidden'; at Powick there were eight 'radmans' who 'mowed for one day a year in the meadows of the lord, and did all the service that was bidden them.' As there are several entries describing the services as 'those which are performed by the other freemen,' we may infer that 'free men' and 'radmans' are here used indifferently. This important conclusion is confirmed by the evidence of the Worcester cartulary. Under the heading *De liberis de Halleg'* (Hallow in Grimley) two tenements are there entered as owing this riding-service.[2] At Grimley itself, it is under *De liberis* that we find payments of $2\frac{1}{2}d.$ a year 'pro equitatura,'[3] and at Charlton it is, similarly, under *De liberis de Cherletun'*, that the payments 'pro equitatura' occur.[4] Archdeacon Hale was doubtless right in identifying this service with Bracton's 'service of riding with the lord or the lady,' or 'from manor to manor.'[5] One unpublished instance, in which such service was due to the sacrist of Evesham, seems decisive on the point.[6] The duty, in short, was that of attendance as escort, but not, in my opinion, of military service.

In addition to that exclusion of the sheriff which appears to have been deemed, in those days, a high and enviable privilege, the Bishop possessed certain rights which seem to have been independent of the special privileges belonging to the Hundred of Oswaldslow. Foremost among these was that *circset* to which the abbots of Pershore, Westminster, and Evesham, and indeed others, were also entitled. Domesday records the county's verdict that the Bishop was entitled at Martinmas to one (horse)load of the best grain from every hide of land belonging to the church of Worcester, whether held in free or in villein tenure (fo. 173*b*). It was also the county's verdict that the church of Pershore was entitled to *circset* from 300 hides (of which 100 were its own and 200 belonged to the abbot of Westminster), that is, Domesday proceeds to

---

[1] Barely five miles, as the crow flies, from Deerhurst. At Deerhurst the 'riding-men' had to reap, mow, plough and harrow (fo. 166). On the great royal manor of Tewkesbury they had to plough and harrow for their lord (fo. 163). This evidence is important for Worcestershire, because at Netherton, a manor of the monks of Worcester, we find that Osbert Guidon, 'for his holding, has to follow the Prior and Cellarer, and any other monks when they will, with his own horse, at their cost; and must plough, twice in the year, half an acre, and sow it with his own seed, and must harrow, and must do three "benrip," and, moreover, must find one man to mow for one day' (Hale, 72*b*). Archdeacon Hale thought that these were villein services, incompatible with 'equitatura,' but this was a misapprehension (*Ibid.* p. lxxvii.).

[2] Hale's *Registrum*, p. 50*a* (cf. p. 47*b*).

[3] *Ibid.* pp. 44*a*, 44*b*.   [4] *Ibid.* 71*b*.   [5] *Ibid.* p. lxxii.

[6] 'In Haccheslench [Atch Lench] . . . Idem Osbertus tenet dimidiam hidam ut equitet cum sacrista in equo proprio' (Cott. MS. Vesp. B. XXIV. fo. 13*d*).

explain, a horseload of grain at Martinmas from each hide held by a free man, though he was not liable to pay on more hides than one (fo. 175). If the grain should not be paid on the day appointed, a twelvefold payment was due, said the county, and a penalty (*forisfactura*) in addition for the default. These provisions applied both to Worcester[1] and to Pershore, but in the case of the latter this penalty was only payable to the Abbot on his own 100 hides, Westminster abbey receiving it, if due, within its own 200 hides. Domesday goes on to explain that the abbot of Evesham had the same right in the case of 'his own land, and all the others the same in the case of their lands.'[2] There was one other right belonging to the bishop of Worcester which is mentioned in the valuable Bishampton entry among his recognised dues: this was 'sepultura' (fo. 173). We find it again in the documents relating to his strife with Evesham, where it is coupled with the *circset* as due to him from Hampton by Evesham.[3] The one other passage in Domesday which should be here compared is that which describes the rights of the bishop of Winchester in his great liberty of Taunton (fo. 87b). Like the bishop of Worcester in Oswaldslow, he possessed, not only special jurisdiction within the bounds of that liberty, but the privilege of sending to the host his own separate contingent;[4] and like him he had 'circieti' and 'sepultura' as his right. For after mentioning those of its members in which he had not 'sepultura,' Domesday observes of the others: 'when the lords of these lands die, they are buried in Taunton.' The burial fees and profits were, of course, what was thus obtained.[5]

This is, perhaps, the fitting point at which to discuss that great dispute between the churches of Worcester and of Evesham, which is so closely connected with the Domesday Survey of the County. The bitterness of the feeling it aroused is shown by the delightful story told by the monks of Worcester and preserved in Heming's Cartulary.[6] According to them the saintly Wulfstan, on the death of the despoiler of their house, Æthelwig abbot of Evesham, was rash enough, in his infinite compassion, to offer special and urgent prayers for the soul of his dead adversary. A sudden attack of gout in his legs and feet was the penalty. It was only

[1] 'Circset' is not mentioned *eo nomine* in the Worcester entry, but the payment is the same; and, indeed, under Bishampton (fo. 173) 'circset' is found among the dues payable to the Bishop. And one of bishop Oswald's charters, granting two hides at Bentley, reserves the payment 'æcclesiastici censi, id est duos modios de mundo grano' (Heming's Cartulary, I. 145).

[2] Peter de Stodley (*alias* Corbizon) gave the 'chirset' of a Worcestershire manor among his endowments of Studley Priory.

[3] The bishop of Coutances, in his certificate, states that the Bishop had proved his right to 'ciricsceat et sepulturam' from Hampton as due to his vill of Cropthorne, and the Conqueror's writ recognises his right to such 'ciricescot et sepulturam' (Heming's Cartulary, I. 77, 78).

[4] 'profectio in exercitu cum hominibus episcopi.' The Exon Domesday, for 'exercitu' has 'expeditione.'

[5] Mr. Eyton observes in his *Shropshire* that 'sepultura' was a right belonging to the mother churches which they were loth to part with.

[6] De conflictu Wlstani episcopi et Agelwii abbatis' (I. 270–272).

when the leeches had given him over that he learnt, by divine revelation, the cause of his severe illness. On ceasing to pray for the soul of Æthelwig, he recovered in a few days ' without human medicine.' To this notable illustration of mediæval, or at least monastic, Christianity one may add the fact that both of these religious houses are suspected with good reason of concocting or altering the charters they produced in support of their rights.

In Heming's Cartulary and the Evesham Chronicle we have the stories of the rival houses, and, in spite of certain contradictions, can form a fair idea of the facts of the case. Abbot Æthelwig and bishop Wulfstan had both enjoyed the favour of Harold ;[1] but both, in Mr. Freeman's opinion, ' were among the first prelates in England to submit to the Conqueror.'[2] It was Æthelwig, however, who secured, we read, ' his lasting favour.'[3] The monks of Worcester insist upon his power,[4] and on their own disadvantage in the disinclination of their saintly Bishop to occupy himself in secular affairs. Æthelwig, they alleged, attracted to himself certain knights and tenants of the Bishop by promising to protect them against the Normans, but ended by defrauding them of their lands. This led to protests from the Bishop, and Æthelwig, though owning at length his rights, retained the lands, they said, till his death. Now these lands, according to them, were two Warwickshire estates, which do not here concern us, and, in Worcestershire, Acton, ' Earesbyri ' ;[5] Bengeworth with several houses in Worcester, Evenlode and Daylesford. Bengeworth will be dealt with separately below ; as to Acton, the monks themselves, in the detailed narrative[6] of their losses, made out rather a weak case against Æthelwig's possession, while Domesday not only ignores their claim (fo. 176), but expressly states that Evesham held it T.R.E. It similarly states, of Evenlode and Daylesford, that Evesham had held them, though recognising Worcester's rights (fo. 173). Its evidence, therefore, is dead against the above story that Æthelwig had only obtained these lands after the Norman Conquest. The story told by the monks of Evesham[7] was that Æthelwig had acquired by fair purchase (*per dignam pecuniam*) all the lands above mentioned except ' Earesbyri.'[8]

But the real battle was over Bengeworth, which formed part, with Hampton by Evesham, of the Bishop's Hundred of Oswaldslow. The first fight for its possession was on the death of abbot Æthelwig (1077). The Evesham story was that these were among the manors acquired by Æthelwig which bishop Odo compelled a great gemot at ' Gildene-

---

[1] Freeman's *Norman Conquest*, III. (1875) 55.

[2] *Ibid.* V. 759.   [3] *Ibid.* IV. (1871) 176.

[4] ' Devicta namque patria hac a Normannis perditisque cunctis melioribus baronibus istius provincie, cepit ipse abbas multum crescere seculari potentia, eo quod ingenio et calliditate et scientia secularium legum qua sola studebat cunctos præcelleret.'

[5] Estbury in Hallow.   [6] Heming's Cartulary, I. 250-1.

[7] Evesham Chronicle, p. 97.

[8] I can throw no light on the case of this estate, which Domesday (fo. 173*b*) represents as having been continuously possessed by Worcester.

beorge' to adjudge to himself on the Abbot's death;[1] but that his successor, abbot Walter, successfully reclaimed Hampton and half Bengeworth for his house.[2] This brings us at once into close relation with Domesday, which tells us of the five hides which formed the half of Bengeworth that ' abbot Walter proved his right (to them) at " Ilde-berga " in (a court of the) four shires '[3](fo. 175b). Bengeworth was a ten-hide manor, and the story told by the monks of Worcester was that bishop Brihtheah had given half of it (5 hides) to ' Atsere' his kinsman and chamberlain, who had been deprived of it, in his lifetime, by Urse the dreaded sheriff. Alarmed by his fate, Ærngrim, the tenant of the other half, had invoked the protection of his powerful neighbour, Æthel-wig abbot of Evesham, and transferred his ' service ' to him, only to be expelled from his land by the unscrupulous abbot.[4] The Evesham Chronicle similarly states that half the manor had been held by 'Erne-grim,' and the other half given to 'Assere' by the Bishop;[5] and Domesday itself records 'Azor' as the previous holder at Bengeworth (fo. 174). Such concurrence of testimony as this deserves notice. The net result, as Domesday shows (fos. 174–175b), was that Urse retained Azor's half of the manor (5 hides), while Evesham Abbey succeeded in retaining Erngrim's half, though one of its five hides was secured by the sheriff Urse, who thus held in all six hides there.[6]

The next struggle was that of the bishop of Worcester to assert his rights, as lord of Oswaldslow, over the lands at Hampton and Benge-worth held by abbot Æthelwig. To this dispute Professor Freeman rightly attached much importance.[7] He held that the great plea re-

---

[1] ' Quasi lupus rapax concilia malignantium in loco qui dicitur Gildenebeorge jubet congregari, quinque videlicet sciras, ibique plus per suam iniquam potentiam quam recto jure ex triginta sex terris quas abbas Agelwius per dignam pecuniam ecclesiæ acquisivit viginti octo villas fecit eidem abjurari et suo iniquo dominio usurpari ' (Evesham Chronicle, p. 97). The Worcester version was that Odo, on Æthelwig's death, obtained from his brother, the King, a grant of all the lands which the Abbot had held and which did not belong to the abbey itself (Heming's Cartulary, I. 273). There is a certain amount of evidence in Domesday (fos. 173, 176, 177b) that Odo did, somehow or other, succeed the abbot of Evesham in several Worcestershire manors, and that, in one case at least, the abbot had lawfully bought a manor from a thegn (fo. 177b), as he is alleged by his monks to have done.

[2] ' De hiis vero Walterus abbas Westune, Hamptune, et medietatem de Beningwrthe (quam Ernegrim tenuit) revocavit, medietatem vero quam Episcopus dedit Assere occupavit Urso' (Evesham Cartulary, p. 97). The Evesham MS. Vesp. B. XXIV. fo. 28 contains a writ of Odo consequent on the 'Gildenbeorge' plea, admitting the abbey's right to certain manors, and a confirmation of it by the King. But I look on them with some suspicion.

[3] I have ventured, in my translation of the text, to identify the place of meeting as the 'Four shire stone' still existing on the border of Evenlode. It is remarkable that, under Warwickshire (fo. 238b), we find bishop Wulfstan asserting that he had proved his right to Alveston, Warwickshire (on which, however, see also Heming's Cartulary, II. 407, 418) ' before Queen Matilda in the presence of four counties.' This is suggestive of another plea held at the 'Four shire stone' (compare p. 307, note 3, below).

[4] Heming's Cartulary, I. 269–270.

[5] See note [2] above.

[6] This explanation is necessary, because, without it, the Domesday text would be obscure.

[7] ' The affairs of the church of Worcester, especially its disputes with the abbey of Evesham, throw great light on both general and local history ' (Norman Conquest, V. 759).

corded in Heming's Cartulary was actually part of the Domesday Survey and held during its progress.[1] I have, however, elsewhere shown that the plea belongs to an earlier date, and have established the sequence of events.[2] We have first a writ, despatched by the Conqueror from Normandy, bidding archbishop Lanfranc and Geoffrey bishop of Coutances settle the dispute, the latter being directed to hear the case.[3] Then we have the wonderfully interesting record of the great plea itself ('Commemoratio placiti'),[4] and next, completing the group, we are given William's writ, directed to 'Urse the sheriff and Osbern "filius Escrob"[5] and all the French and English of Worcestershire,' bidding them observe the decision arrived at before the bishop of Coutances and themselves on the testimony of the county (court).[6] I cannot but suspect that the Worcester monks forged, for production at this very plea, the charter by which Offa is made to grant them Cropthorne[7] (23 Sept. 780). For not only is its language suspicious, but it is also clearly intended to prove the Bishop's right to Hampton and Bengeworth.[8]

Turning to the later group of documents, so strangely confused by Professor Freeman with those we have dealt with above, we find them closely connected with the great Survey. The first in order is the 'testimonium' of Geoffrey bishop of Coutances[9] certifying to the four Domesday commissioners that, when the case had been heard before him, the Bishop had proved the four hides at Bengeworth to be 'of his fee,' and the 15 hides at Hampton[10] to belong to his Hundred of Oswaldslow and to owe it suit and geld and *fyrd*.[11] But the entries in Domesday do not assign these rights to the Bishop ; under

---

[1] 'The Gemót was doubtless held during the taking of the Survey. . . . The Gemót in which the dispute was settled was thus actually a part of the Survey' (*Ibid.* p. 763). (It was) 'held during the progress of the Survey' (*Ibid.* p. 765).

[2] *Domesday Studies* (II.), 542–44.

[3] Heming's Cartulary, I. 77–8.   [4] *Ibid.* pp. 80–2.

[5] See below for this Worcestershire tenant-in-chief, the lord of Richard's castle, Herefordshire.

[6] Heming's Cartulary, I. 78–9, 82–3.   [7] *Ibid.* II. 319–21.

[8] It speaks of a 'comes' and even a 'vice-comes' (!), to say nothing of a 'bibliotheca optima.' After mentioning that the 50 hides of Cropthorne included 'at Hampton 15, at Bengeworth 10,' it adds a special clause empowering the then Bishop to grant half the manor, namely 25 hides, to his kinsmen 'eo tenore ut quisquis habuerit aliquem ex ipsis viculis, venerabili episcopo Tillhere, omnibusque suis successoribus, servitium faciat in vectigalibus, et expeditionibus, omnibusque aliis subjectionibus qualescumque episcopus ipse suique successores michi meisque successoribus persolvere debuerint.' Then follows a provision, in case of any such holder losing his land, for its restoration, without question, 'to the ancient church in Worcester.' Lastly comes the usual denunciation of all offenders against the provisions in the charter, including the 'vice-comes,' a sly hit, perhaps, at Urse himself. I believe that the charter was concocted to account for the 25 hides at Hampton and Bengeworth passing out of Worcester's possession, and to support the claim for their restoration.

[9] A similar 'testimony' to past events by William bishop of Winchester, a generation later, will be found in my *Calendar of Documents preserved in France* (p. 1).

[10] It should be observed that these documents speak throughout of Hampton as of 15 hides, though both the Domesday entries assign 5 hides only. The clue is found in the Henry I. Survey (Heming's Cartulary, I. 315), which mentions that 10 hides there were free from geld by the King's writ (see *Domesday Studies*, p. 545).

[11] Heming's Cartulary, I. 77.

the Evesham fief, in fact, they assign him no rights at all (fo. 175*b*), and under his own fief they vouch the county's statement for the fact that Evesham paid the Bishop T.R.E., in respect of Hampton, nothing but the geld due in his Hundred (fo. 174*b*). The entry of the manors twice over shows us how difficult the question was ; and the Domesday commissioners had, in fact, to arrange a compromise with the Bishop, by which he consented, at their request, to abandon his claim to hold these manors in demesne on the Abbot publicly admitting them to belong to his Hundred of Oswaldslow, and to be liable to geld, suit, and *fyrd* there accordingly.[1] It is an interesting feature of this agreement that among its witnesses are at least two of the dispossessed English tenants of the bishop of Worcester, Edric ' de Hindelep ' and Godric ' de Piria.'[2]

It was explained above that the knight-service due from the bishop of Worcester under the Norman system has to be carefully distinguished from the old English system of liability to *fyrd*.[3] Domesday itself is almost silent on this knight's service, though one knight of the Bishop is referred to incidentally under Crombe.[4] The men (*homines*) also who appear in Domesday as tenants on his great Gloucestershire manor of Westbury (on Trym) are styled knights (*milites*) in a (probably) earlier survey.[5] Again, the return of knights' fees made by the bishop of Worcester in 1166 shows us 37½ fees carved out of the episcopal estates ' antiquitus ' ;[6] and the context shows that this was done in the lifetime of bishop Wulfstan. In short, here as elsewhere,[7] it is clear that knights had been enfeoffed before Domesday, and that the silence of that record is no proof to the contrary. The valuable return of the Bishop's fees *temp*. John[8] shows us where the fees were situate, and its collation with the Domesday Survey and the return of 1166 would throw a great deal of light on the topography and genealogy of the county at that early period.

Here it is only possible to touch upon two points. In 1166 we find William de Beauchamp holding 15 knights' fees, created ' antiquitus,' of the Bishop ;[9] and under John we find a later William de Beauchamp holding these same fees, and are told where they were, the

---

[1] Heming's Cartulary, I. 75, 296. The purport of the ' conventio' is suggestive of the ' fines' of later days.

[2] See, for them, Domesday, fo. 173*b*.

[3] The well-known story of William Rufus calling out the *fyrd* in 1094 as a means of financial extortion (Florence of Worcester, II. 35) proves that the old native host was retained concurrently with the Norman knights (Stubbs' *Const. Hist.*, I. 301).

[4] Similarly incidental mention of enfeoffed knights will be found on fos. 176–176*b*, where Ralf ' miles' holds of Ralf ' de Todeni,' one of Ralf de Mortimer's knights is found holding of him, and 'two knights' hold a manor of Roger de Laci. So too, on fo. 172, ' four knights' hold land of Urse.

[5] See *Feudal England*, p. 294, and Heming's Cartulary, p. 84.

[6] *Red Book of the Exchequer*, p. 300.

[7] See my *Feudal England* for the full argument.

[8] *Testa de Nevill*, pp. 41–2 (see p. 236 above).

[9] £15 had heen remitted to him, in respect of these fees, in 1156 (Rot. Pip. 2 Hen. II.).

places being all in Worcestershire. Now the Beauchamps were the heirs of the sheriff Urse, and the exceptionally large number of their fees is accounted for at once, on turning to Domesday, by the numerous cases in which the sheriff had obtained, as under-tenant, the Bishop's lands.[1]

The important conclusion to be drawn from this is that the church of Worcester obtained a *quid pro quo* from Urse. If it had to give him, as under-tenant, the beneficial occupation of much of its land, he had, in return, to discharge a quarter of the knight-service exacted from it by the Norman kings. The Henry I. survey of the lands of the church of Worcester shows us Walter de Beauchamp holding 100 hides in Oswaldslow and 5 or 6 outside it.[2] A quota of fifteen knights towards the 'service' for which the church was liable was a fairly substantial return for such tenure.

The second point that calls for notice is the curious appearance of the King himself as owing knight-service to the church of Worcester. The list of the Bishop's knights in 1166 opens with the words '(Our) lord the king owes 3 knights.' Here again we find the explanation in the evidence of Domesday Book combined with that of the survey taken under John. The latter return explains that the knights' (fees) in the King's hands[3] are in 'Burleg, Queinhull, et in Broc,' and Domesday shows us 'Burgelege' and 'Cunhille' as then (1086) 'in manu regis' (fo. 173).[4] The very important inference which I draw from this evidence is that the amount of 'knight-service' due from the see must have been fixed before Domesday, and these lands already reckoned as three knights' fees before they came into the King's hands. The inference is subtle, but it seems to be sound.

The other religious houses holding land in Worcestershire do not call for such elaborate discussion as the Bishop's own monastery. According to Domesday (fos. 174*b*, 175), the great estate which Edward the Confessor had bestowed on his new abbey at Westminster, and which was counted as 200 hides (one-sixth of the county), was all appurtenant to the manor of Pershore then in his own hands. Pershore Abbey, however, had certain rights over all of it,[5] and Domesday, having told us, under Westminster Abbey, that the manor of Pershore had been held by Edward, enters next the Pershore fief, and heads it by the statement that Pershore Abbey 'held and holds the manor of Pershore.' Here, therefore, there must have been friction, as there was, we have seen, between Worcester and Evesham. It is singular that Westminster should have been given so great an estate in the West of England as these 200 hides in Worcestershire and the 59 hides of the great manor of Deerhurst

---

[1] His brother, Robert the Despencer, had acquired a few, but those inherited from him by the Beauchamps were comparatively insignificant.

[2] *Feudal England*, pp. 173–4, and p. 325 below.

[3] The *Testa de Nevill* erroneously gives them as 'vii.,' but the Pipe Rolls prove that they were three.

[4] The third manor entered in Domesday as then 'in manu regis' is not 'Broc,' but 'Biselie' (Bushley).   [5] See p. 251 above.

close to the Worcestershire border ; and there must, one would think, have been some reason for Edward bestowing on his new abbey this vast but distant estate. The rights which were exercised over it, as above, by Pershore Abbey prepare one for the definite statement made by William of Malmesbury that much which was bestowed on Westminster had formerly been held by Pershore.[1] This has led to the supposition that king Edward robbed Pershore of the lands that he here bestowed on his own foundation. But this would have been an unheard-of step, nor does Domesday afford any support for that view. There is, however, a faint hint which may put us on another track. Dealing under Herefordshire with what I have identified as the Pull Court estate, Domesday mentions incidentally that it used to form part of 'Langedune a manor of earl Odo.' Now Longdon was the largest of the Worcestershire manors assigned by Domesday to Westminster Abbey, being entered as 30 hides. But the great survey treats it only as appendant to the king's manor of Pershore before Westminster obtained it. We must look elsewhere for 'earl Odo.' And when at last we find him, it is in a suggestive spot. 'At Deerhurst,' writes Florence of Worcester, 'died earl Æthelwine, that is, Odda,' 31 August, 1056, 'having been made a monk before his death by Ealdred bishop of Worcester, but he lies in the monastery of Pershore where he was honourably buried.' At Pershore, according to the abbey's annals, some two centuries later (1259), his bones were found in a leaden chest, beneath the pavement of St. Mary's chapel, with an epitaph to which I shall return. The annals proceed to state that Odda was heir to 'Delfer,' that wicked earl,[2] who had despoiled Pershore of many lands, which were restored by the good 'Odda.'

Now Deerhurst, with which Odda we thus learn was connected, was the head of the Gloucestershire possessions of Westminster Abbey, and is only some five miles, as the crow flies, from Longdon.[3] It is, therefore of importance to observe that Odda's position at Deerhurst is proved by a remarkable inscription found there and now preserved at Oxford, which states that 'Odda dux' caused a 'regia aula' to be constructed there, which was dedicated by Ealdred bishop of Worcester in April, 1056.[4] It states, moreover, that he did this in honour of

---

[1] 'Illud ut cetera quanto succubuerit detrimento miserabile, plus sui medietate diminutum. Partem divitum occupavit ambitio, partem sepelivit oblivio, majusculam portionem reges Edwardus et Willelmus contulere Westmonasterio.' *Gesta Pontificum* (Rolls Series), p. 298. As Brihtheah was abbot of Pershore till he became bishop of Worcester (1038), it is possible, of course, that he was responsible, as at Worcester, for the loss of some lands.

[2] 'Qui Delfero consuli nequissimo jure successerat hereditario.' These annals are known to us by Leland's extracts. (See also *Monasticon*, II. 415.)

[3] It is a singular coincidence that the Deerhurst font, which is, probably, at least as old as Odda's days, was preserved in Longdon church for part of the present century.

[4] *Archæologia*, L. 70. It has been generally supposed that this 'aula' was the well-known church at Deerhurst, and Mr. Freeman wrote of Odda dying 'under the shadow of the minster of his own building' (So also *Norm. Conq.*, V. 612). But it has been suggested, since the discovery of a 'Saxon' chapel in the same parish, that the latter was what Odda built. (*Ibid.*)

his brother Ælfric, who had died there in 1053 and who was similarly buried at Pershore.[1] Having now seen that earl Odda was established at Deerhurst as at Longdon, we may follow up the clue given by the Pershore annals, and ask whether we cannot connect him with the great transfer to Westminster of lands formerly held by Pershore. That 'most wicked earl, Delfer,' of whom, said the monks, he was the heir, was no other than Ælfhere, ealdorman of Mercia (d. 983), who had led the anti-monastic reaction after the death of Eadgar (d. 975), and of whom the Anglo-Saxon Chronicle records that he ' commanded the monasteries to be demolished, which king Eadgar had before commanded the holy bishop Æthelwold to found,'

'and monks expelled
and God's servants persecuted.'[2]

If, as stated in the Pershore annals, it was he who despoiled the abbey of so large a portion of its lands, we understand how Longdon, which Eadgar had confirmed to the house, came to be found in the hands of his heir, earl Odda. It seems therefore to me possible that what really happened was that, on Odda's death (1056), king Edward seized all his lands, as he left no heir, and refused to recognise his undertaking to restore the Pershore manors.[3] The king would thus be able to bestow them on his new foundation. Although Longdon is the only manor that Domesday names as having been Odda's, the great record was not concerned with a man who had died thirty years before it was compiled, and his estates were probably of wide extent. The above suggestion is but tentative, although it is quite in harmony with what we elsewhere read of the fate, especially in Worcestershire, of monastic lands. When they had been held for a time by laymen, the monks' claim had little weight ; possession then, as now, was ' nine points of the law.'

Apart from his distinct connection with Pershore Abbey and its lands, earl Odda has a claim on the historian of Worcestershire if, as Mr. Freeman thought, he was the local earl in the last years of his life.[4] But the fact that he attested three charters of Ealdred bishop of Worcester seems to be insufficient ground for this belief, seeing that, in all three cases, earl Leofric attests before him. Odda obtained his earldom, which was that of the south-western counties, during the ascendancy of the Normanizing party in 1051–2 ; a kinsman of the king he supported him warmly against earl Godwine and was chosen, with earl Ralf of Hereford, to command the king's fleet in 1052. Although sometimes styled ' Odo,' he was doubtless a native, as Mr. Freeman held,[5] though I do not agree with that writer that he bore the

---

[1] Florence of Worcester, I. 211.   [2] Anglo-Saxon Chronicle, II. 99.

[3] The Pershore annals state that he refrained from marriage in order that he might have no heir to claim them. He very possibly bargained that the lands should remain his for life.

[4] ' His connection with the Hwiccian land and its monasteries points to Worcestershire, or possibly Worcestershire and Gloucestershire, as the district under his charge.' (Norman Conquest [1870], II. 565–6.)   [5] Ibid. pp. 564–5.

name of Æthelwine 'after his monastic profession.' The Pershore annals give his epitaph, which speaks of him as originally ' Ædwinus vocatus in baptismo,' and he may have adopted the name Odo (which was Anglicized as ' Odda ') when he joined the foreign party. The English chronicle describes him at his death as ' a good man and pure, and very noble'; and Worcestershire, where he rests, may claim this lord of Longdon as one of the earliest names that adorns its roll of worthies.

It was probably the remoteness of its great estate in this part of the world that led Westminster Abbey to enfeoff almost all its knights there.[1] For the obnoxious duty of providing knights was laid upon it as on Worcester. It is a striking feature of the Domesday survey of the abbey's lands in Worcestershire that the irrepressible sheriff Urse is entered as its tenant in no fewer than fourteen places, holding in all some 50 hides. This holding was represented, eighty years later, by the seven knights' fees which his heir, William de Beauchamp, then held of the abbey.[2] The largest of the abbey's manors held, in Domesday, by Urse was that of 'Newentune' (10 hides), which obtained from his heirs its name of Naunton Beauchamp. Next in importance among the abbey's vassals in 1166 was Hugh 'Puher,' who held three knights' fees,[3] representing some 20 hides which Walter ' Ponther' held of the abbey in 1086.[4] It is remarkable that, as we saw was the case with the Worcester fief, the Westminster return of knights (1166) commences with the statement that the King himself owes the Abbot the service of one knight in respect of ' Stokes in Wirecestrescira,' that is of Severnstoke, which was then in his hands.[5]

Pershore Abbey, in spite of its large holding in the county (100 hides), was only called on to supply two or three knights—the Abbot said two, and he seems to have carried his point.[6] The entry of its Domesday fief, though by no means long, is interesting and instructive. In no fewer than seven cases had Urse, the insatiable sheriff, obtained lands on the fief, while his brother Robert, in addition, had secured 3½ hides at Wadborough. It is clear, however, that the Domesday Commissioners overhauled the claims even of the dreaded Urse. In one case his predecessor, they record, had only a life interest in the land ; in another he was ' the third heir ' under a lease for three lives, so that the land, they record, should revert to the abbey at his death. In two cases he pleaded that the land was given him by the King, and in one of these he admitted that he was bound to render the abbey ' service ' for it. Of his hide at Bransford, the county (court) asserted

---

[1] See the return of its knights in 1166 (*Red Book of the Exchequer*, pp. 188–9). And compare the 1212 return in *Testa de Nevill* (p. 43).

[2] *Ibid.*   [3] *Ibid.*

[4] All in Worcestershire, save one hide in Gloucestershire (Domesday).

[5] *Red Book of the Exchequer*, pp. 59, 132, 188. (It is not identified by the editor.) See also *The Commune of London and other studies*, p. 265.

[6] The 1212 survey states his lands to be free save Beoley and Caldecot, from which two knights were due.

that ' it belonged to the church of Pershore in the time of king Edward, and yet the abbot of Evesham was holding it on the day of king Edward's death, but they knew not how.'   Comparing the case of Acton on the opposite page of Domesday, we shall hardly err in concluding that, as alleged by the monks of Evesham, Bransford was among the manors acquired by abbot Æthelwig,[1] and obtained, on the Abbot's death, by bishop Odo.   The Bishop must then have given it to Urse.   The Pershore lands he held in 1086 amounted only, in all, to $9\frac{1}{4}$ hides ; in 1166 his heir, William de Beauchamp, is returned as holding one of the two knights' fees created on the abbey's lands.

The list of the great Worcestershire houses is closed by Evesham Abbey, which was charged with the service of five knights[2] in respect of a fief comprising, we must remember, not only the 65 hides assigned to it by Domesday in Worcestershire, but lands in three other counties. Although as many as six ' Frenchmen ' (*francigenæ*) are found as tenants on its Worcestershire estate, there is a singular absence of those cases in which Normans had obtained possession, by subinfeudation, of church lands.   Indeed, except for the solitary hide held at Bengeworth by Urse,[3] the only case is at (Abbot's) Morton, of which the 5 hides were held by ' Rannulf,' who was clearly the brother of abbot Walter mentioned in Heming's Cartulary as present at the great plea with Worcester.[4]   This Ranulf also held of the abbey 3 hides at Kinwarton, Warwickshire, and is claimed, apparently with good reason, as the founder of the house of Wrottesley.

The other church lands entered in the Worcestershire Domesday are, comparatively speaking, insignificant.   The bishop of Hereford, at Inkberrow, in addition to the 5 hides which he held there of the bishop of Worcester (fo. 173), had $15\frac{1}{2}$ hides belonging to his see, which ' Earl Harold wrongfully held, but King William restored ' (fo. 174).   The hide that St. Mary of Coventry held at Salwarpe had been virtually absorbed by the sheriff in his park ; St. Peter of Gloucester had rights in Droitwich ; St. Guthlac of Hereford one hide there ; and the priests of the collegiate church of Wolverhampton retained their small estate at Lutley.   Of foreign religious houses the great abbey of St. Denis probably owed its rights at Droitwich to its possession of a large estate in Gloucestershire appendant to its priory at Deerhurst, which would make these rights useful to its monks.   Of the abbey of Cormeilles I have spoken above, so that there remains only the gift by Ralf ' de Todeni ' of 4 hides at Astley to the abbey of St. Taurin at Evreux, the monks of which founded there a cell that became an alien priory.[5]

In Worcestershire we learn practically nothing of the parish churches and their endowments from Domesday.   Of priests, indeed, there is

---

[1] See p. 254 above.   [2] *Feudal England*, pp. 303–4.
[3] See p. 254 above.
[4] See p. 255 above, and *Feudal England*, p. 302.
[5] His gift of Alton in Rock to the abbey of St. Evroul (see my *Calendar of Documents preserved in France*, p. 219, and Heming's Cartulary, p. 255) is not mentioned in Domesday.

frequent mention, but they are normally entered in connection with the ploughs, at the head of the agricultural classes. At Pedmore the priest is even entered between the villeins and the bordars (fo. 177), while in another case (fo. 177*b*) we read of '18 bordars and 1 priest with 1 plough.' At Broughton there are entered '5 villeins and 10 bordars and a church and a priest,' who have between them six ploughs (fo. 177*b*), and at Halesowen the villeins, bordars, 'Radmans,' 'and a church with two priests' have between them $41\frac{1}{2}$ ploughs (fo. 176). It is clear, therefore, that in this county Domesday is only interested in the priests and churches as owners, with the agricultural classes, of the all-important plough-oxen. There is occasional entry, however, of tithes as bestowed on religious houses ; Westminster Abbey had received the tithes of the King's revenues at Droitwich (fo. 174*b*), and William Fitz-Osbern had bestowed on his abbeys of Cormeilles and of Lyre those of his Worcestershire estates (fo. 180*b*).[1]

Of the lay holders of land in the shire earl Roger claims precedence, but his holding is chiefly of interest for his great manor of Halesowen being, in consequence of that tenure, transferred to his own county of Shropshire, only to be restored in modern times.[2] His one other manor, Salwarpe, was secured by Urse as under-tenant, and in its woodland he made his park, which absorbed the church of Coventry's land there, of which also he was under-tenant. Next to earl Roger we must rank William Fitz Ansculf the lord of Dudley, Ralf de Tosni ('Todeni'), Osbern Fitz Richard of Richard's Castle, and the terrible Urse the sheriff. These four had considerable estates, but only the first and fourth need special notice here. For Ralf and Osbern were Herefordshire lords, the former holding Clifford Castle, while his chief seat appears to have been at Flamstead in Hertfordshire. William Fitz Ansculf, whose castle at Dudley and its 'castlery' are mentioned, had succeeded his father Ansculf, who had been sheriff of Surrey, and, apparently, of Bucks, and who belonged to the great Picard house of the *vidames* of Picquigny. From Ansculf's brother Ghilo descended the baronial house of 'Pinkeney,' the head of whose barony was in Northamptonshire. William Fitz Ansculf appears in Domesday as a tenant-in-chief in eleven counties, in some of which, especially in Bucks, he held great estates. His Worcestershire lands were but a small portion of the fief of which Dudley was the head, and which was afterwards held, as the barony of Dudley, by the families of Paynel and of Someri.

The dominant personality revealed to us, in Worcestershire, by Domesday is that of Urse the sheriff. In Mr. Freeman's vigorous words :

> The terrible sheriff . . . Urse of Abetot was only the chief of a whole band of Norman spoilers, who seem to have fallen with special eagerness on the lands of the Church in this particular shire. But the sheriff was the greatest and most daring offender of all. He built his castle in the very jaws of the monks of Worcester so that the foss of the fortress encroached on the monastic burying-ground.[3]

[1] See p. 240 above.   [2] See p. 238 above.   [3] *Norman Conquest* (1871), IV. 171.

He then tells the 'famous tale' of Ealdred, archbishop of York and protector of the see of Worcester, examining the site and denouncing Urse in the grim English lines :

Hightest thou Urse,
Have thou God's curse.[1]

Urse derived the surname which Worcestershire still preserves in Croome d'Abitot and Redmarley d'Abitot from St. Jean d'Abbetot some twelve miles to the east of Havre. In one instance, it is interesting to observe, Domesday gives him the alternative name of Urse 'de Wirecestre' (fo. 169*b*), an illustration of the practice by which sheriffs, in the Norman period, were assigned the names of the capitals of their shires. This is particularly well seen in the case of the sheriffs of Gloucestershire, who held the office by hereditary right, and who, from the Conqueror's reign, took their name from Gloucester till raised to an earldom by the empress Maud in 1141. There can be no question that the shrievalty of Worcestershire also was hereditary, and that Urse was succeeded in it by his son Roger.[2] On the fief passing to Urse's son-in-law, Walter de Beauchamp, he obtained the shrievalty also, and was succeeded in it, as I have elsewhere shown, by his son William.[3]

It seemed desirable to explain this point at some length, because it is asserted by Professor Freeman that Urse was sheriff of Gloucestershire as well as Worcestershire.[4] The statement has been copied by a local writer, but it is without foundation. Durand (de Pîtres), sheriff of Gloucestershire at the time of Domesday, is there styled 'Durandus vice-comes,'[5] and his fief is headed 'Terra Durandi de Glowecestria.' The interest of Urse in that county was limited to the one hide he held, as a tenant-in-chief, at Seisincote ; Worcestershire alone was the scene of his remarkable proceedings.[6] The traces they left upon that county were deep and of long duration. For the acquisition of his wide possessions by his son-in-law, Walter de Beauchamp, founded a great territorial house long mighty in Worcestershire and famous in our feudal history. Although in Worcestershire he held of the Crown a fief at least as large as that of any other lay tenant,[7] his real power, as a land-

---

[1] The authority for this story is William of Malmesbury's *Gesta Pontificum*, and its date, as Mr. Freeman points out, must be anterior to Ealdred's death in Sept. 1069.

[2] The charter of Henry I. in favour of the prior of Worcester and his monks is addressed 'Waltero vicecomiti Gloucest[rie] et Rogero vicecomiti de Wirecestria' (Hale's *Registrum Prioratus Beatæ Mariæ Wigorniensis*, p. 30).

[3] In her charter to William (1141 ?) the Empress says : 'Dedi ei et reddidi vicecomitatum Wigorn[ie] . . . in feodo et hereditarie per eandem firmam quam pater eius Walterus de Bellocampo inde reddebat' (*Geoffrey de Mandeville*, p. 313).

[4] 'We find that the two shires were put under a single sheriff, Urse of Abetot, who stands conspicuous amongst the most oppressive of his class, and whose hand seems to have fallen heavily on clerks and laymen alike' (*Norman Conquest* [1871], IV. 174). 'Urse, Ursus, Urso of Abetot, appears in Domesday as sheriff of both Worcestershire and Gloucestershire ; and we hear much of his evil deeds in both shires' (*Ibid.* [1876], V. 760).

[5] fo. 168*b, et passim*.

[6] He had also, as a tenant-in-chief, holdings of no great consequence in Herefordshire and Warwickshire. [7] About 40 hides.

owner, in the county consisted in the vast extent of land he held as an under-tenant. The baronial houses of Beauchamp 'of Elmley,' Beauchamp 'of Powyk,' and Beauchamp 'of Holt,' all derived their names from places which Urse or his brother Robert the Despencer held as under-tenants of the churches of Westminster and Worcester. It would, indeed, hardly be safe, at this stage of our history, to estimate the amount of church land which thus passed to the Beauchamps, for Urse lived some twenty years beyond the Domesday Survey, and seems to have secured fresh lands between the survey and his death. But we have to remember that he also held, on a small scale, of sundry others, of Nigel the physician, of the bishop of Bayeux, of earl Roger, of Osbern Fitz Richard, and of Ralf 'de Todeni,' besides securing nearly 12 hides on the royal manor of Bromsgrove.

It is clear that Urse obtained several of those manors which the bishop of Bayeux had made his own on the death of abbot Æthelwig.[1] Two of those which he held in chief are the subject, in Domesday, of short narratives. Half a hide at Droitwich had been held, T.R.E., by Evesham Abbey, to which it was given by the father of a youth who was made a monk there in 1047–8. Then the Abbot granted it for life to an uncle of his, on whose death at Stamfordbridge the abbey recovered this land 'before king William came into England.' Abbot Æthelwig held it till his death, and abbot Walter held it after him ' for more than seven years.' But at the time of the survey Urse was in possession. We have here an interesting note of time in connection with the date of Domesday.[2] Of the manor which follows Domesday tells us that the abbot of Evesham held it T.R.E., 'having bought it from a certain thegn who had a right to sell it.' Here we are struck by the close correspondence between the language of Domesday and that of Heming's Cartulary.[3] These two manors are preceded by that of Upton (Warren), which was held by Urse, though 'the county' said that it had been held by abbot Æthelwig, and ought rightfully to belong to the abbey (fo. 177b). Now

---

[1] See p. 261 above.

[2] The chronology of the abbots of Evesham, under the Conqueror, is by no means clear. Abbot Æthelwig died of gout 16 Feb. '1077' (Chron. Evesham, p. 95), and 'tercio quoque mense post discessum patris hujus Agelwii' (Ibid. p. 96, and Harl. MS. 3,763, fo. 171b) there was appointed abbot Walter, whose succession, therefore, is dated in 'May, 1077.' Mr. Freeman reckoned the years of Walter's rule as '1077–1084' (Norman Conquest, IV. 388), and observed of the Domesday entry that 'as Walter succeeded in 1077, the alienation is fixed as late as 1084' (Ibid. V. 765). It is tempting to conclude that Urse had taken advantage of abbot Walter's death to seize the manor. But what the Evesham MS. (Harl. MS. 3,763, fo. 171b) says of Walter is that 'cum fere octo ann[is] isti ecclesie profuisset, diem suum clausit extremum xiii kal. Febr. [20 Jan.] anno vero gracie millesimo LXXXVI.' (sic). And this date is accepted by the editor of the Chronicle (p. 98) as 1086. As this would assign Walter a rule of nearly nine (not 'nearly eight') years, there must, on any hypothesis, be an error somewhere. It is tempting, as I said, to connect the 'fere octo annis' of the Evesham MS. with the 'amplius quam vii annis' of Domesday, and to conclude that abbot Walter died in January '1085' (which may mean 1085 or 1086, just as his accession in '1077' would be 1077 or 1078); but Florence of Worcester, a good authority, dates Walter's death 20 Jan., 1104! In any case, Urse's possession of the land must have been recent at the time of the Survey.

[3] See p. 267 below.

these three manors are all among those of which, the Evesham Chronicle asserts, the abbey was deprived by the bishop of Bayeux on the death of abbot Æthelwig. So also were Acton (Beauchamp) and 'Lenche,' which Domesday enters under 'the bishop of Bayeux's land' (fo. 176). It tells us that the former had belonged to Evesham Abbey T.R.E., and that Urse had received it from the Abbot in exchange for other land, and that, in 1086, he held it 'of the bishop of Bayeux's fee.' The Evesham Chronicle (p. 95) explains this by saying that Acton was the patrimony of Æthelwig, who had given it, with 'Brainesford,' to Urse in exchange for Bengeworth, which he occupied wrongfully,[1] but that 'he detains wrongfully all three.' And Domesday shows him accordingly, on the opposite page (fo. 175*b*), occupying Bransford, which the 'county' said had been held by the abbot of Evesham when king Edward died.[2] The last case is that of 'Lenche' (which I identify with Sheriff's Lench), held in 1086, of the Bishop's fee, by Urse. Domesday tells us that Evesham Abbey 'was seized of it for many years, till the bishop of Bayeux took it from the abbey and gave it to Urse.' The Evesham Chronicle speaks of it as 'Leinch quam Ursini tenent contra Rotulum Winton' (p. 97), which must clearly refer to the above entry in Domesday. In all these cases, therefore, the evidence of the Evesham Chronicle is in virtual harmony with that of Domesday, the entries in which, indeed, it helps to explain.

It should be observed that Urse had extensive rights at Droitwich ; of the sixteen estates he held in chief, no fewer than ten entitled him to a share in the proceeds of its salt, a total of $21\frac{1}{2}$ saltpans and 7 burgesses being entered as his. The existence also of his 'park,' close by, at Salwarpe points to his personal residence, while a careful examination of fos. 172, 172*b*, will show that he 'farmed,' as sheriff, the royal rights at Droitwich, which were important and extensive enough to give him much opportunity for oppression. Here we have the explanation of a passage which has given rise to misapprehension. Domesday states that Sodbury (Gloucestershire), then in the King's hands, had land in (Droit)wich from which it was entitled to receive yearly 25 *sestiers* of salt ; 'but the sheriff Urse has so impoverished (*vastavit*) the tenants that they cannot now render the salt' (fo. 163*b*).

Robert the Despencer, Urse's brother, occurs prominently in Heming's Cartulary as a despoiler of the church of Worcester,[3] and Domesday reveals him also as securing her lands at Piddle, Moor, and Hill, a hide at Knightwick, and a house at Worcester. From Pershore Abbey also he obtained an estate, at Wadborough, where he had his 'park.' His lands, therefore, in the main, lay about Pershore. In this county, however, he was not a tenant-in-chief, as he was in some others. I have elsewhere shown [4] that Robert's fief did not, as has been alleged,

---

[1] The chronicle here adds, 'sicut medietatem iterum postea fecit.' For Bengeworth, and the fate of its two moieties, see p. 254 above. [2] See p. 261 above.
[3] At Lawern (p. 253), Elmley (p. 268), and Charlton (p. 269).
[4] *Feudal England*, pp. 175–6, 179, 194–5.

pass entire to the Marmions, but was divided, especially in Worcestershire, between them and the Beauchamps, the heirs of his brother Urse. As for Urse himself, his rule in Worcestershire must have lasted nearly forty years ; for it began, as we saw above, soon after the Conquest, and he is still found acting as sheriff under Henry I. In the fate of Roger, his son and heir, who incurred that monarch's vengeance, his contemporaries saw the fulfilment of Ealdred's curse, but his daughter brought to Walter de Beauchamp the vast estates of which the history has yet to be largely written from the great cartulary of the Beauchamp family now in the British Museum.[1]

Of the smaller Worcestershire tenants-in-chief, who held from four to six manors (or estates) apiece, Ralf de Mortimer and Roger de Laci were great lords on the Welsh border, and Drogo Fitz Ponz, the collateral ancestor of the Cliffords of Clifford Castle, will, like them, be dealt with, more appropriately, in Herefordshire. Gilbert Fitz Turold, however, though also a tenant on the March, may fairly claim, under Worcestershire, some mention. For in this county we have proof of what had, indeed, been suspected, namely, that Gilbert was one of the followers of the great William Fitz Osbern, earl of Hereford. We read, of Hadsor, in Heming's Cartulary, that ' after the Normans conquered this country, earl William took it from the monastery (of Worcester) and gave it to a certain officer of his, Gilbert by name.'[2] And Domesday shows us Hadsor in possession of Gilbert Fitz Turold. Again, Domesday tells us of Lench (fo. 176) that ' of this land Gilbert Fitz Turold gave two hides to Evesham Abbey for the soul of earl William, by consent of king William.' Gilbert's holding *in capite* within the shire was only some 10 hides, but, as an under-tenant of the churches of Westminster and Worcester, he was a larger holder than this at Comberton, Powick, and Longdon. His seat, which had been given him by earl William, was in Herefordshire on the Welsh border, and there he had a fortified house and ' a great wood for hunting.'

We have now seen something of the Normans, into whose hands there passed the estates of dispossessed Englishmen. The one manor which Domesday shows us retained in English hands is that of Chaddesley, which ' Eddeve ' (Eadgifu) still held as she had done before the Conquest. Of the Normans who had come in under Edward the Confessor, Osbern Fitz Richard had retained a manor he then held, and had succeeded to four others which had been his father's ; Alvred of Marlborough also had retained, and indeed increased his lands at Severnstoke. Otherwise the change was great. Worcestershire, however, had not been a land of great thegns ; the extent of church lands made this impossible. Eadwine, the local earl, had been succeeded by the King, but his local estates were limited, apparently, to the great manor of Bromsgrove and those of Suckley and Dudley. It should be observed that he had established on some 12 hides appurtenant to Bromsgrove six

---

thegns of his, whose names are given, and of whom a remarkable formula records that they could not withdraw themselves from 'the lord of the manor.' Feckenham also, with its 10 hides, was held of him by five thegns, who, on the contrary, 'could betake themselves with (their) land whither they would,'[1] and of whom is made the remarkable statement that they 'had under them four knights (*milites*) as free as they were themselves' (fo. 180*b*). Another of his thegns, 'Simon,' is found on fo. 176*b*, and in my notes on the text I have shown his identity with the 'Simund' who held Crowle, and who, though Domesday does not say so, we know from Heming's Cartulary to have been a Danish thegn of earl Leofric. Two thegns of earl Ælfgar are mentioned on fo. 176. Some English holders are styled 'thegns of king Edward,' as was the case with Bricsmar, who had held Hadsor (fo. 177). A story told in Heming's Cartulary throws a valuable light on the nature of this tenure. We read that Hadsor had been held by Brihtwine, a wealthy man, 'who possessed it by inheritance freely, having, that is, the power of giving it or selling it to whom he would,[2] as (being) his paternal inheritance, for which he owed service to no one but the King.' This Brihtwine, we learn, was succeeded by his son Brihtmar, the 'Bricsmar' of Domesday.

Although Worcestershire lay within the sphere, not of the house of Godwine, but of the house of Leofric, earl Godwine had held there the valuable manor of Wichbold. When we turn from earls to ordinary thegns, it becomes extremely difficult to ascertain their identity, except where a story in Heming's Cartulary comes to our help. In a solitary case, however, Domesday shows us an Englishman, Sawold, holding freely T.R.E. two Worcestershire estates, which had passed in 1086 to Ralph de Mortimer, but on one of which Sawold's son was then farming the land as Ralph's tenant. It is probable also that the Wulfmar who occurs at the end of the survey as holding, at Hilhampton, a wretched little waste virgate, was the man of that name who had preceded Ralf de Todeni and Drogo Fitz Ponz in certain other manors in the same part of the shire. Something may here be said of the English sheriff of the shire, Urse's predecessor, Kineward. He was a principal witness at the great plea between Worcester and Evesham, when he deposed to the practice in Oswaldslow under Edward the Confessor.[3] His home was at Lawern, which the monks of Worcester asserted he had held of them, and had restored to them at his death, having been undisturbed there. But they had not held it long, they said, when Urse's brother, Robert the Despencer, took it from them wrongfully with other lands.[4] Domesday only shows us Robert as his successor

---

[1] That is to say, they could commend themselves to what lord they would.

[2] 'possidebat liberaliter, habens videlicet potestatem donandi sive vendendi eam cuicumque vellet' (I. 263). Compare, at the end of the Worcestershire Survey, abbot Æthelwig's purchase of a manor, 'a quodam taino qui terram suam recte poterat vendere cui vellet' (fo. 177*b*).

[3] Heming's Cartulary, I. 82.   [4] *Ibid.* I. 253.

at 'Laure' (Lawern) and in other lands which I suspect to have been at Elmley (fo. 174). But in another quarter we find him, as 'Kynewardus de Lauro,' witnessing the charter granted, in 1072, by Robert de Stafford to Evesham.[1] If, as there is no reason to doubt, Kineward held Laugherne till his death, it is obvious that the story told by the monks throws back the great plea between Worcester and Evesham to a date several years earlier than that of the Domesday Survey.

If Worcestershire is remarkable in Domesday for the amount of its church land, it has also a peculiar and dominant feature in Droitwich and its salt industry. It is not too much to say that Droitwich pervades the survey of the shire. The actual ownership of the place was divided in a quite peculiar manner between about a dozen tenants-in-chief, who had, each of them, fractional holdings. But, in addition to this, the tenants of many scattered manors possessed there 'burgesses,' saltpans, or rights to a supply of salt. The clue to the Domesday assessment of Droitwich is found in an entry at the foot of fo. 176, that Ralf de Todeni 'holds in (Droit)wich 1 hide, out of 10 hides that pay geld.'[2] A special survey of Droitwich, which was found and printed by me,[3] and which seems to belong to the latter part of Henry I.'s reign, is headed 'Hee sunt x hidæ in Wich.' We have then to recover from Domesday the constituents of 10 hides. They seem to have been as follows :

	Hides	Burgesses
Westminster Abbey . . .	1	31
St. Denis' Abbey	1	18
Coventry Abbey	1	4
St. Guthlac of Hereford . . .	1	9
St. Peter of Gloucester . . .	$\frac{1}{2}$	0
King's Hall at Gloucester . . .	$\frac{1}{2}$	0
Ralf de 'Todeni'	1	0
Harold, son of earl Ralf . . .	1	20
Roger de Laci	$\frac{1}{2}$	11
William, son of Corbucion (in Witton)	2	0
Urse d'Abetot (in Witton) . .	$\frac{1}{2}$	7
	10	100

This would give us exactly 10 hides for Droitwich, a quarter of which (2½) would be in Witton.[4]

[1] Salt (Staffordshire) Arch. Coll., II. 178. In this charter (which is known to us only from an Elizabethan translation) his name is followed by that of 'Harlebaldus,' a leading result under-tenant of Urse. The sheriff Urse also is himself a witness.
[2] This is the entry that Professor Maitland misunderstood (see p. 241 above), with the that he assigned 15½ hides to (Droit)wich and 2½ to Witton.
[3] *Feudal England*, pp. 177, 180. See also p. 330 below.
[4] It is right, however, to observe that Domesday states of Westminster Abbey's hide that it had never paid geld, and that the later survey, though headed (as above) 'these are the 10 hides,' accounts for 11⅜ hides.

THE DOMESDAY SURVEY

In addition to the hundred burgesses accounted for above, there are 13 others definitely assigned to Droitwich, and there are some whose *locale* is not mentioned. The former were appurtenant to Wichbold, and owed there reaping and other service (fo. 176*b*). Houses also are mentioned as held in Droitwich, in two or three cases, by owners of other manors. But it is with the ' salinæ ' that we meet most frequently. Some misapprehension has arisen from the entry of ' salinæ ' under other places, without the explanation that they were situated in Droitwich ; the existence of local saltworks has been wrongly deduced from these entries. As a matter of fact, many places outside Worcestershire possessed ' salinæ ' or rights to salt at Droitwich. That Herefordshire, Gloucestershire, and Warwickshire should supply instances in point may not be surprising ; but so far afield as Oxfordshire we have cases at Bampton[1] and Rollright,[2] while even in Bucks (Prince's) Risborough had its saltworker at Droitwich.[3] It appears to me that these rights, belonging to manors at a distance, must have been due to some extent to their lords having at Droitwich also territorial interests. In Warwickshire, for instance, the Domesday holders of Witton in Droitwich, William son of Corbucion and Urse d'Abetot, held sundry manors. The former's chief seat was at Studley, to which we find appurtenant a saltpan, which must have been at Droitwich,[4] whence also salt was due to another of his Warwickshire manors.[5] A Droitwich saltpan similarly belonged to a Warwickshire manor of Urse.[6] It is probable that Earl Eadwine, who had large interests at Droitwich, had similarly bestowed rights there on distant manors of his own before the Conquest.

Although the process of salt manufacture must be dealt with in the section devoted to industries, it may be mentioned here that Domesday contains several allusions to the process. In addition to the brine-pits, the ' salinæ,' and the somewhat mysterious ' hocci,' we have, under Bromsgrove 3 saltworkers and 6 leaden pans (*plumbi*) for their work ; and two of these leaden pans are mentioned under Tardebigg as distinct from the ' salinæ.' A place for making these pans (*fabrica plumbi*) is mentioned under Northwick (fo. 173*b*), and 4 furnaces (*furni*) stood on the Westminster Abbey estate. The consumption of wood at the saltworks must have been very great. The Bishop's wood at Fladbury, we read (fo. 173), supplied 'ligna ad salinas de Wich,' while Bromsgrove sent yearly

---

[1] ' De . . . salinis de Wic ' (154*b*).   [2] ' III summæ salis ad Wich ' (160*b*).

[3] ' Adhuc unus salinarius de Wicg reddens summas (*sic*) salis ' (143*b*).

[4] ' Salina reddens xix summas salis ' (243). Studley was just over the Worcestershire border, and William's heirs removed thither the religious house they had originally founded at Witton. Thus it was that Studley Priory came to hold St. Peter's, Witton. In addition to Witton, William held, as an under-tenant of Westminster Abbey, the valuable manor of Dormston, Worcestershire, which was represented by the one knight's fee held of the Abbey in 1166 by Peter ' de Stodlega,' William's heir. In the Droitwich survey he holds the two hides at Witton as Peter ' Corbezun,' the family being known by both names.

[5] (Binton): ' de Wich iii summas salis ' (243).   [6] ' Salina in Wich reddens iii solidos ' (243*b*). ' Salters' way ' was the road from Droitwich through Alcester to Stratford-on-Avon. ' Salt Street ' seems to have run south-east towards Stow-on-the-Wold.

300 cartloads, which produced 300 'mits' of salt. This was probably the usual proportion, for a 'salina' of the Bishop is entered as producing '100 "mits" of salt for 100 cartloads of wood' (fo. 173*b*). The monks of Westminster also obtained 100 'mits,' and sent 100 cartloads of wood from (Martin) Hussingtree (fo. 174*b*). Three measures seem to have been used for the salt produced, namely the horse-load (*summa*), the 'sestier' (*sextarium*), and the 'mit' (*mitta*). The meaning of the last, a local word, has been, fortunately, preserved for us by Habington in a passage which explains several of the words used by Domesday in this connection :

> The saltwater drawne out of the wells is in a singular proportion of Justyce conveyghed into seates called anciently *Salinæ* . . . wheare after it is boyled in *leaden pans* and converted to salt, it is dryed in barowes made of twigs and sally, somewhat open, so as the moysture may run from the salt. Foure of these barowes, conteygninge about towe bushells of Salt are named a *Mit*.[1]

The Worcestershire woodlands were of value for more than as a source of fuel for the saltworks. Their uses are suggestively described in the cases of two of the Bishop's manors. At Fladbury, besides the wood for Droitwich, he had the hunting and the honey (as he also had at Bredon) ; in Malvern chase he used to have, in the woods belonging to his manors of Ripple and Upton, the hunting and the honey, and still had 'the pannage and (wood for) firing and for repairs.' In another of his manors it is mentioned that his tenant at Whittington had 'only woodland (sufficient) for firing' (fo. 173). Pannage was a source of substantial profit when great herds of swine were kept to provide the pork of which such large quantities were then salted for food. Stretching back from Hanley (Castle) were woods from which six swineherds brought to their lord the king sixty swine a year (fo. 180*b*). On the other side of the county, at Inkberrow, the bishop of Hereford received a hundred from a broad stretch of woodland (fo. 174). Crowle, in the heart of the county, had 'woodland for a hundred swine' (fo. 176*b*). Honey was a product of more importance in those days than now. The great royal manor of Pershore, under Edward the Confessor, had supplied 50 *sestiers* of honey, in addition to its money-rent. A rent of one *sestier* of honey was still paid at the time of Domesday by a mill at Cleeve (Priors), by a priestly tenant at Witley, and by each of three 'coliberts' at Powick, while a freeman at Wolverley paid two *sestiers* as his rent. Nor was the honey that of wild bees only ; at Suckley (fo. 180*b*) we find a bee-master (*custos apium*) with twelve hives.[2] Mr. Seebohm has

---

[1] Habyngton's Survey, II. 297. In Halliwell's *Dictionary of Archaic Words*, he cites Kennett (MS. Lansd. 1,033) to the effect that 'At Nantwich and Droitwich, the conical baskets wherein they put the salt to let the water drain from it are called barrows. A barrow contained about six pecks.' This would make the 'Mit' about six bushels—a very different reckoning. It should be added that a 'Mit' was considered equivalent to a horse-load according to Hale's *Registrum* (34*a*), 'invenient singulis annis equos diebus Dominicis ad portandum sal de Wich apud Wigorniam . . . quilibet equus portabit unam mittam.'

[2] This was the old English 'beo-ceorl,' on whom see the valuable remarks in Andrews' *Old English Manor*, pp. 205–8.

drawn special attention to the prevalence of honey-rents in Wales and on the Welsh border, and has explained that 'honey had two uses, besides its being the substitute for the modern sugar—one for the making of mead, which was three times the price of beer ; the other for the wax for candles used in the chief's household, and on the altar of the mass.'[1]

In Norman eyes, however, the value of the woodland for hunting was even greater than in those of Edward the Confessor and his thegns. Earl William had installed huntsmen at Feckenham in the east of the county and at Bushley and Hanley (Castle) in the west; king William, his friend and lord, had taken into the royal forest many a stretch of woodland, and the 'huntsman' mentioned under Lippard belonged perhaps to that portion which ran almost, if not quite, up to Worcester on the east.[2] The woods at Chadwick in Bromsgrove, Kidderminster, and Malvern (the Bishop's portion) are specially stated to have been added by the King to the forest, as is half the woodland at Alvechurch, together with that at Woodcote. At Shelve (fo. 176b) the wood had been 'missa in defenso,' and on fo. 180b we read that the woodland of Feckenham, 'foris est missa ad silvam regis,' as had been the 'park for beasts of the chase,' with all the woodland in Holloway adjoining. The great stretch of woodland behind Hanley (Castle) had been taken into Malvern Chase (*missa est foris*), and the King had also laid his hands on the woods of Queenhill near by and of Eldersfield to the south-west (fo. 180b). Thus the forests of Feckenham and of Wyre and the chase of Malvern were all gainers under William. In the woods belonging to Bromsgrove were four 'eyries of hawks,' and in that of Hanley (Castle) one (fo. 180b). The 'hay' or hedged enclosure 'in which wild animals were captured' (fo. 176b) is mentioned at Holt, at 'Chintune,' and at Hanley Castle (fo. 163b). At Lawern, the home of Kineward, the last English sheriff, the survey records '12 oaks,' an entry perhaps unique in Domesday.

In some counties the amount of woodland is reckoned, in the great Survey, by the number of swine that could feed there or that it was worth ; in others it is somewhat obscurely reckoned in leagues (*lewæ*) and furlongs (*quarentenæ*). Worcestershire belonged to the latter class, its woodland being almost exclusively measured in these terms. Mr. Eyton, who devoted to these measures much attention, held strongly that the 'lewa' was equal to 12 'quarentenæ,' that is 2,640 yards, or a mile and a half.[3] So far as Worcestershire, however, is concerned, we never find a higher figure than 3 'quarentenæ' below the 'lewa.' The inference certainly is very strong that this was because the 'lewa' consisted of only 4 'quarentenæ,' that is of half a mile. Such a modification of Mr. Eyton's conclusion[4] would reduce very greatly the amount of

---

[1] *English Village Community*, pp. 207–8, 211, 213.

[2] The woods at Warndon, Cadley, and Pirie (in St. Martin's, Worcester), Bredicot, Churchill, and Aston White Ladies were all 'in the forest' (fo. 173b).

[3] *Key to Domesday : Dorset*, pp. 25–28.   [4] It is also that of other antiquaries.

woodland in the country. On the other hand, it is possible, and even probable, that the woodland then, as in later times, was measured by a larger perch than that which was in common use ; but our knowledge of the measures then prevailing in different districts, and for different purposes, is too slight to enable us to speak with confidence on this point. In any case it will be obvious to intelligent students of the Survey that measurement in such terms as these could be only of a crude nature, and that we cannot accept it as more than a rough estimate.[1]

Several fisheries are mentioned, but their value was not great. Their proceeds, contrary to what might be expected, are always, when mentioned, eels, of which Martley annually supplied nearly three thousand. This number was quite exceptional, and it was more usual to find a mill liable for a small render of eels from the mill pool. There is a curious incidental allusion to the method of fishing, at the time, in the Severn in the story which the monks of Worcester tell of Ribbesford (near Bewdley). The villeins there had been bound, they said, to make for them hedges to capture fish.[2] This ancient practice is described by Mr. Seebohm, who aptly quotes a statute relating to the Severn and Wye fisheries : 'If any person shall make, erect, or set any bank, dam, *hedge*, stank, or net across the same.'[3] He observed that the Tidenham custumal binds the *geneat* (the later 'villein') to do his share of 'weir-building,' and mentions that 'this clumsy process of catching salmon is the ancient traditional method used in the Wye and Severn fisheries,' and was kept up tenaciously.[4]

All sources of revenue, however, were dwarfed in importance by the plough. The *Inquisitio Eliensis* contains what are usually taken to represent the instructions given to the Domesday Commissioners ;[5] and, although this cannot be asserted as a fact,[6] it is probably true in substance. In this passage the Commissioners are described as having inquired ' how many ploughs are in demesne, how many the men have, . . . and if more can be had (from the land) than is (now) had.'[7] The Worcestershire Survey does not tell us, as we are told in many counties, how many 'plough-lands' an estate contained ;[8] but it normally enters the number of ploughs in (the lord's) demesne, and then tells us how many were held by the various tenants. If more ploughs could be employed on the estate, the fact is mentioned, and the

---

[1] The question of forest measures is also dealt with in the introduction to the Domesday Survey in the *Victoria History of Northamptonshire*.

[2] 'Captatorias sepes piscium et alias venatorias instaurare debita lege debebant' (Heming's Cartulary, I. 256).

[3] 1 Geo. I. cap. 18, sec. 14.

[4] *English Village Community*, pp. 153–5.

[5] See Domesday Book (Ed. Record Commission), III. 497 ; Stubbs, *Select Charters* and *Const. Hist.* (1874), I. 385–6 ; Ramsay's *Foundations of England*, II. 129, and other works.

[6] See *Feudal England*, pp. 133–5.

[7] 'quot carruce in dominio, quot hominum, . . . et si potest plus haberi quam habeatur.'

[8] Except in two or three exceptional cases noted in the text.

amount of the arable land thus indicated. A sweeping entry on the fief of the bishop of Worcester tells us that 'In omnibus his Maneriis non possunt esse plus carucæ quam dictum est' (fo. 174).[1] But in the next column we read of Bockelton, a manor of the bishop of Hereford, that 'ibi possunt esse plus iiii carucæ.' There were several manors on the fief of Osbern Fitz Richard short of their complement of ploughs, Elmbridge, for instance, having only ten, though it ought to have had twenty (fo. 176b). At Hagley, a manor of William Fitz Ansculf, there were but six ploughs, eight short of the complement ; and at Churchill, another of his manors, though six ploughs could be employed, there was but one, which was 'in demesne' (fo. 177). One has to render *caruca* by plough, but its really important element was the team of eight oxen,[2] and the stocking of a manor consisted chiefly in providing oxen for its ploughs. A curious entry under Offenham (fo. 175b) informs us that there were there 'oxen for one plough' (*i.e.* a team of eight), 'but they drag stone to the church' ; that is, doubtless, the new buildings which had risen at Evesham under abbot Walter.

When we turn from the land to the men who dwelt on it, we are confronted by a hierarchy of classes bewildering enough in its variety. Indeed, it would be difficult in any county to find a greater variety. Working downwards, we have first the 'barons' or tenants-in-chief, and then their under-tenants,[3] with whom we must group the nameless 'milites,' who would hold of the 'barons' by knight-service. Next would come the class described vaguely as 'Francigenæ.' Beyond the fact that they were Frenchmen by birth, it is not easy to say of whom this class was composed. In Heming's Cartulary we read that the great abbot Æthelwig 'was dreaded even by the Frenchmen themselves,'[4] while the Ely document spoken of above (p. 272) describes the Domesday Survey as made on the oaths 'of the sheriff and of the barons and of their Frenchmen (*francigenarum*), and of the whole county, etc.' The word seems, indeed, to be a 'wide' one, for of the 26 'francigenæ' allotted by Ellis to Worcestershire two (at Snodsbury) are entered as 'francigenæ servientes' (fo. 174b). It is interesting, in connection with this entry, to note that Domesday, at Church Lench, enters one 'francigena' (fo. 175), and that the parallel entry in an Evesham cartulary styles him 'quidam serviens.'[5] It is probable that many of these 'francigenæ' were 'serjeants' of various kinds whose services were rewarded by land.

Of the 'Radchenistres' or 'Radmanni' something has been said

---

[1] Professor Maitland inadvertently states that this entry is found 'at the end of the account of the bishop of Worcester's triple hundred of Oswaldslaw' (*Domesday Book ana Beyond*, pp. 423-4). This is not so ; the entry covers several places outside that Hundred.

[2] Thus the Lippard entry (fo. 174) : '1 caruca et vi boves,' is equivalent to $1\frac{3}{4}$ plough (teams).

[3] These, as in the striking case of Urse, were themselves also, sometimes, tenants-in-chief elsewhere.

[4] 'et ab ipsis Francigenis timebatur' (I. 270).

[5] Cott. MS. Vesp. B. XXIV. fo. 6.

above (pp. 250–251), and it was there suggested that they were some-times here indistinguishable from the free tenants, who are usually termed 'liberi homines,' but in two instances, it should be observed, 'franci homines.'[1] From these there is a sharp drop to the village group and its officers. Ellis allowed but one 'bedellus' and seven 'prepositi' to Worcestershire; but these figures have to be doubled when we include the manors on fo. 180*b*.[2] For then the *bydel* and the *gerefa* of Old English days are found to have respectively, in all, five and eleven repre-sentatives.[3] The village smith, an important functionary, seems to be mentioned eight times, and the miller occasionally. Here, as elsewhere, the villeins (*villani*) were the backbone of the rural community. Ellis reckoned their number at 1,520, but I make it, adding those on fo. 180*b*, to be 1,666. In a somewhat inferior position to them were the class known as bordars (*bordarii*), whom I similarly make, by adding those omitted by Ellis, to have numbered 1,821, not 1,728.

The 'bovarii' are a class deserving of attention, for their occur-rence in Domesday seems to be restricted to a group of adjacent coun-ties:—Worcestershire, Herefordshire, Shropshire, Cheshire, and South Lancashire, the same district (with the exception of Gloucestershire) as that in which occur the 'Radchenistres' and 'Radmans.' On the Evesham Abbey manor of Ombersley we find it the duty of the 'bovarii' to have charge of the oxen, to plough, and to guard any thieves.[4] At Wickhamford, each of the four 'virge bovariorum' sent two men 'ad carucam.'[5] At Hampton (by Evesham), we learn definitely that each of the 'virge bovariorum' found 'two men for the lord's plough,' that is the plough on the lord's demesne.[6] At Blackwell (in Tredington), a manor held by the monks of Worcester, the 'bovarii' similarly held half virgates, and had charge of the Prior's ploughs, and of such prisoners as there were.[7] These 'bovarii' appear to have escaped the notice of Domes-day commentators,[8] but an entry in the Glastonbury Inquisition (1189) tells us that 'Peter the *bovarius* . . . has charge of the lord's oxen, and goes with (*ad*) the plough.'[9] 'Bovarii' also occur in a district even fur-ther from that in which we find them in Domesday; for the Peterborough

---

[1] At the end of Pershore Abbey's lands we read of 'unaquaque hida ubi francus homo manet' (fo. 175*b*); and at the end of those of Westminster Abbey we read of the 'placita francorum hominum' under the Confessor (fo. 175).

[2] See p. 239 above.

[3] For the *gerefa* and the *bydel*, see Andrews' *Old English Manor*, pp. 130–143.

[4] 'Quatuor sunt virge bovariorum. Isti custodiunt boves, et arant per v dies . . . Preter hoc isti debent custodire latrones si fuerint in curia' (Harl. MS. 3,763, fo. 78*d*).

[5] *Ibid.* fo. 72.

[6] 'Per totum annum virga debet invenire duos homines ad carucam domini et autump-no ii homines ad ebdomada et ad Wedhoc,' etc. (*Ibid.* fo. 79).

[7] 'sunt ibi iiij bovatæ terræ, scilicet duæ virgatæ, quarum tenentes tenebunt et fugabunt et custodient carrucas Prioris . . . Bovarii, si non custodient carrucas, et cotarii debent custodire prisones' (Hale, pp. 66*a*, 66*b*).

[8] They are not mentioned in the Indexes to Ellis' *Introduction to Domesday*, Maitland's *Domesday Book and Beyond*, or Seebohm's *English Village Community*.

[9] 'Petrus bovarius . . . custodit boves domini et vadit ad aratrum.'

Liber Niger (*temp.* Henry I.) has some entries on them. At Oundle there were six,[1] who were classed with the villeins ; and on three other manors[2] we find four, six, and eight 'bovarii' connected respectively with two, three, and four ploughs in the lord's demesne, and holding five, nine, and ten acres each on these manors respectively. The abbey's 'bovarii' are found even on its Lincolnshire estate.[3] Here then we have distinct evidence that this class existed in a part of England where Domesday ignores it, and, here again, we draw the inference that the silence of Domesday is no proof of actual non-existence, and that the system of its entries varied according to the district. But we have more than this. The Peterborough evidence distinctly proves that the 'bovarii' were connected with the ploughteams of the lord, each of them consisting of eight oxen, and that to each such team there belonged two 'bovarii.' Now, when we turn to Worcestershire in Domesday, we are able to trace a similar connection. At Ombersley, for instance, Evesham Abbey had five ploughs in the demesne, and there were ' 10 bovarii' ; at Church Lench its ploughs in the demesne were two, and there were four 'bovarii.'[4] But it is when we turn to the Evesham cartulary (Cott. MS. Vesp. B. XXIV.) that the evidence becomes overwhelming. In a 12th century list of its manors (fos. 49*d* and 53) we find in every case 2 'bovarii' to a plough. In the light of this evidence, it becomes highly probable that Domesday uses the terms 'bovarii' and 'servi' alternatively. The Evesham cartulary, for instance, enters under Badby, Northants, 5 ploughs and 10 'bovarii,' where Domesday gives us, in the demesne, ' 4 ploughs and 8 serfs.' Under Badsey, Worcestershire, the former document records 3 ploughs and 6 'bovarii,' while Domesday assigns to its demesne 2 ploughs, and adds that there are 4 'serfs.' There are several other instances in Worcestershire of 2 'bovarii' to the demesne plough.[5] We thus obtain fresh light on a class otherwise obscure and an explanation of its character. While on the subject, I would point out that, in Northamptonshire, there were 8 'bubulci' to the 4 demesne ploughs at Pytchley, and at Aldwincle 4 'bubulci' to the 2 demesne ploughs.[6] This appears to imply clearly the identity of 'bubulci' and 'bovarii,' although this ' is contrary to the usual interpretation.'[7]

[1] It should be added that on this manor there were three ploughs in the demesne.
[2] *Liber Niger*, pp. 162–3.
[3] *Ibid.* pp. 164–5.
[4] See, for both these instances, Domesday, fo. 175*b*.
[5] At 'Hortune' (fo. 177*b*) we read : 'In dominio sunt ii carucæ et iiii bovarii.' At Hadsor there were 4 'bovarii' and 2 demesne ploughs, and at 'Tichenapletreu' (in Hampton Lovett) the same ; at Hampton, 1 demesne plough and 2 'bovarii'; at Clent 1½ demesne ploughs and 3 'bovarii'; at Queenhill, 1 demesne plough and 2 'bovarii'; at Eldersfield 3 demesne ploughs and 6 'bovarii.'
[6] *Liber Niger*, pp. 162, 166.
[7] Dr. Andrews' *Old English Manor*, p. 218. Dr. Andrews, who had specially studied the work of the 'ox-herd,' identified him as the 'bubulcus,' and stated (in error) that this servant is not mentioned in the *Liber Niger*. He considered the duties of the *bovarius* to be distinct.

The 'bovarii' of Worcestershire, to resume, were connected with the plough teams on the lord's demesne, two 'bovarii' having charge of the team of eight oxen. I have rendered 'bovarii,' therefore, by 'oxmen,' forming the word by analogy from the 'horsemen' of the modern farm. They had, probably, small holdings of five to ten acres each (though possibly, in Worcestershire, half a virgate), and we may further gather, from the Peterborough evidence, that some were still of servile status,[1] though others were free and paid 'chevage.'[2] The same evidence suggests that it may have been their wives' duty to winnow the lords' corn.

On the border-land of servitude and freedom was 'the small but interesting class of *buri, burs,* or *coliberti*.'[3] Though Worcestershire, apparently, had only nine of them, the Powick entry concerning them is important as containing the word 'coliberti' interlined above 'buri,' which implies the identity of the two. One should perhaps place next the *cotmanni* and *cotarii* of the Survey, for the typical Domesday cotter, though he held some five acres, appears to have had no concern with the all-important plough-oxen.[4] Professor Maitland has drawn attention to the fact that the Worcester Register distinguishes between the *cotmanni* and *cotarii*, so that the Domesday terms must be slightly different in meaning.[5]

It has been argued, with some elaboration, that the number of serfs and bondwomen ('ancillæ') recorded by Domesday in Worcestershire was due to the proximity of the county to Wales, and that the members of this servile class, especially its female members, had been actually acquired by the monks of Worcester and other holders of land within the shire in the course of 'forays against the Welsh.'[6] But the problems raised by the existence of this servile population require for their solution a wider outlook than a single county can afford. They have to be studied in the light of the valuable Domesday maps compiled for Mr. Seebohm's work[7] from the calculations of Ellis, who gave, in his *Introduction to Domesday*, the number respectively of 'servi' and 'ancillæ' for every county in which they occur. Mr. Seebohm observes that, as shown by his map, the serfs 'were most numerous towards the south-west of England, less and less numerous as the Danish districts were approached, and absent altogether from Yorkshire, Lincolnshire, and bordering districts.'[8] The two best studies on the subject are those

---

[1] Compare the 10th century dialogue of Ælfric : 'Oh, my lord, hard do I work. I go out at daybreak driving the oxen to field, and I yoke them to the plough . . . every day must I plough a full acre or more. . . . Verily then I do more. I must fill the bin of the oxen with hay, and water them, and carry out the dung . . . hard work it is, because I am not free' (Sir E. M. Thompson's Translation).

[2] 'bovarii liberi' are mentioned in Herefordshire (fo. 183*b*).

[3] Maitland's *Domesday Book and Beyond*, pp. 36–8, where the character of this class is discussed.

[4] See, for the cotters, Andrews' *Old English Manor*, pp. 170–5.

[5] *Domesday Book and Beyond*, p. 40. [6] *Architectural Societies' Reports*, XXII. 102–105.

[7] *The English Village Community* (1883). [8] *Ibid.* p. 89.

of Professor Maitland in his *Domesday Book and Beyond*,[1] and of Dr. Andrews in *The Old English Manor*.[2] Both these writers used, of necessity, Mr. Seebohm s maps,[3] but neither they nor Mr. Seebohm himself have drawn attention to the singular constancy, in a large group of counties, of the ratio borne by the serfs to the rest of the population. This ratio, according to the map, was in Worcestershire, Buckinghamshire, Wiltshire, and Gloucestershire 15 per cent., in Hants and Dorset 16 per cent., in Shropshire 17 and in Devon 18 per cent., while in Oxfordshire it was 14 and in Warwickshire and Herefordshire 13 per cent. Here, however, it may be well to observe that the whole of these calculations rest on the figures given by Ellis, and these are affected by a misapprehension from which Ellis suffered. He altogether failed, I find, to understand the Domesday formula ' inter servos et ancillas,' which only meant that the numbers of the class were given jointly, instead of separately. Ellis imagined that, in these cases, no numbers at all were given,[4] and he omitted them accordingly. In Worcestershire this formula occurs on two manors of the church of Worcester which follow one another in the Survey (fo. 174), Wolverley and Alvechurch, on which there were 13 serfs and bondwomen. It is found again at Rushock (fo. 177*b*) and Chaddesley Corbett (fo. 178), which had twelve more between them. But to these we must add the serfs and bondwomen on the Worcestershire manors entered on fo. 180*b*.[5] As these amounted to no fewer than 45; we have to increase the servile population allotted by Ellis to the county by 70 in all, making it 848 instead of 778. It would be only by a careful examination of the whole Survey, county by county, that the effect of his misapprehension on the figures he gives could be determined ; but in Herefordshire it must have excluded, on the lordship of Leominster alone, the 82 ' inter servos et ancillas ' who were there on the eve of the Conquest. The same formula occurs in several cases in Gloucestershire, and as at Tewkesbury alone there were 50 ' inter servos et ancillas,' Ellis' calculations, for that county, must be gravely affected.

Breadth of view, however, is essential in Domesday study, and it is not probable that the necessary correction would materially affect the distribution of the servile population in the country. If, therefore, the proportion of serfs was about the same in Worcestershire as it was in Buckinghamshire and Hampshire, it can scarcely be contended that their numbers in the first of these counties were due to its proximity to the Welsh border. It seems probable that the servile population was recruited from several distinct sources. Capture in warfare was but one ; crime reduced some to serfage, and others voluntarily entered that state,

---

[1] pp. 26–36. Reference may also be made to the chapter on 'The Unfree' in *The History of English Law* by Professors Maitland and Sir F. Pollock ; but this applies mainly to the servitude of a later period.
[2] Macmillan & Co. (1892), pp. 181–201.
[3] *Domesday Book and Beyond*, p. 23 ; *The Old English Manor*, pp. 182–3.
[4] *Introduction to Domesday*, II. 454 (note 4), 500 (note 1).
[5] See p. 239 above.

driven by poverty to take the step. Birth, however, was probably its cause in most cases, for the servile status of the serf's children was rigidly enforced. The recognised existence, at Bristol, of a slave mart was only typical of a traffic that must have prevailed in other places also ; at Lewes, which, it may be pointed out, must then have been a port, the toll on the sale of a man was fourpence. Men thus sold as slaves may obviously have come from anywhere, and there was nothing to prevent slaves from Bristol being brought up the Severn to Worcester. We are told of the Domesday ' servus ' that ' earlier and later documents oblige us to think of him as a slave, one who in the main has no legal rights ; he is the *theów* of the Anglo-Saxon dooms.'[1] The density of the servile population in Devon and Cornwall supports the obvious presumption that the conquered Britons supplied, throughout the West of England, the bulk of the original serfs ; and, in his valuable chapter on the subject, Dr. Andrews pointed out that the earliest gloss for *ancilla* ' is *wyln*, and it is also the most frequent, thus showing the use to which the Welsh women were put who were captured in the conquest.'[2] But this reduction of the conquered race, in the West of England, to slavery needs, of course, to be carefully distinguished from the subsequent acquisition of serfs by purchase or capture in war. Above all is caution needed in dealing with the bondwomen ('ancillæ') of Domesday, of whom Worcestershire is said to contain the largest number. Mr. Eyton, a great Domesday student, argues, possibly with good reason, that the absence of 'ancillæ,' on the pages of the Survey, is no evidence of their non-existence :

> The *Ancilla*, or female serf, is never spoken of in the Somerset Survey, only once in the Dorset Survey, only once in the Survey of Staffordshire. What follows ? Surely . . . that in certain counties the serf-wife was hardly ever reckoned among the agricultural staff of an estate.[3]

It must be remembered that the instructions given, so far as we know them, to the Domesday commissioners[4] directed a return of the ' servi,' but not of the ' ancillæ.' There may therefore have been uncertainty as to whether they ought to be entered or not, and a consequent diversity in practice. Professor Maitland even hints that the serfs themselves may in some districts have been omitted rather than non-existent,[5] while in others their numbers may be swollen by embracing a wider class.[6]

---

[1] Maitland's *Domesday Book and Beyond*, p. 27.
[2] *The Old English Manor*, p. 198.
[3] *Staffordshire Domesday*, p. 6.
[4] See p. 272 above.
[5] *Domesday Book and Beyond*, pp. 23-4.
[6] 'Nor can we be sure that the enumeration of the *servi* is always governed by one consistent principle. In the shires of Gloucester, Hereford, and Worcester we read of numerous *ancillæ*—in Worcestershire of 677 *servi* and 101 *ancillæ*—and this may make us think that in this district all the able-bodied serfs are enumerated, whether or no they have cottages to themselves' (*Ibid.* p. 34). The Professor's figures, as explained above, are those given in error by Ellis.

THE DOMESDAY SURVEY

Apart from the main Domesday classes at which we have glanced above, we have a miscellaneous group comprising the swineherds (fo. 180*b*), with the 'rustici porcarii' at Oldberrow, the cowherd at Bushley, the foresters, of whom we have already heard, and the dairymaid (*daia*), who is found at Bushley and Queenhill. The very irregular mention of such classes as these suggests the need for caution in accepting the number given.[1] Indeed the omissions must be so serious that it would be a futile task to estimate the population of the county on the basis of the Domesday figures. Droitwich, probably, had many salt-workers, though only three or four are mentioned, and the eight burgesses, which is all that Ellis allows to Worcester, is a total obviously absurd. The swine, again, must have needed herds in more than the two or three places where we find them mentioned, and the 'newly-planted vineyard' at Hampton by Evesham must have had its vineyard man.[2]

On agricultural services, the information in Domesday requires to be largely supplemented by the surveys of the monks of Worcester's manors in Archdeacon Hale's *Registrum*, and those of the Evesham manors in the cartularies of that abbey. There is an interesting entry in Domesday (fo. 176*b*) of burgesses of Droitwich owing reaping service at Wichbold ; and although on the Westminster Abbey manors there is mention of some substantial landholders being required to mow for a day yearly in the meadows of their lord, it must be remembered that the labour was due from the land, not from its holder himself. Even villeins could find substitutes, for at Blackwell, in Tredington, the villeins as a body could send six men to mow, at Worcester, the meadow of their lord the Prior.[3]

In discussing the affairs of the local monasteries and their disputes with the new settlers and with one another, we have seen something of the questions raised concerning the title to land. Worcestershire affords numerous illustrations of the risk incurred by leasing church lands to laymen, as was usual, for three lives. Of this practice bishop Oswald had set a dangerous example, and we gather from Heming's Cartulary that another bishop, Brihtheah, had done his best to follow it. It is to this practice that we owe the curious record of a nuncupative will found in the Worcestershire Domesday (fo. 177), the predecessor in possession of William Fitz Ansculf being there alleged to have thus obtained a church manor, and to have exhorted his friends, on his death-bed, to see that the church regained it after his widow's death. Another curious story, which may have escaped notice, is that which accounts

---

[1] The surveys, for instance, of Hanley Castle, on fos. 163*b*, 180*b*, do not tally in details ; and the '6 swineherds' of the latter entry are wholly omitted in the former. The 12th century survey also of the Evesham manors in Cott. MS. Vesp. B. XXIV., strongly suggests the omission of many villagers in Domesday.

[2] The population also must have been increased by the inmates and dependants of the monasteries. A good idea of the officers and servants in the pay of a monastery may be formed from a list of those of the monks of Worcester in Hale's *Registrum* (pp. 119–20).

[3] Hale, p. 65*b*.

for Bushley, though within the Hundred of Oswaldslow, being in the King's hands at the time of the Domesday Survey. The church of Worcester gives its version on fo. 173, and that of the Crown is found on fo. 180*b*. It was alleged on behalf of the latter that the great Tewkesbury thegn, Brihtric son of Ælfgar, had 'bought it of Lyfing bishop of Worcester for three marcs of gold (£18), together with a house in the city of Worcester paying a marc of silver (13*s*. 4*d*.) yearly, . . . all which he so bought and held undisturbed that he did no service for it to any man.'[1] The church of Worcester, on the other hand, alleged that Brihtric used to pay an annual 'ferm' to the Bishop. It would certainly appear that Lyfing, 'the patriot bishop of Worcester,'[2] had no right to alienate the land in perpetuity ; but the fact that he had to recover his see, in 1041, 'at the price, we are told, of money paid to the King'[3] (to be held 'in plurality'), suggests that he may have needed money. The Crown, in any case, retained the manor, as its subsequent history proves.

The only point remaining to be dealt with is the important entry at the very end of the survey of the county stating that the lands at Feckenham and Holloway 'scriptæ sunt in brevi de Hereford,' and that those at Martley and Suckley, although in Dodingtree Hundred for purposes of jurisdiction and taxation, render their ferm at Hereford, 'et sunt scriptæ in breve regis.' The 'breve' here spoken of needs to be carefully distinguished from the ordinary King's writ ('breve regis') placing a man in possession. It was explained by me in *Feudal England* (pp. 135-6) that 'though the word *Breve* in Domesday Book normally means the King's writ, there are passages which seem to have been overlooked, and in which it bears another and very suggestive meaning.' Foremost among these is the passage above, in which the word is used 'of a return, not of a writ.' A similar usage is found in Huntingdonshire (fo. 203), where we read of geld being paid 'secundum hidas in brevi scriptas.' The best parallel, however, is in Cambridgeshire, where we read, 'In Saham habet rex W. vi hidas et xl acras in breve suo' (fo. 189*b*), while a parallel record states, under Kingston, that the King has there $1\frac{3}{4}$ hides 'in brevi suo.'[4] The above Worcestershire passage refers us to the Domesday return of the manor of Hereford, then in the King's hands, in which we accordingly find the surveys of these Worcestershire lands. Their addition to the Worcestershire text, as in the translation below, renders the Domesday Survey of the shire complete.

---

[1] 'ut inde non serviret cuiquam homini.' Compare Brihtwine's tenure of Hadsor, 'nulli inde aliquid servitium nisi regi faciens' (Heming, I. 263).

[2] So styled by Mr. Freeman (*Norm. Conq.*, II. 81), because he was a friend of Godwine.

[3] *Ibid.* I. 509.

[4] *Inquisitio comitatus Cantabrigiensis*, p. 85.

NOTE

The reader should bear in mind throughout that the date of the Domesday Survey is 1086 ; that King Edward, to whose time it refers as 'T.R.E.', died January 5, 1066 ; that the 'hide' was the unit of assessment on which the (Dane)geld was paid, and that the 'virgate' was its quarter. The essential portion of the plough ('caruca') was its team of oxen, eight in number. The 'demesne' was the lord's portion of the manor, the peasantry holding the rest of it under him ; and a 'berewick' was an outlying estate dependent on the chief manor. The woodland measures and the names of the agricultural classes are discussed in the Introduction.

[WIRECESTRESCIRE]

fo. 172.

IN THE CITY OF WORCESTER (*Wirecestre*), king Edward used to have this customary due (*consuetudinem*). When the coinage (*moneta*) was changed, each moneyer gave twenty shillings at London on receiving the dies of the money. When the county paid geld, the city was reckoned at (*se adquietabat pro*) 15 hides. From the said city the King himself used to have ten pounds and earl Eadwine eight pounds. The King took no other due there except the charge (*censum*) on the houses according to the liability of each.

King William has now in demesne both the King's share and the Earl's share. For this the sheriff renders twenty-three pounds and five shillings by weight, for the city ; and for the demesne manors of the King he renders a hundred and twenty-three pounds and four shillings by weight. For the county he renders seventeen pounds by weight ; and he further renders ten pounds of pennies, twenty to the ounce, or a Norway (*Norresc*) hawk ; and to the Queen also a hundred shillings by tale ; and twenty shillings, of twenty (pence) to the ounce, for a sumpter horse. These seventeen pounds by weight and sixteen pounds by tale are for the pleas of the county (court) and for the Hundreds, and if he does not receive (so much) from that source (*inde*), he pays it out of his own (means). In the county there are twelve Hundreds ; seven of these are so exempt (*quieti*), the shire (court) says, that the sheriff has no rights (*nichil*) in them, and therefore, as (he) says, he loses much on the ferm (*in firma*).

In this county, if any one should have wittingly broken the peace given by the King with his (own) hand, he is adjudged an outlaw (*utlaghe*) ; but if any one should have wittingly broken the King's peace given by the sheriff, he shall pay a fine of (*emendabit*) a hundred shillings. He who shall have committed 'forsteal' ('forestellum')[1] shall pay a fine of a hundred shillings ; he who shall have committed 'hámfare' (*heinfaram*) a hundred shillings ; (for him) who shall have committed rape, let there be no amend but corporal punishment (*non sit emendatio alia nisi de corpore justicia*).[2] These forfeitures belong to the

---

[1] 'Forsteal' was waylaying or (attack from) ambush (with malice prepense) ; 'hámfare' (like 'hamsócn') was attack on a man's house. These, like the breach of the peace which precedes them, were the special pleas of the Crown usually reserved. (*History of English Law* [1895], II. 451–56, 466, 491.)

[2] Compare *Ibid.* II. 453, 488–90. This is almost the only mention of the above offence in *Domesday Book*, possibly because where it could not be atoned for by a fine, it did not contribute to the profits of jurisdiction.

King in this county except (in) the land of (the abbey of) St. Peter of Westminster, to which king Edward gave all his rights there, says the county (court).

When the King marches against the enemy, should any one summoned by his edict remain (behind), if he is a man so free that he has his soke and sake, and can go where he will with his land,[1] he is at (*in*) the King's mercy with (*de*) all his land ; but if the free man of another (man who is his) lord should remain (behind), and his lord should bring another man in his place, then he shall pay for his offence (*emendabit*) forty shillings to his lord, as having been summoned ;[2] but if no one at all (*ex toto*) goes in his place, he himself shall give forty shillings to his lord, and his lord shall pay for his offence (*emendabit*) as many shillings to the King.

[1] *i.e.* commend himself to whom he will.

[2] The words 'domino suo qui vocatus fuit emendabit' appear to leave doubtful the very important point whether the summons was addressed to the lord or to his man. Professor Maitland assumes the former, which is probably the right view (*Domesday Book and Beyond*, p. 159). With this definition of free tenure should be compared p. 267, note 2, above.

HERE ARE ENTERED
THE HOLDERS OF LAND
IN WIRECESTRE SCIRE

THE KING'S LAND

King W[illiam] holds in demesne BRE-MESGRAVE [Bromsgrove] with 18 berewicks :—Museleie [Moseley], Nortune [Kingsnorton], Lindeorde [Linthurst], Warthuil [Withall ?], Witeurde [Whitford], Hundesfeld [Houndsfield], Thessale [Tessall farm], Weredeshale   Lea [Lea end ?], Comble [Cobley ?], Bericote [Burcot], Asseberga [   ], Tothehel [Tutnall Cross], Tuneslega [   ], Focheberie [Fochbury], Suruehel [Surehole farm], Vdecote [Woodcote], Timbrehangre [Timberhanger].[2]

Between (them) all, together with the manor (itself), there are 30 hides. Earl E(a)dwine held this manor T.R.E.

In demesne there are now 2 ploughs, and (there are) 20 villeins and the reeve (*prepositus*) and the beadle with the priest and 92 bordars, having between (them) all 77 ploughs.

---

[1] 'Wrehantone.'

[2] There is, admittedly, much difficulty in identifying some of the 'berewicks' (*i.e.* outlying estates) entered above as dependent on Bromsgrove. For some of the identifications in the text I am alone responsible. 'Lindeorde' I make to be Linthurst, 2 miles north-east of Bromsgrove ; 'Thessale' is clearly Tessall (farm) between Chadwick and King's Norton ; and 'Hundesfelde' can be identified as in King's Norton by the Hundred Rolls (ii. 283). We also have a reference in Habington's *Survey* (II. 220) to 'Haunckesfield's Graunge' as 'the syte of the mannor of Hownesfeild' in 36 Hen. VIII., and the *Monasticon* shows us Bordesley Abbey as holding land at 'Houndefeld' when dissolved. Among the five 'chapels' dependent on Bromsgrove were Moseley and Withall, which, therefore, we must recognise in 'Museleie' and 'Warthuil.' Habingdon (ii. 218) wrote of 'Moseley aunciently called Mounsley' in King's Norton, but Moundsley Hall in King's Norton is quite distinct from Moseley. 'Suruehel' appears to me to be Surehole (farm) close to Hall Green. Cobley (Hill) is two miles east of Burcot 'Tutnall and Cobley' are now combined.

There are 9 serfs and 1 bondwoman (*ancilla*), and 3 mills worth (*de*) 13 shillings and 4 pence. The wood(land) is 7 leagues (*lewæ*) long and 4 leagues broad, and 4 eyries (*æiræ*) of hawks are there. To this manor belong 13 saltpans (*salinæ*) in (Droit)wich and 3 salt-workers who render, from these saltpans, 300 'mits' (*mittas*) [1] of salt, for (making) which they used to be given 300 cartloads of wood by the keepers of the wood(land) T.R.E. There are 6 leaden vats (*plumbi*).

To this manor (there) belonged, T.R.E., SUCHELEI [Suckley], a manor of 5 hides, but earl William (of Hereford) took (it) thence and put (it) in the ferm of Hereford.[2]

In all it used to pay, T.R.E., a ferm of 18 pounds. Urse the sheriff paid 24 pounds by weight (*ad peis*) so long as (*dum*) he had the wood.[3]

To this manor (there) belonged and belong GRASTONE [4] [Grafton manor], where are 3½ hides, and COCHESEI [Cooksey] where are 2½ hides, and WILLINGEWIC [Willingwick] where are 2 hides and 3 virgates, and CELDVIC [Chadwick] where are 3 hides; in all 12 hides less 1 virgate.[5]

These lands were held by 5 thegns (*teini*) of earl E(a)dwine, Erniet, Alwin', Brictredus, Frane, Alwold, who could not withdraw (*recedere*) from the lord of the manor.[6] They are now held of Urse the sheriff by 4 knights, (the) 3½ hides by Roger, the 2½ hides by William, the 2 hides and 3 virgates by Walter, (and) the 3 hides by Alvred.

In these lands there are in demesne 5½ ploughs, and (there are) 1 'radchenistre' [7] and 29 bordars who have 11½ ploughs. There are 2 serfs and 6 oxmen (*bovarii*),[8] and there can be (employed) 1 plough more. In Willingewic and Celdwic there are 4 leagues (*lewedes*) of wood, but the King has put (them) in (his) forest. In Droit(wich) there is 1

saltpan worth (*de*) 10 shillings. In all it was worth 6 pounds and 13 shillings T.R.E.; now 100 shillings in all.

Of the land of this manor William Fitz Ansculf holds 3 virgates in Willingewic, and Baldwin (holds) of him.[9] Wulfwine (*Ulwinus*) a thegn of earl E(a)dwine held (it). There is 1 villein with half a plough, and a plough and a half more could be (employed) there. It was worth 5 shillings; now 2 shillings.

King William holds in demesne CHIDE-MINSTRE [Kidderminster] with 16 berewicks: — Wenuerton [Wannerton], Trinpelei [Trimpley], Worcote [Hurcote], Frenesse [Franche], and another Frenesse [Franche], Bristitune [   ], Harburgelei [Habberley], Fastochesfelde [   ], Gurberhale [Wribbenhall?], Ribeford [Ribbesford], and another Ribeford [Ribbesford], Sudtone [Sutton], Aldintone [Oldington], Mettune [Mitton], Teulesberge [   ], Sudwale [   ]. In these lands, together with the manor, there are 20 hides. The whole of this manor was waste.

In (the) demesne is 1 plough, and (there are) 20 villeins and 30 bordars with 18 ploughs, and 20 ploughs more could be (employed) there. There are 2 serfs and 4 bondwomen (*ancillæ*) and 2 mills worth (*de*) 16 shillings, and 2 saltpans worth (*de*) 30 shillings, and a fishery worth (*de*) 100 pence. There is woodland extending to (*de*) 4 leagues (*lewis*). In this manor the reeve holds the land of one 'Radchen[istre']and has there 1 plough and 1 mill worth (*de*) 5 ounces (of silver). To this manor belong a house in (Droit)wich and another in Wirecestre [Worcester] paying 10 pence.

The whole manor used to pay, T.R.E., a ferm of 14 pounds; it now pays 10 pounds and 4 shillings by weight (*ad peis*). The king has put the wood(land) of this manor in (his) forest.

Of the land of this manor William holds 1 hide and the land of one 'Radchenistre,' and has there 1 villein and 8 bordars who have 4½ ploughs. It is worth 11 shillings.

Of the same land Aiulf' holds one virgate. There (are) 1 plough and 2 serfs. It is worth 2 shillings.

In WICH [Droitwich] king Edward had 11 houses, and in 5 brinepits (*puteis*) king Edward used to have his share. In one brine-pit—Upewic [10]—(there are) 54 saltpans

---

[1] See Introduction.

[2] That is to say, among those manors which paid their ferm in a lump sum at Hereford. Suckley, which is on the Herefordshire border, is surveyed accordingly on fo. 180*b*, as will be seen below (see p. 323).

[3] *i.e.* for the saltworks.

[4] The chapels of Grafton and Chadwick were dependent on Bromsgrove.

[5] This, it will be seen, implies the regular Domesday equation : 1 hide = 4 virgates.

[6] That is, could not 'commend' themselves to another lord.

[7] See Introduction.

[8] *Ibid.*

[9] Compare p. 316 below.   [10] Interlined.

and 2 'hocci' (which) pay 6 shillings and 8 pence. In another brine-pit, Helperic, (there are) 17 saltpans. In a third ('iii') brine-pit, MIDELWIC, (there are) 12 saltpans and two-thirds of a 'hoccus' (which) pay 6 shillings and 8 pence. In 5 other brine-pits there are 15 saltpans.[1]

From all these king Edward used to have a ferm (*de firma*) of 52 pounds.

fo. 172b.

In these brine-pits earl E(a)dwine used to have 51½ saltpans (*salinam*), and from the 'Hocci' he used to have 6 shillings and 8 pence. All this used to pay a ferm (*de firma*) of 24 pounds. Now king William has in demesne both what king Edward and what earl E(a)dwine used to have. The sheriff (has) paid thence 65 pounds by weight (*ad peis*) and 2 'mits' (*mittas*) of salt while he has had (the) wood.[2] For without the wood, he says, he could not possibly pay that (amount).

For (*de*) CHENEFARE [Kinver] he pays 100 shillings of twenty (pence) to the ounce. This land is in Stadfordscire, so also is SUINESFORDE [King's Swinford]. For (*de*) this manor and two others which are in Wirecestrescire,—that is Terdesberie [Tardebigg] of 9 hides and Clent of 9 hides,—for these 3 manors the sheriff pays 15 pounds of pennies at (*de*) 20 to the ounce.[3]

IN CAME HUNDRET

King William holds TERDEBERIE [Tardebigg]. King Edward held (it). There are 9 hides. In (the) demesne is 1 plough and another can be employed (*fieri*). There are

2 villeins and 28 bordars with 12 ploughs. In (Droit)wich[4] are 7 saltpans and 2 lead vats (*plumbi*), and they pay 20 shillings and 100 'mits' (mittas) of salt.

The sheriff of Stadfordscire receives, and pays in SUINESFORD [King's Swinford], the ferm of this manor, that is 11 pounds of pennies (at) 20 to the ounce.

IN CLENT HUNDRET

King William holds CLENT [Clent]. King Edward held (it). There are 9 hides. In (the) demesne is a plough and a half and there are 12 villeins and 3 bordars with 9½ ploughs. There are 3 oxmen (*bovarii*), and of wood-(land there are) 2 leagues (*lew*').

The ferm of this manor, 4 pounds, is paid in SUINESFORD [King's Swinford] in Stadfordscire.

In (Droit)wich is half a hide which belongs to the (King's) hall at (*de*) Gloucester.[5]

THE LAND OF THE CHURCH OF WIRECESTRE

II. THE CHURCH OF ST. MARY OF WIRECESTRE [Worcester] has one HUNDRET, called OSWALDESLAW, in which are (*jacent*) 300 hides.[6] In these (*de quibus*) the Bishop of that church has, by ancient (*antiquorum temporum*) custom, all revenue from jurisdiction (*socharum*) and all customary dues there belonging for (his) demesne support (*dominicum victum*) and the King's service and his own, so that no sheriff[7] can have any claim there, either in any plea or in any other matter (*causa*). The whole county (court) testifies to this. These said 300 hides were of the actual (*ipso*) demesne of the church, and if any portion of them was leased (*prestitum*) to any man,[8] for service to be done for it to the Bishop, he who held that land on lease could not retain for himself any customary due from it whatsoever except by permission of (*per*) the Bishop; nor could he retain the land beyond (*nisi usque ad*) the

---

[1] These five brine-pits in three localities can be traced four centuries later, for Habington says in his *Survey* (II. 296) that under Hen. VII. there were 'fyve salt wells springinge in three severall places, one named Upwich, the other Middelwich, the last Neather Wich.' The 'five other brine-pits' of Domesday are somewhat obscure.

[2] For the saltworks.

[3] The entries following show that this sum was made up of 11 pounds from Tardebigg and 4 pounds from Clent. Thus Domesday contradicts itself when it states that the 15 pounds were the proceeds of 'three' manors, of which 'Swinford' was one. From this it follows that the rent of 'Swinford' must be sought elsewhere, namely on fo. 246, where it is seen to be King's Swinford. Old Swinford (Worc.) will be found below on the fief of William Fitz Ansculf.

[4] *i.e.* belonging to this manor.

[5] A blank space follows here in the MS.

[6] In Heming's Cartulary (pp. 287–8) this return of the Bishop's privileges in Oswaldslow is specially entered with the heading, 'Indiculum libertatis de Oswales Lawes Hundred,' and with a few slight additions noted below.

[7] 'Or officer demanding service for the King' (*exactor regalis servitii*) is added here in Heming's Cartulary.

[8] Heming's Cartulary has here : 'howsoever, or to whomsoever, they were leased.'

completion of the term agreed upon between them, or betake himself anywhere [1] with that land.[2]

In this Hundred the Bishop of that church holds CHEMESEGE [Kempsey]. There are 24 hides that (pay) geld. Of these hides 5 hides are waste. In (the) demesne are 2 ploughs and (there are) 15 villeins and 27 bordars with 16 ploughs. There are a priest and 4 serfs and 2 bondwomen and 40 acres of meadow. The wood(land) is a league (*lewa*) long and half a league wide. In (the) demesne are 13 hides. It was worth 16 pounds T.R.E.; now 8 pounds.

Of this manor Urse the sheriff holds 3 berewicks of 7 hides, MUCENHIL [Muckenhill],[3] STOLTUN [Stoulton], ULFRINTUN [Wolverton]. There are 7 ploughs and 7 villeins and 7 bordars and 7 serfs and 16 acres of meadow. For these three estates (*terris*) rent (*firma*) was rendered T.R.E., for they were always assigned to (*de*) the support (of the monks). They are worth 100 shillings.

Of this same manor Roger de Laci holds 2 hides at ULFRINTUN [Wolverton] and Aiulf (holds them) of him. They were in demesne T.R.E., and Alric' was still holding them in the time of king William and was rendering thence all the customary rent (*consuetudines firmæ*) that his predecessors used to render except the peasants' labour (*rustico opere*) as it could be obtained (*deprecari*) from the reeve. There are 2 ploughs with 1 villein and (there are) 2 serfs and a mill worth (*de*) 40 pence. It was worth 50 shillings T.R.E.; now 40 shillings.

Of the same manor Walter Ponther (holds) 2 hides at WIDINTUN [Whittington]. They were in demesne T.R.E., (and) Ailric held them in the same manner (*ratione*) as the above hides.[4] In (the) demesne are 2 ploughs and 4 serfs, and (there are) 3 villeins and 7 bordars with 4 ploughs and a fishery worth (*de*) 4 shillings and 12 acres. The wood(land) is 1 league (*lewa*) long and half (a league) wide. It was worth 30 shillings T.R.E.; now 40 shillings.[5]

In the same hundred the said Bishop holds WICHE [Wyke episcopi].[6] There are 15 hides that (pay) geld. In (the) demesne are 4 hides less a virgate, and 4 ploughs are there; and (there are) 12 villeins and 12 bordars with 12 ploughs, and 2 mills worth (*de*) 12 shillings and 2 fisheries worth 6 shillings and 8 pence and 60 acres of meadow. The wood(land) is 2 leagues (*lewæ*) long and 1 league wide. T.R.E., as now, it was worth 8 pounds.

Of this manor Urse the sheriff holds 5 hides at HOLTE [Holt]. Ailric' held them in the above manner.[7] In (the) demesne are 2 ploughs, and (there are) 12 villeins and 24 bordars with 10 ploughs and a fishery worth (*de*) 5 shillings and, in (Droit)wich 1 saltpan worth 13 pence, and (there are) 12 acres of meadow. The wood(land) is half a league (*lewa*) long and the same in width. There is a hay (*haie*)[8] there.

The said Urse holds one hide at WITLEGE [Witley], and Walter (holds it) of him. In (the) demesne is one plough, and (there is) a priest and 2 bordars with 1 plough. The wood(land) is 3 furlongs (*quar'*) in length and 2 in width. Arnwine the priest[9] held (it and) rendered to the church all the customary rent (*consuetudines firmæ*) and one 'sestier' (*sextarium*) of honey. It is and was worth 10 shillings.

The same Urse holds 1 hide at CHECINWICHE [Kenswick][10] and Walter (holds it) of him. In (the) demesne are 2 ploughs and (there are) 6 bordars and 4 serfs. Wulf-

---

'Ailric' or 'Alric' of the above entries), was a brother of bishop Brihtheah ('Brihtegus'), from Berkshire, who obtained from the Bishop 'Wlfrintun' and 'Hwitintun,' together with Himbleton and Spetchley (see below), but was deprived of them in his lifetime by earl William of Hereford (Heming's Cartulary, p. 266). This is to some extent confirmed by the Domesday statement that Æthelric was still holding them after the Conqueror's accession.

[6] In St. John's, Worcester.

[7] *i.e.* as at Wolverton and Whittington.

[8] A hedge surrounding an enclosure into which animals were driven for capture.

[9] The monks of Worcester stated that this man ('Earnwius') was the priest of the famous Eadric the Wild, at whose request Witley had been given him by Ealdred, then bishop, and Wulfstan, then prior (Heming's Cartulary, I. 256.

[10] A constablewick in Wichenford (Nash).

---

[1] *i.e.* commend himself to another lord.

[2] Heming's Cartulary here adds: 'to retain it by usurping an hereditary right, or claim it as his fee (*feudam*) except in accordance with the Bishop's wish and in accordance with their agreement.'

[3] Now Mucknell Farm.

[4] *i.e.* at Wolverton.

[5] The monks' story was, that Æthelric (the

wine ('Ulwinus') held (it and) rendered all the customary payment to the reeve (in charge) of the 'ferm.' The wood(land) is half a league (*lewa*) long and half (a league) in width. It was worth 20 shillings T.R.E.; now 15 shillings.

The same Urse holds 1 hide at CLOPTUNE [   ]. In (the) demesne is 1 plough and (there are) 1 bordar and 6 acres of meadow. Brictmar held (it and) rendered all that the abovesaid (tenants) did.[1] It was worth 20 shillings T.R.E.; now 15 shillings.

The same Urse holds 3 virgates at LAURE [Lawern]. He has there in demesne 1 plough and 2 bordars. Sawine held it (as) of the Bishop's demesne. There are 6 acres of meadow. It was and is worth 7 shillings. There also Urse (holds) 1 virgate of the Bishop's demesne; (it is) worth 6 shillings.

The same Urse holds 1 hide at GREMANHIL [Grimley], and Godfrey (holds it) of him. There 2 bordars have 1 plough. Eddid held (it and) rendered what the abovesaid tenants rendered. It was and is worth 6 shillings.

Of the same manor Robert the Despencer (*dispensator*) holds half a hide at LAURE [Lawern], where he has 1 plough with 1 bordar and a mill worth (*de*) 5 shillings and 6 acres of meadow and 12 oaks. Keneward held (it) and performed such service as (*deserviebat sicut*) the Bishop willed.[2] It was and is worth 20 shillings.

Of the same manor Osbern Fitz Richard holds 1 hide at CODRIE [Cotheridge], where he has 1 plough in (the) demesne; and (there

are) 6 villeins and 4 bordars with 4 ploughs, and a mill worth (*de*) 5 shillings. There are 12 acres of meadow and 3 'quarentines' of wood(land). Richard[3] held it by such service (*ad servitium*) as the Bishop willed.

In the same Hundred the same Bishop holds FLEDEBIRIE [Fladbury]. There are 40 hides that (pay) geld. In demesne are 7 hides, where are 9 ploughs, and (there are) a priest, who has half a hide, and 23 villeins and 17 bordars with 19 ploughs. There are 16 serfs and 3 bondwomen, and a mill worth (*de*) 10 shillings and 20 'stichs' of eels,[4] and 50 acres of meadow. The wood(land) is 2 leagues (*lewæ*) long and half (a league) in width, and the Bishop has all its proceeds in fo. 173.

hunting and honey and timber (*lignis*) for the saltpans of (Droit)wich, and 4 shillings (also). It was worth £10; now £9.

Of this manor the bishop of Hereford holds 5 hides at INTEBERGE [Inkberrow],[5] where he has a priest and 7 villeins, with 4 ploughs, and meadow for the oxen. Bishop Walter[6] held it T.R.E., performing (*ad*) all the service due to the bishop (*episcopi*) of Wircestre. It was and is worth 30 shillings.

Of the said manor Urse holds 5 hides at ABELENG [Hob Lench][7] where he has 2

---

[1] This was probably the 'Bricsmar' whom Urse is found succeeding at Broughton (fo. 175), for he is said to have obtained all the land of Ælfwine son of Brihtmar (Heming, I. 261).

[2] This Keneward, as is shown in the introduction, was known as Keneward 'of Lawern,' where probably he resided. The monks claimed that Lawern, which had been held by his parents before him of their house, reverted to them at his death, but was wrongfully seized by the above 'Robert, brother of Urse the sheriff' (Heming's Cartulary, p. 253). Whether this wealthy 'Kinwardus,' as they styled him, was the Worcestershire sheriff of that name before the Conquest is, as explained in the Introduction, perhaps doubtful. He was, however, clearly the Keneward who had held of the church of Worcester at Wyre Piddle and at Elmley Castle (which latter similarly passed to Robert the Despencer), for the monks expressly state that he had held other lands of them.

[3] *i.e.* Osbern's father. Of Cotheridge ('Coddarycge') the monks alleged that they had lost it through Arnwig a former and wealthy reeve, who had given it to his dearly loved brother 'Spiritus,' who had been high in favour with Cnut's sons and successors, Harold and Harthacnut. On 'Spiritus' being subsequently expelled from England and exiled, the land was seized by Richard 'Scrob,' and the monastery thus lost it (Heming's Cartulary, p. 254). Domesday, it will be seen, only mentions that Richard (Scrob) had held the land T.R.E., but it contains in another place (fo. 252*b*) a curious reference to the exile of 'Spirtes' ('quum fuisset exsulatus ab Anglia') in Edward's days. Heming's story, therefore, relates to that Spirtes (or Spirites) the priest, the bulk of whose possessions, under William, passed to Nigel the physician (on whom, see p. 308 below).

[4] *i.e.* from the mill pool. There were 25 eels in a 'stich,' according to a Canterbury MS.

[5] He also held land there *in capite* (see below). The above 5 hides were probably Little Inkberrow.

[6] Of Hereford.

[7] Formerly Habbe Lench.

ploughs in (the) demesne, and (there are) 7 villeins and 1 bordar and 1 Frenchman (*francigena*) [1] with 6 ploughs. There are 4 serfs and 2 bondwomen and meadow . . .[2] The wood(land) is 2 furlongs long and 2 furlongs wide. It was and is worth 4 pounds. Godric held (it) doing (such) service for it to the bishop (on such terms) as he could obtain (*deprecari*).

The same Urse holds 7 hides at BISCOPESLENG [Rous Lench] [3] and Alvred holds (them) of him. He has there in (the) demesne 3½ ploughs, and (there are) a priest and 5 villeins and 8 bordars with 5½ ploughs. There are 2 serfs and 2 bondwomen and a mill worth (*de*) 4 shillings and 6 acres of meadow. It was worth 6 pounds; now 7 pounds. Frane held 5 hides performing all the service (due), and the Bishop had 2 hides in demesne.

Of this same manor Robert the Despencer (*dispensator*) holds 5 hides at PIDELE and MORE and HYLLE [Piddle, Moor, and Hill].[4] In (the) demesne are 4 ploughs and (there are) 4 villeins and 1 bordar with 1 plough. There are 3 serfs and 24 acres of meadow. It was and is worth 60 shillings. Keneward held (it) in the same manner as the preceding (*aliam supradictam*).

Of this same manor Ælfric (*Alricus*) the Archdeacon holds 1 hide at BRADELEGE [Bradley] where he has 1 plough in (the) demesne, and there are 3 villeins and 3 bordars, with 1½ ploughs, and 1 serf. It was and is worth 20 shillings. Archbishop Ealdred (*Eldredus*) leased it (*præstitit*) to his reeve T.R.E. and took it from him justly when he would.

Of the same manor Roger de Laci holds 10 hides at BISANTUNE [Bishampton] and two

---

[1] Compare *Domesday Book and Beyond*, p. 46.

[2] A blank in the MS.

[3] It would seem desirable to deal here with the whole question of the Lenches, on which there has been much confusion. As to 'Abeleng' there is no question, for it became 'Habbe Lench' and then 'Hob Lench.' (It has latterly been converted into 'Abbot's Lench,' presumably because it never belonged to an abbot!) 'Biscopesleng' is positively asserted by Nash to be Church Lench (II. 80), although the latter name appears below, under Evesham Abbey, as 'Circelenz.' I hesitated to reject Nash's identification, not knowing what grounds he might have for it, until I traced his assertion as probably derived from a guess by Habington (I. 324), who wrote, under Church Lench, 'This Biscopesleng I thincke was Churchlench.' Oddly enough, it is Habington's work which supplies us with evidence to the contrary. For he elsewhere (I. 317) notes, under Rous Lench, 'that William de Beauchamp, in the Red book of the Bishopricke of Worcester healde seavne Hydes heere of our Byshop,' and again (I. 319) that 'Roger de Lench heald of William Beauchamp seeaune hydes of Land in Lench' (so also II. 171). It is quite clear that these were the 'seven hides' at 'Biscopesleng' held of the Bishop by Urse, whose heirs the Beauchamps were. From Randolf de Lench (compare Heming, p. 291), who held it under them, it took the name of Lench Randolf, and, on passing from his descendants, the Lenches, to the family of Rous, it became Rous Lench.

Church Lench '(Circelenz) will now

present no difficulty,' nor will Atch Lench ('Achelenz'). Both of these were held in Domesday, by Evesham Abbey; and I suspect that Atch Lench was the Lench 'sacriste' that occasionally appears. There remains only the 'Lenche' which Urse had got into his hands as of the bishop of Bayeux' fee (fo. 176). Habington inserted the Domesday entry of it under Rous Lench (I. 316), to which he clearly thought it related. But its subject was evidently the 'Lenz (or Leinch) Bernardi' of the Evesham MS. (Vesp. B. XXIV. fos. 6, 10–11), and I identify it with Sheriffs Lench, of which we read under Edward I. 'Comes Warrewic tenet Shyrreve-lench pro dimidio feodo. Set quia est in manu potentis nichil Abbati facit nisi homagium, et homines de Lench sectam apud Blakehurst,' (Harl MS. 3,763, fo. 168b). Habington observes that 'the Earles of Warwick, descending from the Beauchamps, had within the paryshe of Churchlench a manor called Shreulensh (II. 252). I conclude that the Beauchamps (who inherited the hereditary shrievalty from Urse) kept the above four hides in their own hands, and that this Lench, therefore, took its name from their office.

Among the Lyttelton charters is one, *temp.* Henry III., which brings together the names of Chirchelench, Habbelench, Lench Ranulf and Achelench.

It is perhaps significant that, when Lenchwich is excluded, the Lenches, added together, amount to 25 hides exactly. Lenchwick itself is entered at 10 hides in an early Evesham Survey (Vesp. B. XXIV. fo. 49).

[4] Hill and Moor are a chapelry of Fladbury.

Frenchmen (*francigenæ*) of him. In (the) demesne are 2 ploughs, and (there are) a priest, who has half a hide, and 8 villeins and 2 bordars with 5 ploughs. There are 4 serfs and 4 bondwomen and a mill worth (*de*) 12 pence and 20 acres of meadow. It was worth 12 pounds; now 10 pounds. Four free men held (it) of the Bishop, rendering all proceeds of jurisdiction (*socam et sacam*) and church-scot (*circset*) and (fees for) burials, and service by land and water (*expeditiones et navigia*) and (attendance at) pleas at (the court of) the aforesaid Hundred, and the present holders do likewise.[1]

In the same Hundred the same Bishop holds BREODUN [Bredon]. There are 35[2] hides that (pay) geld. In demesne are 10 hides and 3 ploughs, and (there are) 33 villeins and 13 bordars with 20 ploughs. There are 6 serfs and a mill worth (*de*) 6 shillings and 8 pence and 80 acres of meadow. The wood (land) is 2 leagues (*lewæ*) long and a league and a half wide. The Bishop has from it 10 shillings and all its proceeds in honey and hunting and (all) else. It was worth £10 T.R.E.; now 10 shillings less.

To this manor belong (*jacent*) 3 hides in TEOTINTUNE [Tedington][3] and 1 hide at MITUNE [Mitton],[4] and they belong to (*sunt de*) the support of the monks. There are in (the) demesne 5 ploughs, and (there are) 12 villeins and 6 bordars with 9 ploughs. There

are 10 serfs and 3 bondwomen and 40 acres of meadow and 2 'quarantenes' of wood. It was and is worth £4.

Of this manor Æilric the archdeacon holds 2 hides at CODESTUNE[5] [Cutsdean], and he has there 2 ploughs and a priest, and 4 villeins and 7 bordars, with 3 ploughs. It was and is worth 30 shillings. Bishop Bricsteg[6] had leased (*prestiterat*) this land to Dodo, but archbishop Ealdred (*Ældredus*) proved his right to it in the time of king William.

Of this same manor Urse holds 7 hides at RIDMERLEGE [Redmarley d'Abitot],[7] and William (holds) of him 2 hides out of these. In (the) demesne are 4 ploughs, and (there are) 23 villeins and 9 bordars with 10 ploughs. There are 6 serfs and 2 bondwomen and a mill worth 5 shillings and 8 pence. The wood(land) is 1 league (*lewa*) long and half (a league) wide. It was worth 10 pounds; now 10 shillings less. Azor and Godwine held (it) of the Bishop and performed (their) service (*deserviebant*).

The same Urse holds 2 hides at PEONEDOC[8] [Pendock], where he has 2 ploughs and 3 bordars, and 3 serfs and 1 bondwoman. The wood(land) is half a league (*lewa*) long and half (a league) wide. It was worth 30 shillings; now 4 shillings less. Godwine held it on the same terms as above.[9]

The same Urse holds 3 hides at WASEBURNE [Little Washborne],[10] where he has 2

---

[1] In addition to the places enumerated above Throckmorton, which is not mentioned in Domesday, was a member of Fladbury, and 1 hide was held in Fladbury, of the Bishop *temp.* John (*Testa de Nevill*, p. 41). One virgate of this hide was then held by 'Henricus filius Johannis' (*Ibid.*), who, as 'Henricus filius Johannis de Trochemerton[e],' acknowledged the grant by bishop Mauger (1199–1212) of half a hide claimed by him in Fladbury, the deed being assigned by Mr. Poole to circ. 1200 (14th Report on Hist. MSS., App. 8, p. 194). Another virgate was then held by Adam, son of Robert, possibly the Adam 'de Trokemertun[e]' who occurs in 1220–1221 (Hale's *Register of Worcester Priory*, p. 54*a*). The first of the house, perhaps, to emerge is the 'Reoland Trokemardtune' who appears as a juror for the Hundred of Oswaldslow in the middle of the 12th cent. (Heming, p. 291).

[2] 5 is interlined above 30.

[3] A detached hamlet of Overbury, almost surrounded by Gloucestershire.

[4] A chapelry in Bredon.

[5] A chapelry of Bredon on the Cotswold Hills.

[6] *i.e.* Brihtheah.

[7] Nash says it was 'surnamed D'Abitot, from Robert d'Abitot, steward of the household to William the Conqueror, and brother to Urso d'Abitot the sheriff.' But, like Cromb, it was probably named from the later D'Abitots, who held these manors under the Beauchamps.

[8] This place gave the name to the family of 'de Penedok,' which held the 4 hides at Westmancot for several generations.

[9] The monks' story was that 'Peonedoc' had been given them by a certain 'Northman' with his son, in the time when bishop Wulfstan was dean. They claimed this as an act of restitution, though it was given that Northman's son might be received as a monk. The monastery, they said, held it till Ralf de Bernai ('Rawlfus vicecomes') seized it by the help of William Fitz Osbern, together with other lands, of which he violently deprived them.

[10] A detached hamlet of Overbury surrounded by Gloucestershire.

ploughs, and (there are) 5 villeins and 4 bordars with 2 ploughs. There are 5 acres of meadow. It was and is worth 40 shillings. Elmer held (it) and afterwards became a monk. The Bishop received his land.

The same Urse holds 4 hides at WESTMONECOTE [Westmancot],[1] where he has 3 ploughs, and (there are) 1 villein and 2 bordars with 1 plough. There are 14 serfs and 12 acres of meadow. It was worth 50 shillings; now 60 shillings. Brictuine held it, and did service (*deserviebat*) for it to the Bishop (on such terms) as could be obtained (*deprecari*).

Of the same manor Durand holds 2 hides at NORTUNE [Bredons Norton], where he has 1 plough, and (there are) 2 bordars with 1 plough, and 6 acres of meadow. Leofwine (*Lewinus*) held it and served (*fuit*) for it as Bishop's 'radman.'

Of this same manor Brictic son of Algar[2] held of the Bishop 1 hide at BISELEGE [Bushley][3] and paid rent for it to the Bishop (*inde firmabat ipsum episcopum*) every year; and yet he rendered to the Bishop (*ad socam episcopi*) whatever he owed to the King's service. It is now in the hands of king William.[4] It is and was worth 40 shillings. There are 20 acres of meadow and wood(land) half a league (*lewa*) long and 3 furlongs wide.

In the aforesaid Hundred the same Bishop holds RIPPEL [Ripple] with one (appurtenant) member, UPTUN [Upton-on-Severn]. There are 25 hides that (pay) geld. Of these, 13 are in demesne, where are 4 ploughs; and there are 2 priests who have 1½ hides with 2 ploughs; and (there are) 40 villeins and 16 bordars with 36 ploughs. There are 8 serfs and 1 bondwoman and a mill and 30 acres of meadow. The wood(land) is half a league (*lewa*) long and 3 furlongs wide, (and is) in Malferna [Malvern]; from it (the Bishop) had the honey and the hunting and all profits (*quicquid exibat*), and 10 shillings over and above; it is now in (the King's) forest; but the Bishop has its pannage,[5] and (wood for)

firing and repairs (*domorum emendationem*). It was and is worth 10 pounds.

Of this manor Ordric holds 1 hide at CRUMBE [Earl's Crombe] where he has 3 ploughs and 3 villeins and 5 bordars with 3 ploughs. There are 24 acres of meadow and 3 'quarentenes' of wood. It was worth 20 shillings; now 40. Godric held (it) and performed (his) service to the Bishop (*de episcopo deservivit*). Archbishop Ealdred (*Eldredus*) received it rightfully (*jure*) from him.[6]

There also at CRUMBE [Crombe d'Abitot] Siward holds 5 hides, where he has 1 plough, and (there are) 6 villeins and 4 bordars with 4 ploughs. This land was held of the Bishop, T.R.E., by Sirof, on whose death the Bishop gave his daughter, with this land, to a certain knight of his, who was to support (*pasceret*) her mother and to render the Bishop service (*serviret*) for the land. It was and is worth 40 shillings.

Of this same manor Roger de Laci holds 4 hides at HILCRUMBE [Hill Crombe], where he has 1 plough, and (there are) 8 villeins and 4 bordars with 4 ploughs. There are 30 acres of meadow. The wood(land) is half a league (*lewa*) long and 2 furlongs wide. It was worth 3 pounds; now 4 pounds.

Of the same manor Urse holds 1 hide at HOLEFEST [Holefast],[7] where he has 1 plough

---

[1] A hamlet in Bredon.

[2] This was the great English thegn, Brihtric son of Ælfgar, whose connection with Worcestershire is alluded to in the Introduction.

[3] Formerly Bysseley. It is confused with Bisley (Gloucestershire) in the Index to the *Red Book of the Exchequer* (Rolls Series), and is oddly spoken of by Nash as a 'name now lost' (I. 557).

[4] See further for this estate, Domesday fo. 180*b* (p. 321 below), and the Introduction.

[5] Payment for feeding swine on the mast.

[6] There has evidently, and naturally, been some confusion between the Crombes. Nash makes the one hide held by Ordric to be Crombe d'Abitot (*alias* Crombe Osbern) and the 5 hides held by Siward to be Earl's Crombe (*alias* Crombe Simon). So far as Domesday is concerned, the Crombes are treated as one. There is, however, sufficient evidence even in Nash's pages that Crombe Simon (which took its name from a tenant about a century later) was reckoned at 1 hide, and was not held of the Bishop by the Beauchamps, though it was subsequently obtained by the earls of Warwick, whence it is named Earl's Crombe. On the other hand Crombe d'Abitot (named from Osbern d'Abitot, who held it under the Beauchamps) must have been 5 hides, for the survey *temp.* Henry I. shows us Walter de Beauchamp holding 6 hides 'in Rippel et Uptune.' One of these was at Holefast, for Urse had held it as above, and the other 5 would be at Crombe d'Abitot. This identification, which is the opposite to that of Nash, is in harmony with the feodary *temp.* John, which shows us one Crombe held of the Bishop by Beauchamp, and the other by Adam 'de Crumba' (*Testa de Nevill*, p. 41).

[7] Now 'Holdfast.' A chapelry in Ripple.

and (there are) 7 bordars with 1 plough. There are 5 acres of meadow and 2 'quarentenes' of wood(land). It was and is worth 20 shillings. Two priests held it of the Bishop.

Of this same manor Ralf de Bernai[1] had 1 hide at CUNHILLE [Queenhill].[2] Ailric held it T.R.E., and did service for it to the Bishop. It is now in the King's hand(s). And there are 8 acres of meadow and 2 'quarentenes' of wood(land). It was worth 40 shillings.

Of the same manor Brictric son of Algar[3] held 1 hide at BURGELEGE [Bursley][4] on the same terms as the abovesaid (hide), and it was worth 15 shillings. It is now in the King's hand(s).

In the same Hundred the same Bishop holds BLOCHELEI [Blockley]. There are 38 hides that (pay) geld. Of these, there are in demesne, 25½ hides, where are 7 ploughs; and there are a priest, who has 1 hide, and 4 'radmans,' who have 6 hides, and 63 villeins and 25 bordars; between (them) all they have 51 ploughs. There are 14 serfs and 12 mills, worth (de) 52 shillings less 3 pence, and 24 acres of meadow. The wood(land) is half a league (lewa) in length and in width. It was worth 16 pounds; now 20 pounds.

Of this manor Richard holds 2 hides at DICFORD [Ditchford],[5] where he has 1 plough, and (there are) 2 villeins and 1 bordar and 2 serfs with 1 plough. There are 4 acres of meadow. It was and is worth 30 shillings. Alward held (it) and rendered service (for it).

Ansgot holds 1½ hides of the land appropriated to the villeins (propria terra villanorum), and has 1 plough with 1 bordar. There are 3 acres of meadow. It was and is worth 15 shillings.

To the abovesaid manor belongs (jacet) 1 hide at IACUMBE [Icomb] apportioned (pertinens)

to the support of the monks. There are 2 ploughs and (there are) 4 villeins and 2 bordars and 4 serfs with 2 ploughs. This (estate) is valued in the chief manor (in capite manerii). There are 12 acres of meadow.

Stephen son of Fulchered holds 3 hides at EILESFORD [Dailsford], where he has 2 ploughs and a priest and 6 villeins, with 5 ploughs and 4 serfs and 1 bondwoman. There are 20 acres of meadow. It is and was worth 3 pounds.

Hereward held 5 hides at EUNILADE [Evenlode]. There are 2 ploughs, and (there are) 9 villeins, with 3 ploughs, and 1 serf, and there was a mill worth (de) 32 pence. It is and was worth 3 pounds.

These 2 estates (terras), Eilesford and Eunilade, were held by the abbot of EVESHAM from the bishop of Worcester until the bishop of Bayeux received them from the abbey,[6] and these same lands were assigned to (fuerunt de) the support of the monks.[7]

In the same Hundred the same Bishop holds TREDINCTUN [Tredington] with one (appurtenant) member TIDELMINTUN [Tidmington]. There are 23 hides that (pay) geld. One of these is waste. In the demesne are 5 ploughs;
fo. 173d.
and (there are) 42 villeins and 30 bordars and a priest, who has 1 hide, and 1 'radman.' Between (them) all they have 29 ploughs. There are 10 serfs and 3 mills worth (de) 32 shillings and 6 pence. There are 36 acres of meadow. It was worth 10 pounds; now 12 pounds and 10 shillings.

At BLACHEWELLE [Blackwell][8] are 2 hides assigned (pertinentes) to the support of the monks. In (the) demesne are 3 ploughs, and there are 10 villeins and 6 bordars with 4 ploughs. There are 6 serfs and 1 bondwoman and 10 acres of meadow. It was and is worth 50 shillings.

Of the same manor Gilbert son of Turold

---

[1] A follower of earl William of Hereford, and sheriff, under him, of Herefordshire, and a despoiler of the church of Worcester.
[2] A chapelry in Ripple. The name could be read in Domesday as 'Cumhille' or 'Cunhille.' The monastery's version of the text reads 'Cumhille,' but interlines 'Cynhylle' above it. The 'Chonhelme' on fo. 180b. of Domesday is the same place.
[3] See note above.
[4] This name was preserved till recently on the Ordnance Map in Borley House, half-way between Holefast and Queenhill Chapel. It is also found, apparently, in the 'Borsley Lodge' of an inscription in Nash's *Worcestershire*, II. 447.
[5] In Blockley.

[6] They formed part of the lands involved in the great suit between the Bishop and the Abbot which is discussed in the Introduction.
[7] The monastery's version of the Domesday text (Hearne, p. 304) adds, under Blockley, a marginal note: 'De hoc manerio tenet Urso v hidas in Dorne.' As the Domesday entry on Blockley is complete without it, this holding must have been taken out of Blockley by Urse after the completion of the survey. It is clearly represented by the 5 hides in Blockley held by his representative Walter de Beauchamp *temp.* Henry I. (Hearne, p. 314).
[8] In Tredington.

holds 4 hides at LONGEDUN [Longdon],[1] where he has 2 ploughs; and there are 8 villeins and 2 bordars with 4 ploughs. There are 4 serfs and 4 bondwomen and 8 acres of meadow. It was worth 4 pounds; now 3 pounds. Le(o)fric the reeve held it at the will of the Bishop (*sicut episcopus voluit*).

In the same Hundred the same Bishop holds NORWICHE [Northwick][2] with one (appurtenant) member TIDBERTUN [Tibberton]. There are 25 hides that (pay) geld. Of these 3½ are in demesne, where are 4 ploughs; and there are a reeve, who has 3 virgates, and 1 radman who has 3 virgates, and 13 villeins and 18 bordars. Between (them) all they have 18 ploughs. There are 8 serfs and 3 mills, worth (*de*) 50 shillings, and in (Droit)-wic(h) one saltpan, which renders 100 'mits' of salt for 100 cartloads (*caretedes*) of wood. From (the) fishery (are received) 4 shillings; from the pastures (*pascuis*) 2 shillings. There are 40 acres of meadow. The wood(land) is 1 league (*lewa*) long and 1 in width. To this manor there belong 90 houses in Wirecestre [Worcester]. Of these, the Bishop has in demesne 45, which render nothing but labour at the Bishop's court (*in curia episcopi*). Urse holds 24 houses of these, Osbern Fitz Richard [3] 8, Walter Ponther 11, Robert the Despencer [4] (*dispensator*) 1. The Bishop had the third penny of the borough of Worcester T.R.E., and has it now with the King and the Earl.[5] (It was) then (worth) 6 pounds; now 8 pounds. To the same manor there belong in (Droit)wich 3 houses which render 3 'mits' of salt and 2 shillings from the leadwork (*de fabrica plumbi*). It was worth 13 pounds; now 16 pounds and 10 shillings.

In the market place (*foro*) of Worcester Urse holds of the Bishop 25 houses and renders 100 shillings a year.

Of the same manor Urse holds 5 hides at HINDELEP [Hindlip] and ALCRINTUN [Alfreton],[6] and Godfrey holds (them) of him. In (the) demesne are 2 ploughs, and (there are) a priest, and 3 villeins and 4 bordars with 2 ploughs. There are 24 acres of meadow. The wood(land) is half a league (*lewa*) long and half (a league) wide. It was worth 30

shillings; now 20 shillings. The wood(land) is in (the King's) forest. Eadric (*Edricus*) stirman held (it) and performed his service (*deserviebat*) with the other services belonging to the King and Bishop.

The same Urse holds 1 hide and 3 virgates at WERMEDUN [Warndon] and ESTUN [White Ladies Aston][7] and Robert holds (it) of him. He has there 2 ploughs with 2 serfs and there are 16 acres of meadow. The wood(land) is 2 furlongs long and the same in width, and it is in (the King's) forest. It is and was worth 16 shillings. This land was and is (part) of the villeins' land.

The same Urse holds 1 hide at CUDELEI [Cudeley][8] where he has 2 ploughs and 3 bordars and 2 serfs. The wood(land) is one 'quarentene' (*de una quarentena*), and is in (the King's) forest. It was and is worth 10 shillings. Ælfgifu (*Elgivæ*) the nun held (it on such terms) as could be obtained (*deprecari*).

Of this same manor Ordric holds 3 hides and 1 virgate (*virgam*) at ESTUN [White Ladies Aston] where he has 3 ploughs and (there are) 5 villeins and 4 bordars with 4 ploughs. It was worth 20 shillings; now 40 shillings. This land was and is (part) of the demesne chief (*capitali*) manor.

Ordric holds 1 hide at ODDUNCLEI [Oddingley], where he has 1 plough, and (there are) 1 villein and 3 bordars with 1 plough, and a saltpan worth (*de*) 4 shillings, and 12 acres of meadow. The wood(land) is 2 furlongs long and the same in width, and is in (the King's) forest. Turchil held (it) and did service for it to the Bishop.

Alric the archdeacon holds 1 hide at HUDINTUNE [Huddington], where he has 2 ploughs, and there are 4 villeins and 4 bordars with 2 ploughs. There is a mill which renders 3 (horse) loads (*summas*) of grain. The wood(land is), worth (*de*) 3 shillings and is in (the King's) forest. It is and was worth 30 shillings. Wulfric (*Vluricus*) held it as a villein (*rusticus*) doing service.

Of the same manor Walter Ponther holds 1½ hides at WIDINTUN and RODELEAH [Whittington[9]   ] where he has 1 plough, and there are are 7 bordars, with 2 ploughs, and 2 serfs. There are 16 acres of meadow, and wood(land sufficient) only for firing. It was worth 20 shillings; now 25 shillings. Ailric held it like those above.

The same Walter holds 3 hides at CIRCE-

---

[1] In Tredington.
[2] In Claines.
[3] Lord of Richard's Castle.
[4] Brother of Urse the sheriff.
[5] This appears to mean that he had still his share like the King and Earl (whose share was now the King's).
[6] Now Offerton farm east of Hindlip.

[7] *Alias* Aston Episcopi.
[8] A manor in St. Martin's, two miles east of Worcester.
[9] In St. Peter's, Worcester.

THE HOLDERS OF LANDS

HILLE [Churchhill],[1] where he has 2 ploughs and a priest, and (there are) 3 villeins and 3 bordars with 3 ploughs. There are 3 serfs and a mill worth (*de*) 4 shillings, and 3 acres of meadow, and 2 'quarentenes' of wood(land), which is (*et est*) in (the King's) forest. It was worth 50 shillings ; now 40 shillings. Azor held it on the abovesaid terms (*ut supradict*[*um*]).

The same Walter holds 3 hides at BRADE-COTE [Bredicot], where he has 1 plough with 2 bordars and 2 serfs. There are 16 acres of meadow. (There are) 2 'quarentenes' of wood(land). It was worth 25 shillings ; now 20 shillings. Brictwold the priest held (it) and performed (such) service (*deservivit*) as the Bishop willed. The wood(land) is in (the King's) forest.

Herlebald' holds 1 hide at PIRIAN [Pirie][2] where he has 2 ploughs and 3 villeins and 1 bordar and 3 serfs, with 1 plough. There are 10 acres of meadow. The wood(land) is 2 furlongs long and 1 in width and is in (the King's) forest. It was worth 30 shillings ; now 20 shillings. Godric held (it) at the will of the Bishop.

In the same Hundred this same church[3] holds OVREBERIE [Overbury] with PENEDOC [Pendock]. There are 6 hides that (pay) geld. In (the) demesne are 3 ploughs, and (there are) 15 villeins and 7 bordars with 11 ploughs. There is a priest who has half a hide and 1 plough. There are 6 serfs, and 2 bondwomen, and 10 acres of meadow and wood(land) 1 league (*lewa*) long and 1 (league) wide. T.R.E. it was worth 6 pounds, and now (it is worth) the same.

This same Church holds SEGGESBARUE [Sedgeberrow]. There are 4 hides that (pay) geld. In the demesne are 2 ploughs, and there 11 villeins and 4 bordars with 7 ploughs. There are a priest, who has half a hide, and 4 serfs, and 1 bondwoman, and 2 mills worth (*de*) 10 shillings and 8 acres of meadow. It was and is worth 3 pounds. Dodd' held (it), and it is assigned to (*de*) the support of the monks. Archbishop Ealdred (*Eldredus*) proved their right to it against (*a*) Brictic his son.

This same Church holds SCEPWESTUN [Shipston-on-Stour]. There are 2 hides that (pay) geld. In (the) demesne are 2 ploughs, and there are 15 villeins and 5 bordars with 6 ploughs. There are 4 serfs, and one bondwoman, and a mill worth (*de*) 10 shillings, and 16 acres of meadow. It was and is worth 50 shillings.

This same Church holds HERFERTHUN [Harvington] with WIBURGESTOKE. There are 3 hides that (pay) geld. In (the) demesne are 2 ploughs, and (there are) 12 villeins and 3 bordars with 6 ploughs. There are 4 serfs, and 1 bondwoman, and a mill worth (*de*) 10 shillings, and 24 acres of meadow. It is and was worth 50 shillings.

This same Church holds GRIMANLEH [Grimley]. There are 3 hides that (pay) geld. In (the) demesne are 3 ploughs and (there are) 12 villeins and 15 bordars with 15 ploughs. There are 6 serfs, and 1 bondwoman, and a mill without profit (*sine censu*) and half a fishery, which renders 'stiches' of eels,[4] and 6 acres of meadow. The wood(land) is half a league (*lewa*) long and (the same) in width. It was and is worth 3 pounds.

Robert the Despencer (*dispensator*) holds one of these 3 hides, which is called CNIHTEWIC [Knightwick], where he has 1 plough and 7 bordars, with 2 ploughs and 6 acres of meadow and wood(land) 2 furlongs long and 1 in width. It was and is worth 20 shillings.

This hide rendered in the aforesaid manor sac and soc and all service due to the King (*regis servitium*) ; and it is assigned to (*est de*) the demesne support of the monks, but it was leased (*præstita*) to a certain Eadgyth (*Eadgidæ*), a nun, who was to have it and to perform the service (*deserviret*) so long as the brethren were willing and could dispense with it. On their number (*congregatione*) increasing, under king William (*T.R.W.*),[5] she restored it (to them), and she herself, who is still living, is witness to the fact (*inde*).

This same Church holds HALHEGAN [Hallow in Grimley] with BRADEWESHAM [Broadwas]. There are 7 hides that (pay) geld. In

---

[1] Near Bredicot.
[2] In St. Martin's, Worcester.
[3] The Oswaldslow manors in the monks' hands begin here.

[4] There were 25 eels in a 'stich.' The number of the stiches seems to be omitted in the MS.
[5] With this interesting phrase should be compared a charter of St. Wulfstan (1089), in which he says : 'Nam cum a me paulo plus-quam XII^cim inventi fuissent fratres usque ad quinquaginta a me ibi congregati sunt in eodem monasterio Dei mancipati servicio' (Hale's *Registrum Prioratus Wigorniensis*, p. 84*a*).

demesne there is but 1 hide where are 2 ploughs, and (there are) 10 villeins and 16 bordars with 10 ploughs. There are 4 serfs, and 2 bondwomen, and 2 mills worth (*de*) 10 shillings, and a fishery worth (*de*) 20 'stich(es)' of eels,[1] and 20 acres of meadow, and wood-(land) 1 league long and 1 (league) in width.

To this manor there belong in (Droit)wich 10 houses worth (*de*) 5 shillings, and a saltpan which renders 50 'mits' (*mittas*) of salt.

Of this land 2 'radmanni' hold 2 hides, where they have 2 ploughs.

It was worth 50 shillings T.R.E., and (is worth) the same now.

Of this manor Walter de Burh holds half a hide in ERESBYRIE [Estbury[2] in Hallow], where he has 1 plough. Ælfric (*Alricus*) held (it), and it is (part) of the villeins' land. It is worth 5 shillings.

Of this same manor Roger de Laci holds 3½ hides at HIMELTUN [Himbleton] and SPECLEA [Spetchley]. Himeltun was waste. At Speclea 2 Frenchmen (*francigenæ*) have 4 ploughs, and (there are) 6 bordars with 2 ploughs. There are 16 acres of meadow. Of wood(land there are) 2 'quarentenes.' It was and is worth 50 shillings. Æthelric[3] (*Alricus*) held this land, which is assigned to the demesne support (*de dominico victu*) of the monks, and did service for it to them at their pleasure (*voluntatem*).

fo. 174.

Of this same manor Hugh Grentemaisnil holds half a hide at LAPPEWRTE [Lippard][4] and Baldwin holds (it) of him; and it did and does belong to (*fuit et est de*) the Bishop's soke. There are 3 villeins and 2 bordars. There are a priest and a huntsman. These have 1 plough and 6 oxen.[5] The wood(land) is 1 league (*lewa*) long and half (a league) in width. It was and is worth 20 shillings. From this land is paid (*redduntur*), every year,

8 pence to the church of Worcester for church scot (*cirsette*) and acknowledgment (*recognitione terræ*).[6]

This same church holds CROPETORN [Crop-thorne] with NEOTHERETUNE [Netherton]. There are 50 hides. Of these, (there) are in demesne 14 hides, where are 5 ploughs; and (there are) a priest, who has half a hide with 1 plough, and 18 villeins and 12 bordars with 11 ploughs. There are 10 serfs, and 4 bondwomen, and a mill worth (*de*) 10 shillings and 20 'stiches'[7] of eels, and 20 acres of meadow, and 3 'quarentenes' of wood in all (*inter totum*). There are 5 hides (which are) waste. It was worth 7 pounds, now 6 pounds.

Of this manor Robert the Despencer holds 11 hides, where he has 9 ploughs, and (there are) 10 villeins and 12 bordars with 7 ploughs. There were (*sic*) 8 serfs and 2 bondwomen. It was worth 6 pounds; now 7 pounds. Keneward and Godric held it, and performed service on such terms as (*deserviebant sicut*) they could obtain from the Bishop.[8]

---

[6] This half-hide had been given by bishop 'Brihtegus' [Brihtheah] to a friend, Herlwin by name, for a shilling a year, payable at the Assumption (Heming's Cartulary, p. 267).

[7] There were 25 eels in the 'stich.'

[8] I have shown (*Feudal England*, p. 176) that these 11 hides were Charlton (7 hides) and Elmley (4 hides). Heming's Cartulary gives their history on pp. 267–8. From it we learn that 7 hides at Charlton which had been leased for three lives, were eventually held by (the above) 'Godricus quidam cognomento Finc,' on whose death bishop Wulfstan received it back again, but only to be eventually despoiled of it by 'Rodbertus regis dispensator frater Ursonis vicecomitis,' who relied on the support of the Queen. Elmley, originally alienated by bishop 'Brihtegus,' was regained by bishop Living, who alienated it afresh to Æthelric 'Kiu' his knight. Regained once more, on the latter's death, it was finally seized by 'Rodbertus dispensator regis et frater vicecomitis.' It would seem, however, from the Domesday entry that Elmley had been held by Kineward, as had Charlton by Godric.

On the death of Robert the Despencer the two estates were divided, as were other of his lands. The Henry I. survey shows us Robert Marmion holding the 7 hides at Charlton, while the 4 hides at Elmley had passed to Robert the Despencer's son-in-law, Walter de Beauchamp, the seat of whose descendants they became (see p. 325 below).

---

[1] There were 25 eels in a 'stich.'

[2] Now Eastbury.

[3] This was Æthelric, brother of bishop 'Brihtegus,' who is expressly said in Heming's Cartulary (see p. 288, note 5 above) to have obtained from him these 'members' of Hallow, and to have been deprived of them by earl William. Here, as at Wolverton, he had been succeeded by Roger de Laci.

[4] The name is now represented by 'Leopard's (or Lippards) Grange' to the east of Worcester.

[5] As the plough (*caruca*) of Domesday always implied a team of 8 oxen, the above is equivalent to 1¾ plough teams.

Of this same manor the abbot of Evesham holds 5 hides at HANTUNE [Hampton].[1] From these the bishop of Worcester, T.R.E., only had the geld, (which was due) to his Hundred (*ad suum hund*[*ret*]). From all else it was quit (as belonging) to (*ad*) the church of Evesham, as the county (court) says.[2]

Of the same manor the abbot of EVESHAM holds 4 hides[3] at BENNICWORTE [Bengeworth], and there also Urse the sheriff holds 6 hides, where he has 2 ploughs; and (there are) 12 villeins and 2 bordars with 3½ ploughs. There are 6 serfs, and 1 bondwoman, and 6 acres of meadow. It was worth 60 shillings; now 4 pounds and 10 shillings. Azor held (it) and did service (for it) at the Bishop's pleasure (*ut episcopo placebat*).[4]

IN ESCH HUND[RET]

This same Church holds CLIVE [Cleeve Prior] with LENC [Lench]. There are 10½ hides.[5] In (the) demesne are 2 ploughs and (there are) a priest, who has 1 hide and 2 ploughs, and 9 villeins and 5 bordars with 4 ploughs, and a mill which renders 1 sestier

(*sextarium*) of honey.[6] There are 4 serfs, and 4 bondwomen, and 20 acres of meadow. It was worth 7 pounds; now 6 pounds. Of this land 2 hides, less a virgate, are waste.

This same Church holds FEPSETENATUN [Fepton].[7] There are 6 hides. One of these does not (pay) geld.[8] Walter Ponther holds it. The other five (pay) geld, and on these (*ibi*) there are 2 ploughs, and 2 villeins, with 2 ploughs, and 4 serfs, and 6 acres of meadow. The wood(land) is half a league (*lewa*) long and one furlong in width; and from the saltpans in (Droit)wich[9] (are received) 10 shillings. It was and is worth 10 shillings (*sic*).

To this manor belongs 1 Berewick called CROHLEA [Crowle]. There are 5 hides that (pay) geld. Roger Laci (*sic*) holds (it), and Odo (holds it) of him. In (the) demesne are 2 ploughs, and (there are) 7 villeins and 3 bordars with 4 ploughs. There are 4 serfs, and 1 bondwoman, and a mill worth (*de*) 2 shillings, and a saltpan in (Droit)wich worth (*de*) 3 shillings. There are 16 acres of meadow. The wood(land) is half a league (*lewa*) long and 1 furlong in width; this is in (the King's) forest. Simund held it,—it was (part) of the church's demesne,—and rendered for it to the Bishop all service and geld, and could not betake himself anywhere with this land.[10]

---

[1] Adjoining Evesham.

[2] This estate and that at Bengeworth, which follows it, were the subject of the great suit between the houses of Worcester and Evesham, which is discussed in the Introduction (p. 253).

[3] The detailed survey of these 4 hides, as of the Abbot's Hampton estate, will be found below on the Evesham fief.

[4] It was alleged by the monks of Worcester (Heming's Cartulary, p. 269) that bishop 'Brihtegus' (*i.e.* Brihtheah) gave 5 hides here to 'Atsere,' his kinsman and chamberlain, who was forcibly deprived of them, in his lifetime, by the sheriff Urse. Warned by his fate, his neighbour Ærngrim, who held the other half of Bengeworth (*i.e.* 5 hides), transferred his 'service' to the abbot of Evesham, who was powerful and close at hand. But he was soon, the monks said, tricked out of his land by the Abbot, who secured it for his abbey. One of these 5 hides, however, was obtained by the grasping Urse (Domesday, 175*b*), which accounts for his whole Bengeworth estate being reckoned above at 6 (not 5) hides, and (possibly) for its marked increase in value since it was held by 'Azor,' who, it should be observed, is the 'Atsere' of the monks' story.

[5] The Worcester Cartulary (Ed. Hale) proves that the odd half hide was for Lench, which 'gelded with' Cleeve. As Atch

Lench was 4½ hides it is possible that this half hide had been taken thence; for the original assessment may have been 5 hides.

[6] This is an unusual 'render' for a mill.

[7] In Himbleton; now corrupted to 'Phepson.'

[8] The remaining five were subsequently exempted by Henry I.

[9] *i.e.* belonging to this manor.

[10] *i.e.* could not 'commend' himself, with it to any lord but the Bishop. The story of this estate is told in Heming's Cartulary (fo. 264-5). It is there stated that Crowle was abstracted from the demesne apportioned to the support of the monks (*a dominico victu monachorum*) during the dominion of the Danes, when the above Simund (*i.e.* Siegmund), a Dane by birth and a 'knight' of earl Leofric, who held the other half of Crowle, coveted the monks' half, harried it, was impleaded for doing so, and finally, at the entreaty of earl Leofric, obtained it for his life from prior Æthelwine, agreeing to render certain service for it to the monastery. The 'other' half of Crowle, spoken of in

This same Church holds HAMBYRIE [Hanbury]. There are 14 hides that (pay) geld. In (the) demesne are 2 ploughs, and (there are) 16 villeins and 18 bordars and a priest and a reeve. Between (them) all they have 24 ploughs. There are 4 serfs, and 1 bondwoman, and 20 acres of meadow. The wood(land) is 1 league (*lewa*) in length and half (a) league in width, but it is in the King's forest. (There are received) from the salt-pans in (Droit)wich 105 'mits' (*mittas*) of salt. It was worth 7 pounds; now 6 pounds. Of this land 2 hides are waste.

Urse holds 2 hides of this land, and Ralf (holds them) of him. He has there 1 plough. It was and is worth 5 shillings.

In none of these manors can there be (employed) more ploughs than is stated.[1] The county court (*vicecomitatus*) says that from every hide of land, (whether held by) free or villein (tenure), belonging to the church of Worcester the Bishop ought to have on the feast-day of St. Martin one (horse)load of grain, of the best (*meliori*) that is grown there. But if that day should pass without the grain being rendered, (he) who has kept it back shall render the grain, and shall pay elevenfold (*undecies persolvet*); and the Bishop moreover shall receive such penalty (*forisfacturam*) as he ought to have from his land.

IN CAME HUND[RET]

This same Church holds STOCHE [Stoke PRIOR] with two Berewicks, ESTONE [Aston][2] and BEDINDONE [   ].

There are 10 hides. In (the) demesne are 2 ploughs, and (there are) 13 villeins and 7 bordars and a priest; between (them) all they have 14 ploughs. There are 4 serfs, and 1 bondwoman, and 2 mills which render 7 ounces (of silver). The wood(land) is one league (*lewa*) and a half long. This wood(land) is in (the King's) forest. It was worth 40 shillings; now 100 shillings.

IN CRESSELAU HUND[RET]

This same Church holds HUERTEBERIE

[Hartlebury] with 6 Berewicks. There are 20 hides, and in (the) demesne are 4 ploughs, and (there are) 24 villeins and 3 bordars and a priest; between (them) all they have 21 ploughs. There are 12 serfs, and 3 bondwomen, and 2 mills worth (*de*) 4 shillings and 10 (horse)loads of grain. The wood(land) is 1 league (*lewa*) long and half (a league) in width; and in (Droit)wich there are 5 houses which render 5 mits (*mittas*) of salt. It was worth 16 pounds T.R.E.; now 13 pounds and 10 shillings.

This same Church holds ULWARDELEI [Wolverley]. There are 5 hides. In (the) demesne are 2 ploughs, and (there are) 4 villeins and 5 bordars with 4 ploughs. There are a priest, who has half a plough, and one free man, who has 1 hide and renders 2 sestiers (*sextaria*) of honey. There are 6 serfs, male and female (*inter servos et ancillas*), and a mill worth (*de*) 6 shillings. It was worth 4 pounds T.R.E.; now 30 shillings.

IN CAME HUND[RET]

This same Church holds ALVIEVECHERCHE [Alvechurch] with 4 Berewicks, COSTONE [Coston Hacket], WARSTELLE, TONGE,[3] OVRETONE.

In these, with the manor, are 13 hides. In (the) demesne are 2 ploughs, and (there are) a priest, and a reeve, and a 'Radchen[istre],' and 12 villeins and 7 bordars; between (them) all they have 14 ploughs. There are 7 serfs, male and female (*inter servos et ancillas*), and 4 square leagues (*lewedes*), of (wood)land, of which the King has taken half into his wood. In (Droit)wich there are 8 saltpans; one of these renders 50 'mits' (*mittas*) of salt; the other 7 render 70 'mits' of salt. It was worth 100 shillings T.R.E., and now it is worth the same.

IN DODINTRET HUND[RET]

ST. MARY[4] holds ARDOLVESTONE [Eardiston in Lindridge] and CNISTETONE [Knighton (on Teme)], (which are) assigned to the support (*de victu*) of the monks. The two manors are of 15 hides.[5] In (the) demesne are 8 ploughs, and (there are) a priest and 15 villeins and 10 bordars with 15 ploughs,

---

this story, will be found below, as 'Croelai' on the fief of Osbern Fitz Richard (p. 314).

The above 'Simund' was probably the 'Simund danus' who had held Wolverton (Warw.) T.R.E., and the 'Simon' who had preceded Osbern Fitz Richard at Shelsley (p. 313).

[1] That is, apparently, than the number given as existing.

[2] Aston Fields, south of Bromsgrove.

[3] The name was preserved, according to Habington, in some fields between Alvechurch and Lea end.

[4] The monastery.

[5] There is here a marginal note: 'r[e]-q[uire].'

and 3 more ploughs could be (employed).[1] There are 17 serfs, and a mill worth (*de*) 10 shillings, and a fishery, and 6 acres of meadow. The wood(land) is half a league (*lewa*) long and 3 furlongs in width. It is worth 8 pounds.

THE LAND OF THE BISHOP OF HEREFORD

In Dodintret Hund[ret]

III. The bishop of Hereford holds Boc-LINTUN [Bockleton] of the King. Turchil held it and could betake himself (*ire*) where he would.[2] There are 8 hides that (pay) geld. In (the) demesne are 2 ploughs, and (there are) 2 'radmans' and 4 villeins and 8 bordars with 10 ploughs. There are 12 serfs. The wood(land) is 1 league (*lewa*) and a half long and half a league in width. It was worth 6 pounds; now 4 pounds; and 4 ploughs more can be (employed) there.

The same Bishop holds Cuer [Kyre]. Bishop Walter held it. There are 2 hides that (pay) geld. In (the) demesne is 1 plough, and (there are) 3 bordars and 3 serfs. It was worth 12 shillings; now 10 shillings. Urse holds it of the Bishop, and 2 ploughs more can be (employed) there.

In Esch Hund[ret]

The same Bishop holds INTEBERGA [Ink-berrow]. Earl Harold held it wrongfully, but king William restored it to bishop Walter because it belonged to (*erat de*) the bishopric.[3] There are 15½ hides. Of these, 10 hides (pay) geld, (and) the others not. In (the) demesne are 4 ploughs, and (there are) 15 villeins and 12 bordars with 13 ploughs, and 4 ploughs more could be (employed) there. There are 3 serfs, and a saltpan which renders 15 'mits' (*mittas*) of salt. The wood-(land) is 2 leagues (*lewæ*) long and 1 league in width. For (*de*) the pannage there are rendered 100 swine. It was worth 12

pounds T.R.E., and 10 pounds afterwards;[4] now 12 pounds.

THE LAND OF ST. DENIS

In Clent Hund[ret]

IIII. The church of St. Denis (*Dyonisii*) holds 1 hide in (Droit)wich, where are 18 burgesses, who render 4 shillings and 6 pence, and a saltpan worth (*de*) 20 pence.

THE LAND OF THE CHURCH OF COVENTRY

In Clent Hund[ret]

V. The church of St. Mary of Coventreu [Coventry] holds SALEWARPE [Salwarpe]. There is[5] 1 hide in (Droit)wich. Urse holds (it) of the Abbot, and this land is in his park, and he has 3 burgesses and 6 saltpans in (Droit)wich. It was worth 45 shillings; now 35 shillings.

THE LAND OF THE CHURCH OF CORMEILLES

In Dodintret Hund[ret]

VI. The church of St. Mary of Cormeilles [Cormeliis] holds half a hide at Tametde-BERIE [Tenbury] and (pays) geld. There is a priest with 1 plough, and it is worth 5 shillings. Earl William[6] gave it to the church.

THE LAND OF THE CHURCH OF GLOUCESTER

In Clent Hundred

VII. The church of St. Peter of Gloucester [*Glowecestre*] holds half a hide in (Droit)-WICH with the same dues (*in eadem consuetudine*) as the King's half hide in (Droit)wich that belongs to Gloucester (*Glowec[estre]*).[7]

fo. 174b.
THE LAND OF ST. PETER OF WESTMINSTER

VIII. The church of St. Peter of West-MINSTER holds Persore [Pershore]. King Edward held this manor and gave it to that church as quit and free of all claims as he was holding it in his demesne, the whole county (court) being witness. There are 200

---

[1] This was exceptional on the monastery's estates, as is shown by the entry above, after Hanbury.

[2] *i.e.* choose his lord.

[3] This entry should be compared with several similar ones in Herefordshire (fo. 181*b*, 182). Prof. Freeman (*Norm. Conq.* II., 548), though striving to defend Harold, shows that Edward had called on him, when bishop Walter was appointed (1060), to restore all property alienated from the see.

[4] *i.e.* when the Bishop received it.

[5] *i.e.* belonging to it.

[6] William Fitz Osbern, earl of Hereford.

[7] See p. 287 above.

hides. Of these there are in Pershore 2 hides which never paid geld T.R.E. There, in (the) demesne, are 5 ploughs, and (there are) 10 villeins with 7 ploughs, and 11 serfs, and 1 bondwoman. There (also) 28 burgesses render 30 shillings, and the toll renders 12 shillings. There are 3 mills worth (*de*) 50 shillings, and 100 acres of meadow. The wood(land) is 2 leagues (*lewæ*) long and 3 furlongs in width. (There is) 1 church which renders 16 shillings. It is worth 14 pounds.

In this manor a certain Frenchman (*francigena*) holds the land of Turchil, king Edward's steersman (*stirmanni*) and has 1 plough, and (there are) 2 serfs and 2 villeins with 2 ploughs.

In WICHE [Wick by Pershore] are 6 hides. There, in (the) demesne, is 1 plough, and (there are) 9 villeins and 25 bordars with 12 ploughs, and 1 serf, and a fishery. It is worth 3 pounds. Of these 6 hides, Urse holds 1 hide and Gilbert half a hide. Tor and Osward were the holders. It is worth 25 shillings.

In PENDESHAM [Pensham] are 2 hides, and they are in demesne. There are 2 ploughs, and (there are) 3 villeins and 9 bordars with 4 ploughs. There are 4 serfs and 12 acres of meadow. It is worth 3 pounds.

In BERLINGEHAM [Birlingham] are 3 hides and 1 virgate. There, in (the) demesne, are 2 ploughs, and (there are) 3 villeins and 4 bordars with 4 ploughs, and a fishery and 20 acres of meadow. It is worth 50 shillings.

Of this land Urse holds 2 hides and 1 virgate. Ælfric (*Aluricus*) and Donning held (it). There are 2 ploughs and 2 bordars and 4 serfs and 10 acres of meadow. It was worth 60 shillings; now 40 shillings.

In BRICSTELMESTUNE [Bricklehampton] are 10 hides. There are 10 villeins and 10 bordars with 6 ploughs, and they (have to) plough 6 acres and sow them with their own seed. There are 20 acres of meadow. It is worth 20 shillings.

In DEPEFORDE [Defford] are 10 hides in wood and field (*inter silvam et planum*).[1] There are 8 villeins and 10 bordars with 6 ploughs, and they (have to) plough 4 acres and sow them with their (own) seed. Of this land 2 Frenchmen (*francigenæ*) have 2 hides, and they have 2 ploughs and 4 oxmen

(*bovar'*). There are 10 acres of meadow. It is worth 50 shillings. Of this land Alcot the monk held 1 hide T.R.E., and did the service he was bidden (*precipiebatur*).

In AICHINTUNE [Eckington] are 16 hides. Of these, 9 hides, less 1 virgate, are in demesne. There, in (the) demesne, are 2 ploughs, and (there are) 6 villeins and 2 cottars (*cotarii*).[2] There are 6 coliberts who render, annually, 11 shillings and 2 pence and plough 12 acres and sow them with their own seed. There are 4 serfs and 1 bondwoman. It is worth 100 shillings.

Of this land Urse holds 4 hides less 1 virgate. Dunning held (it). There, in (the) demesne, are 2 ploughs, and (there are) 5 villeins and 8 bordars with 3 ploughs. There are 4 serfs, and 3 bondwomen, and a mill worth (*de*) 10 shillings, and 16 acres of meadow. It is worth 40 shillings.

Of this same land Turstin Fitz Rou holds 3 hides. Brictric held (them). In (the) demesne are 2 ploughs and (there are) 7 villeins and 4 bordars with 1 plough. There are 4 serfs and 3 bondwomen and 16 acres of meadow. These two, Dunning and Brictric,[3] used to mow (*secabant*) in the meadows of their lord for a day as a customary service (*per consuetudinem*).

In BEFORD [Besford] are 10 hides. Of these, 4 hides are in demesne. William the priest holds (them) of the Abbot. There, with his men, he has 1½ ploughs and 10 acres of meadow. The wood(land) is half a league (*lewa*) long and 3 furlongs in width. It is worth 30 shillings.

Of this land Urse holds 5 hides. Edward and Leofric (*Leuricus*) held (them). He has there 2 ploughs, and (there are) 2 villeins and 2 bordars with 1 plough. There are 4 serfs, and 2 bondwomen, and 10 acres of meadow.

Of the same land Walter Ponther holds 1 hide which never (paid) geld. It is and was waste; and yet it was and is worth 16 pence.

In LONGEDUNE [Longdon] are 30 hides. Of these, 11 hides are in demesne. There are 3 ploughs, and (there are) 10 villeins and 17 bordars with a priest who have 6 ploughs. There are 6 serfs, and 2 bondwomen, and 40 acres of meadow. The wood(land) is 3 leagues (*lewæ*) long and 2 leagues in width. It is worth 9 pounds.

Of this land, T.R.E., 9 free men held 18

---

[1] This is a remarkable and rare phrase, which appears to represent the English 'by wode and by felde.' The regular equivalent in Latin charters is 'in bosco et plano.' See *Geoffrey de Mandeville*, p. 241.

[2] A rare word in the Worcestershire Domesday.

[3] The predecessors of Urse and Turstin.

THE HOLDERS OF LANDS

hides, and they used to mow (*secabant*) in the meadows of their lord for one day, and to do such service as was commanded (*eis precipiebatur*). (They were) Elric, Reinbald, Elward', Brictric, Alfric, Godric cloch, and (another) Godric, Alwi, and Alwi blac. What they held was worth in all 11 pounds and 11 shillings.

Of this land king William holds 5 hides and 3 virgates. Reinbald[1] and Alfric were the holders. In (the) demesne are 3 ploughs, and (there are) 12 villeins and 12 bordars with 14 ploughs. There are 7 serfs, and 3 bondwomen, and a mill worth (*de*) 2 shillings.

Of the same land Drogo Fitz Ponz (*filius Ponzii*) holds 1 hide. Godric held (it). There is 1 plough, and (there are) 2 oxmen (*bovarii*) and 6 acres of meadow. It is worth 15 shillings.

Of the same land Urse holds 5 hides. The holders were four of the above (men), Elwar (*sic*), Brictric, Alwi, and Godric. There, in (the) demesne, are 5 ploughs, and (there are) 3 villeins and 9 bordars with 3 ploughs. There (are) 8 serfs, and 3 bondwomen, and 28 acres of meadow. The wood(land) is 3 furlongs long and 2 furlongs in width. It is worth 70 shillings.

Of this same land William Fitz Baderon[2] holds 2½ hides. Alwi held (them). He has there 2 ploughs, and (there are) 4 villeins and 5 bordars with 3 ploughs. It was worth 40 shillings. There are 12 acres of meadow.

Of the same land Roger de Laci holds 5 hides. Alric (*sic*) held (them). He has nothing in demesne. The wood(land) is 1 league (*lewa*) long and half (a league) in width. Of him a 'radman,' Le(o)fric, holds one hide and one virgate, where he has one plough, and (there are) 3 villeins and 8 bordars with 4 ploughs. There are 1 serf, and 3 bondwomen, and a mill worth 8 shillings, and 12 acres of meadow. It is worth 20 shillings.[3]

---

[1] It can scarcely be a coincidence that Eldersfield, close by, had been held, T.R.E. (Domesday, fo. 180*b*), by 'Reinbald canceler' (the latter word is interlined), the chancellor of Edward the Confessor (on whom, see *Feudal England*, pp. 421–426). The name appears to be unique T.R.E.

[2] Of Monmouth, founder of the baronial house, which took its name thence.

[3] It should be observed that the holdings of the above Norman tenants amount to 19¼ hides (at 4 virgates to the hide). This ex-

In Poiwic [Powick] are 3 hides. There, in (the) demesne are 2 ploughs, and (there are) 16 villeins and 5 bordars with 10 ploughs. There are 4 serfs, and 1 bondwoman, and 3 boors (coliberts),[4] who render 3 sestiers (*sextarios*) of honey and 45 pence, and one mill for the use of (*serviens*) the hall. There are 20 acres of meadow, and from a certain rent (*quadam reddita*) 30 shillings (are received). It is worth 20 pounds.

There are a priest who has 1 plough, and 2 oxmen (*bovar'*), and 5 bordars with 2 ploughs. There were 8 'radmans,' Æthelward (*Agelward*), Edward, Brictmer, Saulf, Ælfwine (*Alwinus*), Godric, Ælfwig (*Alwi*), Ketelbert, who had between them 10 ploughs, and many (*plures*) bordars and serfs with 7 ploughs. What they held was worth 100 shillings.

The said (*ipsi*) 'radmans' mowed (*secabant*) for one day a year in the meadows of their lord, and did all the service that they were bidden (*quod eis jubebatur*).

Urse holds the lands which were held by Ælfward (*Ælward*) and Saulf and Brictmer and Ælfwine, and has there 7 ploughs and 22 bordars and 14 serfs. The whole is worth 9 pounds and 5 shillings.

Gilbert Fitz Turold holds what was held by Ælfwig and Ketelbern, and there, in (the) demesne, are 2 ploughs, and (there are) 7 bordars and 3 serfs, with 1 plough, and a mill worth (*de*) 16 pence. It is worth 43 shillings.

Walter Ponther holds what Godric held, and there he has half a plough, and (there are) 1 villein and 6 bordars and 2 serfs with 2 ploughs. It is worth 25 shillings.

A certain Frenchman (*francigena*), Artur, holds what Edward held, and has there 1 plough and 2 oxen.[5]

---

ceeds the 18 hides assigned to their English predecessors, the excess, which is 1¼ hides, being possibly the holding of Leofric the 'radman' (who was not one of them) which is entered at that amount. But, even so, the 11 hides in the monks' demesne would not, with either total, make up exactly 30 hides.

[4] The word 'coliberti' is interlined above 'buri' as a gloss. A similar gloss is found on a Hampshire manor (fo. 38*b*), where 'vel bures' is interlined above 'coliberti' (see also Maitland's *Domesday Book and Beyond*, p. 36).

[5] 1¼ plough teams, the Domesday plough team consisting of 8 oxen.

In SNODESBYRIE [(Upton) Snodsbury][1] are 11 hides. Of these, there are in demesne 7 hides and 1 virgate, one of which hides has never (paid) geld. There, in (the) demesne are 2 ploughs, and (there are) 6 villeins, and 16 cottars, and 2 Frenchmen who serve (*francigenæ servientes*).[2] Between (them) all they have 11 ploughs. There are 4 serfs and 20 acres of meadow. The wood(land) is 1 league (*lewa*) long and the same in width. It is worth 7 pounds and 10 shillings.

Of this land Urse holds 4 hides, less 1 virgate.[3] Ælfward (*Alwardus*) held (them), and, as a customary due (*per consuetudinem*) mowed (for) 1 day the meadows of his lord and did the service he was bidden (*servitia quæ jubebatur*). There is 1 plough and a half, and (there are) 5 cottars and 4 oxmen, with 1 plough and a half, and 6 acres of meadow. The wood(land) is 3 furlongs long and 2 furlongs in width. It is worth 50 shillings.

In HUSENTRE [Martin Hussingtree] are 6 hides. There 11 villeins have 4 ploughs and render annually 100 cartloads of wood for the saltpans of (Droit)wich. He who has the custody of this land has, of it, 1 hide, where he has 1 plough, and (there are) one villein and 6 bordars with 2 ploughs. The whole is worth 30 shillings.

In WICH [Droitwich], there were and are[4] 4 furnaces (*furni*), which rendered annually, T.R.E., 60 shillings and 100 mits (*mittas*) of salt, and 31 burgesses (*burgensis*) who render 15 shillings and 8 pence. There 2 priests hold 1 hide which has never paid geld and is in the Abbot's demesne. And Leofnoth (*Leuenot*) the priest has 1 saltpan, which renders 10 shillings.

All this is worth 112 shillings and 8 pence.

From the King's tithe(s) of Wich [Droitwich] St. Peter (of Westminster) has 8 pounds.[5]

William Fitz Corbuz[ion] holds DORMES-TUN [Dormston]. Waland held (it) T.R.E. There are 5 hides, and in (the) demesne are 2 ploughs, and (there are) 2 villeins and 14 bordars with 3 ploughs. There are 6 serfs, and 1 bondwoman, and 3 acres of meadow. The wood(land) is half a league (*lewa*) long and 3 furlongs in width. Albert holds of William 2 hides, and has there 1 plough and (there is) 1 villein with half a plough. There are 2 serfs. The aforesaid Waland mowed the meadows of his lord and did all the service he was bid. It is worth 4 pounds and 10 shillings.

fo. 175.

Urse the sheriff holds PIDELET [North Piddle].[6] Toli, a free man, held it. There are 5 hides, and in (the) demesne are 2 ploughs, and (there are) 4 villeins and 4 bordars with 3 ploughs. There are 2 serfs and 8 acres of meadow. It was worth 30 shillings; now 60 shillings. The abovesaid Toli did service for (*serviebat de*) this land like the other free men.

The same Urse holds NEWENTUNE [Naunton Beauchamp]. There are 10 hides.[7] Three free men held it T.R.E., Ælfward (*Alwardus*), Saulf, and Elward. In (the) demesne are 4 ploughs, and (there are) 4 villeins with 2 ploughs. There are 8 serfs and 12 acres of meadow. The wood(land) is 2 furlongs long and 1 furlong in width. It was worth 100 shillings; now 4 pounds.

Of these 10 hides, Herbrand holds of Urse 3 hides and 1 virgate, and has there 2 ploughs and 4 serfs, and 2 bondwomen, and 6 acres of meadow, and 2 cottars. It was worth 60 shillings; now 40 shillings. Those who held these lands rendered services (*serviebant*) like the other free men.

The same Urse holds GARSTUNE [Grafton Flyford]. Ælfwine (*Alwinus*), a free man, held (it). There are 2 hides less 1 virgate.[8] In (the) demesne is 1 plough, and (there are) 3 bordars and 2 cottars, and 2 serfs, and 6 acres of meadow. It was worth 40 shil-

---

[1] Upton and Snodsbury were formerly distinct.

[2] This somewhat unusual expression possibly means that they held by 'serjeanty.'

[3] This holding is identified as Cowsdown by a 12th cent. survey (see p. 328 below).

[4] *i.e.* belonging to the abbey.

[5] This is the explanation of the entry which recurs annually, under Worcestershire, in the 12th century Pipe Rolls : 'In decimis constitutis monachis de West[monasterio]

viii li[bras].' The amount, however, appears to exceed considerably a tithe of the revenue received by the King from Droitwich in 1086, though king John let his rights to the burgesses for £100 a year.

[6] I make this to be North Piddle, which is divided from Dormston by Grafton Flyford which follows below.

[7] This clause is added in the margin.

[8] *i.e.* 1¾ hides.

fings; now 30 shillings. He who held this land mowed (*secabat*) in the meadow for one day and performed (*faciebat*) the other services.

The same Urse holds PIDELET [North Piddle].[1] Ælfwine (*Alwinus*) held (it). There are 4 hides, of which 1 never paid geld. In (the) demesne are 2 ploughs, and (there are) 1 villein, and 4 bordars, and 4 oxmen (*bovarii*), and 1 bondwoman. Between (them) all they have 1 plough. It was worth 50 shillings; now 60 shillings.

WALTER Ponther holds PERITUNE [Pirton].[2] Godric held (it). There are 6 hides, and in (the) demesne is 1 plough, and (there are) 3 villeins and 10 bordars with 3½ ploughs. There are 4 serfs and 8 acres of meadow. The wood(land) is 1 league (*lewa*) long and half a league in width. It was worth 4 pounds; now 50 shillings.

In PIPLINTUNE [Peopleton] are 4½ hides in demesne, and there 1 'radman' holds 3 virgates, and 1 Frenchman (*francigena*) holds the land of 1 villein, and (there are) 1 villein and 4 bordars. Between (them) all they have 4 ploughs, and there 2 cottars render 3 shillings.

In the same 'Berewiche'[3] Godric held 3 hides, and half a hide which never (paid) geld; and Ælfwig (*Alwi*) held 1 hide, and 1 virgate which never paid geld; and another Ælfwig (*Alwi*) held 1 hide; and Wulfric (*Vluric*) held 3 virgates, 1 of which did not (pay) geld. These holders (*ipsi*) did their service (*serviebant*) like the other free men. Now Walter ponther holds the land of Godric and of Ælfwig (*Alwi*) and has there 1 plough, and (there are) 3 villeins and 6 bordars with 3 ploughs, There are 4 serfs and 10 acres of meadow. What Walter holds is worth 50 shillings.[4] Urse the sheriff holds the hide which the other Ælfwig (*Alwi*) held. There is nothing there but 2 acres of meadow, and yet it renders 100 pence.[5]

GILBERT Fitz Turold holds CUMBRINTUNE [Comberton]. E(a)dric, a free man, held (it). There are 9 hides, and in (the) demesne is 1 plough, and (there are) a priest and 7 villeins and 2 bordars with 4 ploughs. There are 2 serfs, and 2 bondwomen, and 30 acres of meadow. There a Frenchman (*francigena*) holds 1 hide, and has there 1 plough and 2 serfs and 1 bondwoman. The above (*isdem*) E(a)dric did the same service as the other free men. It was worth 6 pounds; now 70 shillings.

To this (there) belongs a Berewick (*Berewicha*) of 10 hides.[6] Ulf and Ansgot held (it), and mowed (for) one day a year in the lord's meadow, and did their service (*serviebant*) like the others. Now these 10 hides are held by the aforesaid Gilbert, who has there 3 ploughs in (the) demesne; and (there are) 14 villeins and 6 bordars with 11 ploughs. There are 4 serfs and 1 bondwoman, and a mill which renders 30 (horse)loads of grain, and 30 acres of meadow. The wood(land) is 1 league (*lewa*) long and the same in width. The whole was worth 10 pounds; now 100 shillings.

The sheriff (Urse) holds BROCTUNE [Broughton Hackett], and Aiulf (holds it) of him. Bricsmar held (it). There are 3 hides, and in (the) demesne are 1½ ploughs, and (there are) 2 villeins and 2 cottars with 1½ ploughs. There are 2 serfs and 6 acres of meadow. It was worth 40 shillings; now 30 shillings. Bricsmar who held it did his service (*serviebat*) like the others.

In WIRECESTRE SCIRE [Worcestershire] Robert Parler holds of Gilbert Fitz Turold a small piece (*frustrum*) of land called Nadford [Nafford].[7] This land neither pays geld nor owes service at the Hundred court (*pergit ad hun[dret]*). There is a priest without a plough

---

[1] North Piddle lies just between Grafton Flyford and Naunton Beauchamp.

[2] It should be observed that this place is styled 'Pyriton-Power' in 12 Hen. IV.

[3] It should be observed that Peopleton is treated as a mere Berewick (dependency) of Pershore, which seems, therefore, to be the status of the other places among which it occurs.

[4] This clause is inserted two lines lower.

[5] This is a striking instance of the unit of assessment known as the 'hide' representing a

trifling amount of land. It is just possible, however, that Domesday only means 'There is nothing there' which is a source of profit.

[6] In this case, though Comberton must have been deemed, like Peopleton (which precedes it), a mere 'Berewick' of Pershore, it has a dependent 'Berewick' of its own. Great and Little Comberton are, probably, represented by these two entries.

[7] The name is preserved in Nafford mill on the Avon south of Birlingham. Nash asserted of Nafford (which lay south of this mill) that the parish 'is not mentioned in Domesday' (II. 180). It is now one parish with Birlingham.

A HISTORY OF WORCESTERSHIRE

(and) without stock (*pecunia*). It is worth 5 shillings.

ALVRED DE MERLEBERG [1] holds STOCHE [Severn Stoke]. There are 15 hides. The same (Alvred) himself held 12 hides and 1 virgate T.R.E., while two 'Radmanni,' Ælfward and Wulfric (*Alward et Vlfric*) held 3 hides less 1 virgate.[2] Now Alvred holds the whole. He has there in (the) demesne 3 ploughs, and (there are) 10 villeins and 10 bordars, with 5 ploughs and 4 serfs. The priest has 1 plough. There are 20 acres of meadow. The wood(land) is 2 leagues (*lewæ*) in length and 1 league in width.

Of this land 2 'Radmanni' hold 1 hide, where they have 2 ploughs, and they render 10 shillings.

Of the same land, two men, William and Boselin, hold 2 hides and 3 virgates, where they have 2 ploughs (in the demesne), and there are 11 bordars with 3 ploughs.

It was worth in all 13 pounds T.R.E., now 10 pounds.

URSE holds CUMBRINTUNE [Comberton]. There are 2 hides. Azur held (it). There are 4 villeins with 2 ploughs. It was worth 10 shillings, now 20 shillings.

ALL THESE ABOVESAID LANDS BELONGED AND BELONG (*jacuerunt et jacent*) to PERSORE. This Manor, T.R.E., rendered 83 pounds and 50 sestiers (*sextaria*) of honey [3] with all (the profits of) the pleas of the free (*francorum*) men.

THE LAND OF ST. MARY OF PERSORE.

IX. The Church of ST. MARY of PERSORE [4] held and holds the manor itself (of) PERSORE. There are 26 hides that (pay) geld. To it belong (*ibi adjacent*) these Berewicks (*Berewiche*),—Civintone [Chevington], Edbritone [Abberton], Wadberge [Wadborough], Broctune [Broughton], Edbretintune [Abberton], Wicha [Wick by Pershore], Cumbritone [Cumberton]. Of the abovesaid 26 hides the church itself holds 21 hides. In (the) demesne are 5 ploughs, and (there are) 24 villeins and 8 bordars with 22 ploughs. There are 7 serfs, and a mill worth (*de*) 4 shillings,

and at PIDELE [Wyre Piddle] the moiety of a mill (*dimid' molin'*) worth (*de*) 10 shillings and 20 'stiches' of eels.[5] There are 60 acres of meadow. The wood(land) is a league (*lewa*) long and half a league in width. In (Droit)wich is [6] 1 saltpan which renders 30 'mits' (*mittas*) of salt. It was worth 13 pounds T.R.E., now 12 pounds.

Of this land Urse holds 1½ hides, where he has 2 ploughs, and (there are) 2 villeins and 3 bordars with 1 plough. There are 4 serfs and a mill worth (*de*) 10 shillings. It is worth 50 shillings. This land was held by Azor, who did service (*serviebat*) for it to the church (of Pershore), and gave annually to the monks, for acknowledgment, one ferm [7] (*firmam*) or 20 shillings; and the agreement was that, after his death and that of his wife, the land was to revert to the church's demesne. He was living on the day of king Edward's death and was holding the land on these terms (*ita*). After that, his wife being dead, he became an outlaw (*Vtlagh*).

Of the same land the same Urse holds 1 hide at BROCTUNE [Broughton], and says that king William gave it him; and he ought to render service for it to the church. It was and is worth 10 shillings.

Of the same land Robert the Despencer (*dispensator*) holds 3½ hides at WADBERGE [Wadborough], where he has 2 ploughs and 9 bordars and 4 serfs and a park (*parchum*).[8] It is worth 40 shillings. This was land of the demesne (*dominicorum*) villeins with half a hide which was held by a tenant (*ten' unus homo*) of the Abbot.

In the same Wadbergæ [Wadborough] is 1 hide of land in which was the monks' dairy farm (*vaccaria*). It was bought (of them) by a certain Godric, a thegn of king Edward, for three lives (*vita trium heredum*), and he used to give annually to the monks, for acknowledgment, one ferm [9] (*firmam*). The third inheritor (*tercius heres*), namely, Urse who holds it, now has this land. After his death it ought to revert to the church of ST. MARY.[10]

This same Church holds BEOLEGE [Beoley]

---

[5] There were 25 eels in the 'stich.'
[6] *i.e.* appurtenant to Pershore.
[7] *i.e.* a fixed amount in kind.
[8] 'Wadborough Park' preserves the name.
[9] *i.e.* a fixed amount in kind.
[10] This is discussed in the Introduction as a typical case on church lands. The description of Urse as 'heir' of Godric should be observed.

[1] Lord of Ewias (Harold).
[2] *i.e.* 2¾ hides.
[3] 'quatuor xx[ti] libras et iii et 1 sextar' mellis.'
[4] Pershore Abbey.

with one (appurtenant) member GERLEI [Yardley]. There are 21 hides (*hida*) what with field and wood (*inter planum et silvam*).[1] In (the) demesne is 1 plough, and (there are) 8 villeins and 10 bordars and 1 'radman' with 9 ploughs. There is wood(land) 6 leagues (*lewæ*) long and 3 leagues in width, which renders 40 pence. It was worth 8 pounds; now 100 shillings.

This same Church holds STURE [Alderminster].[2] There are 20 hides, and in (the) demesne are 4 ploughs, and (there are) 24 villeins and 8 bordars with 11 ploughs. There are 5 serfs and 2 mills worth (*de*) 17 shillings and 6 pence. There 1 knight[3] (*miles*) holds (*ten'*) 2 hides and 2 'radmans.' There are 20 acres of meadow. It was worth 12 pounds; now 9 pounds. This land (pays) geld.

This same Church holds BRADEWEIA [Broadway]. There are 30 hides that pay geld. In (the) demesne there are 3 ploughs, and (there are) a priest and 42 villeins with 20 ploughs. There are 8 serfs. The whole was worth 12 pounds and 10 shillings T.R.E.; now 14 pounds and 10 shillings.

fo. 175b.

Of this land 2½ hides were held, T.R.E., by one free man, who bought (them) of abbot Edmund. This land belonged to (*erat de*) the demesne. There are now there 2 ploughs in the Abbot's demesne (intended) for (his) support (*ad victum*). Urse claims this land by gift of the King, and says that he exchanged it with (*contra*) the Abbot for a manor which belonged to (*erat de*) the demesne.

This same Church holds at LEGE [Leigh], 3 hides (that pay) geld. The Abbot has 1 of these hides in demesne, and has there 2 ploughs and there are 12 villeins and 32 bordars with 29 ploughs. There are 2 serfs, and 2 mills worth (*de*) 10 shillings and 9 pence, and 30 acres of meadow. The wood-(land) is 3 leagues (*lewæ*) long and 2 leagues in width. It was worth 20 pounds T.R.E.; now 16 pounds.

Of this land aforesaid 2 'radmans' held 1½ hides. Urse the sheriff is the holder now, and has there 2 ploughs; and (there are) 2 villeins and 11 bordars and 1 Frenchman (*francigena*); between (them) all they have 4 ploughs. There are 2 serfs and a mill worth (*de*) 4 shillings. It is worth 50 shillings.

The third hide[4] of this land is held by the same Urse at BRADNESFORDE [Bransford Chapel],[5] where he has in (the) demesne 1 plough, and there are 9 bordars with 4 ploughs, and a mill worth 20 shillings. It is worth 4 pounds. The county (court) says of this hide that it belonged to (*fuit de*) the church of Pershore T.R.E., and yet was held by the church of Evesham on the day of king Edward's death; but it knows not how.

IN DODINTREU HUND[RET]

This same Church holds MATMA [Mathon]. There are 5 hides, but only 3 of them (pay) geld. One of these 5 hides lies in Herefordscire in RADELAU HUND[RET]; it is held by 2 'radmans.' The county (court) of WIRECESTRE [Worcester], has established the right (*diratiocinavit*) of ST. MARY of Pers(h)ore to it, and it belongs to the abovesaid manor. In this same manor there are 2 ploughs in (the) demesne, and (there are) 6 villeins and 20 bordars and 1 smith[6] with 12 ploughs. There is a mill worth (*de*) 30 pence. It was worth 9 pounds; now 100 shillings.

Of this manor Urse holds 3 virgates, and has there 1 plough, and (there are) a priest, and 1 villein, and 3 bordars, and a reeve (*prepositus*). Between them they have 3 ploughs. It is worth 20 shillings.

Of this same land[7] Walter Ponther holds 1 virgate. But the whole of it is waste. It is worth 5 shillings.

The county (court) says that the church of Pershore ought to have 'circset' from all 300 hides;[8] that is from each hide where a free (*francus*) man dwells, one (horse)load of grain

---

[1] See note on p. 300 above.

[2] This is an interesting name. In the valuable *Index to the Charters and Rolls in the British Museum* (1900) the above 'Sture' is one of the places that defied identification, 'Stour' (?) being the equivalent there suggested.

[3] This is an entry of some importance, not only because 'knights' occur somewhat rarely, but also it contrasts sharply the 'knight' with the 'radmans' who seem to be 'held' by him.

[4] Domesday here gives the total as 'three hides' at Leigh, but accounts in detail for three and a half.

[5] A chapelry of Leigh.

[6] The mention of a smith (*faber*) is unusual.

[7] It should be observed that Domesday here employs 'terra' as synonymous with 'manerium,' a point on which I have laid stress in *English Historical Review*, April 1900, pp. 293-4.

[8] *i.e.* the 200 held by Westminster Abbey as well as its own 100.

on the feast day of St. Martin. If he has more hides, let them be free (from the due). And if that day should pass without payment (*fractus fuerit*), he who has kept back the grain shall discharge (the obligation) elevenfold, but shall first pay what he owes. And the abbot of Pershore himself has the forfeit from his (own) 100 hides, as he ought to have from his (own) land; from the other 200 hides he has the (horse)load and the (full) discharge (*persolutionem*), and the abbot of Westminster has the forfeit, because it is his land.[1] And the abbot of Evesham has the same (*similiter*) from his own land, and all the others similarly from their lands.

THE LAND OF THE CHURCH OF EVESHAM

X. In Evesham, the town where is situate (*sedet*) the abbey, are, and always were 3 hides free (from geld). There in (the) demesne are 3 ploughs, and (there are) 27 bordars, servants of the house (*servientes curiæ*), who have 4 ploughs. There is a mill worth (*de*) 30 shillings and 20 acres of meadow. The men dwelling there pay [2] 20 shillings a year. It was worth 60 shillings T.R.E., and 4 pounds afterwards; now 110 shillings.

In Fissesberge [Fishborough] Hund[ret] the church of Evesham has 65 hides; of these hides, 12 are free.[3] In that Hund[ret] there lie 20 hides of Dodentreu (Hundred); and (the) 15 hides of Wirecestre [Worcester] make up the hundred (hides).[4]

This same Church holds Lenchewic [Lenchwick]. There is, and always was, 1 hide free (from geld); and in Nortune [Norton] are 7 hides. In (the) demesne are 5 ploughs, and there are 13 villeins and 11 bordars and 1 Frenchman (*francigena*). Between (them) all they have 11 ploughs; there

are 10 serfs, and 2 mills worth 22 shillings and 6 pence and 2,000 eels.[5] There are 12 acres of meadow. It was worth 7 pounds T.R.E. and 110 shillings afterwards; now 7 pounds.

In Oleberge [Oldberrow] are 12 acres of land, and there are 2 villein (*rustici*) swineherds, and 1 'lewede' of wood. It is worth 5 shillings.

This same Church holds Offenham [Offenham]. There is 1 hide free (of geld); and at Liteltune [Littleton] are 6 hides, and at Bratfortune [Bretforton] 6 hides. In (the) demesne are 3 ploughs; and there are 25 villeins, with 7 ploughs; and 2 'radman' (*sic*), and 2 Frenchmen (*francigenæ*); each of them has 1 plough.[6] There are 25 bordars, and 20 acres of meadow, and a mill worth (*de*) 12 shillings and 6 pence. There are oxen for 1 plough, but they draw stone to the church.[7] It was worth 8 pounds T.R.E., and afterwards; now 6 pounds and 10 shillings.

To this manor belongs (*jacet*) 1 'Berewich,' Aldintone [Aldington]. There is 1 hide free (from geld, belonging) to the church; and in (the) demesne are 2 ploughs, and there are 5 bordars with 1 plough. There are 4 serfs and a mill worth (*de*) 5 shillings. It was and is worth 40 shillings.

This same Church holds Wiquene [Wickhamford]. There are 3 hides free (from geld), and at Bratfortune [Bretforton] 6 hides. In (the) demesne are 4 ploughs; and (there are) 16 villeins and 7 bordars with 10 ploughs. There is a mill worth (*de*) 40 pence, and 10 acres of meadow. It was and is worth 6 pounds.

This same Church holds Badesei [Badsey]. There were 6½ hides T.R.E. In (the) demesne are 2 ploughs; and (there are) 12 villeins with 8 ploughs. There are 4 serfs and 1 widow.[8] It was worth 6 pounds; now 3 pounds and 10 shillings.

---

[1] That is to say that, on the Westminster manors, the abbot of Pershore was entitled to the full discharge of the debt, but the abbot of Westminster received the penalty (*forisfactura*) to which the defaulter became liable.

[2] 'De censu hominum ibi manentium.'

[3] Namely, 3 at Evesham, 1 at Lenchwick, 1 at Offenham, 1 at Aldington, 3 at Wickhamford, and 3 at Ombersley. The abbey claimed to have formerly had 12 hides free at Ombersley alone, but there may have been confusion between this figure and the total entered above.

[4] This is a difficult passage and requires to be discussed in the Introduction (p. 247).

[5] *i.e.* a year.

[6] This passage is literally translated, but is slightly obscure.

[7] This is a remarkable entry. The oxen 'for 1 plough' are, in Domesday, 8 in number. Their employment for other than ploughing purposes is here entered as an exception.

[8] Such mention of a widow is exceedingly rare in Domesday.

This same Church holds LITELTUNE (Littleton). There were 7 hides T.R.E. In (the) demesne are 2 ploughs; and (there are) 15 villeins and 1 Frenchman (*francigena*) with 2 villeins; between (them) all they have 7 ploughs. There are 3 serfs, and 8 acres of meadow. It was worth 4 pounds and 10 shillings; now 70 shillings.

This same Church holds HUNIBURNE [Church Honeybourne]. There were 2½ hides T.R.E. In (the) demesne are 4 ploughs; and (there are) a priest and 10 villeins and 4 bordars with 4 ploughs. There are 4 serfs. It was worth 3 pounds; now 4 pounds. There are 11 acres of meadow.

This same Church holds AMBRESLEGE [Ombersley]. This (land) was of old (*antiquitus*) free for 3 hides,[1] as the charters of the church say, but it was reckoned at (*numerata pro*) 15 hides T.R.E., what with wood and field,[2] and of these, 3 hides are free (of geld). There, in (the) demesne are 5 ploughs, and (there are) 30 villeins and 12 bordars and 2 priests and 2 'radmanni' and 10 oxmen (*bovarii*). Between (them) all they have 20 ploughs. There is a fishery and a half, rendering 2,000 eels, and 2 mills worth (*de*) 8 shillings, and 4 acres of meadow. There are 2 'lewedes' of wood(land), and in (Droit)-wich 1 saltpan. It was worth 18 pounds T.R.E. and afterwards; now 16 pounds.

IN OSWOLDESLAU HUND[RET]

The same Church holds HANTUN [Hampton by Evesham]. There were 5 hides T.R.E. In (the) demesne are 3 ploughs; and there are 15 villeins and 5 bordars, and 1 Frenchman (*francigena*) with 4 bordars. Between (them) all they have 7 ploughs. There are 8 serfs, and 10 acres of meadow; and a newly-planted (*novella*) vineyard is there, and 2 mills worth (*de*) 20 shillings. It was worth 100 shillings; now 6 pounds.

This same Church holds 4 hides at BENINGEORDE [Bengeworth], and a 5th hide is held by Urse. Abbot Walter proved his right to (*diratiocinavit*) these 5 hides at Ildeberga[3] [   ] in (a court of) 4 shires

before the bishop of Bayeux and other barons of the King.[4]

There are 2 ploughs; and (there are) 5 villeins and 2 bordars with 2 ploughs. There are 6 serfs. It was worth 60 shillings T.R.E. and 50 shillings afterwards;[5] now 60 shillings.

IN ESCH HUND[RET]

This same Church holds MORTUNE [Abbot's Morton]. There were 5 hides T.R.E., but a large part of them has been leased out (*prestita foris*). In (the) demesne is 1 plough; and (there are) 7 villeins and 2 oxmen (*bovarii*) with 4 ploughs. There are 15 acres of meadow. The wood(land) is 3 furlongs long and 1 furlong in width. It was and is worth 30 shillings. Rannulf[6] holds it of the Abbot.

This same Church holds ACHELENZ [Atch Lench]. There are 4½ hides. In (the) demesne is 1 plough and (there are) 3 villeins and 4 bordars with 1 plough. There are 2 serfs, and 6 acres of wood(land). It was worth 25 shillings T.R.E., and 20 shillings afterwards; now 15 shillings.

This same Church holds BUINTUN [7] [Bevington]. There is 1 hide and 1 plough and 3 bordars and 3 acres of wood. It was worth 20 shillings, and 15 shillings afterwards; now 10 shillings.

This same Church holds CIRCELENZ [Church Lench]. There were 4 hides T.R.E. In (the) demesne are 2 ploughs; and there are a

hesitated, as to its identity, between Peterborough (the 'Golden Borough') and 'gild beorh,' a boundary mark of Evenlode (Worc.), as the locality. I adopt without hesitation the latter, which is found in a charter of 969 (Heming's Cartulary, p. 214), for I identify it with the 'four shire stone' which marks to this day the northern extremity of Evenlode. The 4 shires which there meet are Worcester, Warwick, Oxford, and Gloucester.

[4] These lands at Bengeworth and Hampton are also mentioned above (p. 297) in the survey of the bishop of Worcester's fief. The story of the dispute concerning them is discussed in the Introduction (pp. 253–6).

[5] Probably when abbot Walter obtained it.

[6] This appears to be Rannulf, abbot Walter's brother, who was enfeoffed by him, according to the Evesham Cartulary (Harl. MS. 3,763), at Littelton and Bretforton.

[7] I make this to be Bevington, in Warwickshire, adjoining Morton and the Lenches.

---

[1] Was quit of paying on more than 3 hides.

[2] See note on p. 300 above.

[3] In the Evesham account of this suit (*Chronicon Abbatiæ Eveshamensis* [Rolls Series], p. 97), this place is called 'Gildeneberga,' Mr. Macray, the editor of the Chronicle,

priest and 3 villeins and 2 bordars and 4 ox-men (*bovarii*) and 1 Frenchman (*francigena*); between (them) all they have 3 ploughs. It was and is worth 30 shillings.

In the city of WIRECESTRE [Worcester] the church of Evesham has 28 dwellings (*masuras*). Of these, 5 are waste, and the others render 20 shillings.

fol. 176.

THE LAND OF THE BISHOP OF BAYEUX

IN DODINTRET HUND[RET]

The bishop of Bayeux held[1] ACTUNE [Acton Beauchamp], and Urse (held it) of him. It belonged to (*fuit de*) the church of ST. MARY of Evesham T.R.E., and Urse received it afterwards from the Abbot in exchange for (some) other land.[2] He holds it now of the bishop of Bayeux's fee. There are 6 hides. Of these, 3 (pay) geld, (and) the other 3 do not (pay) geld. In (the) demesne are 6 ploughs, and (there are) 1 villein and 9 bordars with 4 ploughs. There are 12 serfs. It was worth 70 shillings T.R.E.; now 4 pounds.

IN ESCH HUND[RET]

The same Bishop held (*ten'*) LENCHE [Sheriffs Lench][3] and Urse (held it) of him. There are 4 hides that (pay) geld. Two of these were held by 2 thegns, and the other 2 by a certain woman named Ælfgifu (*Ælveva*). These (holders) could betake themselves (*ire*) where they would, and held (the lands) as 3

manors. In (the) demesne are 2 ploughs; and (there are) 6 villeins and 2 bordars and 4 serfs with 2 ploughs; and 8 ploughs more can be (employed) there. There is wood-(land) which renders 2 shillings. It was worth 110 shillings T.R.E., and 30 shillings afterwards; now 42 shillings.

Of this land, 2 hides were given by Gilbert Fitz Turold to the church of Evesham for the soul of earl William[4] by permission of king William, and 1 monk was placed in (that) church from the proceeds (*proinde*). For the other 2 hides abbot Æthelwig (*Elwi*) gave 1 mark of gold[5] to king William, and the King granted (*concessit*) the said land to the abbey (*æcclesiæ*) for his soul, Gilbert Fitz Turold, who received the gold for the King's use, being witness. This same church was possessed (*seisita*) of these 4 hides many years, until the bishop of Bayeux took them away from the church and gave them to Urse.

THE LAND OF ST. GUTHLAC[6]

IN CLENT HUND[RET]

XII. Of ST. GULLAC (*sic*) Nigel the physician holds 1 hide in WICH [Droitwich]. There are 9 burgesses, who render 30 shillings from the saltpans and for everything.

IN CRESSELAU HUND[RET]

The same Nigel holds DUNCLENT [Dunclent] and Urse (holds it) of him. There are 3 hides. In (the) demesne there is 1 plough; and (there are) 2 bordars and 2 ox-men (*bovarii*); and 5 ploughs can be (employed) there. It was worth 25 shillings; now 10 shillings. Odo held it of St. Guthlac.[7]

XIII. THE priests of Wrehantune [Wolverhampton] hold LUDELEIA [Lutley].[8]
There are 2 hides. They themselves held it T.R.E. They have there 2 villeins and 2 serfs and 1 bordar with 4 ploughs. It is worth 15 shillings.

THE LAND OF EARL ROGER[9]

IN CLENT HUND[RET]

EARL ROGER holds of the King one manor (called) HALA [Halesowen]. There are 10

---

[1] The use of the past tense should be observed.
[2] The title to Acton was much disputed. According to the monks of Worcester (Heming's Cartulary, p. 250), it was an old posses-sion of their monastery, which had been in the hands of a certain Ordwig, who had restored it before his death to St. Wulfstan, then prior. But it had subsequently been taken from them violently by Æthelwig, abbot of Evesham, only to be taken in turn from him by the rapacious Urse, who settled it on his daughter (the ancestress of the Beauchamps). The Evesham monks, on the other hand, asserted (*Chron. Evesham*, p. 95) that it was the patrimony of abbot Æthelwig, who gave it to Urse in exchange for the land which he had wrongfully seized at Bengeworth. The bishop of Bayeux must have owed his tenure to his placing himself in the shoes of the Abbot (so far as his personal possessions were concerned) on the latter's death.
[3] See p. 290 above, note 3.
[4] William Fitz Osbern, earl of Hereford.
[5] Six pounds.
[6] St. Guthlac's Priory, Hereford.
[7] The whole of this entry is added at the foot of the column.
[8] A township of Halesowen.
[9] Roger de Montgomeri, earl of Shrewsbury.

hides. In (the) demesne are 4 ploughs; and (there are) 36 villeins and 18 bordars and 4 'radmans' and a church with 2 priests; between (them) all they have 41½ ploughs. There are 8 serfs and 2 bondwomen. Of this land Roger the huntsman [1] holds of the earl 1½ hides, and has there 1 plough; and (there are) 6 villeins and 5 bordars with 5 ploughs. It is worth 25 shillings.

This manor was worth 24 pounds T.R.E.; now 15 pounds. Olwine held (it) and had in (Droit)wich a saltpan worth (*de*) 4 shillings, and in Wirecester [Worcester] 1 house worth (*de*) 12 pence.

The same Earl holds SALEWARPE [Salwarpe], and Urse (holds it) of him. Ælwine cilt held (it). There are 5 hides. In (the) demesne is 1 plough, and (there are) 6 villeins and 5 bordars with 7 ploughs. There are 3 serfs and 3 bondwomen, and a mill worth (*de*) 10 shillings, and 5 saltpans, worth (*de*) 60 shillings. (There is) half a 'lewa' of wood and a park is there. It was worth 100 shillings T.R.E., now 6 pounds. Two ploughs more can be (employed) there.[2]

---

[1] Of this 'Roger the huntsman' Mr. Eyton wrote: 'He was brother, and probably younger brother, to Norman Venator, the ancestor of the Pichfords; and the two brothers attested earl Roger's foundation-charter of Quatford church, probably in that very year when Domesday was compiled. . . . The Representative of Roger Venator in 1135 is stated on good evidence to have borne the name of Roger, and to have been ancestor, through females, of several Shropshire families. . . . It would seem clear that Roger Venator had a representative in the male line as late as the reign of Henry II. This was Reginald de Pulverbatch, who left a daughter and sole heir Emma. She carried the barony of Pulverbatch to her husband, Herbert de Castello.' (*Antiquities of Shropshire*, VI. 189–190.)

[2] The story told in Heming's Cartulary (ed. Hearne, p. 253) is that this estate was restored to the monastery of Worcester, by Godwine, brother of earl Leofric, on his deathbed, St. Wulfstan, then dean and afterwards bishop, exhorting him to make this restitution. After his death, his son Æthelwine (*Agelwinus*) 'who had his hands cut off by the Danes when a hostage,' repudiated his father's will (*testamentum*), and, by the help of his uncle, the Earl, obtained possession of the land. But not long afterwards, the monks continued, he lost both land

THE LAND OF RALF DE TODENI

IN DODINTREU HUND[RET]

XV. RALF de Todeni holds WERMESLAI [Worsley farm].[3] Eadwig and Æthelnoth (*Edwi et Ælnod*) held it as 2 manors. There are 2 hides that (pay) geld. In (the) demesne are 3 ploughs, and (there are) 2 'radmans' and 8 bordars with 7 ploughs. There are 6 serfs. It was worth 40 shillings, T.R.E., and 20 shillings afterwards; now 4 pounds.

The same Ralf holds LINDE [Lindridge]. Æthelward (*Ælward*) a thegn of earl Ælfgar (*Algari*) held (it). There are 2 hides that (pay) geld. In (the) demesne are 4 ploughs, and (there are) 16 bordars and 6 oxmen (*bovarii*) with 4 ploughs. There are 2 serfs. It was worth 40 shillings, T.R.E., and 20 shillings afterwards; now 16 shillings.

The same Ralf holds HALAC [   ]. Wulfmar (*Vlmer*) a thegn of king Edward held (it). There is 1 hide that (pays) geld. There are 5 bordars who render 5 shillings. It was worth 4 shillings. Two ploughs can be (employed) there.

The same Ralph holds ALVINTUNE [Alton in Rock] Godric a thegn of earl Ælfgar (*Algari*) held it, and could betake himself (*ire*) where he would.[4] There are 2 hides that (pay) geld. In (the) demesne are 4 ploughs, and (there are) a priest and 2 bordars and 2 'radmans,' with 4 ploughs. There are 6 serfs. The wood(land) is 4 leagues (*lewæ*) long and 2 leagues in width. It was worth 40 shillings T.R.E., and 20 shillings afterwards; now 52 shillings.

The same Ralf holds MORE [Moor]. Grim held (it), and could betake himself (*ire*) where he would. There is 1 hide that (pays) geld. There are 2 bordars with 1 plough, and 1 free man with 1 plough. It was and is worth 20 shillings. There is a little wood(land).

The same Ralf holds BETUNE [Bayton]. Eadric and Leofwig (*Edric et Lewi*) held it for 2 manors, and could betake themselves (*ire*) where they would. There are 3½ hides that

---

and life, dying wretchedly in the cottage of his oxman (*bovarii*). He was clearly the Ælwin[us] 'cilt' of the Domesday Survey.

[3] Near Abberley. I have identified it by a 12th century survey (see p. 329 below).

[4] *i.e.* could 'commend' himself to what lord he would.

(pay) geld. In (the) demesne are 3 ploughs, and (there are) 4 villeins and 14 bordars and 1 'radman,' with 12 ploughs. There is a mill worth (*de*) 5 shillings. It was worth 60 shillings T.R.E., and 30 shillings afterwards; now 4 pounds. Rayner holds it of Ralf.

The same Ralf holds MORE [Moor]. Leofnoth (*Leuenot*) held (it), and could betake himself (*ire*) where he would. There is 1 virgate that pays geld. There is 1 villein with 1 plough. The wood(land) is 1 league (*lewa*) long and 3 furlongs in width. It was and is worth 2 shillings.

The same Ralf holds EDBOLDELEGE [Abberley]. Wulfmar (*Vlmer*) held (it), and could betake himself (*ire*) where he would. There are 2½ hides that (pay) geld. In (the) demesne are 2 ploughs, and (there are) 18 villeins and 8 bordars and 1 Frenchman (*francigena*) and 3 cottars with 17 ploughs. There is a priest and 1 serf. It was worth 7 pounds T.R.E., and 4 pounds afterwards; now 10 pounds and 10 shillings.

The same Ralf holds ESLEI [Astley], and the church of St. Taurin (holds it) of him.[1] Ernesi held (it) and could betake himself (*ire*) where he would. There are 6 hides that (pay) geld. Of these, St. Taurin holds 4 hides quit and freed (*solutas*) from all due(s) belonging to the King, as was granted by king William himself, when Ralf gave it to the saint. There in (the) demesne are 2 ploughs, and (there are) a church and a priest and 11 villeins and 3 bordars and 1 'radman'; between (them) all they have 11½ ploughs. There are 3 serfs, and 2 mills worth (*de*) 10 shillings. At Worcester are[2] 2 burgesses worth (*de*) 2 shillings (a year); at (Droit)wich 1 saltpan, which renders 18 'mits' (*mittas*) and 64 pence. There is wood(land), (which) renders nothing.[3] This manor was worth 10 pounds[4] T.R.E., and 100 shillings afterwards, as now.

There Urse holds of Ralph 1 hide, and has

3 ploughs in (the) demesne, and 3 villeins and 15 bordars and 2 free men with 7 ploughs. There are 4 serfs, and 2 mills worth (*de*) 20 shillings. It is worth 3 pounds and 10 shillings.

This same Ralf holds RIDMERLEGE [Redmarley].[5] There are 1½ hides that (pay) geld. Wulfmar and Ulfcytel (*Vlmar et Vlchetel*) held (it) for 2 manors, and could betake themselves (*ire*) where they would. In (the) demesne is 1 plough, and (there are) 14 bordars and 1 smith with 8 ploughs. There are 4 serfs. It was worth 30 shillings T.R.E., and the same amount afterwards; now 40 shillings. Ralf the knight holds it of Ralf.

The same Ralf holds CELDESLAI [Shelsley], and Walter (holds it) of him. Wulfmar (*Vlmarus*) held (it), and could betake himself (*ire*) where he would. There is 1 hide. In (the) demesne are 2 ploughs, and (there are) 2 villeins and 13 bordars with 8 ploughs. There are 2 serfs and a fishery worth (*de*) 2 shillings, and 30 acres of meadow. The wood(land) is half a league (*lewa*) long and 3 furlongs in width. It was worth 50 shillings T.R.E., and 30 shillings afterwards; now 50 shillings.

The same Ralf holds ESTHAM [Eastham] and BESTEWDE [   ],[6] and Herbert holds (them) of him. E(a)dric held (them) as 2 manors. There are 3 hides. In (the) demesne are 2 ploughs, and (there are) a priest and 5 villeins and 8 bordars with 5 ploughs. There are 6 serfs, and one tenant (*homo*) who renders 32 pence, and a mill worth (*de*) 6 shillings and 8 pence, and 60 acres of meadow. The wood(land) is 2 leagues (*lewæ*) long and 1 league in width. It was worth 4 pounds and 5 shillings T.R.E., and 45 shillings afterwards; now 4 pounds.

IN CRESSELAU HUND[RET]

The same Ralph holds ÆLMELEIA [Elmley Lovett], and Walter (holds it) of him. Al-

---

[1] The Benedictine Abbey of St. Taurin at Evreux. See my *Calendar of Documents preserved in France*, p. 106, where Astley is styled 'Heseleia.'

[2] *i.e.* appurtenant to the manor.

[3] A marginal note adds:—'The wood(land) is 1 league (*lewa*) long and half a league in width.'

[4] The monks of Worcester alleged that Astley (*Æstlæge*) had been wrongfully taken from them by a certain Dane, Ocea by name,

who, in turn, had been despoiled of it by Ralf de Bernai supported by his lord William Fitz Osbern, their house being thus finally deprived of it (Heming's Cartulary, pp. 255–6).

[5] In Great Witley.

[6] The monks of Worcester claimed that their house had been despoiled of 'Eastham et Bufawuda' by earl Hakon and his followers in the time of the Danes.

wold held it of queen Eadgyth (*Edded*). There are 11 hides. In (the) demesne are 2 ploughs, and (there are) a priest and 14 villeins and 15 bordars with 8 ploughs. There (are) 3 mills, (which) render 109 shillings and 4 pence, and 4 saltpans (which) render 70 shillings; and at Wich [Droitwich] are (appurtenant) 5 houses worth (*de*) 20 pence; and there 7 villeins render 3 shillings. The wood(land) is 1 league (*lewa*) long and half a league in width. It was worth 10 pounds T.R.E.; now 16 pounds.

The same Ralf holds in WICH [Droitwich] 1 hide—or land [1]—of 10 hides paying geld.[2]

fo. 176b.

THE LAND OF RALF DE MORTEMER

IN DODINTRET HUND[RET]

XVI. RALF de Mortemer holds of the King SUDTUNE [Sodington] [3] and a knight of his (holds it) of him. Æthelsige (*Ælsi*) held it, and could not withdraw himself (*recedere*) from his lord. There is 1 hide, and in (the) demesne is 1 plough, and (there are) 1 smith and 2 bordars with half a plough. There are 3 serfs and 3 'quarentenes' of wood; and one plough more can be (employed) there. It was worth 20 shillings; now 10 shillings.

The same Ralf holds MAMELE [Mamble]. Sawold held (it), and could betake himself (*ire*) where he would. There is half a hide that (pays) geld. In (the) demesne is 1 plough, and (there are) 3 villeins and 6 bordars with 4 ploughs. There are 3 serfs. The wood(land) is half a league (*lewa*) long and 3 furlongs in width. It was worth 30 shillings; now 40 shillings.

The same Ralf holds BROC [   ]. Feche held (it), and could betake himself (*ire*) where he would. There is half a hide that (pays) geld. In (the) demesne are 1½ ploughs, and (there are) 1 villein and 11 bordars with 2½ ploughs. There are 4 serfs and half a fishery. There are 3 'quarentenes' of

wood. It was worth 10 shillings; now 20 shillings.

The same Ralf holds COLINGVIC [   ]. Sawold held (it), and could betake himself (*ire*) where he would. There is 1 hide that (pays) geld. The son of this Sawold has there 1 plough, and 1 bordar is there and 2 serfs. It was and is worth 10 shillings.

THE LAND OF ROBERT DE STATFORD

IN ESCH HUND[RET]

XVII. ROBERT de Stadford holds MORTUNE [Abbot's Morton]. Æthelwig (*Ælwi*) held (it). There are 4 hides that (pay) geld. This Æthelwig (*Elwi*) could betake himself (*ire*) where he would. Ernold holds it of Robert, and has 2 ploughs in (the) demesne, and (there are) 7 villeins and 6 bordars with 4 ploughs. There are 6 serfs, and 1 burgess who renders 10 shillings, and a saltpan that renders 2 shillings and 8 'mits' (*mittas*) of salt. The wood(land) is 1 league (*lewa*) long and half (a league) in width. It was worth 4 pounds T.R.E., and 30 shillings afterwards; now 4 pounds.

THE LAND OF ROGER DE LACI

IN DODINTRET HUND[RET]

XVIII. ROGER de Laci holds STOTUNE [Stockton on Teme]. Godric held (it), and could betake himself (*ire*) where he would. There are 3 hides that (pay) geld. In (the) demesne is 1 plough, and (there are) 3 villeins and 6 bordars with 3 ploughs; and 2 more can be (employed) there. There are 3 serfs, and a mill worth (*de*) 20 shillings, and 3 'quarentenes' of wood(land). It was worth 50 shillings T.R.E.; now 70 shillings.

The same Roger holds STANFORD [Stanford on Teme]. Queen 'Eddied' [4] held (it), and Godric (held it) of her as 2 manors.

---

[1] 'vel terra' is interlined below.

[2] The meaning evidently is that Droitwich was reckoned at 10 hides, one of which was held by Ralf. This is confirmed by a special 12th century survey of Droitwich, printed below (p. 330). It begins, 'Hee sunt x hidæ in Wich,' and one of these 10 hides is assigned by it to Elmley (Lovett).

[3] Although there is a Sutton in Tenbury, to which 'Sudtune' is nearer in form, yet

Sodington (afterwards the seat of the Blounts) must be the place intended. In the *Testa de Nevill* (pp. 40, 43) the Domesday form becomes 'Sutchinton,' 'Sutinton,' 'Suthinton.' Sutton Sturmey (in Tenbury), it may be added, was held of the barony of Richard's Castle, held, in Domesday, by Osbern Fitz Richard. Confusion has been caused by this barony passing subsequently, by marriage, to a branch of the Mortimers.

[4] Wife of Edward the Confessor.

There are 2½ hides that (pay) geld. Hugh holds it of Roger, and has there 1 plough, and (there are) 7 villeins and 2 bordars, and 4 ploughs more can be (employed) there. The wood(land) is half a league long and 2 furlongs in width. It was worth 50 shillings T.R.E.; now 30 shillings.

IN ESCH HUND[RET]

The same Roger holds SCELVES [1] [Shelve], and Herman holds it of him. Ælfwig (*Alwi*) held it as 2 manors, and could betake himself (*ire*) where he would. There is 1 hide that (pays) geld. In (the) demesne is 1 plough, and 2 bordars, and 3 serfs, and 4 saltpans, with wood(land) half a league long and 2 furlongs in width, rendering 60 'mits' (*mittas*) of salt.[2] It was worth 60 shillings T.R.E., and afterwards 30 shillings; now 15 shillings. The wood(land) is cut off (*missa in defenso*).

The same Roger holds CHINTUNE [Kington]. Ælfwig (*Alwi*) and Eilaf and Tori held (it) as 3 manors. There are 5 hides that (pay) geld. These (men) could betake themselves (*ire*) where they would, and (they) had 1 enclosure (*haia*) in which wild animals (*feræ*) used to be captured.[3] There in (the) demesne are 2 ploughs, and (there are) 5 villeins and 7 bordars with 2 ploughs. There are 2 serfs, and wood(land) 1 league (*lewa*) in length and 2 furlongs in width. It was worth 4 pounds T.R.E., and afterwards, as now, 50 shillings. Two knights hold (it) of Roger.

In MERLIE [Martley] Roger has 1 radman (who) pays (*reddit*) him 4 shillings a year.

The same Roger has half a hide in Wich [Droitwich]. Ælfric (*Aluric*) mapesone [4] held it. There are 11 burgesses and 1 saltpan and a half rendering 32 'mits' (*mittas*)

and a half. This manor belongs to his manor of Hereford.[5]

THE LAND OF OSBERN FITZ RICHARD

IN DODINTRET HUND[RET]

XIX. OSBERN the son of Richard scrupe [6] holds BERITUNE [Berrington] [7] of the King. Richard his father held it. There are 2 hides that (pay) geld. In (the) demesne are 2 ploughs, and there are 8 villeins and 4 bordars and a smith and a miller [8] with 9 ploughs; and one plough more can be (employed) there. There are 4 serfs, and 4 bondwomen, and a mill which renders 22 (horse)loads of grain (*annonæ*) and 10 acres of meadow. The wood(land) is a league (*lewa*) and a half long, and a league in width. It was and is worth 20 shillings.

The same Osbern holds TAMEDEBERIE [Tenbury]. His father held it. There are 3 hides that (pay) geld. In (the) demesne is 1 plough, and (there are) 14 villeins and bordars [9] with 12 ploughs; and 2 ploughs more can be (employed) there. There are 2 serfs. The wood(land) there is 2 leagues (*lewæ*) long and 1 league in width. It was worth 60 shillings; now 40 shillings.[10]

The same Osbern holds CLISTUNE [Clifton on Teme]. King Edward held (it). There are 3 hides that (pay) geld. Robert de Olgi [11] holds it of Osbern, and has there 3 ploughs in (the) demesne, and (there are) 6 villeins

---

[1] I take this to be Shelve (*alias* Shell or Selve) in Hanbury and Himbleton, of which the chapel was dependent on Hanbury.

[2] This clause illustrates the difficulty of translating with certainty such passages. The text runs: 'In dominio est i car[uca] et ii bord' et iii servos (*sic*) et iiii salinas (*sic*) cum Silva . . . redd' lx mittas salis.'

[3] They were driven into a hedged enclosure constructed for the purpose (see more in Ellis' *Introduction to Domesday*, I. 114–5).

[4] 'Mapesone' is interlined.

[5] This Droitwich entry is added at the foot of the column.

[6] 'Scrupe' is interlined.

[7] In the extreme angle of the county, south-west of Tenbury.

[8] The mention of a miller is rare in Domesday.

[9] 'xiiii inter vill' et bord'.' Compare the formula 'inter servos et ancillas' (p. 277 above).

[10] It was claimed by the monks of Worcester that Tenbury, Clifton, 'Homme,' and Kyre, which here appear among the manors of Osbern Fitz Richard, had originally belonged to their house, which had been despoiled of them, in the time of the Danes, by earl Hakon and his followers (Heming's Cartulary, p. 251).

[11] This appears to be the only mention of Robert d'Ouilly in Worcestershire. He was a tenant-in-chief in several counties.

and 4 bordars and 4 oxmen (*bovarii*). Between (them) all, with the priest, they have 6 ploughs; and 5 more ploughs could be (employed) there. The wood(land) there is 3 furlongs long and 2 furlongs in width. It was worth 20 shillings T.R.E., and afterwards; now 40 shillings.

The same Osbern holds CHURE [Kyre Wyard].[1] King Edward held (it). There are 3 hides that (pay) geld. In (the) demesne is 1 plough, and (there are) 5 villeins and 4 bordars with 8 ploughs. There are 3 serfs. It was worth 40 shillings T.R.E. and afterwards, as now. There is a mill which renders 10 (horse)loads of wheat (*frumenti*).

The same Osbern holds STANFORD [Stanford]. Brihtric (*Brictric*) a thegn of queen 'Eddid' held (it). There are 1½ hides that (pay) geld. In (the) demesne is 1 plough, and (there are) 1 villein and 1 bordar with 1 plough; and 1 plough more could be (employed) there. There is 1 serf. It was and is worth 20 shillings.

The same Osbern holds CALDESLEI [Shelsley Walsh].[2] Simon, a thegn of earl Eadwine (*Edwini*), held it, and could not withdraw himself (*recedere ab eo*) without his leave (*licentia*).[3] There is 1 hide that (pays) geld. In (the) demesne is 1 plough, and the reeve with 3 villeins and 2 bordars have 2 ploughs. There are 3 serfs, and a fishery that renders

16 'stiches' of eels.[4] There could be (employed) 2 more ploughs there. It was worth 40 shillings T.R.E., and now (is worth) 30 shillings.

The same Osbern holds CUER [Kyre]. His father held (it). There is 1 hide that pays geld. In (the) demesne is 1 plough, and another could be (employed). There are 2 bordars and 1 'radman' with 1 plough. It was worth 15 shillings; now 10 shillings. Herbert holds (it) of Osbern.

The same Osbern holds HAMME [Ham (Castle)].[5] He himself held (it). There is 1 hide that (pays) geld. In (the) demesne is 1 plough, and there are 7 bordars with 5 ploughs; and 1 plough more could be (employed). There are 4 serfs, and a fishery worth (*de*) 2 shillings, and a mill that renders 16 (horse)loads of grain (*annonæ*). It was worth 20 shillings; now 30 shillings.

The same Osbern holds SAPIE [Lower Sapey].[6] He himself held (it). There are 3 hides that (pay) geld. In (the) demesne (there is nothing) but 9 beasts (*animalia*), and (there are) a priest and 9 villeins and 4 bordars with 11 ploughs; and 3 ploughs more could be (employed) there. There is a mill that renders 6 horseloads of grain (*annonæ*). It was worth 45 shillings; now 30 shillings.

The same Osbern holds CARLETUNE [Carton?][7] and Odo holds (it) of him. His father held (it). There are 1 hide and 1 virgate that (pay) geld. In (the) demesne are 2 ploughs, and (there are) 2 villeins and 2 bordars with 1½ ploughs; and 3 ploughs more can be (employed) there. There are 7 serfs. The wood(land) is half a league (*lewa*) long and 3 furlongs in width. It was worth 10 shillings; now 5 shillings.

The same Osbern holds EDEVENT [Edvin

---

[1] So called from the family of Wyard, which held it under his heirs. This was originally a Christian name, for Philip 'filius Wiard' occurs on the Worcestershire Pipe Roll of 1175.

[2] So called from the family of Waleys, which held it under his heirs.

[3] The story told in Heming's Cartulary (p. 251) is that 'Sceldeslæhge' was held by a certain 'Simund' under grant from the brethren of Worcester, to whom it belonged, and to whom he rendered the appointed service for it, 'until the French arrived and deprived him of this estate (*bono*) and of several others.' Nash attributes this story to Great Shelsley, but the name of 'Simund' is decisive in favour of the above 'Caldeslei,' which was rightly identified by Nash as Shelsley Walsh.

The monks' story, it will be observed, is not consistent with the Domesday version of the tenure under Edward. But it is noteworthy that they speak of Simund as deprived of other lands. Now, on page 297

above we read that a 'Simund' had held Crowle of them, and, as this 'Simund' is described in Heming's Cartulary (pp. 264–5) as a Danish thegn of earl Leofric (*miles Leofrici comitis*) he is clearly identical with the above Simund, whom Domesday styles a thegn of earl Eadwine, Leofric's son.

[4] There were 25 eels in the 'stich.'

[5] In Clifton on Teme.

[6] *Alias* Sapey Pitchard, so named from the family which held it under his heirs.

[7] Now a farm in Mamble.

A HISTORY OF WORCESTERSHIRE

Loach].[1] Ulfac held (it), and could betake himself (*ire*) where he would. Herbert holds (it) of Osbern. There is 1 hide that (pays) geld, and in (the) demesne is 1 plough, and there are 1 villein and 5 bordars with 3 ploughs. There are 2 serfs. It was worth 20 shillings; now 28 shillings.

The same Osbern holds WICELBOLD [Wychbold in Dodderhill]. Earl Godwine held it. There are 11 hides. Of these, 4 hides were free (*quietæ*) from geld. In (the) demesne is 1 plough, and 2 ploughs more could be (employed) there; and (there are) 19 villeins and 27 bordars with 18 ploughs. There are 2 serfs, and 5 mills worth (*de*) 4 pounds and 8 shillings, and 26 saltpans which render 4 pounds and 12 shillings, and 13 burgesses in [Droit]wich who cut the crops (*secantes*) for 2 days in August and March and do service at the lord's court (*servientes curiæ*). There is 1 'lewede' of wood. It was worth 14 pounds T.R.E., and afterwards; now 15 pounds.

The same Osbern holds ELMERIGE [Elmbridge]. Ældiet held (it). There are 8 hides. Of these, 3 hides are free (*quietæ*) from geld by the testimony of the county (court). There are 8 villeins and 26 bordars with 10 ploughs, and another 10 ploughs could be (employed) there. There is 1 serf, and a saltpan worth 4 shillings, and 50 acres of meadow. The wood(land) is 1 league (*lewa*) long and half (a league) in width. It was worth 100 shillings T.R.E.; now 50 shillings.

IN ESCH HUND[RET]

The same Osbern holds CROELAI [Crowle], and Urse (holds it) of him. Chetelbert held it, and could betake himself (*ire*) where he would. There are 5 hides that (pay) geld. In (the) demesne are 1½ ploughs, and (there are) 3 bordars and 3 cottars with half a plough, and 3 ploughs more can be (employed) there. There are 3 serfs, and 1 burgess[2] worth (*de*) 2 shillings, and 2 saltpans worth (*de*) 6 shillings. There is half a league (*lewa*) of wood(land sufficient) for 100 swine.[3] It was worth 60 shillings; now 40.

---

[1] So called from the family of Loges, which held it under his heirs.
[2] Probably in Droitwich.
[3] In several counties the woodland is regularly entered in terms of its value for swine. But this is an exception in Worcestershire, where, as a rule, its extent alone is entered.

THE LAND OF GILBERT FITZ TUROLD

IN DODINTRET HUND[RET]

XX. GILBERT son of Turold holds DODEHAM [Doddenham] of the King. Celmar held (it), and could betake himself (*ire*) where he would. There is 1 hide that (pays) geld. In (the) demesne is 1 plough, and (there are) 3 villeins and 8 bordars, and 4 cottars and 1 miller.[4] Between (them) all they have 7 ploughs. There are 2 oxmen (*bovarii*), and a mill worth (*de*) 12 shillings. It was worth 20 shillings; now 42 shillings.

The same Gilbert holds REDMERLEIE [Redmarley].[5] Saward held it, and could betake himself (*ire*) where he would. There are 1½ hides. Ralf holds (it) of Gilbert, and has in (the) demesne 1 plough, and (there are) 11 bordars and 1 Frenchman (*francigena*) with 3 ploughs, and one plough more could be (employed) there. There are 2 serfs. It was worth 30 shillings (T.R.E.), and 15 (shillings) afterwards; now 30 shillings.

The same Gilbert holds HANLEGE [Hanley],[6] and Roger holds it of him. Eadwig (*Edwi*) held (it), and could betake himself (*ire*) where he would. There are 1½ hides that (pay) geld. In the demesne are 2
fo. 177.
ploughs, and (there are) 11 bordars and 1 Frenchman (*francigena*) with 3 ploughs, and 3 more could be (employed) there. There are 2 serfs. It was worth 60 shillings T.R.E., and 20 shillings afterwards; now 40 shillings.

The same Gilbert holds HANLEGE [Hanley][7] and Hugh (holds it) of him. Cheneward and Ulchete held it as 2 manors, and could betake themselves (*ire*) where they would. There are 3 hides that (pay) geld. In the demesne are 2 ploughs, and (there are) 10 bordars and 1 smith and 1 Frenchman (*francigena*) with 3 ploughs, and 5 ploughs more could be (employed) there. It was worth 70 shillings T.R.E.; now 50 shillings.

The same Gilbert holds ALRETUNE [Orle-

---

[4] The mention of millers is rare in Domesday.
[5] In Great Witley.
[6] As Hanley Child and Hanley William were both held by Gilbert, it does not seem possible to distinguish them in Domesday.
[7] See note above.

314

ton], and Hugh (holds it) of him. Eadwig and Eadwine (*Edwi et Edwinus*) held it for 2 manors, and could betake themselves (*ire*) where they would. There are 1½ hides that (pay) geld. In (the) demesne are 3 ploughs, and (there are) 2 villeins and 2 bordars with 1 plough. There are 2 serfs, and 2 fisheries that render 40 stiches[1] of eels. There are 2 'quarentenes' of wood(land). It was worth 40 shillings T.R.E., and afterwards, as now, 30 shillings.

In Clent Hund[ret]

The same Gilbert holds HADESORE [Hadsor], and Walter, his son-in-law, holds it of him. Bricsmar, a thegn of king Edward, held it.[2] There are 2 hides. In (the) demesne are 2 ploughs, and (there are) 2 villeins and 8 bordars and 4 cottars (*cotmanni*) with 2 ploughs, and a third (plough) could be (employed) there. There are 4 oxmen (*bovarii*), and 7 saltpans rendering 111 mits (*mittas*) of salt. It was worth 60 shillings T.R.E.; now 45 shillings.

THE LAND OF DROGO FITZ PONZ

In Dodintret Hund[ret]

XXI. DROGO son of Ponz[3] holds HOLLIM [Hollin][4] of the King. Wulfmar (*Vlmar*) held it, and could betake himself (*ire*) where he would. There is 1 hide that (pays) geld, and 1 plough could be (employed) there. It is and was waste. T.R.E. it used to be worth 5 shillings.

The same Drogo holds STILLEDUNE [Stildon Manor]. Vlchet held (it), and could not withdraw himself (*discedere*) from his lord Wulfmar (*Vlmaro*). There is half a hide that

(pays) geld. The land is (sufficient) for 2 ploughs.[5] It was worth 5 shillings. It is now waste.

The same Drogo holds GLESE [Glashampton].[6] Wulfmar (*Vlmar*) held it, and could betake himself (*ire*) where he would. There is 1 hide that (pays) geld. In (the) demesne is half a plough, and (there are) 1 villein and 3 bordars with 1 plough, and another (plough) could be (employed) there. There is a mill worth (*de*) 4 shillings and 8 pence. It was worth 20 shillings ; now 10 shillings.

The same Drogo holds one virgate in MERLIE [Martley], the King's manor, and pays geld. He has there 1 'radman' who pays him 6 shillings a year. Earnwine (*Ernuin*) held it.

THE LAND OF HERALD SON OF EARL RALF

XXII. HERALD son of earl Ralf[7] holds of the King 1 hide in WICH [Droitwich], and has there 20 burgesses with 7 saltpans rendering 50 'mits' (*mittas*) of salt. It was and is worth 40 shillings.

THE LAND OF WILLIAM FITZ ANSCULF

In Came Hund[ret]

XXIII. William son of Ansculf[8] holds ESCELIE [Selley?][9] of the King, and Wibert (holds it) of him. Wulfwine (*Vlwinus*) held (it). To it (*Ibi*) belongs one 'Berewiche' BERCHELAI [Bartley Green?]. In all (there are) 4 hides. In (the) demesne is half a plough, and (there are) 2 villeins and 9 bordars with 4 ploughs. The wood(land)[10] is 1 league (*lewa*) long.[11] It was worth 100 shillings T.R.E.; now 60 shillings.

---

[1] There were 25 eels in the 'stich.'

[2] According to the interesting narrative in Heming's Cartulary (pp. 263–4), Hadsor was given to the monastery at Worcester by a very wealthy thegn 'Brihtwin' on his grandson Eadwine becoming a monk there. 'Brihtmar' (the 'Bricsmar' of the above entry), the father of Eadwine, confirmed the gift on succeeding his father 'Brihtwin,' but, after the coming of the Normans, earl William of Hereford took it from the monastery and bestowed it on the above Gilbert, 'an officer of his.'

[3] Collateral ancestor of the Cliffords. 'Drogo' was a Latin form representing 'Dru.'

[4] In Rock.

[5] The occurrence of this formula should be noted. It is the one used in several counties, but not in Worcestershire.

[6] In Astley.

[7] Of Hereford, nephew of Edward the Confessor.

[8] De Picquigny ('Pinchengi'). See Introduction.

[9] Selley (better known now as Selley Oak) appears as a township in the early taxation rolls, and appears to me to have been this 'Escelie.'

[10] The word here used is 'nemus' instead of 'silva' as elsewhere.

[11] The width is not mentioned.

The same Wulfwine bought this manor from the bishop of Chester for three lives (*ad ætatem trium hominum*). When he was ill and had come to the end of his life, he called (to him) his son, bishop Li,[1] and his wife and several of his friends, and said : 'Hearken ye, my friends. I desire (*volo*) that my wife hold this land which I bought from the church so long as she lives ; and after her death, let the church from which I received it receive it (back) ; and let him who takes it from the church be excommunicate.'

That this was so is testified by the chief (*meliores*) men of the whole county.

The same William holds NORDFELD [North-field]. Ælfwold (*Alwoldus*) held (it). There are 6 hides. In (the) demesne is 1 plough, and (there are) a priest and 7 villeins and 16 bordars and 6 cottars (*cotmanni*) with 13 ploughs, and 5 more ploughs could be (employed) there. There are 2 serfs, and 1 bond-woman. The wood(land) is half a league (*lewa*) long and 3 furlongs in width. It was worth 8 pounds T.R.E. ; now 100 shillings.

The same William holds FRANCHELIE [Frankley], and Baldwin holds (it) of him. Wulfwine (*Vlwinus*) held (it). There is 1 hide. In (the) demesne is one plough. There are 9 bordars, with 5 ploughs, and 2 serfs. The wood(land) is 1 league (*lewa*) long and half (a league) in width. It was worth 40 shillings T.R.E. ; now 30 shillings.

The same William holds WELINGEWICHE [Willingwick] [2] and Baldwin (holds it) of

him. There are 3 virgates of land. There are one villein and 1 bordar with half a plough. There could be (employed) 2½ ploughs more. It was worth 5 shillings ; now 3 shillings.

The same William holds ESCELIE [Selley ?].[3] Tumi and 'Eleva' held it as 2 manors. Robert holds it of William. There is 1 hide. In (the) demesne is 1 plough, and (there are) 3 villeins and 2 bordars and 2 oxmen (*bovarii*) with 2 ploughs. There is 1 'leuede' of wood(land). It was worth 20 shillings ; now 15 shillings.

The same William holds WERWELIE [Warley Wigorn], and 'Alelm' (holds it) of him. Æthelward (*Æilward*) held (it). There is half a hide. In (the) demesne is 1 plough, and (there are) 2 villeins and 8 bordars with 4½ ploughs. There are 2 serfs. It was worth 17 shillings T.R.E. ; now 10 shillings.

The same William holds CERCEHALLE [Churchill], and Walter (holds it) of him. Wigar held (it). There are 2 hides. In (the) demesne is 1 plough, and 5 ploughs more can be (employed) there. It was worth 60 shillings ; now 8 shillings.

IN CLENT HUND[RET]

The same William holds BELLEM [Belne in Belbroughton]. Leofnoth (*Leuenot*), a thegn of king Edward, held (it). There are 3 hides. Robert holds it of William. In (the) demesne is 1 plough, and (there are) 7 villeins and 4 bordars with 4 ploughs. There are 2 serfs, and a saltpan worth (*de*) 2 ounces (of silver). There could be (employed) 3 ploughs more. It was worth 25 shillings ; now 15 shillings. This manor was held by Ralf Fitz Hubert for more than 5 years, but William Fitz Osbern took it from him wrongfully.[4]

---

[1] The words are 'vocato filio suo ep'o Li.' This name has caused difficulty. It would suggest Lyfing bishop of Worcester, but chronology is against this. Mr. Freeman was doubtless right in holding (*Norm. Conq.*, V. 779) that 'this must mean Leofwine,' bishop of Lichfield (before the see was moved to Chester). But as the Domesday equivalent of Leofwine was 'Lewinus,' the 'Li' might conceivably represent 'Licefelle,' the Domesday Lichfield.

[2] This is identified with (Chadwick and) Willingwick in the royal manor of Broms-grove by the entry above (p. 286), under that manor, which shows us 3 virgates 'in Willingewic' held, as here, by Baldwin of William Fitz Ansculf. The two entries should be carefully compared, as it seems impossible to say positively whether they refer to the same holding or not. If they do, we

have a further instance of discrepancies in Domesday Surveys.

[3] See note 9 on p. 315 above.

[4] This is a difficult passage. Ralf Fitz Hubert may possibly have been the tenant-in-chief of that name, who held land in several counties, but William Fitz Osbern cannot be the celebrated Norman of that name, who is spoken of in Domesday as 'earl William,' and who did not live long enough for the entry to be applicable to him. It looks as if 'William Fitz Osbern' was possibly an error for William Fitz Ansculf.

The same William holds HAGELEIA [Hagley], and Roger (holds it) of him. Godric, a thegn of king Edward, held (it). There are 5½ hides. In (the) demesne is 1 plough, and (there are) a priest and 5 villeins and 10 bordars with 5 ploughs, and 8 ploughs more can be (employed) there. There are 2 serfs. The wood(land) is half a league long and 3 furlongs in width. It was worth 60 shillings T.R.E.; now 50 shillings.

The same William holds DUDELEI [Dudley], and his castle is there. Earl Eadwine (*Eduinus*) held this manor. There is 1 hide. In (the) demesne is 1 plough, and (there are) 3 villeins and 10 bordars and one smith with 10 ploughs. There are 2 serfs, and 2 'lewedes' of wood(land). It was worth 4 pounds T.R.E.; now 3 pounds.

The same William holds SUINEFORDE [Old Swinford], and Acard' (holds it) of him. Wulfwine (*Vlwinus*) held (it). There are 3 hides. In (the) demesne is 1 plough, and (there are) a priest and 5 villeins and 11 bordars with 7 ploughs. There are 2 serfs, and a mill worth (*de*) 5 shillings. There is one 'lewede' of underwood (*silvulæ*).[1] It was worth 6 pounds T.R.E.; now 3 pounds.

The same William holds PEVEMORE [Pedmore], and Acard' (holds it) of him. Turgar held (it). There are 3 hides. In (the) demesne is 1 plough, and (there are) 3 villeins and a priest and 10 bordars and 3 cottars (*cotman*) with 5½ ploughs, and 3 more ploughs can be (employed) there. In Wirecestre [Worcester] there are (appurtenant) 2 messuages worth (*masuræ de*) 2 shillings, and (there is) one 'lew[ede]' of underwood. It was worth 4 pounds T.R.E.; now 50 shillings.

The same William holds CRADELIE [Cradley], and Payn (*Paganus*) holds it of him. Wigar held (it). There is 1 hide. In (the) demesne there is nothing.[2] There are 4 villeins and 11 bordars with 7 ploughs. It was worth 40 shillings; now 24 shillings.

The same William holds BELINTONES [Bellington (House)] in his castlery (*castellaria*). Ælfric (*Elricus*) and Holand held (it) as 2 manors. There are 5 hides. There is land for 5 ploughs.[3] It was and is waste. There

are 4 'quarentenes' of wood(land), but it is in the King's forest. The meadows of this manor are worth 4 pence.

fo. 177b.

THE LAND OF WILLIAM FITZ CORBUCION [4]

IN CLENT HUND[RET]

XXIIII. WILLIAM son of Corbucion holds of the King WITONE IN WICH [Witton in Droitwich]. Tuini, a thegn of king Edward, held it. There are 2 hides. In (the) demesne are 2 ploughs, and (there are) 18 bordars and a priest with 1 plough. There are 4 serfs and one bondwoman, and in Worcester (there is appurtenant) 1 burgess worth (*de*) 2 shillings, and (there are) 3 saltpans (which) render 60 'mits' (*mittas*) of salt; and (he has) part of a saltpan worth 10 'mits' (*mittis*) of salt. There is half a 'lewede' of wood. It was and is worth 3 pounds.

THE LAND OF WILLIAM GOIZEN-BODED

IN CLENT HUND[RET]

XXV. WILLIAM Goizenboded holds CELVESTUNE [Chauson],[5] and William (holds it) of him. Richard the young (*juvenis*) held it T.R.E.[6] There is 1 hide, and there are 4 bordars with 1 plough. It was worth 10 shillings T.R.E.; now 4 shillings.

THE LAND OF URSE DE ABETOT

IN DODINTRET HUND[RET]

XXVI. Urse holds COCHEHI [   ], and Herlebald' (holds it) of him. Godric, a free man, held it. There are 2½ hides that (pay) geld. In (the) demesne is one plough, and (there are) 2 bordars, and 2 ploughs more can be (employed) there. There (are) 2 serfs, and (he has) one burgess (*burgensem*), worth (*de*) 16 pence and 4 'mits' (*mittas*) of salt, and (there are) 3 furlongs in length of wood, and 2 furlongs in width.

---

[1] This is an exceptional word.
[2] *i.e.* no plough-oxen.
[3] On this formula see p. 315 above, note 5.

[4] Of Studley, Warwickshire.
[5] Between Salwarpe and Droitwich. I have identified it through a 12th century survey (see p. 328–9 below).
[6] William had similarly succeeded Richard in a manor in Gloucestershire, in which county lay his chief estate (fo. 167).

In Came Hund[ret]

The same Urse holds OSMERLIE [Osmerley],[1] and Herlebold (holds it) of him. Ælfwold (*Alwoldus*) held (it). There is 1 hide. In (the) demesne is 1 plough, and (there are) 10 bordars with 3 ploughs. There are 2 serfs and 2 bondwomen. In Wirecestre [Worcester] one house worth (*de*) 16 pence (is appurtenant), and in (Droit)wich 1 saltpan which renders 12 'mits' (*mittas*) of salt. There is half a 'lewa' of wood (*Nem'*). It was worth 20 shillings; it is worth 13 shillings.

The same Urse holds COSTONE [Coston Hackett]. Leofgeat and Ælfric and Æthelric (*Leuiet et Aluric et Adelric*) held it as 3 manors. There are 3 hides. Turold holds 2 hides, and Walter 1, of Urse. In (the) demesne are 2 ploughs and (there are) 11 bordars and 3 cottars (*cotmanni*) with 4 ploughs, and 1 plough more can be (employed) there. There is a mill working (*serviens*) for the hall of one of them.[2] The wood(land) is 3 furlongs long and 1 in width, but it is in the King's forest. It was worth 35 shillings T.R.E.; now 27 shillings.

The same Urse holds BENESLEI [Bentley Pauncefote],[3] and William (holds it) of him. Leofric (*Leuric*) held (it) of earl Eadwine (*Edwino*). There is 1 hide. In (the) demesne is 1 plough, and (there are) 4 bordars with 3 ploughs. The wood(land) is 1 league (*lewa*) long and half (a league) in width. It was worth 30 shillings T.R.E.; now 16 shillings.

The same Urse holds UDECOTE [Woodcote], and Herlebald' (holds it) of him. Wulfsige (*Wlsi*), a thegn of king Edward, held (it). There are 1½ hides. There is 1 villein and (there are) 2 bordars with 1 plough. The wood(land) is half a league (*lewa*), but the King has put it in the forest. It was worth 10 shillings T.R.E.; now 5 shillings.

In Cresselau Hund[ret]

The same Urse holds RUSSOCOC [Rushock], and Hunulf' (holds it) of him. Achil held it. There are 5 hides. In (the) desmesne are 1½ ploughs, and there are 13 villeins and 1 bordar and 3 cottars (*cotmanni*) with 6½ ploughs. Of (*inter*) serfs and bondwomen (there are) 4.

(There is appurtenant) a saltpan worth (*de*) 5 ounces (of silver). (There is) 1½ leagues (*lewa*) of wood(land). It was worth 40 shillings T.R.E.; now 30 shillings.

The same Urse holds STANES [Stone]. Tumi and Euchil held (it) as 2 manors. There are 6 hides. Herlebald' holds (it) of Urse. In (the) demesne are 2 ploughs, and (there are) 7 villeins and 15 bordars with 6 ploughs. There are 4 serfs, and a mill worth (*de*) 3 ounces (of silver). It was worth 40 shillings T.R.E.; now 30 shillings.

The same Urse holds LUNVREDELE [Doverdale], and William (holds it) of him. Thurbern (*Turbernus*), a thegn of king Edward, held (it). There are 2 hides. In (the) demesne are 2 ploughs, and (there are) a church and a priest and a smith and 4 villeins and 4 bordars with 4 ploughs. There is a mill worth (*de*) 4 shillings, and a saltpan at (Droit)wich worth (*de*) 4 shillings. It was worth 30 shillings T.R.E.; now 40 shillings.

The same Urse holds HATETE [   ], and Gunfrei (*Gunfridus*) (holds it) of him. Erniet and Eliet held (it) as 2 manors, and could betake themselves (*ire*) where they would. There is 1 hide. In (the) demesne is 1 plough, and another can be (employed). There is a mill worth (*de*) 2 shillings, and 1 bordar who has nothing.[4]

In Clent Hund[ret]

The same Urse holds HAMTUNE [Hampton Lovet],[5] and Robert (holds it) of him. Ælfwold (*Alwold*) held (it). There are 4 hides. In (the) demesne is 1 plough, and (there are) a priest and 5 villeins and 2 bordars with 4 ploughs, and 4 ploughs more can be (employed) there. There 7 saltpans (appurtenant) render 14 ounces (of silver). There are 2 oxmen (*bovarii*). It was worth 4 pounds; now 3 pounds.

The same Urse holds HORTUNE [Horton],[6] and Robert (holds it) of him. Ælfric (*Aluric*) held (it), and could betake himself (*ire*) where he would. There are 2 hides. In (the)

---

[1] In Alvechurch.

[2] *i.e.* of Turold and Walter.

[3] So called from a tenant under the Beauchamps.

[4] *i.e.* no stock.

[5] So called from the family which held it under Urse's heirs. Henry Lovet held 5 hides there of the barony of William de Beauchamp (Habington, I. 265).

[6] In Hampton Lovet, according to British Museum *Index* (as above), p. 384.

demesne are 2 ploughs, and (there are) 4 oxmen (*bovarii*) and 2 bordars. There is a
little (*parva*) wood(land). There is (appurtenant) a saltpan worth (*de*) 40 pence. It was
worth 50 shillings T.R.E.; now 18 shillings.

The same Urse holds COCHESIE [Cooksey],
and Herbrand and William (hold it) of him.
Ælfwine (*Alwinus*) and 'Atilic' held (it) as 2
manors. There are 2 hides. In (the)
demesne is 1 plough, and (there are) 3 bordars
and 2 Frenchmen (*francigenæ*) who have
between them 4 ploughs, and 1 plough more
can be (employed) there. This land is largely
(*ex multa parte*) waste. The wood(land) is
half a league (*lewa*) long and 3 furlongs in
width. It was worth 45 shillings T.R.E.;
now 27 shillings.

The same Urse holds BROTUNE [Brough-
ton Hackett]. Countess Godgifu (*Godeva*)
held (it). There are 2 hides. In (the)
demesne are 2 ploughs, and (there are) 5
villeins and 10 bordars and a church and a
priest; between (them) all they have 6
ploughs. There are 4 serfs. In (Droit)wich
5 (appurtenant) saltpans render 100 'mits'
(*mittas*) of salt and 5 ounces (of silver).
There are 3 'lewedes' of wood(land). It
was worth 4 pounds T.R.E.; now 4 pounds
and 10 shillings.

IN THE SAME HUND[RET]

The same Urse holds 1 hide free (*quietam*)
from geld and every due, and Robert holds (it)
of him. There are 3 bordars who have
nothing.[1] It was and is worth 3 shillings.
Ælfric (*Aluricus*) held (it) T.R.E.

The same Urse holds UPTUNE [Upton
Warren],[2] and Herlebald' (holds it) of him.
Æthelwig (*Alwinus*) abbot of Evesham held[3]
(it), and it ought, rightfully, to be in the
Abbey('s possession) by the witness of the
county (court). There are 3 hides. In (the)
demesne are 2 ploughs, and (there are) 7 villeins and 13 bordars and a priest with 5
ploughs. There are 4 serfs, and a mill worth
(*de*) 4 shillings. In Wirecestre [Worcester]
one burgess worth (*de*) 2 shillings (is appurtenant). In (Droit)wich 3 saltpans render

40 'mits' (*mittas*) of salt. The wood(land) is
3 furlongs long and 2 furlongs in width. It
was worth 60 shillings; now 50 shillings.

The same Urse holds WITUNE [Witton]
in (Droit)wich, and Gunfrei (*Gunfridus*)
(holds it) of him. The church of Evesham
held (it) T.R.E. There is half a hide. In
(the) demesne is 1 plough, and (there are) 2
serfs and 2 bordars, and 7 burgesses in (Droit)-
wich, and 1½ saltpans which render 30 pence.
It was worth 20 shillings; now 15 shillings.

This land was given to the said church of
Evesham by a certain Wulfgeat (*Vluiet*), who
placed (his) gift upon the altar when his son
Ælfgeat (*Aluiet*) was made a monk there.
This was done in the fifth year of the reign
of king Edward. Afterwards, abbot Æthelwig (*Ælwinus*)[4] leased (*præstitit*) this land to
his uncle for life;[5] and the latter died, subsequently, in Harold's battle (*bello*)[6] against the
Northmen, and the church received its land
(back) before king William had come into
England, and the said Abbot held it so long as
he lived,[7] and his successor also, abbot Walter,
held it similarly for more than 7 years.[8]

The same Urse holds HANTUNE [   ].
The abbot of Evesham held it T.R.E. There
are 4 hides. Robert holds (it) of Urse. In
(the) demesne is 1 plough, and (there are) 4
villeins and 6 bordars with 2 ploughs, and 2
ploughs more can be (employed) there. There
are 2 serfs, and a mill worth (*de*) 30 shillings,
and a saltpan which renders 3 ounces (of
silver). It was worth 4 pounds T.R.E.;
now 50 shillings.

The Abbot of the said church bought this
manor from a certain thegn who could rightfully sell his land to whom he would, and
gave it, when bought, to the Abbey (*æcclesiæ*)
by placing a copy of the gospels (*unum textum*)
on the altar, by the witness of the county
(court).

THE LAND OF HUGH LASNE[9]

IN CAME HUND[RET]

XXVII. HUGH the ass (*asinus*) holds

---

[1] *i.e.* no stock.
[2] So named from Warin, who held it of
the Beauchamps.
[3] It is among the manors asserted by the
Evesham monks to have been seized by Odo
on Æthelwig's death.

[4] This also is among the lands alleged to
have been seized by Odo on Æthelwig's
death. Its case is discussed in the Introduction.
[5] 'quamdiu ipse homo viveret.'
[6] The battle of Stamford Bridge.
[7] *i.e.* 1066–1077.
[8] This makes Urse's tenure very recent
(see Introduction, p. 264).
[9] *i.e.* L'Asne (the ass).

TICHENAPLETREU[1] of the King, and William (holds it) of him. Ælfwold (*Alwoldus*) held (it). There are 3 hides. In (the) demesne are 2 ploughs, and (there are) 8 bordars and 1 Frenchman (*francigena*) with 3 ploughs. There are 4 oxmen (*bovarii*), and 1 bondwoman, and 12 acres of meadow. In (Droit)-wich (there is appurtenant) a saltpan which renders 30 'mits' (*mittas*) of salt. It was worth 40 shillings T.R.E. ; now 30 shillings.

fo. 178.

IN CRESSELAU HUND[RET]

XXVIII. EADGIFU (*Eddeve*), a certain woman, holds CEDESLAI [Chaddesley Corbet] of the King. Ѕhe herself held it T.R.E. There, with (its) 8 'Berewiches,' are 25 hides. Of these, 10 hides were free (*quietæ*) from geld, by witness of the county (court). In (the) demesne are 3 ploughs and (there are) 33 villeins and 20 bordars, and 2 priests with 4 bordars ; between (them) all they have 25 ploughs. Of (*inter*) serfs and bondwomen there (are) 8, and (there are) 3 mills which render 12 (horse)loads of grain (*annonæ*). In Wirecestre [Worcester] are (appurtenant) 2 burgesses who render 12 pence, and in (Droit)wich 5 saltpans which render 21 shillings and 4 pence. There is wood(land) of 2 leagues (*lewis*) and other wood(land) of 1 league (in extent). It was worth 12 pounds T.R.E., as now.

Wulfmar (*Wlmarus*) held HILHAMATONE [Hilhampton].[2] There (is) 1 virgate of land, and it is waste. It was worth 12 pence T.R.E.

In ESCH HUND[RET] (there) lie 10 hides in FECHEHAM [Feckenham] and 3 hides in HOLEWEI [Holloway], and they are written (*sic*) in the Hereford return (*brevi*).[3]

In DODINTRET HUND[RET] lie 13 hides of (*de*) MERTELAI [Martley] and 5 hides of SUCHELEI [Suckley], which plead and (pay their) geld here, and render their 'ferm' (*firmam*) at Hereford, and are written (*sic*) in the King's return (*breve*).[4]

---

[1] This was a manor in Hampton Lovet, where the name occurs as 'Taukanapultre' (Nash, I. 536–8).

[2] Adjoining Witley Park on the east.

[3] *i.e.* they are surveyed under Herefordshire (fo. 180*b*), as appurtenant, so far as their rent was concerned, to the royal estate of Hereford. But their assessment for 'geld' had formed part of that of 'Esch' Hundred.

[4] The above note applies here also, but in

[HEREFORDSCIRE]

IN DODINTRET HUND[RET]

fo. 180b.

The King holds MERLIE [Martley]. Queen Eadgyth (*Eddid*)[5] held (it). There are 10 hides and 1 virgate of land.[6] In the demesne are 8 ploughs, and (there are) 47 villeins and 16 bordars and two radmen (*radmanni*) with 43 ploughs. There is a mill worth (*de*) 8 shillings, and two weirs (*Gurgites*) which render two thousand and five hundred eels and 5 'stiches.'[7] The reeve (*prepositus*) and beadle (*bedellus*) have there 2 virgates of land and 2 ploughs. In Wirecestræ [Worcester] are (appurtenant) 3 houses which render 12 pence. The villeins and bordars render 12 shillings in respect of fish (*pro pisce*)[8] and of wood (*lignis*).

This manor renders at Hereford 24 pounds of pence at 20 to the ounce (*in ora*) and 12 shillings for consideration (*de gersumme*).[9]

The church of this manor, with the land appurtenant and with its tithe, and 2 villeins with 2 virgates of land, were given by earl W[illiam][10] to St. MARY of Cormeilles (*Cormeliis*).

This same (*ipse*) Earl gave to Ralf de Bernai 2 'radmans,' and put (*misit*) them outside this manor with the land which they held. They have 2 ploughs.

The same Earl gave to Droard 1 virgate of land, which he still holds.

IN NAISSE[11] HUND[RET]

The King holds FECCHEHAM [Feckenham]. Five thegns held it of earl Eadwine (*Edwino*),

---

this case we have the definite statement that these lands were only appurtenant to Hereford so far as their rents were concerned, and that for jurisdiction and taxation they belonged to 'Dodintret' Hundred.

[5] Wife of Edward the Confessor.

[6] It will be observed that this reckoning does not tally with the assessment recorded above under Worcestershire (13 hides).

[7] As there were 25 eels in the 'stich,' the total annual 'render' would be 2,625 eels.

[8] This is suggestive of the 'fisfe' found as a due payable by villeins on certain Worcestershire manors belonging to the monks of Worcester (see Hale's *Registrum Prioratus Beatæ Mariæ Wigornensis*).

[9] See note 4 on p. 323 below.

[10] William Fitz Osbern earl of Hereford.

[11] Styled 'Esch' Hundred under Worcestershire.

THE HOLDERS OF LANDS

and could betake themselves (*ire*) with (their) land where they would, and (they) had under them 4 knights (*milites*) as free as they themselves were.[1]   There are 10 hides, and in (the) demesne (are) 6 ploughs, and (there are) 30 villeins and 11 bordars, and a reeve (*prepositus*) and a beadle (*bedel*) and a miller and a smith ; between (them) all they have 18 ploughs. There are 12 serfs, and 5 bondwomen, and 1 'radman' who holds half a hide and two-thirds of half a hide,[2] and a croft, and has 1 plough.   There is a mill worth (*de*) 2 shillings.   In (Droit)Wich 4 saltpans are appurtenant.   The wood(land) of this manor is put out of it (*foris est missa*), for the King's forest (*silvam*), and so is 1 hide of land which earl William[3] gave to Gozelin the huntsman.

The tithe(s) of this manor and the church, with the priest, and two virgates of land with 1 villein were given by earl William to the Abbey (*ecclesiæ*) of St. MARY.[4]

Walter de Laci gave to a certain Hubert 1 hide of the demesne land.[5]   This Hubert has half a plough.

The King holds HALOEDE [Holloway].[6] Siward, a thegn and kinsman of king Edward, held it.   There are 3 hides, and in (the) demesne are 3 ploughs, and there are 4 villeins and 1 bordar and a reeve (*prepositus*) and a beadle (*bedel*) with 3 ploughs, and of (*inter*) serfs and bondwomen 6.   There is a park for wild animals (*ferarum*), but it has been put (*missum*) outside the manor with all the

wood(land).   In (Droit)Wich (are appurtenant) 4 saltpans and 1 'hoch.'   In Wirecestre [Worcester] 1 house rend[ers] 2 ploughshares, and 2 other houses, belonging to Feckenham rendered nothing and have been put (*missæ*) outside.

These 2 manors render at Hereford 18 pounds of pennies at (*de*) 20 to the ounce.

IN GLOWECESTRE[7] SCIRE.

The King holds HANLIE [Hanley Castle]. Brictric[8] held (it).   There are 4 hides.   In (the) demesne are two ploughs, and there are 20 villeins and 17 bordars and a reeve ; between (them) all they have 17½ ploughs. Of (*inter*) serfs and bondwomen there are 9 there, and 6 swineherds (*porcarii*) render 60 swine and have 4 ploughs.   There is a mill worth (*de*) 2 shillings.   The wood-(land is) 5 leagues reckoning (*inter*) length and width.   It has been put out of (*missa foris*) the manor.[9]   There is a hawk's eyrie (*airea*).   A forester holds half a virgate of land, and one villein at (*de*) Baldehalle renders to this manor 2 ounces of (silver) pennies (a year).

The King holds FORHELMENTONE [Forthampton].   Brictric held it.[10] . . .

IN WIRECESTRE SCIRE

The King holds BISELIE [Bushley].   Brictric held (it), and he bought it from Lyfing (*Livingo*) bishop of Worcester (*Wirecestre*) for 3 marcs of gold[11] together with (*simul et*) a

---

[1] This is a most exceptional and remarkable entry.

[2] *i.e.* five-sixths of a hide in all.

[3] William Fitz Osbern earl of Hereford.

[4] *i.e.* of La Vieille Lyre, for Nash observes that 'The rectory formerly belonged to the abbey of Lyra in France, and had a large demesne named Astwood attached to it' (I. 442).

[5] The importance of this passage consists in its demonstration that Walter de Laci (who had died shortly before the survey), the father of Roger de Laci the Domesday tenant-in-chief, must have held this manor at some time.

[6] In Feckenham.   It was granted to Bordesley Abbey half a century later.   It is the 'Holewei' of the entry above (fo. 178), and the 'Holeweya' of *Testa de Nevill* (p. 43) where its grant by the Crown to Bordesley Abbey is referred to.   The Abbot and convent speak of it as their manor of Holewey Grange in the county of Worcester, 10 Dec., 1467 (Madox' *Formulare*, p. 286).

[7] *Sic*. But this heading must apply only to the second of the two manors which follow, namely Forthampton, which is in Gloucestershire, though surrounded on three sides by Worcestershire.

[8] The Brictric of this entry and of the two which follow is the great Brihtric son of Ælfgar, the centre of whose power was at Tewkesbury (see Introduction).

[9] This large tract of woodland was part of Malvern Chase running back from Hanley to the Herefordshire border.   Another part was appurtenant to the bishop of Worcester's manor of Upton and Ripple which adjoined Hanley on the south.

[10] Another survey of Hanley Castle and Forthampton will be found below extracted from the Gloucestershire Domesday, where they are entered in the same order as members of Brihtric's great lordship of Tewkesbury.

[11] £18.   Compare the very different story of the transaction in the survey of what seems to be this same estate on p. 292 above, under the lands of the church of Worcester.

house in the city of Worcester (*Wirecestre*) which renders a marc of silver,[1] and (*et simul*) wood(land) one league (*lewa*) long and the same in width. All this he so bought and held undisturbed (*quiete*), that he rendered no service (*non serviret*) for it to any man.[2]

In this manor is one hide and in (the) demesne are 2 ploughs, and there are 4 villeins and 8 bordars and a reeve (*prepositus*) and a beadle (*bedellus*). Between (them) all they have 4 ploughs. Of (*inter*) serfs and bond-women there are 8, and (there are) a cowman and a dairymaid (*vaccarius et daia*). A forester holds half a virgate of land there.

In LAPULE[3] [Pull (Court)] are 3 virgates of land which used to belong to (*jacebant in*) Langedune [Longdon], a manor of earl Odo. Earl William[4] put (*misit*) this land in Biselie [Bushley]. There is 1 plough, and 1 tenant (*homo*) of the monks of Lire[5] holds one virgate of land. Earl William put (*misit*) outside his manors[6] two foresters, one of Hanlie [Hanley Castle] and the other of Biselie [Bushley] for the keeping of the woods.[7]

The King holds CHONHELME [Queenhill].

It was held by Æthelric (*Adelric*) brother of bishop 'Brictrec.' There is 1 hide, and in (the) demesne is 1 plough, and (there are) 7 villeins and 3 bordars with 4½ ploughs. There is 1 swineherd and 2 oxmen (*bovarii*) and a dairymaid (*daia*). The wood(land) is put (*missa*) out of the manor. Earl William gave the tithe(s) of this manor to ST. MARY of Lire with 1 villein who holds half a virgate of land.[8]

Herman holds of this manor 1 villein who has half a virgate of land.

The King holds EDRESFELLE [Eldersfield]. Reinbald canceler[9] held (it) T.R.E. Earl W[illiam][10] obtained it by exchange (*excambiavit illud*) from him. There are 5 hides. In (the) demesne are 3 ploughs, and (there are) 12 villeins and 13 bordars with 11 ploughs. Of serfs and bondwomen there are 5 there, and (there are) 6 oxmen (*bovarii*) and a mill worth (*de*) 2 shillings. The wood-(land) is 2 leagues (*lewæ*) long and the same in width; it has been put (*missa*) outside the manor. Ansgot, a tenant (*homo*) of earl W[illiam] holds half a virgate of land and Wulfgeat (*Vluiet*) 1 hide of free (*liberæ*) land.

ST. MARY[11] has there 1 villein who holds one virgate of land.

---

[1] 13*s.* 4*d.*, a very large sum for a single house in the city.

[2] This seems intended as a direct contradiction to the statements in the Worcestershire entry of this manor.

[3] This name is further disguised by the Domesday scribe as 'Lapvle.' It can be identified with Pull (Court) by the 1212 return in the *Testa de Nevill* (p. 43) and the *Red Book of the Exchequer* (p. 566), in which the name occurs twice over as 'la Pulle.' In spite of this clue, the official editor of the Red Book identifies the place as 'Lapal,' which lies near Halesowen at the opposite extremity of the county. The 1212 return associates 'la Pulle' with the adjacent Bushley as closely as does Domesday, stating that it was held under Henry II. 'pro custod' haya de Busseleg,' and entering the virgate held of Lyre Abbey there as in 'Bisseleg.'

[4] William Fitz Osbern earl of Hereford.

[5] The abbey of La Vieille Lyre.

[6] 'Suos (*sic*) M[aneria].'

[7] The 1212 return records (not one, but) one and a half virgates as held in Hanley 'per serjantiam custod' forestam Malvernie,' and Nash identified this property as Hanley Hall. It also records, like Domesday, half a virgate as held in Bushley 'per serjantiam custod' hayam de Bisseleg.'

[8] 'Chonhelme' is another name which is not easy to identify. I have no hesitation, however, in saying that the place is Queenhill (chapel) adjoining Pull (Court). The *Testa de Nevill* version (p. 43) of the 1212 return assigns to the prior of Lyre (Abbey) half a virgate 'in *Ruhull* de dono Willelmi filii Osberti comitis Glou' (*sic*). This is, clearly, the above half virgate in 'Chonhelme.' In another entry where the *Testa* has 'Ruhulle' (suggestive of Ryall on the opposite bank) the Red Book reads 'Cuhulle,' which approximates to the Worcestershire Domesday form 'Cu[n]hille' (p. above). My conclusion, therefore, is that 'Chonhelme' is the same place as 'Cu[n]hille,' and 'Adelric' the same tenant as 'Ailric,' both representing 'Æthelric.' The two surveys are quite different except as giving the King as the possessor and the assessment as 1 hide.

[9] The chancellor of Edward the Confessor. See my paper on 'Regenbald, priest and chancellor' in *Feudal England*, pp. 421 *et seq.*; and compare p. 301 note 1 above.

[10] William Fitz Osbern earl of Hereford.

[11] *i.e.* the abbey of La Vieille Lyre, which held a virgate at 'Herdewyk' (Hardwick in Eldersfield), as is shown by the 1212 return (*Testa de Nevill*, p. 43).

The King holds SUCHELIE [Suckley]. Earl Eadwine (*Edwinus*) held (it). There are 5 hides. In (the) demesne are 2 ploughs, and (there are) 22 villeins and 24 bordars with 27 ploughs. There are 10 other bordars (who are) poor, and a mill worth (*de*) 6 shillings, and a keeper of the bees, with 12 hives (*vasculorum*). The wood(land) has 5 leagues, reckoning (*inter*) length and width, and (there is) a fishery there. In Wirecestre [Worcester] there is appurtenant 1 burgess, but (he) renders nothing. There is a mill worth (*de*) 6 shillings. ST. MARY holds the tithe(s) of this vill (*villæ*) with 1 villein and half a virgate of land.[1] Earl Roger[2] gave to a certain Richard half a virgate of land in entire freedom (*solida libertate*).

These 6 manors[3] render at Hereford 50 pounds of rent (*de firma*) and 25 shillings for consideration (*gersumma*).[4]

[GLOWECESTRESCIRE]

fo. 163b.

In the same manor of TEODEKESBERIE [Tewkesbury] used to belong 4 hides without (the) demesne[5] which are in HANLEGE

[Hanley (Castle)]. There, T.R.E., were in (the) demesne 2 ploughs, and of (*inter*) villeins and bordars (there were) 40, and of (*inter*) serfs and bondwomen 8, and a mill worth (*de*) 16 pence. (There is) wood(land) in which is a 'Hay.'[6] This land belonged to (*fuit*) earl William;[7] it now is (annexed) to the King's 'ferm' (*firmam*) of Hereford.[8] It was worth 15 pounds T.R.E.; now 10 pounds.

In FORTELMENTONE [Forthampton] 9 hides belonged to this manor (of Tewkesbury). . . .

These 2 estates (*terras*) were held by earl William and paid their geld in (*propter*) Tedekesberie [Tewkesbury].[9]

Forthampton entry, in the Herefordshire version, states that there were 'there 9 hides which were used to (pay) geld for 4 hides' (only). Indeed, Domesday specially mentions (fo. 163b) that, of the 95 hides in the Tewkesbury group of manors, 45 were exempt from 'geld.'

[6] See above, p. 288, note 8.

[7] William Fitz Osbern earl of Hereford. His ownership of Hanley (Castle) is not mentioned in the survey of it given above (p. 321), but is confirmed by the fact mentioned by Nash [I. 562] that 'the parsonage was anciently united to the abbey of Lyra in France, who made it over in fee farm to the prior and convent of Little Malvern.'

[8] *i.e.* to the group of manors of which Hereford was the head and which paid the Crown a joint 'ferm.'

[9] This is the reason of their being entered together under Tewkesbury in the Gloucestershire Survey, just as the Worcestershire manors, including Hanley, entered under Herefordshire, appear there because their rent had been annexed, by earl William, to that of Hereford.

---

[1] This must be the Abbey of Cormeilles for Henry II.'s charter confirms to it the tithes and one (*sic*) virgate of land here.

[2] Roger earl of Hereford, son of William Fitz Osbern.

[3] *i.e.* Hanley Castle, Forthampton, Bushley, Queenhill, Eldersfield, and Suckley.

[4] It should be observed that this represented sixpence on the pound of the rent, exactly the same proportion as at Martley (p. 320 above).

[5] This phrase (*sine dominio*), at first sight, implies a contradiction. But I am inclined to explain it as meaning that the demesne 'hides' were not liable to 'geld.' For the

SOME EARLY WORCESTERSHIRE SURVEYS

In most counties the Domesday Survey is followed by a period of peculiar darkness, for which we have no assistance from documents, and in which the changes of tenure were often great and violent. In Worcestershire, however, we are fortunate in possessing certain surveys which help us to bridge this dark period, especially one of the Hundred of Oswaldslow, which was printed by Hearne in Heming's Cartulary, but the date of which had not been realized till I showed that it belonged to the reign of Henry I. It may safely be dated as having been made between the years 1108 and 1118. A translation of this survey, compared throughout with Domesday, is here appended.

SURVEY OF OSWALDSLAW HUNDRED

These are the 300 hides which belong to Oswaldes Lawes Hundred :

Into KEMESIGE [Kempsey] are 24 hides. Of these Walter de Beauchamp has 9,[1] and Hugh Puiher 2,[2] and the Bishop 13 with his demesnes.

Into WIKE [Wick Episcopi] 15 hides. Of these Walter de Beauchamp (has) 10½,[3] and Nicholas ½ (a hide) at Lawern,[4] and Hugh Fitz Osbern 1 at Kodere [Cotheridge],[5] and the Bishop 3 with his dem[esne].

In FLEDEBYRI [Fladbury] 40 hides. Of these the bishop of Hereford (has) 5 hides,[6] and Walter de Beauchamp 22 hides,[7] and Hugh de Laci 10 hides,[8] and the Bishop 3 with his demesne.

In BREDUNE [Bredon] 35 hides. Of these the monks of Worcester (have) 4 hides,[9] and Walter de Beauchamp 16 hides,[10] and the King 1 hide,[11] and 'Gile' 1 hide, and the Bishop 13 with his dem[esne].[12]

In RIPPEL [Ripple] and UPTUNE [Upton on-Severn] 25 hides. Of these Walter de Beauchamp (has) 6 hides,[13] and Hugh de Laci 3,[14] and the King 2,[15] and the Bishop 14 with his demesne.[16]

---

[1] i.e. the 7 at Mucknell, Stoughton, and Wolverton which had been held by Urse, and the 2 at Wolverton which Roger de Laci had held.

[2] i.e. the 2 at Whittington which Walter 'Ponther' had held.

[3] i.e. the 9¾ which Urse had held, and apparently ¾ hide more.

[4] i.e. the half hide which Robert the Despencer had held there.

[5] Which his father Osbern had held there.

[6] At Inkberrow.

[7] He seems to have secured 5 more in addition to the 12 held by Urse and the 5 held by Robert the Despencer in 1086.

[8] The 10 hides at Bishampton which Roger de Laci had held in 1086.

[9] At Teddington and Mitton.

[10] The 16 hides at Redmarley d'Abitot, Pendock, Little Washbourne, and Westmancote, which Urse had held in 1086.

[11] At Bushley, which was in the King's hands in this survey, as in Domesday.

[12] On this manor the Bishop had gained, for he had only 10 hides in demesne in 1086, Durand having 2 at Bredons Norton, and Æthelric the archdeacon 2 at Cutsdean.

[13] To the '1 hide held by Urse,' in 1086, he had evidently added the 5 hides at Crombe (d'Abitot), which Siward had held at the time of Domesday.

[14] The 3 hides at Hill Crombe, which Roger de Laci had held in 1086.

[15] At Queenhill and the adjoining 'Burgelege' of Domesday, as in 1086.

[16] The Bishop had increased his 13 hides to 14 by regaining the hide at Crombe, which Ordric had held in 1086.

In Bloccelea [Blockley] 38 hides. Of these Walter de Beauchamp (has) 5;[1] (there are) 5 at Deilesford [Daylesford],[2] 3 at Eunilade [Evenlode];[2] the monks have 1,[3] and the Bishop 24 with his demesnes and Dicford [Ditchford].[4]

In Tredinton [Tredington] 23 hides. Of these the monks have 2;[5] at Langedun [Longden] there are 4;[6] the Bishop has 17 with his demesnes.[7]

In Northewike [Northwick in Claines] 25 hides. Of these Walter de Beauchamp has 10 hides, the King 1, Hugh Puiher 7½, the Bishop 6½ with his demesnes.[8]

In Werebyri [Overbury] and Penedoc [Pendock] 6 hides.

In Segesberewe [Sedgeberrow] 4 hides.

At Scepwestune [Shipston-on-Stour] 2.

At Herfortune [Harvington] with Wiburga Stoke 3.

At Grimeleage [Grimley] 3 hides. Walter de Beauchamp has one of these at Cnihtewike [Knightwick].[9]

At Hallhagan [Hallow] with Bradewasse [Broadwas] 7 hides.[10] Of these Walter de Beauchamp (has) 1½ hides,[11] Roger de Laci 3½ hides,[12] the Count of Meulan 1 hide.[13]

At Croppethorne [Cropthorne] 50 hides. Of these the abbot of Evesham has at Hamtun [Hampton by Bengeworth] 5 hides which (pay) geld, and 10 (others which) are free from geld by the King's writ.[14] The same Abbot has 4 hides at Beningwyrde [Bengeworth], and Walter de Beauchamp 9 hides at Beningwrde [Bengeworth] and at Elmelege [Elmley (Castle)],[15] and Robert Marmion 7 hides at Ceorletune [Charlton];[16] the monks 15 hides.

These are (the) 300 hides belonging to Oswaldes lawes Hundret :[17]

The Bishop has in demesne	94
The monks	40
Walter de Beauchamp	[100][18]
Other barons	63
The King	3
	[300]

These (hides) all pay geld, and, besides these, 10 at Hampton are free from the King's geld, as we said above.

De Kinfolka.[19]

In the hundret (sic) of Kerselau[20] the Bishop has in Heortlabyri [Hartlebury] 20 hides. Of these Walter de Beauchamp has

---

[1] At Dorne, acquired by Urse subsequently to 1086 (see p. 293, note 7).

[2] Both these as in Domesday.

[3] At Icombe.

[4] The Bishop, though he had lost Dorne since 1086, had gained the 2 hides that Richard had held at Ditchford, and the 1½ hides that Ansgot had held (of the villeins' land). His demesne, therefore, was only 1½ hides less than in 1086.

[5] At Blackwell, as in Domesday.

[6] Which Gilbert Fitz Turold had held in 1086. William Travers is found holding them of the Bishop temp. John (Testa de Nevill, p. 42).

[7] The division of this manor was unchanged.

[8] Except that Hugh Puiher held the 7½ hides that had been held, in Domesday, by Walter Ponther, there had been a good deal of change here. I expect that the Bishop, whose demesnes had increased by 3 hides, had regained the 3 (or 3¼) hides at Aston, which Domesday entered as held by Ordric, but as forming part of the chief manor. The 7¾ hides held by Urse in 1086 had increased here to 10 hides, the holding of his son-in-law, Walter.

[9] As had Robert the Despencer in 1086.

[10] But according to Domesday 7½.

[11] Urse held nothing here in 1086.

[12] At Himbleton and Spetchley, held also by Roger de Laci in 1086.

[13] Representing, or at least including, the half hide at Lippard ('Lappewrte') held by Hugh de Grentmesnil in 1086.

[14] See p. 255, note 10 above.

[15] i.e. 5 at Bengeworth and 4 at Elmley. But Urse had actually held 6 at Bengeworth, the Abbot's 4 hides completing the 10 (see p. 254 above).

[16] The nameless 11 hides held by Robert the Despencer in 1086 were at Elmley and Charlton. The 4 at Elmley were secured by Beauchamp, and the 7 at Charlton by Marmion (see Feudal England, p. 176). The latter's holding is represented by the two fees (or, as he said, one) which Robert Marmion held of the Bishop in 1166.

[17] This is the Domesday form of 'Hundred.'

[18] This figure is obtained by adding up the hides assigned to him under each manor. Hearne gives the figure as 20, but the MS. is here damaged.

[19] A marginal heading. See p. 244 above for the name.

[20] 'Cresselau' in Domesday.

5 hides at WÆRESLEGE [Waresley].[1] To the Bishop there remain in demesne 15.

In the same hundret (sic) the monks have at WLFWARDILE [Wolverley] 5 hides.[2]

In Kamel [3] hundret (sic) the monks have STOKAN [Stoke Prior]—10 hides; and the Bishop has at ÆLFITHE CYRCE [Alvechurch] 13 hides.[4]

In ÆSC [5] hundret (sic) the monks have at CLIVE [Cleeve Prior] with LENG [Lench] 10 hides;[6] at FEPSINTUNE [Fepton] the same monks have 1 hide;[7] Hugh de Laci, CROHLEA [Crowle] 5 hides.[8]

In the same hundret (sic) the Bishop has at HEANBYRI [Hanbury] 14 hides. Of these Walter de Beauchamp has half a hide.[9]

In Dudintree [10] hundret the monks have 15 hides at EARDULFESTUN [Eardiston] and CNIHTETUN [Knighton].

Total (summa) in Kinefolka. The Bishop has in demesne 41 (hides), the monks 41, Walter de Beauchamp 6, Hugh de Laci 5, Hugh Puiher 1, which does not pay geld.[11]

The total (summa) of the hides which the Bishop has in the whole county (vicecomitatu) is 397, including (cum) those which the abbot of Evesham holds of the Hundred of Oswaldes Lawe.

It will be observed that this document is, like the Domesday Survey itself, largely, or rather exclusively concerned with the liability to geld. Indeed, in Heming's Cartulary, it follows closely on a writ, by which Henry I. directs Walter de Beauchamp and the (geld) 'collectors' of Worcestershire not to exact geld from the Bishop, for his Worcestershire land, thenceforth, on more than $397\frac{1}{2}$ hides.[12]

The totals work out almost exactly right, although we are dealing only with a cartulary transcript. We have seen that the document's own totals give us 300 hides for Oswaldslow, and when we add together the manors, they give us 299 hides, as also do the holdings when added together. That of the Bishop, however, was $93\frac{1}{2}$, not '94,' and that of the barons $62\frac{1}{2}$, not '63' (reckoning the abbot of Evesham's holding as 9 'gelding' hides only). That of the monks also was 39, not '40,' while the King, on the other hand, seems to have held 4, not 3 hides. Outside Oswaldslow, the totals work out as 94, whether we take the manors or the holdings. It is possible that the discrepancy between the grand total and that which is found in the King's writ is connected with the Fepton reduction.

The survey of Oswaldslow in this document runs so closely parallel with that in Domesday itself that we can incidentally learn something of the changes of tenure in the interval. Walter de Beauchamp had not only succeeded his wife's father (Urse) and uncle (Robert) everywhere except at Charlton, but had actually got into his

---

[1] This holding had been carved out of the manor since Domesday.

[2] This survey distinguishes here between the Bishop's manor and that of the monks. Domesday does not.

[3] The 'Came' of Domesday.

[4] See p. 298 above.

[5] The 'Esch' of Domesday.

[6] $10\frac{1}{2}$ hides in Domesday.

[7] In Domesday the monks are entered as liable for geld on 5 hides at 'Fepsetenatun.' The discrepancy here is beautifully accounted for by the writ of Henry I. directed to Walter de Beauchamp and the

other officers of Worcestershire, reducing the assessment of 'Fepsintun' by 4 hides (Hale's Registrum, p. 58b, and compare p. 237 above).

[8] Which had been held by Roger de Laci in 1086.

[9] Which had been held by Urse in 1086.

[10] The 'Dodintret' of Domesday.

[11] This was the hide at Fepton entered in Domesday as held by Walter 'Ponther' and as free from geld.

[12] Vol. I. p. 298. Between this writ and the above survey is extracted a transcript of the relative portion of Domesday 'secundum cartam regis que est in thesauro reg'.'

hands one-third of Oswaldslow (100 hides), his interest in which alone would have made him of importance in the county ; but we shall see below how largely he was holding elsewhere also.

Walter, as I have observed above, had not succeeded his wife's uncle Robert the Despencer at Charlton, which the Survey assigns to Robert Marmion. Thus, of the 17½ hides which Robert had held, in Domesday, of the Bishop, seven had passed to Marmion, and ten and a half to Beauchamp. I have elsewhere shown that in Leicestershire, as in Worcestershire, the Despencer lands were divided between Beauchamp and Marmion,[1] while Scrivelsby and other lands of Robert the Despencer in Lincolnshire fell to the share of Marmion, from whom they passed by female descent to the well-known hereditary champions.[2] A remarkable charter of William Rufus proves that Urse de Abetot had succeeded his brother Robert in at least one Lincolnshire manor,[3] which suggests that Robert himself had died without issue and that the Marmions derived their claim, whatever it was, through Urse.[4]

Further points to be noted in this early survey are that the Walter 'Ponther' of Domesday, the Walter 'Punher' of the Worcester Relief (1095),[5] had been succeeded, as a tenant of the see, by Hugh 'Puher,' and that Roger de Laci had also been succeeded, as in the 1095 list,[5] by Hugh de Laci, except in two cases, in one of which he himself is still named as the tenant, although he had been forfeited and banished in 1088, after being one of the rebel leaders defeated at the battle of Worcester. Hugh de Laci, who remained loyal and who received his lands, was his brother.

We will now pass to the interesting fragment of a Survey rather later in date, which is found in an Evesham cartulary.[6] This fragment begins abruptly at the top of a page, and has no connection with the page preceding it, the text of which it appears to continue.[7] It is, moreover, written in a different hand. Stranger still, it is unconnected with the dorse of its own folio. From internal evidence alone can its date and character be determined.

. . . [in the ?] manor of HAMBYRY [Hanbury], 'Eston Ric[ardi]' half a hide. In the Hundred of Camele : in WARESLEIA [Waresley] 5 hides of the manor of Hertlebery [Hartlebury].[8] Total 93 hides.

In the Hundred of Pershore the church of WESTMINSTER [Westminster Abbey] has these lands, which William de Beauchamp holds :—Hekintona [Eckington] 3 hides and 3 virgates ;[9] Chaddesleia [Chaseley] [10] 2

---

[1] *Feudal England*, p. 214.

[2] *Ibid.* pp. 193–195.

[3] See my *Ancient Charters* (Pipe Roll Society), p. 1.

[4] See *Feudal England*, p. 176.

[5] *Ibid.* pp. 309, 312.

[6] Cott. MS. Vesp. B. XXIV. fo. 8.

[7] The pages preceding it contain a curious abstract of Domesday, arranged in Hundreds, which deserves attention, as its compiler

seems to have possessed some additional information.

[8] These were the two estates held by Walter de Beauchamp of the see, outside Oswaldslaw (see above).

[9] Held by Urse in 1086 as 4 hides less 1 virgate.

[10] In Longdon. Chaddesley Corbett must have been so named to distinguish it from this Chaseley, formerly Chadesley.

hides; Langeduna Osmundi [in Longdon] 1½ hides; Colleduma [Cowsdown][1] 3 hides and 3 virgates; Graftona Ebrandi [Grafton Flyford] 1 hide and 3 virgates;[2] Flavel [Flyford Flavel] and Pidelet [North Piddle] 5 hides;[3] Newentona [Naunton Beauchamp] 10 hides;[4] Brocton Inardi [Broughton Hacket] 3 hides;[5] Pidelet Radulfi [Wyre Piddle] 3 hides;[6] Berford [Besford] 5 hides;[7] Branefford [Bransford Chapel] 1 hide;[8] Wicha Inardi [Wick by Pershore] 3 hides;[9] Burlingeham [Birlingham] 2 hides and 1 virgate;[10] Cumbrintona [Comberton] 2 hides.[10] Poiwica Willelmi de Bellocampo [Beauchampcourt in Powick] 1 hide; Newebolt [   ] 1 hide; Medeleffeld [Madresfield] 1 hide: of Powick; at Berga [Berrow ?] 1 hide; Olendene [   ] 1 hide; Arleia [   ] 1 virgate; Poiwica Inardi [in Powick] 1 hide. Total 60 hides and a half.[11]

In the aforesaid Hundred of Pershore (of) the fief of the abbot of Pershore:—Belega [Beoley] 21 hides; Branefford [Bransford Chapel] 1 hide; Wadberga [Wadborough] 3½ hides; Cumbrientona [Comberton] 1½

hides; Lega Ricardi [Leigh] half a hide; Walecote [Walcote] and Torendune [Thornton] 1½ hides.[12]

In the Hundred of Leisse[13] the same William holds (at) Chirchlench [Churchlench] 4 hides of the abbey of Evesham;[14] (at) Croulega [Crowle] 5 hides of the fief of Osbert Fitz Hugh.[15]

In the Hundred of Clent:—(At) Belna [Belne in Belbroughton] 8 hides of the fief of Fulk (Folwi) Paganel;[16] (at) Salwarpa [Salwarpe] 5 hides of the fief of earl Roger;[17] also (at) Salwarpa 1 hide of the fief of the bishop of Chester;[18] (at) Chalvestona [Chauson] 1 hide of the fee of Robert

---

[1] In Snodsbury. This enables us to identify Urse's Domesday holding of 4 hides less 1 virgate in Snodsbury, which had no name.

[2] The 2 hides less 1 virgate which Urse held at 'Garstune' in 1086.

[3] Held by Urse in 1086 as at 'Pidelet.' The relative entry in the short survey on fo. 6b of this MS. is 'Inter Flavel et Pidelet Robertus Parler habet v hidas et v carucas, et valet lx solidos.' The figures, here, are those of Domesday, which, however, does not mention Robert, who may have been Urse's tenant (see below).

[4] The Domesday holding of Urse there.

[5] Held by (Urse) the sheriff in 1086.

[6] Held in 1086 by Urse as 4 hides, of which one did not pay geld.

[7] Urse's holding there in 1086.

[8] Domesday only mentions the hide he held here of Pershore Abbey (see below).

[9] Domesday only assigns him 1 hide there.

[10] Held by Urse in 1086.

[11] The Powick entries are difficult. Domesday assesses all Powick at 3 hides only, and does not tell us what proportion was represented by Urse's valuable estate there. The version of Domesday in Vesp. B. XXIV. fo. 6b enters Powick as 3 hides, but proceeds to reckon Urse's holding as 5 hides.

[12] In Domesday the great manor of Beoley was held by Pershore Abbey in demesne, but by subsequent enfeoffment Beauchamp held there one of the Abbot's two knight's fees (Testa, p. 40, Liber Rubeus, p. 302). This, however, appears, from the records cited by Habington to have been only 5 hides. Bransford and Comberton had been held by Urse, in 1086, and Wadborough by Robert the Despencer. At Leigh Domesday assigns a hide and a half to Urse, but its figures are not consistent with themselves. The hide and a half at Walcote and Thornton appears to represent the one hide that Domesday assigns to Urse at Broughton (which lay between them). The hide which Urse held at Wadborough and the 2 hides he claimed at Broadwas are not here entered as held by William de Beauchamp.

[13] The 'Esch' of Domesday.

[14] This estate appears in Domesday as held by the Abbey in demesne. The monks accounted for its loss by the statement that Abbot Walter had granted it to Urse 'pro servitio,' for his life only (Harl. MS. 3,763, fo. 168). It is here found held by his grandson William de Beauchamp.

[15] As Urse had held it of his grandfather, Osbern Fitz Richard, in 1086. It was afterwards held, as one knight's fee, by Hacket under Poher, and by Poher under Beauchamp.

[16] Belne, in 1086, was held by William Fitz Ansculf, Fulk's predecessor, as 3 hides. It is not easy to see why it here becomes 8, or why William de Beauchamp held it as under-tenant, unless the Robert who so held it in 1086 was Robert the Despencer.

[17] Which Urse had held of earl Roger in 1086.

[18] Which Urse had held, as of the church of Coventry, in 1086.

Fitz Archembald;[1] at Wich [Droitwich] half a hide (held by) Gunfrei;[2] also at Wich [Droitwich] 1 hide of St. Guthlac's[3] land, which Robert Fitz William holds; there also half a hide of Cormell', which Gilbert holds;[4] (at) Cokehulla [Cookley?] 2½ hides of the King's fief;[5] (at) Hactona [Acton Beauchamp] 3 hides of the fief of the bishop of Bayeux;[6] (at) Escreueleia [Shrawley] 1 hide.[7] Total of the whole: 264½ hides and half a virgate.

[Eastham] 3 hides; Bertona [Bayton] 3 hides and 3 virgates; Alcrintona [Alton in Rock] 2 hides; Linda [Lindridge] 2 hides; and at Halac [   ] 1 hide; Mora Hugonis [Moor in Rock] 1½ hides; Werveslega [Worsley farm][8] 2½ hides; Albodeslega [Abberley] 2½ hides; Rudmerlega [Redmarley in Witley] 1½ hides; Estlega [Astley] 1 hide that pays geld (*geldans*) and 1 hide that is free;[9] Sceldeslega [Shelsley] 1 hide; Almelega Ricardi de Portes [Elmley Lovett] 11 hides.[10]

The land of Roger de Toeney :—Estha

Roughly speaking, the date of the survey of which this is a fragment, is a generation later than that f the Hundred of Oswaldslow. For two great Worcestershire landowⁿers, Walter de Beauchamp and Hugh Fitz Osbern, had been respectively succeeded by their sons, William de Beauchamp and Osbern Fitz Hugh. The name of Roger 'de Toeney' also points to the reign of Stephen. Careful examination proves that all the earlier portion, all, that is, down to 'The land of Roger de Toeney,' is concerned with the holdings of William de Beauchamp in the Hundreds of ('Kerselau'), 'Came,' Pershore, 'Leisse,' Clent and Dodingtree. It is only here, I believe, that the 300 hides, of which the abbey of Westminster was supposed to hold 200, and the abbey of Pershore 100, are definitely termed the Hundred of Pershore, just as the Hundred of Oswaldslow consisted of 300 hides. And the prior rights of Pershore Abbey are thereby confirmed.[11] The object of the Survey seems, as usual, to have been the ascertainment of the liability to 'geld.' But it is a singular feature of the document, that while Roger de Toeney's lands are all of them those which he held as a tenant-in-chief, those of William de Beauchamp are, almost exclusively, lands that he held as under-tenant. It is in the latter's succession to his maternal grandfather Urse (and, at Wadborough, to Urse's brother, Robert) that consists

[1] It lies between Salwarpe and Droitwich, and was held *in capite* by William Goizenboded in 1086. Robert Fitz Archembald was a benefactor to St. Peter's, Gloucester, in 1128 (see its Cartulary in Rolls Series).

[2] It was held of Urse by Gunfrei, as in 'Witone,' in 1086.

[3] It had been held of St. Guthlac by Nigel the leech in 1086.

[4] This entry is obscure. No land at Droitwich is assigned to the Abbey of Cormeilles in Domesday. The probable explanation is that the MS. itself is in fault —and ought, instead of 'also there,' to have read: 'In the hundred of Dodintre,' to which belong the four places which follow. The above half hide would then be that at Tenbury, which was held in 1086 by the abbey of Cormeilles.

[5] Which Urse had held *in capite*, as at 'Cochehi,' in 1086.

[6] These are the 3 'gelding' hides so held there by Urse in 1086.

[7] This would seem to be the first mention of Shrawley, of which the early history is obscure. It was, however, afterwards held by Poher under Beauchamp, and by Beauchamp of 'the heirs of Tony.'

[8] Between Rock and Abberley.

[9] These are the 2 hides that he retained there, after giving 4 to St. Taurin (see Domesday).

[10] The above holdings are identical with those composing the Domesday fief of Ralf de 'Todeni'; and the assessments are the same, except that Bayton is 1 virgate more, Moor 1 virgate more, Worsley half a hide more.

[11] See pp. 251, 257 above.

the chief importance of the Survey for the feudal history of the county.

A very interesting feature of this Survey is its early illustration of a practice prevailing in the 12th century by which manors were distinguished from one another by adding the name of the Norman tenant. In three cases, for instance, we find the word ' Inardi ' appended in this Survey to manors of William de Beauchamp. Now we can trace the ' Inardus ' from whom they derived this name. He, as ' Isnardus,' is the first witness to a charter of William de Beauchamp in favour of the monks of Worcester,[1] and, also as ' Isnardus,' was a benefactor to them, with his wife Emma, at Himbleton.[2] He further, as ' Isnardus,' was a witness to a charter of 1130 to Evesham Abbey, and, as ' Isnardus Parler ' (?), witnessed, with his son Nicholas, the charter granted to William de Beauchamp by the empress Maud (1141 ?).[3] Lastly, in an Evesham cartulary we have an interesting entry on some manors of the Abbey which Urse obtained, including ' Hamtun quam Inard' Parler tenet.'[4] As Hampton was held of Urse by ' Robert ' in 1086, and as Robert ' Parler ' was, at that date, under-tenant of Nafford, there is at least a fair presumption that Urse's tenant was ' Robert Parler,' and that he was Inard's ancestor. And this suggestion is confirmed by the fact that Robert ' Parler ' appears as a tenant on Urse's fief (see p. 328, note 3 above), and that at Powick we read (Vesp. B. XXIV. fo. 6b) of ' pars Roberti Parlere,' as in this survey of Powick ' Inardi.' One is tempted to suggest that Inardestone (or Inarstone) in Redmarley d'Abitot[5] may have derived its name from this tenant, as, in Herefordshire, the name of Walterstone was formed by combining the Norman Walter with the English suffix ' -ton.'

The remaining Survey with which we have to deal is that of Droitwich. This is found on a page of MS. Harl. 3,763 (fo. 82), which has no connection with the pages preceding it or with its own dorse.[6] The text runs as follows :

These are the 10 hides in Wich [Droitwich]. Of Witton 'Petri Corbezun'[7] 2 hides. Of the fee of St. Denis, Richard Corbet (*corvus*) and William son of Oueclinus hold 1 hide.[8] Of St. Guthlac (of Hereford) William Fitz Richard holds 1 hide.[9] Of John de Suthlega, Richard Fitz Robert holds 1 hide.[10] Of Payn Fitz John Godwi holds half a hide. Of Walter de Beauchamp Theobald and Peter hold half a hide.[11] Of the Barton

---

[1] Hale's *Registrum*, p. 92a.
[2] *Ibid.* p. 55b. In both these cases the name has been misread ' Isvardus.'
[3] See *Geoffrey de Mandeville*, pp. 314–5.
[4] Vesp. B. XXIV. fos. 10–11.
[5] Sloane MSS. XXXIII. 48, 64.
[6] On this (fo. 82d) there is a charter of Henry I. confirming to Evesham Abbey the Hundred of ' Blacahurste.' Its date is 1100–1108, and Urse de Abetot is among the witnesses.

[7] Held in 1086, by William Fitz Corbucion, his predecessor.
[8] It was held by the abbey of St. Denis in 1086.
[9] Held of the same house, in 1086, by Nigel the leech.
[10] Held in 1086 by Harold son of earl Ralf (see next page).
[11] This was the half hide in Witton that Gunfrei had held of Urse in 1086.

('Berton') of Gloucester Ralf Fitz Ringulf holds half a hide.[1] Of the monks of Gloucester Baldwin and Lithulf (hold) half a hide.[2] Of the earl of Warwick Randulf and Essulf sons of Ringulf hold 3 virgates. Of Walter del Burc[3] Randulf and Essulf (hold) half a hide. Of Westminster Theobald and Walter Fitz (*fil'*) Thorald (hold) 1 hide.[4] Of Almlega [Elmley Lovett], the son of Aiulf and his mother 1 hide.[5] Of Battona[6] Aiulf the priest (holds) one virgate. Of Wichebold [Wichbold] Roger de Bolles (holds) 1 virgate.[7] Of the monks the son of Grim holds 1 virgate. Of Kinefare [Kinver] and Doverdale 1 virgate. Alewi Caure and his fellows (*socii*) half a virgate.

This Survey is roughly dated by the name of Walter de Beauchamp, and probably belongs to the closing years of the reign of Henry I., when his trusted officer Payn Fitz John was much to the front. It will be observed that the portion of Witton (in Droitwich) held by Peter 'Corbezun'[8] is distinguished by his own name, according to the practice described above (p. 330). The most interesting name in the Survey is that of John de Sudeley ('Suthlega'),[9] for he was that son of Harold, the Domesday tenant at Droitwich, from whom descended, in the male line, the Sudeleys and the Tracys of Toddington. It is just possible that his Droitwich tenant was that Richard who was a younger son of his brother Robert of Ewyas. Although the tenant of St. Guthlac's hide is here given as William Fitz Richard, it is entered in the later Survey (p. 329 above) as held by his son Robert Fitz William of William de Beauchamp. This is probably connected with Urse's position as holding of Nigel the leech, St. Guthlac's under-tenant, at Dunclent; for it was Nigel who had held this hide of St. Guthlac. The few small holdings at the end of the Survey are obscure and difficult to explain. Among the under-tenants, it should be observed, the names of Englishmen still occur.

[1] This was the half hide assigned in Domesday to the King's hall at Gloucester.

[2] As held in 1086 by St. Peter's Abbey, Gloucester.

[3] This was the name of the Domesday under-tenant of Estbury in Hallow.

[4] This hide had been held of Westminster Abbey by 'two priests' in 1086.

[5] This hide immediately follows the entry on Elmley Lovett in Domesday. It was then held *in capite* by Ralf de 'Todeni.'

[6] This name is badly written, and I cannot identify it.

[7] Domesday records several 'burgesses' at Droitwich as appurtenant to Wichbold.

[8] *Alias* Peter de Stodley, founder of Studley Priory (see p. 269, note 4 above).

[9] It must be he who is entered on the Pipe Roll of 1130 (p. 79) as owing 10 marcs for 'his wife's pleas.'

INDEX TO DOMESDAY OF WORCESTER

PERSONAL NAMES

Abitot, Osbern d', *note* 292*b*

Abitot, Robert d', *alias* Robert the Despencer, *note* 291*b*

Abitot, Abetot, Abetoth, Urse d'. See Urse the sheriff

Acard', 317*a*

Achil, 318*a*

Adam brother to Eudo the king's dapifer, 246

Adam 'de Crumba,' *note* 292*b*

Adam son of Robert, *alias* Adam de Trokemertune [?], *note* 291*a*

Adelric [Æthelric], 318*a*

Adelric [Æthelric] brother to bishop 'Brictrec,' 296*a*, 322*b*, *notes* 288*b*, 322*b*

Ædwinus [earl Odda], 260

Æilric the archdeacon, 291*b*, 294*b*. See also Æthelric, Alric

Æilward [Æthelward], 316*b*

Ældiet, 314*a*

Ælfgar [Algar], earl, 267, 309*b*

Ælfgeat [Aluiet], 319*b*

Ælfgifu [Ælveva], 308*a*

Ælfgifu [Elgivæ] the nun, *alias* Eadgyth [Eadgidæ] the nun [?], 294*b*, 295*b*

Ælfhere ealdorman of Mercia, *alias* Delfer, that 'most wicked earl,' 259

Ælfric [Alricus], 296*a*

Ælfric [Alricus] the archdeacon, 290*b*

Ælfric [Aluric, Aluricus, Elricus], 300*a*, 317*a*, 318*a*, 318*b*, 319*a*

Ælfric [Aluric] mapesone, 312*a*

Ælfric brother to earl Odda, 259

Ælfward [Ælward, Alward, Alwardus], 301*b*, 302*a*, 302*b*, 304*a*

Ælfwig [Alwi], 301*a*, 301*b*, 303*a*, 312*a*

Ælfwine [Alwinus], 301*b*, 302*b*, 303*a*, 319*a*

Ælfwine son of Brihtmar, *note* 289*a*

Ælfwold [Alwold, Alwoldus], 316*a*, 318*a*, 318*b*, 320*a*

Ælnod [Æthelnoth], 309*b*

Ælsi [Æthelsige], 311*a*

Ælveva [Ælfgifu], 308*a*

Ælward [Ælfward, Æthelward], 301*b*, 309*b*

Ælwi [Æthelwig], 311*b*

Ælwine cilt, 309*a*

Ærngrim, 254, *note* 297*a*

Æthelflæd lady of the Mercians, 242

Æthelred ealdorman of the Mercians, 242

Æthelred, king, 238

Æthelric [Adelric, Ailric, Alric, Alricus] brother to bishop 'Brictrec,' 296*a*, 322*b*, *notes* 288*b*, 322*b*

Æthelric [Adelric], 318*a*

Æthelric the archdeacon, *note* 324*b*. See also Æilric, Alric

Æthelsige, 'dean,' 238

Æthelward [Æilward], 316*b*

Æthelward [Ælward] thegn of earl Ælfgar, 309*b*

Æthelward [Agelward] 'radman' in Powick, 301*b*

Æthelwig [Ælwinus, Alwinus, Elwi] abbot of Evesham, 252, 253, 254, 261, 264, 265, 273, 308*b*, 319*b*, *notes* 308*a*, 319*a*, 319*b*

Æthelwig [Ælwi, Elwi], 311*b*

Æthelwine [Ælwin(us) cilt, Agelwinus], *note* 309*a*

Æthelwine [Ædwinus, Odo, earl Odda], 258, 260, 322*a*

Æthelwine, prior, *note* 297*b*

Æthelwold, bishop, 259

Ævic [Evic] sheriff of Staffordshire, 239

Agelward [Æthelward], 301*b*

Ailric, 288*a*

Ailric, Alric [Æthelric] brother to bishop Brihtheah, 296*a*, 322*b*, *notes* 288*b*, 322*b*

Aiulf, 286*b*, 288*a*, 303*b*; son and mother of, 331*b*

Aiulf the priest, 331*b*

Albert, 302*b*

Alcot the monk, 300*b*

'Alelm,' 316*b*

Alewi Caure, 331*b*

Alfred, king, 242, 249

Alfric, 301*a*

Algar [Ælfgar], earl, 309*b*

Alric, 288*a*, 301*a*

Alric the archdeacon, 294*b*. See also Æilric, Æthelric

Aluiet [Ælfgeat], 319*b*

Aluric, Aluricus [Ælfric], 300*a*, 318*a*, 318*b*, 319*a*

Aluric [Ælfric] mapesone, 312*a*

Alvred, 290*a*

Alvred, knight, 286*a*

Alvred of Marlborough, de Merleberg, lord of Ewias, 266, 304*a* and *note*

Alward, 293*a*

Alwardus [Ælfward], 302*a*, 302*b*

Alwi [Ælfwig], 301*a*, 301*b*, 303*a*, 312*a*

Alwi blac, 301*a*

Alwin' thegn of earl Eadwine, 286*a*

Alwinus [Ælfwine], 301*b*, 302*b*, 303*a*

Alwold, 310*b*

Alwold thegn of earl Eadwine, 286*a*

Alwold, Alwoldus [Ælfwold], 316*a*, 318*a*, 318*b*, 320*a*

Ansculf de Picquigny [Pinchengi], 262, *note* 315*b*. See also William Fitz Ansculf

Ansgot, 293*a*, 303*b*, 322*b*, *note* 325*a*

Arnwig, *note* 289*b*

Arnwine [Earnwius] the priest, 288*b* and *note*

Artur, 301*b*

Asinus. See Hugh

'Assere,' 254

Atilic, 319*a*

Azor [Atsere], 254, 291*b*, 295*a*, 297*a*, 304*b*, *note* 297*a*

Azur, 304*a*

Baderon. See William Fitz Baderon

PLACE NAMES